A D V A N C E D
S T R U C T U R E D
COBOL

A D V A N C E D
S T R U C T U R E D
COBOL

Edward J. Coburn

Emporia State University

Harcourt Brace Jovanovich, Publishers
and its subsidiary, Academic Press
San Diego   New York   Chicago   Austin   Washington, D.C.
London   Sydney   Tokyo   Toronto

ISBN: 0-15-501873-6
Library of Congress Catalog Card Number: 87-82783
Printed in the United States of America

Material in Appendix C is reprinted from *American National Standard Programming Language* COBOL ANSI X3, 23-1974.

COBOL is an industry language and is not the property of any company or group of companies, or of any organization or group of organizations.

No warranty, expressed or implied, is made by any contributor or by the CODASYL Programming Language Committee as to the accuracy and functioning of the programming system and language. Moreover, no responsibility is assumed by any contributor, or by the committee, in connection therewith.

The authors and copyright holders of the copyrighted material used herein

> FLOW MATIC (trademark of Sperry Rand Corporation), Programming for the UNIVAC® I and II, Data Automation Systems copyrighted 1958, 1959, by Sperry Rand Corporation; IBM Commercial Translator Form No. F 28-8013, copyrighted 1959 by IBM; FACT, DSI 27A5260-2760, copyrighted 1960 by Minneapolis-Honeywell

have specifically authorized the use of this material, in whole or in part, in the COBOL specifications. Such authorization extends to the reproduction and use of COBOL specifications in programming manuals or similar publications.

With an estimated 80 percent of new business computer applications being written in COBOL, it is easy to see that knowledge of COBOL programming will be vital to future business computer graduates. Such widespread usage also makes it apparent that programmers will need to use standardized, structured programming techniques. It is to that end that this book and its companion, *Beginning Structured COBOL*, were written.

Advanced Structured COBOL reviews the basics of COBOL and then progresses into the more advanced concepts used by the professional programmer. Along the way are many student aids.

Each chapter begins with a Chapter Overview and Objectives. Within each chapter, all new terms are highlighted, and these highlighted terms are defined in the Glossary at the end of the chapter. Also at the end of each chapter are a Summary and two groups of questions. The Quick Quiz has 15 true or false, 5 multiple choice, and 5 fill-in-the-blank questions, with all answers listed and explained at the end of the quiz. The Questions to Aid Understanding that follow are geared toward determining if the Objectives expressed at the beginning of the chapter have been fulfilled. An asterisk (*) next to a question in this section indicates that its answer can be found in Appendix E.

Beginning with Chapter 2, each chapter contains several additional groups of exercises of progressive difficulty. (1) First, there are several coding exercises. These are questions for which the student is expected to write single COBOL statements or groups of statements to get a simple, practical start on the coding involved in the various chapter topics. (2) Next is a Maintenance Program, already completely written. The exercise requires the student to examine the program

as it stands and then modify it to fit new specifications. One of the jobs beginning programmers are assigned to most often is program maintenance. These exercises provide excellent preparation for such tasks. (3) Next is an Illustrative Program, which includes the pseudocode and flowchart. The student does the actual programming based on the given design. (4) The fourth level of programming exercise is System Designed Programs. The systems chart, input layouts, and printer spacing charts are provided, and it is up to the student to use them to design and code the programs. There are three of these exercises in each chapter. (5) The final level of exercise is Non-designed Programs. The student designs the input, output, and program and also arranges the test data. After Chapter 4, many of the chapters have a second set of system designed and non-designed programs, for creating interactive programs.

For continuity, sample programs throughout the book deal with the topic at hand as it would apply to *The Record Rack*, a fictitious record and tape store. The programmer for *The Record Rack* goes through the creation process just as the student should, and the examples are completely explained.

This textbook may be used in a variety of ways, but most chapters should be covered in the order presented, since learning a programming language is a cumulative experience. Briefly, the progression is as follows:

- Chapter 1 reviews structured program design. Students look at the idea of structured programming and reexamine many program design tools.

- Chapter 2 reviews all the principal concepts taught in a beginning COBOL course. This chapter, excellent for in-class review, may also serve as a quick reference for students when writing programs outside of class.

- Chapter 3 deals with sequential file updating. Students learn how to use each of the four different files involved in the process and then closely examine a practical program written to illustrate the updating concepts.
- Chapter 4 introduces interactive programming. The majority of COBOL programs being written for modern computers are interactive, so it is imperative that students be exposed to this widely used programming technique. Full-screen processing is discussed, but line-at-a-time processing is mainly used, because its techniques are available in virtually all versions of COBOL and carry over well to the full-screen processing environment.
- Chapter 5 reviews single-level tables and search techniques and then moves on to multi-level tables, supplying many practical examples.
- Chapter 6 covers the COBOL sort in detail. Though most computer systems have sort utilities, the COBOL sort can handle techniques that other sort utilities cannot, such as sorting a file in several different sequences so that it can be displayed on the screen in an interactive program.
- Chapter 7 teaches the student how to process index files in COBOL using ISAM or VSAM. Most actively used computer files are stored as ISAM or VSAM files, and the ability to access such files is beginning to be of prime importance.
- Chapter 8 covers interactive techniques for indexed files. The student is shown straightforward methods of writing programs to add, change, delete, and print or display records from the files.
- Chapter 9 deals with relative files. Though relative files are not used as often as index files, they can be more efficient than index files for certain applications.
- Chapter 10 teaches the student how to program using the Report Writer, a COBOL feature that is gaining attention for its ability to produce simple reports quickly and easily.

- Chapter 11 covers subprograms, data bases, and libraries. The ability to use separately compiled subprograms is essential in the data processing environments programmers encounter. This chapter covers how a subprogram or routine is coded, called, and linked. In addition, because more and more companies are using data base management systems, the student is shown what such systems typically look like and what a programmer might be expected to know in order to use them.

Several appendices cover all the data used for the exercises, the major changes in the 1985 COBOL standards, the standard COBOL statement formats and reserved words, and answers to selected exercises.

The Instructor's Manual to accompany this book includes the following:

1. the objectives for each chapter;
2. an outline of each chapter;
3. a selection of objective questions for each chapter;
4. transparency masters for all coding formats;
5. solutions to all coding exercises, with the output that would be generated by the data given in Appendix A. The data files in Appendix A, the coded programs, and the chapter outlines are also available on diskette for adopters of *Advanced Structured COBOL*.

The author would like to express his thanks to the following persons for their reviews of *Advanced Structured COBOL*: Geoffrey Crosslin, Kalamazoo Valley Community College; George Fowler, Texas A & M University; R. Wayne Headrick, Texas A & M University; Robert C. Tesch, Northeast Louisiana University; and James R. Walters, Pikes Peak Community College.

Also, the author is grateful to the staff members at Harcourt Brace Jovanovich whose untiring efforts helped to produce a quality book.

EDWARD J. COBURN

CONTENTS

CHAPTER 10

REPORT WRITER / 567

CHAPTER 11

LIBRARIES, SUBPROGRAMS, AND DATA BASES / 621

APPENDIXES

ADVANCED
STRUCTURED
COBOL

OBJECTIVES   After completing Chapter 1 you should be able to

1. name the three basic design structures proposed by Dijkstra;
2. describe and draw examples of a systems chart;
3. use structured flowcharts and pseudocode to design any appropriate problem;
4. illustrate the design of the SIMPLE SEQUENCE, DO-WHILE, and IF-THEN-ELSE (and null ELSE) with a flowchart and pseudocode;
5. explain why two input statements are needed in a DO-WHILE when the test is for the end-of-data marker;
6. explain why a program is often broken up into modules;
7. design input and output specifications using the techniques demonstrated in the chapter.

CHAPTER 1

STRUCTURED PROGRAMMING DESIGN

1-1

Introduction

Over the past ten years or so, the computer industry has been going through a transition. Hardware costs continue to plummet while software production costs continue to climb. The reasons for this are many, but the only important thing is that the programmer's time is becoming more and more expensive for the employer. It is therefore imperative that the programmer's time be spent in the most productive way possible. It is no longer necessary to spend time trying to figure out how a program can be made the most creative or most efficiently running program available. What is needed are techniques that allow the programmer to create programs that are easier to understand, code, debug, and modify.

To help achieve this necessary outcome, the concept of **structured programming** becomes ever more important. Structured programming is simply a method of programming that follows a few basic rules that allow for much better code.

The concept of structured programming was proposed by Edsger Dijkstra in the late 1960's. His idea was that any programming problem can be solved using only three basic design structures:

1. the simple sequence of instructions that follow one another in a linear fashion;
2. the selection of one of two program paths based upon a tested condition;
3. an iterative process that allows instructions to be repeated as many times as necessary.

If these structures are used properly, the selection and iteration can be considered as elements in the simple sequence and each problem, at its elementary level, becomes a single linear design. Thus, every program, no matter how complicated, should flow from one task to another in a top-down fashion.

In this chapter, we will look at how structured programs can be designed by using three of the most commonly used design techniques: the systems chart, the structured flowchart, and structured pseudocode. There are many other techniques that might be used, such as HIPO (Hierarchical Input/Processing/Output) charts, Nassi–Shneiderman charts, and Warnier–Orr diagrams. You may actually prefer some of these other techniques. Unfortunately, there is never enough room in a textbook of this type to show the designs in all the available techniques. We therefore limit our designs to the three most widely used.

1-2

The Systems Chart

There are four major functions when we use computers: input, processing, output, and storage. When writing programs, we consider only the first three because storage is actually an element of either the input or the output function. That is, data is input from or output to storage.

In the first design technique we will discuss, the **systems chart**, we generally show one symbol (flowchart symbol) for each of these three functions (see Figure 1-1 for an example). For input, a disk symbol is generally used (Figure 1-2) and labeled as to the type of input file being used. If more than one input file is needed, two or more input symbols are used (Figure 1-3). A process symbol (Figure 1-4) is used to denote the program being created. Finally, a document symbol (Figure 1-5) is used to denote the output from the program if a report is generated. If a disk file is the output from the program, then another disk symbol is used for the output side of the chart.

The systems chart is used to show the overall concept of the program being created: the type of data being input and the type of output being generated. No details about the program or the layout of either the input or the output are specified. This detail design is left to be shown with some of the other design techniques.

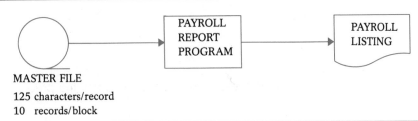

MASTER FILE

125 characters/record
10   records/block

Figure 1-1   An example of a systems chart detailing the input file, the program needed, and the type of output being generated.

MASTER FILE

125 characters/record
10   records/block

Figure 1-2   Illustration of a disk symbol with labeling indicating the disk file contents.

MASTER FILE

125 characters/record
10   records/block

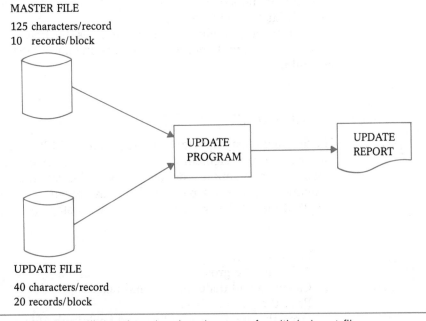

UPDATE FILE

40 characters/record
20 records/block

Figure 1-3   Illustration showing the use of multiple input files.

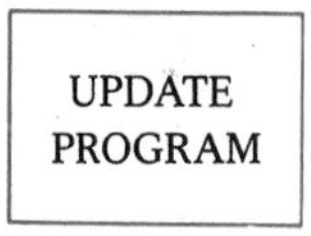

UPDATE
PROGRAM

Figure 1-4　Process symbol used to denote the program to be created.

UPDATE
REPORT

Figure 1-5　Illustration of a document symbol indicating the report to be generated.

1-3
Structured Flowcharts and Pseudocode

We will discuss **structured flowcharts** and **structured pseudocode** in the same section since they are basically the same type of design tool. The only real difference is that a flowchart is a picture of the design that pseudocode states in words only. A flowchart is a symbolic design of the logic necessary to create a program. Pseudocode, on the other hand, is simply the design written out in general, English-language format.

Before we can talk about the structures, we first need to look at the symbols we will be using to design our flowcharts. In Figure 1-6 you can see all the symbols we will use.

1-3-1　The SIMPLE SEQUENCE

The first and most important structure is the SIMPLE SEQUENCE. This is a structure where every element of the structure follows every other element in a top-down fashion. A simple example will best illustrate the concept. Suppose we need a routine to process a payroll check, as shown in the systems chart in Figure 1-7. That means that we need the following steps (shown in pseudocode):

Start
Input the record
Calculate the gross pay
Calculate and deduct FICA and taxes
Print the payroll check
Store the updated payroll record back in the file
End

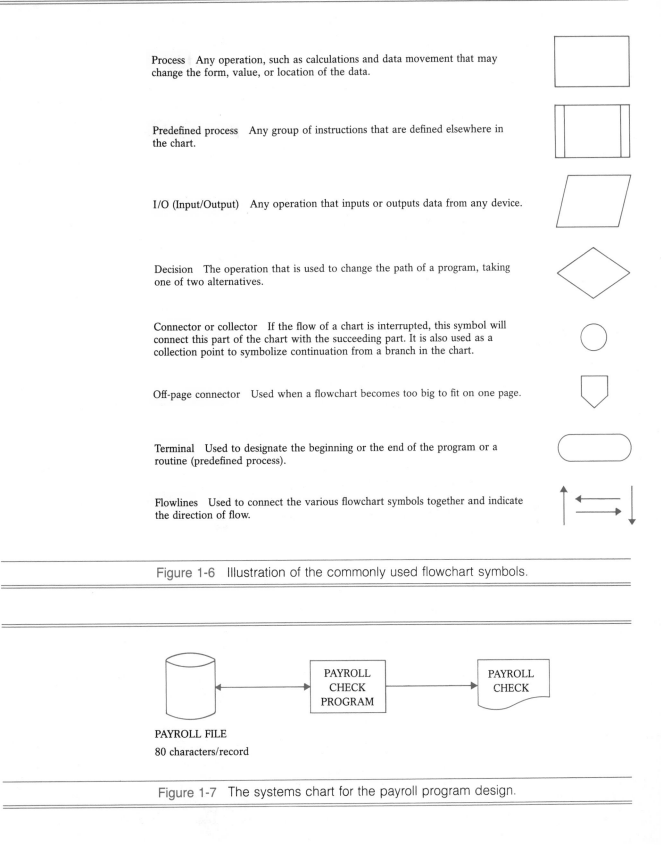

Process   Any operation, such as calculations and data movement that may change the form, value, or location of the data.

Predefined process   Any group of instructions that are defined elsewhere in the chart.

I/O (Input/Output)   Any operation that inputs or outputs data from any device.

Decision   The operation that is used to change the path of a program, taking one of two alternatives.

Connector or collector   If the flow of a chart is interrupted, this symbol will connect this part of the chart with the succeeding part. It is also used as a collection point to symbolize continuation from a branch in the chart.

Off-page connector   Used when a flowchart becomes too big to fit on one page.

Terminal   Used to designate the beginning or the end of the program or a routine (predefined process).

Flowlines   Used to connect the various flowchart symbols together and indicate the direction of flow.

Figure 1-6   Illustration of the commonly used flowchart symbols.

PAYROLL CHECK PROGRAM

PAYROLL CHECK

PAYROLL FILE
80 characters/record

Figure 1-7   The systems chart for the payroll program design.

Figure 1-8 shows the flowchart for this program design. Notice how neither the flowchart nor the pseudocode shows how the calculations are to be done or exactly what is to be printed or stored back into the file. The idea with a program design is that it is generic in nature. That is, it has nothing to do with the particular language you are going to use or the exact way that calculations are to be done. If you specify particular calculations in your design, your design loses all flexibility. It is much better to use a general format such as that shown; then if the percentages used change or something else happens that would change the way the calculations are performed, your design is still correct. Naturally, the program would have to be changed, but your design would not.

1-3-2   The DO-WHILE

The previous example is fine if all you ever want to produce is one payroll check. That's not the way programming works, however. It would be senseless to design a program that would do a particular task only once. It is important to have

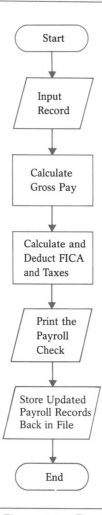

Figure 1-8   The flowchart for the first simple payroll example.

programs that are able to do a particular task any number of times. Thus, we have a need for another structure: one that allows an iterative process, or **loop**.

The most commonly used loop is the DO-WHILE (Figure 1-9). In this loop, the first thing that is done is the test. That is, the processing of the loop is done only when the test is true. When the test fails or is false, the flow passes out of the loop. Also notice the connector symbol at the top of the loop. This is simply used as a point of entry into the structure and a point to branch to for the processes of the loop. It does not represent an actual step in the structure, since the first step is the test.

Notice in Figure 1-9 that there is a dotted line drawn around the entire structure. This illustrates the idea that the entire structure is actually a single procedure and can be considered a single element in a SIMPLE SEQUENCE, as shown in Figure 1-10.

We saw the flowchart for the DO-WHILE; now we need to look at how we would design the pseudocode for the structure. The standard form of the pseudocode is

```
DO-WHILE test
        Processes
END-DO
```

Notice that the first thing in the loop is the test. The processes come after and are wholly contained within the loop. Notice also that the processes are indented to make the loop easier to see. If every element in the pseudocode is lined up, it is difficult to pick out the loops. Finally, at the end of the loop we put an END-DO statement to show us exactly where the loop ends and indicate that any further statements lie outside the loop.

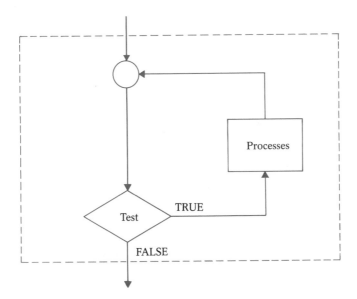

Figure 1-9   Illustration of the DO-WHILE loop. Note the use of the connector symbol to denote the continuation of the loop.

With a loop, we can now redesign our payroll program. If you recall, the pseudocode for the program (the flowchart is back in Figure 1-8) is

```
Start
Input the record
Calculate the gross pay
Calculate and deduct FICA and taxes
Print the payroll check
Store the updated payroll record back in the file
End
```

Now we need to add a loop so that we can process any number of checks. In order to use the loop successfully, we must include a test that determines when the loop is finished. If you recall the systems chart, the data being used in the program came from a disk file. Thus, if we continually read the data off the disk, eventually we will run out of data. In such cases, we will read an **end-of-data marker** that is automatically stored at the end of the records in the file. Since we will get an end-of-data marker when we read off the end of the file, we can test for this in our program. Thus, our test would be

DO-WHILE not end-of-file

That is, we will continue to process the data until we hit the end-of-file marker in the disk file.

Now we need to decide what elements of our original design should be within the loop. Naturally, all the calculation and output commands should be in the loop. Also, if we are going to get new information each time we do the calculations,

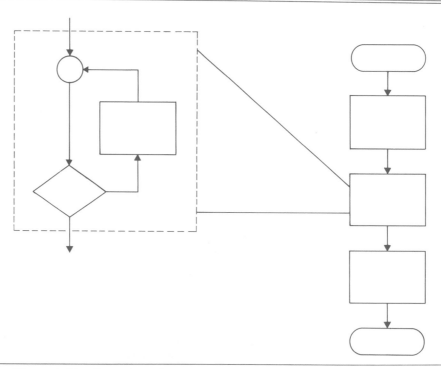

Figure 1-10   Illustration of the concept that every structure should be considered as nothing more than a single element in a SIMPLE SEQUENCE design.

the inputting of the data must be within the loop. Thus, our new design should look like the following (Figure 1-11 shows the flowchart):

Start
DO-WHILE not end-of-file
        Input the record
        Calculate the gross pay
        Calculate and deduct FICA and taxes
        Print the payroll check
        Store the updated payroll record back in the file
END-DO
End

Ah, but we have a problem. We are testing for an end-of-file marker in the DO-WHILE statement without having accessed the file. We can hardly test for something we don't have. We must input the data before we get into the loop.

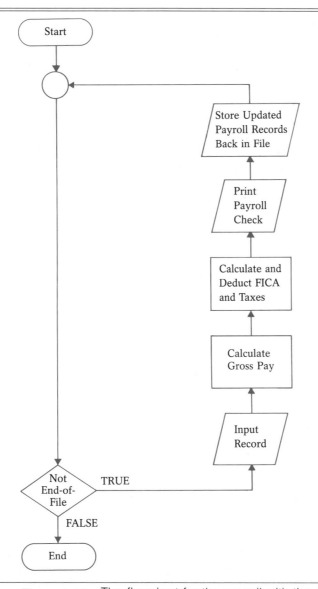

Figure 1-11   The flowchart for the payroll with the added DO-WHILE loop.

To accommodate this need, let's move the input statement outside the loop. The reconstructed design follows (see also Figure 1-12):

```
Start
Input the record  ← — — — — — — — — — — — — — — — — — — — — —  input is moved to here
DO-WHILE not end-of-file
        Calculate the gross pay
        Calculate and deduct FICA and taxes
        Print the payroll check
        Store the updated payroll record back in the file
END-DO
End
```

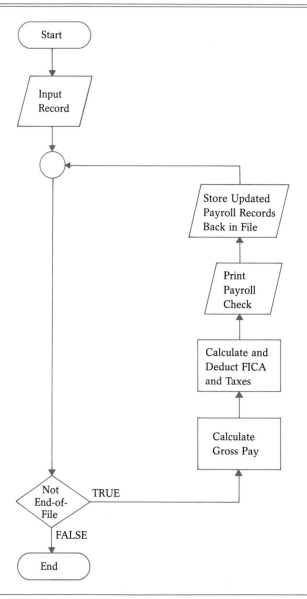

Figure 1-12   The flowchart for the reconstructed DO-WHILE payroll design.

Now we have a new problem. We do not have a file access within the loop anymore. Obviously this won't work. We need to have two input statements—one outside the loop for the first access and one inside the loop to keep the loop going. The proper way to design such a program (flowchart in Figure 1-13):

```
Start
Input the record  ← – – – – – – – – – – – – – – – – – – – – – – – – – – – – – – – – ⌐
DO-WHILE not end-of-file                                                            |
        Calculate the gross pay                                                     |
        Calculate and deduct FICA and taxes                                         |——— two
        Print the payroll check                                                     |    inputs
        Store the updated payroll record back in the file                           |
        Input the record  ← – – – – – – – – – – – – – – – – – – – – – – – – – – – – – ⌐
END-DO
End
```

Notice that the input statement was moved to the end of the loop rather than the beginning where it was before. Naturally we cannot input new data when we first come into the loop. We have just input the data before entering the loop; if we do it again right after we come in, we will lose the first record in the file. We must have the input within the loop at the end of the loop.

A couple more commands are generally needed in a file access program like the one we have been discussing. Before data can be accessed in a disk file, the file must be opened. Then, when you have finished your processing, the file must be closed. Of course, the open and close statements must be placed outside the loop since you only want them to be done once. The final design, with the additional commands (flowchart in Figure 1-14), is

```
Start
Open the file  ← – – – – – – – – – – – – – – – – – – – – – – – – – – – – – – – – – – ⌐
Input the record                                                                    |
DO-WHILE not end-of-file                                                            |
        Calculate the gross pay                                                     |
        Calculate and deduct FICA and taxes                                         |——— new
        Print the payroll check                                                     |    statements
        Store the updated payroll record back in the file                           |
        Input the record                                                            |
END-DO                                                                              |
Close the file  ← – – – – – – – – – – – – – – – – – – – – – – – – – – – – – – – – – – ⌐
End
```

1-3-3   The IF-THEN-ELSE

A third structure, the selection, is often needed. Take our payroll example. Normally, payroll is calculated with overtime pay. Our example doesn't show this. In order to calculate overtime, you need to determine which employees have more than 40 hours. You do this with the selection, or IF-THEN-ELSE, structure. The basic design of the IF-THEN-ELSE structure (Figure 1-15, page 16) is

```
IF test THEN
      True action
ELSE
      False action
END-IF
```

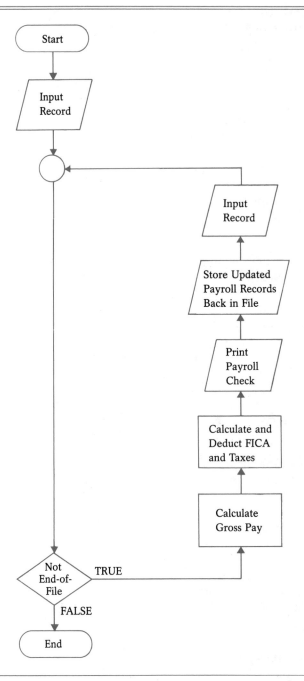

Figure 1-13   The flowchart for the corrected DO-WHILE payroll design.

Notice that there are two possible actions to be taken in the structure. If the test is true (THEN), the right branch is taken and the processes found there are done (of course, the true option does not have to be the right branch). If the test is false (ELSE), the left branch is taken and those processes are done. The connector symbol at the bottom of the flowchart structure serves only to show that the branches are collected at the point where the exit from the structure is taken.

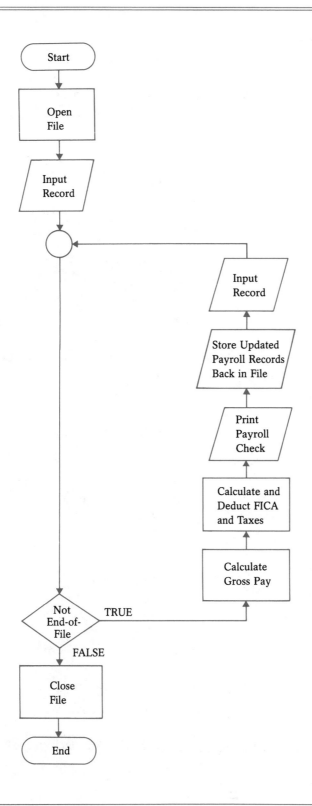

Figure 1-14   The flowchart with the added open and close statements.

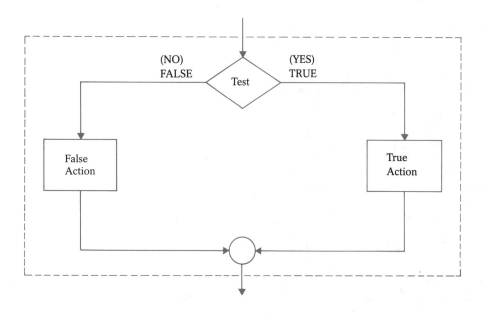

Figure 1-15   Illustration of the basic design for the IF-THEN-ELSE structure.

Once again, there is a dotted line around the structure to illustrate that the entire structure can be thought of as a single step in the SIMPLE SEQUENCE. Also, indentation is used in the pseudocode to allow better visualization of the structure as well as the END-IF.

   If we were to add overtime processing to our example design, it would look like the following (flowchart in Figure 1-16):

```
Start
Open the file
Input the record
DO-WHILE not end-of-file
        IF hours are over 40 THEN                                  ⎫
                Calculate the gross pay and overtime      ⎪ new
        ELSE                                                        ⎬ IF
                Calculate the gross pay                        ⎪ test
        END-IF                                                      ⎭
        Calculate and deduct FICA and taxes
        Print the payroll check
        Store the updated payroll record back in the file
        Input the record
END-DO
Close the file
End
```

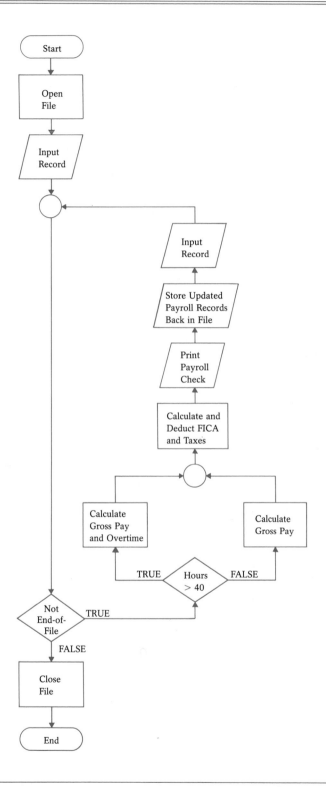

Figure 1-16   The flowchart with an IF-THEN-ELSE.

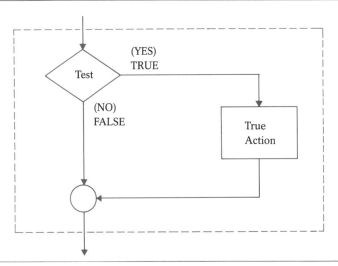

Figure 1-17   Illustration of the standard design for the null ELSE.

Occasionally we have need for an IF-THEN-ELSE test but don't have two actions to carry out. That is, we have no need for the ELSE. In such cases, we have a **null ELSE**. The design of a null ELSE follows (flowchart in Figure 1-17):

```
IF test THEN
      True action
(ELSE)
END-IF
```

We go ahead in the pseudocode and list the ELSE with parentheses around it so that, when we examine the pseudocode, we don't think that maybe we forgot to put in the ELSE. This way we are sure the design is complete.

As an example of how a null ELSE might be used, suppose we have life insurance for our employees and the insurance company wants a list of all the female employees for some studies it is doing. Since our file has a code designating female and male employees, the request is easy to carry out. We merely design a program that tests the code and prints the name on the list if the code designates a female. The design for such a program follows (flowchart in Figure 1-18):

```
Start
Open the file
Input the record
DO-WHILE not end-of-file
      IF sex code is female THEN          null
            Print the name on the list    ELSE
      (ELSE)                              test
      END-IF
      Input the record
END-DO
Close the file
End
```

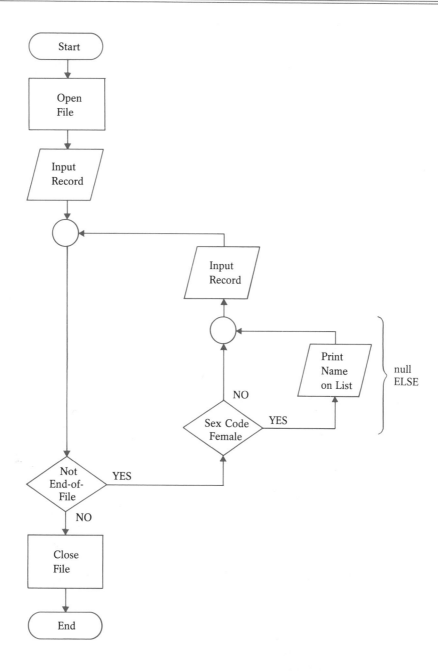

Figure 1-18   Flowchart of the null ELSE test for the female sex code.

Now we have something else that would probably be used for such a program. Most reports that are printed have headings at the top of the report and possibly a total at the bottom. If we needed headings and a count of the number of employees printed on the list, we would need to add four statements as shown below (flowchart in Figure 1-19):

```
Start
Open the file
Print the headings←--------------┐
Initialize the counter←----------┐│
Input the record                 ││        new
DO-WHILE not end-of-file         ││     statements
      IF sex code is female THEN ││
            Print the name on the list
            Increment the counter←----┘│
      (ELSE)                           │
      END-IF                           │
      Input the record                 │
END-DO                                 │
Print the total count←-----------------┘
Close the file
End
```

1-3-4   Modular Design

Another structure technique is to break a program up into **modules**. A module is simply a group of code that is executed by being referenced elsewhere in the program. The previous design problem is a simple example of using a module. We will take the code within the DO-WHILE and make a module out of it as follows (flowchart in Figure 1-20):

```
Start
Open the file
Print the headings
Initialize the counter
Input the record
DO-WHILE not end-of-file
      Perform calc-routine ←----------- where routine was
END-DO
Print the total count
Close the file
End
```

```
Start calc-routine
IF sex code is female THEN
      Print the name on the list
      Increment the counter       the new module created from
(ELSE)                            the calculation routine
END-IF
Input the record
End calc-routine
```

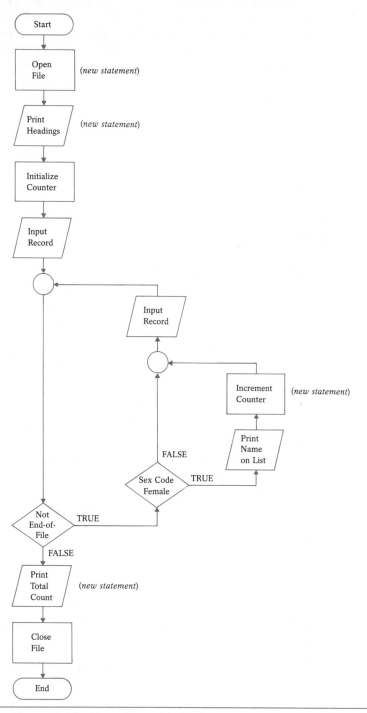

Figure 1-19   Flowchart with the headings and counter added.

If you think that this program is no easier to understand (and possibly more confusing) than the previous one, you may be right. Many times, however, languages are set up so that the easiest way to do a loop is to set it up within a module. COBOL is like that. Also, it is often easier to follow and find errors in programs that are broken up into modules. There is less code to study as a group. Other times, large programs can be broken down into modules with the modules coded separately. This can occasionally make the coding problem a bit more manageable.

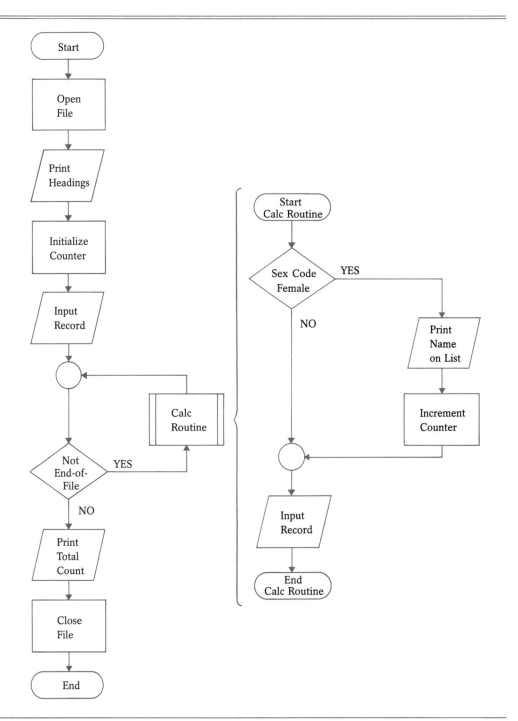

Figure 1-20   Flowchart broken into two separate modules.

1-3-5   Check Your Logic

One of the best ways to reduce the number of logic errors in your programs is to make sure your design is as error free as possible before you translate it into program code. The best way to accomplish this is to **desk check** the design. This is the process of "playing computer" with your design. That is, you set up the type of data to be used in your program and then go through your design as if you were the computer. An illustration will help you understand the concept.

Take the following derivative of the design we have been using. There is a very commonly created error in this design. Study the design for a minute and see if you can find the error before continuing.

```
Start
Open the file
Input the record
DO-WHILE not end-of-file
        IF sex code is female THEN
              Print the name on the list
        ELSE
              Input the record
        END-IF
END-DO
Close the file
End
```

Did you find the error? We shall see. To desk check the design, we need to set up some records to be processed by the program. Let's use the following records set up as a file area, a processing area, and a print area:

File Area	Processing Area	Print Area
Male record		
Male record		
Female record		
Male record		
Female record		
Male record		

Notice that we didn't specify any of the records other than what we actually needed—which records are male and which are female. That's the only thing the program is testing for.

Now, let's start the testing procedure. The first thing the design does is open the file. No problem there. That simply gives us access to the records.

Next is the first input statement. We will move the record out of our file area into the processing area as shown:

File Area	Processing Area	Print Area
	Male record	
Male record		
Female record		
Male record		
Female record		
Male record		

The next step is the DO-WHILE statement. Have we detected the end-of-file? No, of course not. Thus, the loop begins. Now we test the sex code, and since it is a male record, the test is false so we fall through to the false (ELSE) processing. Here we are told to input another record. (Keep in mind that the first male record is no longer in the processing area since the second record will overwrite the area. We generally leave the records in the column for reference.) Our program areas will now become

File Area	Processing Area	Print Area
	Male record	
	Male record	
Female record		
Male record		
Female record		
Male record		

We hit the end of the IF test and then the end of the DO-WHILE so we loop back to the test. No end-of-file yet, so the loop begins again. The test is again false so we get the third record. Our areas become

File Area	Processing Area	Print Area
	Male record	
	Male record	
	Female record	
Male record		
Female record		
Male record		

Now we have a difference. When the loop begins again, the test is true. We will print the record. The areas will now change to

File Area	Processing Area	Print Area
	Male record	
	Male record	
		Female record
Male record		
Female record		
Male record		

Since the test was true, we do not do the ELSE part of the test and thus we hit the end of the test, the end of the loop, and start at the top of the loop again. Notice, however, that when we try to test the record to see if it is the end-of-file, we have no record in the processing area. The problem is that, because we put the input statement in the ELSE part of the IF test, there is no input should the test be true. Thus we would continually process the first female record. Our program would be in a non-ending loop.

What we noticed was that there was no record in the processing area. In reality, of course, the female record is still in the processing area. But moving the record the way we did really points to the fact that something is wrong.

How do we fix the design now that we have discovered the error? Easy. We simply move the input statement out of the IF test and put it between the END-IF and the END-DO where it was before, as shown below:

```
Start
Open the file
Input the record
DO-WHILE not end-of-file
        IF sex code is female THEN
              Print the name on the list
        ELSE
              Input the record    ⟵ ────────── move this statement
        END-IF                                            ↓
        Input the record ⟵ ─────────────── to here
END-DO
Close the file
End
```

Again, this error is very common in programming. Whenever one of your programs becomes caught in a non-ending loop, this is the type of thing to check for first. Of course, if you desk check your design *before* you begin to code it, you will probably catch all errors of this type. Desk checking is probably the most important step in the entire programming process. Those who shortchange this part of the design phase will most likely regret it later on.

1-4
Designing Input and Output Specifications

When you are a programmer, the input and output specifications you will need to create your program will often be designed for you by the systems analyst. Sometimes, however, you will need to design your own. Even if you don't design your own, you should understand how the design is created in order to understand what you are looking at when the specifications are given to you.

1-4-1 Input Specifications

Data that is stored in a disk file must be input precisely as it is stored on the disk; otherwise the fields in your program will not have the proper data in them. In order to lay out the file, you can use a **record layout table** similar to that shown in Figure 1-21.

Sample File					
Field Description	*Position*	*Length*	:	*Dec*	*Type*
Name	1–20	20	:		Non-numeric
Address	21–40	20	:		Non-numeric
City	41–55	15	:		Non-numeric
State	56–57	2	:		Non-numeric
Zip code	58–62	5	:		Non-numeric
Amount	63–70	8	:	2	Numeric
Filler	71–80	10	:		Non-numeric
Record Length = 80					

Figure 1-21   Illustration of how a record layout table is used. Notice that the beginning and ending points of each field are listed, along with the length of the field. Also, the number of decimal positions for the one numeric field is listed. It is also important to list the record length and add up the lengths of the fields to be sure the two agree.

There are a few things of note. First, decimal points themselves are not generally stored in the file; only the number of decimal positions is stored. Second, fields not needed for the particular application you are doing are either left blank or labeled as FILLER. It is important to include the exact length of the entire record and then total the field lengths to be sure they agree. Otherwise, a field might end up specified as the wrong length and errors might occur.

As you might expect, if the output produced by a program is to be disk output, a record layout form is used to design it also.

1-4-2   Output Specifications

A **printer spacing chart** similar to that shown in Figure 1-22 is used to design the printed output a program is going to produce. Notice that the form shows exactly what column each entry is to appear in. It also shows how many lines are to be left blank between each of the printed lines. The labels on the left side (H, D, and T) represent the type of print being shown as heading, detail line, and total line. There are two different types of headings: a page heading and column headings.

A **detail line** is the printing of the information coming from the data file. You should always show at least two detail lines on your chart to show the line spacing. If the detail lines are to be double spaced, you could not tell if only one detail line is specified on the form. Notice that the detail lines are shown with X's rather than with actual data (and that you use a line instead of entering all the X's). This is done because your printer spacing chart should show the maximum size of each of the fields to be printed, and if you used actual data, it would generally not fill up the field.

The chart shows a continuation mark (wavy line) under each of the fields in the detail lines. This is to indicate that the report continues indefinitely.

Finally, in the total line, only the fields to be totaled are shown. It would make no sense to show fields on the total line that were not to be totaled.

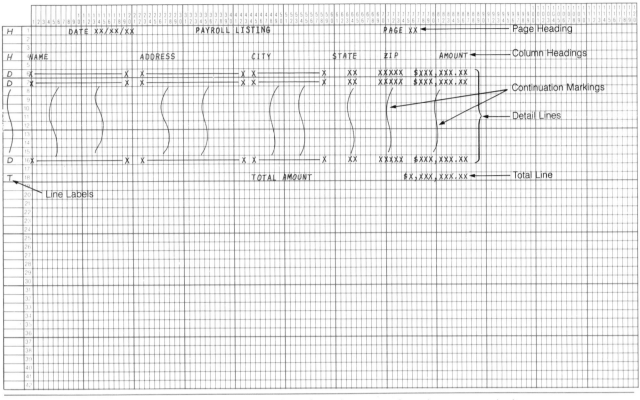

Figure 1-22   Illustration of a printer spacing chart report design.

1-5

Summary

1. In recent history, computer costs have gone down while personnel costs have skyrocketed. It is important now to have programmers who are familiar with structured programming techniques so that programs will be well designed and easy to maintain.

2. Structured programming is built around three basic design structures: the simple sequence, the selection, and the iterative procedure.

3. When we are designing programs we use several tools, the first of which is the systems chart. This is a chart which shows what input is brought into the program and what output is generated. There are no specifics about the I/O or the processing to be carried out on that I/O.

4. Structured flowcharts are a pictorial representation of the logic flow in the program. Structured pseudocode, on the other hand, is the same design written out in general, English-language format.

5. The first programming structure we need to understand is the SIMPLE SEQUENCE. The elements in this structure simply follow each other in a top-down fashion.

6. The DO-WHILE is the loop, or iterative structure. The first thing done in the loop is the test. If the test is true, the loop continues; if it is false, the loop terminates. When using the end-of-file marker to determine the end of the loop, it is imperative that you have an input statement before the loop and another within the loop.

7. The third structure is the IF-THEN-ELSE, or selection structure. This is simply a test in which the processing is directed to take one of the two program paths, depending upon the result of the test. If the test is true, the THEN part of the structure is used; if it is false, the ELSE is used. If there is no need for the ELSE part of the structure, we have what is called a null ELSE.

8. A program is often broken up into smaller groups of code called modules. Sometimes this is done because the programming language dictates it, but it is also done because it makes the programs easier to understand and modify.

9. Input specifications for what input is to be used in a program are depicted in a record layout table. Output specifications are created using a printer spacing chart.

1-6

Glossary

Desk checking   The process of checking through your program design manually to detect any errors before you code the design into a programming language.

Detail line   The line on a report that shows the data input from the file.

DO-WHILE   The most commonly used structure to create a loop.

End-of-data marker   The marker put on the end of a data file by the operating system. This can be checked for when inputting records from a file.

IF-THEN-ELSE   The selection structure used to determine which of two possible paths the program will take.

Loop   A process in which instructions are reused an indefinite number of times.

Modules   Small sections of a program that are executed from another area of the program.

Null ELSE   The IF-THEN-ELSE structure when there is no ELSE needed.

Printer spacing chart   The form used for designing printed output for a program.

Record layout table   The form used for designing input for a program.

SIMPLE SEQUENCE   The structure in which every function follows every other function in a top-down, linear fashion.

Structured pseudocode   Generic, English-language formatted statements used to design the logic in a program.

Structured flowcharts   Symbols used to illustrate the flow of logic in a program.

Structured programming   A method of programming that follows a few simple rules that allow a programmer to write much better code.

Systems chart   A design technique used to show the overall concept of the program to be written. It generally shows the type of input and output to be used in the program without getting specific about what the I/O actually looks like.

1-7
Quick Quiz

Cover the answers with a blank sheet of paper and test yourself. Questions 1–15 are true or false questions, 16–20 are multiple choice, and 21–25 are fill-in-the-blank.

T F **1.** Structured programming was an idea first formulated by Edsger Dijkstra.

T F **2.** A disk symbol is generally used for systems charts rather than regular flowcharts.

T F **3.** A process symbol is generally used to depict the output in a systems chart.

T F **4.** A flowchart is basically a picture of the program structure.

T F **5.** Program design should be very specific so that translation to COBOL is as easy as possible.

T F **6.** The IF-THEN-ELSE structure is the implementation of the loop structure.

T F **7.** We drew a dotted line around the structures in the book to show that each structure can be thought of as a single step in the simple sequence.

T F **8.** Every DO-WHILE loop that inputs data from a file must have two input statements.

T F **9.** If we are going to use a counter in our loop, it should be initialized outside the loop.

T F **10.** If we do not need both paths on an IF-THEN-ELSE, we would use the null THEN structure.

T F **11.** Systems charts are usually designed by a systems analyst.

T F **12.** Empty fields on the printer spacing chart are generally labeled as FILLER.

T F **13.** There are two types of headings.

T F **14.** The idea of structured programming is a fairly recent development.

T F **15.** A parallelogram is the shape used to depict I/O in a flowchart.

_____ **16.** Which of the following is not a type of print line typically found on a printer spacing chart?

    (a) heading   **(c)** detail

    (b) total   **(d)** All are found.

_____ **17.** Which symbol is not part of the typical DO-WHILE flowchart?

    (a) connector   **(c)** decision

    (b) I/O   **(d)** They all are.

_____ **18.** Which of the following structures does not directly use the decision test?

    (a) SIMPLE SEQUENCE   **(c)** DO-WHILE

    (b) IF-THEN-ELSE   **(d)** They all do.

_____ **19.** Which of the following commands is always necessary when processing records from a disk file?

    (a) open   **(c)** input

    (b) output (or store)   **(d)** All are necessary.

_____ **20.** When pseudocoding an IF test, which of the following statements is not always needed?

    (a) IF   **(c)** ELSE

    (b) END-IF   **(d)** They all are needed.

21. The systems chart generally uses three flowchart symbols: the _____ symbol for input, the _____ symbol for indicating the program, and the _____ symbol for output.
22. When accessing data from a disk file, we can determine when we run out of data by checking for the _____ .
23. The DO-WHILE is the _____ structure, while the IF-THEN-ELSE is the implementation of the _____ structure.
24. When you use a disk file, the file must be _____ before processing of the records can begin and must be _____ when processing is finished.
25. An input specification is depicted using a _____ and an output specification is shown using a _____ .

══════ 1-8 ══════════════════
Answers to Quick Quiz

1. T
2. T
3. F (The document symbol is typically used for output.)
4. T
5. F (Design should be as general as possible so that, when program changes are necessary, the design will not have to be redone.)
6. F (The DO-WHILE is the loop; the IF-THEN-ELSE is the selection.)
7. T
8. F (Only if the test for the loop is for the end-of-data marker.)
9. T (At least most of the time. Remember, however, that there are very few absolutes in programming.)
10. F (The null ELSE.)
11. T
12. F (That is done on the record layout table. Blank spaces on the printer spacing charts are simply left blank.)
13. T (Page and column.)
14. F (But it is only recently that many programmers have begun using structured programming techniques.)
15. T
16. d
17. d
18. a (The SIMPLE SEQUENCE can contain the other structures but does not directly use the test.)
19. a (Only the open statement is always needed. If we are creating a new file, we do not input, and if we are simply printing a report, we do not output to the file.)
20. d (You always need all three. Even the null ELSE uses the (ELSE) notation.)
21. disk, process, document
22. end-of-file marker
23. loop, selection
24. opened, closed
25. record layout table, printer spacing chart

1-9
Questions to Aid Understanding

1. Name the three basic design structures originally proposed by Dijkstra and the formal structures they have become.
2. Illustrate the basic design of the SIMPLE SEQUENCE, DO-WHILE, IF-THEN-ELSE, and null ELSE with a flowchart and pseudocode.
*3. Explain why two input statements are needed for a DO-WHILE when the test is for the end-of-data marker.
4. Explain how modules can be a useful programming technique.
*5. Explain why structured programming is such a good technique.
6. List and describe the use of at least five flowchart symbols.
*7. Explain why it is important to be able to consider an IF-THEN-ELSE structure as a part of the SIMPLE SEQUENCE.
8. Explain why a loop is generally needed in a program.
9. Explain how an end-of-data marker can be useful.
*10. Explain why desk checking is important.

1-10
Design Problems

In the following design problems, if you are asked to design a program, do it using both a flowchart and pseudocode unless your instructor specifies otherwise.

1. Using a record layout table, design a record of employee information that contains the following fields with the specified lengths:

Employee ID	4
Employee name	20
Address	20
City	15
State	2
Zip code	5
Amount due	6
Date of last purchase	6

*2. Using a record layout table, design a record of student information that contains the following fields with the specified lengths:

Social security number	9
Name	20
Major	3
GPA	1.2 (two decimal positions)
Number of hours taken	3.1 (one decimal position)
Status flag	1 (1 for frosh, 2 for soph, etc.)
Veteran flag	1 (1 if veteran, 0 if not)
Filler	20 (left for later expansion)

3. Using a printer spacing chart, design a report for the data file you would create with the record layout in exercise 1. Use a total line for the appropriate field(s).

*4. Using a printer spacing chart, design a report for the data file you would create with the record layout in exercise 2. Use a total line for the appropriate field(s).

5. Show the systems chart that would depict the program for exercise 4.

6. Design a program to print the report you would create using the printer spacing chart in exercise 3. Use both pseudocode and flowcharting techniques.

*7. Design a program that will input records from the user who is keying the data into a terminal. The data should be input and then stored in a file. (Hint: The user should indicate to the program to halt execution of the input by keying some type of exit code. Your design should test for this exit code.)

8. Design a printer spacing chart and a program that will input the file created from the layout in exercise 1 and print it out in three-across, mailing label format. The labels should look like the following:

```
Name 1                    Name 2                    Name 3
Address 1                 Address 2                 Address 3
City 1, State 1  Zip 1    City 2, State 2  Zip 2    City 3, State 3  Zip 3
```

9. Use the printer spacing chart designed in Figure 1-23 to design another printer spacing chart switching the locations of the name and customer number fields. In between the zip code and the credit limit fields add an amount field (XX,XXX.XX) and create a total line at the bottom of the report.

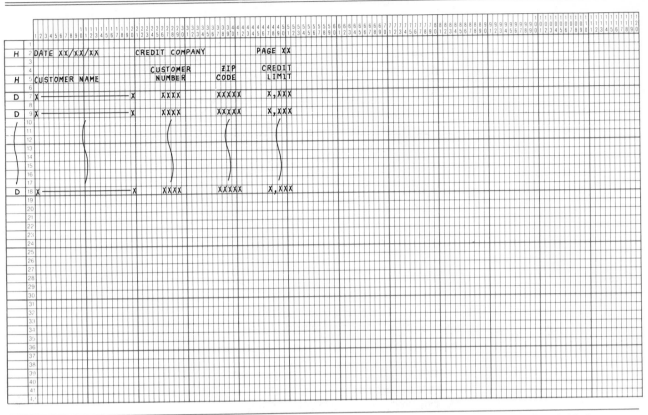

Figure 1-23   The printer spacing chart to be modified for exercise 1-10-9.

OBJECTIVES After completing Chapter 2 you should be able to

1. describe the format and usage of the
   (a) OPEN statement
   (b) CLOSE statement
   (c) READ statement (and READ . . . INTO)
   (d) WRITE statement (and WRITE . . . FROM)
   (e) PERFORM statement (three forms)
   (f) MOVE statement
   (g) ADD statement
   (h) SUBTRACT statement
   (i) MULTIPLY statement
   (j) DIVIDE statement
   (k) IF statement
   (l) READY TRACE statement
   (m) DISPLAY statement
   (n) EXHIBIT statement
   (o) INSPECT statement
2. explain the purpose of the AT END clause of the READ statement;
3. explain the purpose of data editing;
4. demonstrate by creating PIC clauses the usage of the different editing features shown in the chapter;
5. explain the purpose of redefining a field;
6. explain the purpose of the REMAINDER, ROUNDED, and ON SIZE ERROR clauses;
7. explain why a programmer might choose to use the COMPUTE statement rather than the more explanatory keyword calculations;
8. explain what happens if you do not mark a field to store a positive or negative sign;
9. explain what logic errors are and why they are so difficult to find;
10. explain the purpose of the NEXT SENTENCE clause;
11. explain what a control break program is and how the control field and hold field are used;
12. list at least four statements that are needed in a control break routine;
13. explain the purpose of the READY TRACE, EXHIBIT, and DISPLAY statements.

CHAPTER 2

REVIEW OF STRUCTURED COBOL CONCEPTS

2-1
Introduction

Before you begin any advanced programming course, it is always a good idea to review the concepts and techniques you learned in the past. This chapter will reintroduce you to all the COBOL concepts you should have learned in a beginning course. It can also act as a reference should you need a quick reminder of any topics in the future.

We will begin this chapter with a brief look at the standard COBOL command format. Then we will do a quick overview of the four divisions that make up each COBOL program. Next we will systematically cover all the instructions that the beginning COBOL programmer should be familiar with. Along the way we will look at several techniques that can make your COBOL programming better.

2-2
Standard COBOL Command Format

COBOL is a standardized language, and the presentation of its command syntax has also been standardized. This book will follow the standard conventions for presenting command formats, as shown in the following examples.

Illustration 1:

> SELECT file-name ASSIGN TO external-name

Illustration 2:

$$\text{MOVE} \left\{ \begin{array}{l} \text{field-name-1} \\ \text{literal} \\ \text{figurative constant} \end{array} \right\} \text{TO field-name-2, [field-name-3, } \ldots \text{]}$$

Reserved words will be shown in uppercase letters. If they are required for the command, they will also be underlined. In Illustration 1, SELECT and ASSIGN are required while TO, since it is not underlined, is optional.

Lowercase words signify the parts of the command that the programmer must supply. In Illustration 1, a file-name and an external-name must be included and are to be supplied by the programmer. When file-names and other programmer-chosen field-names are used, they must be constructed according to the following guidelines:

- They must not be spelled like reserved words. For example, a file-name of ASSIGN would not be allowed.
- They must be 1 to 30 characters long.
- The only valid characters are letters, numeric digits, and the dash. No other characters are allowed, including the blank. A blank imbedded in a field-name would cause the field-name to be treated as two field-names.
- All names must contain at least one letter, with the exception of paragraph and section names (programmer supplied), which may be all numbers.
- Names may not begin or end with a dash.

Square brackets, [ ], are used to indicate optional entries. In Illustration 2, field-name-2 must be there, but inclusion of field-name-3 is the programmer's choice.

When one of several different clauses may be used, whether required or not, the clauses are enclosed with braces, { }. For example, Illustration 2 shows that field-name-1, a literal, or a figurative constant may be used as the object of the MOVE statement. Any of them may be used. But, since there are no square brackets, *one* of them *must* be used.

Some punctuation may be required, such as most periods, while other punctuation may be optional—commas and semicolons always are. Ellipsis points (. . .) indicate that as many additional options may be used as are needed. Illustration 2 shows ellipsis points after field-name-3, which indicates that field-name-4 and as many more fields as are needed are allowed.

2-3
The Four COBOL Divisions

COBOL requires the use of four divisions: the IDENTIFICATION DIVISION, the ENVIRONMENT DIVISION, the DATA DIVISION, and the PROCEDURE DIVISION. Each has specific entries and rules that must be followed.

2-3-1   The IDENTIFICATION DIVISION

The IDENTIFICATION DIVISION, which has no effect on the execution of the program, is used to supply information to the computer system and comments to the programmer. The IDENTIFICATION DIVISION is divided into the following paragraphs:

```
IDENTIFICATION DIVISION.
PROGRAM-ID.            program-name.
[AUTHOR.               [comment] . . . ]
[DATE-WRITTEN.         [comment] . . . ]
[DATE-COMPILED.        [comment] . . . ]
[INSTALLATION.         [comment] . . . ]
[SECURITY.             [comment] . . . ]
```

Only the division name and the PROGRAM-ID paragraph are required. Most programmers, instead of using the other entries in the IDENTIFICATION DIVISION, will code a section at the beginning of the program using an asterisk in column 7 to create comment lines. Frequently used comments include the author of the program, the purpose of the program, the date the program was put into production, the date of the last change, who made the last change, and other notations. For student programs, it is useful to have a detailed comment layout, such as Figure 2-1, drawn out on a COBOL coding form. We suggest that all students use this layout when turning in their programs.

2-3-2   The ENVIRONMENT DIVISION

The ENVIRONMENT DIVISION supplies information concerning the hardware being used for the program. Its entries depend upon the type of computer equipment being used at the installation. All example programs in this textbook will use entries for an IBM OS type of computer. This is the only division where there will be any compiler differences. All other entries follow the ANS standards and can be used in any compiler that follows those standards.

The ENVIRONMENT DIVISION has two sections: the CONFIGURATION SECTION and the INPUT–OUTPUT SECTION. The CONFIGURATION SECTION is used to name the computer that the program was created and used on. Its format is

CONFIGURATION SECTION.
SOURCE-COMPUTER.   computer-name.
OBJECT-COMPUTER.   computer-name.

COBOL Coding Form

SYSTEM		PUNCHING INSTRUCTIONS / PAGE OF
PROGRAM		GRAPHIC
PROGRAMMER	DATE	PUNCH / CARD FORM #

SEQUENCE / COBOL STATEMENT / IDENTIFICATION

```
01  ***                                                                  ***
02  ***                                                                  ***
03  *
04  *
05  *
06  *   PROGRAM NAME:
07  *
08  *   PROGRAMMER NAME:
09  *
10  *   SOCIAL SECURITY NUMBER:
11  *
12  *   DUE DATE:
13  *
14  *   DESCRIPTION:
15  *
16  *
17  *
18  ***                                                                  ***
19  ***                                                                  ***
20
```

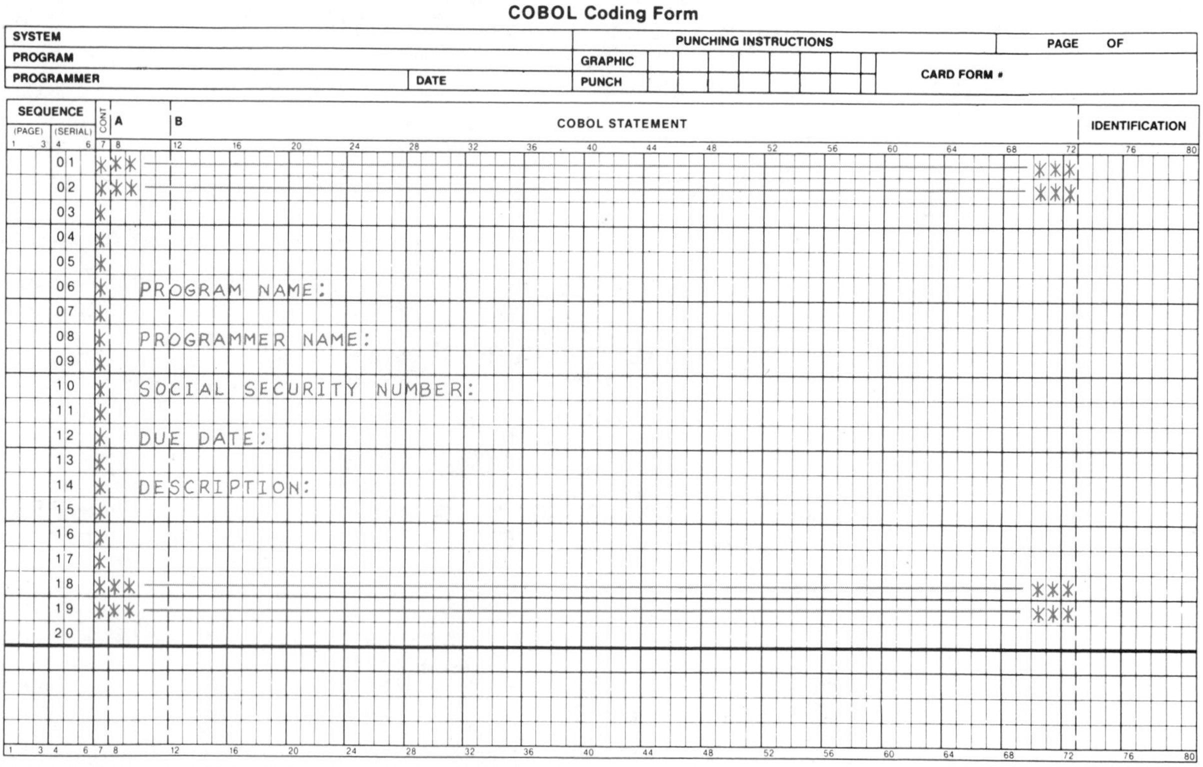

Figure 2-1   Illustration of suggested comment section to be used at the beginning of all programming assignments.

Some computer systems allow the CONFIGURATION SECTION to be omitted.

The **INPUT–OUTPUT SECTION**, which is optional but rarely omitted, is used to specify the input and output files in the program. If this section is used, the FILE-CONTROL paragraph is required.

In the **FILE-CONTROL** paragraph we identify the input and output files using a **SELECT** clause. The form of the SELECT clause is generally of two types, one as simple as

> SELECT file-name ASSIGN TO external-name.

or the other, with a more extensive external-name,

Symbolic device—device type—device number—organization [—programmer-name]

The symbolic device is the SYS number, such as SYS001 or SYS006. The device type is the two-digit code UR for unit-record, UT for utility, or DA for direct access. The device number, supplied by the computer manufacturer, might be 1403 printer or 3340 disk drive or the like. The organization is the type of file being accessed—an S for sequential, an I for indexed, an R for random, or a D for direct access. The programmer-name is optional on most computer systems. A sample of the external-name might be SYS001-UT-3340-S.

On IBM OS systems (as used throughout this book), a simpler external-name is used. We simply need the device type, the organization, and the external file-name. A sample would be UT-S-PAYROLL.

2-3-3 The DATA DIVISION

The **DATA DIVISION**, which describes and defines all the data fields you are going to use in your program, contains four sections: the FILE SECTION, the WORKING-STORAGE SECTION, the REPORT SECTION, and the LINKAGE SECTION. We will discuss the FILE SECTION and WORKING-STORAGE SECTION here. The other two sections are discussed in Chapters 10 and 11, respectively.

FILE SECTION Every file that is listed in a SELECT clause must be listed in the **FILE SECTION**. The characteristics of the files are described in the FILE SECTION, along with each type of record and all the fields in the records.

Each file listed in the FILE SECTION begins with an FD, or **file description** sentence. The beginning clause of the FD sentence is the FD itself. It is followed (in any order) by,

- the required LABEL RECORD(S) clause, which is either STANDARD or OMITTED. It describes the type of labels that are used for magnetic media. If you are not using magnetic media, the clause must be OMITTED.
- the RECORD CONTAINS clause, which is optional and specifies the number of characters found in the record.
- the optional BLOCK CONTAINS clause, which specifies the number of records to be stored as a block.
- the final clause in the FD, which is the optional DATA RECORD(S) clause. It is used as documentation to assign a name to the record format or formats used.

The FD defines the file to the computer. To describe the record, we use a record description, which begins with a level number of 01. All fields are considered subordinate to the record itself and are coded on levels with numbers higher than 01—from 02 to 49. The level number is followed by a record-name.

Two types of data items may be listed: elementary items and group items. An elementary item is one that is not subdefined into different, smaller fields and so has no levels below it. If the item is a group item, it is subdefined, thus having levels below it.

All elementary items must be defined as to type and length of field. A PIC-TURE (or, more commonly, PIC) clause is used to define the type of field: A for alphabetic (seldom used), X for non-numeric, or 9 for numeric. The number of symbols shown in the PIC clause designates the length of the field; for example, PIC XXXX [or PIC X(4)] means a non-numeric field four characters long. The total of the lengths of all the fields must add up to the number in the RECORD CONTAINS clause (if it is used). The reserved word FILLER can be used to designate any fields in the record being read that are not going to be accessed in any way in the program.

Numeric fields that have decimal positions contain a V at the location of the decimal. This V requires no storage space in the computer; it is only an implied decimal point.

When fields are defined for printing, typically the field will be edited or coded so that, among other things, decimal points line up, commas are printed, and leading zeros are dropped. The most frequently used editing features:

■ Zero suppression, or **truncation** of leading zeros, is accomplished with the Z edit character.

■ Commas and decimal positions are indicated by a comma and a decimal point being placed in the appropriate position in the PIC clause.

■ Either a fixed or a floating dollar sign may be used. The fixed dollar sign is indicated by one dollar sign being placed in the PIC clause. The floating dollar sign is created by several dollar signs being used. The dollar sign will print one character to the right of the right-most signficant digit.

■ Check protection allows the asterisk (*) to be used as a fill character to keep anyone from changing the amount of a check.

■ Signs can be printed when the number is either positive or negative. If we use a negative sign in the PIC clause (on either end of the field) a negative sign will be printed if the number is negative, but a positive sign will not print. If we use a plus for the edit character, the plus sign will print whether the number is negative or positive. The sign can be used as a floating edit character like the floating dollar sign.

If we are going to use a sign in our output field definition, the field containing the data must include the S character in its definition, causing it to retain the sign. Without this sign designation, the field will be unsigned and will always print as positive.

■ The DB or CR can be printed for negative numbers.

■ Other insertion characters are the ƀ for a blank, the / for a slash, and the 0 for printing a zero.

■ The BLANK WHEN ZERO clause will cause the field to print as blanks when the field being printed is zero.

■ A field can be filled with any literal by using the ALL figurative constant; for example, PIC X(20) ALL '*' would fill with asterisks.

■ With the JUSTIFIED RIGHT **clause**, a non-numeric field can be set up to store data on the right side of the field. Any excess blanks will appear on the left.

(Note: in the following discussion and in the future, interpret a lowercase b with a slash through it, such as ƀ, as a blank. Thus ƀƀ32 should be interpreted as blank, blank, 32.)

WORKING-STORAGE SECTION

The **WORKING-STORAGE SECTION,** which must follow the FILE SECTION in the DATA DIVISION, is used to define any fields that are needed by the program but are not defined in the FILE SECTION. Within the section, we define fields just like we do in the FILE SECTION. We can use group or elementary items as we need them.

A convenient feature allowed in the WORKING-STORAGE SECTION but not in the FILE SECTION is the VALUE clause, which may be used to give a field an initial value.

2-3-4 The PROCEDURE DIVISION

The fourth COBOL division, the PROCEDURE DIVISION, does all the calculations, data movement, and reading and writing of files.

This division is broken up into modules called **paragraphs**. When a paragraph is encountered in a program, execution begins with the first statement of the paragraph and ends when another paragraph-name is found.

Some programmers prefer to use numbers on their paragraph-names to mark the location of the routine in the program. In this text we will use sequentially numbered paragraph-names such as 0100-CALCULATION-ROUTINE and 0200-INPUT-MODULE.

After the paragraph-name, the rest of the paragraph is made up of sentences. A **sentence** is a statement or group of statements that is executed as a unit. The sentence continues until a period is found, no matter how many statements are in it.

2-4
Types of Data

In COBOL, we use two types of data: constant data, or data that doesn't change, and variable data, or data that changes as the program executes. Variable data is represented in the program by a field since the value of a field can change. Constants fall into three categories:

- **numeric literals** that are numeric constants, like the number 5. They are used primarily for mathematical operations.
- **non-numeric literals**, also known as alphanumeric literals, which are constants used for any purpose other than a mathematical process. These are enclosed in quotation marks and may be up to 120 characters long.
- **figurative constants**—COBOL reserved words that have a special meaning to the compiler. You should be familiar with the use of the following figurative constants:

ZEROS ZEROES ZERO	Used to fill a field with zeros.
SPACES SPACE	Used to fill a field with blank spaces.
QUOTES QUOTE	Used to allow printing of quotation marks.
HIGH-VALUES HIGH-VALUE	Used to fill a field with the highest possible value.
ALL	Used to fill a field with a specified literal.

2-5

Using the REDEFINES Clause

When we need to overlay one type of data on another, we can use the REDEFINES clause. Its format is

> level number field-name-1 <u>REDEFINES</u> field-name-2.

All it does is set up a second definition for the same storage area. A few rules must be followed when we are using the REDEFINES clause:

1. The level numbers of field-name-1 and field-name-2 must be the same.
2. We can use level number 01–49, but the record description entry (01 level) in the FILE SECTION cannot be redefined. We redefine the record layout by using a second record layout.
3. The total number of characters specified by the first field specification must be used in the second field specification.
4. The field-name being redefined must be followed by the field-name redefining it.

For example, let's suppose we are setting up a record layout (in WORKING-STORAGE) of

```
01   RECORD-IN.
     10   FIELD-A            PIC 9999.
     10   FIELD-B            PIC XXXX.
     10   FIELD-C            PIC X(25).
```

FIELD-A is the field we want to redefine. To do so, we specify another field on level 10 as follows:

```
01   RECORD-IN.
     10   FIELD-A                           PIC 9999.
     10   FIELD-RE REDEFINES FIELD-A        PIC XXXX.
     10   FIELD-B                           PIC XXXX.
     10   FIELD-C                           PIC X(25).
```

Now FIELD-RE redefines the PIC 9999 of FIELD-A to PIC XXXX. As the example shows, FIELD-RE has the same level number as FIELD-A (10), follows immediately after it, and has the same field length.

2-6

File Processing Statements

One of the primary purposes of any programming language is to aid in the processing of data stored in files. To process such data, we must gain access to it with a variety of processing statements, which will now be discussed separately.

2-6-1 The OPEN Statement

To process records from a file, we must first open the file to allow the program access to the records. The form of the OPEN statement is

$$\text{OPEN} \begin{Bmatrix} \underline{\text{INPUT}} & \text{file-name-1 [file-name-2} & \text{. . .]} \\ \underline{\text{OUTPUT}} & \text{file-name-3 [file-name-4} & \text{. . .]} \end{Bmatrix}$$

The OPEN statement must be executed in the program before any other statement tries to access the records. The file-names listed are the same file-names used on the SELECT and FD clauses.

2-6-2 The CLOSE Statement

After we finish processing the records, we must close the file using the CLOSE statement. The form of the CLOSE statement is

CLOSE file-name-1
[file-name-2 . . .]

2-6-3 The READ Statement

After the file is opened as an input file, we can input the data into the program. This is accomplished with a READ statement. Every READ statement brings exactly one record into the input storage area. The READ statement has the following format:

READ file-name [INTO record-layout] [AT END statement]

The file-name listed is the same one used in the SELECT clause, the FD clause, and the OPEN statement. The AT END clause is used by the program to determine when the end of the file is reached. You can make any legal COBOL statement the subject of the AT END clause, but generally the simple setting of a switch is used, such as

```
READ INPUT-FILE
     AT END MOVE 1 TO END-OF-FILE-MARKER.
READ INPUT-FILE
     AT END MOVE 'END' TO EOF.
```

2-6-4 The WRITE Statement

Printing reports and storing the data in a file are both done with the WRITE statement. The format for the WRITE is

$$\text{WRITE record-name} \begin{Bmatrix} \underline{\text{BEFORE}} \\ \underline{\text{AFTER}} \end{Bmatrix} \text{ADVANCING} \begin{Bmatrix} \text{integer} \\ \underline{\text{PAGE}} \end{Bmatrix} \begin{bmatrix} \underline{\text{LINE}} \\ \underline{\text{LINES}} \end{bmatrix}$$

Notice that we WRITE a record-name, rather than using a file-name as we do with the READ statement. Remember to

READ A FILE, WRITE A RECORD

The BEFORE ADVANCING and AFTER ADVANCING clauses, which are optional, are used for spacing on printed reports. PAGE is a reserved word that tells the machine to skip to the top of the next page BEFORE or AFTER printing.

When we use ADVANCING integer LINES, we can use any number of lines from 0 to 99; the keywords ADVANCING and LINES or LINE, though optional, are generally added for clarity. On some machines, if 0 lines are used no line feed is generated, which allows a line to be overprinted. On other machines, specifically most IBM machines, 0 lines will cause a page feed just as if the PAGE option had been used. Using 1 line will cause single spacing, as if the ADVANCING option had not been used at all. ADVANCING 2 LINES will cause double spacing, which means one blank line will appear between two printed lines.

When we set up multiple layouts in the WORKING-STORAGE SECTION, we can print them from the output FD by using the WRITE . . . FROM option, which has the form

WRITE record-name [FROM record layout]

2-7
The PERFORM Statement

In COBOL a loop is generally accomplished with the PERFORM . . . UNTIL **statement**:

PERFORM module-name [UNTIL condition]

The PERFORM statement itself simply transfers program execution control to the named module (paragraph). After that named module finishes executing, control returns to the next statement after the PERFORM statement. When we are creating a loop, however, we need to continue to PERFORM the module UNTIL a certain condition occurs, such as an end-of-file. The form of such a statement might be

```
PERFORM 0200-CALC-ROUTINE
        UNTIL END-OF-FILE-MARKER = 1.
```

This statement would be paired with the READ statement

```
READ INPUT-FILE
    AT END MOVE 1 TO END-OF-FILE-MARKER.
```

As long as the condition we are testing for on the UNTIL clause is not met, the module called for (0200-CALC-ROUTINE in our example) will continue to be executed. When the named module is finished, control is returned to the UNTIL clause instead of to the statement following the PERFORM. Then the test is performed; if it is not met, control goes back to the module.

It is important to realize that the condition on the PERFORM . . . UNTIL statement is tested *before* the routine is performed. The condition can be met before the routine is ever performed. The named paragraph may not be performed at all.

If we are processing records from a file, we need to be sure to read the file before the loop begins (before the PERFORM statement) and then again within the loop (inside the module being performed). If we use a PERFORM . . . UNTIL statement in place of a DO-WHILE loop, the program code might look like this:

```
      :  :  :
      READ INPUT-FILE
            AT END MOVE 'END' TO EOF.
      PERFORM 0200-CALC-ROUTINE
            UNTIL EOF = 'END'.
      :  :  :
  0200-CALC-ROUTINE.
      :  :  :
      READ INPUT-FILE
            AT END MOVE 'END' TO EOF.


  0300-NEXT-PARAGRAPH.
```

The READ statement prior to the PERFORM . . . UNTIL statement gets the initial record. Then the PERFORM statement tests for the end-of-file marker of 'END' in the variable EOF. If 'END' is not found, the module 0200-CALC-ROUTINE is executed. At the end of the module is the second READ statement. After the internal READ statement is executed, control returns to the PERFORM statement and the condition is tested again. If it is still false (EOF is not 'END'), the loop will continue to execute.

It is important to note that the logic of the condition for the UNTIL test and the logic for the condition for the DO-WHILE test are reversed. That is, in our design for the DO-WHILE we would say

DO-WHILE not end-of-file

but our UNTIL clause reads

```
      PERFORM 0200-CALC-ROUTINE
            UNTIL EOF = 'END'.
```

The DO-WHILE says to continue to process *while* (as long as) the condition is true. The UNTIL says the opposite; we process *until* the condition is true. You will need to remember this important point when translating your design into a COBOL program.

2-7-1 PERFORM . . . VARYING

The PERFORM . . . UNTIL is only one form of the PERFORM statement. Another form that can prove useful is the PERFORM . . . VARYING, which has the form

PERFORM module-name VARYING field-name-1 FROM $\begin{Bmatrix} \text{field-name-2} \\ \text{integer-1} \end{Bmatrix}$

BY $\begin{Bmatrix} \text{field-name-3} \\ \text{integer-2} \end{Bmatrix}$ UNTIL condition

The statement works in a fashion similar to the PERFORM . . . UNTIL except that it will automatically initialize field-name-1 to the value in field-name-2 (or integer-1) and increase it by the value in field-name-3 (or integer-2) until the condition is true. A sample statement might be

```
PERFORM 0200-LIST-LOOP
          VARYING LOOP-COUNTER FROM 1 BY 5
          UNTIL LOOP-COUNTER > 15.
```

In this statement the field LOOP-COUNTER will be initialized to 1 (FROM 1), will be incremented by 5 (BY 5) each time the 0200-LIST-LOOP module is performed, and will continue until LOOP-COUNTER is 16 or more. In this case, 0200-LIST-LOOP would be performed three times: LOOP-COUNTER would start as 1, would then be 6 (or 5 + 1), then 11 (or 6 + 5), and finally 16, which would be just larger than 15, causing the loop to stop functioning.

2-7-2   PERFORM . . . TIMES

Yet another form of the PERFORM statement, the PERFORM . . . TIMES, will cause a routine to be performed a specified number of times. The form of the statement is

$$\underline{\text{PERFORM}} \text{ module-name} \begin{Bmatrix} \text{field-name} \\ \text{integer} \end{Bmatrix} \underline{\text{TIMES}}$$

An example of this form is

```
PERFORM 0200-LIST-LOOP 10 TIMES.
```

This statement will simply make the 0200-LIST-LOOP be performed ten times. The form is useful when you need to perform a routine that doesn't necessarily need a counter. You can code your own counter, of course, but if you're going to do that, you might as well use the PERFORM . . . VARYING.

2-7-3   The THRU Clause

Every form of the PERFORM statement can perform multiple paragraphs because the actual form of all the PERFORM statements is

$$\underline{\text{PERFORM}} \text{ module-name-1} \begin{Bmatrix} \underline{\text{THRU}} \\ \underline{\text{THROUGH}} \end{Bmatrix} \text{ module-name-2}$$

(the remainder of each form of the PERFORM statement comes after the second module name). What this statement says is that the program should do all the statements in the first module (paragraph) and continue to process statements until it finishes all the statements in the second module. This means that many different (not just two) paragraphs may be performed with each invocation of the PERFORM statement. For example,

```
PERFORM 0200-LIST-LOOP THRU 0500-LIST-END
          UNTIL EOF = 'YES'
```

would cause 0200-LIST-LOOP, 0500-LIST-END, and all paragraphs in between to be performed until the end-of-file is found.

2-8

The MOVE Statement

To move data from one field to another we use the MOVE **statement**, with the form

$$\text{MOVE} \begin{Bmatrix} \text{literal} \\ \text{figurative-constant} \\ \text{field-name-1} \end{Bmatrix} \underline{\text{TO}} \text{ field-name-2, [field-name-3 } \dots \text{]}$$

We can move a literal, a figurative constant, or a data field to one or more data fields. There are several main categories of COBOL moves:

- A *non-numeric move* is used to move either numeric or alphanumeric data to an alphanumeric field. The data is moved one character at a time, beginning with the left-most character of the sending field and working from left to right. If the receiving field is the same size as the sending field, all the data is transferred from one field to the other. If the sending field is larger than the receiving field, the sending field is truncated (shortened) to fit in the receiving field. If the receiving field is larger than the sending field, the receiving field will get all the characters in the sending field and the remainder of the receiving field will be filled with blanks.

- *Numeric moves* are made only when both fields are numeric. The integer portion of the number is moved from the decimal point, one character at a time, to the left. The decimal portion is moved from the decimal point, one character at a time, to the right. If the sending and receiving fields are the same length, the move is a character-by-character duplication. If the receiving field is larger, the data in the sending field is moved and the remaining storage positions are filled with zeros. The receiving field should never be smaller than the sending field. If it is, digits of the number being sent will be truncated, changing the value of the field.

- *Group moves* are used to move an elementary item to a group item, a group item to an elementary one, or a group item to another group item. They are always treated as non-numeric moves. You can also move constants to a group item, such as moving spaces to a group item to initialize all the elementary items defined within it.

2-9

The STOP Statement

The logical end of a COBOL program is indicated with the STOP RUN **statement**, which signals to the computer that the program is finished. Control then returns to the operating system.

═══ 2-10 ═══

COBOL Calculations

There are two basic methods of performing calculations in COBOL: independent calculation statements and the COMPUTE statement. Each of the calculation statements has at least two different forms. For the **ADD statement**, which is used to add two or more numbers together, the two basic forms are

$$\underline{ADD} \begin{Bmatrix} \text{field-name-1} \\ \text{literal-1} \end{Bmatrix} \begin{bmatrix} \text{field-name-2} & \cdots \end{bmatrix} \underline{TO} \text{ field-name-3 [field-name-4} \quad \cdots \text{]}$$

and

$$\underline{ADD} \begin{Bmatrix} \text{field-name-1} \\ \text{literal-1} \end{Bmatrix} \begin{Bmatrix} \text{field-name-2} \\ \text{literal-2} \end{Bmatrix} [\ldots] \underline{GIVING} \text{ field-name-3 } [\ldots]$$

The difference between the two is that in the first form, one or more fields (or literals) are added to one or more result fields. The second form allows two or more fields to be added together, the result being placed into a result field and the previous contents of that field being discarded.

The **SUBTRACT statement** also has two forms:

$$\underline{SUBTRACT} \begin{Bmatrix} \text{field-name-1 [field-name-2} & \cdots \text{]} \\ \text{literal-1} & \text{[literal-2} & \cdots \text{]} \end{Bmatrix} \underline{FROM} \text{ field-name-3 } [\ldots]$$

and

$$\underline{SUBTRACT} \begin{Bmatrix} \text{field-name-1 [field-name-2} & \cdots \text{]} \\ \text{literal-1} & \text{[literal-2} & \cdots \text{]} \end{Bmatrix} \underline{FROM} \begin{Bmatrix} \text{field-name-3} \\ \text{literal-3} \end{Bmatrix}$$
$$\underline{GIVING} \text{ field-name-4 } [\ldots]$$

Again the main difference between the two is that the first form changes the result field while the second form uses a separate field to store the result of the calculation.

The **MULTIPLY statement** has two forms:

$$\underline{MULTIPLY} \begin{Bmatrix} \text{field-name-1} \\ \text{literal-1} \end{Bmatrix} \underline{BY} \text{ field-name-2 [field-name-3} \quad \cdots \text{]}$$

and

$$\underline{MULTIPLY} \begin{Bmatrix} \text{field-name-1} \\ \text{literal-1} \end{Bmatrix} \underline{BY} \begin{Bmatrix} \text{field-name-2} \\ \text{literal-2} \end{Bmatrix} \underline{GIVING} \text{ field-name-3 } [\ldots]$$

Again, in the first form the fields following the BY verb are simultaneously the calculated and result fields; the second form uses a separate result field.

The **DIVIDE statement** has three forms:

$$\underline{DIVIDE} \begin{Bmatrix} \text{field-name-1} \\ \text{literal-1} \end{Bmatrix} \underline{INTO} \text{ field-name-2 } [\ldots]$$

or

$$\text{DIVIDE } \begin{Bmatrix} \text{field-name-1} \\ \text{literal-1} \end{Bmatrix} \underline{\text{BY}} \begin{Bmatrix} \text{field-name-2} \\ \text{literal-2} \end{Bmatrix} \underline{\text{GIVING}} \text{ field-name-3 [. . .]}$$

or

$$\text{DIVIDE } \begin{Bmatrix} \text{field-name-1} \\ \text{literal-1} \end{Bmatrix} \underline{\text{INTO}} \begin{Bmatrix} \text{field-name-2} \\ \text{literal-2} \end{Bmatrix} \underline{\text{GIVING}} \text{ field-name-3 [. . .]}$$

As in other statements, the first form uses for its result field one of the fields being calculated. The second and third forms are virtually identical, the only difference being that the field being divided switches places with the field doing the dividing, based upon the keyword BY or INTO. Of course, the result field comes after the GIVING in both of the latter forms.

The **REMAINDER clause** takes the remainder of the division and places it in a separate field.

The **ROUNDED clause** can be added to the result field of any calculation to keep from losing the significance of unneeded decimal positions.

The **ON SIZE ERROR clause** is useful for capturing any truncation or division-by-zero errors.

The **COMPUTE statement** is for calculations more complicated than simple addition or subtraction. We still use the same four calculation types—addition, subtraction, multiplication, and division—but can now do exponentiation and can combine many calculations into a mathematical format, allowing complicated formulas to be written as one statement instead of several.

2-11
The IF Test

The conditional test in COBOL is the **IF test**, which has the form

```
IF condition
    imperative statement-1 [ . . . ]
[ELSE
    imperative statement-2 [ . . . ]].
```

The *condition* is the part of the statement that performs the test. Three simple relational tests can be used:

$$\underline{\text{IF}} \begin{Bmatrix} \text{field-name-1} \\ \text{literal-1} \end{Bmatrix} \begin{Bmatrix} \text{IS } \underline{\text{EQUAL}} \text{ TO} \\ \text{IS } \underline{\text{LESS}} \text{ THAN} \\ \text{IS } \underline{\text{GREATER}} \text{ THAN} \end{Bmatrix} \begin{Bmatrix} \text{field-name-2} \\ \text{literal-2} \end{Bmatrix} \begin{matrix} \text{(can use =)} \\ \text{(can use <)} \\ \text{(can use >)} \end{matrix}$$

We can also use the logical operators AND, OR, and NOT with our IF test. We use the AND operator when we want to test two conditions and want the statement to be true only if *both* of the tests are true. We use the OR logical operator when we want the statement to be true if *either or both* conditions are true. We use the NOT operator when we want the statement to be evaluated exactly the opposite of the way the conditional is listed. That is, NOT GREATER THAN is evaluated as *less than or equal to* because that is what is left after GREATER THAN is eliminated.

An IF test can have another IF test for the action that takes place depending on whether the result of the test was true or false. In such cases, the statement is called a **nested IF statement**. When we use nested IF tests we need to be careful where we place the ELSE clauses. In COBOL, the ELSE is related to the *immediately preceding* IF test whether that's what you intended or not. The following statement does not have the correct indentation for the way the statement would function:

```
IF FIELD-A = FIELD-B
    ADD 1 TO LINE-CTR
    IF LINE-CTR > 59
        PERFORM HEADINGS-ROUTINE
ELSE
    ADD 3 TO LINE-CTR.
```

By the indentation, it would appear that we intended to add 3 to the line-counter when FIELD-A and FIELD-B are not equal. However, if the line-counter is not greater than 59 (the second IF test), *then* the program will add 3 to the line-counter. If FIELD-A and FIELD-B are not the same, *nothing* will happen and control will fall through the statement. The proper indentation for the way the statement will function is

```
IF FIELD-A = FIELD-B
    ADD 1 TO LINE-CTR
    IF LINE-CTR > 59
        PERFORM HEADINGS-ROUTINE
    ELSE
        ADD 3 TO LINE-CTR.
```

But what if we wanted the ELSE to be paired with the *first* IF test? We can make this happen, but we need to use the **NEXT SENTENCE clause**, which simply tells the computer to skip the rest of the test and jump out to the sentence following the IF test. The coding for the previous example would be

```
IF FIELD-A = FIELD-B
    ADD 1 TO LINE-CTR
    IF LINE-CTR > 59
        PERFORM HEADINGS-ROUTINE
    ELSE
        NEXT SENTENCE
ELSE
    ADD 3 TO LINE-CTR.
```

Now, when the sentence is executed, if FIELD-A and FIELD-B are not the same we will add 3 to the line-counter because the ELSE is properly paired with the first IF test. On the inside IF test, if the line-counter is not greater than 59 the ELSE is performed, and the IF test ends as program control jumps out of the sentence.

Other Types of Conditionals

There are two types of conditional tests that fall into a category called **data validation**. These are

- the **class test**, to determine if a field is numeric or alphabetic. The form is

    IF field name IS $\left\{ \begin{array}{l} \text{NUMERIC} \\ \hline \text{ALPHABETIC} \end{array} \right\}$ imperative statement [. . .]
    [ELSE imperative statement [. . .]]

- the **sign test**, to test for a positive or negative value. The form is

    IF field-name IS $\left\{ \begin{array}{l} \text{POSITIVE} \\ \hline \text{NEGATIVE} \end{array} \right\}$ imperative statement [. . .]
    [ELSE imperative statement [. . .]]

The INSPECT **statement** in the 1976 and 1985 versions of COBOL lets us replace one character in a field with another character, or simply to count occurrences of certain characters. The INSPECT statement has lots of options and two forms. The first form is

INSPECT field-name-1 TALLYING field-name-2 FOR

$\left\{ \begin{array}{l} \text{ALL} \\ \hline \text{LEADING} \\ \hline \text{CHARACTERS} \end{array} \right\} \left\{ \begin{array}{l} \text{field-name-3} \\ \text{literal-1} \end{array} \right\} \left\{ \begin{array}{l} \text{BEFORE} \\ \hline \text{AFTER} \end{array} \right\}$ INITIAL $\left\{ \begin{array}{l} \text{field-name-4} \\ \text{literal-2} \end{array} \right\}$

Using this form of the statement, we can count (TALLY) the number of occurrences of a particular character within a field. The second form lets us change characters:

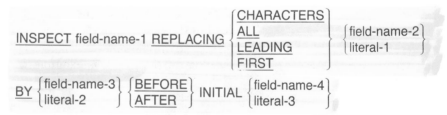

INSPECT field-name-1 REPLACING $\left\{ \begin{array}{l} \text{CHARACTERS} \\ \hline \text{ALL} \\ \hline \text{LEADING} \\ \hline \text{FIRST} \end{array} \right\} \left\{ \begin{array}{l} \text{field-name-2} \\ \text{literal-1} \end{array} \right\}$

BY $\left\{ \begin{array}{l} \text{field-name-3} \\ \text{literal-2} \end{array} \right\} \left\{ \begin{array}{l} \text{BEFORE} \\ \hline \text{AFTER} \end{array} \right\}$ INITIAL $\left\{ \begin{array}{l} \text{field-name-4} \\ \text{literal-3} \end{array} \right\}$

About the only difference between this form and the other is that, instead of counting the occurrences, we replace each with another character. Once again we are dealing with characters, not groups of characters.

If you happen to be using a 1968 compiler, you cannot use the INSPECT statement. There is a similar statement available, however—the EXAMINE **statement**, which also has two forms. The first is

EXAMINE field-name-1 REPLACING $\left\{ \begin{array}{l} \text{ALL} \\ \hline \text{LEADING} \\ \hline \text{FIRST} \\ \hline \text{UNTIL FIRST} \end{array} \right\}$ literal-1 BY literal-2

The options of this statement follow the same rules as those of the INSPECT statement.

The second form of the EXAMINE statement uses the TALLYING clause and requires you to set up a field called TALLY in the WORKING-STORAGE SECTION with a PIC clause (again required) of 9(4). After the statement is executed, the TALLY field will contain the count of the characters tallied. The form of the statement is

$$
\text{EXAMINE field-name-1 } \underline{\text{TALLYING}} \left\{ \begin{array}{l} \underline{\text{UNTIL FIRST}} \\ \underline{\text{ALL}} \\ \underline{\text{LEADING}} \end{array} \right\}
$$

literal-1 [REPLACING BY literal-2]

2-13

Condition Name

When you want to use field-names to test for codes, you can use condition names by using 88 levels:

88 condition-name VALUE literal-1 [THRU literal-2] [. . .]

These condition names are coded immediately after the field that they refer to. There are no PICTURE clauses on the 88-level entries, as they are used only to establish possible values for the field. A marital status field might be set up as

```
10   MARITAL-STATUS          PIC X.
     88   SINGLE             VALUE 'S'.
     88   MARRIED            VALUE 'M'.
     88   DIVORCED           VALUE 'D'.
```

Now, with these definitions, we can test for the condition of MARITAL-STATUS simply by testing the 88-level fields. An ordinary IF test to determine the value of MARITAL-STATUS would look like

```
IF  MARITAL-STATUS = 'S'
    PERFORM 0600-SINGLE-ROUTINE.
```

But, using the condition names, we can simplify this:

```
IF  SINGLE
    PERFORM 0600-SINGLE-ROUTINE.
```

2-14
Control Break Programming

Although control break programs would not usually be included in a discussion of COBOL coding standards, it is important that the advanced student understand how to write such programs. A **control break program** is simply a program that prints a report that details file information and shows subtotals along the way. These subtotals are created by separating the detail lines upon the changing of a control field. Thus, the subtotals are sometimes called control totals.

For a single-level control break program, the file must be sorted into control field order. Then we begin the program by moving the control field into a hold field, which will be compared against future control fields. When a control field is greater than the hold field, we perform the control break routine.

The real control break functions, which are done in the control break routine, include

- printing the control total,
- adding the control total to the grand total,
- zeroing out the control total,
- moving the new control field to the hold field.

At the end of the file, we need to print the subtotals since there can be no control break generated without more records. We also print the grand totals for the entire report.

When we need to subdivide our report into groups within groups, we use a multiple-level control break program designating a major control field, and a minor control field, and possibly some intermediate control fields. Each of these fields is checked separately and each controls its own control break routine. The difference between single- and multiple-level programs is that when we have a major control break, as we do in multiple-level control break programs, it is necessary to perform the minor control break routine as well. We don't want a change in a major control total to print without first printing the minor control totals, that go with it, whether they have changed or not.

Occasionally, management will want to see the results of a control break program without the detail lines having been printed. What they want is a summary report showing just the totals. You can change most control break programs into summary reports by simply removing the line or lines that print the details.

2-15
Program Debugging

Since this is an advanced book, we will assume you have done enough programming to understand compiler errors. It is quite possible, however, that those ever-elusive logic errors are still troubling you. We offer the following discussion of tools and techniques to help you locate logic errors.

2-15-1 The READY TRACE

Of the several commands available in COBOL to help you track down your errors, the first is the READY TRACE. The statement simply causes the computer to print out a list of the paragraph-names as they are encountered during the execution of the program. This listing begins after the READY TRACE statement is encountered in the program. For example, suppose we had a program composed of paragraphs:

```
PROCEDURE DIVISION.
0100-MAIN-MODULE.
  :  :  :
0200-CALC-ROUTINE.
  :  :  :
0300-PRINT-ROUTINE.
  :  :  :
0400-HEADING-ROUTINE.
  :  :  :
0500-DETAIL-PRINTING.
```

If we placed a READY TRACE statement before the MAIN-MODULE paragraph, we might see results like the following:

```
0100-MAIN-MODULE.
0400-HEADING-ROUTINE.
0200-CALC-ROUTINE.
0300-PRINT-ROUTINE.
0500-DETAIL-PRINTING.
0300-PRINT-ROUTINE.
0500-DETAIL-PRINTING.
0300-PRINT-ROUTINE.
0500-DETAIL-PRINTING.
```

What has probably occurred is that the 0100-MAIN-MODULE called the 0400-HEADING-ROUTINE paragraph to print the headings at the top of the page and then read a record and used a PERFORM to start executing the 0200-CALC-ROUTINE paragraph. The 0200-CALC-ROUTINE paragraph in turn called the 0300-PRINT-ROUTINE paragraph, which called the 0500-DETAIL-PRINTING paragraph upon each execution. Notice that the 0200-CALC-ROUTINE paragraph was printed only once. Even when a paragraph is continually in use, the name of that paragraph is not listed unless the paragraph is reentered by the program. That is, the 0200-CALC-ROUTINE paragraph is probably performing the 0300-PRINT-ROUTINE paragraph, which means that program control continually returns to the PERFORM statement in the 0200-CALC-ROUTINE paragraph. But, since the PERFORM statement is in the middle of the paragraph, the 0200-CALC-ROUTINE paragraph-name will not continue to print. Only the paragraphs being executed from the beginning (0300-PRINT-ROUTINE and 0500-DETAIL-PRINTING) are shown.

Some computers help overcome this minor problem by printing, beside the paragraph-name, the number of times the paragraph was executed:

```
0200-CALC-ROUTINE (25 times)
```

The READY TRACE can come in handy for programs that ABEND (have an ABnormal END). It can indicate how many times a particular routine functioned, information that can be useful in tracking down the offending data record that is causing the program to ABEND.

Sometimes you may wish to use the READY TRACE for only a part of your program. You can turn off the READY TRACE by using the **RESET TRACE** command. When the program encounters the RESET TRACE command, the tracing ceases until another READY TRACE is found.

2-15-2   The DISPLAY Statement

The READY TRACE statement can be useful for tracking through your program. However, all the READY TRACE statement does is print the paragraph-names. If you have long paragraphs in your program, you might need a more detailed examination of them than the READY TRACE statement can give you. Also, if your program is causing an ABEND, the READY TRACE statement may get you to the paragraph where the ABEND is occurring but, if that paragraph contains a long series of calculations, you will still not know which calculation is causing the problem.

Another COBOL statement can help us in this respect. The **DISPLAY statement** will allow us to print on the screen certain data so that we can determine exactly where we are in our program and what values are contained in specified fields. The form of the statement is

$$\underline{\text{DISPLAY}} \left\{ \begin{array}{l} \text{field-name-1} \ [\ \ldots\ ] \\ \text{literal-1} \ [\ \ldots\ ] \end{array} \right\} [\underline{\text{UPON}} \text{ mnemonic-name}]$$

Most computers do not require that you use the mnemonic-name when simply displaying on the screen. Without the mnenomic-name, the displayed output is sent to the default output device, which is usually the display screen. If your installation uses the printer as the default device, you may wish to determine how to use the mnemonic-name to display the data.

We can display either fields or literals. Often we will need to print the value of a field; at other times a simple literal will tell us what we need to know. Let's suppose we have a string of calculations and we are getting an ABEND. We have looked carefully at the data we are using for the calculations, but we still cannot find any problem. We need to localize the error to a specific statement so we can determine exactly which data field is causing the problem. For example, suppose the statements in question are the following:

```
ADD FIELD-A TO FIELD-B GIVING FIELD-C.
DIVIDE FIELD-D BY FIELD-E.
MOVE FIELD-C TO FIELD-C-OUT.
ADD FIELD-A TO FIELD-A-TOTAL.
ADD FIELD-B TO FIELD-B-TOTAL.
ADD FIELD-D TO FIELD-D-TOTAL.
```

To verify that we have indeed reached the calculations, we might want to display a message before the calculations start:

```
DISPLAY 'BEFORE-CALCULATIONS'.
ADD FIELD-A TO FIELD-B GIVING FIELD-C.
DIVIDE FIELD-D BY FIELD-E.
MOVE FIELD-C TO FIELD-C-OUT.
ADD FIELD-A TO FIELD-A-TOTAL.
ADD FIELD-B TO FIELD-B-TOTAL.
ADD FIELD-D TO FIELD-D-TOTAL.
```

This statement will not display anything but "BEFORE-CALCULATIONS" on the screen, but its doing so will tell us that we have reached the calculations. Next we might want to be sure the ABEND is in fact in the calculations. We can do this by installing a DISPLAY statement at the end of the calculations:

```
DISPLAY 'BEFORE-CALCULATIONS'.
ADD FIELD-A TO FIELD-B GIVING FIELD-C.
DIVIDE FIELD-D BY FIELD-E.
MOVE FIELD-C TO FIELD-C-OUT.
ADD FIELD-A TO FIELD-A-TOTAL.
ADD FIELD-B TO FIELD-B-TOTAL.
ADD FIELD-D TO FIELD-D-TOTAL.
DISPLAY "AFTER CALCULATIONS".
```

If we see both statements displayed when we execute the program, we know that there is no problem in the calculations. On the other hand, if the first message prints but not the second, we know for sure that the error is in the calculations.

Suppose we do get the first message but not the second. We would need to localize the error further. We might want to add a few more DISPLAY statements:

```
DISPLAY 'BEFORE-CALCULATIONS'.
ADD FIELD-A TO FIELD-B GIVING FIELD-C.
DISPLAY 'FIRST-CALC  ' FIELD-A FIELD-B FIELD-C.
DIVIDE FIELD-D BY FIELD-E.
DISPLAY 'SECOND-CALC  ' FIELD-D FIELD-E.
MOVE FIELD-C TO FIELD-C-OUT.
ADD FIELD-A TO FIELD-A-TOTAL.
DISPLAY 'THIRD-CALC  ' FIELD-A-TOTAL.
ADD FIELD-B TO FIELD-B-TOTAL.
ADD FIELD-D TO FIELD-D-TOTAL.
DISPLAY "AFTER-CALCULATIONS".
```

If these new statements don't do the trick, we can insert even more. Notice that we have now begun to display a literal and a field on the same DISPLAY statement. When the statement

```
DISPLAY 'FIRST-CALC  ' FIELD-A FIELD-B FIELD-C.
```

is executed by the program, it will display first the message FIRST-CALC and then the values of the three fields.

Now, what do you suppose would happen if we tried to display the field that is the cause of the ABEND we are looking for? That's right, the statement would ABEND. But we will have narrowed the problem greatly. Suppose, for example, that the following results are printed on the terminal upon execution of the program:

```
BEFORE-CALCULATIONS
FIRST-CALC  0010005000100
DATA EXCEPTION
```

Since the data exception (the ABEND) happened after the first calculation but before the DISPLAY for the second calculation, it stands to reason that the error must be in the second calculation or in the displaying of the results. Of course, since we are trying to track down an ABEND that is already happening, the statement that is causing the ABEND must be the calculation rather than the DISPLAY statement. Thus, we discover that the ABEND is being caused by the statement

```
DIVIDE FIELD-D BY FIELD-E.
```

Such a conclusion doesn't tell us precisely what is wrong, but it tells us which statement is causing the problem. Armed with that specific information, we should be able to figure out what is causing the error.

You may have noticed that the output from the second display statement made it a little difficult to tell just what field was what:

```
FIRST-CALC   0010005000100
```

The problem is that we told the computer to print three numeric fields without any spacing—so we got the three fields printed back to back, making them difficult if not impossible to read. What we need to do to clarify this output is put some spaces between the fields:

```
DISPLAY 'FIRST-CALC   ' FIELD-A ' ' FIELD-B ' ' FIELD-C.
```

Now when this statement is executed, the display will look like

```
FIRST-CALC   0010  0050  00100
```

which is much easier to understand.

The DISPLAY statement has a limitation. Most computers limit you to a display width of 120 characters. Others allow you to display only the size that is allowed for the particular device being used, such as 80 columns on a terminal screen. Still others have virtually no limit to the width of the display statement and will simply wrap the displayed data around the edge of the displayed line.

2-15-3 The EXHIBIT Statement

The DISPLAY statement is useful as far as it goes. Most compilers, however, also have the EXHIBIT statement.

The **EXHIBIT statement** is a lot like the DISPLAY statement except that it can print only on the default output device. Though the default device is usually the display screen, if it's the printer, we must EXHIBIT to the printer.

The full form of the EXHIBIT statement is

$$\text{EXHIBIT} \left\{ \begin{array}{l} \text{NAMED} \\ \text{CHANGED} \\ \text{CHANGED \underline{NAME}} \end{array} \right\} \left\{ \begin{array}{l} \text{field-name-1} \ [\ldots] \\ \text{literal-1} \ [\ldots] \end{array} \right\}$$

We can use the EXHIBIT statement just like we used the DISPLAY statement. As an example, let's change one of our DISPLAY statements

```
DISPLAY 'FIRST-CALC   ' FIELD-A ' ' FIELD-B ' ' FIELD-C.
```

to an EXHIBIT:

```
  EXHIBIT 'FIRST-CALC   'FIELD-A ' ' FIELD-B ' ' FIELD-C.
```

The output produced by both statements would be exactly the same. However, it is unclear which printed field is which. For example, the output from the statement is

```
  FIRST-CALC   0010  0050  00100
```

If we were using a series of such statements, it would be difficult to determine which fields are being printed.

The EXHIBIT statement has the NAMED option so that the field-name can be displayed with the data:

```
  EXHIBIT NAMED 'FIRST-CALC   ' FIELD-A.
```

The result will be

```
  FIRST-CALC   FIELD-A = 0010
```

This option has another advantage in that it will print the names of all the fields listed on the statement

```
EXHIBIT NAMED 'FIRST-CALC   ' FIELD-A ' ' FIELD-B ' ' FIELD-C.
```

with the output of

```
FIRST-CALC   FIELD-A = 0010  FIELD-B = 0050  FIELD-C = 00100
```

Sometimes it might be handy to have our values displayed only when they have changed. To do this we use another option of the EXHIBIT statement, the CHANGED verb:

```
  EXHIBIT CHANGED 'FIRST-CALC   ' FIELD-A.
```

Now the EXHIBIT statement will function only if the value of FIELD-A changes from what it was when the last EXHIBIT statement that printed that field was encountered. The only problem with using this option is that the FIRST-CALC literal will print only when FIELD-A is changed. And if we want to use one EXHIBIT statement to print more than one field, all the fields and the literals on the statement will be printed if any of the values of the fields change. Therefore, if you want to use the CHANGED option, you would be wise to use several different EXHIBIT statements. We might change our one statement

```
EXHIBIT CHANGED 'FIRST-CALC   ' FIELD-A '  ' FIELD-B '  ' FIELD-C.
```

to three statements:

```
    EXHIBIT CHANGED 'FIRST-CALC   ' FIELD-A.
    EXHIBIT CHANGED 'FIRST-CALC   ' FIELD-B.
    EXHIBIT CHANGED 'FIRST-CALC   ' FIELD-C.
```

Now the problem is that the fields will print on separate lines instead of on the same line. And notice that we included the FIRST-CALC literal on each statement so that, no matter which statement printed, we could refer to the printed literal to determine the area of the program that the EXHIBIT was in.

You can combine the NAMED and CHANGED options as in

```
    EXHIBIT CHANGED NAMED 'FIRST-CALC   ' FIELD-A.
```

Now the statement will execute only when FIELD-A changes, but it will also display the field-name when the value is printed.

2-15-4 Cross-reference Listings

There are many different types of syntax errors, such as field-names that are misspelled, missing, or misused. With large programs it is sometimes difficult to track down all such errors. To aid in determining just where your variables are in your programs, you may want to use a **cross-reference listing** of all the variables you have used in your program and the lines they are found on. A partial example of such a listing follows:

CROSS-REFERENCE DICTIONARY

DATA NAMES	DEFN	REFERENCE		
CUSTOMERS-IN	000034	000112	000123	000129
		000155		
LIST-OUT	000035	000112	000120	000121
		000127	000129	000151
CUSTOMER-RECORD	000043			
CUSTOMER-NUMBER-IN	000044	000136		
LAST-NAME-IN	000045	000137		
FIRST-NAME-IN	000046	000138		
ADDRESS-IN	000047			
CITY-IN	000048			
STATE-IN	000049			
ZIP-CODE-IN	000050			
AMOUNT-DUE-IN	000051	000139	000142	000144
CREDIT-LIMIT-CODE	000052	000140	000144	
SALESMAN-NUMBER	000053			
LIST-OUT-RECORD	000059	000120	000121	000127
		000151		

The list shows you the field-names (DATA NAMES), the line the field is first defined on (DEFN), and the other (PROCEDURE DIVISION) statements where the field may be found (REFERENCE). Some fields are not referenced anywhere else in the program (such as ADDRESS-IN and CITY-IN). Generally, the names are not in alphabetical order (though they would be on some computers). They are listed here in the order they appear in the programs DATA DIVISION.

2-16
The Record Rack Control Break Program

At the end of each of the following chapters, we will present a sample program using the techniques discovered in the chapter. This program will be written for a fictional company called *The Record Rack*, a store that sells records, tapes, and other items. Roger Barnell is the owner and Cindy Harrison is the programmer he has hired to write the programs. Each program will first be thoroughly designed and then examined as necessary. The program will be tested with sample data and the generated reports will be presented.

For this chapter, Roger Barnell is in the process of calculating the value of his inventory for the end-of-month balance sheet report. His inventory contains several products, and each product contains a different number of product types. He has instructed Cindy to prepare a control break report with the following details:

1. product number
2. product type
3. inventory amount of each product type
4. cost per unit for each product type
5. total cost of each product type
6. total cost for each product number (control total)
7. total cost of the inventory

She designed the program to print the report as shown in the printer spacing chart in Figure 2-2. Her systems design is shown in Figure 2-3, the flowchart is in Figure 2-4, and her pseudocode design for the program follows:

```
Start
Open the files
Initialize totals, line-counter, page-counter
Print headings
Read a record at end mark end-of-file
Move product number to hold field
DO-WHILE not end-of-file
        IF product number < > hold field THEN
                Do Control Break Routine
        (ELSE)
        END-IF
        Calculate total cost of the product type
        Print detail line
        Increment line-counter by 1
```

IF line-counter > 59 THEN
      Print headings
(ELSE)
END-IF
Accumulate cost of product number
Read a record at end mark end-of-file

END-DO
Do Control Break Routine
Print out total inventory cost
Close the files
End

Start Control Break Routine
Accumulate total inventory
Print out total product cost
Increment line-counter by 2
IF line-counter > 59 THEN
      Print headings
(ELSE)
END-IF
Zero out total product cost
Move product number to hold field
End Control Break Routine

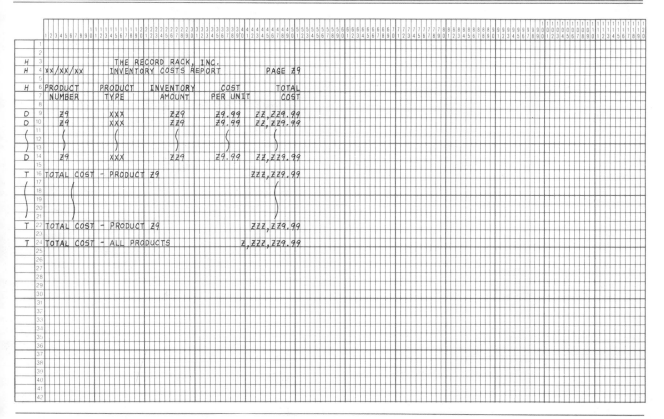

Figure 2-2   The layout for the inventory costs report.

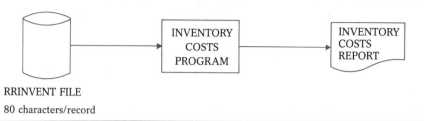

Figure 2-3   The systems chart for *The Record Rack* costs report.

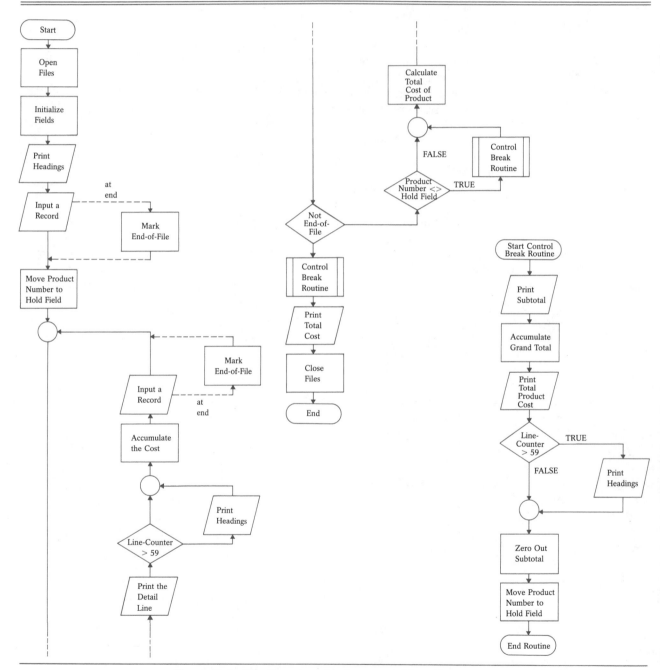

Figure 2-4   The flowchart for the control break program.

The record layout for the RRINVENT file is shown in Figure 2-5. The sample data Cindy used is

Product	Product Type	Inventory Amount	Cost per Unit
01	12C	453	2.00
01	14D	301	4.50
01	76F	90	11.99
01	81R	33	6.22
02	J09	700	10.00
02	KL1	43	34.67
02	MN5	27	15.48
02	PO8	51	17.99
02	TZ3	89	14.90
03	RT6	76	12.00
03	S6L	56	9.87
03	ZEF	84	4.09

RRINVENT File					
Field Description	*Position*	*Length*	:	*Dec*	*Type*
Product number	1–2	2	:	0	Numeric
Product type	3–5	3	:		Non-numeric
Product quantity	6–8	3	:	0	Numeric
Unit cost	9–12	4	:	2	Numeric
Filler	13–80	68	:		Non-numeric
Record Length = 80					

Figure 2-5   The RRINVENT file for the inventory costs report program.

Cindy's program:

```
****************************************************************
****************************************************************
*
*
*
*   PROGRAM NAME: INV-COST
*
*   PROGRAMMER NAME:  CINDY HARRISON
*
*   SOCIAL SECURITY NUMBER:  999-99-9999
*
*   DUE DATE: FEBRUARY 10, 1988
*
*   DESCRIPTION: THIS PROGRAM WILL PRODUCE A CONTROL BREAK INVENTORY
*                COST REPORT DETAILING THE QUANTITY, COST, AND TOTAL
*                COST OF THE INVENTORY.  THE REPORT WILL SHOW THE
*                CONTROL TOTAL ON THE PRODUCT NUMBERS.
*
*
****************************************************************
****************************************************************
```

```
IDENTIFICATION DIVISION.
PROGRAM-ID.    INV-COST.
AUTHOR.        CINDY HARRISON.

ENVIRONMENT DIVISION.

CONFIGURATION SECTION.
SOURCE-COMPUTER. IBM-4331.
OBJECT-COMPUTER. IBM-4331.

INPUT-OUTPUT SECTION.
FILE-CONTROL.
    SELECT INVENTORY-IN ASSIGN TO UT-S-RRINVENT.
    SELECT LIST-OUT     ASSIGN TO UT-S-SYSPRINT.

DATA DIVISION.
FILE SECTION.


FD  INVENTORY-IN
    LABEL RECORDS ARE OMITTED
    RECORD CONTAINS 80 CHARACTERS.
01  INVENTORY-RECORD.
    05   PRODUCT-NUMBER          PIC 99.
    05   PRODUCT-TYPE            PIC XXX.
    05   PRODUCT-QUANTITY        PIC 999.
    05   UNIT-COST               PIC 99V99.
    05   FILLER                  PIC X(68).

FD  LIST-OUT
    LABEL RECORDS ARE OMITTED
    RECORD CONTAINS 133 CHARACTERS.
01  LIST-OUT-RECORD             PIC X(133).

WORKING-STORAGE SECTION.

01  WORK-AREAS.
    05   EOF                     PIC XXX          VALUE 'NO '.
         88   WE-ARE-OUT-OF-DATA                  VALUE 'YES'.

    05   LINE-CTR                PIC 99           VALUE ZERO.
    05   PAGE-CTR                PIC 99           VALUE 1.
    05   TOTAL-COST              PIC 9(6)V99      VALUE ZERO.
    05   SUB-TOTAL-COST          PIC 9(6)V99      VALUE ZERO.
    05   GRAND-TOTAL-COST        PIC 9(6)V99      VALUE ZERO.
    05   HOLD-PRODUCT-NUMBER     PIC 99.

    05   MACHINE-DATE            PIC X(6).
    05   DATE-WORK REDEFINES MACHINE-DATE.
         10   DATE-YY            PIC XX.
         10   DATE-MM            PIC XX.
         10   DATE-DD            PIC XX.

01  PAGE-HEADING-1.
    05   FILLER                  PIC X(36)        VALUE
         '                  THE RECORD RACK, INC.'.

01  PAGE-HEADING-2.
    05   FILLER                  PIC X            VALUE SPACES.
```

```
        05  HEADING-MONTH              PIC XX.
        05  HEADING-DAY                PIC /XX/.
        05  HEADING-YEAR               PIC XX.
        05  FILLER                     PIC X(29)         VALUE
            '      INVENTORY COSTS REPORT'.
        05  FILLER                     PIC X(12)         VALUE
            '        PAGE '.
        05  PAGE-CTR-OUT               PIC Z9.

    01  COLUMN-HEADING-1.
        05  FILLER                     PIC X(52)         VALUE
            ' PRODUCT     PRODUCT   INVENTORY    COST        TOTAL'.

    01  COLUMN-HEADING-2.
        05  FILLER                     PIC X(52)         VALUE
            ' NUMBER      TYPE      AMOUNT    PER UNIT       COST'.

    01  DETAIL-LINE.
        05  FILLER                     PIC X(4)          VALUE SPACES.
        05  PRODUCT-NUMBER-OUT         PIC Z9.
        05  FILLER                     PIC X(8)          VALUE SPACES.
        05  PRODUCT-TYPE-OUT           PIC XXX.
        05  FILLER                     PIC X(9)          VALUE SPACES.
        05  PRODUCT-QUANTITY-OUT       PIC ZZ9.
        05  FILLER                     PIC X(6)          VALUE SPACES.
        05  PRODUCT-COST-OUT           PIC Z9.99.
        05  FILLER                     PIC X(3)          VALUE SPACES.
        05  TOTAL-COST-OUT             PIC ZZ,ZZZ.99.

    01  SUB-TOTAL-LINE.
        05  FILLER                     PIC X(22)         VALUE
            ' TOTAL COST - PRODUCT '.
        05  HOLD-PRODUCT-OUT           PIC Z9.
        05  FILLER                     PIC X(18)           VALUE SPACES.
        05  SUB-TOTAL-COST-OUT         PIC ZZZ,ZZ9.99.

    01  GRAND-TOTAL-LINE.
        05  FILLER                     PIC X(40)         VALUE
            ' TOTAL COST - ALL PRODUCTS            '.
        05  GRAND-TOTAL-OUT            PIC Z,ZZZ,ZZ9.99.


PROCEDURE DIVISION.

0100-MAIN-MODULE.

    OPEN INPUT   INVENTORY-IN
         OUTPUT  LIST-OUT.

    ACCEPT MACHINE-DATE FROM DATE.
    MOVE DATE-YY TO HEADING-YEAR.
    MOVE DATE-MM TO HEADING-MONTH.
    MOVE DATE-DD TO HEADING-DAY.

    PERFORM 0300-HEADING-ROUTINE.

    READ INVENTORY-IN
         AT END MOVE 'YES' TO EOF.
    MOVE PRODUCT-NUMBER TO HOLD-PRODUCT-NUMBER.
```

```
        PERFORM 0200-LIST-LOOP
                UNTIL WE-ARE-OUT-OF-DATA.

        MOVE SUB-TOTAL-COST        TO    SUB-TOTAL-COST-OUT.
        MOVE HOLD-PRODUCT-NUMBER TO    HOLD-PRODUCT-OUT.
        WRITE LIST-OUT-RECORD      FROM SUB-TOTAL-LINE
                AFTER ADVANCING 2 LINES.

        ADD SUB-TOTAL-COST     TO GRAND-TOTAL-COST.
        MOVE GRAND-TOTAL-COST TO GRAND-TOTAL-OUT.
        WRITE LIST-OUT-RECORD FROM GRAND-TOTAL-LINE
                AFTER ADVANCING 2 LINES.

        CLOSE INVENTORY-IN
                LIST-OUT.
        STOP RUN.


    0200-LIST-LOOP.

        IF PRODUCT-NUMBER NOT = HOLD-PRODUCT-NUMBER
            PERFORM 0400-PRODUCT-CONTROL-BREAK.

        MOVE PRODUCT-NUMBER     TO PRODUCT-NUMBER-OUT.
        MOVE PRODUCT-TYPE       TO PRODUCT-TYPE-OUT.
        MOVE PRODUCT-QUANTITY TO PRODUCT-QUANTITY-OUT.
        MOVE UNIT-COST          TO PRODUCT-COST-OUT.

        MULTIPLY UNIT-COST     BY PRODUCT-QUANTITY GIVING TOTAL-COST.

        MOVE TOTAL-COST        TO TOTAL-COST-OUT.
        ADD  TOTAL-COST        TO SUB-TOTAL-COST.

        WRITE LIST-OUT-RECORD FROM DETAIL-LINE
                AFTER ADVANCING 1 LINE.

        ADD 1 TO LINE-CTR.

        IF LINE-CTR > 59
            PERFORM 0300-HEADING-ROUTINE.

        READ INVENTORY-IN
                AT END MOVE 'YES' TO EOF.


    0300-HEADING-ROUTINE.

        MOVE PAGE-CTR TO PAGE-CTR-OUT.
        WRITE LIST-OUT-RECORD FROM PAGE-HEADING-1
                AFTER ADVANCING PAGE.
        WRITE LIST-OUT-RECORD FROM PAGE-HEADING-2
                AFTER ADVANCING 1 LINE.

        WRITE LIST-OUT-RECORD FROM COLUMN-HEADING-1
                AFTER ADVANCING 2 LINES.
        WRITE LIST-OUT-RECORD FROM COLUMN-HEADING-2
                AFTER ADVANCING 1 LINE.

        MOVE 6 TO LINE-CTR.
        ADD 1 TO PAGE-CTR.
```

0400-PRODUCT-CONTROL-BREAK.

```
    MOVE SUB-TOTAL-COST      TO SUB-TOTAL-COST-OUT.
    MOVE HOLD-PRODUCT-NUMBER TO HOLD-PRODUCT-OUT.
    WRITE LIST-OUT-RECORD FROM SUB-TOTAL-LINE
          AFTER ADVANCING 2 LINES.

    ADD SUB-TOTAL-COST TO GRAND-TOTAL-COST.

    MOVE ZEROS TO SUB-TOTAL-COST.
    MOVE PRODUCT-NUMBER TO HOLD-PRODUCT-NUMBER.

    ADD 2 TO LINE-CTR.
```

The output generated by Cindy's program looks like the following:

```
                    THE RECORD RACK, INC.
      05/23/88      INVENTORY COSTS REPORT         PAGE  1

      PRODUCT    PRODUCT   INVENTORY     COST        TOTAL
      NUMBER     TYPE       AMOUNT     PER UNIT       COST

         1        12C         453        2.00       906.00
         1        14D         301        4.50     1,354.50
         1        76F          90       11.99     1,079.10
         1        81R          33        6.22       205.26

      TOTAL COST - PRODUCT  1                      3,544.86

         2        J09         700       10.00     7,000.00
         2        KL1          43       34.67     1,490.81
         2        MN5          27       15.48       417.96
         2        P08          51       17.99       917.49
         2        TZ3          89       14.90     1,326.10

      TOTAL COST - PRODUCT  2                     11,152.36

         3        RT6          76       12.00       912.00
         3        S6L          56        9.87       552.72
         3        ZEF          84        4.09       343.56

      TOTAL COST - PRODUCT  3                      1,808.28

      TOTAL COST - ALL PRODUCTS                   16,505.50
```

2-17
Summary

1. COBOL is made up of four program divisions: the IDENTIFICATION DIVISION, the ENVIRONMENT DIVISION, the DATA DIVISION, and the PROCEDURE DIVISION. Each of these has different clauses and sections that may be used to define or perform COBOL elements.
2. The PROCEDURE DIVISION is divided into groups of code called paragraphs. The paragraphs are made up of many separate sentences which are, in turn, made up of one or several statements.

3. The OPEN statement allows our program to access a data file for inputting or outputting data. Every file that is opened should subsequently be closed after the program no longer needs it. Data is input into the program storage areas with the READ statement. Generally an extra clause, AT END, is used on the READ statement to sense when the file has no more data left to input. After data is processing in the program, it is written to a file or some type of output device, such as a printer, with the WRITE statement. If the data being output is to be printed, the ADVANCING clause can be used to skip a specified number of lines or to advance to the top of the next page.

4. In COBOL the DO-WHILE loop is accomplished with the PERFORM . . . UNTIL statement, which will perform a named paragraph until the stated condition is true. If the paragraph to be performed is to be executed only once, the optional UNTIL clause is not needed. The PERFORM . . . VARYING and the PERFORM . . . TIMES are other forms of the PERFORM statement. Any variation of the PERFORM statement can use the THRU option, which lets us perform multiple paragraphs with one PERFORM statement.

5. Three different types of data can be moved in a program: literals, figurative constants, and data fields. Also, there are three ways to MOVE data in a program: non-numeric moves, numeric moves, and group moves.

6. When editing reports we can generally arrange to do the following:

   (a) print decimal points, commas, and dollar signs;
   (b) suppress leading zeros;
   (c) print asterisks for check protection;
   (d) print plus or minus signs as value indicators;
   (e) print the accounting indicators CR and DB;
   (f) print blanks when the value of the field is zero;
   (g) fill a cell with specified characters.

7. We can redefine a field to have a second layout by using the REDEFINES clause.

8. Since COBOL is basically a business language, only a few calculations are generally needed in a typical COBOL program. COBOL has commands for addition (ADD), subtraction (SUBTRACT), multiplication (MULTIPLY), division (DIVIDE), and, with the use of a special statement (COMPUTE), exponentiation.

9. The REMAINDER clause takes the remainder of the division and places it in a separate field. The ROUNDED clause can keep your result field from losing the significance of unneeded decimal postions. The ON SIZE ERROR clause is useful for capturing any truncation errors that might occur if a result field is not created large enough. It can also be used to capture any division-by-zero error.

10. When using negative numbers in COBOL, you must add a special symbol (S) to the beginning of the PIC clause to notify COBOL that the numbers are to be signed. If you do not use the S in the PIC clause, the numbers are considered to be unsigned; in calculations, an unsigned number functions as if it were positive.

11. One of COBOL's most important capabilities is of comparing items and then taking one of two possible paths through the program depending on the results of the comparision. The COBOL statement to accomplish this is the IF test. The IF test has an ELSE clause. Also, three basic conditionals—EQUAL, LESS THAN, and GREATER THAN—and three logical operators—NOT, AND, and OR—may be used with it.

12. If we use one IF test as the true or false action of another IF test, we are said to be using a nested IF test. In nested IF tests, the ELSE clause always is paired with the immediately preceding IF test. Sometimes this can cause problems, requiring the use of the NEXT SENTENCE clause, in which control of the program jumps out of the IF statement. We can simplify some IF tests by using PERFORM statements as the action. We can also use implied IF tests to shorten the conditional statements themselves.

13. A control break program prints a report that details the file information and shows subtotals along the way. The subtotals are created by separating the detail lines upon the changing of a control field; thus, the subtotals are sometimes called control totals.

14. The real control break functions, which are done in the control break routine, include

- printing the control total,
- adding the control total to the grand total,
- zeroing out the control total,
- moving the new control field to the hold field.

2-18
Glossary

ABEND   An acronym for "ABnormal END", referring to when a program stops executing because of a program error.

ADD statement   The keyword command that allows two or more numbers to be added together.

AT END   A clause used on the READ statement to allow the program to detect when there are no more records in the file that is being read.

BLOCK CONTAINS   The file description clause that specifies the number of records in the block.

Class test   The test for the type (NUMERIC or ALPHABETIC) of data being used.

CLOSE statement   The command that allows the closing of a file that has been used to process data.

COMPUTE statement   The statement that allows the mathematical operations to be performed in a calculation format instead of through keywords being used for the commands.

CONFIGURATION SECTION   The ENVIRONMENT DIVISION section that specifies the computer used to compile and execute the program.

Control break program   A program that prints group subtotals along with grand totals at the end of the program.

Cross-reference listing   A JCL command that causes the compiler to show the locations of all the fields in the program.

DATA DIVISION   The division that specifies all the input and output files used in the program and their associated records and fields.

DATA RECORD(S)   The file description clause that specifies the name(s) of the records being used.

Data validation   The process of using various COBOL tests to determine if the input data is valid for the operations that are to be performed.

DISPLAY statement   The command for printing specified data to the default device, which is generally the display screen.

DIVIDE statement   The keyword command for dividing one number by another.

ENVIRONMENT DIVISION   The COBOL division that describes the hardware to be used by the program.

EXAMINE statement   The statement from the 1968 standard that allows the programmer to count or change the occurrence of characters in a field. (See also INSPECT.)

EXHIBIT statement   The statement that allows a list of items to be displayed on the default device.

FD, or File Description   Several clauses that list the name of the file and give information about how the file is set up.

Figurative constant   A COBOL reserved word that has special meaning to the compiler. SPACES and ZEROS were discussed in the chapter as being examples of figurative constants.

FILE-CONTROL   The paragraph in the ENVIRONMENT DIVISION that lists the SELECT clauses.

FILE SECTION   The FILE DIVISION section that describes the characteristics of the files used in the program.

IDENTIFICATION DIVISION   The COBOL division that supplies information about the installation and the author of the program.

IF test   The command that tests a specified condition and then executes one of two possible commands depending upon the results of the test.

INPUT-OUTPUT SECTION   The ENVIRONMENT DIVISION section that contains the FILE-CONTROL paragraph, which in turn lists the SELECT clauses.

INSPECT statement   The statement from the 1976 and 1985 standards that allows the programmer to count or change the occurrence of characters in a field.

JUSTIFIED RIGHT clause   The clause on a PIC statement that allows the stored literal to be moved to the right side of the storage area.

LABEL RECORD(S)   The file description clause that indicates whether the file is to have labels (STANDARD) or not (OMITTED).

MOVE statement   The command that allows data in one storage area of the machine to be copied to one or more other storage areas.

MULTIPLY statement   The keyword command for multiplying numbers.

NEXT SENTENCE   The clause that allows one action of the IF test to skip out of the test without the use of any other imperative statements.

Non-numeric literals   Quotation-enclosed constants used for purposes other than mathematical calculations.

Numeric literals   Constants used primarily for mathematical calculations.

OPEN statement   The command that allows a file to be available to the program for processing. No data can be processed from a file that has not been opened.

Paragraph   A group of sentences and statements that defines a particular procedure to be performed.

PERFORM statement   The statement that allows a procedure to be executed one or more times.

PERFORM . . . TIMES   The form of the PERFORM statement that allows the named module to be executed a specified number of times.

PERFORM . . . UNTIL   The form of the PERFORM statement that allows the named module to be executed until a specified condition is met.

PERFORM . . . VARYING   The form of the PERFORM statement that allows initialization and automatic updating of a field that can be used as a subscript or simply as a counter.

PROCEDURE DIVISION   The COBOL section in which all the processing in the program takes place.

READ **statement**   The statement that inputs data from a file to the program storage area.

READY TRACE   The command that causes the computer to begin producing a listing of the paragraph-names as they are executed in the program.

RECORD CONTAINS   The file description clause that specifies how many characters long the record is.

Record description   The clause that gives the name of the record. It is always listed on an 01 level.

REDEFINES   The clause that allows a field to be defined with two or more different layouts.

REMAINDER **clause**   A clause that can be added to the DIVIDE statement to store the remainder of the division operation.

RESET TRACE   The command to turn off the tracing function (READY TRACE).

ROUNDED **clause**   A clause that can be used to cause the decimal portion of the result field of a calculation to be rounded instead of truncated.

SELECT   The clause that gives a name to the file and indicates to the machine what type of file it is.

Sentence   One or more statements specifying a certain action to be executed.

Sign test   The clause in the IF test that allows you to test for the sign of a number with a POSITIVE or NEGATIVE option.

STOP RUN   The statement that indicates the logical end of the program. When STOP RUN is encountered, the program ends and control returns to the operating system.

SUBTRACT **statement**   The keyword command for subtracting one number from another.

THRU   The clause that allows a PERFORM statement to continue processing through several paragraphs.

Truncation   The process of shortening a field when it is moved to an area too small to hold all its data.

UNTIL   An option of the PERFORM statement that allows the PERFORM to function until some condition is reached.

WORKING-STORAGE SECTION   The FILE DIVISION section that defines any fields in the program that were not previously defined in the FILE SECTION.

WRITE **statement**   The statement that allows data to be transferred from the program storage areas to a data file or the printed page.

2-19
Quick Quiz

Cover the answers with a blank sheet of paper and test yourself. Questions 1–15 are true or false questions, 16–20 are multiple choice, and 21–30 are fill-in-the-blank.

T F **1.** It is okay to end the program without closing the files as long as none of them is an output file.

T F **2.** The AT END clause on the READ statement is optional.

T F **3.** Though the ADVANCING clause is optional, it is on almost every WRITE statement.

T F   **4.** The PERFORM statement without the UNTIL clause is useful for modular programming.

T F   **5.** We can MOVE a figurative constant to a group item.

T F   **6.** Data editing is basically a numeric field function.

T F   **7.** When the GIVING option is used on any of the calculation forms, the result field is not part of the calculation itself.

T F   **8.** Most logic errors are detected during the compile process.

T F   **9.** You can always change the form of the IF test so that you won't need the NEXT SENTENCE clause.

T F   **10.** Data fields compared on the IF statement must be the same size.

T F   **11.** The ELSE test is always related to the immediately preceding IF.

T F   **12.** It is not necessary for input data to be in sequence when a control break program is being executed.

T F   **13.** To determine when the control field changes, we compare it against a hold field.

T F   **14.** We typically do not zero out subtotals in the control break routine.

T F   **15.** In the statement

```
PERFORM LIST-LOOP-FIRST THRU LIST-LOOP-END UNTIL EOF = 1.
```

all the paragraphs located between LIST-LOOP-FIRST and LIST-LOOP-END will be performed.

_____   **16.** Which of the following cannot be moved to a numeric variable?

    (a) literal   **(c)** figurative constant

    (b) numeric field   **(d)** All are valid to MOVE.

_____   **17.** Given

```
ADD FIELD-A TO FIELD-B.
MULTIPLY FIELD-C BY FIELD-B.
DIVIDE FIELD-B BY 25 GIVING FIELD-D.
```

which of the following COMPUTE statements is equivalent?

    (a) COMPUTE FIELD-D = (FIELD-C * (FIELD-A + FIELD-B)) / 25.

    (b) COMPUTE FIELD-B = (FIELD-C * (FIELD-A + FIELD-D)) / 25.

    (c) COMPUTE FIELD-D = (FIELD-A + (FIELD-C * FIELD-B)) / 25.

    (d) None of them.

_____   **18.** Which of the following statements will give you the most information about field values?

    (a) TRACE   **(c)** EXHIBIT NAMED

    (b) EXHIBIT   **(d)** DISPLAY

_____   **19.** Which of the following is not necessary in a control break routine?

    (a) printing the control total

    (b) moving the control field to the hold field

    (c) zeroing out the control total

    (d) advancing to a new page

_____   **20.** In a multiple-level control break, the first item in the detail loop is always

    (a) the IF test

    (b) the move control to hold statement.

    (c) the READ statement.

    (d) the detail WRITE statement.

21. A group move is always considered to be a _____ move.
22. Using one PERFORM within another PERFORM is called _____ .
23. The three types of moves are _____, _____, and _____ . .
24. The clause used to fill a cell with a specified literal is the _____ .
25. If you attempt to do any calculation with a numeric field that does not have valid data in it, the program will _____ .
26. All four keyword calculation statements have the use of one keyword clause in common. It is _____ .
27. When you are using a nested IF test and need an ELSE clause but the ELSE clause will be paired with the wrong IF test, the _____ clause can be very handy.
28. Control totals are sometimes referred to as _____ .
29. The field that is used to determine when a control break is to be performed is called a (an) _____ .
30. The command to print information on the screen is _____ .

2-20

Answers to Quick Quiz

1. F (All files should be closed, though there is a special problem with output data files.)
2. T
3. F (The ADVANCING option is used only for print files, and there are a lot of output files besides print files.)
4. T (Along with reusing a module in several places in the program.)
5. T (SPACES is commonly used.)
6. T (There are only a few editing symbols that are used on non-numeric fields.)
7. T (The result is calculated and then placed in the result field.)
8. F (The compiler cannot find logic errors. The programmer has to uncover them.)
9. F (You usually can, but there are times in nested IF tests when the NEXT SENTENCE clause becomes a necessity.)
10. F (The computer will make them the same size.)
11. T (That's why a NEXT SENTENCE is sometimes necessary.)
12. F (It must always be in sequence; otherwise the matching won't work.)
13. T
14. F (We must zero out subtotals in the control break routine; otherwise the subtotal will keep accumulating and will be the same as the grand total.)
15. T
16. d (As long as a numeric literal is used and ZEROS are used for the figurative constant.)
17. a (This can be figured out by writing out each statement in COMPUTE form, such as

```
COMPUTE FIELD-B = FIELD-A + FIELD-B
COMPUTE FIELD-B = FIELD-C * FIELD-B
COMPUTE FIELD-D = FIELD-B / 25
```

Now substitute the calculation from the first statement for FIELD-B in the second statement to get

```
COMPUTE FIELD-B = FIELD-C * (FIELD-A + FIELD-B)
```

Then substitute this calculation for FIELD-B in the third statement to get answer a:

```
COMPUTE FIELD-D = (FIELD-C * (FIELD-A + FIELD-B)) / 25.
```

18. c (Because it also prints the field-name.)
19. d (We sometimes do it, but it isn't imperative.)
20. a (The IF test is always first, whether the break is multiple-level or not.)
21. non-numeric
22. nesting
23. non-numeric, numeric, group
24. ALL
25. ABEND
26. GIVING
27. NEXT SENTENCE
28. subtotals
29. control field
30. DISPLAY

2-21
Questions to Aid Understanding

1. Describe the format and usage of the
  (a) OPEN statement
  (b) CLOSE statement
  (c) READ statement (mention READ . . . INTO)
  (d) WRITE statement (mention WRITE . . . FROM)
  (e) PERFORM statement (all three forms)
  (f) MOVE statement
  (g) ADD statement
  (h) SUBTRACT statement
  (i) MULTIPLY statement
  (j) DIVIDE statement
  (k) IF statement
  (l) READY TRACE statement
  (m) DISPLAY statement
  (n) EXHIBIT statement
  (o) INSPECT statement

2. Explain why a file that is being output to must be closed before the program concludes.
3. Explain the purpose of the AT END clause of the READ statement.
*4. Using the following DATA DIVISION, explain what is wrong with each of the statements below it (if anything; some have no errors):

```
DATA DIVISION.
FILE SECTION.
FD   FILE-IN
     LABEL RECORDS ARE OMITTED.
01   RECORD-IN.
     05   NAME-IN                      PIC X(20).
     05   ADDRESS-IN                   PIC X(20).
     05   CITY-IN                      PIC X(15).
     05   STATE-IN                     PIC XX.
     05   ZIP-CODE-IN                  PIC X(5).
     05   AMOUNT-IN                    PIC 9(5)V99.
FD   FILE-OUT
     LABEL RECORDS ARE OMITTED.
01   RECORD-OUT                        PIC X(133).

WORKING-STORAGE SECTION.
01   WORK-AREAS.
     05   EOF                          PIC XXX    VALUE 'NO'.
01   PRINT-RECORD.
     05   NAME-OUT                     PIC X(20).
     05   FILLER                       PIC XXX.
     05   ADDRESS-OUT                  PIC X(20).
     05   FILLER                       PIC XXX.
     05   CITY-OUT                     PIC X(15).
```

```
*(a) READ RECORD-IN
         AT END MOVE 'YES' TO EOF.
 (b) PERFORM CALC-ROUTINE
             WHILE EOF NOT = 'YES'.
*(c) MOVE ZIP-CODE-IN TO ZIP-CODE-OUT.
 (d) READ FILE-IN
         AT END MOVE 9 TO EOF
*(e) WRITE FILE-OUT.
 (f) MOVE SPACES TO RECORD-IN.
*(g) PERFORM CALC-ROUTINE
             UNTIL EOF = 'NO'.
 (h) WRITE PRINT-RECORD
         AFTER ADVANCING 2 LINES.
*(i) WRITE RECORD-OUT
         UNTIL EOF = 'YES'.
 (j) WRITE RECORD-OUT
         AFTER ADVANCING 2 PAGES.
```

*5. Explain the purpose of data editing.
*6. For the following questions, fill in the missing entry. The caret (ˆ) represents the location of the decimal point.

	SENDING-FIELD		RECEIVING-FIELD	
	PIC clause	Contents	PIC clause	Contents
(a)	99V99	12^44	ZZ.99	_____
(b)	9999V999	0234^120	_____	ƀƀ234.1
(c)	S999V99	000^06 (+)	$$$.00	_____
(d)	999	123 (−)	$ZZZ.99	_____
(e)	S99	00 (−)	+++	_____
(f)	S999V99	123^45 (+)	$$$$.99	_____
(g)	S99	01 (−)	_____	ƀ1ƀƀ
(h)	S99	22 (+)	_____	22ƀDB
(i)	S99V99	00^01 (+)	$ZZ.99CR	_____
(j)	S999V9	123^45 (−)	_____	$123.40
(k)	S9999V99	1234^45	_____	−1,234.45
(l)	9999	1234	$*,***.99	_____
(m)	XXXX	1234	XX/XX	_____
(n)	XXXXX	12345	XX/XXBX	_____
(o)	S99999	00022 (−)	$$,$$9.99−	_____
(p)	S99999	00001 (+)	$$,$$$.99+	_____
(q)	S9999V99	0000.13 (−)	$Z,ZZZ.ZZCR	_____
(r)	9999V99	0001^23	_____	$1.23
(s)	99V99	11^22	_____	+11.22
(t)	S99	00 (+)	−−−	_____
(u)	S99	00 (−)	+++	_____

7. Explain the purpose of the REMAINDER, ROUNDED, and ON SIZE ERROR clauses.

*8. Explain why a programmer might choose to use the COMPUTE statement rather than the more explanatory keyword calculations.

9. Explain why a field that might end up as a negative value must be given special treatment in the PIC clause and what that special treatment is.

*10. For the next set of exercises, assume the following field sizes and values:

```
10   FIELD-A        PIC 999V99  VALUE 10.
10   FIELD-B        PIC 9999V9  VALUE 20.
10   FIELD-C        PIC 99      VALUE  5.
10   FIELD-D        PIC 9       VALUE  3.
```

Calculate the results of each of the following statements, listing the field(s) that would get the result and the value of that result. Always assume the original values shown above on subsequent questions.

* **(a)** ADD FIELD-A, FIELD-B TO FIELD-C.
  (b) DIVIDE FIELD-C BY 5 GIVING FIELD-D.
* **(c)** COMPUTE FIELD-A ROUNDED = FIELD B * .25.
  (d) MULTIPLY 25 BY FIELD-A.
* **(e)** ADD 25 TO FIELD-D.
  (f) COMPUTE FIELD-A = (FIELD-C + 5) * FIELD-D / 3
* **(g)** COMPUTE FIELD-A = (FIELD-A - 18) / (FIELD-B * 5)

*11. Assuming the field-names and paragraph-names referenced below are properly defined, explain what is wrong (if anything) with each of the following:

* **(a)** ADD 1 TO FIELD-A.
  (b) ADD FIELD-A TO FIELD-B GIVING FIELD-C.
* **(c)** COMPUTE FIELD-A / FIELD-B.
  (d) ADD FIELD-A FIELD-B GIVING FIELD-C ROUNDED.
* **(e)** SUBTRACT -100 FIELD-A FROM FIELD-B.
  (f) ADD -100 FIELD-B FIELD-C TO FIELD-D.
* **(g)** ADD 1 FIELD-A TO FIELD-A.
  (h) MULTIPLY FIELD-A BY FIELD-B.
* **(i)** MULTIPLY FIELD-A INTO FIELD-C.
  (j) DIVIDE FIELD-A BY FIELD-D FIELD-C GIVING FIELD-E.
* **(k)** DIVIDE ZERO INTO FIELD-A.
  (l) DIVIDE FIELD-A BY FIELD-B GIVING FIELD-R ROUNDED.
* **(m)** DIVIDE FIELD-A INTO FIELD-B ROUNDED GIVING FIELD-R.
  (n) DIVIDE FIELD-A BY FIELD-B GIVING FIELD-R REMAINDER.
* **(o)** SUBTRACT 400 FROM FIELD-D.
  (p) COMPUTE FIELD-A = (FIELD-A*5) - FIELD-B.
* **(q)** COMPUTE REMAINDER FIELD-A = FIELD-B / FIELD-C.
  (r) COMPUTE FIELD-A = -1.
* **(s)** COMPUTE = FIELD-A + FIELD-B / FIELD-C * FIELD-D.
  (t) COMPUTE FIELD-A = FIELD-B / FIELD-C ROUNDED.
* **(u)** COMPUTE FIELD-A = FIELD-B / FIELD-C REMAINDER FIELD-D.

12. Write PROCEDURE DIVISION statements for the following:

(a) Write both an ADD statement and a COMPUTE statement to add 15 to FIELD-A.

(b) Write an ADD statement to add the fields FIELD-A, FIELD-B, and FIELD-C and store the result in FIELD-D.

(c) Write a single COBOL statement to subtract a discount of 25% from FIELD-A and then add that discount to FIELD-D.

(d) Write the COBOL statements to accomplish the following formula without a COMPUTE statement:

$$RESULT = \frac{AMOUNT * 35}{(FIELD\text{-}A + FIELD\text{-}B) / 25} + (45\ FIELD\text{-}E) / 3$$

(e) Write a COMPUTE statement to accomplish the above formula.

*13. Explain what logic errors are and why they are so difficult to find.

14. Explain what the TRACE is and how it can be valuable in tracking down program errors. Also give the statements that are used to turn the statement on and off.

15. Explain what the DISPLAY statement is and how it is used.

16. Explain what the EXHIBIT statement is, how it is used, and what capabilities it has that the DISPLAY statement doesn't.

17. Describe how a cross-reference listing can help you debug your programs.
*18. List the three logical operators and explain how they are used.
19. Design a nested IF test. Then show another method to accomplish the same processing.
*20. Explain the purpose of the NEXT SENTENCE clause and show how it would be used in a nested IF test.

Find what (if anything) is wrong with each of the statements 21 through 26 and explain how to correct it.

*21. IF FIELD-A IS LESS THAN OR EQUAL TO FIELD-B
        PERFORM ROUTINE-1.
22. IF FIELD-A NOT = FIELD-B OR FIELD-C AND FIELD-D
        PERFORM ROUTINE-1.
*23. IF FIELD-A NOT = FIELD-B = FIELD-C
        PERFORM ROUTINE-1.
24. IF FIELD-A = 'ABC'
        PERFORM ROUTINE-1.
*25. IF FIELD-A OR FIELD-B = 5
        PERFORM ROUTINE-1.
26. IF FIELD-A = 'ABC' OR FIELD-B = 123
        PERFORM ROUTINE-1.

27. Explain the purpose of a control break and how the break works.
*28. Explain how the hold field is used in conjunction with the control field.
29. What is typically done in a control break routine?

2-22
Coding Exercises

1. Write the PIC clause necessary to cause an 8-(significant) digit number to be printed with commas, two decimal positions, and a floating dollar sign.
2. Write the PIC clause needed to print a 5-digit field (plus two decimal positions) as a check protected field.
3. Write a single COMPUTE statement to add AMOUNT-1, AMOUNT-2, and AMOUNT-3, multiply that sum by MULTIPLICATION-FACTOR, subtract 25 from that, and divide the entire calculation by the field called DIVISOR. Put the result in the CALCULATED-RESULT field.
4. Change the COMPUTE statement produced in exercise 3 to as many separate calculation statements as are needed. Use other fields if necessary for intermediate totals.
5. Write the IF statement to determine if the value in a field called ACCOUNTS-RECEIVABLE-AMOUNT is equal to the value in a field called ACCOUNT-BALANCE. If they are equal, add 1 to the IN-BALANCE field. If they are not the same, add 1 to the OUT-OF-BALANCE field.
6. Write an IF test to determine if NUMBER-INPUT is greater than NUMBER-CALCULATED. If it is not, don't do anything. If it is, add 1 to NUMBER-COUNTER and test to see if NUMBER-COUNTER exceeds 25. If it does, perform 0800-ERROR-ROUTINE.

7. Write the coding necessary for a control break module that will print out a customer's name, address, and telephone number. Customers are divided into areas (AREA AND AREA-HOLD) for the control test. Make the control break routine name CONTROL-BREAK-ROUTINE. All that is needed is the IF test and the control break routine itself.

2-23
Maintenance Program

The Widget Works has several manufacturing facilities around the country that receive raw materials from several different warehouses. The company has a report that details these shipments by what products are received and when they are received. You are assigned the task of modifying the regular detail report into a control break program so that it breaks on the warehouse that the products are shipped from. The original systems chart is shown in Figure 2-6. The file layout that was used for the SHIPPING file is shown in Figure 2-7. The printer spacing chart in Figure 2-8 shows the report as it looks now, and Figure 2-9 shows it as it should look. Virtually the only difference is the use of the control totals. The original design of the program is shown in Figure 2-10. The pseudocode is

```
Start
Open the files
Initialize totals, line-counter, page-counter
Print headings
Read a record at end mark end-of-file
DO-WHILE not end-of-file
        Calculate total value of the product
        Print detail line
        Increment line-counter by 2
        IF line counter > 59 THEN
            Print headings
        (ELSE)
        END-IF
        Accumulate total product value
        Read a record at end mark end-of-file
END-DO
Print out total product value
Close the files
End
```

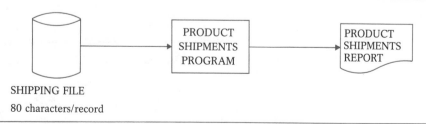

SHIPPING FILE

80 characters/record

Figure 2-6   The systems chart for the maintenance program.

SHIPPING File					
Field Description	*Position*	*Length*	:	*Dec*	*Type*
Warehouse	1–2	2	:		Non-numeric
Product number	3–7	5	:		Non-numeric
Filler	8–33	26	:		Non-numeric
Product value	34–40	7	:	2	Numeric
Filler	41–45	5	:		Non-numeric
Date received	46–51	6	:		Non-numeric
Quantity received	52–56	5	:	0	Numeric
Filler	57–80	24	:		Non-numeric
Record Length = 80					

Figure 2-7   The file layout for the SHIPPING file.

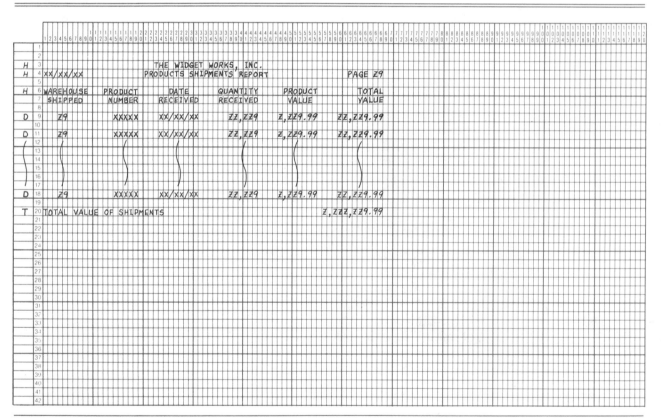

Figure 2-8   The original look of the products shipments report.

```
            111111111122222222223333333333444444444455555555556666666666777777777788888888889999999999000000000011111111112
 123456789012345678901234567890123456789012345678901234567890123456789012345678901234567890123456789012345678901234567890
1
2
H 3                         THE WIDGET WORKS, INC.
H 4 XX/XX/XX               PRODUCTS SHIPMENTS REPORT                        PAGE Z9
5
H 6 WAREHOUSE   PRODUCT      DATE      QUANTITY    PRODUCT        TOTAL
H 7 SHIPPED     NUMBER     RECEIVED    RECEIVED    VALUE          VALUE
8
D 9 Z9          X---X      XX/XX/XX    ZZ,ZZ9     Z,ZZ9.99     ZZ,ZZ9.99
10
D 11 Z9         X---X      XX/XX/XX    ZZ,ZZ9     Z,ZZ9.99     ZZ,ZZ9.99
12
13
14
15
16
17
D 18 Z9         X---X      XX/XX/XX    ZZ,ZZ9     Z,ZZ9.99     ZZ,ZZ9.99
19
T 20 TOTAL VALUE OF SHIPMENTS FOR WAREHOUSE Z9            Z,ZZZ,ZZ9.99
21
22
23
24
25
26
T 27 TOTAL VALUE OF SHIPMENTS FOR WAREHOUSE Z9            Z,ZZZ,ZZ9.99
28
T 29 TOTAL VALUE OF ALL SHIPMENTS                        ZZ,ZZZ,ZZ9.99
30
31
32
33
34
35
36
37
38
39
40
41
42
```

Figure 2-9 The layout of the products shipments report after it has been changed to a control break program.

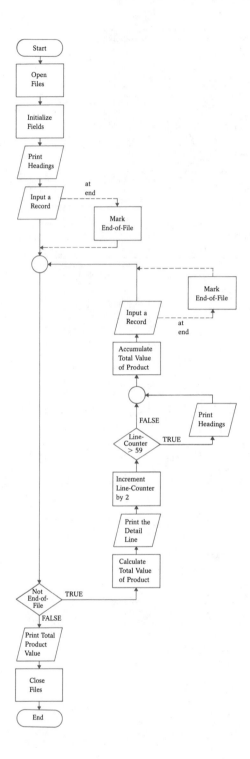

Figure 2-10   The flowchart for the products shipments report.

The original program:

```
****************************************************************
****************************************************************
*
*
*
*   PROGRAM NAME: PROD-SHP
*
*   PROGRAMMER NAME:  EDWARD J. COBURN
*
*   SOCIAL SECURITY NUMBER:  999-99-9999
*
*   DUE DATE: FEBRUARY 10, 1988
*
*   DESCRIPTION: THIS PROGRAM WILL PRODUCE A REPORT SHOWING
*                THE SHIPMENTS TO THE WAREHOUSE INCLUDING THE
*                QUANTITY AND PRODUCT VALUES.
*
****************************************************************
****************************************************************

IDENTIFICATION DIVISION.
PROGRAM-ID.    PROD-SHP.
AUTHOR.        EDWARD J. COBURN.

ENVIRONMENT DIVISION.

CONFIGURATION SECTION.
SOURCE-COMPUTER. IBM-4331.
OBJECT-COMPUTER. IBM-4331.

INPUT-OUTPUT SECTION.
FILE-CONTROL.
    SELECT SHIPPING-IN ASSIGN TO UT-S-SHIPPING.
    SELECT LIST-OUT    ASSIGN TO UT-S-SYSPRINT.

DATA DIVISION.
FILE SECTION.

FD  SHIPPING-IN
    LABEL RECORDS ARE OMITTED
    RECORD CONTAINS 80 CHARACTERS.
01  SHIPPING-RECORD.
    05   WAREHOUSE            PIC 99.
    05   PRODUCT-NUMBER       PIC XXXXX.
    05   FILLER               PIC X(26).
    05   PRODUCT-VALUE        PIC 9(5)V99.
    05   FILLER               PIC X(5).
    05   DATE-RECEIVED        PIC X(6).
    05   QUANTITY-RECEIVED    PIC 9(5).
    05   FILLER               PIC X(56).

FD  LIST-OUT
    LABEL RECORDS ARE OMITTED
    RECORD CONTAINS 133 CHARACTERS.
01  LIST-OUT-RECORD          PIC X(133).
```

```
WORKING-STORAGE SECTION.

01   WORK-AREAS.
     05   EOF                      PIC XXX           VALUE 'NO '.
          88  WE-ARE-OUT-OF-DATA                     VALUE 'YES'.
     05   LINE-CTR                 PIC 99            VALUE ZERO.
     05   PAGE-CTR                 PIC 99            VALUE 1.
     05   TOTAL-VALUE              PIC 9(5)V99       VALUE ZERO.
     05   GRAND-TOTAL-VALUE        PIC 9(7)V99       VALUE ZERO.
     05   MACHINE-DATE             PIC X(6).
     05   DATE-WORK REDEFINES MACHINE-DATE.
          10   DATE-YY             PIC XX.
          10   DATE-MM             PIC XX.
          10   DATE-DD             PIC XX.

01   PAGE-HEADING-1.
     05   FILLER                   PIC X(45)         VALUE
          '                              THE WIDGET WORKS, INC.'.
01   PAGE-HEADING-2.
     05   FILLER                   PIC X             VALUE SPACES.
     05   HEADING-MONTH            PIC XX.
     05   HEADING-DAY              PIC /XX/.
     05   HEADING-YEAR             PIC XX.
     05   FILLER                   PIC X(37)         VALUE
          '                  PRODUCTS SHIPMENTS REPORT'.
     05   FILLER                   PIC X(21)         VALUE
          '                PAGE '.
     05   PAGE-CTR-OUT             PIC Z9.

01   COLUMN-HEADING-1.
     05   FILLER                   PIC X(44)            VALUE
          ' WAREHOUSE    PRODUCT        DATE        QUANTITY'.
     05   FILLER                   PIC X(25)            VALUE
          '     PRODUCT        TOTAL'.

01   COLUMN-HEADING-2.
     05   FILLER                   PIC X(44)            VALUE
          '  SHIPPED        NUMBER     RECEIVED        RECEIVED'.
     05   FILLER                   PIC X(25)            VALUE
          '      VALUE         VALUE'.

01   DETAIL-LINE.
     05   FILLER                   PIC X(4)          VALUE SPACES.
     05   WAREHOUSE-OUT            PIC Z9.
     05   FILLER                   PIC X(9)          VALUE SPACES.
     05   PRODUCT-NUMBER-OUT       PIC XXXXX.
     05   FILLER                   PIC X(4)          VALUE SPACES.
     05   DATE-RECEIVED-OUT        PIC XX/XX/XX.
     05   FILLER                   PIC X(6)          VALUE SPACES.
     05   QUANTITY-RECEIVED-OUT    PIC ZZ,ZZZ.
     05   FILLER                   PIC X(4)          VALUE SPACES.
     05   PRODUCT-VALUE-OUT        PIC Z,ZZ9.99.
     05   FILLER                   PIC X(4)          VALUE SPACES.
     05   TOTAL-VALUE-OUT          PIC ZZ,ZZ9.99.

01   TOTAL-LINE.
     05   FILLER                   PIC X(25)         VALUE
          ' TOTAL VALUE OF SHIPMENTS'.
     05   FILLER                   PIC X(32)         VALUE SPACES.
     05   GRAND-TOTAL-VALUE-OUT    PIC Z,ZZZ,ZZ9.99.
```

```
PROCEDURE DIVISION.

0100-MAIN-MODULE.

    OPEN INPUT  SHIPPING-IN
        OUTPUT LIST-OUT.

    ACCEPT MACHINE-DATE FROM DATE.
    MOVE DATE-YY TO HEADING-YEAR.
    MOVE DATE-MM TO HEADING-MONTH.
    MOVE DATE-DD TO HEADING-DAY.

    PERFORM 0300-HEADING-ROUTINE.

    READ SHIPPING-IN
        AT END MOVE 'YES' TO EOF.
    PERFORM 0200-LIST-LOOP
            UNTIL WE-ARE-OUT-OF-DATA.

    MOVE GRAND-TOTAL-VALUE TO GRAND-TOTAL-VALUE-OUT.

    WRITE LIST-OUT-RECORD FROM TOTAL-LINE
        AFTER ADVANCING 2 LINES.

    CLOSE SHIPPING-IN
        LIST-OUT.
    STOP RUN.

0200-LIST-LOOP.

    MULTIPLY QUANTITY-RECEIVED BY PRODUCT-VALUE
            GIVING TOTAL-VALUE.

    MOVE WAREHOUSE          TO WAREHOUSE-OUT.
    MOVE PRODUCT-NUMBER     TO PRODUCT-NUMBER-OUT.
    MOVE DATE-RECEIVED      TO DATE-RECEIVED-OUT.
    MOVE QUANTITY-RECEIVED  TO QUANTITY-RECEIVED-OUT.
    MOVE PRODUCT-VALUE      TO PRODUCT-VALUE-OUT.
    MOVE TOTAL-VALUE        TO TOTAL-VALUE-OUT.

    WRITE LIST-OUT-RECORD FROM DETAIL-LINE
        AFTER ADVANCING 2 LINES.

    ADD TOTAL-VALUE TO GRAND-TOTAL-VALUE.

    ADD 2 TO LINE-CTR.

    IF LINE-CTR > 59
        PERFORM 0300-HEADING-ROUTINE.

    READ SHIPPING-IN
        AT END MOVE 'YES' TO EOF.

0300-HEADING-ROUTINE.

    MOVE PAGE-CTR TO PAGE-CTR-OUT.
    WRITE LIST-OUT-RECORD FROM PAGE-HEADING-1
            AFTER ADVANCING PAGE.
    WRITE LIST-OUT-RECORD FROM PAGE-HEADING-2
            AFTER ADVANCING 1 LINE.
```

```
WRITE LIST-OUT-RECORD FROM COLUMN-HEADING-1
     AFTER ADVANCING 2 LINES.
WRITE LIST-OUT-RECORD FROM COLUMN-HEADING-2
     AFTER ADVANCING 1 LINE.

MOVE 6 TO LINE-CTR.
ADD 1 TO PAGE-CTR.
```

A sample of the output from the program:

```
                        THE WIDGET WORKS, INC.
05/23/88              PRODUCTS SHIPMENTS REPORT              PAGE  1

WAREHOUSE    PRODUCT     DATE      QUANTITY     PRODUCT        TOTAL
SHIPPED      NUMBER    RECEIVED    RECEIVED      VALUE         VALUE

    1        A1345     01/25/88     1,225       426.18     22,070.50

    1        A3485     02/25/88     1,317        71.29     93,888.93

    1        BB908     02/12/88       176       418.59     73,671.84

    1        BR988     02/15/88       994       728.75     24,377.50

    7        A4569     02/18/88     1,377       931.78     83,061.06

    7        B8498     02/01/88       818     1,200.66     82,139.88

    7        DDD98     03/15/88        26       493.75     12,837.50

    8        B948R     04/12/88       216       364.84     78,805.44

    8        DD838     05/18/88       174        83.02     14,445.48

    8        R8477     01/18/88        20       473.27      9,465.40

    8        ZZ837     03/21/88       481       327.94     57,739.14

   12        AA948     04/25/88       742     1,190.42     83,291.64

   12        AB948     05/16/88       268     1,007.04     69,886.72

   12        ACC98     12/15/87     1,071       727.54     79,195.34

   12        ACG99     01/14/88       551       785.14     32,612.14

   12        BR88A     02/30/88        39         4.03        157.17

   15        GHIH0     05/25/88       234        48.57     11,365.38

TOTAL VALUE OF SHIPMENTS                                   829,011.06
```

2-24

Illustrative Program

Write a program to validate data coming in from the donations file called DONATE, found in Appendix A. Use the file layout shown in Figure 2-11 to check that

■ numeric data is valid in the fields of
   (a) contributor's number
   (b) date of previous contribution
   (c) amount of previous contribution
   (d) date of current contribution
   (e) amount of current contribution
■ the file is in sequence by the contributor's number.

Figure 2-12 shows the printer spacing chart for the program. Notice that it shows the various error messages that are to be used if one of the fields is not valid or if the file is not in sequence. Figure 2-13 shows the systems chart for the program; the flowchart is in Figure 2-14; the pseudocode follows:

```
Start
Open the files
Initialize total, line-counter, page-counter
Print headings
Move 0 to hold field.
Move 'NO' to line printed field
Read a record at end mark end-of-file
DO-WHILE not end-of-file
        IF previous date is not numeric THEN
                Move error message to detail line
                Do error message routine
        (ELSE)
        END-IF
        IF previous amount is not numeric THEN
                Move error message to detail line
                Do error message routine
        (ELSE)
        END-IF
        IF current date is not numeric THEN
                Move error message to detail line
                Do error message routine
        (ELSE)
        END-IF
        IF current amount is not numeric THEN
                Move error message to detail line
                Do error message routine
        (ELSE)
        END-IF
        IF previous date is older than previous year THEN
                Move error message to detail line
                Do error message routine
```

```
(ELSE)
END-IF
IF current date is older than previous year THEN
        Move error message to detail line
        Do error message routine
(ELSE)
END-IF
IF contributor's number < = hold field THEN
        Move error message to detail line
        Do error message routine
ELSE
        Move contributor's number to hold field
END-IF
IF line printed field = 'NO'
        Print detail line
ELSE
        Move 'NO' to line printed field
END-IF
Read a record at end mark end-of-file
END-DO
Print total errors line
Close the files
End

Start error message routine
        Print detail line
        Move 'YES' to line printed field
        Add 1 to error counter
End error routine
```

Notice that the program will print any number of errors for each input record. It is also set up so that if an error message is printed, no additional detail line will be printed; if no error is found for a particular record, a detail line will be printed. Finally, we keep a counter of the number of errors and print the total number of errors at the end of the report.

DONATE File					
Field Description	Position	Length	:	Dec	Type
Contributors number	1–4	4	:		Non-numeric
Date of previous cont.	5–10	6	:		Non-numeric
Amount of prev. cont.	11–17	7	:	2	Numeric
Date of current cont.	18–23	6	:		Non-numeric
Amount of curr. cont.	24–30	7	:	2	Numeric
Filler	31–80	50	:		Non-numeric
Record Length = 80					

Figure 2-11   The record layout for the DONATE file.

If the records are out of sequence, we print an error message, but we keep the same hold field because we are assuming that the current record is the one causing the sequence error. This processing could be done by moving the new contributor's number into the hold field when the error is found, but we choose to assume that the current record is in error, not the previous one.

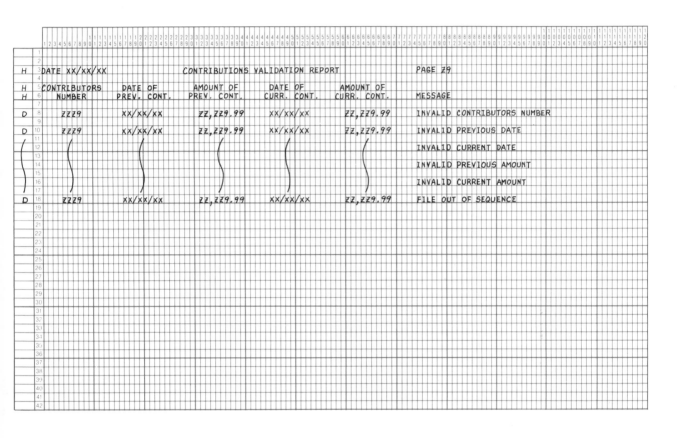

	CONTRIBUTORS NUMBER	DATE OF PREV. CONT.	AMOUNT OF PREV. CONT.	DATE OF CURR. CONT.	AMOUNT OF CURR. CONT.	MESSAGE
H	DATE XX/XX/XX		CONTRIBUTIONS VALIDATION REPORT			PAGE Z9
D	ZZZ9	XX/XX/XX	ZZ,ZZ9.99	XX/XX/XX	ZZ,ZZ9.99	INVALID CONTRIBUTORS NUMBER
D	ZZZ9	XX/XX/XX	ZZ,ZZ9.99	XX/XX/XX	ZZ,ZZ9.99	INVALID PREVIOUS DATE
						INVALID CURRENT DATE
						INVALID PREVIOUS AMOUNT
						INVALID CURRENT AMOUNT
D	ZZZ9	XX/XX/XX	ZZ,ZZ9.99	XX/XX/XX	ZZ,ZZ9.99	FILE OUT OF SEQUENCE

Figure 2-12   The layout for the contributions validation report.

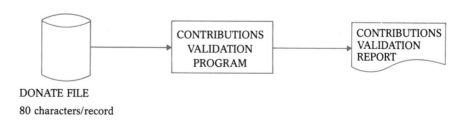

DONATE FILE
80 characters/record

Figure 2-13   The systems chart for the contributions validation program.

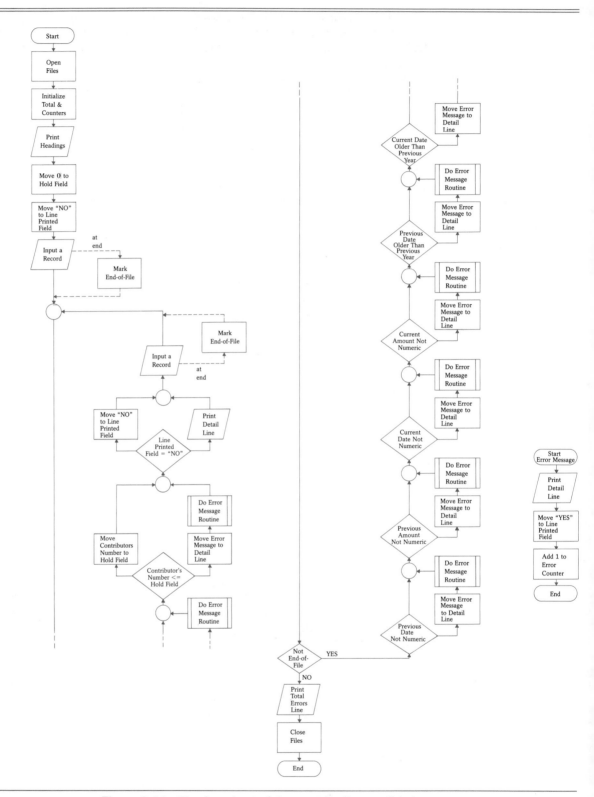

Figure 2-14   The flowchart of the contributions validation program.

2-25

System Designed Programs

For the following programs, all the design elements typically furnished to a programmer by the systems analyst are furnished. It is up to you, as programmer, to design and code the program. The files to be used are found in Appendix A.

1. Prepare a sales commission report. Your data should come from the SALES file shown in Figure 2-15. The commission is to be calculated on the total sales from the record (add up the five product totals) and figured on the basis of years of service:

   - 1 year   = 3%
   - 2 years   = 5%
   - 3 years   = 6%
   - 4 to 6 years   = 8%
   - 7 to 9 years   = 9%
   - 10 years or more = 10%

   This commission rate is paid only if the total sales amount is at least $1,000. If it is less, no commission is paid. The systems chart can be seen in Figure 2-16 and the report layout is shown in Figure 2-17. Notice in the latter that there are column totals on the sales amount and the commission.

SALES File					
Field Description	*Position*	*Length*	:	*Dec*	*Type*
Salesman number	1–4	4	:		Non-numeric
Salesman name	5–24	20	:		Non-numeric
Sales territory	25–26	2	:		Non-numeric
Filler	27–28	2	:		Non-numeric
Sales of product 1	29–35	7	:	2	Numeric
Sales of product 2	36–42	7	:	2	Numeric
Sales of product 3	43–49	7	:	2	Numeric
Sales of product 4	50–56	7	:	2	Numeric
Sales of product 5	57–63	7	:	2	Numeric
Years of service	64–65	2	:	0	Numeric
Filler	66–80	15	:		Non-numeric
Record Length = 80					

Figure 2-15   The record layout for the SALES file for exercise 2-25-1.

SALES FILE

80 Characters/record

Figure 2-16   The systems chart for the sales commission program, exercise 2-25-1.

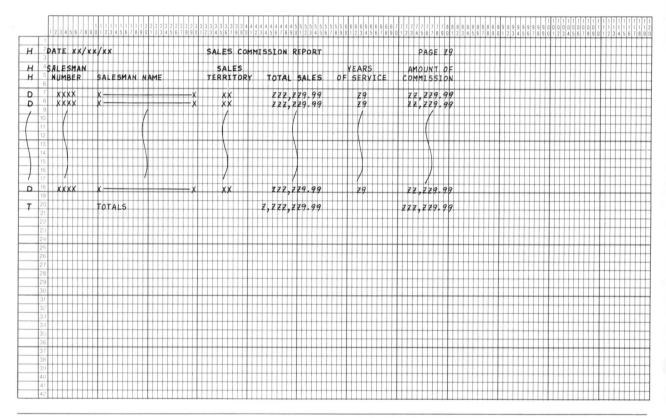

Figure 2-17   The layout for the sales commission report, exercise 2-25-1.

2. A credit card company is in the process of determining the total amount of debt charged by its card holders during a given month. Write a program to show each card holder's charge account purchases during one month, using the file input layout shown in Figure 2-18 for the CHARGE file. Print the date, place, type, and amount of purchase under the card holder's account number. At the end of each card holder's records, print the total amount of purchases made by that card holder. At the end of the report, print a grand total of all purchases made by all the card holders. The printer spacing chart is shown in Figure 2-19 and the system design in Figure 2-20.

CHARGE File					
Field Description	Position	Length	:	Dec	Type
Account number	1–5	5	:		Non-numeric
Date of purchase	6–11	6	:		Non-numeric
Place of purchase	12–31	20	:		Non-numeric
Description of purchase	32–46	15	:		Non-numeric
Amount of purchase	47–52	6	:	2	Numeric
Filler	53–80	28	:		Non-numeric
Record Length = 80					

Figure 2-18   The record layout for the CHARGE file, exercise 2-25-2.

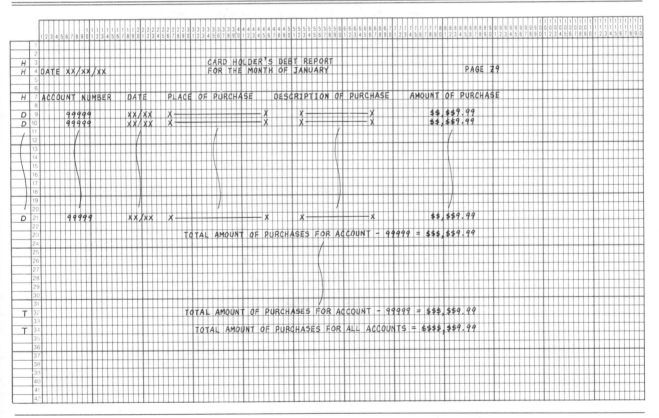

Figure 2-19   The layout for the charge card debt report, exercise 2-25-2.

CHARGE FILE

80 characters/record

Figure 2-20   The systems chart for exercise 2-25-2.

3. Because of advanced automation, a single factory can produce many different products. A large factory in Texas is divided into several manufacturing facilities. Each manufacturing facility contains a different number of machines. Each machine produces a different product. The factory wants a report showing the efficiency percent of each machine. This is computed by dividing the number of good products, which is the total products less those that are defective, by the total number of products produced by each machine. This number is then multiplied by 100 to give the efficiency percent. Also, the factory wants to know the efficiency percent for each manufacturing facility as well as the overall efficiency percent for the entire factory. The record layout for the MANUFACT file is shown in Figure 2-21, the printer spacing chart is shown in Figure 2-22, and the system design is shown in Figure 2-23. Arrange the program so that it can be used for printing either all the details or just a summary report.

MANUFACT File					
Field Description	*Position*	*Length*	:	*Dec*	*Type*
Facility	1–2	2	:	0	Numeric
Machine	3–4	2	:	0	Numeric
Total production	5–9	5	:	0	Numeric
Defective products	10–13	4	:	0	Numeric
Filler	14–80	67	:		Non-numeric
Record Length = 80					

Figure 2-21   The record layout for the MANUFACT file, exercise 2-25-3.

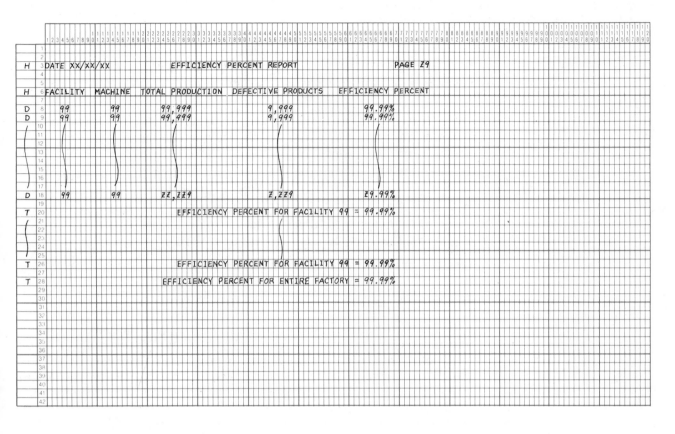

Figure 2-22   The layout for the efficiency report, exercise 2-25-3.

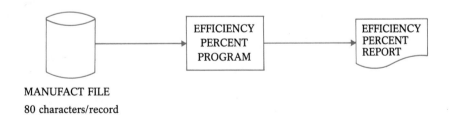

MANUFACT FILE

80 characters/record

Figure 2-23   The systems chart for exercise 2-25-3.

2-26

Non-designed Programs

In the following programs you will need to design the systems chart, the input files (record layout), the printer spacing chart, the program design, and the data with which to test the program.

1. Write a program to print out the charges for tuition and fees at your school. The file is to contain the ID (Social Security number), name, residency code (resident or non-resident), and credit hours for each student. The tuition is to be calculated as follows:

    < 12 hours = \$45 per credit for residents
    $> = 12$ hours = \$540 total for residents
    < 12 hours = \$118 per credit for non-residents
    $> = 12$ hours = \$1416 total for non-residents

    The fees are the same for residents and non-residents:

    < 12 hours = \$3 per credit
    $> = 12$ hours = \$36 total

    Your report should list the student ID with dashes, the name, the hours, the tuition charge, the fees charge, and a total charge. There should be report totals of the hours and of each of the charge columns. Also, you should have counts of the number of resident students and the average charge, the number of non-resident students and the average charge, and the total number of students and the average charge.

2. A large general merchandise store keeps track of the amount of sales each of its employees makes. Every time an employee makes a sale, a record is prepared showing the department number, employee number, and revenue from the sale. Each department has a different number of employees. Every employee is entitled to a 5% commission. Write a program that prints all the sales records by department, with a control total for each employee. Compute and print the commission during the printing of the control total. At the end of each department, print the total sales made and commissions earned. Also, print a grand total, for the entire store of both sales and commissions.

3. On the first of every month, a newspaper company creates a file with all the home deliveries it expects to make in that month. Write a program that determines the amount of revenue the newspaper company expects to receive from its home deliveries in the month under study. The newspaper has divided its entire service area into zones. Each zone has a different number of areas, and each area is divided into a different number of routes. The file was created in sequence by zone, area, and route. The total number of houses in each route has already been totaled on the file. The newspaper charges a standard fee of $6.90 a month per house for deliveries Monday thru Saturday. If a house receives a Sunday paper, an extra $1.50 is charged. The report should show the total number of houses in each route, the number of houses that receive the Sunday paper, and the total revenue expected from that route. Then, appropriate totals should show the expected revenue from each area within a zone. A total should also be generated for each zone and for the entire report.

OBJECTIVES After completing Chapter 3 you should be able to

1. explain the process of creating a sequential file and list three different methods of creating one;
2. list the four different files you use when doing a sequential update and explain the purpose of each;
3. list the three different types of update transactions and explain how they are accomplished;
4. list the three different reports that are printed during the update procedure and explain the purpose of each;
5. explain what is printed on the transaction report for each type of transaction;
6. list the three different possibilities when record keys are compared and explain what type of processing occurs during each possibility;
7. explain the purpose of HIGH-VALUES;
8. explain the processing differences that arise when you use rewriting instead of regular processing.

CHAPTER 3

SEQUENTIAL FILE HANDLING

3-1
Introduction

Thus far we have dealt with the topic of files and file processing in general terms only. We have never specifically addressed just how files are created and maintained on a disk. Well, in this chapter we will discuss how sequential files are handled on both tape and disk.

Sequential files are the only type of file that are used on tapes, since a tape drive is strictly a sequential storage device. Other types of files are used on disk; the discussion of those file types is left for Chapters 8 and 10.

In this chapter, then, we will begin by looking at the way sequential files are *created* on tape (or disk). Though we will seldom mention tape or disk by name, keep in mind that most of the file handling techniques are the same whether your sequential file is on tape or on disk. We will also look at several of the ways that sequential files can be processed.

3-2
Creation of a Sequential File

Creating a sequential file is not much different from printing a report. About the only differences are that you do not edit any of the data before writing it to the file, that the records you write are not designed with spaces and blank lines as they are on a report, and, of course, that there are no headings or totals.

Sequential files are created in a variety of ways.

■ The user may input the data directly using some type of on-line processing technique (see Chapter 4).
■ The data may be input from an existing sequential file created with some type of keypunching device such as a key-to-disk or key-to-tape device.
■ The data may be created using internal processing in our program.

Regardless of the method used to receive the data into our program, the sequential output file is processed the same way. We simply follow the same steps we have been using to create reports:

1. get the data for outputting (however this is accomplished);
2. move the data to our output record;
3. write the record to the output file.

This entire three-step procedure is repeated continuously until all the needed data is processed and the entire output file is created.

3-3
Files Used in a Sequential Update

One of the major processes on a sequential file (other than printing a report) is updating. **Updating** is the process of changing one or more records in the file in some manner. The problem with updating a sequential file is that all the records in the entire file must be processed. For example, if we want to change a record in the middle of the file, there is no way to get to the middle of the file without processing all the records previous to the record we need to change.

As you will see shortly, if we are going to modify records in a sequential file, the file must be in some type of order. Here we may have a problem of semantics. When we call a file *sequential,* we do not necessarily mean that the file is in sequence. We mean that all the records are stored, and must be processed, one at a time from the first record to the last. But, when we are going to update the records, it becomes necessary for the file to be in sequence, in sorted order by the field that we are going to process against, in much the same manner as the files we used for control break processing.

Now, when we are doing sequential file updating, we really use four different files:

1. First of all, there is the file we are updating, generally called the **old master file**. This file is made up of the records that are going to be changed during the update procedure.
2. Next there is the **new master file**, the file we create when we change the records in the old master file. If we are using tape files, we cannot write the records back to the same tape, so we must create a new master file for the updated records. That is, each record we read from the old master file is modified and then stored in the new master file (except for those that are deleted). This process is depicted in Figure 3-1.

   If we are updating a sequential disk file, we can use a special process called **rewriting**, which we will deal with later in the chapter. For now, however, just assume that we cannot update a master file without creating a distinct, new master file.

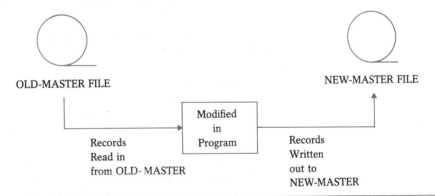

Figure 3-1   Illustration of how the records are processed from the OLD MASTER file to the NEW MASTER file.

3. Next there is the **transaction file**. This is the file of the records that contain the data to be changed. Generally there are three different types of transaction records to match the three different types of changes to the old master file:

    (a) Records can be added to the old master file. These transaction records must contain all the data necessary to put the entire record into the new master file. If there are ten different fields of data in the old master file, the transaction record must contain all ten of these fields in order for the new master file to contain all the needed data.

        Sometimes not all of the fields are put into the new master file from the transaction record. On occasion, a subsequent program is used to put some of the fields into the new master file. Possibly some calculations are made to create the fields. This is not generally the case, however, as most transaction updates put all the data into the new master file in the add routine.

    (b) Records can be deleted from the old master file. When records are deleted, the processing of the records is very easy: they are simply not written to the new master file. Remember that the new master file is being created from the old master file. Thus, if we want to remove a record from the old master file, we can do so by simply not writing that particular record to the new master file.

    (c) Records can be changed, a fairly easy procedure. We simply determine which field in the record needs to be changed, move the new data from the transaction record into the corresponding field in the old master record, and then write that record to the new master file.

4. The last file we will use for sequential updating is not really a file, though COBOL processes all output, including printed output, as files. When we update a file, it is a good idea to keep a printed record of what transactions have been processed. Thus, the fourth file is a print file. We print a report showing all the updates as they occur. Generally, when doing an update procedure, we generate three separate reports in the program:

    (a) We print out the file as it currently exists. Not all installations do this, but it is a fairly common procedure. It is generally skipped, to save paper and processing time, when the file being processed is especially long.

    (b) We print out a record of the transactions as they are processed. Recall that there are three types of transactions to keep track of:

    ▪ If a record is added, we print the new record information so that we know what data was added to the file.

    ▪ If a record is deleted, we print the data that was removed from the file as a safeguard against having deleted the wrong record. If it is discovered that the wrong record was deleted, we have a printed record of what data the file contained, and it can be replaced. Without the printout we might not know what data was deleted, especially if we have not printed the file *before* we update it.

    ▪ If a record is changed, we print the record the way it is now, but we also print the field data that was there before. Again, this is done in case we have made a mistake and changed the wrong field or changed the right field in the wrong record. Based on the information in the printout, we can go back to the file and repair our mistake.

    (c) The third report is generally a printout of the file in its new, updated form.

3-4
Designing the Update Program

We've already mentioned that, in order to do sequential updating, we must see that the master file is in order by some key field. Well, since we are going to update the master file using a transaction file, it stands to reason that the transaction file would have to be in order also. That is, if the master file is sorted by the employee number, then the transaction file must be sorted by the employee number also.

Once the files are both in order, they can be compared on the fields that were used to put them in order. This is done to find those records that can be added, changed, or deleted. When the files are compared, there are always three possibilities:

- the key fields in the master record and the transaction record are the same;
- the key field in the master record is less than the key field in the transaction record;
- the key field in the master record is greater than the key field in the transaction record.

Now, certain things can happen during each one of these posssible conditions.

3-4-1 When Both Key Fields Are the Same

We will begin by looking at what can happen when both key fields have the same value. If such is the case, it would be okay to delete the record from the old master file. Keep in mind that you delete a record by simply not writing it to the new file.

It is also okay to change the record. We do this by storing the new data from the transaction record in the input area for the old master file. Then, when we move it to be stored in the new master file, we will be storing the updated record.

If both of the key fields have the same value, for the transaction record to specify the transaction as an add is an error. Since the record is already in the file, we don't want another to be put into the file. Although we could set up our program so it would allow addition of any number of records with the same record key, such files, as we mentioned earlier, would be unusable.

The design for a module in which the key fields match (the flowchart in Figure 3-2 is incomplete since this is only a module) would be as follows:

```
IF master-key = trans-key THEN
      IF trans-code = change THEN
           Change the appropriate field
           Print change transaction detail line
           Input transaction record
      ELSE IF trans-code = delete THEN
           Print delete transaction detail line
           Input master record
           Input transaction record
      ELSE
           Print error message (invalid add)
           Input transaction record
      END-IF
```

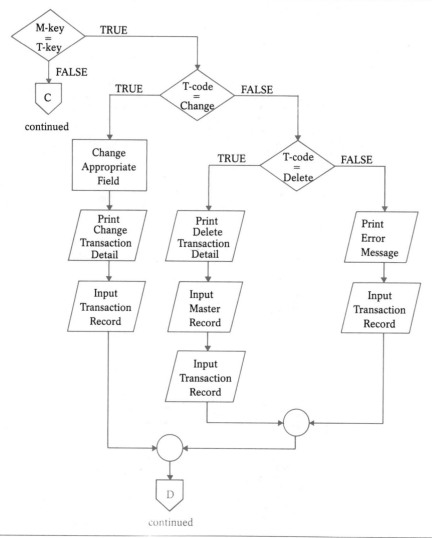

Figure 3-2 Flowchart for when both keys are the same. Note that the entire chart is incomplete since it is only one module of the entire routine.

Notice that when the transaction code is for a change, the design specifies that we "Change the appropriate field." In the typical data record, there are many different fields that can be changed. Therefore, some other type of code is usually found on the transaction record indicating a specific field to be changed. The simple "change the appropriate field" would need to be expanded to reflect the particular fields and codes to be processed but, since this is a general design, we do not know what fields there are to change; we will simply state that we are changing whatever field the field code dictates.

All three of the actions have the statement "Input transaction record," because, in all three cases, we have finished with the transaction record and need another. But we can simplify the design slightly—by moving the input statement to the end of the IF test—so that there is only one input statement instead of three. The new design (redrawn flowchart in Figure 3-3) would be

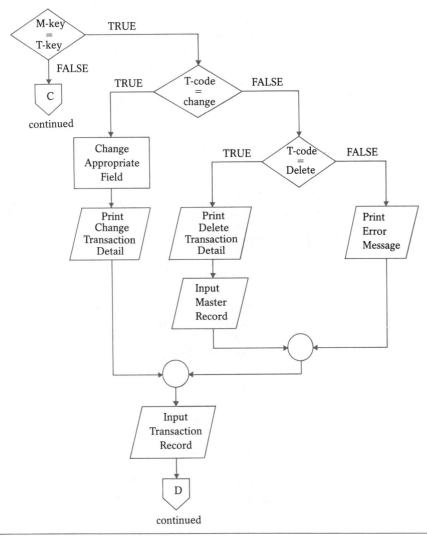

Figure 3-3   Redrawn flowchart for when both keys are the same (incomplete).

```
IF master-key = trans-key THEN
     IF trans-code = change THEN
          Change the appropriate field
          Print change transaction detail line
     ELSE IF trans-code = delete THEN
          Print delete transaction detail line
          Input master record
     ELSE
          Print error message (invalid add)
     END-IF
     Input transaction record
```

Now, regardless of what type of transaction code is on the transaction record, we will input a new transaction record.

3-4-2 When the Master Key Is Greater Than the Transaction Key

When the record keys are the same, the processing is pretty easy to understand. When the keys are not the same, however, the processing is a bit more confusing. We need to decide what is valid when the master key is greater than the transaction key.

Let's start by looking at what happened to the records when the keys were the same. In all cases, regardless of the transaction type, we read another transaction record. In none of the cases did we read a master record without reading a transaction record. (That's why we could move the input statement to the end of the IF test.) Thus, the only way a transaction key could be less than a master key is if a new master record is read. Suppose the new master record is larger than the transaction record: since the master records are in order, there is no way to get a master record to be equal to the transaction record. That means that the transaction record we are trying to process must be one that does not exist on the master file, in which case the only valid type of transaction would be to add the transaction record to the new master file. Any other type of transaction code would be an error; we cannot change or delete a record that doesn't exist. Thus, the design for this module (flowchart in Figure 3-4) would be the following:

```
ELSE IF master-key > trans-key THEN
      IF trans-code = add THEN
           Add the record to the new master file
           Print the detail record
      ELSE
           Print an error message
      END-IF
      Input a transaction record
```

Notice that this IF test is on an ELSE. Recall that we are simply continuing the original IF test (where the keys are equal) with a second option. Again, we have the situation where each option of the internal IF test requires reading a new transaction record. If the transaction code is an add, we add the record; then we are through with the transaction record, so we need to input another. If the transaction code is anything else, we have an error—but we are still through with the transaction record and need another. Since both parts require the input of a new transaction record, we simply put it after the IF test instead of on both actions.

You may have noticed something else. This pair of IF tests could actually be simplified by creating a compound conditional:

```
ELSE IF master-key > trans-key AND trans-code = add THEN
```

We wrote the IF test the other way only for the sake of consistency. Since the first IF test was split apart into several IF tests, it seems appropriate to do the same thing with this one.

3-4-3 When the Master Key Is Less Than the Transaction Key

The final possibility is that the master key is less than the transaction key. Since the transaction file is in the same order as the master file, if the transaction key is past the master key there is no possibility of this particular master key ever equaling the current transaction key. Thus, when this happens we know we are

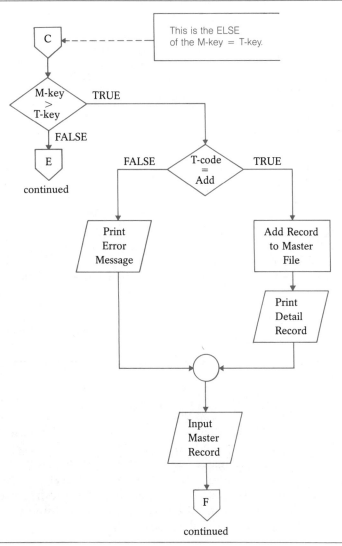

Figure 3-4   Flowchart for when the master key is greater than the transaction key (incomplete).

finished with the master record and ready to input a new one. We may have already changed the record, or not. It really doesn't matter at this point. All we are concerned with is that we are finished with the master record and ready to write it out to the new master file. And, after writing the old master record to the new master file, we need another master record to process, so we input another from the old master file. The design for this module is pretty simple (the flowchart is in Figure 3-5):

```
ELSE
      Write the new master record from the old master record
      Print the detail record
      Input a master record
END-IF
```

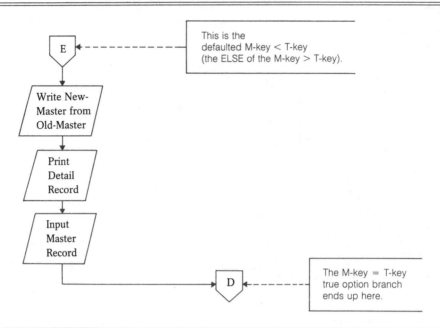

Figure 3-5   The flowchart for when the master key is less than the transaction key (incomplete).

This module was the only one in which we did not need to input another transaction record—because we did not process the transaction record. We simply recognized the fact that we were finished with the master record, wrote it out to the new master file, and input another.

This module signals the end of the entire IF test. All three cases have been covered. This part didn't even require the IF test because we had already tested for the other two conditions. If neither of the other two possibilities was true, the master was less and the IF test for that condition was not necessary. The test simply defaulted to the third possibility.

3-4-4   The Design of the Entire Program

Now that we know what the three modules look like, let's lay out the entire program. Remember that this program doesn't simply read records and print them out. This program is a lot more sophisticated. We begin with a routine to print the file out in its current form. This is the first report, which we discussed earlier (the flowchart will be shown when we put the entire design together):

```
Start
Open the old master file and the print file
Print the headings for the first report
Input a master record at end mark end-of-file
DO-WHILE not end-of-file
        Print the detail line
        Input a master record at end mark end-of-file
END-DO
Close the old master file
```

After this report is printed, we must close the master file. Why do we do this when we need the file open in order to process the records against the transactions? The master file is a sequential file. If it is also a tape file, the tape will have passed all the records; we need to rewind the tape to get back to the beginning. On a disk file, the machine keeps an internal pointer pointing to the current record. After we read through the file, that pointer is pointing past the end of the file. By closing the file, we reposition the pointer back to the beginning of the file.

Notice that we closed only the master file. We did not close the print file. If on your machine the printed file goes automatically to the printer instead of to a disk file, you could close the print file and then reopen it for the next report (even though it would be unnecessary). But most of us work on machines where the print file is stored on disk. When we are ready, we can print the stored file. However, when you close this type of file, the file pointer returns to the beginning of the file; whatever you print next will be added to the beginning of the file. In other words, you will have just wiped out your print file. You should never close your print file until the end of the program.

Now, to begin the next module we need to reopen the old master file, the new master file, and the transaction file:

```
Open the old master, new master, and transaction files
Print the headings for the second report
Input a master record at end mark end-of-file
Input a transaction record at end mark end-of-file
DO-WHILE not end-of-file on both files
        DO Check-module
END-DO
Close old master, new master, and transaction files

Start Check-module
IF master-key = trans-key THEN
        IF trans-code = change THEN
            Change the appropriate field
            Print change transaction detail line
        ELSE IF trans-code = delete THEN
            Print delete transaction detail line
            Input master record at end mark end-of-file
        ELSE
            Print error message (invalid add)
        END-IF
        Input transaction record at end mark end-of-file
ELSE IF master-key > trans-key THEN
        IF trans-code = add THEN
            Add the record to the new master file
            Print the detail record
        ELSE
            Print an error message
        END-IF
        Input a transaction record at end mark end-of-file
ELSE
        Write the new master record from the old master record
        Print the detail record
        Input a master record at end mark end-of-file
END-IF
End Check-module
```

Most of this module consists of the three IF tests we constructed in the last section. Notice that we did close all three of the files we opened. We are finished with the old master and the transaction files at this point, and we need to close the new master so we can reopen it to print. Again we did not close the print file.

The next module is almost a repeat of the first section of the program, since we just print the new master file (the third report). This routine would follow the DO-WHILE of the last routine:

```
Open the new master file
Print the headings for the third report
Input a master record at end mark end-of-file
DO-WHILE not end-of-file
        Print the detail line
        Input a master record at end mark end-of-file
END-DO
Close the new master file and the print file
End
```

Now, at the end of the entire program, we close the print file. The flowchart for the entire program design may be seen in Figure 3-6. The check module is split up into several pieces; Figure 3-7 (page 117) shows how the entire module looks when put together.

3-5
Using HIGH-VALUES

Let's look again at a section of our design:

```
Input a master record at end mark end-of-file
Input a transaction record at end mark end-of-file
DO-WHILE not end-of-file on both files
```

Notice that we specify marking the end-of-file when we input the records and then we test for the end-of-file on the DO-WHILE. Well, there is a problem with this. Obviously we are not finished processing the records until both files (the transaction and master files) have reached the end-of-file. Thus, we do want our loop to continue until we have reached the end-of-file on both files. The problem is with subsequent input statements. If we have reached the end of one of the files, and then later on we inadvertently try to input another record from that file, we will get an ABEND in our program from trying to read past the end-of-file.

One way to fix this problem is to put IF tests on all the input statements so they will input only new records if the end-of-file has not been reached. One of the statements might look like this:

```
IF not end-of-file THEN
        Input a transaction record at end mark end-of-file
(ELSE)
END-IF
```

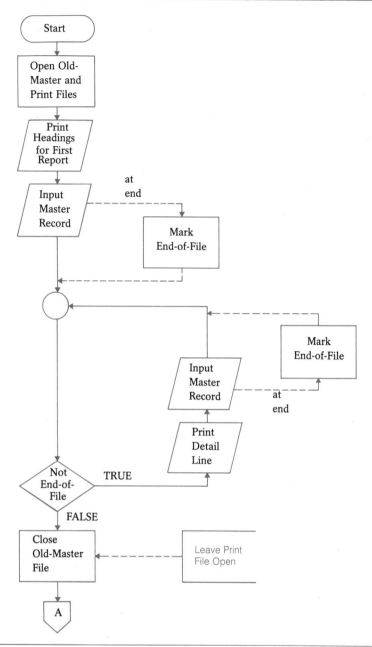

Figure 3-6   The entire flowchart for the sequential update program.

Such handling might create another problem: the value of the transaction key would always be less than any new master record key—which would indicate, according to our program design, that the only valid processing would be to add the transaction record to the new master file. But if we have run out of transaction records, we want to simply move the rest of the old master records into the new master file. Since there are no more transactions, there can be no changes or deletions to the master record. The only valid thing to do is simply move all the records.

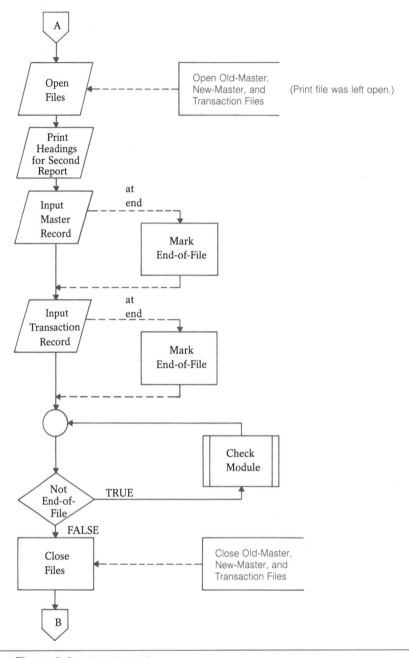

Figure 3-6   (continued)

What we need is some way to tell the program, when we run out of transaction records, to use the routine that says the master record key is less (not greater) than the transaction key. We need to be able to make the transaction key always greater than the master key.

Fortunately, COBOL has an easy method of accomplishing just that. With the COBOL reserved word HIGH-VALUES we can force a field to have the highest value possible. We simply move HIGH-VALUES to the key field when we find the end-of-file; from then on, every field compared to it will automatically be less.

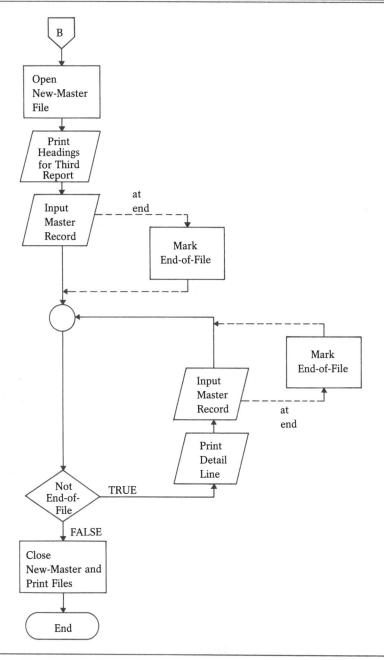

Figure 3-6 (continued)

What HIGH-VALUES does is set all the storage bits of the key to 1's. Recall that every field is made up of a group of characters and that each character is stored as a group of on–off storage bits. Well, moving HIGH-VALUES to a field simply tells the computer to "turn on" all the storage bits of the entire key. Since no character that can be entered from the keyboard can have a value equivalent to the one HIGH-VALUES creates, all other fields will have to be less than the one stored as HIGH-VALUES. If one of the keys is set to HIGH-VALUES, the other key will automatically test out as less than it.

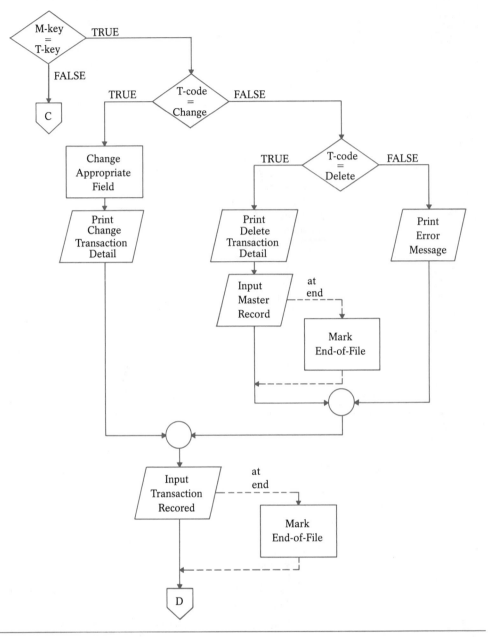

Figure 3-6 (continued)

We need to use HIGH-VALUES on all the READ statements so that when we reach the end-of-file on either the master file or the transaction file, the HIGH-VALUES will get moved into the key. Such a statement might look like

```
READ MASTER-FILE
     AT END MOVE HIGH-VALUES TO MASTER-KEY.
```

Let's quickly examine our program design and see the results of using HIGH-VALUES. If either of the files runs out of data and gets the key set to HIGH-

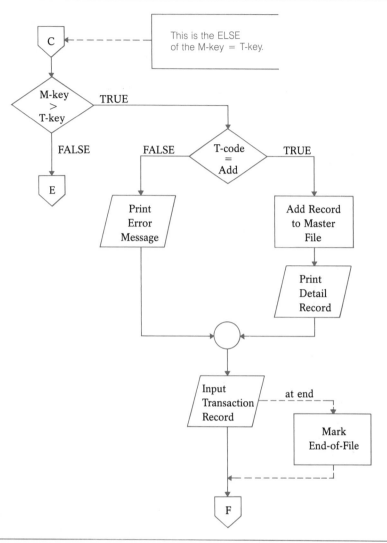

Figure 3-6   (continued)

VALUES, the test for the keys being equal can never be true. Thus, we will be left with only the other two options—less than and greater than.

Let's suppose that the first file to run out of records is the transaction file. This will make the transaction key larger than the master key. Thus, what remains is the master-key < trans-key option, which was the third option of the three IF tests:

ELSE
    Write the new master record from the old master record
    Print the detail record
    Input a master record at end move high-values to key
END-IF

Notice that this writes the new master record from the old master record and then inputs a new master record. Nowhere did we say we were inputting another

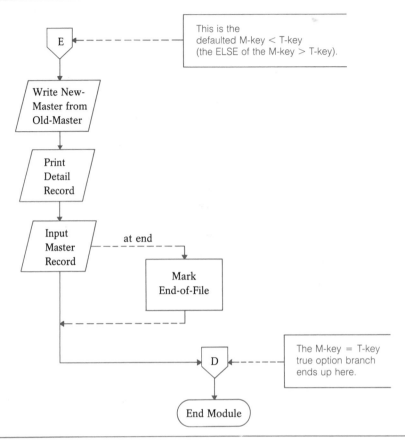

Figure 3-6   (continued)

transaction record. This is just what we wanted. Naturally, if we have found the end of the transaction file, we don't want to read any more of the transaction records. Thus, our design seems to work properly if we set HIGH-VALUES into the trans-key. Notice that we changed the "at end" clause on the input statement to reflect using "high-values" instead of "mark end-of-file." We would need to change this throughout the design.

On the other side of the end-of-file idea, we might run out of records in the master file first. If this happens, then the only option that could possibly work is the one in which the master-key is greater than the trans-key:

```
ELSE IF master-key > trans-key THEN
     IF trans-code = add THEN
         Add the record to the new master file
         Print the detail record
     ELSE
         Print an error message
     END-IF
Input a transaction record at end move high-values to key
```

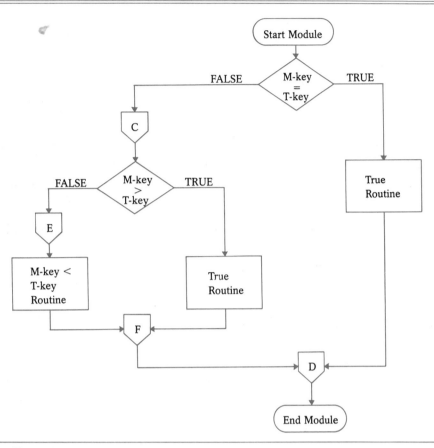

Figure 3-7   Illustration of how the entire check module fits together.

Now the transaction records are processed. If we are past the end of the master file, only an add could be valid because there are no master records left to change or delete. Notice that we again changed the "at end" to "move high-values to key." As we said earlier, this would need to be done to all the input statements in the entire design. One place in particular is important:

> Input a master record at end move high-values to key
> Input a transaction record at end move high-values to key
> DO-WHILE not high-values on both files

Now we are testing for "high-values" on both of the files, and the loop does not end until they are both "high-values." This makes sense, since we would not want the program to quit until all the records in both the transaction file and the master file were processed.

An important point to remember is that HIGH-VALUES can be used only on non-numeric fields. Since numeric fields must contain only valid numeric data and a HIGH-VALUES field would not be numeric characters (remember that what is stored there is not something that can be entered from a keyboard), the computer gives us an error when we try to move HIGH-VALUES to a numeric field. Thus, our record keys for sequential updates must be non-numeric.

3-6

A Sample Program

Now that we have discussed in general terms, the process of sequentially updating a file, it is time to write a sample program as a demonstration of the update technique. Let's suppose we have a contributions file that contains only four fields; the customer number that we will use as the key field, the customer name, the date of last contribution, and the amount of last contribution. In our update program we want to be able to delete records of those contributors who have moved out of town or the like, add new contributors, and change records to reflect new contributions. Thus, our program will need all three of our transaction types. Our file has the layout shown in Figure 3-8.

The customer number will be used for the record key; thus the transaction record will also lead off with the customer number. In each transaction record there must be four elements:

1. the record key. This is the key field that is to be matched against the record key found in the master file.
2. the transaction code. This is used to determine what type of transaction we are processing. In our example we will use three codes: A for adding records, C for changing records, and D for deleting records. Remember that these are the standard types of update transactions.
3. another code to designate which field in the master record we need to change. This code will be 2 for a change to the customer name, 3 for a new date, and 4 for a new amount. Note that there is no 1 for the customer number. Since we are processing sequential files, we generally do not change the customer number. If we did, the file would not necessarily still be in sequence. We could change the key and then, after processing all the records, resort the file. This is sometimes done, but, for our example programs, we will assume that we are not permitted to change the key field. Thus, there will be no code of 1.
4. the data that is to be changed or added. If the transaction is a change there will be only one field. If the change is an add, all three of the new fields must be on the transaction record.

CONTRIB **File**					
Field Description	*Position*	*Length*	:	*Dec*	*Type*
Customer number	1–3	3	:		Non-numeric
Customer name	4–23	20	:		Non-numeric
Date of last cont.	24–29	6	:		Non-numeric
Amount of last cont.	30–35	6	:	2	Numeric
Filler	36–80	45	:		Non-numeric
Record Length = 80					

Figure 3-8   The layout for the CONTRIB file.

Why, if we have three fields that might be changed, can a change transaction record have only one field? Why not put all the changes on one record? Well, in the case of our small file, we could. But doing so would be impractical if there were many different fields. Why should we reserve extra long records for each change transaction when most transactions are to change only one field? As we said, impractical. Therefore, each change transaction is put on a separate data record, which means we may have multiple transaction records making changes to the same master record. Does this bother the logic of our design? No, not at all. Remember we designed the program so that it will not write the new master record until the transaction key is larger than the master key. In such a situation, we are finished processing the master record because no more transaction records can have a key less than or equal to the master key. But, even more important, this is the only time the new master record is written. We did not write the record every time we made a change to it; thus we can make as many changes as necessary without affecting the new master file until we are finished with all the transaction records for that master record.

Now, if the add transactions have all the data, why can't the change records have it all? Wouldn't they be the same length? In fact, they would. Generally, however, when you have large records in a file, you don't do an add transaction with only one record. Each add transaction requires the input of two or more data records so that all the fields necessary to add the record to the master file can be input. In our example, however, we have only a few fields, and one data record will be enough to hold all the fields.

Since we have three different transaction types, we will need three slightly different record layouts. Actually, we will create one layout with the possibility of there being different data in some of the fields. The layout will look like the one in Figure 3-9.

The "Change field code" is used only when the "Trans. code" is a C for change. Then the 2, 3, or 4 is used to determine the type and length of the data found in the fourth field. If the transaction is an add, the entire length of 32 characters is needed since all three fields (name, date, and amount) must be input there. On a delete no data is needed because all the delete does is remove the record from the file.

Remember that this program will use three different reports. We will print the master file out before the updates are done, as the updates are done, and then again after the updates. The reports before and after can use exactly the

TRANS File					
Field Description	*Position*	*Length*	:	*Dec*	*Type*
Customer number	1–3	3	:		Non-numeric
Trans. code (A, C, D)	4–4	1	:		Non-numeric
Change field code (2–4)	5–5	1	:		Non-numeric
Date for add or change	6–37	32	:		Non-numeric
Filler	38–80	43	:		Non-numeric
Record Length = 80					

Figure 3-9   The layout for the transaction file.

same format, shown in Figure 3-10. The transaction report, however, needs to show not only the data from the file, but also the transactions themselves. The format for the transaction report is shown in Figure 3-11.

Notice in the figure the area that is labeled "TRANSACTION INFORMATION." This is where we will print the information about what type of transaction we processed and how the data was affected. The left part of the report is the same as the other report format so that the file information in all three reports will print in the same format. The transaction report will simply add the transaction information onto the right side of the report. The information we will print for the transactions will fall into four categories:

1. If the transaction is an add, we will print all the new fields being added to the file as if the record was already in the file. We will simply place a message in the "TRANSACTION INFORMATION" area that says "ADD."
2. If the transaction is a delete, all the fields from the record being deleted will be printed on the left side of the report and the "TRANSACTION INFORMATION" area will simply say "DELETE."
3. If the transaction is a change, we will print the record, with the new data in it already, on the left side of the report. The "TRANSACTION INFORMATION" area will show the transaction type as "CHANGE," then the name

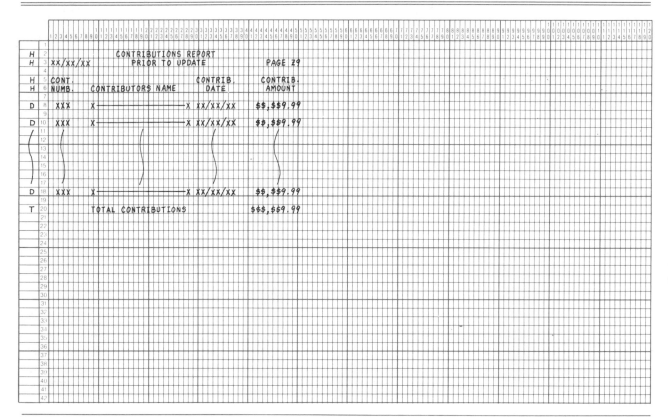

Figure 3-10   The layout for the first and third report formats for the CONTRIBUTIONS file update.

of the field being changed—"NAME," "DATE," or "AMOUNT"—and finally, the old data that was in the file before the change. For example, suppose the master record contained the name "SAM SMITH" and we needed to change it to "FRED SMITH." The transaction report detail line would look like

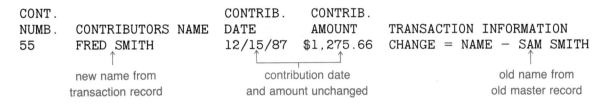

```
CONT.                               CONTRIB.   CONTRIB.
NUMB.    CONTRIBUTORS NAME          DATE       AMOUNT     TRANSACTION INFORMATION
55       FRED SMITH                 12/15/87   $1,275.66  CHANGE = NAME - SAM SMITH
```

        new name from   contribution date   old name from
        transaction record   and amount unchanged   old master record

4. The fourth category of transaction detail line is an error. Basically we can have three errors while processing these transactions:

■ We can cause an error by trying to add a record that is already on file. The "TRANSACTION INFORMATION" for this error should look like

```
ADD = ERROR - RECORD ALREADY ON FILE
```

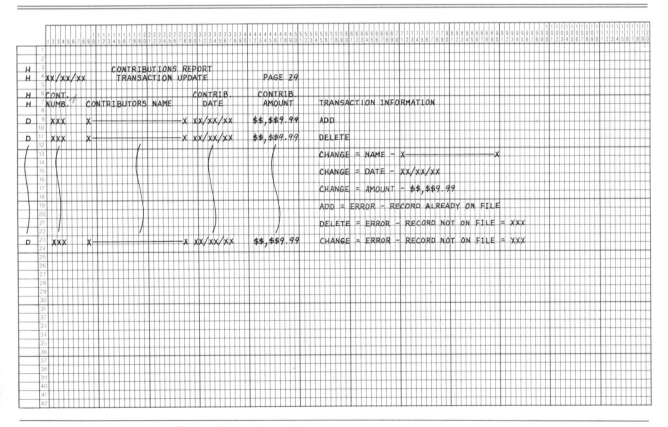

Figure 3-11   The layout of the transaction update report.

In the detail area (the left side of the report) you would print the data from the old master record, not the data on the transaction record. Naturally, since the transaction code is for an add, the fields that are to be added will be on the transaction record. They will, unfortunately, have to be ignored in favor of printing the current master record on the report.

■ We can cause an error by trying to change a record that is not on file. Here the "TRANSACTION INFORMATION" should be

```
CHANGE = ERROR - RECORD NOT ON FILE = XXX (key)
```

Now we will print nothing on the left side of the report: the transaction record has only one field and that field is meaningless since the record we were supposed to change doesn't exist. The record key that we tried to match is printed on the end of the "TRANSACTION INFORMATION" so that we know which key field we didn't find.

■ If we try to delete a record not on file we will print basically the same "TRANSACTION INFORMATION" and, again, no detail will be printed. The error message should be

```
DELETE = ERROR - RECORD NOT ON FILE = XXX (key)
```

3-6-1 Setting Up the File Layouts

Now that we know how the data files should look, it's time to set up the file layouts we are going to need. The specifications for the old master file are easy:

```
FD   OLD-MASTER
     LABEL RECORDS ARE OMITTED
     RECORD CONTAINS 80 CHARACTERS.
01   OLD-MASTER-RECORD.
     05   MASTER-KEY                PIC XXX.
     05   MASTER-NAME               PIC X(20).
     05   DATE-OF-CONTRIBUTION      PIC X(6).
     05   AMOUNT                    PIC 9(4)V99.
     05   FILLER                    PIC X(45).
```

And for the new master file we change only the file- and field-names:

```
FD   NEW-MASTER
     LABEL RECORDS ARE OMITTED
     RECORD CONTAINS 80 CHARACTERS.
01   NEW-MASTER-RECORD.
     05   NEW-MASTER-KEY            PIC XXX.
     05   NEW-MASTER-NAME           PIC X(20).
     05   NEW-DATE                  PIC X(6).
     05   NEW-AMOUNT                PIC 9(4)V99.
     05   FILLER                    PIC X(45).
```

The transaction layout is a bit more complicated. We will need to define several different layouts for the input area after the change code. The layout follows:

```
FD  TRANSACTION-IN
    LABEL RECORDS ARE OMITTED
    RECORD CONTAINS 80 CHARACTERS.
01  TRANS-RECORD.
    05  TRANS-KEY                 PIC XXX.
    05  TRANS-KEY CODE            PIC X.
        88  ADD-CODE              VALUE 'A'.
        88  CHANGE-CODE           VALUE 'C'.
        88  DELETE-CODE           VALUE 'D'.

    05  TRANS-CHANGE-CODE         PIC X.
        88  NAME-CODE             VALUE '2'.
        88  DATE-CODE             VALUE '3'.
        88  AMOUNT-CODE           VALUE '4'.

    05  FILLER                    PIC X(75).

01  CHANGE-2.
    05  FILLER                    PIC X(5).
    05  CHANGE-NAME               PIC X(20).
    05  FILLER                    PIC X(55).

01  CHANGE-3.
    05  FILLER                    PIC X(5).
    05  CHANGE-DATE               PIC X(6).
    05  FILLER                    PIC X(69).

01  CHANGE-4.
    05  FILLER                    PIC X(5).
    05  CHANGE-AMOUNT             PIC 9(4)V99.
    05  FILLER                    PIC X(69).

01  ADD-FIELDS.
    05  FILLER                    PIC X(5).
    05  ADD-NAME                  PIC X(20).
    05  ADD-DATE                  PIC X(6).
    05  ADD-AMOUNT                PIC 9(4)V99.
    05  FILLER                    PIC X(43).
```

Notice how we used several different layouts for the same input area. Then, in the PROCEDURE DIVISION, we simply determine which of the data fields we need to access based upon the transaction and change codes.

Note also that we used 88-level definitions for the transaction and change codes. Now, instead of using an IF test like

```
IF TRANS-CODE = 'A'
```

we can use a more direct reference, such as

```
IF ADD-CODE
```

Some programmers prefer to use the conditional IF tests rather than the 88-level defined codes.

3-6-2 The WORKING-STORAGE SECTION

A few things need to be looked at in the matter of setting up the output layouts. Since there are three different reports with basically the same layout, we will use only one set of headings and will simply move appropriate information into them. This will occur in two places: The first page heading will simply say "CONTRI-BUTIONS REPORT" on all three reports. The second page heading will vary. The first report will say "PRIOR TO UPDATE" and the whole heading layout will be

```
01  PAGE-HEADING-2.
        05  FILLER                   PIC X           VALUE SPACES.
        05  HEADING-MONTH            PIC XX.
        05  HEADING-DAY              PIC /XX/.
        05  HEADING-YEAR             PIC XX.
        05  VARIABLE-HEAD            PIC X(31).      VALUE
            '        PRIOR TO UPDATE           '.
        05  FILLER                   PIC X(9)        VALUE
            '     PAGE '.
        05  PAGE-CTR-OUT             PIC Z9.
```

Notice the field VARIABLE-HEAD in the second heading. The other fields are simply the date and page number. On the second report we will move the heading "TRANSACTION UPDATE" into the VARIABLE-HEAD field. Then, on the third report we will move in the heading "AFTER UPDATE." This procedure is much easier then setting up three different headings, for two reasons. First, it requires less keypunching. Second, and more important, in the PROCEDURE DIVISION we will use one performed heading routine for all three headings. If we had used different headings for each of the page headings, the heading layout names would have been different and we would have had to have a different page heading routine for each report.

The second place we use a variable heading is on the second column heading, where we need to print "TRANSACTION INFORMATION" over the information being printed about what transaction we are processing. We specify the second column heading as

```
01  COLUMN-HEADING-2
    05  FILLER                   PIC X(54)       VALUE
        ' NUMB.   CONTRIBUTORS NAME        DATE        AMOUNT     '.
    05  TRANS-HEAD               PIC X(23)       VALUE SPACES.
```

On the first execution of the heading routine, we want the TRANS-HEAD field to be SPACES as specified, since the transaction area of the report will not show anything on the first report. Then, before we print the headings for the second report, we move "TRANSACTION INFORMATION" into the TRANS-HEAD field. Finally, before we print the headings for the third report, we move SPACES into the TRANS-HEAD field again because the third report also has no transaction data. This manipulation will again eliminate the need for three separate heading routines.

One final point needs to be examined in the WORKING-STORAGE SECTION. When we set up the detail line for the reports, we set up a field, MESSAGE-OUT, where we will print the transaction information. On the first and third reports, the field is filled with spaces. On the transaction update report, however, we need many different layouts for this message area. We will specify each of them in a separate group item. The detail line will be

```
01   DETAIL-LINE.
     05   FILLER              PIC X(2)            VALUE SPACES.
     05   MASTER-KEY-OUT      PIC XXX.
     05   FILLER              PIC X(4)            VALUE SPACES.
     05   MASTER-NAME-OUT     PIC X(20).
     05   FILLER              PIC X              VALUE SPACES.
     05   DATE-OUT            PIC XX/XX/XX.
     05   FILLER              PIC X(4)            VALUE SPACES.
     05   AMOUNT-OUT          PIC $$,$$9.99.
     05   FILLER              PIC X(3)            VALUE SPACES.
     05   MESSAGE-OUT         PIC X(50)           VALUE SPACES.
```

Notice that the last field is MESSAGE-OUT. The separate group items that will be moved to MESSAGE-OUT, given the appropriate conditions, will be three for changes:

```
01   CHANGE-MESSAGE-NAME.
     05   FILLER              PIC X(16)           VALUE
          'CHANGE = NAME - '.
     05   MESSAGE-NAME        PIC X(20).

01   CHANGE-MESSAGE-DATE.
     05   FILLER              PIC X(16)           VALUE
          'CHANGE = DATE - '.
     05   MESSAGE-DATE        PIC XX/XX/XX.

01   CHANGE-MESSAGE-AMOUNT.
     05   FILLER              PIC X(18)           VALUE
          'CHANGE = AMOUNT - '.
     05   MESSAGE-AMOUNT      PIC $$,$$9.99.
```

and three for errors:

```
01   CHANGE-MESSAGE-ERROR.
     05   FILLER              PIC X(54)           VALUE SPACES.
     05   FILLER              PIC X(38)           VALUE
          'CHANGE = ERROR - RECORD NOT ON FILE = '.
     05   CHANGE-ERROR-KEY    PIC XXX.

01   ADD-MESSAGE-ERROR       PIC X(36)           VALUE
     'ADD = ERROR - RECORD ALREADY ON FILE'.

01   DELETE-MESSAGE-ERROR.
     05   FILLER              PIC X(54)           VALUE SPACES.
     05   FILLER              PIC X(38)           VALUE
          'DELETE = ERROR - RECORD NOT ON FILE = '.
     05   DELETE-ERROR-KEY    PIC XXX.
```

Since the transaction information will simply be the word "ADD" or "DELETE" when we add or delete a record, we will not set up group items for the transaction information. We simply move it into the MESSAGE-OUT field. Again a savings of keypunching.

You may have noticed a difference between the add error group and the change and delete groups: The latter have a filler length of 54 spaces before the error message. This filler will bypass the detail information. When there is a change or delete error (record not on file), no detail information can be printed; instead, we print spaces in the detail area. These two errors will not be moved to the message area; instead they will be printed as entire detail lines.

3-6-3 The PROCEDURE DIVISION

Most of the modules in the PROCEDURE DIVISION require a little explanation. We have previously designed each of them, and you may wish to backtrack a little to refresh your memory as to what each of them is going to accomplish.

The main module is pretty straightforward. Basically, all it contains are the PERFORM statements for the three modules we will use to print the reports. The first section, which will give us the first report, looks like this:

```
PROCEDURE DIVISION.

0100-MAIN-MODULE.

     OPEN INPUT  OLD-MASTER
          OUTPUT LIST-OUT.

     ACCEPT MACHINE-DATE FROM DATE.
     MOVE DATE-YY TO HEADING-YEAR.
     MOVE DATE-MM TO HEADING-MONTH.
     MOVE DATE-DD TO HEADING-DAY.

     PERFORM 0900-HEADING-ROUTINE.

     READ OLD-MASTER
          AT END MOVE 'YES' TO EOF.
     PERFORM 0200-LIST-OLD-MASTER
             UNTIL WE-ARE-OUT-OF-DATA.

     MOVE TOTAL-AMOUNT TO TOTAL-AMOUNT-OUT.

     WRITE LIST-OUT-RECORD FROM TOTAL-LINE
           AFTER ADVANCING 2 LINES.

     CLOSE OLD-MASTER.
```

Notice that we use the standard end-of-file test for the PERFORM statement. Then we close the OLD-MASTER file without closing the LIST-OUT file, as we discussed before.

The second report requires the opening of three files:

```
OPEN INPUT  OLD-MASTER
            TRANSACTION-IN
     OUTPUT NEW-MASTER.
```

We input the OLD-MASTER, match it against the TRANSACTION-IN, and generate the NEW MASTER. The headings are set up as

```
MOVE '       TRANSACTION UPDATE        ' TO VARIABLE-HEAD.
MOVE 'TRANSACTION INFORMATION' TO TRANS-HEAD.

PERFORM 0900-HEADING-ROUTINE.
```

We have moved the heading information into the fields, as we discussed before. The processing of the data begins with

```
PERFORM 1000-READ-OLD-MASTER.
PERFORM 1010-READ-TRANSACTION-RECORD.
PERFORM 0300-TRANSACTION-UPDATE
        UNTIL MASTER-KEY = HIGH-VALUES
        AND   TRANS-KEY  = HIGH-VALUES.
```

Notice that we must use PERFORM statements for reading the files since we are going to be reading them within an IF test. As we have discussed in the past, doing so can cause problems on some computers, and so it is best avoided. By using a procedure, we don't end up with an AT END clause on an IF test. The two routines contain only the READ statement with an AT END clause of HIGH-VALUES. Then the PERFORM statement tests both file keys against HIGH-VALUES. After we process the report, we close the files

```
CLOSE OLD-MASTER
      NEW-MASTER
      TRANSACTION-IN.
```

and open the NEW-MASTER again to print the third report:

```
OPEN INPUT NEW MASTER.
```

The LIST-OUT file is still open. We have to set up the headings again (remember they change for every report):

```
MOVE '         AFTER UPDATE           ' TO VARIABLE-HEAD.
MOVE SPACES TO MESSAGE-OUT TRANS-HEAD.
PERFORM 0900-HEADING-ROUTINE.
```

Special caution needs to be used here. Since we will simply read the NEW-MASTER file until we run off the end of the file, we have to be sure that we initialize the end-of-file marker field if we use the same one. We used it earlier, so it will contain 'YES' now and we need to set it back to 'NO':

```
MOVE 'NO ' TO EOF.
```

Then the file processing is as usual:

```
READ NEW-MASTER
     AT END MOVE 'YES' TO EOF.
PERFORM 0800-LIST-NEW-MASTER
        UNTIL WE-ARE-OUT-OF-DATA.

MOVE TOTAL-AMOUNT TO TOTAL-AMOUNT-OUT.

WRITE LIST-OUT-RECORD FROM TOTAL-LINE
      AFTER ADVANCING 2 LINES.

CLOSE NEW-MASTER
      LIST-OUT.
STOP RUN.
```

This completes the main module. The 0200-LIST-OLD-MASTER and 0800-LIST-NEW-MASTER modules are nothing special. They simply move the fields and print the detail lines, as always, so we will not show them here (the entire program is shown at the end of this discussion). We will instead move on to the 0300-TRANSACTION-UPDATE module.

When we discussed the COBOL IF test, we mentioned that there are occasions when we may have problems getting the IF test to fit what we need to do because of the way the statement works. Well, in this program, we actually have to break the 0300-TRANSACTION-UPDATE module into several separate modules because of the difficulty with the IF test. Doing so might be considered an advantage this time, however, because we will break the module up into the three logical choices of equal to, less than, and greater than. Thus, the 0300-TRANSACTION-UPDATE module is basically three PERFORM statements:

```
0300-TRANSACTION-UPDATE.

    IF MASTER-KEY = TRANS-KEY
        PERFORM 0400-EQUAL-ROUTINE
    ELSE
        IF MASTER-KEY > TRANS-KEY
        PERFORM 0500-MASTER-GREATER-ROUTINE
    ELSE
        PERFORM 0600-MASTER-LESS-ROUTINE.
```

Then we have the module for the 0400-EQUAL-ROUTINE:

```
0400-EQUAL-ROUTINE.

    IF CHANGE-CODE
      IF NAME-CODE
          MOVE MASTER-NAME TO MESSAGE-NAME
          MOVE CHANGE-MESSAGE-NAME TO MESSAGE-OUT
          MOVE CHANGE-NAME TO MASTER-NAME
          PERFORM 0700-TRANSACTION-PRINT
          MOVE 1 TO CHANGE-PRINT-CODE
```

```
            ELSE
                IF DATE-CODE
                    MOVE DATE-OF-CONTRIBUTION TO MESSAGE-DATE
                    MOVE CHANGE-MESSAGE-DATE TO MESSAGE-OUT
                    MOVE CHANGE-DATE TO DATE-OF-CONTRIBUTION
                    PERFORM 0700-TRANSACTION-PRINT
                    MOVE 1 TO CHANGE-PRINT-CODE
                ELSE
                    IF AMOUNT-CODE
                        MOVE AMOUNT TO MESSAGE-AMOUNT
                        MOVE CHANGE-MESSAGE-AMOUNT TO MESSAGE-OUT
                        MOVE CHANGE-AMOUNT TO AMOUNT
                        PERFORM 0700-TRANSACTION-PRINT
                        MOVE 1 TO CHANGE-PRINT-CODE
                    ELSE NEXT SENTENCE

        ELSE
            IF DELETE-CODE
                MOVE 'DELETE' TO MESSAGE-OUT
                PERFORM 0700-TRANSACTION-PRINT
                PERFORM 1000-READ-OLD-MASTER
        ELSE

            MOVE ADD-MESSAGE-ERROR TO MESSAGE-OUT
            PERFORM 0700-TRANSACTION-PRINT.
    PERFORM 1010-READ-TRANSACTION-FILE.
```

Remember that we set up the 88-levels so we could construct our IF tests as you see them. For example,

```
IF CHANGE-CODE
```

is used instead of

```
IF TRANS-CODE = 'C'
```

Notice that we had to use a NEXT SENTENCE clause so that the IF DELETE-CODE test would correspond to the IF CHANGE-CODE test rather than the IF AMOUNT-CODE test. Without the NEXT SENTENCE, the IF DELETE-CODE test would have become the ELSE of the IF AMOUNT-CODE test. Also, we had to use an ELSE on the IF DELETE-CODE test; otherwise it would have followed the NEXT SENTENCE as another part of the ELSE action and would never have been done because the NEXT SENTENCE would have caused the program to jump out of the test.

The second major ELSE is the default of all codes that are not change or delete (usually add). Here we have an error that we process with an error message.

One final point needs to be examined. Since printing the detail line is virtually the same in most cases, we set up a procedure called 0700-TRANSACTION-PRINT. Why do we have this procedure in each of the code groups instead of just once at the end? Well, if we put it at the end of the entire procedure, where we have the READ statement for the transaction file, the detail line will print the data currently in the old master file. But if you look at the test for deleting records (DELETE-CODE) you will notice that we print and then input another old master record. Since we are inputting another old master record, if we print at the end of the routine we will be printing the data from the freshly input record, instead of the old record like we should. Thus, we have to use the print routine in each of the code sections to get the proper sequence of statements in the delete routine.

The second performed routine is the 0500-MASTER-GREATER-ROUTINE:

```
0500-MASTER-GREATER-ROUTINE.

    IF ADD-CODE
        MOVE TRANS-KEY   TO NEW-MASTER-KEY, MASTER-KEY-OUT
        MOVE ADD-NAME    TO NEW-MASTER-NAME, MASTER-NAME-OUT
        MOVE ADD-DATE    TO NEW-DATE, DATE-OUT
        MOVE ADD-AMOUNT  TO NEW-AMOUNT, AMOUNT-OUT
        WRITE NEW-MASTER-RECORD

        MOVE 'ADD' TO MESSAGE-OUT
        WRITE LIST-OUT-RECORD FROM DETAIL-LINE
            AFTER ADVANCING 2 LINES
        ADD 2 TO LINE-CTR
        IF LINE-CTR > 59
            PERFORM 0900-HEADING-ROUTINE
        ELSE
            NEXT SENTENCE

    ELSE
        IF CHANGE-CODE
            MOVE TRANS-KEY TO CHANGE-ERROR-KEY
            WRITE LIST-OUT-RECORD FROM CHANGE-MESSAGE-ERROR
                AFTER ADVANCING 2 LINES
        ELSE
            MOVE TRANS-KEY TO DELETE-ERROR-KEY
            WRITE LIST-OUT-RECORD FROM DELETE-MESSAGE-ERROR
                AFTER ADVANCING 2 LINES.

    PERFORM 1010-READ-TRANSACTION-FILE.
```

When we add the record, we need to move the data to the new master record and also to the print area, as the move statements at the beginning of the routine show.

Here we cannot use the 0700-TRANSACTION-PRINT routine because the add must print the detail data from the transaction record and the change and delete errors print no detail data.

The third performed routine is the 0600-MASTER-LESS-ROUTINE:

```
0600-MASTER-LESS-ROUTINE.

    MOVE MASTER-KEY           TO NEW-MASTER-KEY.
    MOVE MASTER-NAME          TO NEW-MASTER-NAME.
    MOVE DATE-OF-CONTRIBUTION TO NEW-DATE.
    MOVE AMOUNT               TO NEW-AMOUNT.
    WRITE NEW-MASTER-RECORD.
```

```
MOVE SPACES TO MESSAGE-OUT.
IF CHANGE-PRINT-CODE = 0
    PERFORM 0700-TRANSACTION-PRINT
ELSE
    MOVE 0 TO CHANGE-PRINT-CODE.
PERFORM 1000-READ-OLD-MASTER.
```

This is the simplest of the routines: all we do is move the data from the old master record to the new master record, write the new master record, print the detail line, and then read another old master record. There is one slight addition, however. When we were printing the change records in the "equal" module, we set a CHANGE-PRINT-CODE that is used to determine if a detail record has already been printed for the record being processed at that moment. Remember that every time we change the master record, we print a detail line. Thus, we cannot arbitrarily print each detail line as we write it to the new file; if we do we will have several detail records printed twice. So we set a code for when the change record is printed. When we get to this routine, if the code is still zero we know that there was no change record and that we need to print the detail line. If the code has been set, on the other hand, we simply reset the code and don't print the detail line since it was printed in the change routine.

3-6-4 The Whole Program

We have looked at all the sections of the program. Now let's look at the whole thing:

```
****************************************************************
****************************************************************
*
*
*
*   PROGRAM NAME: CONTRIB
*
*   PROGRAMMER NAME:   EDWARD J. COBURN
*
*   SOCIAL SECURITY NUMBER:  999-99-9999
*
*   DUE DATE: FEBRUARY 10, 1988
*
*   DESCRIPTION: THIS PROGRAM WILL DO A TRANSACTION UPDATE ON
*                THE CONTRIBUTIONS FILE PRINTING BEFORE, DURING,
*                AND AFTER REPORTS.
*
****************************************************************
****************************************************************

IDENTIFICATION DIVISION.
PROGRAM-ID.    CONTRIB.
AUTHOR.        EDWARD J. COBURN.

ENVIRONMENT DIVISION.

CONFIGURATION SECTION.
SOURCE-COMPUTER. IBM-4331.
OBJECT-COMPUTER. IBM-4331.
```

```
        INPUT-OUTPUT SECTION.
        FILE-CONTROL.
             SELECT OLD-MASTER      ASSIGN TO UT-S-CONTRIB.
             SELECT NEW-MASTER      ASSIGN TO UT-S-MASTOUT.
             SELECT TRANSACTION-IN ASSIGN TO UT-S-TRANS.
             SELECT LIST-OUT        ASSIGN TO UT-S-SYSPRINT.


        DATA DIVISION.
        FILE SECTION.

        FD  OLD-MASTER
            LABEL RECORDS ARE OMITTED
            RECORD CONTAINS 80 CHARACTERS.
        01  OLD-MASTER-RECORD.
             05  MASTER-KEY              PIC XXX.
             05  MASTER-NAME             PIC X(20).
             05  DATE-OF-CONTRIBUTION    PIC X(6).
             05  AMOUNT                  PIC 9(4)V99.
             05  FILLER                  PIC X(45).

        FD  NEW-MASTER
            LABEL RECORDS ARE OMITTED
            RECORD CONTAINS 80 CHARACTERS.
        01  NEW-MASTER-RECORD.
             05  NEW-MASTER-KEY          PIC XXX.
             05  NEW-MASTER-NAME         PIC X(20).
             05  NEW-DATE                PIC X(6).
             05  NEW-AMOUNT              PIC 9(4)V99.
             05  FILLER                  PIC X(45).

        FD  TRANSACTION-IN
            LABEL RECORDS ARE OMITTED
            RECORD CONTAINS 80 CHARACTERS.
            01  TRANS-RECORD.
                 05  TRANS-KEY           PIC XXX.
                 05  TRANS-CODE          PIC X.
                     88  ADD-CODE        VALUE 'A'.
                     88  CHANGE-CODE     VALUE 'C'.
                     88  DELETE-CODE     VALUE 'D'.

                 05  TRANS-CHANGE-CODE   PIC X.
                     88  NAME-CODE       VALUE '2'.
                     88  DATE-CODE       VALUE '3'.
                     88  AMOUNT-CODE     VALUE '4'.

                 05  FILLER              PIC X(75).

            01  CHANGE-2.
                 05  FILLER              PIC X(5).
                 05  CHANGE-NAME         PIC X(20).
                 05  FILLER              PIC X(55).

            01  CHANGE-3.
                 05  FILLER              PIC X(5).
                 05  CHANGE-DATE         PIC X(6).
                 05  FILLER              PIC X(69).
```

```
01  CHANGE-4.
    05  FILLER                      PIC X(5).
    05  CHANGE-AMOUNT               PIC 9(4)V99.
    05  FILLER                      PIC X(69).

01  ADD-FIELDS.
    05  FILLER                      PIC X(5).
    05  ADD-NAME                    PIC X(20).
    05  ADD-DATE                    PIC X(6).
    05  ADD-AMOUNT                  PIC 9(4)V99.
    05  FILLER                      PIC X(43).

FD  LIST-OUT
    LABEL RECORDS ARE OMITTED
    RECORD CONTAINS 133 CHARACTERS.
01  LIST-OUT-RECORD                 PIC X(133).

WORKING-STORAGE SECTION.

01  WORK-AREAS.
    05  EOF                         PIC XXX           VALUE 'NO '.
        88  WE-ARE-OUT-OF-DATA                        VALUE 'YES'.

    05  LINE-CTR                    PIC 99            VALUE ZERO.
    05  PAGE-CTR                    PIC 99            VALUE 1.
    05  TOTAL-AMOUNT                PIC 9(5)V99       VALUE ZERO.
    05  CHANGE-PRINT-CODE           PIC 9             VALUE ZERO.

    05  MACHINE-DATE                PIC X(6).
    05  DATE-WORK REDEFINES MACHINE-DATE.
        10  DATE-YY                 PIC XX.
        10  DATE-MM                 PIC XX.
        10  DATE-DD                 PIC XX.

01  PAGE-HEADING-1.
    05  FILLER                      PIC X(34)         VALUE
        '                  CONTRIBUTIONS REPORT'.

01  PAGE-HEADING-2.
    05  FILLER                      PIC X             VALUE SPACES.
    05  HEADING-MONTH               PIC XX.
    05  HEADING-DAY                 PIC /XX/.
    05  HEADING-YEAR                PIC XX.
    05  VARIABLE-HEAD               PIC X(31)         VALUE
        '           PRIOR TO UPDATE        '.
    05  FILLER                      PIC X(9)          VALUE
        '   PAGE '.
    05  PAGE-CTR-OUT                PIC Z9.

01  COLUMN-HEADING-1                PIC X(51)         VALUE
    ' CONT.                      CONTRIB.   CONTRIB.'.

01  COLUMN-HEADING-2.
    05  FILLER                      PIC X(54)         VALUE
        ' NUMB.    CONTRIBUTORS NAME        DATE        AMOUNT      '.
    05  TRANS-HEAD                  PIC X(23)         VALUE SPACES.

01  DETAIL-LINE.
    05  FILLER                      PIC X(2)          VALUE SPACES.
```

```
        05   MASTER-KEY-OUT           PIC XXX.
        05   FILLER                   PIC X(4)           VALUE SPACES.
        05   MASTER-NAME-OUT          PIC X(20).
        05   FILLER                   PIC X              VALUE SPACES.
        05   DATE-OUT                 PIC XX/XX/XX.
        05   FILLER                   PIC X(4)           VALUE SPACES.
        05   AMOUNT-OUT               PIC $$,$$9.99.
        05   FILLER                   PIC X(3)           VALUE SPACES.
        05   MESSAGE-OUT              PIC X(50)          VALUE SPACES.

    01  CHANGE-MESSAGE-NAME.
        05   FILLER                   PIC X(16)          VALUE
             'CHANGE = NAME - '.
        05   MESSAGE-NAME             PIC X(20).

    01  CHANGE-MESSAGE-DATE.
        05   FILLER                   PIC X(16)          VALUE
             'CHANGE = DATE - '.
        05   MESSAGE-DATE             PIC XX/XX/XX.

    01  CHANGE-MESSAGE-AMOUNT.
        05   FILLER                   PIC X(18)          VALUE
             'CHANGE = AMOUNT - '.
        05   MESSAGE-AMOUNT           PIC $$,$$9.99.

    01  CHANGE-MESSAGE-ERROR.
        05   FILLER                   PIC X(54)          VALUE SPACES.
        05   FILLER                   PIC X(38)          VALUE
             'CHANGE = ERROR - RECORD NOT ON FILE = '.
        05   CHANGE-ERROR-KEY         PIC XXX.

    01  ADD-MESSAGE-ERROR            PIC X(36)          VALUE
        'ADD = ERROR - RECORD ALREADY ON FILE'.

    01  DELETE-MESSAGE-ERROR.
        05   FILLER                   PIC X(54)          VALUE SPACES.
        05   FILLER                   PIC X(38)          VALUE
             'DELETE = ERROR - RECORD NOT ON FILE = '.
        05   DELETE-ERROR-KEY         PIC XXX.

    01  TOTAL-LINE.
        05   FILLER                   PIC X(9)           VALUE SPACES.
        05   FILLER                   PIC X(32)          VALUE
             'TOTAL CONTRIBUTIONS          '.
        05   TOTAL-AMOUNT-OUT         PIC $$$,$$9.99.

PROCEDURE DIVISION.

0100-MAIN-MODULE.

    OPEN INPUT  OLD-MASTER
         OUTPUT LIST-OUT.

    ACCEPT MACHINE-DATE FROM DATE.
    MOVE DATE-YY TO HEADING-YEAR.

    MOVE DATE-MM TO HEADING-MONTH.
    MOVE DATE-DD TO HEADING-DAY.
```

```
PERFORM 0900-HEADING-ROUTINE.

READ OLD-MASTER
     AT END MOVE 'YES' TO EOF.
PERFORM 0200-LIST-OLD-MASTER
        UNTIL WE-ARE-OUT-OF-DATA.

MOVE TOTAL-AMOUNT TO TOTAL-AMOUNT-OUT.

WRITE LIST-OUT-RECORD FROM TOTAL-LINE
        AFTER ADVANCING 2 LINES.

CLOSE OLD-MASTER.

OPEN INPUT  OLD-MASTER
            TRANSACTION-IN
     OUTPUT NEW-MASTER.

MOVE '       TRANSACTION UPDATE         ' TO VARIABLE-HEAD.
MOVE 'TRANSACTION INFORMATION' TO TRANS-HEAD.
PERFORM 0900-HEADING-ROUTINE.

PERFORM 1000-READ-OLD-MASTER.
PERFORM 1010-READ-TRANSACTION-FILE.
PERFORM 0300-TRANSACTION-UPDATE
        UNTIL MASTER-KEY = HIGH-VALUES
        AND   TRANS-KEY  = HIGH-VALUES.

CLOSE OLD-MASTER
      NEW-MASTER
      TRANSACTION-IN.

OPEN INPUT NEW-MASTER.

MOVE '         AFTER UPDATE              ' TO VARIABLE-HEAD.
MOVE SPACES TO MESSAGE-OUT, TRANS-HEAD.
PERFORM 0900-HEADING-ROUTINE.

MOVE 'NO ' TO EOF.

READ NEW-MASTER
     AT END MOVE 'YES' TO EOF.
PERFORM 0800-LIST-NEW-MASTER
        UNTIL WE-ARE-OUT-OF-DATA.

MOVE TOTAL-AMOUNT TO TOTAL-AMOUNT-OUT.

WRITE LIST-OUT-RECORD FROM TOTAL-LINE
        AFTER ADVANCING 2 LINES.

CLOSE NEW-MASTER
      LIST-OUT.

STOP  RUN.
```

```
0200-LIST-OLD-MASTER.

    ADD AMOUNT TO TOTAL-AMOUNT.

    MOVE MASTER-KEY             TO MASTER-KEY-OUT.
    MOVE MASTER-NAME            TO MASTER-NAME-OUT.
    MOVE DATE-OF-CONTRIBUTION TO DATE-OUT.
    MOVE AMOUNT                 TO AMOUNT-OUT.

    WRITE LIST-OUT-RECORD FROM DETAIL-LINE
         AFTER ADVANCING 2 LINES.

    ADD 2 TO LINE-CTR.


    IF LINE-CTR > 59
       PERFORM 0900-HEADING-ROUTINE.

    READ OLD-MASTER
         AT END MOVE 'YES' TO EOF.


0300-TRANSACTION-UPDATE.

    IF MASTER-KEY = TRANS-KEY
       PERFORM 0400-EQUAL-ROUTINE
    ELSE
       IF MASTER-KEY > TRANS-KEY
       PERFORM 0500-MASTER-GREATER-ROUTINE
    ELSE
       PERFORM 0600-MASTER-LESS-ROUTINE.


0400-EQUAL-ROUTINE.

    IF CHANGE-CODE
       IF NAME-CODE
          MOVE MASTER-NAME TO MESSAGE-NAME
          MOVE CHANGE-MESSAGE-NAME TO MESSAGE-OUT
          MOVE CHANGE-NAME TO MASTER-NAME
          PERFORM 0700-TRANSACTION-PRINT
          MOVE 1 TO CHANGE-PRINT-CODE
       ELSE
          IF DATE-CODE
             MOVE DATE-OF-CONTRIBUTION TO MESSAGE-DATE
             MOVE CHANGE-MESSAGE-DATE TO MESSAGE-OUT
             MOVE CHANGE-DATE TO DATE-OF-CONTRIBUTION
             PERFORM 0700-TRANSACTION-PRINT
             MOVE 1 TO CHANGE-PRINT-CODE
          ELSE
             IF AMOUNT-CODE
                MOVE AMOUNT TO MESSAGE-AMOUNT

                MOVE CHANGE-MESSAGE-AMOUNT TO MESSAGE-OUT
                MOVE CHANGE-AMOUNT TO AMOUNT
                PERFORM 0700-TRANSACTION-PRINT
                MOVE 1 TO CHANGE-PRINT-CODE
             ELSE NEXT SENTENCE
```

```
        ELSE
           IF DELETE-CODE
               MOVE 'DELETE' TO MESSAGE-OUT
               PERFORM 0700-TRANSACTION-PRINT
               PERFORM 1000-READ-OLD-MASTER

        ELSE

               MOVE ADD-MESSAGE-ERROR TO MESSAGE-OUT
               PERFORM 0700-TRANSACTION-PRINT.

        PERFORM 1010-READ-TRANSACTION-FILE.


0500-MASTER-GREATER-ROUTINE.

        IF ADD-CODE
           MOVE TRANS-KEY    TO NEW-MASTER-KEY, MASTER-KEY-OUT
           MOVE ADD-NAME     TO NEW-MASTER-NAME, MASTER-NAME-OUT
           MOVE ADD-DATE     TO NEW-DATE, DATE-OUT
           MOVE ADD-AMOUNT   TO NEW-AMOUNT, AMOUNT-OUT
           WRITE NEW-MASTER-RECORD

           MOVE 'ADD' TO MESSAGE-OUT

           WRITE LIST-OUT-RECORD FROM DETAIL-LINE
              AFTER ADVANCING 2 LINES

           ADD 2 TO LINE-CTR
           IF LINE-CTR > 59
              PERFORM 0900-HEADING-ROUTINE
           ELSE
              NEXT SENTENCE

        ELSE

           IF CHANGE-CODE
               MOVE TRANS-KEY TO CHANGE-ERROR-KEY
               WRITE LIST-OUT-RECORD FROM CHANGE-MESSAGE-ERROR
                   AFTER ADVANCING 2 LINES
           ELSE
               MOVE TRANS-KEY TO DELETE-ERROR-KEY
               WRITE LIST-OUT-RECORD FROM DELETE-MESSAGE-ERROR
                   AFTER ADVANCING 2 LINES.

        PERFORM 1010-READ-TRANSACTION-FILE.


0600-MASTER-LESS-ROUTINE.

        MOVE MASTER-KEY            TO NEW-MASTER-KEY.
        MOVE MASTER-NAME           TO NEW-MASTER-NAME.
        MOVE DATE-OF-CONTRIBUTION  TO NEW-DATE.
        MOVE AMOUNT                TO NEW-AMOUNT.
        WRITE NEW-MASTER-RECORD.
```

```
        MOVE SPACES TO MESSAGE-OUT.
        IF CHANGE-PRINT-CODE = 0
            PERFORM 0700-TRANSACTION-PRINT
        ELSE
            MOVE 0 TO CHANGE-PRINT-CODE.
        PERFORM 1000-READ-OLD-MASTER.


    0700-TRANSACTION-PRINT.

        MOVE MASTER-KEY            TO MASTER-KEY-OUT.
        MOVE MASTER-NAME           TO MASTER-NAME-OUT.
        MOVE DATE-OF-CONTRIBUTION  TO DATE-OUT.
        MOVE AMOUNT                TO AMOUNT-OUT.

        WRITE LIST-OUT-RECORD FROM DETAIL-LINE
            AFTER ADVANCING 2 LINES.

        ADD 2 TO LINE-CTR.

        IF LINE-CTR > 59
            PERFORM 0900-HEADING-ROUTINE.

    0800-LIST-NEW-MASTER.

        ADD NEW-AMOUNT TO TOTAL-AMOUNT.

        MOVE NEW-MASTER-KEY   TO MASTER-KEY-OUT.
        MOVE NEW-MASTER-NAME  TO MASTER-NAME-OUT.
        MOVE NEW-DATE         TO DATE-OUT.
        MOVE NEW-AMOUNT       TO AMOUNT-OUT.

        WRITE LIST-OUT-RECORD FROM DETAIL-LINE
            AFTER ADVANCING 2 LINES.

        ADD 2 TO LINE-CTR.

        IF LINE-CTR > 59
            PERFORM 0900-HEADING-ROUTINE.

        READ NEW-MASTER
            AT END MOVE 'YES' TO EOF.


    0900-HEADING-ROUTINE.

        MOVE PAGE-CTR TO PAGE-CTR-OUT.
        WRITE LIST-OUT-RECORD FROM PAGE-HEADING-1
            AFTER ADVANCING PAGE.
        WRITE LIST-OUT-RECORD FROM PAGE-HEADING-2
            AFTER ADVANCING 1 LINE.

        WRITE LIST-OUT-RECORD FROM COLUMN-HEADING-1
            AFTER ADVANCING 2 LINES.
        WRITE LIST-OUT-RECORD FROM COLUMN-HEADING-2
            AFTER ADVANCING 1 LINE.

        MOVE 6 TO LINE-CTR.
        ADD 1 TO PAGE-CTR.
```

```
1000-READ-OLD-MASTER.
    READ OLD-MASTER
        AT END MOVE HIGH-VALUES TO MASTER-KEY.


1010-READ-TRANSACTION-FILE.
    READ TRANSACTION-IN
        AT END MOVE HIGH-VALUES TO TRANS-KEY.
```

When we run the program we will get the three different reports:

```
                    CONTRIBUTIONS REPORT
06/02/88              PRIOR TO UPDATE              PAGE  1

CONT.                             CONTRIB.      CONTRIB.
NUMB.      CONTRIBUTORS NAME        DATE         AMOUNT

 002      ABLE BAKER            01/01/88        $70.00

 003      JOHN CARTWELL         01/01/88        $77.12

 004      SAMUAL DORSEY         01/01/88       $330.11

 006      JERMIA NOLTE          01/02/88       $120.12

 007      LISA REDFORD          01/02/88       $833.12

 008      FRED JOHNKE           02/01/88        $55.12

 010      HARRISON MARSHALL     02/01/88        $40.12

 011      TOM EISEN             02/01/88        $40.13

 013      HARROLD STERN         02/02/88        $10.08

 014      FREDERICK SUMMERS     02/02/88        $10.03

 016      SALLY JOHNSON         03/01/88        $10.14

 017      BARBARA NOLAN         03/01/88        $50.05

 018      FRANCIS CANTWELL      03/02/88        $56.00

 019      GEORGE SMITH          03/02/88        $57.68

 020      MARK HAMMEL           03/02/88        $90.12

          TOTAL CONTRIBUTIONS                $1,849.94
```

****

```
                        CONTRIBUTIONS REPORT
      06/02/88          TRANSACTION UPDATE              PAGE  2

      CONT.                               CONTRIB.   CONTRIB.
      NUMB.    CONTRIBUTORS NAME            DATE      AMOUNT     TRANSACTION INFORMATION

      001      RICHARD ADAMSON           01/01/88     $2.00     ADD

      002      ABLE BAKER                01/01/88    $70.00     ADD = ERROR - RECORD ALREADY ON FILE

      002      JAMIE STEVENS             01/01/88    $70.00     CHANGE = NAME - ABLE BAKER

      002      JAMIE STEVENS             01/01/88    $22.22     CHANGE = AMOUNT -    $70.00

      003      JOHN CARTWELL             01/01/88    $77.12

      004      SAMUAL DORSEY             01/01/88   $330.11     DELETE

      005      NICK HAMMOND              01/02/88    $15.00     ADD

      006      TOMMY TOMPSON             01/02/88   $120.12     CHANGE = NAME - JERMIA NOLTE

      006      TOMMY TOMPSON             06/15/87   $120.12     CHANGE = DATE - 01/02/88

      006      TOMMY TOMPSON             06/15/87    $66.66     CHANGE = AMOUNT -   $120.12

      007      LISA REDFORD              01/02/88   $833.12

      008      FRED JOHNKE               02/01/88    $55.12     DELETE

                                                               CHANGE = ERROR - RECORD NOT ON FILE = 009

      010      HARRISON MARSHALL         02/01/88    $40.12

      011      TOM EISEN                 02/01/88    $12.34     CHANGE = AMOUNT -    $40.13

                                                               DELETE = ERROR - RECORD NOT ON FILE = 012

      013      HARROLD STERN             02/02/88    $10.08

      014      FREDERICK SUMMERS         02/02/88    $10.03

      015      TOM JONES                 03/01/88     $4.50     ADD

      016      SALLY JOHNSON             03/01/88    $10.14

      017      BARBARA NOLAN             03/01/88    $50.05

      018      FRANCIS CANTWELL          03/02/88    $56.00

      019      GEORGE SMITH              03/02/88    $57.68

      020      MARK HAMMEL               03/02/88    $90.12

                                                               CHANGE = ERROR - RECORD NOT ON FILE = 022
```

****

```
                    CONTRIBUTIONS REPORT
06/02/88               AFTER UPDATE              PAGE   3

CONT.                              CONTRIB.        CONTRIB.
NUMB.      CONTRIBUTORS NAME        DATE           AMOUNT

 001     RICHARD ADAMSON          01/01/88          $2.00

 002     JAMIE STEVENS            01/01/88         $22.22

 003     JOHN CARTWELL            01/01/88         $77.12

 005     NICK HAMMOND             01/02/88         $15.00

 006     TOMMY TOMPSON            06/15/87         $66.66

 007     LISA REDFORD             01/02/88        $833.12

 010     HARRISON MARSHALL        02/01/88         $40.12

 011     TOM EISEN                02/01/88         $12.34

 013     HARROLD STERN            02/02/88         $10.08

 014     FREDERICK SUMMERS        02/02/88         $10.03

 015     TOM JONES                03/01/88          $4.50

 016     SALLY JOHNSON            03/01/88         $10.14

 017     BARBARA NOLAN            03/01/88         $50.05

 018     FRANCIS CANTWELL         03/02/88         $56.00

 019     GEORGE SMITH             03/02/88         $57.68

 020     MARK HAMMEL              03/02/88         $90.12

         TOTAL CONTRIBUTIONS                    $3,207.12
```

A total is printed only on the first and last reports; a total on the transaction report would be meaningless.

3-7

Using the REWRITE Statement

We have mentioned that sequential tape processing and sequential disk processing are handled basically the same way. Well, that's not correct in all cases. Sometimes we modify our update procedure for sequential disk files so that we can update the records without needing a new master file. That is, we use only two files—the master file and the transaction file.

In order to process the records in place, we use not a WRITE statement but a REWRITE. When we are ready to write the changed records into the new master file, we actually REWRITE them into the old master file. This does not require any special processing by the computer: in a disk file, the computer knows where the record was retrieved from and can put it back without any difficulty.

In this type of processing, the file OPEN statement must specify the master file as opened for **I–O** (Input and Output) since we will be reading, writing, and rewriting the file.

This type of processing has a couple of problems. When we add records to the file we still WRITE them, and the records are stuck on the end of the file. The problem is that the file is no longer in sequence, so unless we are careful our program will no longer work.

Also, when we are deleting records, we have to put some kind of mark in the file because the machine will not (in most computers) delete records from a sequential file. So we set up a special field called RECORD-STATUS or some such and put a "D" in the field if it is to be deleted. Then, all subsequent programs would need to check this status field to see whether the field was still active.

The third problem is possibly worse than the other two. If we update the records in place without creating a new master file, we lose the automatic backup file we had left over (the old master). Since we are making changes directly to the old master file, if we make a mistake—by deleting the wrong record or changing the wrong data—we generally have to reconstruct the file instead of simply rerunning the update program with changed transactions.

It is for these reasons especially that most sequential disk updating of the old and new master files is done as was demonstrated in this chapter.

3-8

The Record Rack Sequential Update Program

Roger Barnell needs a report to show the changes made to his payroll file (file layout in Figure 3-12) when transactions to the file are being performed. He needs the report to detail the following:

1. employee number and name
2. rate of pay
3. number of deductions
4. type of transaction
5. transaction done

There are three types of transactions: add new record, delete old record, and change the record. All Roger wants the program to be able to do is change the rate of pay. The file layout for the transaction file is in Figure 3-13. He assigned the project to Cindy and she designed the report to look like the one shown in Figure 3-14. Her systems chart is shown in Figure 3-15, the design of the program is shown in Figure 3-16, and the pseudocode appears below.

PAYROLL **File**					
Field Description	*Position*	*Length*	:	*Dec*	*Type*
Employee number	1–4	4	:		Non-numeric
Employee name	5–24	20	:		Non-numeric
Filler	25–27	3	:		Non-numeric
Rate of pay	28–31	4	:	2	Numeric
Deductions	32–33	2	:	0	Numeric
Filler	34–80	47	:		Non-numeric
Record Length = 80					

Figure 3-12   The payroll file for the *The Record Rack* sequential update program.

RRTRANS **File**					
Field Description	*Position*	*Length*	:	*Dec*	*Type*
Employee number	1–4	4	:		Non-numeric
Transaction code	5–5	1	:		Non-numeric
Filler	6–6	1	:		Non-numeric
Data fields	7–32	26	:		Various
Filler	33–80	48	:		Non-numeric
Record Length = 80					

For the change function, "Data fields" will be defined as

New rate	7–10	4	:	2	Numeric
Filler	11–32	22	:		Non-numeric

For the add function, "Data fields" will be defined as

Name	7–26	20	:		Non-numeric
Rate	27–30	4	:	2	Numeric
Deductions	31–32	2	:	0	Numeric

Figure 3-13   The record layout and the additional layouts needed for the transaction file for *The Record Rack* payroll update program.

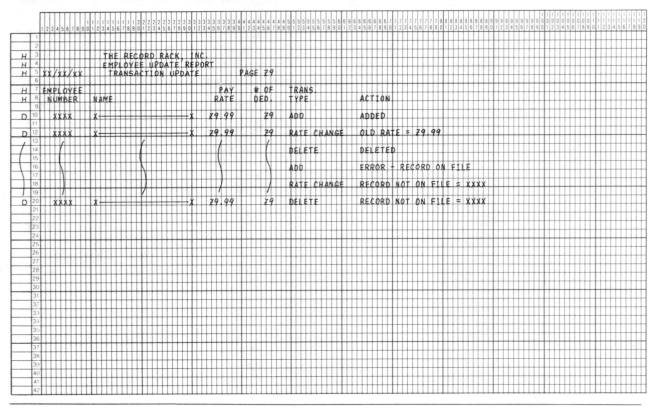

Figure 3-14   The layout for all three forms of the report for *The Record Rack*.

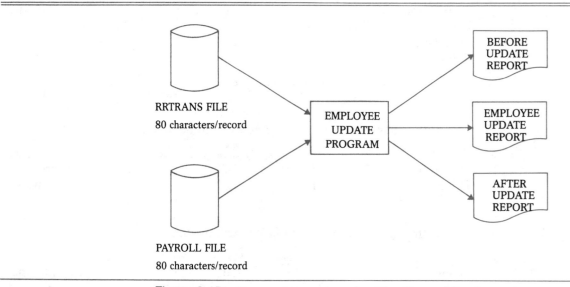

Figure 3-15   The systems chart for *The Record Rack* employee update report program.

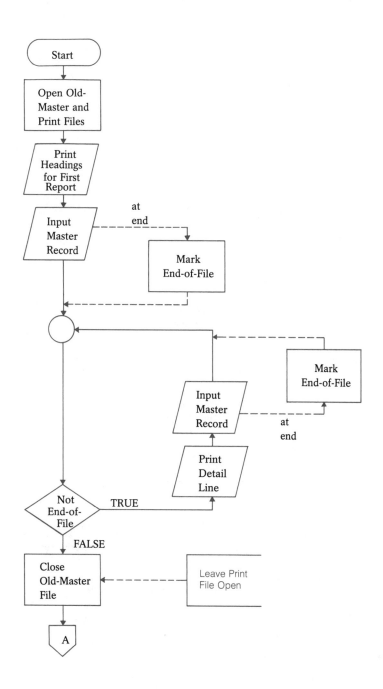

Figure 3-16   The entire flowchart for the sequential update program.

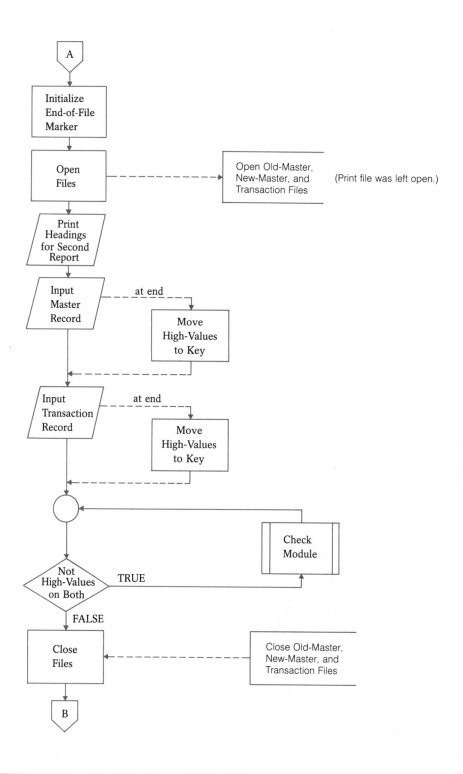

Figure 3-16   (continued)

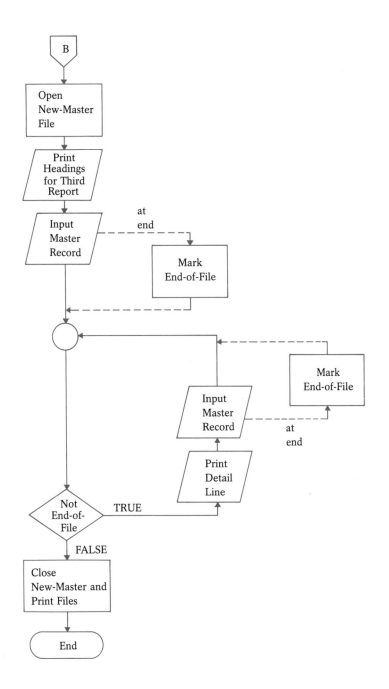

Figure 3-16   (continued)

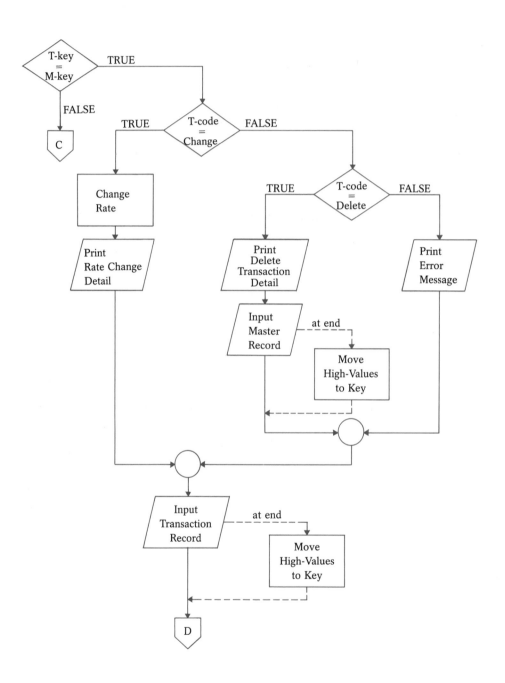

Figure 3-16   (continued)

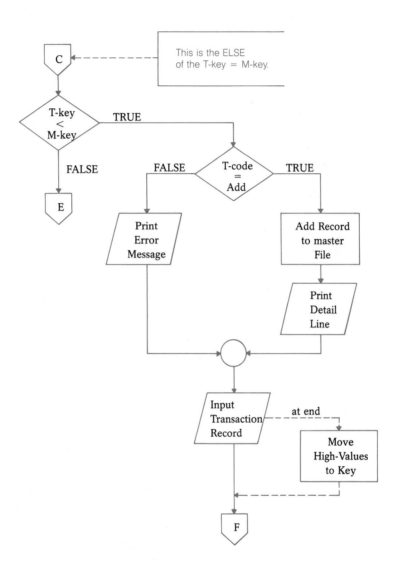

Figure 3-16   (continued)

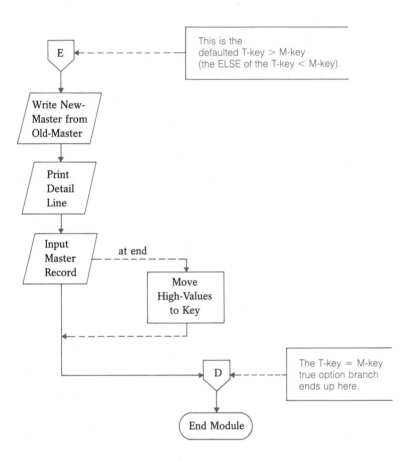

Figure 3-16   (continued)

Start
Open old master file and print file
Print the headings for the first report
Input a master record at end mark end-of-file
DO-WHILE not end-of-file
       Print detail line
       Input a master record at end mark end-of-file
END-DO
Close the old master file
Initialize the end-of-file marker
Open the old master file, transaction file, and new master file
Print headings for the second report
Input a master record at end move high-values to key
Input a transaction record at end move high-values to key
DO-WHILE not high values on both files
       IF trans employee number = master employee number THEN
              IF transaction = change rate THEN
                  Change the rate
                  Print the detail line
              ELSE IF transaction = delete THEN
                  Print delete detail line
                  Input old master record at end move high-values to key
              ELSE
                  Print error message
              END-IF
              Input a transaction record at end move high-values to key
       ELSE IF trans employee number < master employee number THEN
              IF transaction = add THEN
                  Write trans record to new master file
                  Print the detail line
              ELSE
                  Print error message
              END-IF
              Input a transaction record at end move high-values to key
       ELSE
              Write master file to new master file
              Print the detail line
              Input a master record at end move high-values to key
       END-IF
END-DO
Close the old master file, new master file, and transaction file
Open the new master file
Print the headings for the third report
Input a new master record at end mark end-of-file
DO-WHILE not end-of-file
       Print detail line
       Input a new master record at end mark end-of-file
END-DO
Close the new master file and print file
End

After the program was keypunched and debugged, the following master file data was used to test it.

Emp. No.	Name	Rate	Deductions
0001	JOHN SMITH	5.12	1
0002	SAMANTHA JOHNSON	3.65	4
0010	FRED HARRIS	10.85	3
0015	ED COBURN	15.85	4
0025	CINDY HARRISON	12.25	3
0026	JOHN JONES	10.35	2
0030	SUSAN SMITH	13.90	3
0032	MARK HEIDER	9.80	2
0035	TOM LONG	8.90	1

Then the transaction file input was created, with the transactions codes of A for add, C for change, and D for delete. The following data was used:

Emp. No.	Trans. Code	Name	Rate	Deductions
0001	A	TONY SMITH	1.30	10
0002	D	—	—	—
0004	A	JEFF HAMMEL	8.40	1
0010	C	—	12.60	—
0012	A	KAREN WHITE	7.50	2
0030	D	—	—	—
0035	C	—	10.75	—
0045	D	—	—	—

Cindy's program:

```
****************************************************************
****************************************************************
*
*
*
*  PROGRAM NAME: RATE-UP
*
*  PROGRAMMER NAME:  CINDY HARRISON
*
*  SOCIAL SECURITY NUMBER:  999-99-9999
*
*  DUE DATE: FEBRUARY 10, 1988
*
*  DESCRIPTION: THIS PROGRAM WILL PERFORM A SEQUENTIAL UPDATE TO
*               THE PAYROLL FILE, ADDING, DELETING, AND CHANGING
*               THE RATE OF PAY.
*
*
****************************************************************
****************************************************************
```

```
IDENTIFICATION DIVISION.
PROGRAM-ID.     RATE-UP.
AUTHOR.         CINDY HARRISON.

ENVIRONMENT DIVISION.

CONFIGURATION SECTION.
SOURCE-COMPUTER. IBM-4331.
OBJECT-COMPUTER. IBM-4331.

INPUT-OUTPUT SECTION.
FILE-CONTROL.
    SELECT OLD-MASTER ASSIGN TO UT-S-PAYROLL.
    SELECT NEW-MASTER ASSIGN TO UT-S-NEWPAY.
    SELECT TRANS-IN   ASSIGN TO UT-S-RRTRANS.
    SELECT LIST-OUT   ASSIGN TO UT-S-SYSPRINT.

DATA DIVISION.
FILE SECTION.

FD  OLD-MASTER
    LABEL RECORDS ARE OMITTED
    RECORD CONTAINS 80 CHARACTERS.
01  OLD-MASTER-RECORD.
    05  MASTER-KEY              PIC XXXX.
    05  MASTER-NAME             PIC X(20).
    05  FILLER                  PIC X(3).
    05  PAY-RATE-IN             PIC 99V99.
    05  DEDUCTIONS-IN           PIC 99.
    05  FILLER                  PIC X(50).

FD  NEW-MASTER
    LABEL RECORDS ARE OMITTED
    RECORD CONTAINS 80 CHARACTERS.

01  NEW-MASTER-RECORD.
    05  NEW-MASTER-KEY          PIC XXXX.
    05  NEW-MASTER-NAME         PIC X(20).
    05  NEW-PAY-RATE            PIC 99V99.
    05  NEW-DEDUCTIONS          PIC 99.
    05  FILLER                  PIC X(50).

FD  TRANS-IN
    LABEL RECORDS ARE OMITTED
    RECORD CONTAINS 80 CHARACTERS.
01  TRANS-RECORD.
    05  TRANS-KEY               PIC XXXX.
    05  TRANS-CODE              PIC X.
        88  ADD-CODE            VALUE 'A'.
        88  CHANGE-CODE         VALUE 'C'.
        88  DELETE-CODE         VALUE 'D'.

    05  FILLER                  PIC X.
    05  DATA-FIELD              PIC X(74).

01  DATA-RATE.
    05  FILLER                  PIC X(6).
    05  CHANGE-RATE             PIC 99V99.
    05  FILLER                  PIC X(70).
```

```
01   ADD-FIELDS.
     05   FILLER                    PIC X(6).
     05   ADD-NAME                  PIC X(20).
     05   ADD-RATE                  PIC 99V99.
     05   ADD-DEDUCTIONS            PIC 99.
     05   FILLER                    PIC X(48).

FD   LIST-OUT
     LABEL RECORDS ARE OMITTED
     RECORD CONTAINS 133 CHARACTERS.
01   LIST-OUT-RECORD               PIC X(133).

WORKING-STORAGE SECTION.

01   WORK-AREAS.
     05   EOF                       PIC XXX              VALUE 'NO '.
          88   WE-ARE-OUT-OF-DATA                        VALUE 'YES'.

     05   LINE-CTR                  PIC 99               VALUE ZERO.
     05   PAGE-CTR                  PIC 99               VALUE 1.
     05   CHANGE-PRINT-CODE         PIC 9                VALUE ZERO.

     05   MACHINE-DATE              PIC X(6).
     05   DATE-WORK REDEFINES MACHINE-DATE.
          10   DATE-YY              PIC XX.
          10   DATE-MM              PIC XX.
          10   DATE-DD              PIC XX.

01   PAGE-HEADING-1.
     05   FILLER                    PIC X(35)            VALUE

          '              THE RECORD RACK, INC.'.

01   PAGE-HEADING-2.
     05   FILLER                    PIC X(35)            VALUE
          '         EMPLOYEE UPDATE REPORT'.

01   PAGE-HEADING-3.
     05   FILLER                    PIC X                VALUE SPACES.
     05   HEADING-MONTH             PIC XX.
     05   HEADING-DAY               PIC /XX/.
     05   HEADING-YEAR              PIC XX.
     05   VARIABLE-HEAD             PIC X(27)            VALUE
          '        PRIOR TO UPDATE       '.
     05   FILLER                    PIC X(9)             VALUE
          '     PAGE '.
     05   PAGE-CTR-OUT              PIC Z9.

01   COLUMN-HEADING-1.
     05   FILLER                    PIC X(50)            VALUE
          ' EMPLOYEE                          PAY   # OF     '.
     05   TRANS-HEAD-1              PIC X(6)             VALUE SPACES.

01   COLUMN-HEADING-2.
     05   FILLER                    PIC X(50)            VALUE
          '  NUMBER    NAME                 RATE    DED.'.
     05   TRANS-HEAD-2              PIC X(23)            VALUE SPACES.

01   DETAIL-LINE.
     05   FILLER                    PIC X(3)             VALUE SPACES.
     05   MASTER-KEY-OUT            PIC XXXX.
```

```
      05   FILLER                     PIC X(4)            VALUE SPACES.
      05   MASTER-NAME-OUT            PIC X(20).
      05   FILLER                     PIC XXX             VALUE SPACES.
      05   PAY-RATE-OUT               PIC Z9.99.
      05   FILLER                     PIC X(6)            VALUE SPACES.
      05   DEDUCTIONS-OUT             PIC ZZ.
      05   FILLER                     PIC X(3)            VALUE SPACES.
      05   TRANS-TYPE-OUT             PIC X(14)           VALUE SPACES.
      05   TRANS-ACTION-OUT           PIC X(50)           VALUE SPACES.

 01   CHANGE-MESSAGE.
      05   FILLER                     PIC X(11)           VALUE
           'OLD RATE = '.
      05   OLD-PAY-RATE               PIC Z9.99.

 01   CHANGE-OR-DELETE-ERROR-MESSAGE.
      05   FILLER                     PIC X(50)           VALUE SPACES.
      05   ERROR-TYPE                 PIC X(14)           VALUE SPACES.
      05   FILLER                     PIC X(21)           VALUE
           'RECORD NOT ON FILE = '.
      05   ERROR-KEY                  PIC XXXX.

 01   ADD-MESSAGE-ERROR              PIC X(22)           VALUE
      'ERROR - RECORD ON FILE'.

 PROCEDURE DIVISION.

 0100-MAIN-MODULE.

     OPEN INPUT  OLD-MASTER
          OUTPUT LIST-OUT.

     ACCEPT MACHINE-DATE FROM DATE.
     MOVE DATE-YY TO HEADING-YEAR.
     MOVE DATE-MM TO HEADING-MONTH.
     MOVE DATE-DD TO HEADING-DAY.

     PERFORM 0900-HEADING-ROUTINE.

     READ OLD-MASTER
          AT END MOVE 'YES' TO EOF.
     PERFORM 0200-LIST-OLD-MASTER
             UNTIL WE-ARE-OUT-OF-DATA.

     CLOSE OLD-MASTER.

     OPEN INPUT  OLD-MASTER
                 TRANS-IN
          OUTPUT NEW-MASTER.

     MOVE '      TRANSACTION UPDATE' TO VARIABLE-HEAD.
     MOVE 'TRANS.' TO TRANS-HEAD-1.
     MOVE 'TYPE            ACTION' TO TRANS-HEAD-2.
     PERFORM 0900-HEADING-ROUTINE.

     PERFORM 1000-READ-OLD-MASTER.
     PERFORM 1010-READ-TRANS-FILE.
     PERFORM 0300-TRANSACTION-UPDATE
             UNTIL MASTER-KEY = HIGH-VALUES
             AND   TRANS-KEY  = HIGH-VALUES.
```

```
        CLOSE OLD-MASTER
              NEW-MASTER
              TRANS-IN.

        OPEN INPUT  NEW-MASTER.

        MOVE '         AFTER UPDATE' TO VARIABLE-HEAD.
        MOVE SPACES TO TRANS-TYPE-OUT TRANS-ACTION-OUT,
                       TRANS-HEAD-1   TRANS-HEAD-2.
        PERFORM 0900-HEADING-ROUTINE.

        MOVE 'NO ' TO EOF.

        READ NEW-MASTER
             AT END MOVE 'YES' TO EOF.
        PERFORM 0800-LIST-NEW-MASTER
              UNTIL WE-ARE-OUT-OF-DATA.

        CLOSE NEW-MASTER
              LIST-OUT.
        STOP RUN.


    0200-LIST-OLD-MASTER.

        PERFORM 0700-TRANSACTION-PRINT.
        PERFORM 1000-READ-OLD-MASTER.


    0300-TRANSACTION-UPDATE.

        IF MASTER-KEY = TRANS-KEY
            PERFORM 0400-EQUAL-ROUTINE
        ELSE
            IF MASTER-KEY > TRANS-KEY
            PERFORM 0500-MASTER-GREATER-ROUTINE
        ELSE
            PERFORM 0600-MASTER-LESS-ROUTINE.


    0400-EQUAL-ROUTINE.

        IF CHANGE-CODE
            MOVE 'RATE CHANGE'  TO TRANS-TYPE-OUT
            MOVE PAY-RATE-IN    TO OLD-PAY-RATE
            MOVE CHANGE-MESSAGE TO TRANS-ACTION-OUT
            MOVE NEW-PAY-RATE   TO PAY-RATE-IN
            PERFORM 0700-TRANSACTION-PRINT
            MOVE 1 TO CHANGE-PRINT-CODE

        ELSE
            IF DELETE-CODE
            MOVE 'DELETE'  TO TRANS-TYPE-OUT
            MOVE 'DELETED' TO TRANS-ACTION-OUT
            PERFORM 0700-TRANSACTION-PRINT
            PERFORM 1000-READ-OLD-MASTER
```

```
    ELSE
        MOVE 'ADD'                TO TRANS-TYPE-OUT
        MOVE ADD-MESSAGE-ERROR TO TRANS-ACTION-OUT
        PERFORM 0700-TRANSACTION-PRINT.

    PERFORM 1010-READ-TRANS-FILE.


0500-MASTER-GREATER-ROUTINE.

    IF ADD-CODE
        MOVE TRANS-KEY        TO NEW-MASTER-KEY, MASTER-KEY-OUT
        MOVE ADD-NAME         TO NEW-MASTER-NAME, MASTER-NAME-OUT
        MOVE ADD-RATE         TO NEW-PAY-RATE, PAY-RATE-OUT
        MOVE ADD-DEDUCTIONS TO NEW-DEDUCTIONS, DEDUCTIONS-OUT
        WRITE NEW-MASTER-RECORD

        MOVE 'ADD'   TO TRANS-TYPE-OUT
        MOVE 'ADDED' TO TRANS-ACTION-OUT

        WRITE LIST-OUT-RECORD FROM DETAIL-LINE
           AFTER ADVANCING 2 LINES

        ADD 2 TO LINE-CTR
        IF LINE-CTR > 59
           PERFORM 0900-HEADING-ROUTINE
        ELSE
           NEXT SENTENCE

    ELSE IF CHANGE-CODE
        MOVE 'RATE CHANGE' TO ERROR-TYPE
        MOVE TRANS-KEY        TO ERROR-KEY
        WRITE LIST-OUT-RECORD FROM CHANGE-OR-DELETE-ERROR-MESSAGE
             AFTER ADVANCING 2 LINES

    ELSE
        MOVE 'DELETE'  TO ERROR-TYPE
        MOVE TRANS-KEY TO ERROR-KEY
        WRITE LIST-OUT-RECORD FROM CHANGE-OR-DELETE-ERROR-MESSAGE
             AFTER ADVANCING 2 LINES.

    PERFORM 1010-READ-TRANS-FILE.


0600-MASTER-LESS-ROUTINE.

    MOVE MASTER-KEY       TO NEW-MASTER-KEY.
    MOVE MASTER-NAME      TO NEW-MASTER-NAME.
    MOVE PAY-RATE-IN      TO NEW-PAY-RATE.
    MOVE DEDUCTIONS-IN TO NEW-DEDUCTIONS.
    WRITE NEW-MASTER-RECORD.

    MOVE SPACES TO TRANS-TYPE-OUT, TRANS-ACTION-OUT.
    IF CHANGE-PRINT-CODE = 0
        PERFORM 0700-TRANSACTION-PRINT
    ELSE
        MOVE 0 TO CHANGE-PRINT-CODE.
    PERFORM 1010-READ-OLD-MASTER.
```

```
0700-TRANSACTION-PRINT.

    MOVE MASTER-KEY     TO MASTER-KEY-OUT.
    MOVE MASTER-NAME    TO MASTER-NAME-OUT.
    MOVE PAY-RATE-IN    TO PAY-RATE-OUT.
    MOVE DEDUCTIONS-IN  TO DEDUCTIONS-OUT.

    WRITE LIST-OUT-RECORD FROM DETAIL-LINE
        AFTER ADVANCING 2 LINES.

    ADD 2 TO LINE-CTR.

    IF LINE-CTR > 59
       PERFORM 0900-HEADING-ROUTINE.

0800-LIST-NEW-MASTER.

    MOVE NEW-MASTER-KEY   TO MASTER-KEY-OUT.
    MOVE NEW-MASTER-NAME  TO MASTER-NAME-OUT.
    MOVE NEW-PAY-RATE     TO PAY-RATE-OUT.
    MOVE NEW-DEDUCTIONS   TO DEDUCTIONS-OUT.

    WRITE LIST-OUT-RECORD FROM DETAIL-LINE
        AFTER ADVANCING 2 LINES.

    ADD 2 TO LINE-CTR.

    IF LINE-CTR > 59
       PERFORM 0900-HEADING-ROUTINE.

    READ NEW-MASTER
        AT END MOVE 'YES' TO EOF.

0900-HEADING-ROUTINE.

    MOVE PAGE-CTR TO PAGE-CTR-OUT.
    WRITE LIST-OUT-RECORD FROM PAGE-HEADING-1
        AFTER ADVANCING PAGE.
    WRITE LIST-OUT-RECORD FROM PAGE-HEADING-2
        AFTER ADVANCING 1 LINE.
    WRITE LIST-OUT-RECORD FROM PAGE-HEADING-3
        AFTER ADVANCING 1 LINE.

    WRITE LIST-OUT-RECORD FROM COLUMN-HEADING-1
        AFTER ADVANCING 2 LINES.
    WRITE LIST-OUT-RECORD FROM COLUMN-HEADING-2
        AFTER ADVANCING 1 LINE.

    MOVE 7 TO LINE-CTR.
    ADD 1 TO PAGE-CTR.

1000-READ-OLD-MASTER.
    READ OLD-MASTER
        AT END MOVE HIGH-VALUES TO MASTER-KEY.

1010-READ-TRANS-FILE.
    READ TRANS-IN
        AT END MOVE HIGH-VALUES TO TRANS-KEY.
```

From the data shown earlier, her program generated the following three reports:

```
                    THE RECORD RACK, INC.
                  EMPLOYEE UPDATE REPORT
       06/16/88        PRIOR TO UPDATE          PAGE   1
```

EMPLOYEE NUMBER	NAME	PAY RATE	# OF DED.
0001	JOHN SMITH	5.12	1
0002	SAMANTHA JOHNSON	3.65	4
0010	FRED HARRIS	10.85	3
0015	ED COBURN	15.85	4
0025	CINDY HARRISON	12.25	3
0026	JOHN JONES	10.35	2
0030	SUSAN SMITH	13.90	3
0032	MARK HEIDER	9.80	2
0035	TOM LONG	8.90	1

****

```
                THE RECORD RACK, INC.
              EMPLOYEE UPDATE REPORT
   06/16/88       TRANSACTION UPDATE        PAGE   2
```

EMPLOYEE NUMBER	NAME	PAY RATE	# OF DED.	TRANS. TYPE	ACTION
0001	JOHN SMITH	5.12	1	ADD	ERROR - RECORD ON FILE
0001	JOHN SMITH	5.12	1		
0002	SAMANTHA JOHNSON	3.65	4	DELETE	DELETED
				RATE CHANGE	RECORD NOT ON FILE = 0003
0004	JEFF HAMMEL	8.40	1	ADD	ADDED
0010	FRED HARRIS	8.40	3	RATE CHANGE	OLD RATE = 10.85
0012	KAREN WHITE	7.50	2	ADD	ADDED
0015	ED COBURN	15.85	4		
0025	CINDY HARRISON	12.25	3		
0026	JOHN JONES	10.35	2		
0030	SUSAN SMITH	13.90	3	DELETE	DELETED
0032	MARK HEIDER	9.80	2		
0035	TOM LONG	9.80	1	RATE CHANGE	OLD RATE = 8.90
				DELETE	RECORD NOT ON FILE = 0045

****

```
                        THE RECORD RACK, INC.
                       EMPLOYEE UPDATE REPORT
          06/16/88           AFTER UPDATE              PAGE  3

          EMPLOYEE                               PAY      # OF
           NUMBER    NAME                        RATE      DED.

            0001     JOHN SMITH                  5.12        1

            0004     JEFF HAMMEL                 8.40        1

            0010     FRED HARRIS                 8.40        3

            0012     KAREN WHITE                 7.50        2

            0015     ED COBURN                  15.85        4

            0025     CINDY HARRISON             12.25        3

            0026     JOHN JONES                 10.35        2

            0032     MARK HEIDER                 9.80        2

            0035     TOM LONG                    9.80        1
```

3-9
Summary

1. This chapter looked at how sequential files are created and maintained on disk and tape. A tape drive can contain only sequential files since a tape is strictly a sequential device. Disk drives, on the other hand, can process several different types of files.

2. A sequential file may be created by inputting data through an on-line procedure, some type of keypunching device, or internal program processing.

3. One of the procedures used most frequently when working with sequential files is changing, deleting, and adding new records—*updating* the file. For this type of processing we use three files: the old master file, the transaction file, and the new master file.

4. We also use a fourth file—a print file—and we generally print three different reports: one before we update the records, so we have a record of what the file looked like before the updating; another as the records are updated, to show us what changes were made; and a new printout of the master file, after the changes have been made.

5. In order to match the master and transaction records for updating, it is important that both files be in sorted order by the key field we are going to match against.

6. There are three different matching possibilities: the key fields are the same, the master key is greater than the transaction key, and the master key is less than the transaction key. If the key fields are equal, we can change or delete the master records. If the master key is greater than the transaction key, we

■

can only add a new record. If the master key is less than the transaction key, we do no processing and the old master record is simply written to the new master file.

7. We can update by rewriting the records directly in the old master file instead of writing them to a new master file. This type of processing has several problems, however. We generally cannot delete records; rather, we have to mark them some way. Also, we cannot add new records in the file where they need to be; they must be added on the end, which can cause processing problems if the program is not carefully constructed. Finally, without the new master file to put the updated records into, we lose the automatic backup that the intact old master file would provide and that we might need to check errors in processing.

3-10
Glossary

HIGH-VALUES The reserved word that specifies storing the maximum possible value into a field. It is used to mark the end-of-file for inputting key fields during the sequential update procedure.

I–O The type of processing specified on the OPEN statement for updating in place with the REWRITE statement.

New master file The updated records from the old master file. The records in the file are stored in the new master file as they are changed or added.

Old master file The original file during a sequential update procedure.

Rewriting The process of updating records in place in the file.

Transaction file The file that contains the records to be used to update the old master file in a sequential update procedure.

Updating The process of modifying a file by using transaction records.

3-11
Quick Quiz

Cover the answers with a blank sheet of paper and test yourself. Questions 1–15 are true or false questions, 16–20 are multiple choice, and 21–25 are fill-in-the-blank.

T F **1.** Creating a sequential file is just like printing a report, except that we write to a file without using edit symbols and blanks.

T F **2.** When doing an update, we must use three files: the old master, the transaction, and the new master.

T F **3.** The three transactions that we typically do to a master file are delete, add, or change a record.

T F **4.** Both the old master file and the transaction file need to be in sequence by a key field in order for updating to be performed.

T F **5.** If both key fields are the same, we are finished with the master record and may write it to the new master file.

T   F   **6.** If the master key is greater than the transaction key, we are finished with the master record and may write it to the new master file.

T   F   **7.** If the master key is less than the transaction key, we have a new record that needs to be added—if the code does in fact indicate an add.

T   F   **8.** We should check for an add code only when the transaction key is less than the master key.

T   F   **9.** If both key fields are equal and the transaction code indicates a delete, then the transaction record is in error.

T   F   **10.** The purpose of HIGH-VALUES is to set the bits of the key of the record being read to all 1's so that the key field in the other file will always be greater than the key field of the file that has no more records.

T   F   **11.** Before we enter the main loop that will perform all the changes necessary to our master file, we typically have only to input a transaction record; we need not be worried about inputting a master record because the transaction record indicates what needs to be done in the loop.

T   F   **12.** If the master key is greater than the transaction key and the transaction record indicates an add, then the transaction record is in error.

T   F   **13.** If the master key is less than the transaction key and the transaction record indicates a change, then the transaction record is in error.

T   F   **14.** The new master file resulting from an update will probably have to be resorted by key field, since we have no way of being positive that the records were written in sequence.

T   F   **15.** The REWRITE statement can be used to update a record, whether the master file is in sequence or not.

_____ **16.** The creation of a sequential file requires

     (a) that we do not write to the file with edit symbols and blank lines.
     (b) that we do not write to the file with headings and totals.
     (c) that it always be in some sequence by a key field.
     (d) a and b.

_____ **17.** Which of the following groups of files is absolutely necessary to perform a sequential file update?

     (a) a new master file, a print file, and a transaction file
     (b) a master file, a new master file, and a print file
     (c) a new master file, a master file, and a transaction file
     (d) a master file, a transaction file, and a print file

_____ **18.** Which of the following must be true before we can test for "add a record" in a sequential file update?

     (a) The master key must be less than the transaction key.
     (b) The master key must be equal to the transaction key.
     (c) The master key must be greater than the transaction key.
     (d) We must always test for a new record because of the uncertainty involved in using keys.

_____ **19.** When the master key is equal to the transaction key, the transaction key might indicate a change, but what other code would be legal on the transaction record?

     (a) an add
     (b) a delete
     (c) a rewrite
     (d) Only a change code is possible when the master key is equal to the transaction key.

20. When the master key is less than the transaction key, which of the following is permissible?

    (a) Write the old master record to the new master record.
    (b) Add the transaction record if its code indicates an add.
    (c) Delete the current master record if the transaction key indicates a delete.
    (d) Change the master record indicated by the change on the transaction file.

21. The updating of a sequential file typically uses four files: the master file, the new master file, the transaction file, and the _____ .
22. When the master key equals the transaction key, we can either change the master record or _____ the master record.
23. Before the main loop of the update program is entered, it is necessary to input a record from the master file and the _____ file.
24. To allow the processing of records left in the master file when the transaction file runs out of data, or vice versa, we can assign the transaction key the highest possible value by using _____ .
25. The only time we should write the old master record to the new master record is when the master key is _____ the transaction key.

3-12
Answers to Quick Quiz

1. T (Also, we do not use headings and totals.)
2. T (However, we typically use a print file to see what was performed.)
3. T
4. T
5. F (When they are equal we have either a change or a delete.)
6. F (We possibly have an add.)
7. F (Now we can write the old master file record to the new master file.)
8. T
9. F (When they are equal we have found the master record that corresponds to the transaction record, which could indicate a delete.)
10. T (Thus, the highest value possible is assigned to the key.)
11. F (Both a transaction record and a master record must be input.)
12. F (This is the correct setup to test for an add.)
13. F (Because the master key is less than the transaction key, we are finished with the master record and may write it to the new master file. However, the transaction record could still indicate a change, because we have not yet reached a master key that is equal to the transaction key.)
14. F (The records are written to the new master file in the same sequence they are input.)
15. T (It simply writes the record back to where it came from.)
16. d
17. c (The print file is not necessary but is recommended.)
18. c
19. b
20. a (For c and d to be true, the master key must equal the transaction key. For b to be true, the master key must be greater than the transaction key.)

21. print file
22. delete
23. transaction
24. HIGH-VALUES
25. less than

══ 3-13 ══
Questions to Aid Understanding

1. Explain how a sequential file is created, giving three examples.
2. What four files are used when updating a sequential file? What is the purpose of each of them?
*3. Why is the print file not necessary but recommended for a sequential file update?
4. What three possible transactions are generally considered during an update procedure?
5. What three different reports are often printed during an update procedure?
6. What is meant by the master key being equal to the transaction key?
*7. What is meant by the master key being less than the transaction key?
8. What is meant by the master key being greater than the transaction key?
9. What is the purpose of HIGH-VALUES?
10. Explain how the processing of the records is different when you are using the REWRITE statement.
11. Explain why both the master record and the transaction record must be input before we enter the main loop for an update procedure.

══ 3-14 ══
Coding Exercises

1. Write the select statements necessary for a sequential file update. Include the select for writing a report.
2. Write the coding necessary for a module that will test for the three different possibilities of master key and transaction key agreement.
3. Write the FD statements for a transaction file with multiple record layouts as needed for

Field Description	Position	Length	:	Dec	Type
Customer number	1–3	3	:		Non-numeric
Trans. code (A, B, C)	4–4	1	:		Non-numeric
Change field code	5–5	1	:		Numeric
Data for add or change	6–37	32	:		Non-numeric
Filler	38–80	43	:		Non-numeric

The master file contains the following information:

Field Description	Position	Length	:	Dec	Type
Customer number	1–3	3	:		Non-numeric
Customer name	4–23	20	:		Non-numeric
Salary	24–29	6	:		Numeric
Dependents	30–30	1	:		Numeric
Job code	31–31	1	:		Numeric

All fields except Customer number can be changed.
4. Look back in the chapter to the design for the sample program (pages 108–117). Rewrite the design to allow the program to use the REWRITE statement. (The changes are minor.)

3-15
Maintenance Program

Roger Barnell decides that the sequential update program that Cindy designed needs to be updated to allow changes to the name and number of deductions. You are assigned the task of updating the program. Look back at section 3-8 for the details of the program. Use transaction messages similar to the change message already used in the program.

3-16
Illustrative Program

A large magazine company needs a report to show the changes made to its master customer file. The subscription update report to be generated is shown in Figure 3-17. Only one report is necessary because any changes to the file will simply be recorded by the report. Figure 3-18 shows the systems chart for the program.

The record layout for the master file, SUBSCRIB, is in Figure 3-19. The transaction file, used to update the master file, has the record layout shown in Figure 3-20.

There are three possible transactions: cancel, renewal, and new account. For the renewal you need to add the number of months of renewal to the number of months left on the subscriber's record. On the report, any new subscribers will show the number of months they have subscribed for in the renewal column. The number of months each customer has left is reduced each time a monthly issue

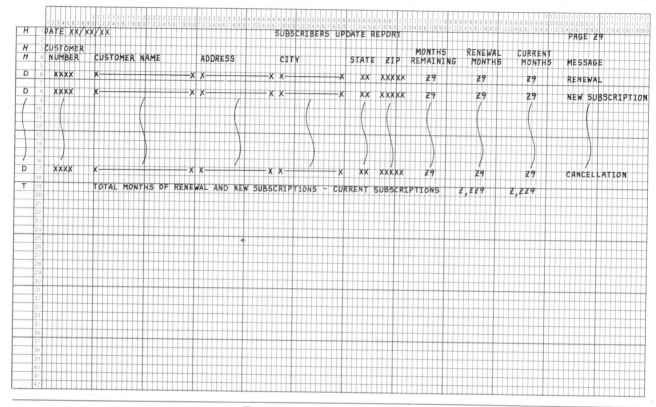

Figure 3-17 The layout for the subscription update report.

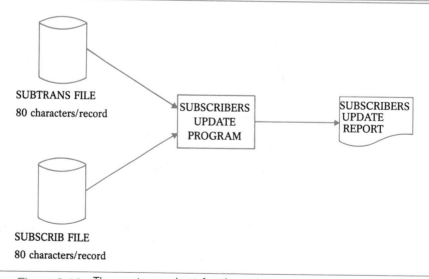

Figure 3-18 The systems chart for the subscription update report program.

SUBSCRIB File					
Field Description	*Position*	*Length*	:	*Dec*	*Type*
Customer number	1–4	4	:		Non-numeric
Customer name	5–24	20	:		Non-numeric
Address	25–39	15	:		Non-numeric
City	40–52	13	:		Non-numeric
State	53–54	2	:		Non-numeric
Zip code	55–59	5	:		Non-numeric
Months of subscription	60–61	2	:	0	Numeric
Filler	62–80	19	:		Non-numeric
Record Length = 80					

Figure 3-19   The record layout for the SUBSCRIB file.

SUBTRANS File					
Field Description	*Position*	*Length*	:	*Dec*	*Type*
Customer number	1–4	4	:		Non-numeric
Transaction code	5–5	1	:		Non-numeric
Data fields	6–62	57	:		Various
Filler	63–80	18	:		Non-numeric
Record Length = 80					

For the renewal function, "Data fields" will be defined as

Number of months	6–7	2	:	0	Numeric
Filler	8–62	55	:		Non-numeric

For the new account function (add), "Data fields" may be moved as a group and will not have to be subdefined.

Figure 3-20   The record layout and the additional layout needed for the transaction file for the SUBSCRIB file update program.

is sent. The flowchart design for this program is shown in Figure 3-21. The pseudocode follows:

```
Start
Open old master file, transaction file, new master file, and print file
Print headings for the second report
Input a transaction record at end move high-values to key
Input a master record at end move high-values to key
DO-WHILE not high-values on both
        IF trans subscribers number = master subscribers number THEN
                IF transaction = renewal THEN
                    Update number of months
                    Print the detail line
                ELSE IF transaction = cancel THEN
                    Print the cancel detail line
                    Input a master record at end move high-values to key
                ELSE
                    Print error message
                END-IF
                Input a transaction record at end high-values
        ELSE IF trans subscribers number < master subscribers number THEN
                IF transaction = new account THEN
                    Write trans record to new master file
                    Print the new account detail line
                ELSE
                    Print error message
                END-IF
                Input a transaction record at end high-values
        ELSE
                Write master file to new master file
                Print the detail line
                Input a master record at end high values
        END-IF
END-DO
Close old master file, transaction file, new master file, and print file
End
```

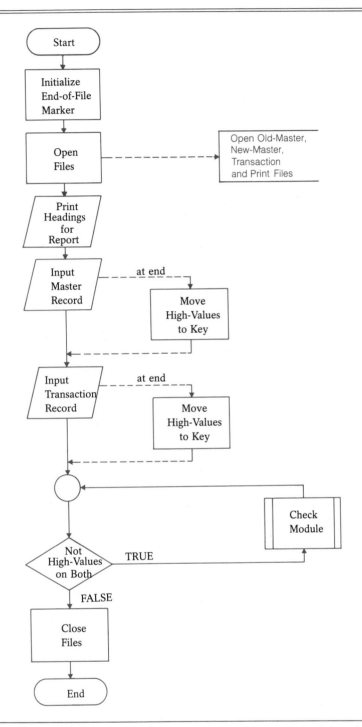

Figure 3-21   The entire flowchart for the sequential update program.

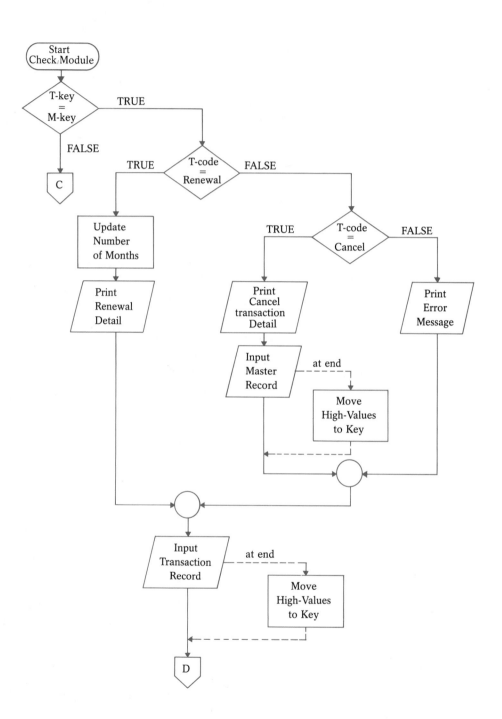

Figure 3-21 (continued)

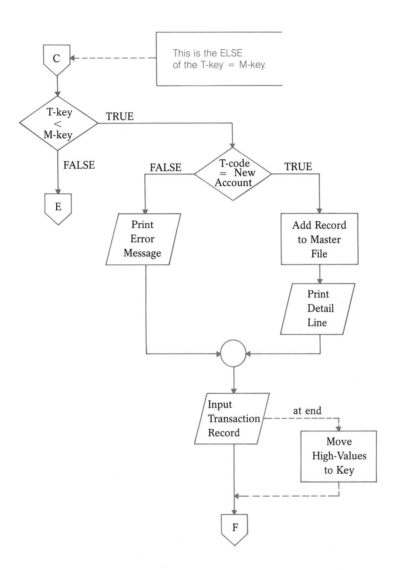

Figure 3-21   (continued)

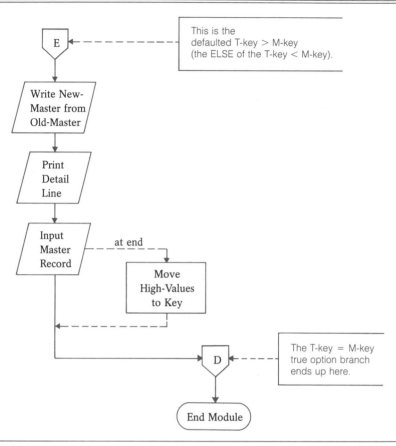

Figure 3-21   (continued)

3-17
System Designed Programs

For the following programs, all the design elements typically furnished to a programmer by the systems analyst are furnished. It is up to you, as programmer, to design and code the program. The files to be used are found in Appendix A.

1. *Sales Incorporated* has a master file (SALES) that contains the salesman's number and name, current amount of sales, commission, and commission rate for each of its employees, as shown in Figure 3-22.

   At the end of each month the company reads in a transaction file to update the master file with the current amount of sales. The transaction file simply contains the employee's number and amount of sales, as shown in Figure 3-23.

   Both files are in sequence by salesman number. Write a program to update the master file by replacing last month's sales with the amount from the transaction record.

SALES File					
Field Description	*Position*	*Length*	:	*Dec*	*Type*
Salesman number	1–4	4	:		Non-numeric
Salesman name	5–24	20	:		Non-numeric
Filler	25–26	2	:		Non-numeric
Commission rate	27–28	2	:	0	Numeric
Current sales	29–35	7	:	2	Numeric
Filler	36–80	45	:		Non-numeric
Record Length = 80					

Figure 3-22   The record layout for the SALES file, exercise 3-17-1.

SALETRANS File					
Field Description	*Position*	*Length*	:	*Dec*	*Type*
Salesman number	1–4	4	:		Non-numeric
Current amount of sales	5–11	7	:	2	Numeric
Filler	12–80	69	:		Non-numeric
Record Length = 80					

Figure 3-23   The record layout for the SALESTRAN file, exercise 3-17-1.

There is no need to print the contents of the file before the update or during, since there are only changes to the records. But after the records have been updated, you will need to print the report to show the new commission earned. Multiply the amount of sales by the commission rate in the record to determine the amount of commission earned. Print out a report as shown in the printer spacing chart in Figure 3-24. Also, total all the monthly commissions and print out a total line. The systems design is shown in Figure 3-25.

2. A small bank has developed a master file called BANK, as shown in Figure 3-26. The file contains all the information about the bank's charge customers who owe money. At the end of each month, the bank receives a list of the charges and payments made to the charge accounts. This list is in the form of the UPDATE file shown in Figure 3-27.

Write a program that generates a report like the one shown on the printer spacing chart in Figure 3-28. If the payment reduces the balance to zero, drop the record from the file. (Doing so is not actually practical since another transaction record might have a new charge to the account. This is only a practice program, however, so we can take a few liberties.) At the end of the report, print the total number of records that were dropped from the file. The systems design for this program is shown in Figure 3-29.

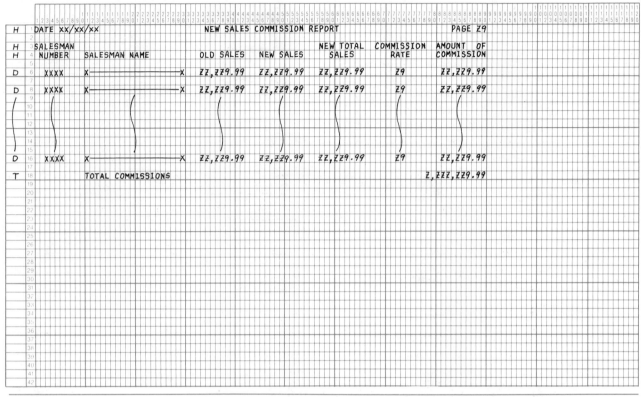

Figure 3-24 The layout for the news sales commission report, exercise 3-17-1.

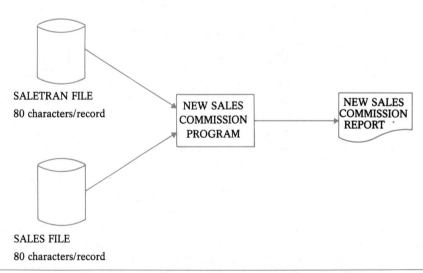

Figure 3-25 The systems chart for the new sales commission report program, exercise 3-17-1.

BANK File					
Field Description	*Position*	*Length*	:	*Dec*	*Type*
Customer number	1–4	4	:		Non-numeric
Customer name	5–24	20	:		Non-numeric
Charge card code	25–25	1	:	0	Numeric
Balance	26–32	7	:	2	Numeric
Date of last payment	33–38	6	:		Non-numeric
Amount of last payment	39–45	7	:	2	Numeric
Filler	46–80	35	:		Non-numeric
Record Length = 80					

Figure 3-26   The record layout for the BANK file, exercise 3-17-2.

UPDATE File					
Field Description	*Position*	*Length*	:	*Dec*	*Type*
Customer number	1–4	4	:		Non-numeric
Transaction type	5–5	1	:		Non-numeric
Amount	6–12	7	:	2	Numeric
Filler	13–80	68	:		Non-numeric
Record Length = 80					

Figure 3-27   The record layout for the UPDATE file, exercise 3-17-2.

3. At the end of each day, the department store where you work determines the quantity sold for each of the items in its inventory. A file, INVSALES, is then created that contains each item code and its quantity sold. Write a program to update the current inventory on the master inventory file, INVENT. Both files are in sequence by item code. The record layout for the INVENT file is in Figure 3-30 and the layout for INVSALES is in Figure 3-31.

When you are matching the records, if the item code on the INVSALES is less than the item code on the INVENT file, print out an error message indicating that the item code on the INVSALES file does not exist. If they match, subtract the quantity sold in the INVSALES file from the amount on hand in the INVENT file and create a new record. If the item code from the master file is greater than the item code from the update file, then indicate that none of the item has been sold, as shown in the printer spacing chart in Figure 3-32. The system design for this program is shown in Figure 3-33.

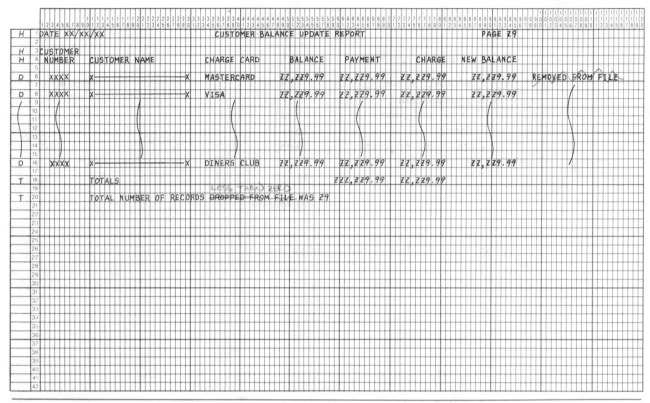

Figure 3-28   The layout for the customer balance update report, exercise 3-17-2.

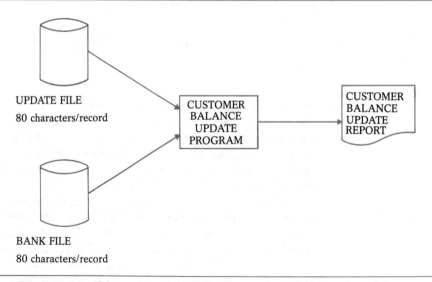

UPDATE FILE
80 characters/record

BANK FILE
80 characters/record

CUSTOMER BALANCE UPDATE PROGRAM

CUSTOMER BALANCE UPDATE REPORT

Figure 3-29   The systems chart for the customer balance update report program, exercise 3-17-2.

INVENT File					
Field Description	*Position*	*Length*	:	*Dec*	*Type*
Item number	1–4	4	:		Non-numeric
Current quantity	5–10	6	:	0	Numeric
Filler	11–80	70	:		Non-numeric
Record Length = 80					

Figure 3-30   The layout for the INVENT file, exercise 3-17-3.

INVSALES File					
Field Description	*Position*	*Length*	:	*Dec*	*Type*
Item number	1–4	4	:		Non-numeric
Quantity sold	5–10	6	:	0	Numeric
Filler	11–80	70	:		Non-numeric
Record Length = 80					

Figure 3-31   The record layout for the INVSALES file, exercise 3-17-3.

3-18

Non-designed Programs

In the following programs, you will need to design the systems chart, the input files (record layout), the printer spacing chart, the program design, and the data with which to test the program.

1. Under federal law, an employer must match, dollar for dollar, the amount of Social Security taxes paid by its employees. Write a program to update a company's master file that contains each employee's Social Security number and the amount of Social Security taxes that person has paid so far this year. Read in an update file that contains the employee's Social Security number and the amount of Social Security taxes paid for this pay period. Add the amount from the update file to the cumulative total in the master file record and write the updated record to a new file. Print out an error message if an update record does not have a corresponding master file record. Also, since some employees will not pay Social Security taxes because of layoffs, extended illness, or income that exceeds the maximum to be withheld for Social Security, some master file records will not be updated. These records should be listed on the report with a special notation indicating that no Social Security was withheld for this period.

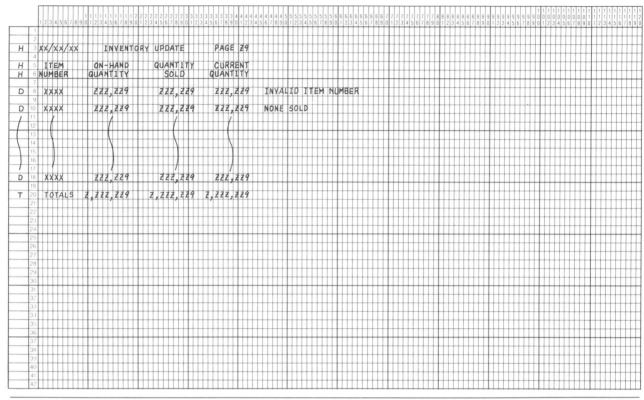

Figure 3-32   The layout for the inventory update program, exercise 3-17-3.

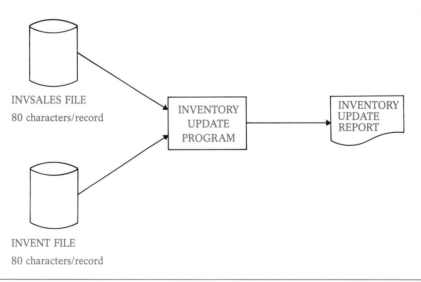

Figure 3-33   The systems chart for the inventory update report program, exercise 3-17-3.

2. The electric company maintains a master file showing each of its customer's current balance due. The record layout for the file shows the customer's number, current balance, and the last date of payment (in Julian calendar form). Write a program that will read an update file that contains the customer's account number and amount of payment. If no update record exists for a particular account, indicate on the report that the account is delinquent. Also, verify that the current balance due equals the payment received. If it does not, indicate on the report that the full amount has not been paid and show the amount still owed. The report should show the totals for all amounts paid, all amounts overdue, and the number of customers who have delinquent accounts.

3. The investment company you own buys stock in many other companies. You have a file that contains the name of the stock, the purchase price per share, and the number of shares purchased for each of the different companies invested in. It is updated every month in order to produce a balance sheet report. Thus, an update file containing the name of the stock and the current value per share is matched against the master file to update the value of the stock. New investment records may be added during this transaction procedure. If a particular master record has no update record, indicate that the price per share has not changed. Otherwise, compute the new current value of the stock and show it on the report.

OBJECTIVES After completing Chapter 4 you should be able to
1. explain the difference between batch and interactive processing;
2. list the three basic methods of using the screen and keyboard for interactive programs;
3. list and describe at least four screen design techniques;
4. list and describe at least four of the screen design guidelines;
5. explain what the DISPLAY statement is used for;
6. explain what the ACCEPT statement is used for and describe at least one difference between the various implementations;
7. explain what the STRING and UNSTRING statements are used for and the difference between them;
8. explain how the STRING and UNSTRING statements are used to help verify input data;
9. show how to use the screen guidelines to design sample screens.

CHAPTER 4

INTERACTIVE PROCESSING

4-1
Introduction

There are two basic methods of working with data in a computer system: batch and interactive (the latter is sometimes called **on-line**). In a **batch** environment, all the data is collected into a *batch* and then submitted to the computer. Batch systems often have several programs that execute one after another, guided by appropriate JCL.

An **interactive** system, on the other hand, enables the user to communicate directly with the computer system, updating files and generating reports. Typically, the computer will present the user with a **prompt**, which is simply a message on the terminal screen, and the user will respond by typing the appropriate answer. Then the computer will do whatever the response directed it to do.

Most computer systems are made up of both batch and interactive applications. These systems allow the user to update files interactively during the day and then print reports through batch processing at night.

All the programs we have written thus far have been batch programs. We have printed reports and created and updated files. Since most computer departments are moving more and more to interactive applications, it is important that the modern COBOL student be exposed to the way interactive programming is accomplished. The problem is that there are virtually no provisions in standard COBOL for interactive programming. Most computer vendors have added extensions to the standard COBOL statements to allow for it, but there is little consistency in these extensions. There are, however, many basic design elements of interactive programming common among programming systems. These common elements are the subject of this chapter.

4-2
Screen Design

In interactive applications, one of the most important program elements is the display screen. Depending upon the particular vendor implementation of COBOL, there are three basic methods of using the screen and keyboard for interactive programs:

- full-screen input and output with all the screen information defined in the WORKING-STORAGE SECTION. The commands to accomplish this are very much machine (or compiler) specific.
- input and output done with cursor positioning commands that are specific to the particular COBOL version. These are also machine specific.
- input and output using line-at-a-time processing that works with virtually any COBOL version (what we will be doing).

4-2-1 Full-screen Specifics

In full-screen processing, the screen layouts and necessary cursor handling commands are generally set up with an auxiliary program outside the application program. Most computer vendors have some type of programming system to set up screen designs that can be input into the COBOL programs and then used in an interactive fashion. This capability is necessary because COBOL itself has virtually no provisions for interactive programming. Though we will not discuss any of these programming systems, we will briefly look at the screen design techniques most of them allow the programmer to use. The most common are

- cursor positioning—the cursor may be positioned so that data can be displayed and input at specified screen locations.
- screen blanking—the information displayed on the screen can be erased from the current cursor position to the end of the display, or the entire screen can be cleared and the cursor moved to the upper left-hand corner (known as the **home position**).
- area protection—areas of the screen can be specified as being protected, and subsequent cursor movements will automatically skip over those areas. Information can be written into the protected areas by the system as the screen is set up; then that information will be protected from change.
- special display characteristics—the user has available highlighting (displaying as brighter than the rest of the display), reverse video (exchanging the background and character colors, for example, switching to black on white rather than white on black), blinking, underlining, and (for those machines that use color screens) using different colors for different areas of the screen.
- field length designations—the user can see how many characters long the entry is allowed to be. Some systems allow the designation character to be specified, using perhaps an asterisk for non-numeric entries, a number symbol (#) and decimal points for numeric entries, and even special markings for such fields as dates (which typically use markings like MM/DD/YY).
- special keys—function keys (marked on terminals as F1 for function key 1, or maybe PF1 or PA1) or control keys (the user presses another key while holding down a control key) can be used for special functions, such as jumping backward or forward among fields.

Displays are typically designed with field designations, followed by the field area to be input. As an example, we might design a screen to allow the input of the following information:

```
EMPLOYEE NUMBER #####
EMPLOYEE NAME.. ********************
ADDRESS........ *******************
CITY.......... *******************
STATE......... **
ZIP CODE...... #####
HIRE DATE..... MM/DD/YY
```

On such a screen, the entry information (EMPLOYEE NUMBER, EMPLOYEE NAME, and so on) might be displayed with normal intensity and the information actually entered shown with high intensity (or a different color). Only the input areas would be unprotected, which would cause the cursor to jump from one input area to the next as it advanced past all the protected areas. On a normal display screen, not all the input areas would be shown as we have depicted them. The entry markers would display only when the cursor moved to the field. For example, the first two fields would be displayed as

```
EMPLOYEE NUMBER #####
EMPLOYEE NAME..
```

with the cursor on the first # symbol. Then, after the user entered the EMPLOYEE NUMBER, the cursor would automatically jump down to the next unprotected area, the EMPLOYEE NAME, and the input area designators would appear as

```
EMPLOYEE NUMBER 12345
EMPLOYEE NAME.. ********************
```

As each field was entered, the cursor would move down the screen, indicating each field entry. Naturally, the user could return the cursor to the previously entered character by pressing the backspace key; also there is generally some function key that would allow the user to go back to a previously entered field to repair any errors.

4-2-2 Screen Design Guidelines

When setting up the screens to be used in your programs, there are several things you can do that can prove helpful to the eventual user:

1. If at all possible, get the user involved in the design of the system. Since the system is being designed for the user, it makes sense that the user should be allowed some input.
2. Use a menu system approach whenever possible. Such programs are among the most friendly to the user. They let the user simply choose from several choices on a menu of items to select the task to be performed. A sample menu:

```
1) ADD A RECORD
2) CHANGE A RECORD
3) DELETE A RECORD
4) PRINT A LIST OF THE RECORDS

SELECT OPTION:
```

In this example, the user is given a choice of four options and is simply requested to select the option by number. This is easier for the user than having to enter a command, such as ADD or DELETE.

3. Always put some type of heading and date on the screen so users will know exactly what is occurring in the program at each moment. If several screens look similar, a heading becomes vital; you may even want to put numbers on the screens to further clarify them.
4. Don't clutter up the screen. If there is more data to be displayed than will comfortably fit on one screen, use two or more. If you try to fit too much information onto one screen, users can become confused and frustrated. If you do use multiple screens, make the transition between them as smooth as possible.

5. Be consistent in the use of your screens. If similar items appear on several screens, put them in the same location on each screen. Any prompting of the user should always be done in the same location on the screen. Many programmers prefer to put the prompt at the bottom of the screen. Also, the use of any special keys should be standardized throughout your program; better yet, standardize it in your program system and in all the other systems produced by your department. For example, if the function key PF1 is used to backup from one field to the previous one in one part of your program, don't use the PF1 key for some other function in another part of the program.

6. Error messages should be informative yet as brief as possible. Avoid trying to be funny, or sarcastic: error messages should only be helpful. Here again, error messages should be printed in a consistent location, such as the bottom of the screen, so the user will not have to search for them.

7. Use the available features of the terminal, such as highlighting, color, and field protection. As mentioned earlier, such devices can help convey information to the user. You do, however, need to avoid overusing the special features. Too much use can diminish their value and make them more distracting than helpful.

4-2-3 Line-at-a-Time Processing

Since screen layouts are generally implemented with systems beyond the COBOL program itself, each with its own commands and structures, we will not deal with such systems for our programs in this book. We will also not deal with cursor positioning commands since they are also nonstandard. Instead, we will handle our interactive programming by displaying and inputting information one line at a time. We won't use a design system to create our screens, but that doesn't mean we won't follow our basic screen guidelines. We can use many of the same techniques. The only difference is that the displays are put to the screen one line at a time, instead of the screen displayed in its entirety with one command.

To do screen processing one line at a time, we use several simple commands. These commands may or may not be the ones used when you are doing full-screen processing (some systems suspend the use of these line-at-a-time commands in favor of others specially designed for full-screen processing), but the techniques we will be discussing in the next few sections are universally applicable.

4-3
The DISPLAY Statement

Undoubtedly, you have used the **DISPLAY statement** in the past. In Chapter 2 we reviewed it and showed how to use it for debugging a program. It is simply a command that causes information to be displayed on the terminal. Its form is

$$\underline{\text{DISPLAY}} \begin{Bmatrix} \text{field-name-1} [\ldots] \\ \text{literal-1} [\ldots] \end{Bmatrix} [\underline{\text{UPON}} \text{ mnemonic-name}]$$

The mnemonic-name allows us to direct the output from the statement to some device other than the default device, which in most systems is the display terminal. When doing interactive applications, we want the output to show up on the display terminal; thus we generally do not need to use the mnemonic-name.

The display statement can be used to display either literals or variables. When formatting screens, we need both of these potentials. Recall the simple menu shown earlier:

```
1) ADD A RECORD
2) CHANGE A RECORD
3) DELETE A RECORD
4) PRINT A LIST OF THE RECORDS

SELECT OPTION:
```

According to our guidelines, this is not enough information for the user. We need to add a heading to the screen so the user will know what the program is and what part of it is currently being accessed:

```
MAIN MENU     THE WIDGET WORKS, INC.    DATE: 10/15/88

              MASTER RECORD UPDATE SYSTEM

              1) ADD A RECORD
              2) CHANGE A RECORD
              3) DELETE A RECORD
              4) PRINT A LIST OF THE RECORDS

              SELECT OPTION:
```

Now the screen not only has the menu, but also informs the user that it is the "MASTER RECORD UPDATE SYSTEM" and the "MAIN MENU" of that system.

Such a menu can be displayed on the screen in several different ways. We can set up the lines in the WORKING-STORAGE SECTION:

```
WORKING-STORAGE SECTION.

01  SCREEN-SETUP.

    05  FIRST-LINE.
        10  HEADING-1-1              PIC X(40)       VALUE
            'MAIN MENU          THE WIDGET WORKS, INC. '.
        10  HEADING-1-2              PIC X(13)       VALUE
            '        DATE: '.
        10  DISPLAY-DATE             PIC X(8).
        10  FILLER                   PIC X(19).
    05  SECOND-LINE                  PIC X(80)       VALUE
        '                   MASTER RECORD UPDATE SYSTEM'.
    05  FILLER                       PIC X(80)       VALUE SPACES.
    05  MENU-LINE-1                  PIC X(80)       VALUE
        '                    1) ADD A RECORD'.
    05  FILLER                       PIC X(80)       VALUE SPACES.
    05  MENU-LINE-2                  PIC X(80)       VALUE
```

```
        '                     2) CHANGE A RECORD'.
05  FILLER                        PIC X(80)        VALUE SPACES.
05  MENU-LINE-3                   PIC X(80)        VALUE
        '                     3) DELETE A RECORD'.
05  FILLER                        PIC X(80)        VALUE SPACES.
05  MENU-LINE-4                   PIC X(80)        VALUE
        '                     4) PRINT A LIST OF THE RECORDS'.
05  FILLER                        PIC X(80)        VALUE SPACES.
05  FILLER                        PIC X(80)        VALUE SPACES.
05  OPTION-LINE                   PIC X(80)        VALUE
        '                     SELECT OPTION:'.
```

and then display them all at once with the statement

```
DISPLAY SCREEN-SETUP.
```

Notice that each of the screen lines is set up to have a length of 80. The standard width for a display terminal is 80 columns; by displaying 80 characters, we will fill up the line on the screen with each of the defined lines. This will not work on all terminals, however. Some will force one or two characters at the end of each displayed line so that, though the physical width of the screen is still 80 characters, the actual usable width may only be 78 or 79. If this is the case, each of your displayed lines would have to be 78 or 79.

Printing the screen with one command is not recommended because adjusting it is difficult if it is off by one or two characters. For example, suppose we have an extra character on the first line we are printing. Since all the lines are 80 characters, this one extra character affects all the subsequent lines. Often it is easier to adjust the screen display if each line is displayed separately such as:

```
DISPLAY FIRST-LINE.
DISPLAY BLANK-LINE.
DISPLAY SECOND-LINE.
DISPLAY BLANK-LINE.
DISPLAY MENU-LINE-1.
DISPLAY MENU-LINE-2.
DISPLAY MENU-LINE-3.
DISPLAY MENU-LINE-4.
DISPLAY BLANK-LINE.
DISPLAY BLANK-LINE.
DISPLAY OPTION-LINE.
```

Most computer systems that use interactive programs don't have a single terminal communicating with the computer. Generally there are dozens if not hundreds of terminals. Because of this, it is quite possible that two different users may be using the same program at the same time. Ordinarily this would require each user to have a completely different copy of the program in the computer's memory. However, it would seem wasteful for there to be two exact copies of the same program in memory at the same time (or many copies, since there may be many users using the same program at the same time).

In a COBOL program, all the data is stored in the DATA DIVISION or, more precisely, the area of memory set up to hold the DATA DIVISION. The PROCEDURE DIVISION uses the data for calculations and data movement, but all the results of these manipulations are stored back into the DATA DIVISION area. Thus, even though more than one person is using a program, the only part of the program that each user needs is the DATA DIVISION. For example, suppose user #1 is accessing the record of employee 0001 and user #2 is accessing the record of employee 0002. All the data being accessed by user #1 is for record 0001; likewise, all the data that user #2 is accessing is for record 0002. But all this data is stored in the DATA DIVISION, not the PROCEDURE DIVISION. Thus, for users #1 and #2 to use the same program requires only that the computer keep two copies of the DATA DIVISION, not of the entire program.

Given this, computer storage is used more effectively if we write our programs so that all literals (headings and such) show up only in the PROCEDURE DIVISION. We use the DATA DIVISION only for the actual data that we are processing.

Therefore, we come to the third method of handling the screen display: using all the literals in DISPLAY statements. The following code would cause the display of the same screen we have been discussing, but now all the displaying is done strictly with literals:

```
DISPLAY 'MAIN MENU            THE WIDGET WORKS, INC.          DATE: '
        DISPLAY-DATE.
DISPLAY '              MASTER RECORD UPDATE SYSTEM'.
DISPLAY ' '.
DISPLAY '                 1) ADD A RECORD'.
DISPLAY '                 2) CHANGE A RECORD'.
DISPLAY '                 3) DELETE A RECORD'.
DISPLAY '                 4) PRINT A LIST OF THE RECORDS'.
DISPLAY ' '.
DISPLAY ' '.
DISPLAY '              SELECT OPTION:'.
```

═══ Ч-Ч ═══
The ACCEPT Statement

Along with displaying information so the user will know what is going on, it is important for the computer to be able to input data from the user. To do that we use the **ACCEPT statement**, which has the form

ACCEPT field-name-1 FROM [mnemonic-name]

As in the DISPLAY statement, the mnemonic-name is generally not necessary because the systems are usually set up to receive data from the terminal. Unlike the DISPLAY statement, which functions virtually the same on all computers (since it simply displays data to the screen), the ACCEPT statement functions somewhat differently on the various computers.

The basic idea with the ACCEPT statement is that we will display some type of prompt on the screen and then input the user's response. For example, we might want to display the following:

```
DISPLAY 'ENTER EMPLOYEE NAME'.
```

Then, to get that "EMPLOYEE NAME" from the user, we would use an ACCEPT statement, like

```
ACCEPT EMP-NAME.
```

This will work with virtually all compilers. The difference is in the way that data is input through the ACCEPT statement. Let's suppose that the field EMP-NAME is defined as follows:

```
10  EMP-NAME          PIC X(10).
```

Now the statement:

```
ACCEPT EMP-NAME.
```

Most computers allow the user to type up to 10 characters but no more. That is, the computer will not accept 12 characters. As soon as the user has pressed the tenth key, the computer inputs the data and the program moves on to the next command. If not all 10 characters are needed, the user can press the RETURN key before the end of the field to terminate the entry. A few computers will terminate the field only if the RETURN key is pressed. That is, if the field is 10 characters long and the user enters 12 before pressing RETURN, the computer will input all the characters. But then, since the field can hold only 10 characters, the last two (the right-hand most) get truncated.

The newly input data, of course, overlays whatever data was in the field to begin with. When you do not fill the field, the extra characters in the stored area may be filled with blanks or zeros, may be left as is, or may be garbage—or the machine may simply indicate that you need to enter more data, though this is not common. For example, let's suppose our EMP-NAME field contains

T	O	M		S	M	I	T	H	E

Now, on some machines, if the user entered the new name "AL MIRA", the storage of EMP-NAME would be filled out with blanks and become

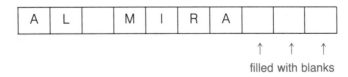

filled with blanks

On other machines, the extra characters would be left as they were:

left as they were

On these latter machines, the logical thing to do is blank out the entry before the ACCEPT statement:

```
MOVE SPACES TO EMP-NAME.
DISPLAY 'ENTER EMPLOYEE NAME'.
ACCEPT EMP-NAME.
```

Then the extra characters at the end of the field are already blanks.

4-5

The STRING Statement

Many times, especially when using interactive programs, we need to combine two separate fields into one. The most frequent example is storing the last and first names in two separate fields and then combining them into one for displaying or printing. The two fields might be defined as

```
10   FIRST-NAME          PIC X(6).
10   LAST-NAME           PIC X(6).
```

Assuming the fields contained the data

A	L	L	E	N	

FIRST-NAME

S	M	I	T	H	

LAST-NAME

what we would like to be able to do is combine the fields so that they would be stored as

A	L		S	M	I	T	H					

WHOLE-NAME

with the WHOLE-NAME field for this illustration defined as

```
10   WHOLE-NAME          PIC X(13).
```

COBOL has a statement that allows just such manipulations: the **STRING statement**. Its form is

$$\text{STRING} \begin{Bmatrix} \text{field-name-1} \\ \text{literal-1} \end{Bmatrix} [\dots] \text{ DELIMITED BY} \begin{Bmatrix} \text{field-name-2} \\ \text{literal-2} \\ \text{SIZE} \end{Bmatrix} \text{INTO field-name-3}$$

[ON OVERFLOW imperative statement]

The form specifies that there may be one or more sending fields (the ones shown in front of the DELIMITED clause) and one receiving field (field-name-3). The data is transferred from the sending field(s) and stored in the receiving field just as if we had used a MOVE statement—except for two differences. First, the receiving field is not filled with blanks if it is larger than the sending fields. The remaining characters in the receiving field are left as they were.

The other difference is the DELIMITED BY clause. Field-name-2 or literal-2, which must be a single character, is used to indicate when to terminate the transfer of the sending fields. That is, unlike the MOVE statement, the STRING statement transfers the characters only until the specified delimiter character is found. Suppose that we set up the STRING statement with the fields we used before, namely,

```
STRING FIRST-NAME LAST-NAME DELIMITED BY ' '
       INTO WHOLE-NAME.
```

The STRING statement moves the characters from FIRST-NAME to WHOLE-NAME, one by one from the left side, until the character listed as the delimiter, a blank in this case, is found:

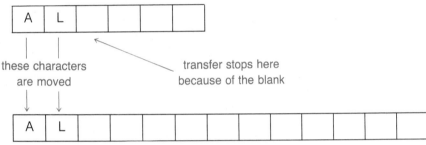

Notice that the delimiter was not moved. Transfer stops when the delimiter is found, not after it has been passed.

After the first field is used, the statement moves to the next sending field:

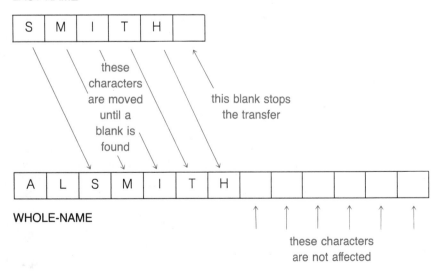

Since the data transfer stops as soon as the delimit character is found, the characters at the end of the field are not affected. Thus, whatever is contained in the field (WHOLE-NAME) in those characters will not be changed.

You might have noticed that this STRING statement movement did not give us a blank between the first name and the last name. Since the delimiter was a blank and we didn't move a blank into the receiving field, there is no blank there. This is where the SIZE clause comes in. Whenever we want to move a field as is, we delimit it by SIZE. Thus, for our STRING statement to have the desired result of first name, blank, and last name, we will have to change it to

```
STRING FIRST-NAME DELIMITED BY ' '
       ' '         DELIMITED BY SIZE
       LAST-NAME   DELIMITED BY ' '
       INTO WHOLE-NAME.
```

Now a blank will be placed between the first name and the last name in the receiving field.

It is generally a good idea to have a result field that is large enough to contain all the possible characters from all the fields you are stringing together. In the example, our result field, WHOLE-NAME, is 13 characters long because each of the name fields is 6 characters long and the blank between them required an additional one.

There are times, however, when it will be inconvenient or impossible to use a field that long. In such cases, the *ON OVERFLOW* clause can prove valuable. It will simply execute the listed imperative statement if the number of characters being strung together exceeds the length of the receiving field. If WHOLE-NAME were only 10 characters long, we might want to change our STRING statement again to include the ON OVERFLOW clause:

```
STRING FIRST-NAME DELIMITED BY '
       ' '         DELIMITED BY SIZE
       LAST-NAME   DELIMITED BY ' '
       INTO WHOLE-NAME
       ON OVERFLOW PERFORM 0900-ERROR-ROUTINE.
```

Now, if the statement attempts to write a seventeenth character into WHOLE-NAME, the program will perform the error routine.

Let's do another example of the STRING statement just to be sure you're clear on exactly what is happening. We will define four fields:

```
10   FIELD-1          PIC XXX.
10   FIELD-2          PIC XXX.
10   FIELD-3          PIC XX.
10   FIELD-4          PIC X(8).
```

The STRING statement will look like the following:

```
STRING FIELD-1 DELIMITED BY '-'
       FIELD-2 DELIMITED BY '/'
       FIELD-3 DELIMITED BY ' '
       INTO    FIELD-4.
```

The fields will contain the following data and the transfer will be done as shown:

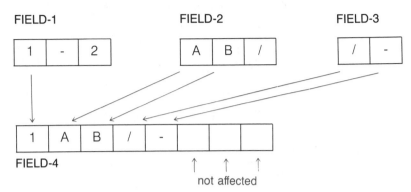

On FIELD-1, only the 1 is moved since the '-' is the second character. Then the first two characters of FIELD-2 are moved. Finally, both characters of FIELD-3 are moved since there wasn't a blank in the field. Notice that the characters in FIELD-3 were the two delimiters for the other fields. This, of course, makes no difference, since the only delimiter for FIELD-3 was a blank. Remember, the data will be moved until the delimit character is found; if one is not found, all the characters in the sending field will be moved.

If we need more than one delimiter for one field, we can use a compound conditional, much like we used for the IF statement. We can change the previous STRING statement to something like this:

```
STRING FIELD-1 DELIMITED BY '-'
       FIELD-2 DELIMITED BY '/'
       FIELD-3 DELIMITED BY ' ' OR '-' OR '/'
       INTO    FIELD-4.
```

Then no characters will be transferred from FIELD-3 because the first character in the field is one of the delimiters.

══ 4-6 ══
The UNSTRING Statement

In interactive programs, it is sometimes more important to be able to split one field into two or more than to combine multiple fields into one. We can divide a field with the **UNSTRING statement**, which has the form

UNSTRING field-name-1 DELIMITED BY [ALL] $\begin{Bmatrix} \text{field-name-2} \\ \text{literal-1} \end{Bmatrix}$ INTO field-name-3 . . .

[ON OVERFLOW imperative statement]

With this statement we can use only one sending field (field-name-1), and that field is split into multiple fields around the delimit character, if one is used. The simplest way to use the UNSTRING statement is to split the sending field by letting it fall into the receiving fields, without delimiting, as dictated by the size of the receiving fields. For example, suppose we define the fields

```
10  FIELD-1          PIC XXX.
10  FIELD-2          PIC XXX.
10  FIELD-3          PIC XX.
10  FIELD-4          PIC X(10).
```

and FIELD-4 contains the data

1	2	3	4	5	6	7	8	9	0

FIELD-4

Using the UNSTRING statement

```
UNSTRING FIELD-4 INTO FIELD-1 FIELD-2 FIELD-3.
```

causes the following result:

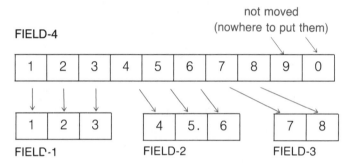

Notice that the first three characters of FIELD-4 were transferred to FIELD-1. Since FIELD-1 was then full, the next three characters were moved to FIELD-2. The next two characters filled FIELD-3, and the leftover two characters (in FIELD-4) were not transferred because there was nowhere to put them.

The DELIMITED BY clause allows the programmer to designate where the sending field is divided. Transfer of the characters begins with the first character and terminates when the receiving field is full or the delimiter is found. The following is a simple example of the use of the delimiter. The fields are defined as

```
10  FIELD-1          PIC 999.
10  FIELD-2          PIC 99.
10  FIELD-3          PIC 9999.
10  FIELD-4          PIC X(11).
```

With data of

1	2	3	-	4	5	-	6	7	8	9

FIELD-4

the UNSTRING statement

```
UNSTRING FIELD-4 DELIMITED BY '-' INTO FIELD-1 FIELD-2 FIELD-3.
```

would cause the following transfer:

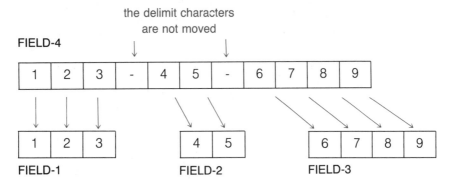

Notice that we changed the PIC clauses of the three receiving fields. The UNSTRING—and the STRING statement, for that matter—can use either non-numeric or numeric fields for sending or receiving fields, though non-numeric fields are generally used.

If you have to divide up a field that has multiple adjacent delimit characters, you can use the ALL clause to treat them all as one delimiter. Suppose we have the name fields defined as

```
10   FIRST-NAME        PIC X(6).
10   LAST-NAME         PIC X(6).
10   WHOLE-NAME        PIC X(13).
```

and the WHOLE-NAME contains

A	L				S	M	I	T	H			

WHOLE-NAME

There are three blanks between "AL" and "SMITH." With the ALL clause we can use all three blanks as one delimiter (notice that we use the figurative constant SPACES instead of a literal this time):

```
UNSTRING WHOLE-NAME DELIMITED BY ALL SPACES
         INTO FIRST-NAME LAST-NAME.
```

The transfer would be done as

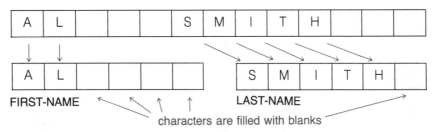

As you can see from the example, if the receiving field is not filled by the sending field, non-numeric receiving fields are padded with blanks. Numeric receiving fields are padded with zeros.

If there are two or more delimiters in adjacent positions in the sending field, the receiving field that gets no characters from the sending field is filled with blanks if it is non-numeric and zeros if it is numeric. Assume the following field definitions:

```
10   FIELD-1        PIC XXXX.
10   FIELD-2        PIC XXX.
10   FIELD-3        PIC XXX.
10   FIELD-4        PIC X(11).
```

with data of

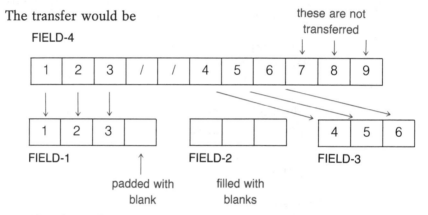

The UNSTRING statement is

```
UNSTRING FIELD-4 DELIMITED BY '/' INTO FIELD-1 FIELD-2 FIELD-3.
```

The transfer would be

If we have characters left over in the sending field, as in the previous example, and have used the ON OVERFLOW clause, it will be activated. It will also be activated should there be any result fields that get no data.

4-7
Verifying the Input Data

Now that we have seen how to handle data if it needs to be put together or split apart, it is time to further discuss inputting information using an interactive program. We have already discussed how to get the data into the program using the ACCEPT statement, but now we need to look at what to do with the data after it comes into the program from the user.

Non-numeric entries present no real difficulties. We may wish to STRING or UNSTRING them, but that is pretty basic processing. Numeric entries, on the other hand, have their own problems. If users enter the wrong data into a non-numeric field, the program won't have any problem with it. The wrong data will be stored, of course, but the program will function properly. With numeric data, however, if the user enters the wrong data into a field, the program might ABEND. For example, suppose the program requests data for the field defined as

```
10   SALARY          PIC 99999.
```

As long as the user responds with numeric digits, such as 15000, everything will be fine. But what if the user accidentally types 15P00 (the P is just below the zero key on most keyboards)? Now the SALARY field is receiving non-numeric data into a numeric field and the program might ABEND. Also, if the user doesn't fill out the field, the ACCEPT statement will, on most systems, fill with blanks, which, of course, are not valid in a numeric field. Some systems will not ABEND upon acceptance of the data. But afterward, if the data is manipulated in any fashion—for example, if we do calculations with it—the program will crash with a data exception (bad data in a numeric field).

Can we reasonably expect users to not make any typing mistakes as they input data and to always completely fill each field they enter? Of course not. Then how do we keep our programs from ABENDing when users do enter bad or incomplete data? First, we input the data into non-numeric fields instead of numeric ones. Then, if there is any bad data, we inform the users and let them enter their data again. If the field is entered properly on this try, we simply move the data to the numeric field and let the program continue.

(By the way, some interactive systems are set up so that, if a field is defined to the system as being numeric, the program will not accept anything into the field except numbers or a decimal point. We will assume throughout our discussion that our systems are not that sophisticated.)

Let's begin by setting up our fields for accepting the data. As we said, we will accept the data into a non-numeric field:

```
10   SALARY-INPUT          PIC X(6).
```

Now, as we accept the data into the field, the characters will be left-justified. We will need some way to move them back to the right since we are trying to create a numeric field. This is where the STRING statement comes in. We will STRING the SALARY-INPUT field into another non-numeric field so the field can be right-justified. Then we will redefine that second field into a numeric format. Thus, our other two fields would be

```
10   NON-NUMERIC-SALARY                    PIC X(6)
     JUSTIFIED RIGHT.
10   SALARY REDEFINES NON-NUMERIC-SALARY   PIC 9(6).
```

Note that we right-justified the NON-NUMERIC-SALARY field. We will use the REDEFINES statement as shown only if the field is used in the WORKING-STORAGE SECTION. If we need both fields defined in the FILE SECTION, we will use two 01-level record definitions.

The PROCEDURE DIVISION code to get the field would be made up of the statements

```
DISPLAY 'ENTER THE SALARY'
DISPLAY '######'
ACCEPT SALARY-INPUT.
```

which would display the message and the markers on the screen as

```
ENTER THE SALARY
######
```

The markers are printed so that the user will know how many characters are allowed for the entry. Then, after accepting SALARY-INPUT, we will need to STRING it to the NON-NUMERIC-SALARY field:

```
STRING SALARY-INPUT DELIMITED BY SPACE INTO NON-NUMERIC-SALARY.
```

This command will create an internal field that the program will transfer the data to. This field will be only as long as the data. Then, when the temporary field is moved to the receiving field, it can be right-justified properly. It would be pictured as

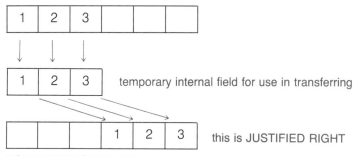

SALARY-INPUT

NON-NUMERIC-SALARY

Before we can verify the field for accuracy, we need to get rid of the blanks on the left side of the field. We can do this with the **INSPECT statement** in the following form:

```
INSPECT NON-NUMERIC-SALARY REPLACING ALL SPACES BY ZEROS.
```

This will cause the data in the field to be changed to

0	0	0	1	2	3

NON-NUMERIC-SALARY

Now that there aren't any blanks left, we can check the field for the validity of the user's input. This is also pretty simple. The statement we would use is

```
IF NON-NUMERIC-SALARY IS NOT NUMERIC
    DISPLAY ' '
    DISPLAY 'ENTRY NOT NUMERIC.  PLEASE TRY AGAIN.'
    DISPLAY ' '.
```

There is a problem with this setup: There is no way to let the user enter the data again. We input the data, check it, and print an error on the screen if the data is bad, but then the program will simply continue on to the next part. We could put another prompt and an ACCEPT statement after the error routine, but doing so would give the user only one more chance to enter correct data. What we need is a way to let the user keep trying as many times as are necessary. We can do it with a routine like the following:

```
MOVE SPACES TO NON-NUMERIC-SALARY.
PERFORM SALARY-CHECK
        UNTIL NON-NUMERIC-SALARY IS NUMERIC.
: : :
: : :

SALARY-CHECK.

    DISPLAY 'ENTER THE SALARY'
    DISPLAY '######'
    ACCEPT SALARY-INPUT.
    STRING SALARY-INPUT DELIMITED BY SPACE INTO NON-NUMERIC-SALARY.
    INSPECT NON-NUMERIC-SALARY REPLACING ALL SPACES BY ZEROS.
    IF NON-NUMERIC-SALARY IS NOT NUMERIC
        DISPLAY ' '
        DISPLAY 'ENTRY NOT NUMERIC.  PLEASE TRY AGAIN.'
        DISPLAY ' '.
```

Now the program will start the entry by performing the SALARY-CHECK routine. If the data is invalid, the NON-NUMERIC-SALARY field will cause the message to be printed and the PERFORM statement will send the program back into the SALARY-CHECK routine until the user enters correct data.

══════ 4-8 ══════
What About the Decimal Point?

A decimal point in our numeric entry can cause some special problems. Again, some computers will accept numeric fields properly, including the decimal point. Some won't, however. To handle the decimal point, we will use most of the techniques we have already discussed, but we will add the UNSTRING statement and a different field layout. We will still use a field to originally input the data into:

```
10 HOURLY-RATE-INPUT          PIC X(6).
```

We have specified the field as having six characters so that we can have a range up to 999.99, which requires six characters. Now we will specify the fields that the data is to end up in (again, not in the FILE SECTION):

```
10   HOURLY-RATE               PIC 999V99.
10   NON-NUMERIC-HOURLY-RATE   REDEFINES HOURLY-RATE.
    20   DOLLARS               PIC XXX   JUSTIFIED RIGHT.
    20   CENTS                 PIC XX.
```

We right-justified the DOLLARS field for the same reason we did so before. We didn't right-justify the cents field, however, because the decimal positions should be left-justified (or justified around the decimal point).

We will also need to change our handling of the input. Instead of using the STRING statement, we will UNSTRING the HOURLY-RATE-INPUT field:

```
UNSTRING HOURLY-RATE-INPUT DELIMITED BY SPACES OR '.'
          INTO DOLLARS CENTS.
```

Notice that we used a compound clause for the delimiter. We did this because the user may enter the data in a variety of formats. Suppose the user simply entered the numeral 1. The field would look like this:

1					

HOURLY-RATE-INPUT

If we delimited by only the decimal point, the DOLLARS field would receive

1		

DOLLARS

because the blanks would be a legitimate part of the field. Thus, by using SPACES as an additional delimiter, we ensure that only actual characters get transferred. When the data is transferred, it must be right-justified, and this can happen only if the spaces on the right side of the field are dropped.

How would our statement work if the user entered a decimal point? We'll set it up as

1	5	.	1		

HOURLY-RATE-INPUT

Since we have delimited by the decimal point, the movement will be

HOURLY-RATE-INPUT

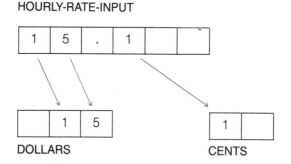

Then we will need to change the blanks to zeros:

```
INSPECT NON-NUMERIC-HOURLY-RATE REPLACING ALL SPACES BY ZEROS.
```

and verify the entry with

```
IF NON-NUMERIC-HOURLY-RATE IS NOT NUMERIC
    DISPLAY ' '
    DISPLAY 'ENTRY NOT NUMERIC.  PLEASE TRY AGAIN.'
    DISPLAY ' '.
```

Just as with the salary entry, we would need to set this up in a performed procedure so the user could continually retype the field until valid data was entered.

4-9
Do We Edit Non-numeric Fields?

Thus far we have looked only at how to edit numeric fields. But what about non-numeric fields? Can they be edited? The answer is yes, but generally they're not. That is, we can test a non-numeric entry to be sure that it is alphabetic, or that there are no leading blanks, or that several other, similar things are correct. But, generally speaking, these tests are unnecessary.

Our major concern with editing data has to be with getting data into our program that will not cause an ABEND. No non-numeric field entry will cause a program to ABEND, because anything is acceptable in a non-numeric field. We do need to edit our fields when they are supposed to have certain values, but checking an address to be sure it is alphabetic, for example, is a risky business. The input "1400 SOUTH STREET" is not alphabetic, but it is a perfectly valid address.

As we said, we would edit a non-numeric field that is supposed to contain a certain group of values. Suppose, for example, that the user is asked to enter the two-digit state code. Since our company deals with only four states, the state code would have to be one of four. We could easily set up a test for that:

```
IF STATE-CODE NOT EQUAL TO 'TX' AND
                          'CA' AND
                          'NM' AND
                          'OK'

    DISPLAY ' '
    DISPLAY 'STATE CODE IN ERROR.  IT MUST BE TX, CA, NM, OR OK.'
    DISPLAY 'PLEASE ENTER IT AGAIN.'
    DISPLAY ' '.
```

Our PERFORM statement could have a similar test:

```
PERFORM STATE-CHECK
        UNTIL STATE-CODE = 'TX' OR
                          'CA' OR
                          'NM' OR 'OK'.
```

4-10

The Record Rack Customer File Entry Program

Roger Barnell recently had a couple of interactive terminals installed on *The Record Rack* computer. He wants Cindy to write an interactive program so that new customers can be added to the CUSTOMER file. Her program must allow the entry of all the fields in the record layout in Figure 4-1.

Her systems chart is shown in Figure 4-2. She decides she will write the program so that, after the user enters all the data fields (with appropriate editing), the program will redisplay them on the screen and let the user verify that they are correct. If any are incorrect, they can be chosen by number and reentered. Then the program will display the fields again and wait for the user to accept the record or modify another one of the fields. Cindy draws the initial screen layout (Figure 4-3) and another layout for the field maintenance display, Figure 4-4. The pseudocode design of the program is shown next. The flowchart is in Figure 4-5. She has shortened the pseudocode a bit by not showing all the input modules. She shortened the flowchart as well, by using sample routines instead of all of the modules.

CUSTOMER File					
Field Description	*Position*	*Length*	:	*Dec*	*Type*
Customer number	1–4	4	:		Non-numeric
Name Last	5–14	10	:		Non-numeric
First & initial	15–24	10	:		Non-numeric
Address	25–39	15	:		Non-numeric
City	40–52	13	:		Non-numeric
State	53–54	2	:		Non-numeric
Zip code	55–59	5	:		Non-numeric
Amount of sale	60–65	6	:	2	Numeric
Filler	66–80	15	:		Non-numeric
Record Length = 80					

Figure 4-1 The record layout for the CUSTOMER file.

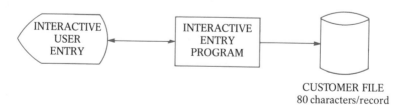

CUSTOMER FILE
80 characters/record

Figure 4-2 The systems chart for the interactive customer file entry program.

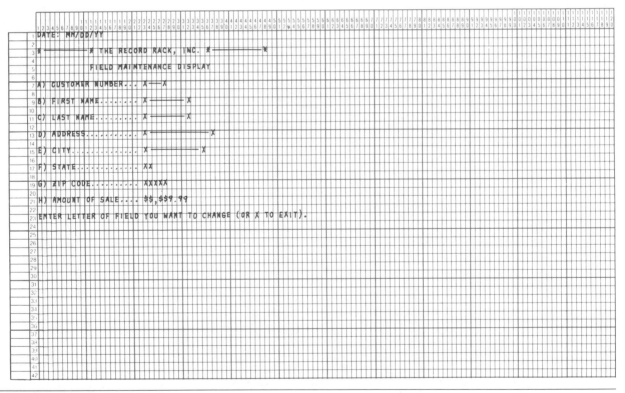

```
DATE: MM/DD/YY

*———————* THE RECORD RACK, INC. *————— **

       CUSTOMER FILE RECORD ADDITION PROGRAM

      IF YOU WISH TO ADD RECORDS, PRESS Y .......

      IF YOU ARE FINISHED ADDING RECORDS, PRESS X





ENTER EITHER A Y TO ADD OR X TO EXIT PROGRAM ...
```

Figure 4-3 The display layout for the initial screen for the customer file entry program.

```
DATE: MM/DD/YY

*———————* THE RECORD RACK, INC. *————— *

          FIELD MAINTENANCE DISPLAY
A) CUSTOMER NUMBER... X———X
B) FIRST NAME......... X———————X
C) LAST NAME......... X———————X
D) ADDRESS........... X———————————X
E) CITY.............. X———————————X
F) STATE............. XX
G) ZIP CODE.......... XXXXX
H) AMOUNT OF SALE.... $$,$$9.99
ENTER LETTER OF FIELD YOU WANT TO CHANGE (OR X TO EXIT).
```

Figure 4-4 The display layout for the field maintenance screen for the customer file entry program.

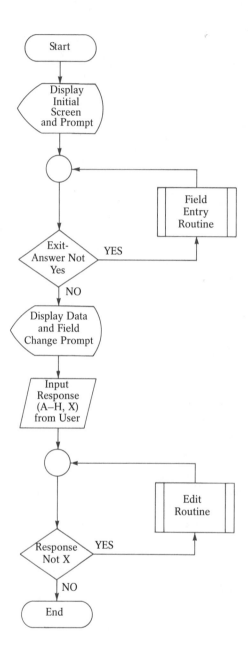

Figure 4-5 The flowchart for the program to add customer records (part 1).

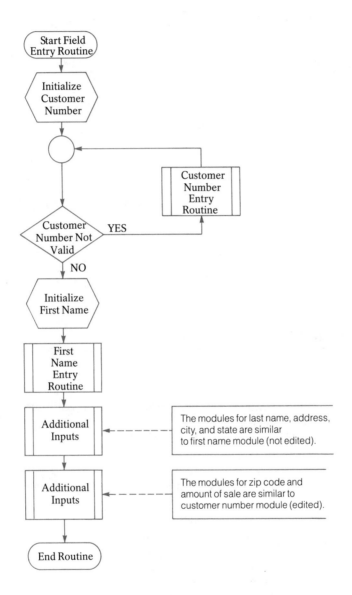

The modules for last name, address, city, and state are similar to first name module (not edited).

The modules for zip code and amount of sale are similar to customer number module (edited).

Figure 4-5 (continued)   Field entry routine.

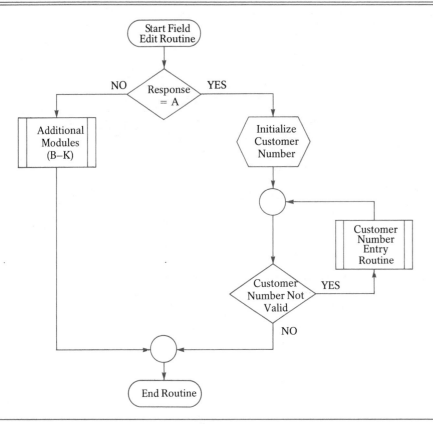

Figure 4-5 (continued)   Field edit routine.

Start
Display initial screen and prompt user to continue or exit
Input exit-response
DO-WHILE exit-response not yes
      Initialize customer number
      DO-WHILE customer number not valid (numeric)
          Do customer number entry routine
      END-DO
      Initialize first name
      Do first name entry routine (no edit)
      Initialize last name
      Do last name entry routine (no edit)
      Initialize address
      Do address entry routine (no edit)
      Initialize city
      Do city entry routine (no edit)
      Initialize state
      Do state entry routine (no edit)
      Initialize zip code
      DO-WHILE zip code not valid (numeric)
          Do zip code entry routine
      END-DO

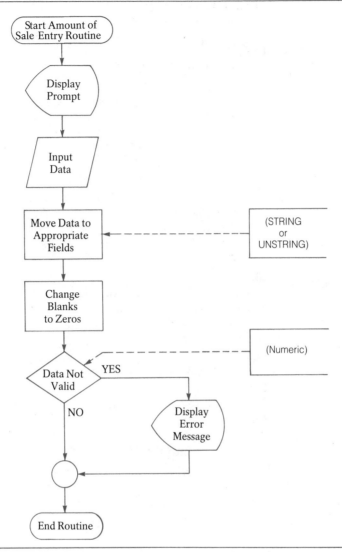

Figure 4-5 (continued)   Amount of sale routine.

Initialize amount of sale
DO-WHILE amount of sale not valid (numeric)
        Do amount of sale entry routine
END-DO
Display all the data and field change prompt on the screen
Input the response (A–H, X) from the user
DO-WHILE response not X
    IF response = A THEN
        Initialize customer number
        DO-WHILE customer number not valid (numeric)
            Do customer number entry routine
        END-DO
    ELSE-IF response = B THEN
        Initialize first name
        Do first name entry routine (no edit)

```
                    ELSE IF response = C THEN
                        Initialize last name
                        Do last name entry routine (no edit)
                    ELSE IF response = D THEN
                        Initialize address
                        Do address entry routine (no edit)
                    ELSE IF response = E THEN
                        Initialize city
                        Do city entry routine (no edit)
                    ELSE IF response = F THEN
                        Initialize state
                        Do state entry routine (no edit)
                    ELSE IF response = G THEN
                        Initialize zip code
                        DO-WHILE zip code not valid (numeric)
                                Do zip code entry routine
                    END-DO
                    ELSE IF response = H THEN
                            Initialize amount of sale
                            DO-WHILE amount of sale not valid (numeric)
                                    Do amount of sale entry routine
                            END-DO
                    ELSE
                            Display error message
                    END-IF
                    Display all the data and field change prompt on the screen
                    Input the response (A–H, X) from the user
                END-DO
                Write the record into the file
                Display initial screen and prompt user to continue or exit
                Input exit-response
        END-DO
        Display exit message
        End
```

Each of the entry routines will simply display a message and then input the data, verifying the numeric data and the credit code. Naturally Cindy designed each of the routines, but in the interest of space we will show the design for the amount of sale field only (this is also the only one in the flowchart):

```
        Start amount of sale entry routine
        Display prompt
        Input data
        Move the data to appropriate fields (STRING or UNSTRING)
        Change blanks to zeros
        IF data not valid (numeric) THEN
            Display error message
            Initialize amount of sale field
        (ELSE)
        END-IF
        End routine
```

Cindy's program:

```
*****************************************************************
*****************************************************************
*
*
*
*   PROGRAM NAME: CUST-ADD
*
*   PROGRAMMER NAME:  CINDY HARRISON
*
*   SOCIAL SECURITY NUMBER:  999-99-9999
*
*   DUE DATE: FEBRUARY 10, 1988
*
*   DESCRIPTION: THIS INTERACTIVE PROGRAM WILL ALLOW THE ADDITION
*                OF RECORDS TO THE CUSTOMER FILE.
*
*
*
*****************************************************************
*****************************************************************

    IDENTIFICATION DIVISION.
    PROGRAM-ID.   CUST-ADD.
    AUTHOR.       CINDY HARRISON.

    ENVIRONMENT DIVISION.

    CONFIGURATION SECTION.
    SOURCE-COMPUTER. IBM-4331.
    OBJECT-COMPUTER. IBM-4331.

    INPUT-OUTPUT SECTION.
    FILE-CONTROL.
        SELECT CUSTOMER-OUT ASSIGN TO UT-S-CUSTOMER.
    DATA DIVISION.
    FILE SECTION.

    FD  CUSTOMER-OUT
        LABEL RECORDS ARE OMITTED
        RECORD CONTAINS 80 CHARACTERS.
    01  CUSTOMER-RECORD.
        05  CUSTOMER-NUMBER         PIC X(4) JUSTIFIED RIGHT.
        05  CUSTOMER-NAME.
            10  LAST-NAME           PIC X(10).
            10  FIRST-NAME          PIC X(10).
        05  CUS-ADDRESS             PIC X(15).
        05  CITY                    PIC X(13).
        05  STATE                   PIC XX.
        05  ZIP-CODE                PIC X(5).
        05  AMOUNT-OF-SALE          PIC 9(4)V99.
        05  FILLER                  PIC X(15).

    01  CUSTOMER-RECORD-2.
        05  FILLER                  PIC X(59).
        05  NON-NUMERIC-SALE.
            10  SALE-DOLLARS        PIC X(4) JUSTIFIED RIGHT.
            10  SALE-CENTS          PIC XX.
        05  FILLER                  PIC X(15).
```

```
WORKING-STORAGE SECTION.

01   WORK-AREAS.

     05    DATE-IN.
           10    DATE-YY           PIC XX.
           10    DATE-MM           PIC XX.
           10    DATE-DD           PIC XX.

     05    SALE-IN                 PIC X(7).
     05    EDIT-OPTION             PIC X.
     05    OPTION                  PIC X.
     05    AMOUNT-OF-SALE-EDITED    PIC $$,$$9.99.
     05    CUSTOMER-IN             PIC XXXX.

     05    DISPLAY-DATE.
           10    DISPLAY-MM        PIC XX.
           10    DISPLAY-DD        PIC /XX/.
           10    DISPLAY-YY        PIC XX.


PROCEDURE DIVISION.

MAIN-MODULE.

    OPEN OUTPUT CUSTOMER-OUT.

    MOVE SPACES TO STATE.
    PERFORM 0800-STATE-ROUTINE.

    MOVE SPACES TO ZIP-CODE.
    PERFORM 0900-ZIP-CODE-ROUTINE UNTIL ZIP-CODE IS NUMERIC.

    MOVE SPACES TO NON-NUMERIC-SALE.
    PERFORM 1000-SALE-ROUTINE UNTIL NON-NUMERIC-SALE IS NUMERIC.

    MOVE SPACES TO EDIT-OPTION.
    PERFORM 0300-FIELD-EDITS UNTIL EDIT-OPTION = 'X'.

    WRITE CUSTOMER-RECORD.


0300-FIELD-EDITS.

    DISPLAY 'DATE: ' DISPLAY-DATE.
    DISPLAY ' '.
    DISPLAY '*********** THE RECORD RACK, INC. *************'.
    DISPLAY ' '.
    DISPLAY '              FIELD MAINTENANCE DISPLAY'.
    DISPLAY ' '.
    DISPLAY 'A) CUSTOMER NUMBER... ' CUSTOMER-NUMBER.
    DISPLAY ' '.
    DISPLAY 'B) FIRST NAME........ ' FIRST-NAME.
    DISPLAY ' '.
    DISPLAY 'C) LAST NAME......... ' LAST-NAME.
    DISPLAY ' '.
    DISPLAY 'D) ADDRESS........... ' CUS-ADDRESS.
    DISPLAY ' '.
```

h

```
DISPLAY 'E) CITY.............. ' CITY.
DISPLAY ' '.
DISPLAY 'F) STATE............. ' STATE.
DISPLAY ' '.
DISPLAY 'G) ZIP CODE.......... ' ZIP-CODE.
DISPLAY ' '.
MOVE AMOUNT-OF-SALE TO AMOUNT-OF-SALE-EDITED.
DISPLAY 'H) AMOUNT OF SALE.... ' AMOUNT-OF-SALE-EDITED.
DISPLAY ' '.
DISPLAY 'ENTER LETTER OF FIELD TO CHANGE (OR X TO EXIT).'

ACCEPT EDIT-OPTION.

IF EDIT-OPTION = 'A'
    MOVE SPACES TO CUSTOMER-NUMBER
    PERFORM 0400-CUSTOMER-NUMBER-ROUTINE
            UNTIL CUSTOMER-NUMBER IS NUMERIC

ELSE IF EDIT-OPTION = 'B'
    MOVE SPACES TO FIRST-NAME
    PERFORM 0500-FIRST-NAME-ROUTINE
ACCEPT DATE-IN FROM DATE.
MOVE DATE-YY TO DISPLAY-YY.
MOVE DATE-MM TO DISPLAY-MM.
MOVE DATE-DD TO DISPLAY-DD.

PERFORM 0100-INITIAL-DISPLAY
        UNTIL OPTION = 'X'.

CLOSE CUSTOMER-OUT.
STOP RUN.


0100-INITIAL-DISPLAY.

    PERFORM 1400-DISPLAY-BLANK-LINE 2 TIMES.
    DISPLAY 'DATE: ' DISPLAY-DATE.
    DISPLAY ' '.
    DISPLAY '*********** THE RECORD RACK, INC. *************'.
    DISPLAY ' '.
    DISPLAY '     CUSTOMER FILE RECORD ADDITION PROGRAM'.
    DISPLAY ' '.
    DISPLAY ' '.
    DISPLAY '     IF YOU WISH TO ADD RECORDS, PRESS Y .......'.
    DISPLAY ' '.
    DISPLAY '     IF YOU ARE FINISHED ADDING RECORDS, PRESS X'.
    PERFORM 1400-DISPLAY-BLANK-LINE 10 TIMES.
    DISPLAY 'ENTER EITHER A Y TO ADD OR X TO EXIT PROGRAM ...'.
    ACCEPT OPTION.

    IF OPTION = 'Y'
        PERFORM 0200-ADD-THE-RECORD
    ELSE IF OPTION NOT = 'X'
        DISPLAY ' '
        DISPLAY 'ONLY A Y OR X ARE VALID.  PLEASE TRY AGAIN ..'
        DISPLAY 'PRESS ANY KEY TO CONTINUE.'
        ACCEPT OPTION.
```

```
0200-ADD-THE-RECORD.

    MOVE SPACES TO CUSTOMER-NUMBER.
    PERFORM 0400-CUSTOMER-NUMBER-ROUTINE
            UNTIL CUSTOMER-NUMBER IS NUMERIC.

    MOVE SPACES TO FIRST-NAME.
    PERFORM 0500-FIRST-NAME-ROUTINE.

    MOVE SPACES TO LAST-NAME.
    PERFORM 0550-LAST-NAME-ROUTINE.

    MOVE SPACES TO CUS-ADDRESS.
    PERFORM 0600-ADDRESS-ROUTINE.

    MOVE SPACES TO CITY.
    PERFORM 0700-CITY-ROUTINE.

    ELSE IF EDIT-OPTION = 'C'
        MOVE SPACES TO LAST-NAME
        PERFORM 0550-LAST-NAME-ROUTINE

    ELSE IF EDIT-OPTION = 'D'
        MOVE SPACES TO CUS-ADDRESS
        PERFORM 0600-ADDRESS-ROUTINE

    ELSE IF EDIT-OPTION = 'E'
        MOVE SPACES TO CITY
        PERFORM 0700-CITY-ROUTINE

    ELSE IF EDIT-OPTION = 'F'
        MOVE SPACES TO STATE
        PERFORM 0800-STATE-ROUTINE

    ELSE IF EDIT-OPTION = 'G'
        MOVE SPACES TO ZIP-CODE
        PERFORM 0900-ZIP-CODE-ROUTINE
                UNTIL ZIP-CODE IS NUMERIC

    ELSE IF EDIT-OPTION = 'H'
        MOVE SPACES TO NON-NUMERIC-SALE
        PERFORM 1000-SALE-ROUTINE
                UNTIL NON-NUMERIC-SALE IS NUMERIC

    ELSE IF EDIT-OPTION NOT = 'X'
        DISPLAY ' '
        DISPLAY 'ENTRY IS NOT CORRECT.  ENTER ONLY A - H OR X.'
        DISPLAY 'PLEASE TRY AGAIN.'
        DISPLAY ' '.


0400-CUSTOMER-NUMBER-ROUTINE.

    PERFORM 1400-DISPLAY-BLANK-LINE 5 TIMES.
    DISPLAY 'ENTER CUSTOMER NUMBER...'.
    DISPLAY '####'.
    ACCEPT CUSTOMER-IN.

    STRING CUSTOMER-IN DELIMITED BY SIZE
            INTO CUSTOMER-NUMBER.
```

```
        INSPECT CUSTOMER-NUMBER REPLACING ALL SPACES BY ZEROS.

        IF CUSTOMER-NUMBER NOT NUMERIC
            DISPLAY ' '
            DISPLAY 'CUSTOMER NUMBER MUST BE ALL NUMERIC DIGITS.'
            DISPLAY ' '
            MOVE SPACES TO CUSTOMER-IN.

    0500-FIRST-NAME-ROUTINE.

        PERFORM 1400-DISPLAY-BLANK-LINE 5 TIMES.
        DISPLAY 'ENTER FIRST NAME...'.
        DISPLAY '**********'.
        ACCEPT FIRST-NAME.


    0550-LAST-NAME-ROUTINE.

        PERFORM 1400-DISPLAY-BLANK-LINE 5 TIMES.
        DISPLAY 'ENTER LAST NAME...'.
        DISPLAY '**********'.
        ACCEPT LAST-NAME.


    0600-ADDRESS-ROUTINE.

        PERFORM 1400-DISPLAY-BLANK-LINE 5 TIMES.
        DISPLAY 'ENTER ADDRESS...'.
        DISPLAY '***************'.
        ACCEPT CUS-ADDRESS.


    0700-CITY-ROUTINE.

        PERFORM 1400-DISPLAY-BLANK-LINE 5 TIMES.
        DISPLAY 'ENTER CITY...'.
        DISPLAY '*************'.
        ACCEPT CITY.


    0800-STATE-ROUTINE.

        PERFORM 1400-DISPLAY-BLANK-LINE 5 TIMES.
        DISPLAY 'ENTER STATE...'.
        DISPLAY '**'.
        ACCEPT STATE.


    0900-ZIP-CODE-ROUTINE.

        PERFORM 1400-DISPLAY-BLANK-LINE 5 TIMES.
        DISPLAY 'ENTER ZIP CODE...'.
        DISPLAY '#####'.
        ACCEPT ZIP-CODE.

        IF ZIP-CODE NOT NUMERIC
            DISPLAY ' '
            DISPLAY 'ZIP CODE MUST BE ALL NUMERIC DIGITS.'
            DISPLAY ' '
            MOVE SPACES TO ZIP-CODE.
```

```
1000-SALE-ROUTINE.

    PERFORM 1400-DISPLAY-BLANK-LINE 5 TIMES.
    DISPLAY 'ENTER AMOUNT OF SALE (INCLUDING DECIMAL POINT)...'.
    DISPLAY '#######'.
    ACCEPT SALE-IN.

    UNSTRING SALE-IN DELIMITED BY '.' OR SPACES
          INTO SALE-DOLLARS SALE-CENTS.

    INSPECT NON-NUMERIC-SALE REPLACING ALL SPACES BY ZEROS.

    IF NON-NUMERIC-SALE NOT NUMERIC
        DISPLAY ' '
        DISPLAY 'AMOUNT OF SALE INCORRECT.  TRY AGAIN.'
        DISPLAY ' '
        MOVE SPACES TO SALE-IN.


1400-DISPLAY-BLANK-LINE.

    DISPLAY ' '.
```

4-11

Summary

1. There are two types of computer programs: batch and interactive. Most computer systems have some of each type of program and so are called hybrid systems.
2. There are three basic methods of creating interactive programs: full-screen I/O, I/O done with cursor positioning, and line-at-a-time I/O.
3. Most computer systems have some type of auxiliary system to allow the use of screen layouts and cursor positioning commands. These systems are not dealt with in this book but a few basic techniques that are common were discussed in this chapter. Typically found in such a programming system are cursor positioning, screen blanking, special display characteristics, field length designations, and special keys.
4. Some ways of setting up screens can be helpful to the user. These include

   - getting the user involved in designing the system;
   - using a menu system in your program;
   - using headings on your screens;
   - being consistent in the use of your screens;
   - using informative error messages;
   - using any available terminal features.

5. To do line-at-a-time processing, we begin by using the DISPLAY statement to display the prompts on the screen for the user. It is generally best to set up

the screen designs in the PROCEDURE DIVISION using literals, instead of in the DATA DIVISION, because of the way most computer systems handle interactive programs.

6. The ACCEPT statement is used to input data from the user.

7. The STRING statement can be used to move one or more fields into another field, eliminating excess characters.

8. The UNSTRING statement does just the opposite of the STRING statement, splitting one field into several different fields.

9. The purpose of the STRING and UNSTRING statements in our discussion is to help verify the data as the user inputs it. We can STRING one field into another to right-justify it. Then we can INSPECT the field and change any blanks to zeros. Finally we can use the class test (NUMERIC) to determine if the field contains any bad data. If it does, we simply report this to the user and reprompt for another entry.

10. A decimal point in the entry of a number creates a situation for the UNSTRING statement. We simply UNSTRING the field into two separate fields—one for the integer part and one for the decimal part—to eliminate the decimal point and align our field properly.

11. Typically, non-numeric fields are not edited unless the entry should be within a certain range of entries. If the entry should be, the field is tested against the allowable range.

4-12
Glossary

ACCEPT statement   The statement that allows data to be input from a device outside the program, such as a terminal keyboard.

Batch   A type of processing in which all the data is gathered together and then submitted to the computer in a batch.

DISPLAY statement   The statement that allows data to be printed on a device other than the printer, typically the terminal screen.

Home position   The upper lefthand corner of the display screen.

INSPECT statement   The statement that allows the program to examine a data field and count or replace specified characters.

Interactive   A type of program that will print information on the display screen and then input data from the program user.

On-line   See **Interactive**.

Prompt   A message displayed on the screen, giving the program user certain information.

STRING statement   The statement that allows the program to move the data of two or more fields into one field.

UNSTRING statement   The statement that allows a single field to be split into two or more fields.

4-13

Quick Quiz

Cover the answers with a blank sheet of paper and test yourself. Questions 1–15 are true or false questions, 16–20 are multiple choice, and 21–25 are fill-in-the-blank.

T   F   **1.** Most batch programs use a lot of prompts.

T   F   **2.** All the programs we have written thus far in this book have been batch programs.

T   F   **3.** The typical DISPLAY statement has provisions for cursor positioning.

T   F   **4.** The upper lefthand corner of the screen is known as the home position.

T   F   **5.** It's always a good idea to indicate to your user the length of entry you expect.

T   F   **6.** You should design your new system and then show the specifications to the user for approval.

T   F   **7.** It is sometimes a good idea to have sequential numbers on your program screens.

T   F   **8.** If you can put all the data onto one screen, you should avoid using additional screens. A single screen is easier for the user.

T   F   **9.** We can use the DISPLAY command to print on the printer as well as on the screen.

T   F   **10.** The DISPLAY statement will display field data as well as literals.

T   F   **11.** The standard width for a display terminal is 80 characters.

T   F   **12.** The ACCEPT statement functions the same way in all versions of COBOL.

T   F   **13.** We can use the STRING statement to move one field into another.

T   F   **14.** The ON OVERFLOW clause on the STRING statement is used to execute a statement when there is more data in the sending fields than there is room for in the receiving field.

T   F   **15.** It would be helpful if the INSPECT statement would allow us to change all non-numeric characters to zeros to correct any bad entries.

_____   **16.** If we are inputting a field with a decimal point, which of the following statements would we probably not use?

(a) STRING   (c) UNSTRING
(b) INSPECT   (d) IF NUMERIC

_____   **17.** Which of the following functions is most concerned with the home position?

(a) cursor positioning   (c) screen blanking
(b) function keys   (d) field length designations

_____   **18.** Which of the following display characteristics is most dependent upon the type of computer you are using?

(a) cursor positioning   (c) special keys
(b) highlighting   (d) color

_____   **19.** Considering the way most computers handle interactive programs, which of the following methods of using the DISPLAY statement is considered to be the best?

(a) Display the information stored in the DATA DIVISION with one DISPLAY statement.

(b) Display the information stored in the DATA DIVISION with several DISPLAY statements.

(c) Display the information using literals in the PROCEDURE DIVISION.

(d) All methods are equally valuable.

____ **20.** When you use the UNSTRING statement to input a number that has a decimal position, which of the following delimit clauses should be used?

    (a) DELIMITED BY "."
    (b) DELIMITED BY " "
    (c) DELIMITED BY " " AND "."
    (d) DELIMITED BY " " OR "."

21. The upper left-hand corner of the screen is called the _____ .

22. The STRING statement has an extra clause that can be used to print an error message when the result field is not large enough. That clause is _____ .

23. The message printed on the screen to inform the user of what is expected is called a _____ .

24. With the _____ clause, we can have the UNSTRING statement use multiple adjacent characters as the delimiter.

25. We can use the _____ statement to replace spaces with zeros.

4-14
Answers to Quick Quiz

1. F (The prompt is basically an interactive program tool, though some batch programs do occasionally ask for small amounts of input from the program operator—such as a date or code.)

2. T

3. F (That's why we used line-at-a-time processing—because there are no standard cursor positioning commands.)

4. T

5. T

6. F (You should check with the user before designing anything, since the user is the one who knows how the system should be designed. Involving the user in the beginning can help you avoid having to redesign your programs.)

7. T (If you have a program with a large number of screens, numbering them can help the user avoid being confused.)

8. F (Not if you have crammed too much information onto one screen. The user's job is easier if the screens are informative without being cluttered. Use multiple screens if necessary.)

9. T (With the use of the mnemonic-name.)

10. T

11. T

12. F (In some versions, any characters the user doesn't fill with the entry are filled with blanks; other versions leave the characters that were already in the field.)

13. T (That's how we right-justify a field that does not have a decimal point.)

14. T

15. F (That would be of little value, since changing all bad characters to zero would not necessarily result in a correct entry. It is much safer to simply change any spaces to zero and let the user correct any other errors.)

16. a (We would need the UNSTRING statement to split the field around a decimal point.)

17. c (The home position is where the cursor goes when we blank the entire screen.)

18. d (Color displays are available only on machines that have that capability.)
19. c (This is so because the system must keep multiple copies of the DATA DIVISION but only one copy of the PROCEDURE DIVISION.)
20. d (We need to delimit by either the blank or the decimal point but not by both, as in choice c.)
21. home position
22. ON OVERFLOW
23. prompt
24. ALL
25. INSPECT

4-15
Questions to Aid Understanding

1. Explain the difference between a batch program and an interactive program.
*2. List the three basic methods of using the screen and the keyboard for interactive programs. Explain why we used only one type in our examples in the chapter.
3. List and describe at least four different screen design techniques.
4. List and describe at least four of the screen design guidelines.
*5. Explain what the DISPLAY statement is used for. List three different ways of using the statement and explain why you might choose one method over the others.
6. Explain what the ACCEPT statement is used for and describe at least one difference between the various implementations.
7. Explain what the STRING and UNSTRING statements are used for and what the difference is between them. Explain what the ON OVERFLOW is used for.
*8. Explain how the STRING and UNSTRING statements are used to help verify input data. How does verification of a field with a decimal point differ from verification of a field without one?
9. Design a screen layout that has 15 different fields of differing lengths to be input.
10. Design a menu screen with the following screen choices:

- add a record
- change a record
- delete a record
- display a list
- print a list in name sequence
- print a list in employee number sequence
- print a list in zip code sequence

*11. Given the following data fields, show the results of each STRING statement below.

FIELD-1   PIC X(4).

1	2	-	3		4

FIELD-2   PIC X(6).

X	Y		-	Z	-

FIELD-3   PIC X(6).

FIELD-4   PIC X(10) VALUE SPACES.

*(a) STRING FIELD-1 FIELD-2 INTO FIELD-4.
 (b) STRING FIELD-1 DELIMITED BY ' '
         FIELD-2 DELIMITED BY '-'
         INTO FIELD-4.
*(c) STRING FIELD-2 DELIMITED BY ' '
         FIELD-3 DELIMITED BY '-'
         FIELD-1 DELIMITED BY '-'
         INTO FIELD-4.
 (d) STRING FIELD-3 DELIMITED BY ' '
         FIELD-3 DELIMITED BY '-'
         FIELD-1 DELIMITED BY ' '
         INTO FIELD-4.
*(e) STRING FIELD-1 DELIMITED BY '-'
         FIELD-2 DELIMITED BY '-'
         FIELD-3 DELIMITED BY '1'
         INTO FIELD-4.
 (f) STRING FIELD-2 DELIMITED BY '3'
         FIELD-3 DELIMITED BY 'X'
         FIELD-1 DELIMITED BY SIZE
         INTO FIELD-4.

*12. Given the following data fields, show the results of each UNSTRING statement below.

A	B	C	-	D		1	*	2	3

FIELD-4   PIC X(10).

FIELD-1   PIC X(3).

FIELD-2   PIC X(4).

FIELD-3   PIC X(4).

```
    (a) UNSTRING FIELD-4 INTO FIELD-1 FIELD-2.
   *(b) UNSTRING FIELD-4 DELIMITED BY '-'
                INTO FIELD-1 FIELD-2 FIELD-3.
    (c) UNSTRING FIELD-4 DELIMITED BY '-' OR ' '
                INTO FIELD-3 FIELD-1 FIELD-2.
   *(d) UNSTRING FIELD-4 DELIMITED BY '*'
                INTO FIELD-1 FIELD-2 FIELD-3.
    (e) UNSTRING FIELD-4 DELIMITED BY ALL SPACES
                INTO FIELD-2 FIELD-3.
```

4-16
Coding Exercises

1. Design a screen display to allow the user to enter five fields into a file: employee number, employee name, hourly rate, hours worked, and union code (1 or 2). Use an appropriate heading on the screen design. Write the code that would be used to display the screen.

2. Write the code that could be used to input the data from exercise 1 above. The hourly rate should be verified as being less than or equal to $15 per hour, the hours worked should not be more than 50, and the union code can be only 1 or 2.

3. Suppose you have a field that has the data stored as first name, middle initial, and last name. Write the code to transform the field so that is has last name, a comma, first name, and middle initial.

4. Write the code to input a date, letting the user enter the slashes, and verify that each part of the date is valid. That is, the month must be larger than 0 but less than 13, the day cannot be larger than 31, and the year should be larger than 85 but less than 90. For extra practice you might want to set up the code to test for the maximum number of days allowed for each month. For example, January can have 31 but April can have only 30 and February can have only 28 (leap year is an additional problem you can try to solve if you wish).

5. Write the code to input a name, address, city, state, and zip code. Follow these with the code to display them on the screen in mailing label format. String the city, state, and zip code together for the third line of the label.

6. Write the code to input a field that will contain either a dash or a slash in two different locations. Unstring the field into three other fields.

4-17
Maintenance Program

More information has been added to the customer file for *The Record Rack*. Now the interactive program Cindy created needs to be modified to incorporate these new fields: amount due, credit limit, and salesman number. The new record layout is shown in Figure 4-6. The amount due should not exceed $500, and the credit limit is a one-character code of 0 through 4. The salesman number, like the customer number that is already part of the file, is to be all numeric digits, even though it is stored as a non-numeric field. Also, Cindy realized that her prompts for the first name don't say anything about the middle initial, and her code would not work if there were an initial. The program needs to be modified to allow the entry of the middle initial on the first-name field (no separate field.)

Modify the program design so it fits the new needs, and then change the program to accomplish the desired results. The new field maintenance display layout is shown in Figure 4-7. Change the program to use the new layout (with the added fields).

4-18
Illustrative Program

You work as a programmer for *The Hamster*, a magazine about the care and feeding of hamsters. The master file of subscriptions is updated with a sequential update program. Since the terminal system was installed at the company about a year ago, the data to update the file has been entered into the system using a simple interactive editor. It is your job to write an interactive program to allow the creation of transaction records.

The records must be of three types: add, renewal, and cancel. The layout for the records you are to create is shown in Figure 4-8.

CUSTOMER File					
Field Description	*Position*	*Length*	:	*Dec*	*Type*
Customer number	1–4	4	:		Non-numeric
Name Last	5–14	10	:		Non-numeric
First & initial	15–24	10	:		Non-numeric
Address	25–39	15	:		Non-numeric
City	40–52	13	:		Non-numeric
State	53–54	2	:		Non-numeric
Zip code	55–59	5	:		Non-numeric
Amount of sale	60–65	6	:	2	Numeric
Amount due	66–71	6	:	2	Numeric
Credit limit	72–72	1	:		Non-numeric
Salesman number	73–76	4	:		Non-numeric
Filler	77–80	4	:		Non-numeric
Record Length = 80					

Figure 4-6   The modified record layout for the CUSTOMER file.

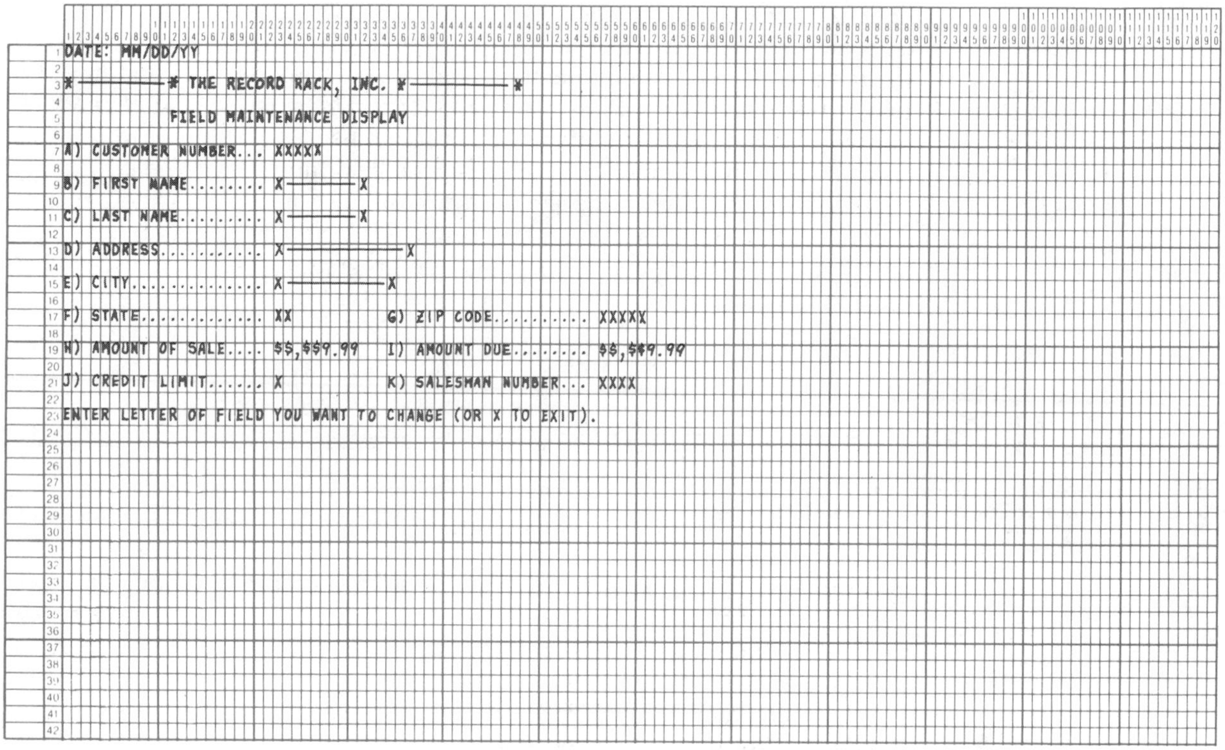

Figure 4-7   The new field maintenance screen display. Note that there are now two fields on some of the lines.

The systems design for the program is shown in Figure 4-9. Figure 4-10 shows the initial screen for the program and Figure 4-11 shows the field maintenance screen to be used after all the data has been entered during the add record function. On the renewal record, you should redisplay the entry and let the user verify that it is correct. The flowchart can be seen in Figure 4-12. The pseudocode design for the program follows.

```
Start
Display initial screen and prompt user (A, C, R, X)
Input user initial-response
DO-WHILE initial-response not X (for exit)
        IF initial-response is A THEN
                Do add record routine
        ELSE IF initial-response is C THEN
                Do cancel record routine
        ELSE IF initial-response is R THEN
                Do renewal record routine
        ELSE
                Display error message
        END-IF
        Display initial screen and prompt user (A, C, D, X)
        Input user initial-response
END-DO
```

SUBTRANS File					
Field Description	*Position*	*Length*	:	*Dec*	*Type*
Customer number	1–4	4	:		Non-numeric
Transaction code	5–5	1	:		Non-numeric
Data fields	6–62	57	:		Various
Filler	63–80	58	:		Non-numeric
Record Length = 80					

For the renewal function, "Data fields" will be defined as

Number of months	6–7	2	:	0	Numeric
Filler	8–62	55	:		Non-numeric

For the new account function (add), "Data fields" will be defined with all the needed fields as follows:

Customer name	6–25	20	:		Non-numeric
Address	26–40	15	:		Non-numeric
City	41–53	13	:		Non-numeric
State	54–55	2	:		Non-numeric
Zip code	56–60	5	:		Non-numeric
Months of subscription	61–62	2	:	0	Numeric
Filler	63–80	18	:		Non-numeric

Figure 4-8 The record layouts needed for the transaction file.

```
Start add record routine
Initialize customer number
DO-WHILE customer number not valid (numeric)
        Do customer number entry routine
END-DO
Initialize name
Do name entry routine (no edit)
Initialize address
Do address entry routine (no edit)
Initialize city
Do city entry routine (no edit)
Initialize state
Do state entry routine (no edit)
Initialize zip code
DO-WHILE zip code not valid (numeric)
        Do zip code entry routine
END-DO
```

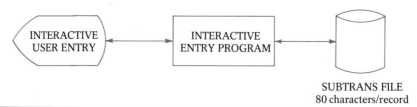

SUBTRANS FILE
80 characters/record

Figure 4-9   The systems chart for the interactive transaction file entry program.

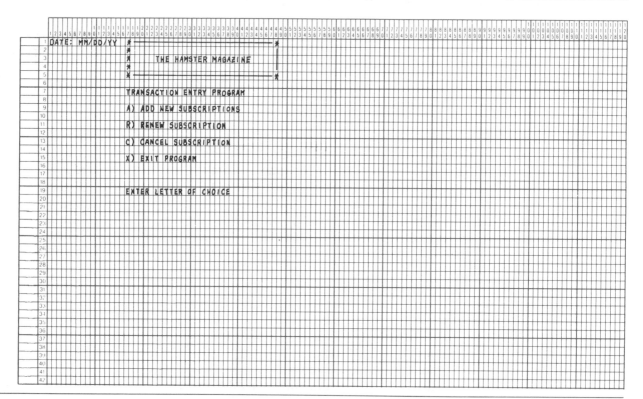

Figure 4-10   The display layout for the initial screen for the transaction file entry program.

```
Initialize months of subscription
DO-WHILE months of subscription not valid (numeric)
        Do months of subscription entry routine
END-DO
Display all the data and field change prompt on the screen
Input the response (0–7) from the user
DO-WHILE response not 0 (quit)
        IF response = 1 THEN
                Initialize customer number
```

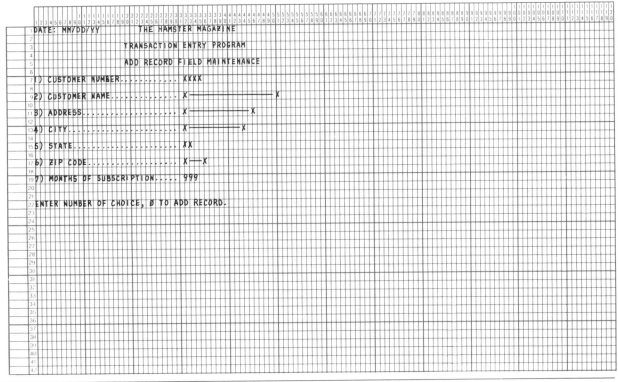

Figure 4-11   The display layout for the field maintenance screen for the transaction file entry program.

```
          DO-WHILE customer number not valid (numeric)
                Do customer number entry routine
          END-DO
     ELSE IF response = 2 THEN
          Do name entry routine (no edit)
     ELSE IF response = 3 THEN
          Do address entry routine (no edit)
     ELSE IF response = 4 THEN
          Do city entry routine (no edit)
     ELSE IF response = 5 THEN
          Do state entry routine (no edit)
     ELSE IF response = 6 THEN
          Initialize zip code
          DO-WHILE zip code not valid (numeric)
                Do zip code entry routine
          END-DO
     ELSE IF response = 7 THEN
          Initialize months of subscription
          DO-WHILE months of subscription not valid (numeric)
                Do months of subscription entry routine
          END-DO
     ELSE
          Display error message
```

```
                            END-IF
                            Display all the data and field change prompt on the screen
                            Input the response (0–7) from the user
                    END-DO
                    Write the record into the file
                    End add record routine


                    Start renewal record routine
                    Initialize customer number
                    DO-WHILE customer number not valid (numeric)
                            Do customer number entry routine
                    END-DO
                    Initialize months of subscription
                    DO-WHILE months of subscription not valid (numeric)
                            Do months of subscription entry routine
                    END-DO
                    Display the two fields change prompt on the screen
                    Input the response (0–2) from the user
                    DO-WHILE response not 0 (quit)
                            IF response = 1 THEN
                                    Initialize customer number
                                    DO-WHILE customer number not valid (numeric)
                                            Do customer number entry routine
                                    END-DO
                            ELSE IF response = 2 THEN
                                    Initialize months of subscription
                                    DO-WHILE months of subscription not valid (numeric)
                                            Do months of subscription entry routine
                                    END-DO
                            ELSE
                                    Display error message
                            END-IF
                            Display all the data and field change prompt on the screen
                            Input the response (0–2) from the user
                    END-DO
                    Write the record into the file
                    End renewal record routine


                    Start cancel record routine
                    Initialize customer number
                    DO-WHILE customer number not valid (numeric)
                            Do customer number entry routine
                    END-DO
                    Display verification prompt on the screen
                    Input the response (Y–N) from the user
                    IF response = Y THEN
                            Write the record into the file
                    ELSE
                            Display record not written message
                    END-IF
                    End cancel record routine
```

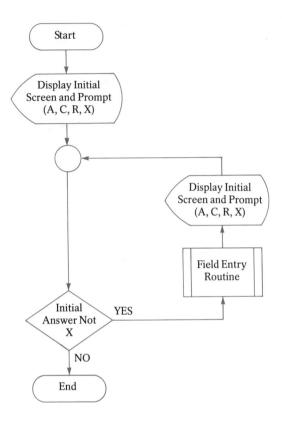

Figure 4-12 The flowchart for the transaction file entry program (part 1).

Each of the entry routines will simply display a message and then input the data, verifying the numeric fields. In the interest of space, we will show only the design for the customer entry routine (this is also the only one in the flowchart):

```
Start customer number entry routine
Display prompt
Input data
Move the data to appropriate fields (STRING or UNSTRING)
Change blanks to zeros
IF data not valid (numeric) THEN
    Display error message
    Initialize customer number field
(ELSE)
END-IF
End routine
```

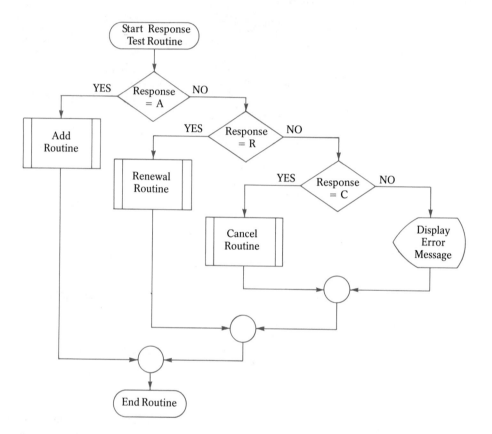

Figure 4-12 (continued)   Part 2.

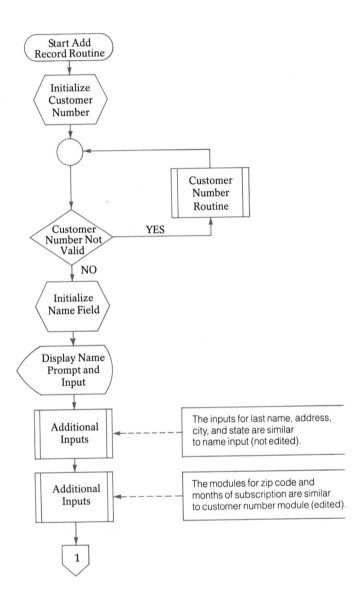

Figure 4-12 (continued)   Part 1 of add record entry routine.

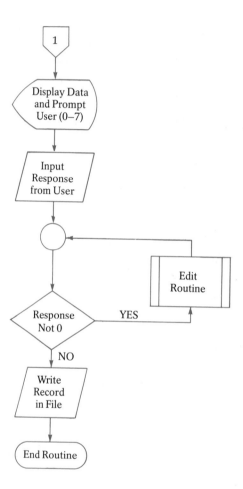

Figure 4-12 (continued)   Part 2 of add record entry routine.

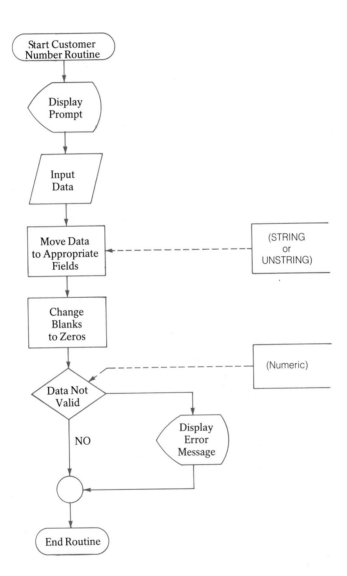

Figure 4-12 (continued) Field edit routine.

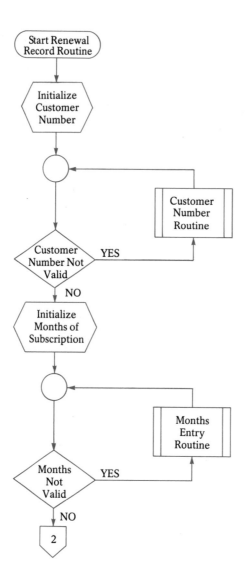

Figure 4-12 (continued)   Part 1 of renewal record entry routine.

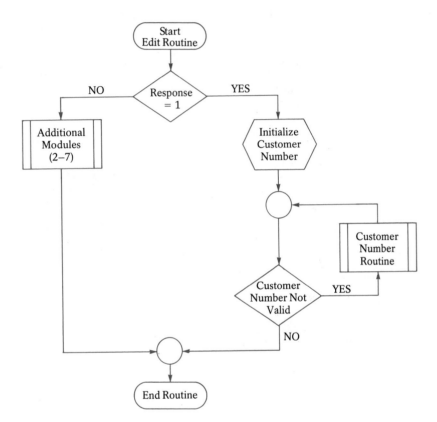

Figure 4-12 (continued)   Part 2 of renewal record entry routine.

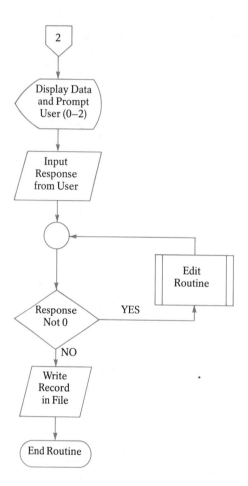

Figure 4-12 (continued)   Field edit routine for renewal.

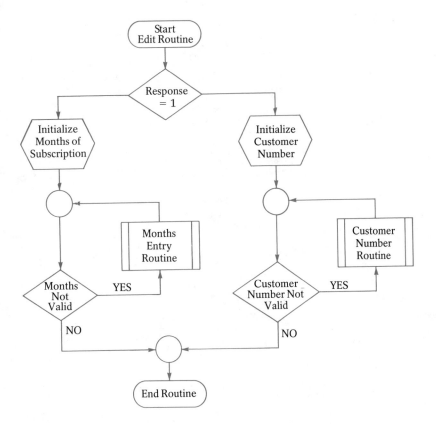

Figure 4-12 (continued)   Cancel record routine.

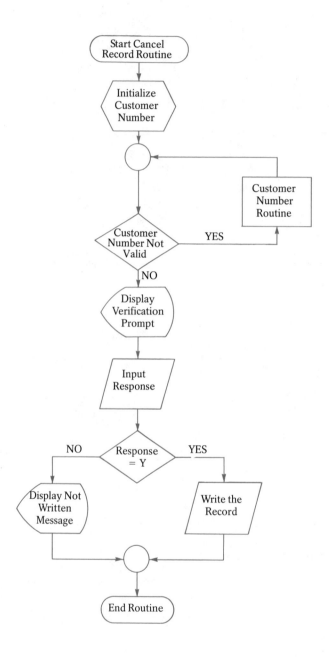

Figure 4-12 (continued) Customer number routine.

4-19

System Designed Programs

For the following programs, all the design elements typically furnished to a programmer by the systems analyst are furnished. It is up to you, as programmer, to design and code the program. The files to be used are found in Appendix A.

1. *The Record Rack* needs to send an overdue-payment letter to each customer who has an overdue balance. Use the STRING command to create a form letter that can be sent to these customers. The form of the letter can be seen in Figure 4-13. The underlined areas of the letter are those that need to be extracted from the CUSTOMER file, the layout of which is shown in Figure 4-14. The systems chart for the program is shown in Figure 4-15.

    For the name line in the heading, string together the first and last names; for the last line of the heading, string together the city, state, and zip code.

2. Write an interactive program to display and print records from the SALES file shown in Figure 4-16. The initial menu is shown in Figure 4-17. The single record display is shown in Figure 4-18. The report format for either the screen or the printer is shown in Figure 4-19. The systems chart for the program is shown in Figure 4-20.

    In order to do these various functions, you will have to close and reopen the file between tasks. That is, after you display one record you will have to close the file and reopen it (for input) to list the whole file.

3. Write an interactive program to add records to the sequential INVENT file containing the data shown in Figure 4-21. The initial program display should look like the one in Figure 4-22. After all the fields are input, display them all so the user can modify any that are incorrect. This field maintenance display should look like the one shown in Figure 4-23. Notice that three fields displayed on the screen are calculated. The sytems chart for the program is shown in Figure 4-24.

4-20

Non-designed Programs

In the following programs, you will need to design the systems chart, the input files (record layout), the printer spacing chart (or display design), the program design, and the data with which to test the program.)

1. Write an interactive entry program to create a transaction file to update an inventory master file. Five different types of transactions are needed:

    (a) sale of item
    (b) receipt of item
    (c) new item
    (d) delete item
    (e) change field of item

The Record Rack
1500 South Street
Cincinnati, Ohio 98978

First name Last name
Address
City, State Zip code

Dear Mr. or Ms. Last name,

It has come to our attention that your charge
account payment is well overdue. According to our
records, you owe us amount due. We're sure it is simply
an oversight and it is your intention to pay your bill
promptly. As a matter of fact, the check is probably in
the mail already. If such is the case, please ignore
this letter.

Please be aware that The Record Rack is like any
other business: we need money to keep us going.
Unfortunately, that means that people like you, first
name, must pay their bills in a timely fashion. Thus, if
we do not hear from you in the next two weeks, we will
have to hand this account over to our collection agency.
None of us wants this to happen, so please, first name,
pay the bill.

If you need help in arranging a method of payment,
please contact us and tell us what bank in city you do
business with. We will contact them to help you make
arrangements. We will do all we can do to help you keep
a good payment record with us, because we value good
customers.

Thanks for your help in this matter.

Sincerely,

Your name here
The Record Rack

Figure 4-13   The design of the form letter for exercise 4-20-1.

| CUSTOMER File | | | | | |
Field Description	Position	Length	:	Dec	Type
Customer number	1–4	4	:		Non-numeric
Name Last	5–14	10	:		Non-numeric
First & initial	15–24	10	:		Non-numeric
Address	25–39	15	:		Non-numeric
City	40–52	13	:		Non-numeric
State	53–54	2	:		Non-numeric
Zip code	55–59	5	:		Non-numeric
Amount due	60–65	6	:	2	Numeric
Filler	66–80	15	:		Non-numeric
Record Length = 80					

Figure 4-14   The record layout for the CUSTOMER file for exercise 4-20-1.

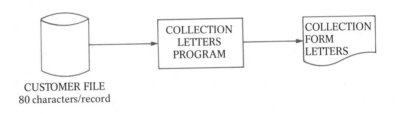

CUSTOMER FILE
80 characters/record

Figure 4-15   The systems chart for exercise 4-20-1.

| SALES File | | | | | |
Field Description	Position	Length	:	Dec	Type
Salesman number	1–4	4	:		Non-numeric
Salesman name	5–24	20	:		Non-numeric
Sales territory	25–26	2	:		Non-numeric
Commission rate	27–28	2	:	0	Numeric
Sales of product 1	29–35	7	:	2	Numeric
Sales of product 2	36–42	7	:	2	Numeric
Sales of product 3	43–49	7	:	2	Numeric
Filler	50–80	31	:		Non-numeric
Record Length = 80					

Figure 4-16   The record layout for the SALES file, exercise 4-20-2.

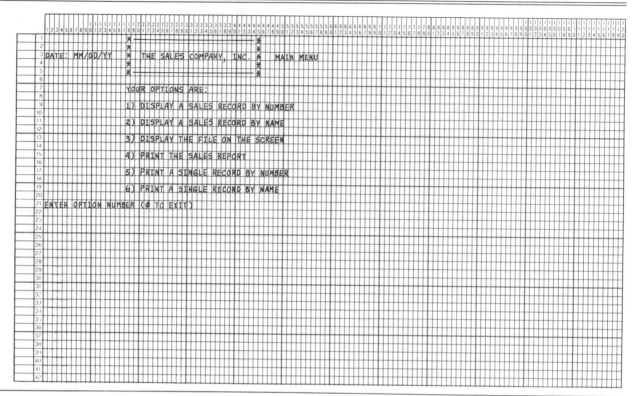

Figure 4-17   The initial menu screen for exercise 4-20-2.

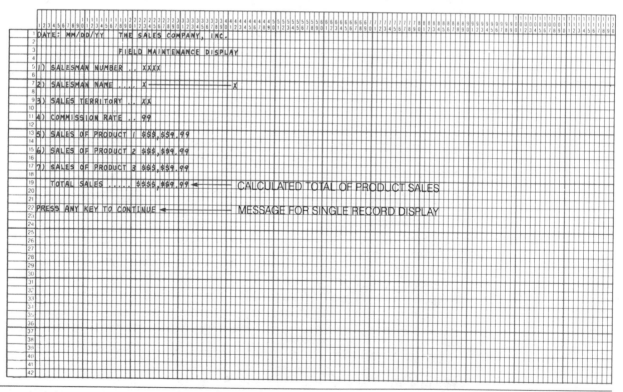

Figure 4-18   The field update screen for exercise 4-20-2. Notice that there is a different prompt for the update versus the single-record display.

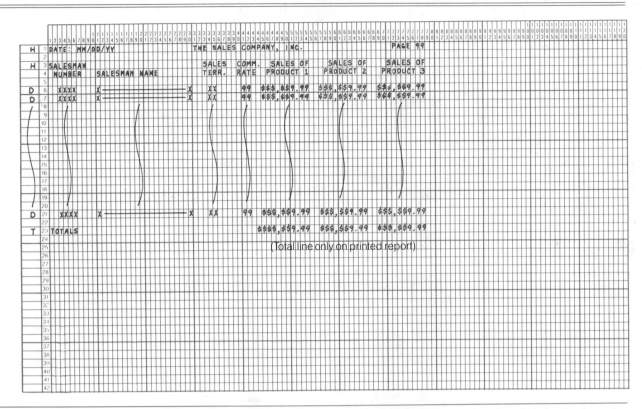

Figure 4-19   The report layout for the screen display or the printed report for exercise 4-20-2.

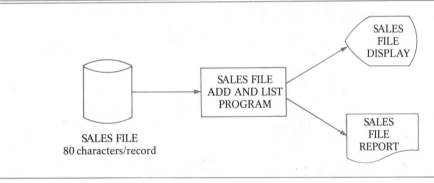

Figure 4-20   The systems chart for exercise 4-20-2.

2. Write an interactive program that will read a customer record and display it on the screen. Then, using a purchase date stored in the record, the user is to visually determine if the account is 30, 60, or 90 days overdue. Input a code from the user (for days overdue) and write the input record into one of three different output files, one each for each number of days overdue. Then create a second program to print a report that specifies whether each record on the list is 30, 60, or 90 days overdue.

INVENT File					
Field Description	Position	Length	:	Dec	Type
Item number	1–4	4	:		Non-numeric
Last count	5–10	6	:	0	Numeric
Current count	11–16	6	:	0	Numeric
Unit cost	17–24	8	:	2	Numeric
Unit price	25–32	8	:	2	Numeric
Amount received	33–38	6	:	0	Numeric
Amount sold	39–44	6	:	0	Numeric
Filler	45–80	36	:		Non-numeric
Record Length = 80					

Figure 4-21   The record layout for the INVENT file, exercise 4-20-3.

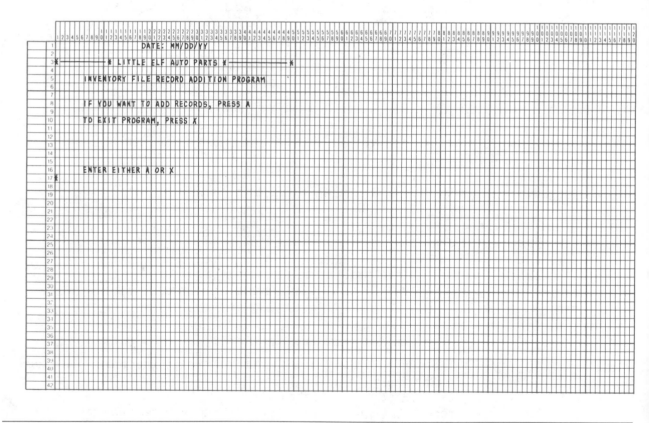

Figure 4-22   The initial screen display for exercise 4-20-3.

```
 1 MM/DD/YY        LITTLE ELF AUTO PARTS
 2
 3          FIELD MAINTENANCE DISPLAY
 4
 5 A) ITEM NUMBER .......  XXXX
 6
 7 B) LAST COUNT ........  ZZZ,ZZ9
 8                             COUNT DIFFERENCE -ZZZ,ZZ9  ◄───────── (LAST-CURRENT)
 9 C) CURRENT COUNT ....  ZZZ,ZZ9
10
11 D) UNIT COST .........  ZZZ,ZZ9.99
12                             UNIT PROFIT    -ZZZ,ZZ9.99 ◄───────── (PRICE-COST)
13 E) UNIT PRICE .......  ZZZ,ZZ9.99
14
15 F) AMOUNT RECEIVED ..  ZZZ,ZZ9
16                             AMOUNT DIFFERENCE -ZZZ,ZZ9 ◄───────── (RECEIVED-SOLD)
17 G) AMOUNT SOLD .......  ZZZ,ZZ9
18
19
20
21
22 ENTER OPTION (A - G, X TO EXIT)
```

Figure 4-23   The field maintenance display for exercise 4-20-3.

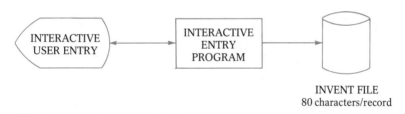

INVENT FILE
80 characters/record

Figure 4-24   The systems chart for the interactive INVENT file entry program, exercise 4-20-3.

3. Write an interactive program to read student grade records and display them on the screen based upon

- student name (single record display);
- a particular score (A–F) on any of 6 exams (list of all records that meet grade requirements). In other words, let the user pick a score (A–F) and an exam (1–6) and display all the records that have a score above the one chosen for the particular exam chosen. If any request doesn't produce any records, your program should display an error message detailing that fact.

Be sure to list all the students in the file.

OBJECTIVES   After completing Chapter 5 you should be able to
1. explain what a table is and how it can be useful;
2. explain the difference between single- and multi-level tables;
3. explain the use of the OCCURS clause;
4. explain how to access data stored in a table;
5. explain the difference between the OCCURS clause and the OCCURS . . . DEPENDING clause;
6. explain the purpose and show an example of the SEARCH statement;
7. explain the differences between an index and a subscript;
8. explain why the SET statement is necessary;
9. explain the difference in the way COBOL uses the SEARCH statement versus the SEARCH ALL statement;
10. list at least three differences in the rules for using the SEARCH and SEARCH ALL statements;
11. explain why the ASCENDING and DESCENDING KEY clause is necessary;
12. explain why we use the index names GROUP and ITEM for the two levels of a table;
13. explain how to set up and use a two-level table when all the data is not of the same type.

CHAPTER 5

MULTI-LEVEL TABLES

5-1
Introduction

Because two- and three-level tables exist in virtually all COBOL compilers, we need to be able to use multi-level tables. The 1985 standards allow up to seven levels, and though we will primarily focus on two- and three-level tables, we will briefly discuss tables with more levels.

Before we begin discussing two-level tables, it would be a good idea to review single-level tables and the techniques involved in creating them.

5-2
Review of Single-level Tables

As you will recall, a **table** is simply a group of like data items, stored together, that can be referenced by number. In other programming languages and in mathematics in general, such groupings are called **arrays**, a name which may be more familiar to you. A table is similar to an array, especially when we are dealing with **single-level tables**. When we move to on to multi-level tables, we will see that tables and arrays differ in concept.

There are many uses for tables in programming. We use tax tables, payroll rate tables, tables of states and abbreviations, tables of zip codes, and many hundreds of different translation tables, all allowing us to change a code to a more meaningful description.

A table must be defined to the program with an **OCCURS clause**, which is put on the PIC clause. It looks like this:

OCCURS integer TIMES

It is used to tell the program that a certain field OCCURS an integer number of times. With a normal field, there is simply one item. With a table, however, we use the OCCURS clause to specify how many items there are going to be.

Only a few rules apply to the use of this clause:

■ The integer must be larger than zero and must be a numeric literal. A field-name cannot be used, even if it is an integer.

■ An OCCURS clause cannot be used on either an 01 or an 88 level. It must be used on the level numbers 02–49.

■ The OCCURS clause can be used on either an elementary item or a group item.

■ An OCCURS clause cannot have a VALUE clause on it (except in the 1985 version).

An OCCURS clause might look like this:

```
10   PHONE—NUMBER OCCURS 10 TIMES      PIC X(13).
```

This would give us ten (OCCURS 10 TIMES) separate storage locations, all related to PHONE-NUMBER:

PHONE—NUMBER (1) ◄————— first field

PHONE—NUMBER (2) ◄————— second field

: : :

PHONE—NUMBER (10) ◄————— tenth field

If we would like to load data into the table, the REDEFINES clause gives us an easy method:

```
WORKING STORGAE SECTION.

01  WORK-AREAS.
    10  TABLE-SETUP.
        20  FILLER              PIC X(14)  VALUE 1-800-305-3798.
        20  FILLER              PIC X(14)  VALUE 1-800-335-3897.
        20  FILLER              PIC X(14)  VALUE 1-800-496-9384.
        20  FILLER              PIC X(14)  VALUE 1-800-857-8587.
        20  FILLER              PIC X(14)  VALUE 1-800-858-8476.
        20  FILLER              PIC X(14)  VALUE 1-800-858-8577.
        20  FILLER              PIC X(14)  VALUE 1-800-333-3333.
        20  FILLER              PIC X(14)  VALUE 1-800-838-8487.
        20  FILLER              PIC X(14)  VALUE 1-800-839-8474.
        20  FILLER              PIC X(14)  VALUE 1-800-849-9848.
    10  PHONE-NUMBERS REDEFINES TABLE-SETUP
            OCCURS 10 TIMES     PIC X(14).
```

Notice that we redefined the group field TABLE-SETUP, which was defined with ten different FILLER fields each containing a phone number.

When accessing one of the defined elements of the table, we use a numeric **subscript** that points to the individual element we need from the table. For example,

```
MOVE PHONE-NUMBERS (5) TO PHONE-NUMBER-OUT.
```

would move the fifth element of the table into the other field.

There are only a few things to be concerned about when using subscripts:

- We must be sure to use only subscripts that lie within the range of the table as we defined it with our OCCURS clause. We would get an error if we tried to access PHONE-NUMBERS (25) and our table only contained ten elements.
- There is no zero element in any table (on most compilers). Thus, if we used PHONE-NUMBERS (0), we would get an error.
- On most compilers, spacing must be precise. There should be at least one space between the table name and the left parenthesis and one space between the right parenthesis and whatever follows (with the exception of a period

or comma). Within the parentheses there should be no spaces at all. The following two examples show possible coding problems:

```
MOVE PHONE-NUMBERS(5) TO PHONE-NUMBER-OUT.
MOVE PHONE-NUMBERS ( 5 ) TO PHONE-NUMBER-OUT.
```

In the first example, there should be a space between PHONE-NUMBERS and (5). In the second example, the spaces around the subscript, (5), are not allowed.

A subscript does not have to be a literal. We can use field-names to access elements of the table. For example, the statement

```
MOVE PHONE-NUMBERS (5) TO PHONE-NUMBER OUT.
```

can be changed to

```
MOVE PHONE-NUMBERS (SUB) TO PHONE-NUMBER-OUT.
```

Now, depending upon the value of SUB, we can access any element of the table. As mentioned, we must make sure that SUB is never zero or any number larger than the specified size of the table.

5-2-1   OCCURS . . . DEPENDING

Normally, when specifying the number of elements in a table, we cannot use a variable size (that is, we cannot define with a field-name). The size specification must be an integer literal. Well, there are occasions when we do not know how many elements are going to be needed. In such cases we can use the **DEPENDING ON** option of the OCCURS clause. The form of the option is

OCCURS integer-1 TO integer-2 TIMES DEPENDING ON field-name

The DEPENDING ON option makes the number of elements in the table vary between the two limits of integer-1 and integer-2, depending on the value in field-name. Integer-1 must have a value less than integer-2.

This use of the DEPENDING ON clause doesn't save any memory when the program is compiled. All the space listed in integer-2 is set aside for storage even though it may not be needed. If this is the case, why not just use a table of integer-2 size and forget the DEPENDING ON option? If there are any extra elements in the table when we're searching it, they have to be searched every time the search is executed. Thus, if we're not sure how many elements are going to be needed in the table, we use the DEPENDING ON clause. Any elements not put into the table aren't searched and time is not wasted.

5-2-2   Searching a Table

If we need to look up a certain item in our table, we can use the SEARCH **command**:

```
SEARCH table-name [AT END imperative-statement-1]
       WHEN condition-1 imperative-statement-2
       [WHEN condition-2 imperative-statement-3] [ . . . ]
```

This statement allows the computer to search the table until the condition following the WHEN clause is satisfied. If it is not satisfied before the end of the file is found, the AT END clause takes effect. Although the AT END clause is optional, it is always a good idea to use it—because if you don't and the end-of-table is found, the program will ABEND. Though we are allowed to use multiple WHEN clauses, it is seldom necessary. One WHEN clause usually accomplishes what we need. An example of the SEARCH statement would be

```
SEARCH NUMBER-TABLE
      AT END PERFORM 0800-ERROR-ROUTINE
      WHEN NUMBER-TABLE (SUBSCRIPT) = ITEM-NUMBER
      PERFORM 0500-CALC-ROUTINE.
```

This statement will cause the computer to search the table called NUMBER-TABLE for an element that matches the field ITEM-NUMBER. If it does, then it will perform the 0500-CALC-ROUTINE. If it doesn't, then the 0800-ERROR-ROUTINE will be performed.

We cannot use ordinary subscripts in the SEARCH statement. Instead, we have to define special subscripts, called **indexes**, that must be specified on the OCCURS clause. The form of the clause becomes

OCCURS integer TIMES [INDEXED BY index-name]

We use an index much like a subscript, with just a couple of changes. Instead of us having to define the index ourselves, the computer does it for us automatically. In other words, we do not set up a field for the index. The computer will automatically set it up with the appropriate size. For example, if we use the statement

```
10   NUMBER-TABLE OCCURS 100 TIMES
                INDEXED BY TABLE-INDEX PIC 999V99.
```

the compiler will set up a field (actually just a storage location) called TABLE-INDEX. The PIC clause will be 999 because, at most, 100 elements will require a three-digit index.

Since the index is not an ordinary subscript, using "INDEX" as part of the field name is considered good practice. This way you are always informed that you are using an index.

Generally, a table is searched when we need to use a paired element. That is, we use two tables subdefined under a group item, searching one to get the index so we can point to an element from the other table. We might do it as

```
01   WORK-AREAS.
     10   TWIN-TABLES OCCURS 20 TIMES
                   INDEXED BY TABLE-INDEX.
         20    NUMBER-TABLE              PIC X(12).
         20    COST-TABLE               PIC 999V99.
```

Now we have both tables set up and indexed by TABLE-INDEX.

Unlike the value of an ordinary subscript, the value of an index cannot be changed with an ADD or a MOVE statement. Because the index is a special field, it requires special handling when the value is being changed. You must use the

SET statement to modify the contents of the index. The form of the **SET statement** is

$$\underline{\text{SET}} \text{ index-name} \begin{Bmatrix} \underline{\text{TO}} \\ \underline{\text{UP}} \ \underline{\text{BY}} \\ \underline{\text{DOWN}} \ \underline{\text{BY}} \end{Bmatrix} \text{ integer}$$

There are three different forms of the SET statement. The first one is used to assign (or reassign) an initial value to the index, such as

```
SET TABLE-INDEX TO 1.
```

UP BY and DOWN BY are used to increment and decrement the index:

```
SET TABLE-INDEX UP BY 1.
```

or

```
SET TABLE-INDEX DOWN BY 1.
```

The SET statement is necessary in a couple of instances. When you do a search, the SEARCH statement will automatically begin at the current value of the index. That is, the index is not automatically set back to 1 every time you search. Therefore, you need to SET the value of the index to 1 (or whatever other number might be appropriate) before you begin the search procedure. An example:

```
SET TABLE-INDEX TO 1.
SEARCH TWIN-TABLES
        AT END PERFORM 0900-ERROR-ROUTINE
        WHEN NUMBER-TABLE (TABLE-INDEX) = ITEM-NUMBER
        PERFORM 0600-CALC-ROUTINE.
```

Notice that the table name after the SEARCH verb is not the same as the one following the WHEN. When we search, we must always search the field defined with the OCCURS clause. If you recall, we defined the table as

```
01  WORK-AREAS.
    10  TWIN-TABLES OCCURS 20 TIMES
                    INDEXED BY TABLE-INDEX.
        20  NUMBER-TABLE              PIC X(12).
        20  COST-TABLE                PIC 999V99.
```

Given this layout, we must search TWIN-TABLES, not NUMBER-TABLE, since TWIN-TABLES is the element that has the OCCURS clause. But the WHEN clause needs to specify the NUMBER-TABLE part of the table, since that is what is being matched against the field being looked up.

There is one final consideration. If you need to manipulate a table that has been defined with an index, you must use the SET UP and SET DOWN statements. You can, however, use a PERFORM . . . VARYING without worrying about the SET statements. The PERFORM . . . VARYING takes care of its own initialization and incrementation and does not require the use of the SET statements.

Even though we can use the PERFORM . . . VARYING without the SET, it is absolutely imperative that you use either the SET . . . TO or the PERFORM . . . VARYING statement to initialize the index value before using a SEARCH statement. Otherwise, you will get unpredictable and, no doubt, incorrect results.

5-2-3 The SEARCH ALL Statement

The SEARCH statement is only one way to do a search. It is a serial search, so it begins at the position in the file that the index is set to and looks at each entry until either the correct one or the end of the table is found. The steps in a **serial search** are as follows:

1. The entry pointed to by the index in the table is examined.
2. If the search condition is met, the search is complete.
3. If the condition is not met, the index is incremented by 1 and the next table entry is examined.
4. This procedure continues until either the condition is met or the table entries are exhausted.

This search technique always begins with the record pointed to by the index and continues to search until the condition is met. Given this, some conditions will be met as soon as one or two entries are read. Other times, the search will continue until near the end of the table. On average, the routine will search through half of the table before meeting the condition.

If the table you are searching is not in any type of sequence, you will have to use a serial search. And, as long as the table is relatively small, a serial search will function okay. When you need to search larger tables, however, a serial search is just too slow.

The **SEARCH ALL statement** allows COBOL to do a **binary search** instead of a serial search. To use a binary search, the table must be in sequence by the field being used for the search.

The computer begins a binary search at the middle element in the table, determining if the element it is looking for is less than or greater than that middle element. Based on what it finds, it then moves to the midpoint of the lower or upper group. Taking the following table of numbers as an example:

1
4
8
12
15
18
22
26

let's search for the number 18. We begin with the middle entry in the table, entry 4, which has the value of 12. (If there is no "middle" item, the computer will pick the item either just larger or just smaller than the middle, depending on the method written into the system.) Our number is larger so we use the larger four entries left in the table, find the middle element of those, and end up with entry 6, which just happens to be 18, the number we were searching for.

Binary searches of much larger tables work the same way and are much faster than serial searches. If we had used a serial search on our list of numbers, we would have had to test six numbers before finding 18. The binary search took only two tests.

In COBOL the binary search is done with the SEARCH ALL statement. The form of the statement is virtually the same as that of the SEARCH statement:

> SEARCH ALL table-name [AT END imperative-statement-1]
>   WHEN condition imperative-statement-2

However, besides the method of search, there are a number of differences between the SEARCH and SEARCH ALL statement:

- The SEARCH ALL can test only for an equal condition, while the SEARCH can use any of the conditionals we have discussed, such as LESS THAN or GREATER THAN.
- The only compound conditional allowed with the SEARCH ALL statement is the AND. The OR is not allowed. Again, any valid conditional can be used with the SEARCH statement.
- Only one WHEN clause can be used with the SEARCH ALL statement; the SEARCH is allowed as many as are necessary.
- We must SET the index to the beginning value when doing a SEARCH, but we do not use the SET before the SEARCH ALL. The SEARCH ALL does not start at the beginning or at any particular location. It always begins in the middle of the list, so setting the pointer to a particular value serves no purpose.
- And, of course, the major difference is that the SEARCH ALL table must be in sequence.
- Since we must have the file in sequence for the SEARCH ALL statement, we need to specify the order that the table is in. Keep in mind that it could be in either ascending (A–Z) or descending (Z–A) order and that the computer must know the order to know how to perform the binary search. We specify the order with the KEY clause on the OCCURS clause as follows:

> OCCURS integer TIMES $\left\{ \begin{array}{l} \text{ASCENDING} \\ \text{DESCENDING} \end{array} \right\}$ KEY is field-name
>
> [INDEXED BY index-name]

The field-name specified as the key must be one of the fields found in the table specification. It is generally the same one that is used in the WHEN clause, but it doesn't have to be. Continuing our previous example, our new definition would look like this:

```
01   WORK-AREAS.
     10   TWIN-TABLES OCCURS 20 TIMES
                 ASCENDING KEY IS NUMBER-TABLE
                 INDEXED BY TABLE-INDEX.
          20   NUMBER-TABLE            PIC X(12).
          20   COST-TABLE              PIC 999V99.
```

This now stipulates that NUMBER-TABLE is the field that is in ascending sequence. This field, then, becomes the object field for the binary search. That is, the binary search is performed using the fields found in NUMBER-TABLE.

5-3
A Few Sample Uses

Tables have many uses. To further your understanding, we will present a few of them.

5-3-1 Using Tables for Output

A table can be useful when you have similar items to be printed across a page. A common need in modern business organizations is the printing of mailing labels. Labels are typically printed three or four across the page. We will construct four-across labels that contain the name on the first line, the street address on the second line, and the city, state, and zip code on the third line, with three extra lines between each set of labels. We could define three separate print areas, each containing four fields, such as

```
01  WORK-AREAS.

    10   LABEL-LINE-1.
         20   NAME-1          PIC X(20).
         20   FILLER          PIC X(10).
         20   NAME-2          PIC X(20).
         20   FILLER          PIC X(10).
         20   NAME-3          PIC X(20).
         20   FILLER          PIC X(10).
         20   NAME-4          PIC X(20).
         20   FILLER          PIC X(10).
```

This is the definition of only the first line, but each of the other three lines would be similar. Each would have four areas defined.

If we use a table, on the other hand, the definition can be much simpler:

```
01  WORK-AREAS.

    10   LABEL-LINE-1 OCCURS 4 TIMES.
         20   NAME-TABLE         PIC X(20).
         20   FILLER             PIC X(10).
```

Now the line is set up as a table. The other lines would be defined the same way. Of course, using a table helps to do more than just simplify the definitions. The PROCEDURE DIVISION coding can be shortened considerably. Consider the following coding we can use because of tables:

```
READ INPUT-FILE
     AT END MOVE 'YES' TO EOF.
PERFORM 0400-SETUP-LOOP
        UNTIL EOF = 'YES'.
  : : :
  : : :
```

```
0400-SETUP-LOOP.

    MOVE 1 TO TABLE-SUBSCRIPT.
    PERFORM 0500-LOAD-TABLE.

    IF EOF NOT = 'YES'
        MOVE 2 TO TABLE-SUBSCRIPT
        PERFORM 0500-LOAD-TABLE

        IF EOF NOT = 'YES'
            MOVE 3 TO TABLE-SUBSCRIPT
            PERFORM 0500-LOAD-TABLE

            IF EOF NOT = 'YES'
                MOVE 4 TO TABLE-SUBSCRIPT
                PERFORM 0500-LOAD-TABLE.

    WRITE DETAIL-LINE FROM LABEL-LINE-1.
    WRITE DETAIL-LINE FROM LABEL-LINE-2.
    WRITE DETAIL-LINE FROM LABEL-LINE-3
        BEFORE ADVANCING 3 LINES.

    MOVE SPACES TO WORK-AREAS.

0500-LOAD-TABLE.

    MOVE NAME-IN    TO NAME-TABLE (TABLE-SUBSCRIPT).
    MOVE ADDRESS-IN TO ADDRESS-TABLE (TABLE-SUBSCRIPT).
    MOVE CITY-IN    TO CITY-TABLE (TABLE-SUBSCRIPT).
    MOVE STATE-IN   TO STATE-TABLE (TABLE-SUBSCRIPT).
    MOVE ZIP-IN     TO ZIP-TABLE (TABLE-SUBSCRIPT).
    READ INPUT-FILE
        AT END MOVE 'YES' TO EOF.
```

Without the use of tables, each PERFORM 0500-LOAD-TABLE statement would have been six statements, including the READ statement. We could not have used the performed procedure. And this is only printing four-across labels. This technique is useful for printing other items across the page—other routines with more than just four elements. Naturally, the more elements there are, the more coding can be saved.

Notice that we moved SPACES to the WORK-AREAS. This is necessary when the last group of labels is not full, which happens when the number of records is not evenly divisible by four. If we don't blank out all the lines, whichever label doesn't get new data moved in will end up displaying the data from the previous group of labels.

5-3-2 Searching for a Maximum and a Minimum Value

There are many times when we need to determine the largest or smallest value in a list of items. For example, we might have a list of quoted prices for a particular inventory item we need to purchase. Naturally we want to pay the least amount possible. Thus, we want to search the list to find the item with the smallest value—

the lowest cost. Let's suppose we have two tables, one with the names of companies that quoted prices and the other with the current price each company quoted for the item we need to order. The tables would be defined as

```
01  WORK-AREAS.

    10  INVENTORY-TABLE OCCURS 100 TIMES.
        20  COMPANY-TABLE              PIC X(20).
        20  COST-TABLE                PIC 9(6)V99.
```

To determine which of the costs in the COST-TABLE is the smallest, we need to use a field we will call MINIMUM-COST. We will load into it the largest possible value so that the first comparison will yield a value less than that. We will also define a field to store the name of the company that has the minimum cost:

```
    10  MINIMUM-COST      PIC 9(6)V99 VALUE 999999.99.
    10  COMPANY-NAME      PIC X(20).
```

Now, using this value, we will perform a search procedure:

```
        PERFORM 0400-TABLE-SEARCH
                VARYING SUBSCRIPT FROM 1 BY 1
                UNTIL SUBSCRIPT > 100.
        : : :
        : : :


0400-TABLE-SEARCH.
        IF MINIMUM-COST > COST-TABLE (SUBSCRIPT)
            MOVE COST-TABLE (SUBSCRIPT) TO MINIMUM-COST
            MOVE COMPANY-TABLE (SUBSCRIPT) TO COMPANY-NAME.
```

In the procedure, we compare the minimum cost field to the values in the table. If a value in the table is less than the value in the minimum cost field, that first value is moved to the minimum cost field. In addition, the corresponding company name is moved from the table to the special company name field. After the routine has examined all the fields in the table, the value in the minimum field will be the smallest.

A similar procedure could be used to find the maximum value in a list.

5-3-3 Using a Table for Accumulating Totals

Suppose a company has 25 different sales areas throughout the country, and we want to print a total of the sales for each of the different areas. But because the sales information for different areas comes in at different times and is entered into the file as it comes in, the file is not in sequence by sales areas. A table can be set up to handle this type of problem. Our file is set up as

```
    FD  SALES-IN
        LABEL RECORDS ARE OMITTED.
    01  SALES-RECORD.
        10  SALES-AREA           PIC XX.
        10  AMOUNT-OF-SALES      PIC 9(6)V99.
```

We need a table that will allow up to 25 different sales areas. You may have noticed that the sales areas that are read in are not numeric. That is, we cannot use the sales area to point to the table element we want to total into. We would prefer to use a setup like

```
ADD AMOUNT-OF-SALES TO TOTAL (SALES-AREA).
```

so that, if the SALES-AREA were 12, the program would add the AMOUNT-OF-SALES to the twelfth item in the table. But, since the SALES-AREA is non-numeric, we must instead set up two concurrent tables, one for the totals and one for the sales areas, which will be loaded with the areas codes:

```
01  WORK-AREAS

    10  AREA-CODES                          PIC X(50) VALUE
        'AABBCCDDEEFFGGHHIIJJKKLLMMNNOOPPQQRRSSTTUUVVWWXXYY'.
    10  AREA-TABLE REDEFINES AREA-CODES
                OCCURS 25 TIMES
                INDEXED BY AREA-INDEX  PIC XX.
    10  AREA-TOTALS OCCURS 25 TIMES         PIC 9(6)V99.
```

Now we need a procedure to read the data from the file and look up the input sales area in the AREA-TABLE. Then we can use the index of that element to point to the total element to add the amount into. The code would look like this:

```
        READ SALES-IN
            AT END MOVE 'YES' TO EOF.
        PERFORM 0500-TABLE-TOTAL
                UNTIL EOF = 'YES'.
        : : :
        : : :


0500-TABLE-TOTAL.

        SET AREA-INDEX TO 1.
        SEARCH AREA-TABLE
            AT END PERFORM 0900-ERROR-ROUTINE
            WHEN AREA-TABLE (AREA-INDEX) = SALES-AREA
            ADD AMOUNT-OF-SALES TO AREA-TOTAL (AREA-INDEX).
        : : :
        : : :
        READ SALES-IN
            AT END MOVE 'YES' TO EOF.
```

The 0500-TABLE-TOTAL routine may or may not have any additional code after the SEARCH statement. That will depend upon what the program is supposed to do. The code that is shown is all that is needed to search the table and add to the total fields.

5-4
Two-level Tables

As we said at the beginning of this chapter, there are many times when a single-level table is just not suitable for what we need to accomplish. A simple example of this is a tax table. To look up the amount of tax we owe, we look down a column of numbers that represents our income. When we find the appropriate number, we move across that row to the column for the type of filing we are doing. At the intersection of the row and the column is the amount of tax we owe. A sample tax table might look like the following (this is highly simplified, and any income over $46,000 must use another rate schedule that's calculated):

Income Range	Filing Type			
	Single	Married Filing Joint Return	Married Filing Separate Return	Head of Household
0– 1,999	0	0	0	0
2,000– 3,999	90	24	127	87
4,000– 7,999	445	325	512	405
8,000–12,999	877	642	1,045	840
13,000–18,999	1,609	1,205	1,906	1,443
19,000–28,999	2,978	2,300	3,709	2,765
29,000–45,999	5,518	4,876	7,006	5,818

Let's assume that the income we are going to tax is $17,432 and that we are filing single. We would look up the income in the first column (13,000–18,999), then move across that row to the "single" column (second column), and thus determine that we owe $1,609 in taxes.

Obviously the capability to look up something in this type of table is a powerful feature. Single-level tables are fine for simple applications, but for more complicated tasks, a two-level table can prove to be invaluable.

5-4-1 Defining a Two-level Table

Two-level tables can be conceptualized with a row–column setup as shown in the example above. That is, the rows are created with the amount and the individual entries are actually the column entries (or where the rows and columns intersect). This is the way conventional mathematics views arrays. The problem with this is that it's not really the way the data is stored in the computer. Computers store data in a linear fashion, one item after another. A mathematical picture of our previous table would be an array of seven rows of five columns, or a seven-by-five array. The one difficulty with this idea is that the first column of the tax table isn't a number but a range of numbers. However, it can be handled, since the income range indicates the row entries to be used when the income amount is below the low point of the next range. That is, our tax amount is to be found in the first row if our income is at or below 2,000. Thus, the first column of our array would be 2,000, 4,000, 8,000, and so on, as shown here:

2,000	0	0	0	0
4,000	90	24	127	87
8,000	445	325	512	405
13,000	877	642	1,045	840
19,000	1,609	1,205	1,906	1,443
29,000	2,978	2,300	3,709	2,765
46,000	5,518	4,876	7,006	5,818

The computer, however, will store all the data in a simple column (by rows), separated logically into groups:

Group 1
2,000
0
0
0
0

Group 2
4,000
90
24
127
87

Group 3
8,000
445
325
512
405

Group 4
13,000
877
642
1,045
840

Group 5
19,000
1,609
1,205
1,906
1,443

Group 6
29,000
2,978
2,300
3,709
2,765

Group 7
   46,000
    5,518
    4,876
    7,006
    5,818

This type of image is perfect for the storage definition COBOL uses. As we have seen, a table is defined on a level as an item. Well, a two-level table is defined as elementary items within a group table, or one level of table defined as an element of another table. To define the table we were just describing, we would set it up using an OCCURS on two levels, as in the following:

```
01   WORK-AREA.

   10   INCOME-GROUP   OCCURS 7 TIMES.
      20   TAX-TABLE OCCURS 5 TIMES        PIC 9(5).
```

Notice that we use an OCCURS clause on both the first subdefined level and the second but a PIC clause on only the second level. We are trying to set up a table with elementary table items grouped within another table level. Thus we define two OCCURS levels, but only the second level is defined with a PIC clause since this level contains the elementary items. This definition specifies that we have seven groups with five elementary items in each group, just like the linear layout we showed on page 258. An illustration of this table layout could look like the following (continued on page 260):

INCOME-GROUP (1)	TAX-TABLE (1) TAX-TABLE (2) TAX-TABLE (3) TAX-TABLE (4) TAX-TABLE (5)
INCOME-GROUP (2)	TAX-TABLE (1) TAX-TABLE (2) TAX-TABLE (3) TAX-TABLE (4) TAX-TABLE (5)
INCOME-GROUP (3)	TAX-TABLE (1) TAX-TABLE (2) TAX-TABLE (3) TAX-TABLE (4) TAX-TABLE (5)
INCOME-GROUP (4)	TAX-TABLE (1) TAX-TABLE (2) TAX-TABLE (3) TAX-TABLE (4) TAX-TABLE (5)

	TAX-TABLE (1)
INCOME-GROUP (5)	TAX-TABLE (1) TAX-TABLE (2) TAX-TABLE (3) TAX-TABLE (4) TAX-TABLE (5)
INCOME-GROUP (6)	TAX-TABLE (1) TAX-TABLE (2) TAX-TABLE (3) TAX-TABLE (4) TAX-TABLE (5)
INCOME-GROUP (7)	TAX-TABLE (1) TAX-TABLE (2) TAX-TABLE (3) TAX-TABLE (4) TAX-TABLE (5)

The labeling of this example is not quite correct, because it was meant not as program usage but only to illustrate the way the table is laid out. First, when using a two-level COBOL table correctly, we reference only the elementary items; the labeling of INCOME-GROUP (X) is not correct because we should not reference the group level. Second, the labeling of the elementary items of TAX-TABLE is not proper either. If we were to use the single subscript reference shown, the computer would not be able to determine which of the seven groups the particular elementary item was in. Thus, we must use two subscripts, such as TAX-TABLE (1, 3), which would represent the third item in the first group (group 1, item 3).

We have a few simple rules to follow about two-level tables:

■   The field for the second-level OCCURS must be on a level subordinate to the field for the first OCCURS. In our example, TAX-TABLE is on the 20 level while INCOME-GROUP is on the 10 level.

■   The field-name used on the first level of the table is not accessible in our code (as we mentioned). We can only access, by subscript, the second-level field-name. That means that we access TAX-TABLE, not INCOME-AMOUNT. We can, however, access WORK-AREA to affect the entire table if we need to (in most compilers). For example, we can initialize the entire table by moving zeros to WORK-AREA.

■   As we pointed out, since this is a two-level table we must use two subscripts to access any element. Thus, to access any element in the table, we would use a specification such as TAX-TABLE (1, 4) which would yield the element in row 1, column 4.

■   The first subscript always refers to the first level that is defined in the table. In our example, the first subscript refers to the OCCURS defined with seven elements.

■   Subscripts must always be either positive integer literals or fields that contain positive integers. There can be no negative nor zero elements (with most compilers).

5-4-2 Loading a Two-level Table

As with one-level tables, we cannot use a VALUE clause to load data into a two-level table. We can use a REDEFINES clause to assign the data, but a two-level table is more often loaded from a file. To load the tax table we have been discussing, we would have to read the data out of the file and then move it into the table elements.

Remember that we defined the table as

```
01   WORK-AREA.

     10   INCOME-GROUP  OCCURS 7 TIMES.
          20   TAX-TABLE OCCURS 5 TIMES      PIC 9(5).
```

The file we need to read will be defined as

```
FD   TAX-FILE
     LABEL RECORDS ARE OMITTED.
01   TAX-RECORD.
     10   TAX-FIELD OCCURS 5 TIMES          PIC 9(5).
```

Each record in the file is set up with the appropriate number of data items to fill one row of the tax table. We would use a PERFORM . . . VARYING to load this file into the table, such as

```
PERFORM 0200-READ-FILE
        VARYING GROUP-SUBSCRIPT FROM 1 BY 1
        UNTIL GROUP-SUBSCRIPT > 7.
```

Within the 0200-READ-FILE procedure, coded below, we will read the file and then perform another procedure to put the data into the table. Notice that the READ statement has an error routine for the AT END clause. This is because, under normal circumstances, we will know exactly how much data is in our file; and should there not be enough to fill in the entire table, we will want to be notified with an error message. The routine is

```
0200-READ-FILE.

     READ TAX-FILE
          AT END PERFORM 0900-ERROR-ROUTINE.
     PERFORM 0500-LOAD-TABLE
             VARYING ITEM-SUBSCRIPT FROM 1 BY 1
             UNTIL ITEM-SUBSCRIPT > 5.
```

Notice that we have set up the first-level subscript as GROUP-SUBSCRIPT, simply because the first subscript is used to point to the group level of the table. The second subscript is the item within that group, so we call it ITEM-SUBSCRIPT. Now, to actually load the data into the table, we would use the procedure

```
0500-LOAD-TABLE.

     MOVE TAX-FIELD (ITEM-SUBSCRIPT) TO
          TAX-TABLE (GROUP-SUBSCRIPT, ITEM-SUBSCRIPT).
```

The entire procedure would be

```
PERFORM 0200-READ-FILE
        VARYING GROUP-SUBSCRIPT FROM 1 BY 1
        UNTIL GROUP-SUBSCRIPT > 7.


0200-READ-FILE.

    READ TAX-FILE
        AT END PERFORM 0900-ERROR-ROUTINE.
    PERFORM 0500-LOAD-TABLE
        VARYING ITEM-SUBSCRIPT FROM 1 BY 1
        UNTIL ITEM-SUBSCRIPT > 5.


0500-LOAD-TABLE.

    MOVE TAX-FIELD (ITEM-SUBSCRIPT) TO
        TAX-TABLE (GROUP-SUBSCRIPT, ITEM-SUBSCRIPT).
```

Let's look at the first two records read from the file to see how this procedure would load the data into the table:

Income Amount	Filing Type			
	Single	Married Filing Joint Return	Married Filing Separate Return	Head of Household
2,000	0	0	0	0
4,000	90	24	127	87

Now, the procedure starts by performing the 0200-READ-FILE routine. It reads the first record, loading the TAX-FIELD table with the first row of the above table as follows:

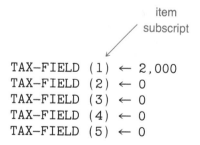

```
TAX-FIELD (1) ← 2,000
TAX-FIELD (2) ← 0
TAX-FIELD (3) ← 0
TAX-FIELD (4) ← 0
TAX-FIELD (5) ← 0
```

Then the 0200-READ-FILE routine performs the 0500-LOAD-TABLE five times, with the ITEM-SUBSCRIPT varying from 1 to 5. That means that the TAX-TABLE table will be loaded with the elements

```
      group                    item
    subscript                subscript

 TAX-TABLE (1, 1) ← TAX-FIELD (1) ← 2,000
 TAX-TABLE (1, 2) ← TAX-FIELD (2) ← 0
 TAX-TABLE (1, 3) ← TAX-FIELD (3) ← 0
 TAX-TABLE (1, 4) ← TAX-FIELD (4) ← 0
 TAX-TABLE (1, 5) ← TAX-FIELD (5) ← 0
```

After 0500-LOAD-TABLE has executed five times, ITEM-SUBSCRIPT will be 6 and the UNTIL condition will be satisfied. This will cause the 0200-READ-FILE routine to be completed, and control will return to the first PERFORM statement, which will increment the GROUP-SUBSCRIPT. Then 0200-READ-FILE will be performed again to load the second record from the file into the TAX-FIELD table:

```
                    item
                  subscript

 TAX-TABLE (1) ← 4,000
 TAX-TABLE (2) ← 90
 TAX-TABLE (3) ← 24
 TAX-TABLE (4) ← 127
 TAX-TABLE (5) ← 87
```

Again the 0500-LOAD-TABLE will be executed five times, causing TAX-FIELD elements to be moved into TAX-TABLE elements:

```
      group                    item
    subscript                subscript

 TAX-TABLE (2, 1) ← TAX-FIELD (1) ← 4,000
 TAX-TABLE (2, 2) ← TAX-FIELD (2) ← 90
 TAX-TABLE (2, 3) ← TAX-FIELD (3) ← 24
 TAX-TABLE (2, 4) ← TAX-FIELD (4) ← 127
 TAX-TABLE (2, 5) ← TAX-FIELD (5) ← 87
```

The rest of the table would be loaded in a like fashion.

5-4-3 Searching a Two-level Table

A search can be performed on a two-level table just as easily as on a one-level table. Since we are going to search, we need to modify our table definition to include an index:

```
01  WORK-AREA.

    10  INCOME-GROUP  OCCURS 7 TIMES
                      INDEXED BY GROUP-INDEX.
        20  TAX-TABLE OCCURS 5 TIMES
                      INDEXED BY ITEM-INDEX    PIC 9(5).
```

To search this table requires that we search the lowest level, TAX-TABLE. We will set up a routine to read a client record, get the gross pay, and look that pay up in the table to determine its group level on the tax table. We determine the item within the table group using a marital status code in the record—1 for single, 2 for married filing joint return, 3 for married filing separate return, and 4 for head of household. Our routine would look like the following:

```
READ PAYROLL-FILE
     AT END MOVE 'YES' TO EOF.
PERFORM 0200-PAYROLL-READ
     UNTIL EOF = 'YES'.
: : :
: : :


0200-PAYROLL-READ.

SET GROUP-INDEX TO 1.
ADD 1 TO MARITAL-STATUS GIVING STATUS-CODE.
SEARCH TAX-TABLE
     AT END PERFORM 0900-ERROR-ROUTINE
     WHEN TAX-TABLE (GROUP-INDEX, 1) > TAXABLE-INCOME
     MOVE TAX-TABLE (GROUP-INDEX, STATUS-CODE) TO AMOUNT-OF-TAX.
: : :
: : :
READ PAYROLL-FILE
     AT END MOVE 'YES' TO EOF.
```

This routine will read the payroll file and then search the table, starting the item index at 1. Notice that we don't search the entire table, only item 1 in each group. That's because item 1 is where the income amount is found. After the table entry is greater than the income from the record, we use that group index to indicate the group, while the marital status points to the particular item entry within that group. We have to add 1 to the marital status because the table items for the marital status start with item 2 while the marital status codes are 1 through 4. The amount of the tax is then moved to another field that we will use later in the routine. Naturally, the last thing in the routine is the reading of the file.

5-5

An Example of a Two-level Table

The tax table example is useful because it covers most of the techniques involved in using tables, but to get an in-depth understanding it is important to see several different ways of using tables. Otherwise it can be difficult to picture just how to use a table for a certain application. The following example shows several different methods of handling a two-level table.

Frequently, data would be perfect for a table application, but will not be all the same. Remember that to be put into a table, all the data must be of the same type—all non-numeric or all numeric and the same length. Take a student grading system, for example. We might have a setup like the following:

Student Name	Exam 1	Exam 2	Exam 3	Exam 4
Ed Coburn	50	75	78	69
Sam Jones	89	96	99	87
Sara Smith	80	75	89	92
Fred Harrison	89	88	79	85
(table continues for many other students)				

We want to be able to store all the grades in a table so that we may display them on the screen. We would also like to be able to search the table for things like the maximum or minimum grade on a particular exam and the grades for a particular student. Setting up this table so that we can access the data by the student name as well as by any of the grades is not as difficult as it might sound. We simply set up two tables—one a one-level and the other a two-level.

We can set up the tables two different ways. The most obvious would be this:

```
01   WORK-AREAS.

     10   NAME-TABLE OCCURS 100 TIMES
                   INDEXED BY NAME-INDEX PIC X(20).
     10   GRADES-TABLE OCCURS 100 TIMES
                   INDEXED BY GROUP-INDEX.
          20   TABLE-OF-GRADES OCCURS 4 TIMES
                      INDEXED BY ITEM-INDEX PIC 999.
```

This structure would store the data in memory—the names first and then the grades. The memory would look like the following (there would be first 100 names and then 100 student groups):

Ed Coburn Sam Jones Sara Smith Fred Harrison	all the names (100 of them, actually)
050 075 078 069	grades for the first student
089 096 099 087	grades for the second student
080 075 089 092	grades for the third student
089 088 079 085	grades for the fourth student

To use this setup to search for a record by name, we would have to search the NAME-TABLE and then move the NAME-INDEX into the GROUP-INDEX so we could access that particular group in the TABLE-OF-GRADES table.

Another way to set it up for easier access would be this:

```
01  WORK-AREAS.

    10  GRADES-TABLE OCCURS 100 TIMES
                    INDEXED BY GROUP-INDEX.
        20  NAME-TABLE                   PIC X(20).
        20  TABLE-OF-GRADES OCCURS 4 TIMES
                        INDEXED BY ITEM-INDEX PIC 999.
```

This setup would put all the names in front of their respective grades:

Ed Coburn 050 075 078 069	name and grades for the first student
Sam Jones 089 096 099 087	name and grades for the second student
Sara Smith 080 075 089 092	name and grades for the third student
Fred Harrison 089 088 079 085	name and grades for the fourth student

This structure will set up NAME-TABLE as a one-level table and allow the program to access it with GROUP-INDEX. When the name is found in NAME-TABLE, we can simply use the GROUP-INDEX to point to the row that contains the grade we need.

How do we load the data from a file into this table? The technique is virtually the same as the one for the tax table, except that now we have to manipulate the single-level table as well as the two-level table.

Since each student record must have a name with four grades, we could set up the file like this:

```
FD  GRADES-FILE
    LABEL RECORDS ARE OMITTED.
01  GRADES-RECORD.
    20  NAME-IN                      PIC X(20).
    20  GRADES-IN OCCURS 4 TIMES     PIC 999.
```

Then, to read the file into the other tables, we would use the following code (0800-NOT-ENOUGH-RECORDS is an error routine):

```
    READ GRADES-FILE
        AT END PERFORM 0800-NOT-ENOUGH-RECORDS.
    PERFORM 0300-LOAD-TABLE
        VARYING GROUP-INDEX FROM 1 BY 1
        UNTIL GROUP-INDEX > 100.
    : : :
    : : :


0300-LOAD-TABLE.

    MOVE NAME-IN TO NAME-TABLE (GROUP-INDEX).
    PERFORM 0400-LOAD-GRADES
        VARYING ITEM-INDEX FROM 1 BY 1
        UNTIL ITEM-INDEX > 4.
    READ GRADES-FILE
        AT END PERFORM 0800-NOT-ENOUGH-RECORDS.


0400-LOAD-GRADES.

    MOVE GRADES-IN (ITEM-INDEX) TO
        TABLE-OF-GRADES (GROUP-INDEX, ITEM-INDEX).
```

Since the NAME-TABLE is a one-level table, we simply use the GROUP-INDEX as the pointer into the table because it points to the element where the data should be stored. Then we perform another routine in which the grades that were read in are loaded into the grades table using both the group index and the item index.

Once the data is in the table, there is a lot we can do with it. One thing that we said we want to be able to do is display the data for a particular student. The code to allow this would look like the following:

```
DISPLAY 'WHAT IS THE STUDENT NAME YOU WANT TO DISPLAY?'.
DISPLAY '********************'.
ACCEPT STUDENT-NAME.
PERFORM 0600-SEARCH-FOR-NAME.
DISPLAY 'STUDENT NAME .... ' NAME-TABLE (GROUP-INDEX).
DISPLAY ' '.
DISPLAY 'EXAM 1 GRADE  ... ' TABLE-OF-GRADES (GROUP-INDEX, 1).
DISPLAY 'EXAM 2 GRADE  ... ' TABLE-OF-GRADES (GROUP-INDEX, 2).
DISPLAY 'EXAM 3 GRADE  ... ' TABLE-OF-GRADES (GROUP-INDEX, 3).
DISPLAY 'EXAM 4 GRADE  ... ' TABLE-OF-GRADES (GROUP-INDEX, 4).
: : :
: : :


0600-SEARCH-FOR-NAME.

    SET GROUP-INDEX TO 1.
    SEARCH GRADES-TABLE
        AT END PERFORM 0900-ERROR-ROUTINE
        WHEN NAME-TABLE (GROUP-INDEX) = NAME-IN
        NEXT SENTENCE.
```

The display of the data, while not very fancy, is functional. If this were the actual program, we would create some type of heading for the display, and, of course, there would be more program following the display of the data. Notice that, in the SEARCH statement, our only objective was to find the particular group the student was in. Thus, there was nothing that the routine needed to do and we just used the NEXT SENTENCE.

Another thing we might want to search for using this table setup is the maximum or minimum score for a particular exam. Let's try to create a routine for displaying the maximum score for each exam and the name of the student who had the score.

The easiest way to do this is to find the maximum score for each exam and then store the group pointer for that score. That way we can get the score and the student name. We will have to store the pointer in order to create one routine to look up all four scores. Otherwise, we would have to have four routines, one for each exam.

To begin with, we will need one field to hold the maximum value and one to hold the index (put in our WORK-AREAS):

```
10   MAXIMUM-VALUE          PIC 999.
10   MAXIMUM-GROUP          PIC 999.
```

Now we will need a routine to look up the scores. Notice that we are traversing the table through the items and then the groups. Typically a table is traversed the other way around. It generally doesn't matter which way you travel if you are searching the entire table. Since we are looking for the maximum value of a particular exam and the exams are related to the item number, not the group number, we have to change the item number only after we have examined that item in each group. The routine is

```
     DISPLAY 'THE MAXIMUM GRADES FOR THE EXAMS ARE:'.
     DISPLAY ' '.
     PERFORM 0700-COUNTER-LOOP
             VARYING ITEM-COUNTER FROM 1 BY 1
             UNTIL ITEM-COUNTER > 4.
     : : :
     : : :

0700-COUNTER-LOOP.
     SET ITEM-INDEX TO ITEM-COUNTER.
     MOVE ZERO TO MAXIMUM-VALUE.
     PERFORM 0800-LOOK-UP-ROUTINE
             VARYING GROUP-COUNTER FROM 1 BY 1
             UNTIL GROUP-COUNTER > 100.
     SET GROUP-INDEX TO MAXIMUM-GROUP.
     DISPLAY 'THE MAXIMUM SCORE FOR EXAM ' ITEM-COUNTER ' IS '
             TABLE-OF-GRADES (GROUP-INDEX, ITEM-INDEX) ' AND THE '
             'STUDENT WHO HAD IT IS ' NAME-TABLE (GROUP-INDEX) '.'.
     DISPLAY ' '.
```

```
0800-LOOK-UP-ROUTINE.

    SET GROUP-INDEX TO GROUP-COUNTER.
    IF MAXIMUM-VALUE < TABLE-OF-GRADES (GROUP-INDEX, ITEM-INDEX)
       MOVE GROUP-COUNTER TO MAXIMUM-GROUP
       MOVE TABLE-OF-GRADES (GROUP-INDEX, ITEM-INDEX) TO MAXIMUM-VALUE.
```

You may have noted that this routine uses a few statements that may seem unnecessary. Why, for example, do we perform the loop varying GROUP-COUNTER and then set the GROUP-INDEX to the value of GROUP-COUNTER? Why not just use GROUP-INDEX in the routine and forget the GROUP-COUNTER? Well, as it turns out, since GROUP-INDEX is, in fact, an index, we have to handle it carefully. You already know that we can't move a value to an index, but most computers will not allow us to move an index value to another field either. Also, in the 0700-COUNTER-LOOP we need to display the item pointer. We could have just used ITEM-INDEX, but, once again, most computers will not allow us to use an index in a DISPLAY statement. Thus, we had to use a different field as a sort of dummy counter, just to circumvent the techniques that the computer would not allow. Finally, we need to use the MAXIMUM-GROUP for the row pointer in the DISPLAY statement. This time we are restricted to using only indexes as the subscripts. We had to move MAXIMUM-GROUP to the GROUP-INDEX so we could use it as a subscript. Such extra coding is not especially difficult; it's just a bit clumsy.

The final possibility we will explore using this table is searching for the highest (or lowest) score on any of the exams. We will construct a routine that will determine the highest score, the exam it was scored on, and the student who made the score.

To accomplish this, we will need to retain not only the group pointer but the item pointer as well. Therefore we need another field:

```
    10  MAXIMUM-ITEM           PIC 999.
```

Our code will look like the following one (notice that we once again traverse the table by changing the item index first, and we use the extra item and group counters):

```
MOVE ZERO TO MAXIMUM-VALUE.
PERFORM 1000-MAXIMUM-SEARCH
        VARYING ITEM-COUNTER
        FROM 1 BY 1 UNTIL ITEM-COUNTER > 4.
SET ITEM-INDEX TO MAXIMUM-ITEM.
SET GROUP-INDEX TO MAXIMUM-GROUP.
DISPLAY 'THE MAXIMUM SCORE ON ALL EXAMS WAS '
        TABLE-OF-GRADES (GROUP-INDEX, ITEM-INDEX)
        ' ON EXAM NUMBER ' ITEM-INDEX
        ' AND THE STUDENT WHO GOT THE SCORE IS '
        NAME-TABLE (GROUP-INDEX).
    : : :
    : : :
```

```
1000-MAXIMUM-SEARCH.

    SET ITEM-INDEX TO ITEM-COUNTER.
    PERFORM 1100-GROUP-SEARCH
            VARYING GROUP-COUNTER FROM 1 BY 1
            UNTIL GROUP-COUNTER > 100.

1100-GROUP-SEARCH.

    SET GROUP-INDEX TO GROUP-COUNTER.
    IF MAXIMUM-VALUE < TABLE-OF-GRADES (GROUP-INDEX, ITEM-INDEX)
        MOVE GROUP-COUNTER TO MAXIMUM-GROUP
        MOVE ITEM-COUNTER TO MAXIMUM-ITEM
        MOVE TABLE-OF-GRADES (GROUP-INDEX, ITEM-INDEX) TO MAXIMUM-VALUE.
```

5-6
Multi-level Tables

Thus far we have discussed tables with one and two levels. Most COBOL compilers also allow tables with three levels, and the 1985 standard allows for tables with up to seven levels.

In **multi-level tables**, the COBOL description of tables becomes ever more important. A mathematical description of a two-dimensional array is visualized as a simple flat table with rows and columns and two subscripts:

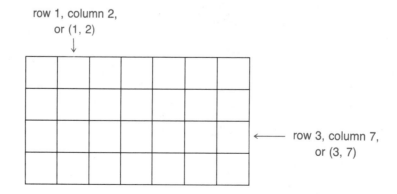

COBOL modifies this description into a table of groups and items:

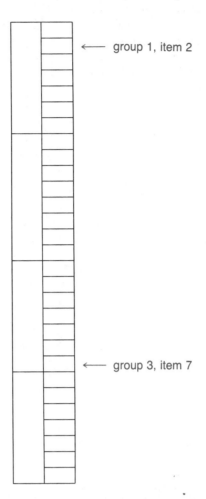

With a mathematical approach, a three-level table can be visualized as a series of these flat tables stacked on top of each other. A reference to individual elements requires three subscripts (the third level, depth, is sometimes referred to as the page, as in pages of a book, so you have subscripts of page, row, column):

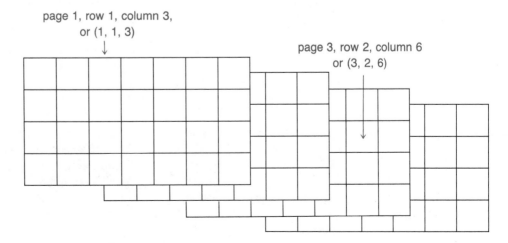

This type of definition may be fine for three dimensions, but what of a fourth or a fifth dimension? As we mentioned, COBOL 1985 allows tables with up to seven levels. How would you picture a table with seven dimensions? Well, the way we have described a table, the explanation can easily be expanded to any number of levels. A three-level table simply uses elementary items inside one group that is subordinate to another group. A table that is defined as

```
01   WORK-AREAS.

     10   LEVEL-1            OCCURS 3 TIMES.
          20   LEVEL-2       OCCURS 2 TIMES.
               30   ITEMS-LEVEL OCCURS 4 TIMES PIC 9(5).
```

would look like this:

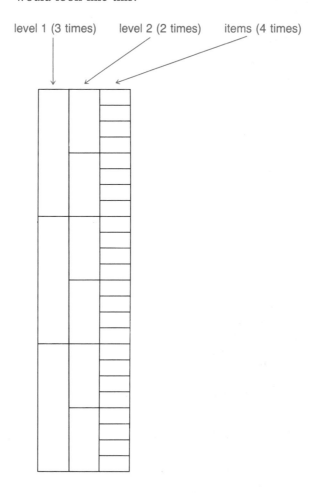

This could easily be expanded into more levels if necessary.

As an example of how to set up and access a three-level table, assume we have a company with five different manufacturing plants. Since all the plants are constructed basically the same way, each has eight different warehouses for storage of raw materials, works-in-progress, and finished goods. The inventory is broken down into 127 categories: 13 raw materials, 94 works-in-progress, and 20 finished goods.

To visualize how a table would be set up to hold all this data, think of the five plants as level 1. Level 2 would be the eight warehouses at each plant, and the categories would be the items since they are the most elementary. Thus, our table should be laid out like this:

```
01  WORK-AREAS.

    10   PLANT-TABLE             OCCURS 5 TIMES
                                 INDEXED BY LEVEL-1-IDX.
         20   WAREHOUSE-TABLE    OCCURS 8 TIMES
                                 INDEXED BY LEVEL-2-IDX.
              30   CATEGORY-TABLE OCCURS 127 TIMES
                                 INDEXED BY ITEM-IDX PIC 9(6).
```

Just as when we use two-level tables, each successive subscript requires a different OCCURS level on a lower level (higher-level number). This table defines 5080 storage locations in memory (5 * 8 * 127). In order to access the data in the table, we must use the lowest level field-name; in this case, we would access CATEGORY-TABLE. Since it is a three-level table we must use three subscripts; the first would refer to the plant, the second to the warehouse, and the third to the category. Thus (3, 4, 27) would refer to plant 3, warehouse 4, category 27.

Now let's experiment with how to access this table. We want to display on the screen the total amount of any category throughout all the plants and warehouses. This capability would be useful for determining when a particular raw material would need to be reordered for distribution throughout all the plants, when there are too many of a particular work-in-progress item, or when there are enough warehoused finished goods of a particular product for production to be temporarily halted.

To get this total, we will need a field to total into and a category to search for (the item number needed):

```
    10   TOTAL-FIELD            PIC 9(8).
    10   CATEGORY               PIC 9(3).
```

In the PROCEDURE DIVISION we will begin by prompting the user for the particular category of interest:

```
    DISPLAY 'WHAT CATEGORY DO YOU WANT TO TOTAL?'.
    DISPLAY '###'.
    ACCEPT CATEGORY.
```

Then we will need to move through the various plants and warehouses, totaling up the particular category by first performing a loop to vary the plant subscript (LEVEL-1-IDX). After the program comes back from this (the outermost loop) PERFORM, we will be ready to display the total:

```
PERFORM 0300-PLANT-LOOP
        VARYING LEVEL-1-IDX FROM 1 BY 1
        UNTIL LEVEL-1-IDX > 5.
DISPLAY 'THE TOTAL OF CATEGORY ' CATEGORY ' IS ' TOTAL-FIELD.
:::
:::
```

Then, in the plant loop we will perform another loop varying the warehouse subscript (LEVEL-2-IDX):

```
0300-PLANT-LOOP.

    PERFORM 0400-WAREHOUSE-LOOP
            VARYING LEVEL-2-IDX FROM 1 BY 1
            UNTIL LEVEL-2-IDX > 8.
```

In the warehouse loop we will need to total up the particular category. This loop (one statement, actually) will function 40 times since it will run through all eight warehouses in each of the five plants:

```
0400-WAREHOUSE-LOOP.

    ADD CATEGORY-TABLE (LEVEL-1-IDX, LEVEL-2-IDX, CATEGORY)
        TO TOTAL-FIELD.
```

This entire procedure would look like the following:

```
DISPLAY 'WHAT CATEGORY DO YOU WANT TO TOTAL?'.
DISPLAY '###'.
ACCEPT CATEGORY.

PERFORM 0300-PLANT-LOOP
        VARYING LEVEL-1-IDX FROM 1 BY 1
        UNTIL LEVEL-1-IDX > 5.
DISPLAY 'THE TOTAL OF CATEGORY ' CATEGORY ' IS ' TOTAL-FIELD.
:::
:::


0300-PLANT-LOOP.

    PERFORM 0400-WAREHOUSE-LOOP
            VARYING LEVEL-2-IDX FROM 1 BY 1
            UNTIL LEVEL-2-IDX > 8.


0400-WAREHOUSE-LOOP.

    ADD CATEGORY-TABLE (LEVEL-1-IDX, LEVEL-2-IDX, CATEGORY)
        TO TOTAL-FIELD.
```

Another thing this particular table might be useful for is even distribution of materials. Suppose that one warehouse has received a new shipment of raw materials but has nowhere to store it. We would need to determine which warehouse has the smallest amount of that particular raw material so we could transfer some of it. To do this, we would need one field to keep track of the minimum amount, one for the category to be searched, and one for each of the levels where the entry is found. Also, we will need extra counters to handle the indexes:

```
         10   LEVEL-1-CTR              PIC 9.
         10   LEVEL-2-CTR              PIC 9.
         10   MINIMUM-VALUE            PIC 9(6).
         10   CATEGORY                 PIC 9(3).
         10   MIN-LEVEL-1              PIC 9(3).
         10   MIN-LEVEL-2              PIC 9(3).
```

Then we will have to prompt the user for the category:

```
         DISPLAY 'WHAT CATEGORY DO YOU WANT THE MINIMUM OF?'.
         DISPLAY '###'.
         ACCEPT CATEGORY.
         SET ITEM-INDEX TO CATEGORY.
```

Now we will need a routine to search for the lowest value:

```
MOVE 999999 TO MINIMUM-VALUE.
PERFORM 0600-PLANT-LOOP-2
        VARYING LEVEL-1-CTR FROM 1 BY 1
        UNTIL LEVEL-1-CTR > 5.
DISPLAY 'THE EXCESS MATERIAL SHOULD BE TRANSFERRED TO '
        'WAREHOUSE NUMBER ' MIN-LEVEL-2 ' AT PLANT NUMBER '
        MIN-LEVEL-1.
: : :
: : :

0600-PLANT-LOOP-2.

    SET LEVEL-1-IDX TO LEVEL-1-CTR.
    PERFORM 0700-WAREHOUSE-LOOP-2
            VARYING LEVEL-2-CTR FROM 1 BY 1
            UNTIL LEVEL-2-CTR > 8.

0700-WAREHOUSE-LOOP-2.

    SET LEVEL-2-IDX TO LEVEL-2-CTR.
    IF MINIMUM-VALUE > CATEGORY-TABLE (LEVEL-1-IDX, LEVEL-2-IDX, ITEM-IDX)
       MOVE LEVEL-2-CTR  TO LEVEL-2-ROW
       MOVE LEVEL-1-CTR TO MIN-LEVEL-1
       MOVE CATEGORY-TABLE (LEVEL-1-IDX, LEVEL-2-IDX, ITEM-IDX)
            TO MINIMUM-VALUE.
```

5-7

The Record Rack Interactive Inventory

Since *The Record Rack* has installed a few interactive terminals, Roger Barnell has decided he would like to have access to the amount of sales made by his staff in each of the five product categories, as shown by the file layout in Figure 5-1.

SALES File					
Field Description	*Position*	*Length*	:	*Dec*	*Type*
Salesman number	1–4	4	:		Non-numeric
Salesman name	5–24	20	:		Non-numeric
Filler	25–26	2	:		Non-numeric
Commission rate	27–28	2	:	0	Numeric
Sales of product 1	29–35	7	:	2	Numeric
Sales of product 2	36–42	7	:	2	Numeric
Sales of product 3	43–49	7	:	2	Numeric
Sales of product 4	50–56	7	:	2	Numeric
Sales of product 5	57–63	7	:	2	Numeric
Years of service	64–65	2	:	0	Numeric
Filler	66–80	15	:		Non-numeric
Record Length = 80					

Figure 5-1   The record layout for the SALES file.

Each of the sales figures is sales year-to-date. Roger explains to Cindy that he wants to be able to access the data in the following ways:

■ display the sales for a particular salesman, including the commission paid;
■ display the total sales for all the products by all the salesmen, including the total commissions paid;
■ display the largest and smallest amounts of sales for any of the five product groups, the total commissions paid, and the salesmen involved.

To generate these various displays, Cindy designed the display shown in Figure 5-2 for the main menu to access the various options of the program. Figure 5-3 is the display for the individual salesman, Figure 5-4 is the display for the total sales for all products, and Figure 5-5 is the display for the maximum and minimum sales amounts. Figure 5-6 shows the system chart for the program.

Cindy's pseudocode design for the program follows. The flowchart can be seen in Figure 5-7.

```
Start
Open file
Input record from file at end EOF
Initialize group counter
DO-WHILE not EOF
        Store record in table using group counter
        Input record from file at end EOF
        Increment group counter
END-DO
Display main menu and prompt for option
Input response
DO-WHILE response not = 9
        IF response = 1 or 2 THEN
                Do salesman routine
```

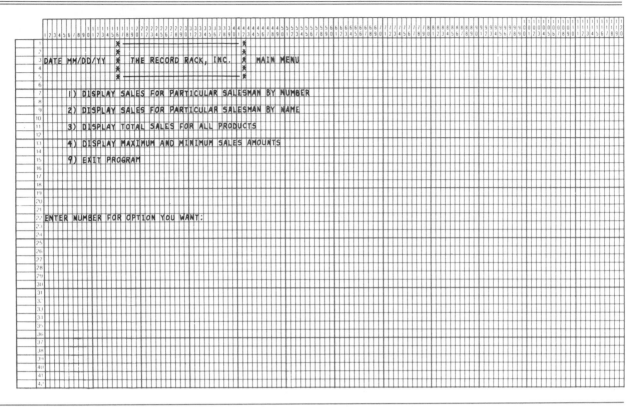

Figure 5-2   Display of the main menu.

ELSE IF response = 3 THEN
        Do total sales routine
ELSE IF response = 4 THEN
        Prompt for product number
        Input product number
        DO-WHILE product number > 5 or < 0
                Display error message
                Prompt for product number
                Input product number
        END-DO
        Do maximum and minimum sales routine
ELSE
        Display error message
END-IF
Display main menu and prompt for option
Input response
END-DO

Start salesman routine
IF response = 1 THEN
        Display prompt for salesman number
        Input number
        Search table using number

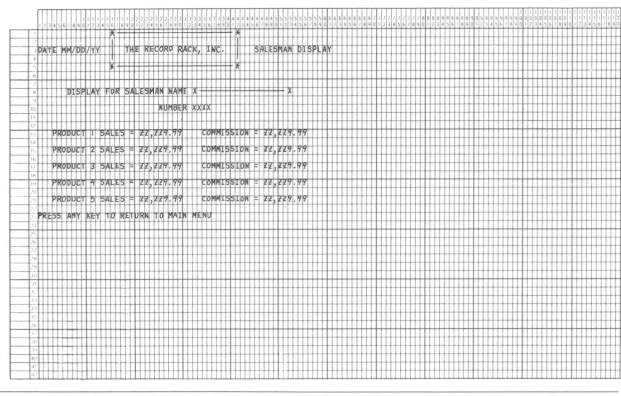

Figure 5-3   Display of the salesman record.

```
                    DO-WHILE search not found
                         Display error message
                         Display prompt for salesman number
                         Input number
                         Search table using number
                    END-DO
               ELSE
                    Display prompt for salesman name
                    Input name
                    Search table using name
                    DO-WHILE search not found
                         Display error message
                         Display prompt for salesman name
                         Input name
                         Search table using name
                    END-DO
               END-IF
               Display data and prompt (any key)
               Accept any key
               End routine
```

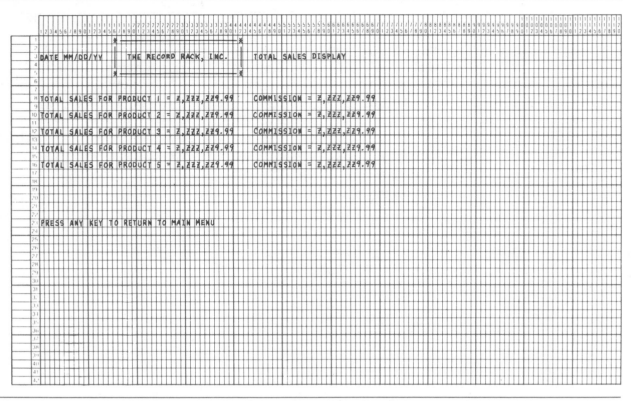

Figure 5-4   Display of the total sales.

Start total sales routine
Initialize group counter to 1
DO-WHILE group counter < 21 (number of records)
    Initialize item counter to 1
    DO-WHILE item counter < 6
        Add product sales amount (group, item) total
        Calculate commission amount
        Add commission to commission total
        Increment item counter by 1
    END-DO
    Display total of product and commission
    Increment group counter by 1
END-DO
Display continuation prompt
Input any key
End routine

Start maximum and minimum sales routine
Initialize minimum and maximum fields
DO-WHILE group counter < 21 (number of records)
    IF sales amount (group, product) < minimum THEN
        Move sales amount (group, product) to minimum
        Calculate commission amount
        Save group number

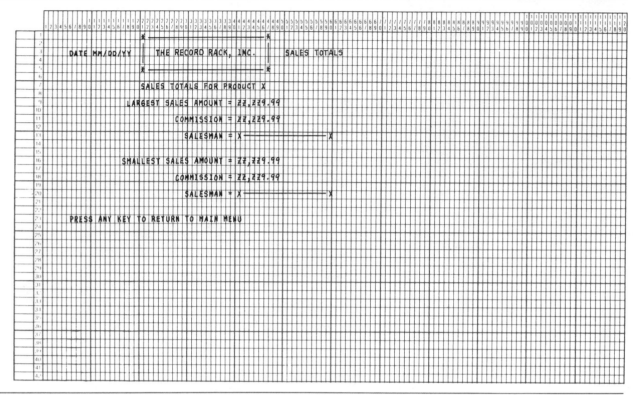

Figure 5-5   Display of the largest and smallest sales amounts.

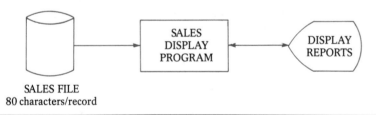

Figure 5-6   The systems chart for *The Record Rack* program.

```
                ELSE IF sales amount (group, product) > maximum THEN
                        Move sales amount (group, product) to maximum
                        Calculate commission amount
                        Save group number
                (ELSE)
                END-IF
                Increment group counter by 1
        END-DO
        Display sales data using group number for salesman name
        Display continuation prompt
        Input any key
        End routine
```

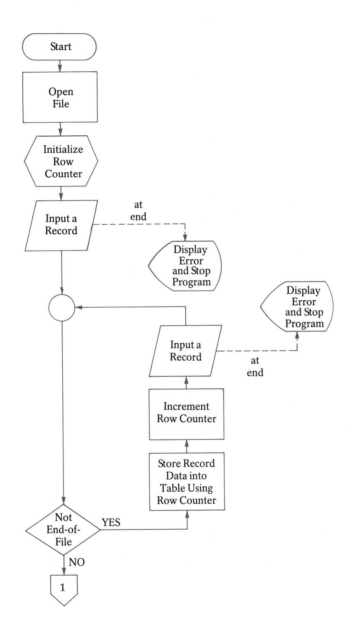

Figure 5-7   The flowchart for *The Record Rack* program.

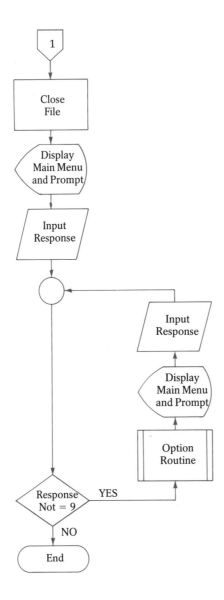

Figure 5-7 (continued)

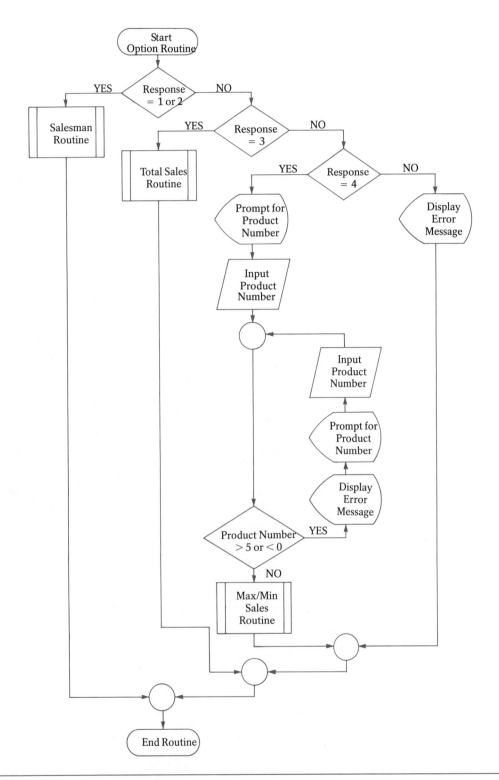

Figure 5-7 (continued)

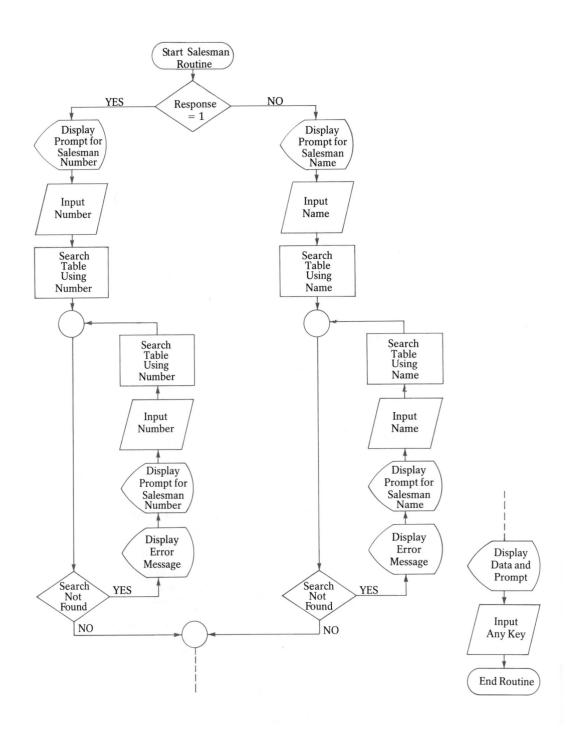

Figure 5-7 **(continued)**

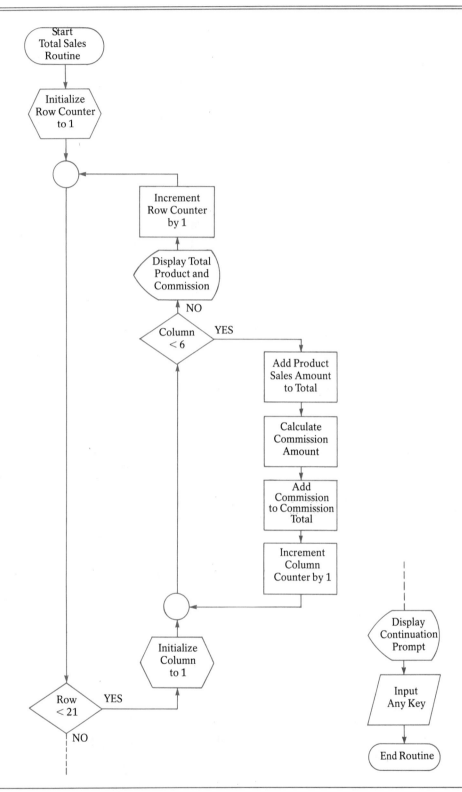

Figure 5-7 **(continued)**

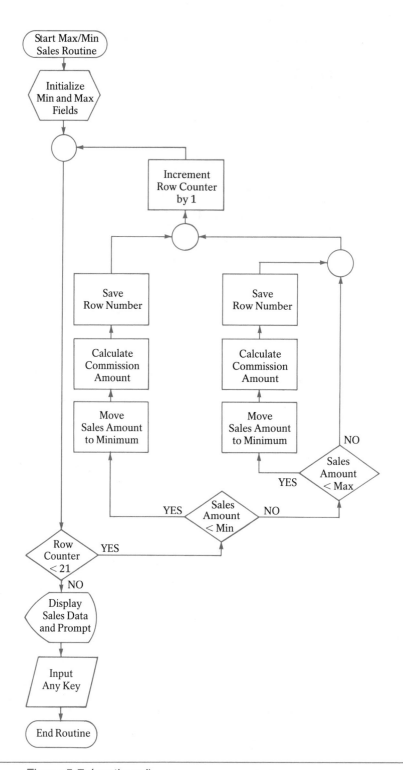

Figure 5-7 (continued)

Cindy's program:

```
****************************************************************
****************************************************************
*
*
*
*   PROGRAM NAME: SALE-DSP
*
*   PROGRAMMER NAME:  CINDY HARRISON
*
*   SOCIAL SECURITY NUMBER:  999-99-9999
*
*   DUE DATE: FEBRUARY 10, 1988
*
*   DESCRIPTION: THIS PROGRAM WILL DISPLAY VARIOUS LISTS OF
*                THE SALESMAN DATA ON THE SCREEN.
*
*
*
****************************************************************
****************************************************************

    IDENTIFICATION DIVISION.
    PROGRAM-ID.    SALE-DSP.
    AUTHOR.        CINDY HARRISON.

    ENVIRONMENT DIVISION.

    CONFIGURATION SECTION.
    SOURCE-COMPUTER. IBM-4331.
    OBJECT-COMPUTER. IBM-4331.

    INPUT-OUTPUT SECTION.
    FILE-CONTROL.
        SELECT SALES-FILE ASSIGN TO UT-S-SALES.

    DATA DIVISION.
    FILE SECTION.

    FD  SALES-FILE
        LABEL RECORDS ARE OMITTED
        RECORD CONTAINS 80 CHARACTERS.
    01  SALES-RECORD.
        05    SALES-NUMBER              PIC XXXX.
        05    SALES-NAME                PIC X(20).
        05    FILLER                    PIC XX.
        05    COMMISSION                PIC V99.
        05    PRODUCTS OCCURS 5 TIMES   PIC 9(5)V99.
        05    YEARS-OF-SERVICE          PIC 99.
        05    FILLER                    PIC X(15).
```

```
WORKING-STORAGE SECTION.

01  WORK-AREAS.

    05   SALES-TABLE OCCURS 20 TIMES INDEXED BY ROW-IDX.
         10   SALESMAN-NUMBER      PIC XXXX.
         10   SALESMAN-NAME        PIC X(20).
         10   SALES-COMMISSION     PIC V99.
         10   SALES-PRODUCTS OCCURS 5 TIMES
                            INDEXED BY COLUMN-IDX PIC 9(5)V99.

    05   MAXIMUM                  PIC 9(5)V99.
    05   MINIMUM                  PIC 9(5)V99.
    05   SAVE-MAXIMUM-GROUP       PIC 99.
    05   SAVE-MINIMUM-GROUP       PIC 99.
    05   GROPU-CTR                PIC 99.

    05   PRODUCT-TOTAL            PIC 9(7)V99.
    05   COMMISSION-TOTAL         PIC 9(7)V99.
    05   CALC-COMMISSION          PIC 9(5)V99.

    05   OPTION                   PIC X.
    05   ANY-KEY                  PIC X.
    05   ANY-KEY-N REDEFINES ANY-KEY PIC 9.
    05   LOOP-COUNTER             PIC 9.
    05   FOUND                    PIC XXX.

    05   DISPLAY-PRODUCT          PIC ZZ,ZZ9.99.
    05   DISPLAY-COMMISSION       PIC ZZ,ZZ9.99.
    05   DISPLAY-PRODUCT-TOTAL    PIC Z,ZZZ,ZZ9.99.
    05   DISPLAY-COMM-TOTAL       PIC Z,ZZZ,ZZ9.99.

    05   DATE-IN                  PIC X(6).
    05   DATE-WORK REDEFINES DATE-IN.
         10   DATE-YY             PIC XX.
         10   DATE-MM             PIC XX.
         10   DATE-DD             PIC XX.

    05   HEADING-DATE.
         10   HEADING-MONTH       PIC XX.
         10   HEADING-DAY         PIC /XX/.
         10   HEADING-YEAR        PIC XX.

    05   HEADING-INFO             PIC X(19).

PROCEDURE DIVISION.

0100-MAIN-MODULE.

    OPEN INPUT SALES-FILE.

    ACCEPT DATE-IN FROM DATE.
    MOVE DATE-YY TO HEADING-YEAR.
    MOVE DATE-MM TO HEADING-MONTH.
    MOVE DATE-DD TO HEADING-DAY.
```

```
READ SALES-FILE
    AT END PERFORM 1000-ERROR-ROUTINE.
PERFORM 0200-READ-FILE
        VARYING GROUP-IDX FROM 1 BY 1
        UNTIL GROUP-IDX > 20.

CLOSE SALES-FILE.

PERFORM 0150-INITIAL-ENTRY
        UNTIL OPTION = '9'.

STOP RUN.


0150-INITIAL-ENTRY.

    MOVE 'MAIN MENU' TO HEADING-INFO.
    PERFORM 0300-HEADING-ROUTINE.

    DISPLAY '      1) DISPLAY SALES FOR PARTICULAR SALESMAN '
        'BY NUMBER'.
    DISPLAY ' '.
    DISPLAY '      2) DISPLAY SALES FOR PARTICULAR SALESMAN '
        'BY NAME'.
    DISPLAY ' '.
    DISPLAY '      3) DISPLAY TOTAL SALES FOR ALL PRODUCTS'.
    DISPLAY ' '.
    DISPLAY '      4) DISPLAY MAXIMUM AND MINIMUM SALES AMOUNTS'.
    DISPLAY ' '.
    DISPLAY '      9) EXIT PROGRAM'.
    PERFORM 1500-BLANK-LINE 6 TIMES.
    DISPLAY 'ENTER NUMBER FOR OPTION YOU WANT:'.

    ACCEPT OPTION.

    IF OPTION = '1' OR '2'

        MOVE 'NO' TO FOUND
        PERFORM 0400-GET-SALESMAN
                UNTIL FOUND = 'YES'
        PERFORM 0300-HEADING-ROUTINE.
        DISPLAY ' '
        DISPLAY '        DISPLAY FOR SALESMAN NAME '
            SALESMAN-NAME (GROUP-IDX)
        DISPLAY ' '
        DISPLAY '                          NUMBER '
            SALESMAN-NUMBER (GROUP-IDX)
        DISPLAY ' '
        DISPLAY ' '

        PERFORM 0500-DISPLAY-PRODUCT VARYING
                LOOP-COUNTER FROM 1 BY 1
                UNTIL LOOP-COUNTER > 5
```

```
              DISPLAY 'PRESS ANY KEY TO RETURN TO MAIN MENU'

              ACCEPT ANY-KEY

          ELSE IF OPTION = '3'

              MOVE 'TOTAL SALES DISPLAY' TO HEADING-INFO
              PERFORM 0300-HEADING-ROUTINE

              PERFORM 0600-DISPLAY-TOTALS
                      VARYING LOOP-COUNTER
                      FROM 1 BY 1 UNTIL LOOP-COUNTER > 5

              PERFORM 1500-BLANK-LINE 6 TIMES

              DISPLAY 'PRESS ANY KEY TO RETURN TO MAIN MENU'

              ACCEPT ANY-KEY

          ELSE IF OPTION = '4'

              MOVE 'SALES TOTALS' TO HEADING-INFO
              PERFORM 0300-HEADING-ROUTINE

              PERFORM 0700-GET-PRODUCT-NUMBER
                      UNTIL ANY-KEY > '0' AND < '6'

              SET COLUMN-IDX TO ANY-KEY-N

              MOVE ZEROS     TO MAXIMUM
              MOVE 999999.99 TO MINIMUM

              PERFORM 0800-MAX-MIN-ROUTINE
                      VARYING GROUP-IDX FROM 1 BY 1
                      UNTIL GROUP-IDX > 20

              PERFORM 0300-HEADING-ROUTINE.
              DISPLAY '               SALES TOTALS FOR PRODUCT '
                      ANY-KEY-N
              DISPLAY ' '
              SET GROUP-IDX TO SAVE-MAXIMUM-GROUP
              MOVE SALES-PRODUCTS (GROUP-IDX, ITEM-IDX) TO
                      DISPLAY-PRODUCT
              DISPLAY '               LARGEST SALES AMOUNT = '
                      DISPLAY-PRODUCT
              DISPLAY ' '
              MULTIPLY SALES-PRODUCTS (GROUP-IDX, ITEM-IDX) BY
                      SALES-COMMISSION (GROUP-IDX) GIVING
                      DISPLAY-COMMISSION
              DISPLAY '                        COMMISSION = '
                      DISPLAY-COMMISSION
              DISPLAY ' '
              DISPLAY '                          SALESMAN = '
                      SALESMAN-NAME (GROUP-IDX)
              DISPLAY ' '
```

```
            DISPLAY ' '
            SET GROUP-IDX TO SAVE-MINIMUM-GROUP
            MOVE SALES-PRODUCTS (GROUP-IDX, ITEM-IDX) TO
                 DISPLAY-PRODUCT

            DISPLAY '             SMALLEST SALES AMOUNT = '
                    DISPLAY-PRODUCT
            DISPLAY ' '
            MULTIPLY SALES-PRODUCTS (GROUP-IDX, ITEM-IDX) BY
                    SALES-COMMISSION· (GROUP-IDX) GIVING
                    DISPLAY-COMMISSION
            DISPLAY '                         COMMISSION = '
                    DISPLAY-COMMISSION
            DISPLAY ' '
            DISPLAY '                      SALESMAN = '
                    SALESMAN-NAME (GROUP-IDX)
            DISPLAY ' '
            DISPLAY ' '
            DISPLAY 'PRESS ANY KEY TO RETURN TO MAIN MENU'

            ACCEPT ANY-KEY

        ELSE IF OPTION NOT = '9'

            DISPLAY ' '
            DISPLAY 'ERROR ON ENTRY.'
            DISPLAY ' '
            DISPLAY 'PLEASE ENTER AGAIN'.


    0200-READ-FILE.

        PERFORM 0210-MOVE-PRODUCTS
                VARYING ITEM-IDX FROM 1 BY 1
                UNTIL ITEM-IDX > 5.
        MOVE SALES-NUMBER TO SALESMAN-NUMBER (GROUP-IDX).
        MOVE SALES-NAME    TO SALESMAN-NAME (GROUP-IDX).
        MOVE COMMISSION    TO SALES-COMMISSION (GROUP-IDX).
        READ SALES-FILE
             AT END PERFORM 1000-ERROR-ROUTINE.


    0210-MOVE-PRODUCTS.

        MOVE PRODUCTS (ITEM-IDX) TO
             SALES-PRODUCTS (GROUP-IDX, ITEM-IDX).


    0300-HEADING-ROUTINE.

        PERFORM 1500-BLANK-LINE 4 TIMES.
        DISPLAY '            **************************'.
        DISPLAY '            *                        *'.
        DISPLAY 'DATE ' HEADING-DATE '  *   THE RECORD '
                'RACK, INC.  * ' HEADING-INFO.
        DISPLAY '            *                        *'.
        DISPLAY '            **************************'.
        DISPLAY ' '.
```

```
0400-GET-SALESMAN.

    PERFORM 1500-BLANK-LINE 4 TIMES.

    IF OPTION = 1
        DISPLAY 'WHAT SALESMAN NUMBER DID YOU WANT TO '
                'SEARCH FOR?'
        DISPLAY '####'
        ACCEPT SALES-NUMBER

    ELSE

        DISPLAY 'WHAT SALESMAN NAME DID YOU WANT TO SEARCH FOR?'
        DISPLAY '********************'
        ACCEPT SALES-NAME.

    SET GROUP-IDX TO 1.

    IF OPTION = 1
        SEARCH SALES-TABLE
            AT END MOVE 'NO' TO FOUND
            WHEN SALESMAN-NUMBER (GROUP-IDX) = SALES-NUMBER
            MOVE 'YES' TO FOUND.

    IF OPTION NOT = 1
        SEARCH SALES-TABLE
            AT END MOVE 'NO' TO FOUND
            WHEN SALESMAN-NAME (GROUP-IDX) = SALES-NAME
            MOVE 'YES' TO FOUND.

    IF FOUND = 'NO '
        DISPLAY ' '
        DISPLAY 'INCORRECT SALESMAN.  PLEASE TRY AGAIN.'
        DISPLAY ' '.


0500-DISPLAY-PRODUCT.

    SET ITEM-IDX TO LOOP-COUNTER.
    MOVE SALES-PRODUCTS (GROUP-IDX, ITEM-IDX) TO
        DISPLAY-PRODUCT.
    MULTIPLY SALES-PRODUCTS (GROUP-IDX, ITEM-IDX) BY COMMISSION
            GIVING DISPLAY-COMMISSION.
    DISPLAY '   PRODUCT ' LOOP-COUNTER ' SALES = '
            DISPLAY-PRODUCT
            '   COMMISSION = ' DISPLAY-COMMISSION.
    DISPLAY ' '.


0600-DISPLAY-TOTALS.

    SET ITEM-IDX TO LOOP-COUNTER.
    MOVE ZEROS TO PRODUCT-TOTAL COMMISSION-TOTAL.
    PERFORM 0610-CALCULATE-TOTALS
            VARYING GROUP-IDX FROM 1 BY 1
            UNTIL GROUP-IDX > 20.
    MOVE PRODUCT-TOTAL    TO DISPLAY-PRODUCT-TOTAL.
    MOVE COMMISSION-TOTAL TO DISPLAY-COMM-TOTAL.
```

```
        DISPLAY ' '.
        DISPLAY 'TOTAL SALES FOR PRODUCT ' LOOP-COUNTER ' = '
                DISPLAY-PRODUCT-TOTAL '     COMMISSION = '
                DISPLAY-COMM-TOTAL.


    0610-CALCULATE-TOTALS.

        ADD SALES-PRODUCTS (GROUP-IDX, ITEM-IDX) TO PRODUCT-TOTAL.
        MULTIPLY SALES-PRODUCTS (GROUP-IDX, ITEM-IDX) BY
                SALES-COMMISSION (GROUP-IDX) GIVING CALC-COMMISSION.
        ADD CALC-COMMISSION TO COMMISSION-TOTAL.


    0700-GET-PRODUCT-NUMBER.

        DISPLAY ' '.
        DISPLAY ' '.
        DISPLAY 'ENTER PRODUCT NUMBER YOU WANT TO DISPLAY (1 - 5)'.

        ACCEPT ANY-KEY.


        IF ANY-KEY < '0' OR > '5'
           DISPLAY 'INCORRECT PRODUCT NUMBER.  TRY AGAIN.'.

    0800-MAX-MIN-ROUTINE.

        SET GROUP-IDX TO GROUP-CTR.
        IF SALES-PRODUCTS (GROUP-IDX, ITEM-IDX) < MINIMUM
           MOVE SALES-PRODUCTS (GROUP-IDX, ITEM-IDX) TO MINIMUM
           MOVE GROUP-CTR TO GROUP-IDX.
        IF SALES-PRODUCTS (GROUP-IDX, ITEM-IDX) > MAXIMUM
           MOVE SALES-PRODUCTS (GROUP-IDX, ITEM-IDX) TO MAXIMUM
           MOVE GROUP-CTR TO GROUP-IDX.


    1000-ERROR-ROUTINE.

        PERFORM 1500-BLANK-LINE 20 TIMES.
        DISPLAY 'THERE ARE NOT ENOUGH RECORDS IN THE FILE.'.
        DISPLAY ' '.
        DISPLAY 'PROGRAM TERMINATING.'.
        DISPLAY ' '.
        DISPLAY 'PRESS ANY KEY TO TERMINATE PROGRAM.'.
        ACCEPT OPTION.
        STOP RUN.


    1500-BLANK-LINE.

        DISPLAY ' '.
```

5-8

Summary

1. In certain applications, a single-level table is unsuitable, but two- or three-level tables might prove useful. This chapter discussed these two- and three-level tables, beginning with a review of table terminology and techniques.

2. We define a table with an OCCURS clause, which is generally used with a PIC clause. We have to be sure that we use only an integer size specification on the OCCURS and that it is placed on an 02–49 level.

3. We can access data from a table by referencing the item by subscript number. For example, if we need to access the fifth element in a table, we do so by requesting item 5, such as table-name (5). This subscript can be either a literal or a field.

4. If we need to be able to specify a flexible size for our table, we can use the DEPENDING ON clause.

5. Many times we will use two tables, accessed by the same subscript, when we need to get information from one table based upon the contents of another table.

6. Table pairs are handy for use with the table SEARCH statement. The SEARCH statement will begin at the beginning of the table and search until the condition stated in the WHEN clause is met. If no match is found, an AT END clause can be specified.

7. In order for a SEARCH to be done, the table must be INDEXED BY an index field. This index is simply a special subscript that the computer automatically sets up for us. But, because it is special, we cannot use ordinary calculations with it. If the value of the index needs to be initialized or changed, we have to use the SET statement. Before the SEARCH statement can be used, the value of the index must be SET to a beginning value, which is usually 1 but can be any appropriate number.

8. The normal SEARCH statement works well for tables that are small or cannot be put into sequence. But, if you have a large table that can be put in order, a SEARCH ALL is much better. The regular SEARCH is a serial search. The SEARCH ALL, on the other hand, does a binary search, which in most cases is much faster.

9. There a few differences between the two search types. The SEARCH ALL can test only for an equal condition, is allowed only the AND operator, and can use only one WHEN clause. The SEARCH ALL doesn't require the use of the SET statement like the SEARCH does.

10. For the SEARCH ALL to know which direction the table should be searched in, you need to specify either an ASCENDING KEY or a DESCENDING KEY.

11. Most versions of COBOL allow tables to be used with two and three levels. The 1985 standard allows for tables with as many as seven levels.

12. A two-level table is set up with data pictorially arranged into groups and elementary items. To define a two-level table requires that the second level be set up subordinate (higher level number) to the first level. Also, the field-name on the first level is not accessible; we always access the lowest level field-name (the elementary items).

13. A two-level table is generally loaded from a file by changing the first subscript in an outside loop and the second subscript in an inside loop. This way the data is put into the table one group at a time.

14. A three-level table uses three subscripts: the first two generally are referred to as levels and the third is the item itself. Again, the third subscript is listed on a level number subordinate to the other two subscripts.

5-9
Glossary

Arrays   Another name for **table**. Most other languages use tables but call them arrays. COBOL tables are handled differently than mathematical arrays.

Binary search   The method of searching a table that starts in the middle of the table and moves to the middle of the upper or lower half of the table depending upon the test of the field being compared. This movement continues either until the field is found or until there are no more fields to check.

DEPENDING ON   The optional clause on the OCCURS clause that allows the number of elements assigned to the table to be variable.

Indexes   Special subscripts used on tables that are to be searched.

KEY   The field in the table that is used to specify whether the table is in ASCENDING or DESCENDING order.

Multi-level tables   Tables that have more than one level. They have elementary items within groups rather than just elementary items.

OCCURS clause   The clause added to the field assignment to allow definition of a table.

SEARCH statement   The statement that allows the computer to automatically examine the entries in a table by way of a serial search until a certain condition is met.

SEARCH ALL statement   Similar to the SEARCH statement, except that a binary search is used and the table being searched must be in sequence.

Serial search   The type of search that begins with the first element of the table and continues one by one until either the field is found or the end of the table is reached.

SET statement   The statement necessary to change the value of an index. The index can be SET UP, SET DOWN, or simply SET (initialized).

Single-level tables   Tables that have only one series of numbers.

Subscript   The number that is used to point to the item to be accessed in the table.

Table   A group of like items that are arranged together so that they can be accessed by referencing the item number.

5-10
Quick Quiz

Cover the answers with a blank sheet of paper and test yourself. Questions 1–15 are true or false questions, 16–20 are multiple choice, and 21–25 are fill-in-the-blank.

T F **1.** In a three-level table, the most elementary level is generally referred to as the item because this level is the one that actually refers to the items.

T F **2.** The COBOL statement that defines a table is the OCCURS clause.

T F **3.** When loading a two-level table, we have to use two nested loops to get the data into the appropriate table elements.

T F **4.** Subscripts must always be integers, never field names.

T F **5.** The AT END clause is required on the SEARCH statement.

T F **6.** The SET statement is not necessary if we are using a PERFORM . . . VARYING.

T F **7.** A table requires special setup and handling when it is used directly for output.

T F **8.** In the statement

```
01   TABLE OCCURS 10 TO 10000 TIMES DEPENDING ON S1 PIC X(20)
```

if S1 turned out to be 10, we would have significantly cut down on the amount of storage used by the program.

T F **9.** In the SEARCH statement, a key data field must be in either ascending or descending sequence.

T F **10.** We must use an index when we use the search statement to search a table.

T F **11.** When initializing an index, we treat it like any other data field.

T F **12.** When we search for a maximum value, the comparison field (generally called MAXIMUM) is initially set to the largest possible value.

T F **13.** In accumulating totals into a table, a field that is read in from the record cannot be used as the pointer into the total table.

T F **14.** A major limitation of the SEARCH ALL statement is that we can test only for an equal condition.

T F **15.** In the SEARCH ALL statement, multiple WHEN clauses are permissible.

_____ **16.** All of the following are true of the INDEXED BY clause except the statement that

(a) indexes are defined in the OCCURS clause.
(b) the computer automatically sets up an index with the proper size.
(c) one index can be used on many tables.
(d) an index is used with either the SEARCH statement or the SEARCH ALL statement.

_____ **17.** Which of the following is true when we are using the DEPENDING ON clause?

(a) It requires less storage than a regular table that is defined with the same number of elements as the top-end number on the DEPENDING ON clause.
(b) If the table is defined as numeric, the table elements not within the range of the DEPENDING ON clause will automatically be loaded with zeros.
(c) The field-name defining the size of the table is uninitialized; it is assumed to be zero.
(d) It is useful in table searching because it doesn't require the search to examine all the table locations.

_____ **18.** Which of the following is not true for the SEARCH ALL statement?

(a) It is typically used when a large table must be searched.
(b) The table being searched must be in sequence by a field.
(c) Only one WHEN clause is permitted.
(d) The conditional can test for inequalities.

_____ **19.** A binary search

(a) is performed by using the SEARCH statement.

(b) can access a table only if it has been defined by an ASCENDING or a DESCENDING KEY clause.

(c) usually takes more time than a serial search.

(d) is typically not used because of its many limitations.

____ **20.** The SET statement is used

(a) when a subscript must be initialized, incremented, or decremented.

(b) when an index must be initialized, incremented, or decremented.

(c) when either a subscript or an index must be initialized, incremented, or decremented.

(d) None of the above.

21. COBOL 1985 standards allow for _____ table levels.

22. When searching for a maximum or minimum amount in a table, we don't use a SEARCH statement because a simple _____ statement does the trick.

23. When a SEARCH statement is simply trying to establish a pointer to the particular item and we don't have any statement that needs to be done after the WHEN clause, we can use the _____ statement to cause the program to continue.

24. The SEARCH and SEARCH ALL statements must have a(an) _____ clause defined in the OCCURS statement.

25. The ASCENDING or DESCENDING KEY clause is specified in the OCCURS statement when a _____ will be performed.

5-11
Answers to Quick Quiz

1. T

2. T

3. T (Unless you use a literal assignment.)

4. F (They can be either.)

5. F (But it is strongly recommended; without it, if the search runs off the end of the table the program will ABEND in most computers.)

6. T (Because the PERFORM . . . VARYING initializes the index automatically.)

7. F (It can be printed exactly as it is stored in memory because it is always stored in a serial fashion—exactly the way you need it to be printed.)

8. F (Storage for 10,000 records will be set aside regardless of the amount actually needed by the program.)

9. F (It is only necessary with the SEARCH ALL statement.)

10. T

11. F (We must use the SET statement to initialize, increment, or decrement the index, and we don't define the field because COBOL does it automatically.)

12. F (It is set to the smallest possible value so that any field it is compared against will be larger.)

13. F (We didn't in our example on pages 255–56 because our field wasn't numeric. But if you have a numeric field that can be used to point to the appropriate total field, by all means use it.)

14. T (We cannot test for a condition that is greater than or less than the item we are looking up.)
15. F (Only one WHEN clause can be used.)
16. c (An index can only be defined on one OCCURS clause.)
17. d (Any storage areas not designated within the table are not accessed in the search. The DEPENDING ON clause does require the same amount of storage (answer a). For both b and c, COBOL doesn't initialize anything automatically; that is always the programmer's responsibility.)
18. d (The WHEN clause can test only for a condition that is equal to the one being looked up.)
19. b
20. b (The SET statement is used with indexes.)
21. seven
22. IF
23. NEXT SENTENCE
24. INDEXED BY
25. SEARCH ALL or binary search

══════ 5-12 ══════
Questions to Aid Understanding

1. Explain how we define a table in COBOL.
*2. What is the difference between a single-level table and a two-level table?
3. Write the DATA DIVISION statements necessary to define a table that contains 1000 identical items.
4. What is the purpose of the OCCURS . . . DEPENDING?
*5. Explain why you might wish to use two tables at the same time.
6. What is the purpose of the SEARCH statement?
7. Explain the difference in the way COBOL handles the functioning of a SEARCH and a SEARCH ALL.
*8. What is the difference between a subscript and an index?
9. Why must we use the ASCENDING or DESCENDING KEY clause when we are going to perform a binary search?
10. Explain what the SET statement is used for and list the different forms the statement can take.
11. List at least three differences in the rules for using the SEARCH and SEARCH ALL statements.
12. Why do we use the names GROUP and ITEM for the two level subscripts on a two-level table?
13. Explain why you might want to set up two or more concurrent tables. Show how to set up a two-level table in conjunction with two single-level tables.
14. Explain why you store the smallest possible number in the maximum field you are searching a table with.

5-13
Coding Exercises

1. Write the DATA DIVISION statements necessary to define a table that looks like the following:

```
01   DAY-TIME-TABLE.
     05  DAY1        PIC 9(7).
     05  TIME1       PIC 9(4).
     05  DAY2        PIC 9(7).
     05  TIME2       PIC 9(4).
     05  DAY3        PIC 9(7).
     05  TIME3       PIC 9(4).
     05  DAY4        PIC 9(7).
     05  TIME4       PIC 9(4).
     05  DAY5        PIC 9(7).
     05  TIME5       PIC 9(4).
     05  DAY6        PIC 9(7).
     05  TIME6       PIC 9(4).
     05  DAY7        PIC 9(7).
     05  TIME7       PIC 9(4).
```

2. Write the DATA DIVISION statements necessary to define a table that looks like the following:

```
01   DAY-TABLE.
     05  DAY1.
         10  HOUR1   PIC 9(7).
         10  HOUR2   PIC 9(7).
         10  HOUR3   PIC 9(7).
     05  DAY2.
         10  HOUR1   PIC 9(7).
         10  HOUR2   PIC 9(7).
         10  HOUR3   PIC 9(7).
     05  DAY3.
         10  HOUR1   PIC 9(7).
         10  HOUR2   PIC 9(7).
         10  HOUR3   PIC 9(7).
     05  DAY4.
         10  HOUR1   PIC 9(7).
         10  HOUR2   PIC 9(7).
         10  HOUR3   PIC 9(7).
     05  DAY5.
         10  HOUR1   PIC 9(7).
         10  HOUR2   PIC 9(7).
         10  HOUR3   PIC 9(7).
     05  DAY6.
         10  HOUR1   PIC 9(7).
         10  HOUR2   PIC 9(7).
         10  HOUR3   PIC 9(7).
```

```
            05  DAY7.
                10  HOUR1    PIC 9(7).
                10  HOUR2    PIC 9(7).
                10  HOUR3    PIC 9(7).
```

3. Write the coding necessary to intialize an index called INDEXCODE, to 1.

4. Write the coding necessary to increment INDEXCODE by 4.

5. Write the SEARCH statement necessary to look up the field ZIPCODE-LOOKUP in the ZIPCODE-TABLE. Use the table defined below:

```
        01  POSTAL-TABLE.
            05  RATE-AMOUNT OCCURS 50 TIMES
                            INDEXED BY S1.
                10  ZIPCODE-TABLE       PIC 9(5).
                10  RATE-TABLE          PIC 99V99.
```

6. Write the code necessary to find the maximum value in the INCOME-TABLE defined below:

```
        01  TAX-TABLE.
            05  INCOME-TAX       OCCURS 1000 TIMES.
                10  INCOME-TABLE OCCURS 25 TIMES PIC 9(6).
```

7. Write the code necessary to find the value of the field BOOK-LOOKUP in the BOOK-TABLE shown below. Write the code so that it will display the author and copyright date on the screen when the value is located.

```
        01  BOOK-SHELVE-TABLE.
            05  ROWS OCCURS 1000 TIMES
                     INDEXED BY GROUP-IDX.
                15  BOOK-TABLE        PIC X(20).
                15  AUTHOR-TABLE      PIC X(20).
                15  COPYRIGHT-TABLE   PIC 9(4).
```

8. Write the code necessary to load data from a file into the following defined tables. Each input data record has exactly one zip code and ten addresses.

```
        01  STATE-TABLE.
            05  CITY-TABLE            OCCURS 500 TIMES.
                10  ZIP-CODE-TABLE    OCCURS 50 TIMES.
                    20  ADDRESS-TABLE OCCURS 10 TIMES.
```

9. Assuming your computer will not allow you to zero out a table with a simple reference to the 01 level (some won't), write a routine to zero out the following table:

```
        01  STUDENT-TABLE.
            05  BUILDING-TABLE        OCCURS 10 TIMES.
                10  CLASSROOM-TABLE   OCCURS 30 TIMES.
                    10  STUDENT-GRADES OCCURS 20 TIMES PIC 999V9.
```

10. Assuming the table defined for question 9 above, write a routine to initialize all first items with 1's, all second items with 2's, and so on all the way to the twentieth items initialized with 20's.
11. Given the table designed for question 9 above, write a routine that could be used to display the 20 student grades on a report, using a table to print each row with one WRITE statement.
12. Given the table designed for question 9 above, write a routine to calculate what the grades were and how many times they occurred. For example, you need to display whether there was a grade of 55 and how many times it occurred throughout the entire table.
13. Write the definition for two tables of 20 groups each with 30 elements in each group. Then write the code to move all the elements of the first table to the elements of the second table.
14. Write the definition for two tables of 20 groups each with 30 elements in each group. Then write the code to compare each element with its corresponding element in the other table and to display a message every time the elements match. Keep track of how many elements match and then display that number after the routine is finished.
15. Write the definition for three tables of 20 groups each with 30 subgroups and 40 elements in each subgroup. Write the code to add the like elements of the first two tables and put the result into the same element of the third table.

5-14
Maintenance Program

Roger Barnell of *The Record Rack* liked the program Cindy created for him detailing the salesman information (see section 5-7). He decides, however, that he wants the program to do more. First he wants the program to print a sequential listing of the salesmen, as shown in the printer spacing chart in Figure 5-8. This will become option 5 on the main menu for the program (Figure 5-2). Then he wants both the salesman display (Figure 5-3) and the total sales display (Figure 5-4) updated to show the total sales and commissions for all the products.

Redraw Figures 5-2, 5-3, and 5-4, to reflect these changes. Also, change the program design to incorporate the new report and the additional calculations.

5-15
Illustrative Program

You are an employee of the government in the city where you live. A preliminary election is coming up soon, and you are assigned the task of writing a program to tabulate the number of votes each candidate receives. The government has a special machine that will read the ballots and store each ballot's information in one record, according to the layout shown in Figure 5-9. Notice that the first position in the record is to be filled with a number for the party declaration: 1 for Democrat, 2 for Republican, and 3 for Independent or undeclared. Following that will be four one-digit numbers representing the votes for the particular candidates in the various races. These represent the following races and candidates:

Position	Race	Candidate Number/Name/Party
2	Mayor	1 = GIFFORD—Democrat 2 = HARRISON—Republican 3 = SIMMONS—Republican 4 = FRANKS—Independent 5 = FIVERS—Independent
3	City Council, place 1	1 = DE LEON—Democrat 2 = COLLINS—Democrat 3 = DAVIS—Republican 4 = MCNUTT—Independent
4	City Council, place 2	1 = MORALES—Democrat 2 = RUSSEL—Democrat 3 = ANDERSON—Republican 4 = GONZALEZ—Republican 5 = DE LA CRUZ—Republican
5	County Judge	1 = BOND—Democrat 2 = PEDRIGON—Democrat 3 = SHAGNASTY—Republican 4 = CARSNER—Republican 5 = GREEN—Republican 6 = COBURN—Independent

The program will need to read the ballot records and tabulate the votes for the particular candidates, including the party declaration of the voter. You will need one table to tabulate the votes (two-level) and another with the candidates names (single-level) so they may be printed on the report. The report you are to generate, shown in Figure 5-10, is basically a control break report since you are to print totals for each office (for example, the number of votes for mayor) and a grand total of all the votes.

The systems design for the program is shown in Figure 5-11 and the flowchart in Figure 5-12. The pseudocode appears below. The program design is relatively simple. Deciding how to set up the tables for storing the data and then getting the data into the tables for storage are the real problems.

```
Start
Open file
Initialize total fields
Print report headings
Read ballot record at end EOF
DO-WHILE not EOF
        Add 1 vote to the appropriate counter for each race
        Read ballot record at end EOF
```

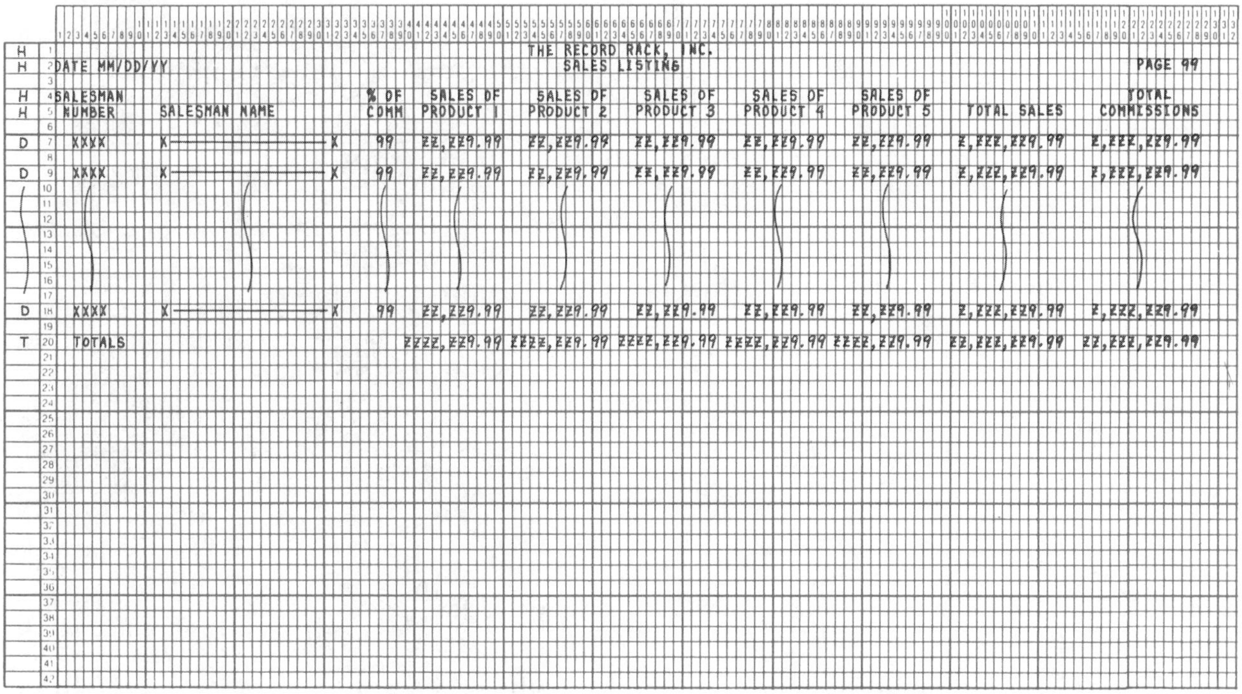

Figure 5-8 The report program for *The Record Rack* maintenance program.

BALLOT **File**					
Field Description	*Position*	*Length*	:	*Dec*	*Type*
Party declaration	1–1	1	:	0	Numeric
Race/Candidate	2–5	4	:	0	Numeric
Filler	6–80	75	:		Non-numeric
Record Length = 80					

Figure 5-9 The BALLOT file containing election information.

```
END-DO
Initialize group counter to 1
Put race into hold field
DO-WHILE group number < 20 (20 candidates)
        IF race (group) not = hold field THEN
                Print subtotals
                Add subtotals to grand totals
                Zero out subtotals
                Move race into hold field
        (ELSE)
        END-IF
        Print the detail line
        Accumulate subtotals
```

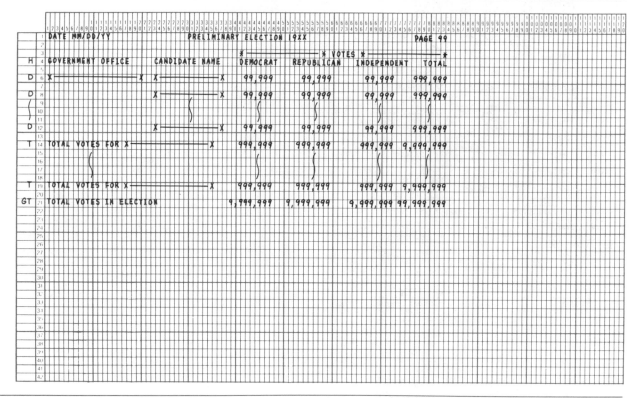

The report layout table:

	GOVERNMENT OFFICE	CANDIDATE NAME	* VOTES *			
			DEMOCRAT	REPUBLICAN	INDEPENDENT	TOTAL
H	DATE MM/DD/YY	PRELIMINARY ELECTION 19XX				PAGE 99
D	X———————X	X————X	99,999	99,999	99,999	999,999
D		X————X	99,999	99,999	99,999	999,999
D		X————X	99,999	99,999	99,999	999,999
T	TOTAL VOTES FOR X————X		999,999	999,999	999,999	9,999,999
T	TOTAL VOTES FOR X————X		999,999	999,999	999,999	9,999,999
GT	TOTAL VOTES IN ELECTION		9,999,999	9,999,999	9,999,999	99,999,999

Figure 5-10   The report layout for the election summary report.

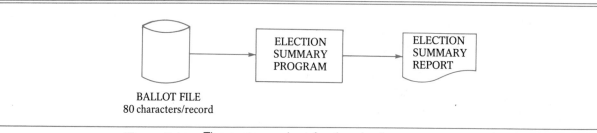

BALLOT FILE
80 characters/record

ELECTION SUMMARY PROGRAM

ELECTION SUMMARY REPORT

Figure 5-11   The systems chart for the election summary report program.

```
END-DO
Print the subtotals
Add subtotals to grand totals
Print grand totals
End
```

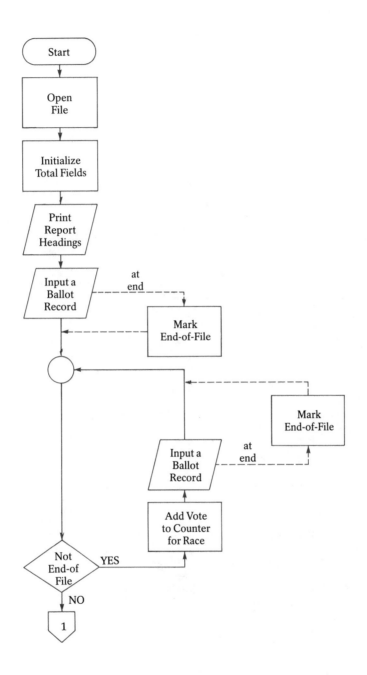

Figure 5-12   The flowchart for the election summary report.

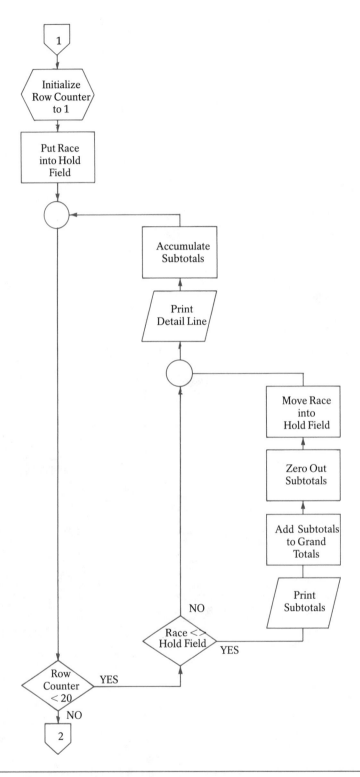

Figure 5-12 (continued)

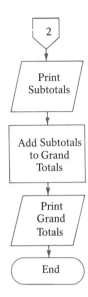

Figure 5-12 (continued)

5-16

System Designed Programs

For the following programs, all the design elements typically furnished to a programmer by the systems analyst are furnished. It is up to you, as programmer, to design and code the program. The files to be used are found in Appendix A.

1. A large warehouse uses the INVENT file, with the record layout shown in Figure 5-13, to store the identification number, unit price, and inventory quantity of its merchandise. Because this file is accessed every time a product is sold, at the end of each month, management randomly selects several identification numbers in order to check the integrity of the price that was charged. A file has been prepared with only selected identification numbers and associated prices. This ITEMNO file layout is shown in Figure 5-14. Write a program to read this ITEMNO file into a table and then, as the INVENT records are read in, look up the item number in the table. If the item number is not in the table, print nothing. If it is in the table, match the unit prices to see if they agree. Print an agreement message if they do agree; print the difference and an appropriate message if they do not. The form for the report is shown in the printer spacing chart in Figure 5-15. The systems design is shown in Figure 5-16.

2. As the programmer for the *Little House Construction Company*, you are assigned the task of writing a report summarizing construction information. You will be using the CNSTRUCT file as shown in Figure 5-17. The data stored in the file is classified by regions (1, 3, 7, 9, and 10) of the country, with each

INVENT File					
Field Description	*Position*	*Length*	:	*Dec*	*Type*
Item number	1–4	4	:		Non-numeric
Quantity	5–10	6	:	0	Numeric
Filler	11–24	14	:		Non-numeric
Unit price	25–32	8	:	2	Numeric
Filler	33–80	48	:		Non-numeric
Record Length = 80					

Figure 5-13   The record layout for the INVENT file, exercise 5-16-1.

ITEMNO File					
Field Description	*Position*	*Length*	:	*Dec*	*Type*
Item number	1–4	4	:		Non-numeric
Unit price	5–12	8	:	2	Numeric
Filler	13–80	68	:		Non-numeric
Record Length = 80					

Figure 5-14   The record layout for the ITEMNO file, exercise 5-16-1.

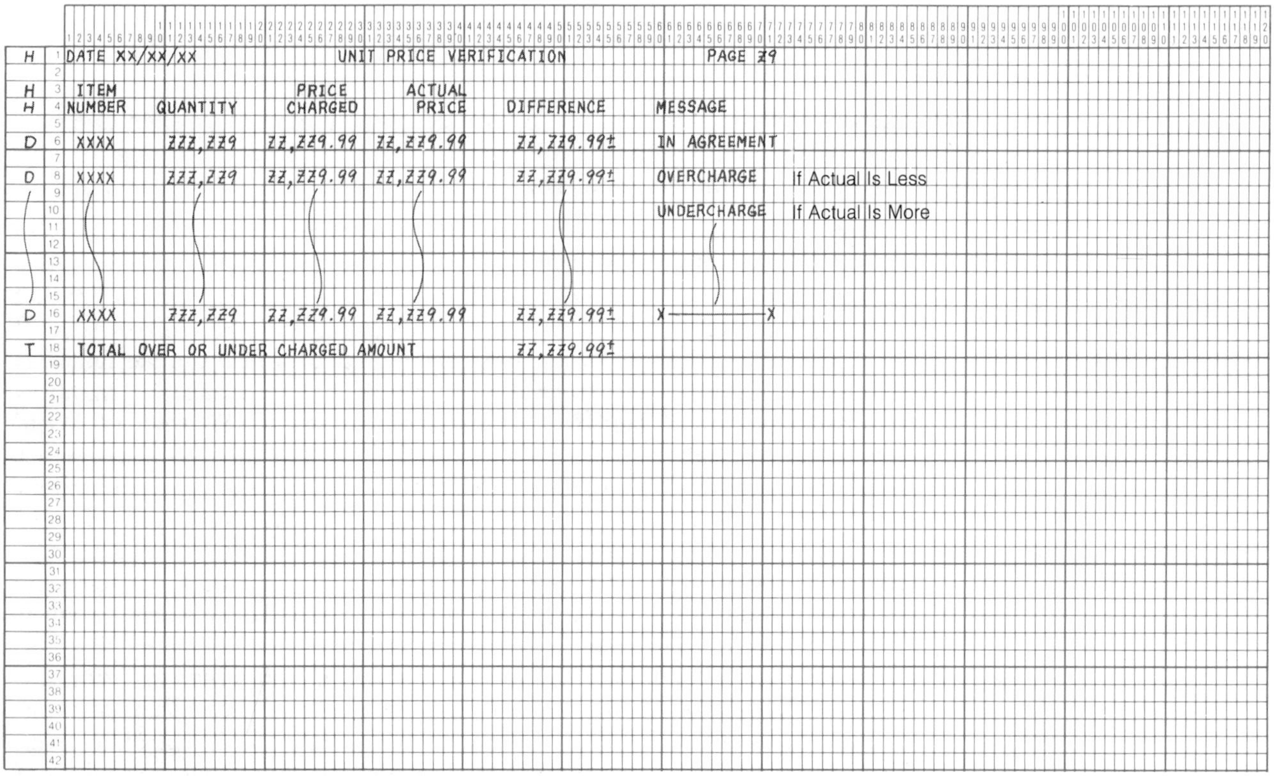

Figure 5-15   The report layout for the price verification report program, exercise 5-16-1.

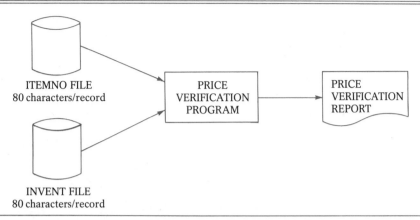

Figure 5-16   The systems chart for the price verification report program, exercise 5-16-1.

CNSTRUCT File					
Field Description	*Position*	*Length*	:	*Dec*	*Type*
Region	1–2	2	:	0	Numeric
Section	3–4	2	:	0	Numeric
Project number	5–9	5	:		Non-numeric
Type of project	10–24	15	:		Non-numeric
Budget amount	25–33	9	:	0	Numeric
Actual amount	34–42	9	:	0	Numeric
Filler	43–80	38	:		Non-numeric
Record Length = 80					

Figure 5-17   The record layout for the CNSTRUCT file, exercise 5-16-2.

region divided up into eight possibile sections. You will need to read the data in and then total the budgeted amounts and the actual amounts into two two-levels tables (one for budget and one for actual). From this data, you will need to prepare the report shown in Figure 5-18. The variance is the budgeted amount minus the actual amount. Naturally, if there is no section designated in a particular region, it will not be printed (as zero). Print only those regions and sections that are in the data. Notice that you will also need to print a total of the various types of projects (house, office building); there are 11 different ones. The systems design for the program is shown in Figure 5-19.

3. You work for a large manufacturing company that produces various finished goods on many different machines at several different facilities on the plant grounds. The workers prepare daily reports as to how many products are produced on each machine and how many of those products are defective. It is your job to write a program to read the file of these reports (MACHINE—Figure 5-20) and produce the report, as in Figure 5-21, that shows the production efficiency of the facilities and the machines. The facilities are numbered 1, 3, 7, 9, and 10 and there are up to eight machines in each facility.

```
      H  1                                    LITTLE HOUSE CONSTRUCTION COMPANY
      H  2  DATE MM/DD/YY                     REGIONAL SUMMARY REPORT                  PAGE 99
      H  3
      H  4  REGION        SECTION                    TOTAL              TOTAL              TOTAL
      H  5                                    BUDGETED AMOUNT      ACTUAL AMOUNT         VARIANCE
         6
      D  7    Z9              Z9              ZZZ,ZZZ,ZZ9        ZZZ,ZZZ,ZZ9       ZZZ,ZZZ,ZZ9 ±
         8
      D  9    Z9              Z9              ZZZ,ZZZ,ZZ9        ZZZ,ZZZ,ZZ9       ZZZ,ZZZ,ZZ9 ±
        10
        11
        12
      D 13    Z9              Z9              ZZZ,ZZZ,ZZ9        ZZZ,ZZZ,ZZ9       ZZZ,ZZZ,ZZ9 ±
        14
      T 15  TOTALS FOR REGION Z9      Z,ZZZ,ZZZ,ZZ9        ZZZ,ZZZ,ZZ9       ZZZ,ZZZ,ZZ9 ±
        16
        17
        18
      T 19  TOTALS FOR REGION Z9      Z,ZZZ,ZZZ,ZZ9      Z,ZZZ,ZZZ,ZZ9       ZZZ,ZZZ,ZZ9 ±
        20
      T 21  GRAND TOTALS             Z,ZZZ,ZZZ,ZZ9      Z,ZZZ,ZZZ,ZZ9       ZZZ,ZZZ,ZZ9 ±
        22
        23
      T 24  TOTALS FOR PROJECT TYPES
        25
      T 26  X-----------X            Z,ZZZ,ZZZ,ZZ9      Z,ZZZ,ZZZ,ZZ9       ZZZ,ZZZ,ZZ9 ±
        27
      T 28  X-----------X            Z,ZZZ,ZZZ,ZZ9      Z,ZZZ,ZZZ,ZZ9       ZZZ,ZZZ,ZZ9 ±
        29
        30
        31
      T 32  X-----------X            Z,ZZZ,ZZZ,ZZ9      Z,ZZZ,ZZZ,ZZ9       ZZZ,ZZZ,ZZ9 ±
```

Figure 5-18   The record layout for the construction summary report, exercise 5-16-2.

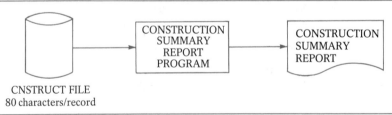

CNSTRUCT FILE
80 characters/record

Figure 5-19   The systems chart for the construction summary report program, exercise 5-16-2.

MACHINE **File**					
Field Description	*Position*	*Length*	:	*Dec*	*Type*
Facility	1–2	2	:	0	Numeric
Machine	3–4	2	:	0	Numeric
Total production	5–9	5	:	0	Numeric
Defective products	10–13	4	:	0	Numeric
Filler	14–80	67	:		Non-numeric
Record Length = 80					

Figure 5-20   The record layout for the MACHINE file, exercise 5-16-3.

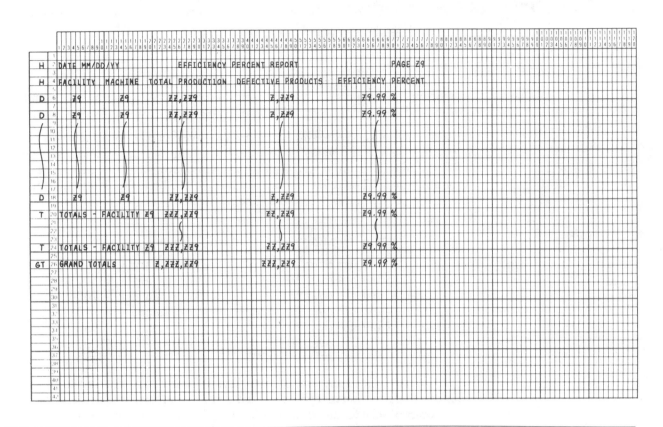

Figure 5-21   The report layout for the produce efficiency percentage report, exercise 5-16-3.

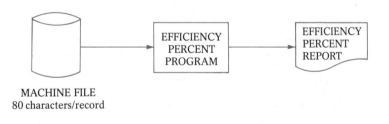

MACHINE FILE
80 characters/record

Figure 5-22   The systems chart for exercise 5-16-3.

The report should show only a detail line for those facilities and the machines each has. You calculate the efficiency by dividing the number of good products (total minus defective) by the total production. The report should show totals of each facility and then a grand total at the end of the report. The systems chart for this program is shown in Figure 5-22.

5-17

Interactive System Designed Programs

For the following programs, all the design elements typically furnished to a programmer by the systems analyst are furnished. It is up to you, as programmer, to design and code the program. The files to be used are found in Appendix A.

1. At the end of the year, *Oil, Incorporated*, gives its employees a bonus based on their salary and years of service. Depending on the years of service, a bonus percent is multiplied against an employee's salary to determine part of the bonus. Then a flat amount is added to the bonus to determine the full amount of the bonus. The table for such figuring is listed below:

Years of Service	Amount of Bonus
not over 5	2% of salary + $ 0
over 5 but not over 10	2% of salary + $ 500
over 10 but not over 14	2% of salary + $ 700
over 14 but not over 21	3% of salary + $ 800
over 21 but not over 30	3% of salary + $ 950
over 30	4% of salary + $1000

To help speed the end-of-year payroll processing, you are to write an interactive program that will allow the user to input the name of the employee, the years of service, and the salary, after which the program will automatically calculate the amount of bonus and print the bonus check on the printer. You can use the data from the PAYROLL file (layout shown in Figure 5-23) to test your program, though you enter the information interactively rather than by reading the file. The checks you print should look like the sample shown in Figure 5-24. Notice that each check is 18 lines long. The systems chart for the program is shown in Figure 5-25.

PAYROLL File					
Field Description	*Position*	*Length*	:	*Dec*	*Type*
Employee number	1–4	4	:		Non-numeric
Employee name	5–24	20	:		Non-numeric
Filler	25–33	9	:		Non-numeric
Years of service	34–35	2	:	0	Numeric
Annual salary	36–41	6	:	0	Numeric
Filler	42–80	39	:		Non-numeric
Record Length = 80					

Figure 5-23   The PAYROLL file used for interactive entry in exercise 5-17-1.

2. You work for the *Wonderful Lake Tour Company*, which runs a cruise ship that travels up and down the length of Wonderful Lake for a week at a time. The company needs an interactive program to display all the cabin numbers (45 of them) on the screen for a particular cruise and let the user enter a name for each cabin as it is booked. This way, the user can monitor the phone calls and book a cabin as soon as a customer calls in. The screen design for the cabin display is shown in Figure 5-26. The program should hold two months worth of bookings (eight weeks, eight screen displays) so that the user can book any available cabin on any cruise during the two-month period.

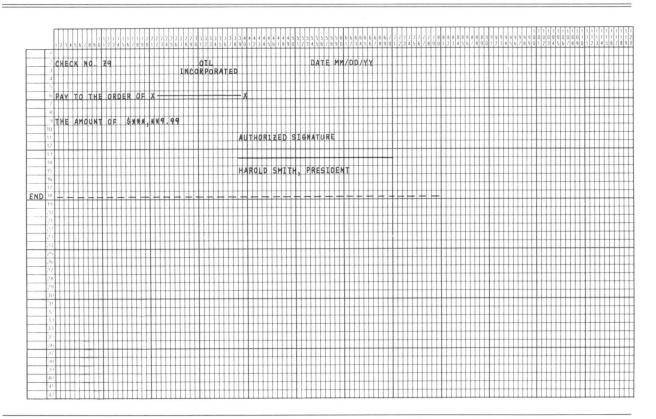

Figure 5-24   The design of the checks to be printed in exercise 5-17-1.

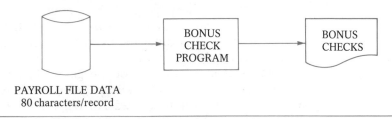

PAYROLL FILE DATA
80 characters/record

Figure 5-25   The systems chart for exercise 5-17-1.

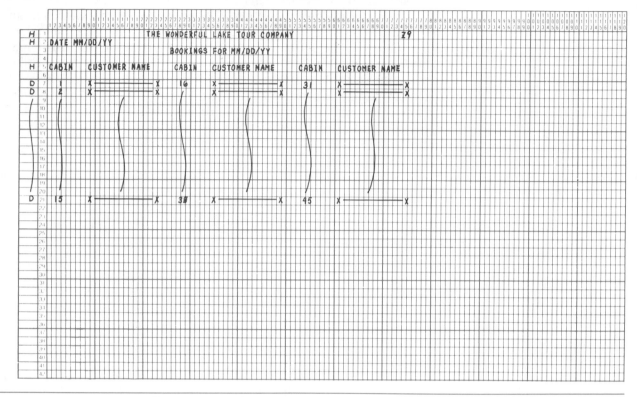

Figure 5-26 The display layout for the bookings display program, exercise 5-17-2.

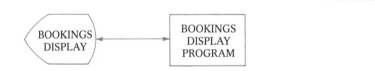

Figure 5-27 The systems chart for the bookings program, exercise 5-17-2.

The systems chart for the program is shown in Figure 5-27. (There is no file for this program although in reality the bookings would be stored in a file.)

3. You work for a bookie in Las Vegas (legal). He wants you to write an interactive program to keep track of the amounts of money being bet on the various football games going on across the country. Since the program will need to be used throughout the year, the games will simply be numbered consecutively and a current list will be kept beside the machine, indicating the number assigned to each of the games being played that week. The program will need to display all the game numbers and the amount being bet on each, as shown in Figure 5-28. When the user enters a game number and the amount being bet, the program should automatically update the amount displayed for that game and then redisplay the entire table of bets. There is no file for this program since you will simply be adding amounts to the totals. The system design is shown in Figure 5-29.

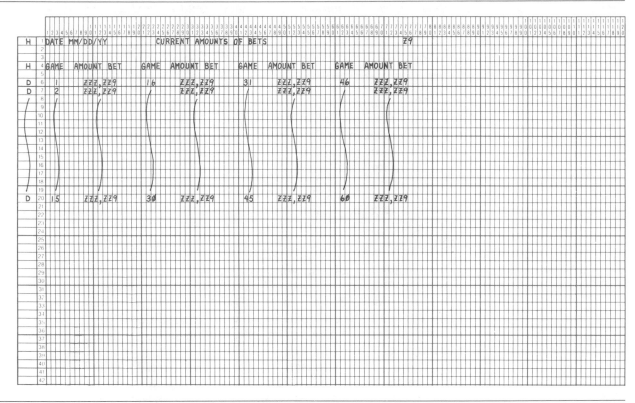

Figure 5-28   The display layout for the betting program, exercise 5-17-3.

Figure 5-29   The systems chart for the betting program, exercise 5-17-3.

5-18
Non-designed Programs

In the following programs, you will need to design the systems chart, the input files (record layout), the printer spacing chart, the program design, and the data with which to test the program.

1. A magazine company charges $37.50 a year for one of its magazine subscriptions. Depending on the year the subscription was first begun, a subscriber is entitled to pay only a percent of the full $37.50. The following

table shows the amount a subscriber would have to pay when renewing a subscription:

Year Subscribed	Code Used	Percent of Total
1961 and earlier	1	45
1962 through 1963	2	50
1964 through 1968	3	69
1969 through 1970	4	70
1970 through 1972	5	71
1973 through 1976	6	78
1977 through 1979	7	81
1980 through 1981	8	83
1982 through 1984	9	90
1985 through 1988	10	100

Establish a table in your program with the rates shown. Then read in another file that contains each subscriber's number, name, date first subscribed, and number of years the renewal is for. Print out a report showing the amount to be charged for renewal of each subscription. You will have to match the subscription year against the ranges and then use the associated percentage.

2. You are a teaching assistant. The professor you work for wants you to produce a program that will allow records to be read in that contain each student's name, class, exam number (exam 1, exam 2, etc.), and exam grade. That data will need to be stored so that, after all the records are read, a report can be produced detailing—for each class the professor teaches—the students, the exams taken, and the grades received. The students' grades should be listed across the page (a row). At the end, an average grade and a letter grade should be shown. The letter grade is based on the following scale:

A is 90 or greater
B is 80 up to 90
C is 70 up to 80
D is 60 up to 70
F is anything less than 60

At the end of the list for each class, there should be a total of the number of A's, B's, C's, D's, and F's. Then, at the end of the entire report, there should be a grand total for each letter grade.

3. You work for a company that has salesman all over the country. Their sales areas are broken down by region (eight different ones) and by states within the region. Write a program that will input the data from sales orders and tabulate the amount of orders for each region and each state. After all the records have been read, produce a report detailing the total sales for each region and state.

5-19

Interactive Non-designed Programs

In the following programs, you will need to design the systems chart, the input files (record layout), the printer spacing chart, the program design, and the data with which to test the program.

1. You work for the city tourist bureau, and they need to have a program written that will allow visitors to determine the distance between various cities. The program should display a screenful of cities (20 or so), let the user pick two of the cities by number, and then display the distance between those cities. You could expand the program to give information about the best highways to take, interesting places to visit, and anything else a tourist might like to know.

2. In beautiful Ocean City, a boat rental company rents out boats for one to several days at a time. There are five sizes of boats and several boats of each size. The company needs an interactive program that stores and displays one month's (one day at a time) data about all of the boats, so that when a potential renter calls, the user can instantly determine whether a particular boat will be available when the customer wants it.

   Your program will need to be able to prompt the user for the date of interest, then display the information for that day on the screen. The display should include all the boats and whether they're booked or not. You should use the customer's name as the marker that indicates the boat is booked. That way you store the name of the customer at the same time you mark the booking. The program should be able to accept input from the user to book a particular boat on the date in question for the number of days needed and automatically book all the days.

   The five types and number of different boats are listed below:

Size	Number of Boats
Mini	5
Tug	3
Midsize	8
Yacht	3
Macro	2

3. The clothing store you work for wants an interactive program that will display data about their various products on the screen so that the on-hand inventory amount for a given item may be updated as a sale of that item is made. Have the program display the data and then prompt the user for the clothing sold and the quantity. With this input, you will update the inventory for the item and redisplay all the data.

OBJECTIVES   After completing Chapter 6 you should be able to

1. explain what a sort is and what ascending and descending mean;
2. explain what EBCDIC and ASCII are and what they have to do with a sort;
3. describe the major parts of the SORT statement and how they are used by the program;
4. explain what an SD is and what significance it has to a sort;
5. list the seven steps that are automatically handled by the computer when using the USING and GIVING clauses;
6. explain what INPUT and OUTPUT PROCEDUREs are and how they are used;
7. explain the purpose of the RETURN and RELEASE statements and what other COBOL statements they are similar to;
8. explain the purpose of the EXIT paragraph and why it is necessary;
9. give one example of when you would use an INPUT PROCEDURE and one example of when an OUTPUT PROCEDURE would be preferable;
10. explain what the MERGE statement is and how it can prove useful.

CHAPTER **6**

THE COBOL SORT

6-1
Introduction

One of the procedures most commonly used on a computer is putting files into some type of sequence. For a sequential update, the files, both master and transaction, must be in sequence. For a control break report, the file must be in sequence. To get cheaper mailing rates, flyers and other publications that are sent out thousands at a time must be given to the postal service in zip code sequence. Then there are the thousands of reports that are simply easier to read when the file is put into sequence before the report is printed.

To put these files into sequence, we need to use some type of sort. A **sort** is simply a procedure used to put a file into an ordered sequence by some key field. Though most modern computer systems have a sort utility that allows sorting to be done outside of any regular programming, most versions of COBOL have their own sort feature. Sort utility programs can generally sort files quicker and easier than a COBOL program can be written to do the sorting. If we need to process any records immediately before or after the sorting, however, a COBOL sort takes on more importance. It is this internal COBOL sort feature that is the concern of this chapter.

6-2
The Idea of a Sort

Before we begin looking at how a sort is handled in COBOL, it is a good idea to take a quick look at just what a sort is. As we said, a sort is simply a method of getting a list of data into some type of order by a key field. Take the following list, for example:

0456	GEORGE	P. O. BOX 1610	ANTHONY	NM	88021
1111	VIRAMONTE	333 ROSEWOOD	SANTA TERESA	NM	88022
1234	PINON	234 TEXAS DR	EL PASO	TX	79935
2223	MCDOWELL	2323 TRUTH	SARASOTA	FL	24234
2248	HANSON	242 CHISHOLM	ANTHONY	TX	48234

This is a small section of the CUSTOMER file. As you can see, the records are already in sequence by the first field, the customer number. If we need to look up one of the customers by name, however, having the list in customer number order is of little value. We need to sort the list down into customer name order to make looking up the name easier. If we sort the file by name, we will have a list like the following:

0456	GEORGE	P. O. BOX 1610	ANTHONY	NM	88021
2248	HANSON	242 CHISHOLM	ANTHONY	TX	48234
2223	MCDOWELL	2323 TRUTH	SARASOTA	FL	24234
1234	PINON	234 TEXAS DR	EL PASO	TX	79935
1111	VIRAMONTE	333 ROSEWOOD	SANTA TERESA	NM	88022

Now the list is in name sequence (the second field), and the sort key (or **key field**) is the customer name.

But we are not finished with the list yet. We need to send a mailing to all our customers, and to get the bulk mailing rates, we need to put the list in zip code sequence. We will sort the file and it will look like this:

2223	MCDOWELL	2323 TRUTH	SARASOTA	FL	24234
2248	HANSON	242 CHISHOLM	ANTHONY	TX	48234
1234	PINON	234 TEXAS DR	EL PASO	TX	79935
0456	GEORGE	P. O. BOX 1610	ANTHONY	NM	88021
1111	VIRAMONTE	333 ROSEWOOD	SANTA TERESA	NM	88022

The sample sorts we have been showing have all been in **ascending sequence**. This means in A-to-Z sequence. Most of the time this is the order we want. Occasionally we do want the list sorted into **descending**, or Z-to-A, **sequence**. If we sorted the list by zip code into descending sequence, it would be

1111	VIRAMONTE	333 ROSEWOOD	SANTA TERESA	NM	88022
0456	GEORGE	P. O. BOX 1610	ANTHONY	NM	88021
1234	PINON	234 TEXAS DR	EL PASO	TX	79935
2248	HANSON	242 CHISHOLM	ANTHONY	TX	48234
2223	MCDOWELL	2323 TRUTH	SARASOTA	FL	24234

The list is exactly the reverse of what it was previously.

Sometimes our list will be so large that sorting it down by one field still doesn't give us everything we need. If we need to print a control break on two control fields, sorting the file by one key field is not sufficient. We need to sort it by multiple keys. Suppose the file we are working with now looks like

03	02	25056	STORE RENOV.
01	01	08187	BUILDING
03	01	06829	PRIVATE HOME
01	03	06875	PRIVATE HOME
03	01	17079	OFFICE BUILDING
01	03	25209	RR TERMINAL
01	02	07251	OFFICE BUILDING
03	04	28193	HEATING PLANT
01	01	07476	SHOPPING CENTER
03	06	00048	TENNIS COURT
03	04	31107	BUILDING DEMOL.

This is the small section of a construction company file. The first field is the region of the country where the project is being built, and the second field is the section within that region. We need to print a control break program using this file information, but it is useless to us the way it is. It needs to be sorted, but not by just the first field. Within each of the regions, the sections must also be in order. This requires a two-level sort. After we run it, we will have the following list:

01	01	08187	BUILDING
01	01	07476	SHOPPING CENTER
01	02	07251	OFFICE BUILDING
01	03	25209	RR TERMINAL
01	03	06875	PRIVATE HOME
03	01	06829	PRIVATE HOME
03	01	17079	OFFICE BUILDING
03	02	25056	STORE RENOV.
03	04	31107	BUILDING DEMOL.
03	04	28193	HEATING PLANT
03	06	00048	TENNIS COURT

Now, within the 01 region, the sections are sorted into 01, 02, and 03. Within the 03 region, they are sorted into 01, 02, 04, and 06.

6-3

The Collating Sequence

Two main storage codes are used in modern computers. Most IBM computers and a few others use **EBCDIC,** which stands for **Extended Binary Coded Decimal Interchange Code.** All the other computers, including all microcomputers, use **ASCII,** which stands for the **American Standard Code for Information Interchange.** In these codes, each character is automatically assigned a decimal storage code by the computer. These decimal codes are not the same in the two schemes, so the characters are not stored in the same sequence.

The sequences that EBCDIC and ASCII use are called **collating sequences** because they are used for **collating,** or putting in sequence, the fields that are sorted. Simplified, the two collating sequences are

EBCDIC	ASCII
1. Blanks	1. Blanks
2. Special characters	2. Special characters
3. Lowercase letters	3. Numeric digits
4. Uppercase letters	4. Special characters
5. Numeric digits	5. Uppercase letters
	6. Special characters
	7. Lowercase letters

All that really needs to concern us about the collating sequences is the location of the specific groups of characters in relationship to each other. That is, in EBCDIC, numeric digits are considered to be the largest characters, and lowercase letters (a–z) are less than uppercase letters (A–Z). In ASCII, the order is very different.

This is important if we are sorting, for example, an address field. In EBCDIC, "Box 495" would be sorted before "1400 South Street" because "B" is lower in the collating sequence than "1." In ASCII, the opposite is true. As long as we are sorting zip codes, numeric fields like customer numbers, and non-numeric fields like names that don't mix numbers and letters, we will not have any problems because ASCII and EBCDIC both sort similar fields the same way. A-to-Z is A-to-Z in both collating sequences.

6-4

The COBOL SORT Statement

Now that we understand what a sort is and have briefly looked at the collating sequences, it is time to move on to the **COBOL SORT statement** itself. The form of the statement is

SORT sort-file-name

ON $\left\{\begin{array}{l}\text{DESCENDING}\\ \text{ASCENDING}\end{array}\right\}$ KEY field-name-1

[ON $\left\{\begin{array}{l}\text{DESCENDING}\\ \text{ASCENDING}\end{array}\right\}$ KEY field-name-2 . . .]

USING file-name-3

GIVING file-name-4

The first line of the statement is the SORT verb itself. Following that is the sort-file-name, which we will discuss later.

The second and third lines of the statement are for the ASCENDING or DESCENDING KEY clause. This is where you designate what field(s) you want to sort the file on and what order you want the file to be in. You can use as many KEY clauses as you wish, but after two or three, you reach the limit of practicality. Generally no more than two are necessary.

The next clause, the USING clause, designates the input file into the sort. If you are trying to sort the CUSTOMER file, you would list it here.

The final clause, the GIVING clause, is for the output file. COBOL will bring in the input file (USING), sort the records using the sort-file-name, and then store the sorted record back into the file designated on the GIVING clause.

It is possible to use the same file-name on the USING AND GIVING clauses. Doing this will cause the program to load the original file, sort it, and store it back where it came from. This is not desirable when you need to keep the original file in the order it's in or when you cannot write to the original file for some reason or other (such as in indexed files, discussed in the next chapter).

A sample sort statement would be

```
SORT SORT-FILE
     ON ASCENDING KEY SORT-NAME
     USING CUSTOMER-FILE
     GIVING SORTED-CUSTOMER-FILE.
```

This statement would sort the CUSTOMER-FILE on the name field (SORT-NAME) and store the sorted file into a new file called the SORTED-CUSTOMER-FILE.

6-4-1 The SD Statement

Since it is a file, the sort file must be defined to the program, but it is not defined exactly like other files. Every time we have defined a file, we have used the FD, or File Description statement. And we continue to define the USING and GIVING files with the FD, just as we have in the past. But the sort file is not a normal file. It is a temporary file that the program will abandon as soon as the sort is completed, so it must be defined in a slightly different way.

Instead of an FD, we must use an **SD**, or Sort Description. The LABEL REC-ORDS clause that is required on an FD is not allowed on the SD. The BLOCK CONTAINS clause is not allowed either, but the RECORD CONTAINS clause is, and it is still a good idea to use it. The record is defined the same way for an SD as it was for an FD, with the fields laid out in precisely the same manner. An SD for the file SORT-FILE used in the previous example would look like the following:

```
SD  SORT-FILE.
01  SORT-RECORD.
    10  FILLER          PIC XXXX.
    10  SORT-NAME       PIC X(20).
    10  FILLER          PIC X(66).
```

Notice that the ASCENDING KEY field we used on the SORT statement is defined in the SORT-FILE, not in the FD of either the input file or the output file. The reasoning behind this is obvious: If we are sorting on the SORT-NAME, it needs to be defined in the SORT-FILE because it is the SORT-FILE that is going to be sorted, not the input or output file.

Though the sort file is set up in an SD, in most computers the SELECT statement requires no special handling. Some systems, however, require the sort file to be assigned to some special systems file, such as SYSWORK for the external file-name. You will need to check with your instructor or lab assistant to discover if the external file-name requires any special handling on your computer.

6-4-2   The USING and GIVING Files

As we said, the USING and GIVING files are defined with FD's in the normal manner, but they are not handled in the sort procedure in the normal manner. As a matter of fact, most of the file handling is done automatically by the sort procedure, which will automatically do all the following:

- open the input and output files;
- read the records from the input file;
- write the input records into the sort file;
- sort the sort file according to the directions given in the KEY clause(s);
- read the sorted records back from the sort file;
- write the sorted records to the output file;
- close the input and output files and erase the sort file (remember that the sort file is only a temporary file that is erased after the sort is completed).

Given all this, you need to remember to not try to open or close any of the files associated with the sort. If you do, you will get an error. The entire procedure necessary to sort a file is the simple SORT statement.

After the file has been sorted and all the sorted data is in the output file, the output file can be opened (by your command) for input and the data can be read into the same program and processed to create a control break report, a sequential file update, mailing labels, or a simple sequential report.

6-4-3   Multiple Sort Files

We mentioned earlier that there are occasions when sorting on one field doesn't give us everything we need. Sometimes we need to sort on two or more fields. All this requires on the SORT statement is an additional KEY clause (along with the fields being defined in the SD). Let's suppose we want to sort the customer file by zip code and then by name within zip code. The sort file will need to be set up like

```
SD   SORT-FILE.
01   SORT-RECORD.
     10   FILLER              PIC XXXX.
     10   SORT-NAME           PIC X(20).
     10   FILLER              PIC X(30).
     10   SORT-ZIP-CODE       PIC X(5).
     10   FILLER              PIC X(21).
```

We have added the description of the SORT-ZIP-CODE field to the field descriptions. Now the SORT statement will be changed to

```
SORT SORT-FILE
     ON ASCENDING KEY SORT-ZIP-CODE
     ON ASCENDING KEY SORT-NAME
     USING CUSTOMER-FILE
     GIVING SORTED-CUSTOMER-FILE.
```

The statement now tells the computer to read the file CUSTOMER-FILE into the SORT-FILE, sort it down by SORT-ZIP-CODE and then SORT-NAME, and, after the sort is finished, store the file in SORTED-CUSTOMER-FILE.

6-4-4   Variations

As we said, we can use the same file-name for both the input and output names. To do this requires only a simple change to the previous example:

```
SORT SORT-FILE
     ON ASCENDING KEY ZIP-CODE
     ON ASCENDING KEY SORT-NAME
     USING CUSTOMER-FILE
     GIVING CUSTOMER-FILE.
```

Now the file will be read from CUSTOMER-FILE, and after it is sorted it will be stored back into CUSTOMER-FILE.

Another possibility, though not available on all compilers, is to sort multiple files using one SORT statement. We can change the statement so it reads like the following:

```
SORT SORT-FILE
     ON ASCENDING KEY ZIP-CODE
     ON ASCENDING KEY SORT-NAME
     USING CUSTOMER-FILE NEW-CUSTOMER-FILE
     GIVING CUSTOMER-FILE.
```

Now the statement will take all the records from CUSTOMER-FILE, combine them with the records from NEW-CUSTOMER-FILE, and sort and store them back in CUSTOMER-FILE. This is a simple way to add records to an existing file and still keep the file in sequence.

6-4-5 An Example

To help you better understand just how easy a sort is to write and use, we will prepare an entire program. The program will simply sort the CUSTOMER file down into last-name sequence so a mailing list can be printed. The CUSTOMER file was recently upgraded with additional names purchased from an outside company. Thus the list is being printed so that names and addresses can be checked, any misspellings fixed, and duplicates removed.

The first thing we will need to concern ourselves with in the program is the SELECT statements. We will need four files: the input file, the sort file, the output file, and the print file. The INPUT-OUTPUT SECTION for the program will look like the following:

```
INPUT-OUTPUT SECTION.
FILE-CONTROL.
    SELECT CUSTOMER-IN   ASSIGN TO UT-S-CUSTOMER.
    SELECT CUSTOMER-OUT  ASSIGN TO UT-S-SORTCUST.
    SELECT SORT-FILE     ASSIGN TO UT-S-SORTFILE.
    SELECT LIST-OUT      ASSIGN TO UT-S-SYSPRINT.
```

Notice that the external name for the sort file is simply SORTFILE. As we mentioned, the systems will sometimes require a special external name, but most won't.

Next we need to design the file layouts. As we said, we are sorting the CUSTOMER file (layout in Figure 6-1) by the last name, so our SD (for the sort file) must have the last-name field defined as the field to sort on. No other fields need to be defined in the SD:

```
SD  SORT-FILE.
01  SORT-RECORD
    RECORD CONTAINS 80 CHARACTERS.
    05  FILLER               PIC X(4).
    05  SORT-LAST-NAME       PIC X(10).
    05  FILLER               PIC X(66).
```

CUSTOMER File					
Field Description	*Position*	*Length*	:	*Dec*	*Type*
Customer number	1–4	4	:		Non-numeric
Name Last	5–14	10	:		Non-numeric
First & initial	15–24	10	:		Non-numeric
Address	25–39	15	:		Non-numeric
City	40–52	13	:		Non-numeric
State	53–54	2	:		Non-numeric
Zip code	55–59	5	:		Non-numeric
Filler	60–80	21	:		Non-numeric
Record Length = 80					

Figure 6-1　The record layout for the CUSTOMER file.

Since we are not going to be accessing any of the fields in the input file, we can simply define the record, without worrying about the individual fields:

```
FD   CUSTOMER-IN
     LABEL RECORDS ARE OMITTED
     RECORD CONTAINS 80 CHARACTERS.
01   CUSTOMER-RECORD              PIC X(80).
```

For the output file, however, we need to define all the fields that we are going to print. After the sort, we are going to open the output file so information can be input and the listing printed. Thus, we will define the output file as

```
FD   CUSTOMER-OUT
     LABEL RECORDS ARE OMITTED
     RECORD CONTAINS 80 CHARACTERS.
01   CUSTOMER-OUT-RECORD.
     10   CUSTOMER-NUMBER         PIC X(4).
     10   CUSTOMER-NAME           PIC X(20).
     10   CUS-ADDRESS             PIC X(15).
     10   CITY                    PIC X(13).
     10   STATE                   PIC XX.
     10   ZIP-CODE                PIC X(5).
     10   FILLER                  PIC X(21).
```

The final file to be defined is the print file, which we will call LIST-OUT:

```
FD   LIST-OUT
     LABEL RECORDS ARE OMITTED
     RECORD CONTAINS 133 CHARACTERS.
01   LIST-OUT-RECORD             PIC X(133).
```

In the WORKING-STORAGE SECTION we define our EOF field and the layout for the report itself. You can check the actual program listing (pages XXX–XX) if you want to see those.

The program is very easy to process. We simply call the sort procedure before we do anything else (remember that we don't open any of the files when we were using the USING and GIVING for input and output):

```
PROCEDURE DIVISION.

0100-MAIN-MODULE.

    SORT SORT-FILE ←————————————————— this is the SD file
        ON ASCENDING KEY SORT-LAST-NAME ← the field defined in the SD
        USING  CUSTOMER-IN
        GIVING CUSTOMER-OUT.
```

After the sort has processed, we simply open the output file (CUSTOMER-OUT) for input and then read and print the records:

```
OPEN INPUT  CUSTOMER-OUT
     OUTPUT LIST-OUT.

ACCEPT DATE-IN FROM DATE.
MOVE DATE-YY TO HEADING-YEAR.
MOVE DATE-MM TO HEADING-MONTH.
MOVE DATE-DD TO HEADING-DAY.

PERFORM 0300-HEADINGS-ROUTINE.

READ CUSTOMER-OUT
     AT END MOVE 'YES' TO EOF.
PERFORM 0200-LIST-LOOP
        UNTIL EOF = 'YES'.

CLOSE CUSTOMER-OUT
      LIST-OUT.
STOP RUN.

0200-LIST-LOOP.

MOVE CUSTOMER-NUMBER   TO NUMBER-OUT.
MOVE CUSTOMER-NAME     TO NAME-OUT.
MOVE CUS-ADDRESS       TO ADDRESS-OUT.
MOVE CITY              TO CITY-OUT.
MOVE STATE             TO STATE-OUT.
MOVE ZIP-CODE          TO ZIP-CODE-OUT.

WRITE LIST-OUT-RECORD FROM DETAIL-LINE
      AFTER ADVANCING 2 LINES.

ADD 2 TO LINE-CTR.

IF LINE-CTR IS GREATER THAN 59
   PERFORM 0300-HEADINGS-ROUTINE.

READ CUSTOMER-OUT
     AT END MOVE 'YES' TO EOF.
```

As you can see, this is just an ordinary report program once the sort is done. The entire program follows.

```
****************************************************************
****************************************************************
*
*
*
*   PROGRAM NAME: CUS-SORT
*
*   PROGRAMMER NAME:  ED COBURN
*
*   SOCIAL SECURITY NUMBER:  999-99-9999
*
*   DUE DATE: FEBRUARY 10, 1988
*
*   DESCRIPTION: THIS PROGRAM WILL SORT THE CUSTOMER FILE AND
*                PRODUCE A LISTING THAT CAN BE HAND EDITED.
*
*
*
****************************************************************
****************************************************************

    IDENTIFICATION DIVISION.
    PROGRAM-ID.    CUS-SORT.
    AUTHOR.        ED COBURN.

    ENVIRONMENT DIVISION.

    CONFIGURATION SECTION.
    SOURCE-COMPUTER. IBM-4331.
    OBJECT-COMPUTER. IBM-4331.

    INPUT-OUTPUT SECTION.
    FILE-CONTROL.
        SELECT SORT-FILE     ASSIGN TO UT-S-SORTFILE.
        SELECT CUSTOMER-IN   ASSIGN TO UT-S-CUSTOMER.
        SELECT CUSTOMER-OUT  ASSIGN TO UT-S-SORTCUST.
        SELECT LIST-OUT      ASSIGN TO UT-S-SYSPRINT.


    DATA DIVISION.
    FILE SECTION.

    SD  SORT-FILE
        RECORD CONTAINS 80 CHARACTERS.
    01  SORT-RECORD.
        05   FILLER                    PIC X(4).
        05   SORT-LAST-NAME            PIC X(10).
        05   FILLER                    PIC X(66).

    FD  CUSTOMER-IN
        LABEL RECORDS ARE OMITTED
        RECORD CONTAINS 80 CHARACTERS.
    01  CUSTOMER-RECORD               PIC X(80).
```

```
FD    CUSTOMER-OUT
      LABEL RECORDS ARE OMITTED
      RECORD CONTAINS 80 CHARACTERS.
01    CUSTOMER-OUT-RECORD.
      10    CUSTOMER-NUMBER          PIC X(4).
      10    CUSTOMER-NAME            PIC X(20).
      10    CUS-ADDRESS              PIC X(15).
      10    CITY                     PIC X(13).
      10    STATE                    PIC XX.
      10    ZIP-CODE                 PIC X(5).
      10    FILLER                   PIC X(21).

FD    LIST-OUT
      LABEL RECORDS ARE OMITTED
      RECORD CONTAINS 133 CHARACTERS.
01    LIST-OUT-RECORD               PIC X(133).


WORKING-STORAGE SECTION.

01    WORK-AREAS.
      05    EOF                      PIC XXX          VALUE 'NO '.
      05    LINE-CTR                 PIC 99           VALUE ZERO.
      05    PAGE-CTR                 PIC 99           VALUE 1.

      05    DATE-IN                  PIC X(6).
      05    DATE-WORK REDEFINES DATE-IN.
            10    DATE-YY            PIC XX.
            10    DATE-MM            PIC XX.
            10    DATE-DD            PIC XX.

01    PAGE-HEADING.
      05    FILLER                   PIC X(6)         VALUE ' DATE '.
      05    HEADING-MONTH            PIC XX.
      05    HEADING-DAY              PIC /XX/.
      05    HEADING-YEAR             PIC XX.
      05    FILLER                   PIC X(45)        VALUE
            '                   CUSTOMER SORTED LISTING REPORT'.
      05    FILLER                   PIC X(16)        VALUE SPACES.
      05    FILLER                   PIC X(5)         VALUE 'PAGE '.
      05    PAGE-COUNTER-OUT         PIC Z9.

01    COLUMN-HEADING-1.
      05    FILLER                   PIC X(9)         VALUE
            ' CUSTOMER'.
      05    FILLER                   PIC X(67)        VALUE SPACES.
      05    FILLER                   PIC X(3)         VALUE
            'ZIP'.

01    COLUMN-HEADING-2.
      05    FILLER                   PIC X(42)        VALUE
            ' NUMBER    CUSTOMER NAME          ADDRESS'.
      05    FILLER                   PIC X(37)        VALUE
            '           CITY          STATE    CODE'.
```

```
01   DETAIL-LINE.
     05   FILLER                      PIC XXX          VALUE SPACES.
     05   NUMBER-OUT                  PIC XXXX.
     05   FILLER                      PIC X(5)         VALUE SPACES.
     05   NAME-OUT                    PIC X(20).
     05   FILLER                      PIC XXX          VALUE SPACES.
     05   ADDRESS-OUT                 PIC X(15).
     05   FILLER                      PIC XX           VALUE SPACES.
     05   CITY-OUT                    PIC X(13).
     05   FILLER                      PIC XXXX         VALUE SPACES.
     05   STATE-OUT                   PIC XX.
     05   FILLER                      PIC XXXX         VALUE SPACES.
     05   ZIP-CODE-OUT                PIC XXXXX.


PROCEDURE DIVISION.

0100-MAIN-MODULE.

     SORT SORT-FILE
          ON ASCENDING KEY SORT-LAST-NAME
          USING  CUSTOMER-IN
          GIVING CUSTOMER-OUT.

     OPEN INPUT  CUSTOMER-OUT
          OUTPUT LIST-OUT.

     ACCEPT DATE-IN FROM DATE.
     MOVE DATE-YY TO HEADING-YEAR.
     MOVE DATE-MM TO HEADING-MONTH.
     MOVE DATE-DD TO HEADING-DAY.

     PERFORM 0300-HEADINGS-ROUTINE.

     READ CUSTOMER-OUT
          AT END MOVE 'YES' TO EOF.
     PERFORM 0200-LIST-LOOP
          UNTIL EOF = 'YES'.

     CLOSE CUSTOMER-OUT
           LIST-OUT.
     STOP RUN.


0200-LIST-LOOP.

     MOVE CUSTOMER-NUMBER    TO NUMBER-OUT.
     MOVE CUSTOMER-NAME      TO NAME-OUT.
     MOVE CUS-ADDRESS        TO ADDRESS-OUT.
     MOVE CITY               TO CITY-OUT.
     MOVE STATE              TO STATE-OUT.
     MOVE ZIP-CODE           TO ZIP-CODE-OUT.

     WRITE LIST-OUT-RECORD FROM DETAIL-LINE
           AFTER ADVANCING 2 LINES.
```

```
ADD 2 TO LINE-CTR.

IF LINE-CTR IS GREATER THAN 59
    PERFORM 0300-HEADINGS-ROUTINE.

READ CUSTOMER-OUT
    AT END MOVE 'YES' TO EOF.


0300-HEADINGS-ROUTINE.

    MOVE PAGE-CTR TO PAGE-COUNTER-OUT.
    WRITE LIST-OUT-RECORD FROM PAGE-HEADING
        AFTER ADVANCING PAGE.
    WRITE LIST-OUT-RECORD FROM COLUMN-HEADING-1
        AFTER ADVANCING 2 LINES.
    WRITE LIST-OUT-RECORD FROM COLUMN-HEADING-2
        AFTER ADVANCING 1 LINE.

    MOVE 6 TO LINE-CTR.
    ADD  1 TO PAGE-CTR.
```

Upon running the program, you will get a report printed in last-name sequence:

```
DATE 01/08/87               CUSTOMER SORTED LISTING REPORT              PAGE  1

CUSTOMER                                                                 ZIP
NUMBER     CUSTOMER NAME              ADDRESS          CITY        STATE  CODE

 2423      FIORETTI  GODDELL      234 WEST WAY      EL PASO         TX   79936

 0456      GEORGE    MONICA L     P. O. BOX 1610    ANTHONY         NM   88021

 2248      GESPIN    BRENDA       242 CHISHOLM      ANTHONY         TX   48234

 2323      GRONDIN   GEORGE       1290 HAWKINS      EL PASO         TX   79936

 2223      MCDOWELL  HARRY        2323 TRUTH        SARASOTA        FL   24234

 2345      MUNIZ     FRANK        24 OHARA RD       ANTHONY         NM   88021

 1234      PINON     TONY         234 TEXAS DR      EL PASO         TX   79935

 1111      VIRAMONTE ARNOLD       333 ROSEWOOD      SANTA TERESA    NM   88022
```

6-5

Processing the Sort Data

There are many occasions when we need to process the data being sorted. Suppose we want to sort a customer file into zip code sequence for mailing out some flyers, but we don't want to mail the flyer to everyone. We want to mail it to only one or two of the zip codes in the file. We could sort the entire file and then, as we print the labels, eliminate the records we don't want by simply not printing them, but there are three things wrong with this approach:

1. The sort has to sort all the records, not just the ones we want to use. If the file is large, this might slow the processing significantly.

2. The output file must contain all the records and will therefore require more disk space than is actually necessary for our specific project.

3. In order to eliminate the records as we print the labels, we first have to read those records from the file to determine that they are the ones we do not want—another processing of many unneeded records.

We can eliminate this excess storage and unnecessary processing by using the additional options allowed in the SORT statement.

6-5-1   The INPUT PROCEDURE

First of all, we can process the records *prior* to the sort. This is accomplished with an **INPUT PROCEDURE** that we use *instead* of the USING clause on the SORT statement. The form of this clause is

$$\underline{\text{INPUT PROCEDURE}} \text{ IS section-name-1 } \begin{Bmatrix} \underline{\text{THRU}} \\ \underline{\text{THROUGH}} \end{Bmatrix} \text{ section-name-2}$$

Since this clause *replaces* the USING clause, a sample SORT statement becomes

```
SORT SORT-FILE
     ON ASCENDING KEY SORT-LAST-NAME
     INPUT PROCEDURE IS 0500-ELIMINATE-ZIP-CODES
     GIVING CUSTOMER-OUT.
```

This is the same SORT statement we used in the previous program, except that we replaced the USING with the INPUT PROCEDURE.

In the 0500-ELIMINATE-ZIP-CODES procedure, we can do any preliminary data processing we need to *before* the sort file receives it to be sorted. We may, as the name of the procedure hints, want to eliminate certain zip codes before we sort. We might also want to check for blank fields, count records, or change the records in some manner.

You may have noticed that on the form of the INPUT PROCEDURE clause we listed section names. A **section** is simply a series of paragraphs that is executed as a unit, just as sentences are executed in a paragraph. One section ends when another section is found or when the program ends. The rules for naming sections are the same as the rules for naming paragraphs, with the exception that a section name must have the word SECTION following it, as in WORKING-STORAGE SECTION.

How sections are used in COBOL varies from compiler to compiler. Some require all paragraphs to be within sections if there are any sections in the program. Some require only that the INPUT PROCEDURE be a section. You will have to check with your instructor or lab assistant to determine the needs of your system.

What Must Be in the INPUT PROCEDURE? With a USING clause, the computer will automatically open the file, read the records from the input file, move them to the sort file before they are sorted, and, when finished reading the records, close the input file. When using an INPUT PROCEDURE, however, since we want to process the records, we will have to do all this file handling ourselves. That is, the program will no longer open the input file, read the records from the input file, write them to the sort file, or close the input file after the sort is completed. All these tasks will have to be done in the INPUT PROCEDURE.

It is very important to remember that even though we open and close the input file, we do nothing with either the sort file or the output file. Those files are still handled automatically by the computer.

The RELEASE Statement

As we just said, when using an INPUT PROCEDURE, we have to handle all the input file processing ourselves. But since the input file is just an ordinary file, most of the processing is of the same type that we have become accustomed to. That is, the OPEN statement is used the same way we have used it in the past. We still READ the records from the file and use the AT END clause. The difference comes when we transfer the records to the sort file. The sort file is not an ordinary file and requires special handling.

First, to get the records to the sort file for processing, the record is read from the input file (after the file is opened, of course). Then we have to move the data to the sort file record. The last step is to put the records into the sort file itself. With a normal file, we would WRITE the record to the file. But with the sort file, we have to RELEASE the record to the file. When we RELEASE the records, they become available for sorting. The actual sorting doesn't begin until all the records have been released into the file. And we only RELEASE the records that we want sorted.

The form of the **RELEASE statement** is simple:

RELEASE record-name

Notice that we use the record-name on the statement instead of the file-name. Since the RELEASE statement is basically a WRITE statement, we use the record-name the way we would if we were using a WRITE statement. Also like the WRITE statement, we can use a slightly different form of the statement that allows us to eliminate the move of the data from the input record:

RELEASE record-name-1 [FROM record-name-2]

The second record-name (record-name-2) is the record layout of the input file. If the input record layout is named INPUT-RECORD and the sort record layout is called SORT-RECORD, we could use the statement

RELEASE SORT-RECORD FROM INPUT-RECORD.

An INPUT PROCEDURE

We do have one other point to discuss about the INPUT PROCEDURE, but we will leave it until after we develop a procedure. This last point will be easier to understand after you see an entire procedure.

We want to eliminate certain zip codes from our processing before we print mailing labels. As we said previously, the best way to do this is with an INPUT PROCEDURE.

We will begin by setting up our sort file and the input file so that the use of the field-names in the procedure will not be confusing—even though we will be using the same files we used in the earlier sample program. The SD will be

```
SD   SORT-FILE.
01   SORT-RECORD
     RECORD CONTAINS 80 CHARACTERS.
     05   FILLER                   PIC X(54).
     05   SORT-ZIP-CODE            PIC X(5).
     05   FILLER                   PIC X(21).
```

```
FD  CUSTOMER-IN
    LABEL RECORDS ARE OMITTED
    RECORD CONTAINS 80 CHARACTERS.
01  CUSTOMER-RECORD.
    10  FILLER                    PIC X(54).
    10  ZIP-CODE-IN               PIC X(5).
    10  FILLER                    PIC X(21).
```

Next, the SORT statement will look like the following:

```
SORT SORT-FILE
     ON ASCENDING KEY SORT-ZIP-CODE
     INPUT PROCEDURE IS 0900-ELIMINATE-ZIP-CODES
     GIVING CUSTOMER-OUT.
```

Now we need the procedure itself. Remember that the INPUT PROCEDURE must be a section. We also put a paragraph-name directly after the section heading. This is not necessary in all compilers, but all will accept it and it's not a bad idea to include it. The code follows:

```
0900-ELIMINATE-ZIP-CODES SECTION.

0910-ZIP-CODE-PARAGRAPH.

    OPEN INPUT CUSTOMER-IN.

    READ CUSTOMER-IN
         AT END MOVE 'YES' TO EOF.
    PERFORM 0920-ZIP-CODE-ROUTINE
         UNTIL EOF = 'YES'.

    CLOSE CUSTOMER-IN.
    GO TO 0930-EXIT-ELIMINATE-ZIP-CODES.

0920-ZIP-CODE-ROUTINE.

    IF ZIP-CODE-IN = '79922' OR '79968'
         RELEASE SORT-RECORD FROM CUSTOMER-RECORD.

    READ CUSTOMER-IN
         AT END MOVE 'YES' TO EOF.

0930-EXIT-ELIMINATE-ZIP-CODES.
    EXIT.
```

First, we need to notice that the processing of the input records is virtually identical to the processing we would have used if we were simply printing a report. We open the file, read one record, and then perform a procedure that reads the records until the end of the file is reached. Within that procedure we write the data of the file (in this case we RELEASE the data instead). Of course, we also use the procedure to eliminate any of the zip codes we don't want, by releasing only those that match our condition.

Then we come to end of the looping procedure. After all the records have been read, we close the file. But remember that we are processing a section, not just a paragraph, and the program will not branch out of a section without finding another section. Thus, after the file is closed, the program would simply continue on into the next paragraph. Unfortunately, that next paragraph is the paragraph we used to perform the reading of the file. We cannot allow the program to continue on into the routine; if we do, it will crash because we will be trying to read a file that is no longer open.

This is where the **GO TO statement** comes in. We use it to branch around the performed paragraph. But if we are going to branch around the paragraph, we have to have someplace to branch to. Thus we also have need for the EXIT paragraph.

The **EXIT paragraph** is a special paragraph that must contain nothing more than the single command EXIT, positioned at the end of the section. The next thing in the program will be the physical end of the program or another section, either of which will cause the control of the program to exit from the section. It is important to realize that the EXIT paragraph doesn't actually cause an exit from the section; it is simply a marker. Thus, we can't just use the EXIT statement at the end of the first paragraph to avoid using the GO TO statement and the EXIT paragraph. If we do that, program control will still fall into the performed paragraph since the EXIT paragraph doesn't actually exit. For example,

```
0900-ELIMINATE-ZIP-CODES SECTION.

0910-ZIP-CODE-PARAGRAPH.

    OPEN INPUT CUSTOMER-IN.

    READ CUSTOMER-IN
        AT END MOVE 'YES' TO EOF.
    PERFORM 0920-ZIP-CODE-ROUTINE
            UNTIL EOF = 'YES'.

    CLOSE CUSTOMER-IN.
    EXIT.   ←──────────────────────── note that the EXIT is here

0920-ZIP-CODE-ROUTINE.

    IF ZIP-CODE-IN = '79922' OR '79968'
        RELEASE SORT-RECORD FROM CUSTOMER-RECORD.

    READ CUSTOMER-IN
        AT END MOVE 'YES' TO EOF.
```

This won't work: the EXIT statement is simply a marker, so the program would continue on into the 0920-ZIP-CODE-ROUTINE where it would crash when it tried to read the CUSTOMER-IN file.

It's also important to remember that if we want to add more code in our program after the EXIT paragraph, it will have to begin with a section name. Otherwise the program won't exit the procedure but will simply continue on into the next paragraph.

One final point should be made about the EXIT paragraph. We could (with most compilers) set up the exit routine without using the EXIT statement. We could use the CLOSE statement instead of the EXIT statement, simply by moving it from after the PERFORM statement to the EXIT paragraph. The code could look like

```
0900-ELIMINATE-ZIP-CODES SECTION.

0910-ZIP-CODE-PARAGRAPH.

    OPEN INPUT CUSTOMER-IN.

    READ CUSTOMER-IN
        AT END MOVE 'YES' TO EOF.
    PERFORM 0920-ZIP-CODE-ROUTINE
        UNTIL EOF = 'YES'.

    GO TO 0930-EXIT-ELIMINATE-ZIP-CODES.

0920-ZIP-CODE-ROUTINE.

    IF ZIP-CODE-IN = '79922' OR '79968'
        RELEASE SORT-RECORD FROM CUSTOMER-RECORD.

    READ CUSTOMER-IN
        AT END MOVE 'YES' TO EOF.

0930-EXIT-ELIMINATE-ZIP-CODES.
    CLOSE CUSTOMER-IN.
```

We mention this only as a point of interest. Such coding is not suggested, because the standard method of coding is to use the EXIT statement. You should learn to code according to standard techniques so that your programs may be easily understood by other programmers.

6-5-2 The OUTPUT PROCEDURE

Just as we can substitute the INPUT PROCEDURE for the USING clause if we want to process the records before they are sorted, we can also substitute the OUTPUT PROCEDURE for the GIVING clause if we want to process the records *after* they have been sorted and *before* they are stored in the output file. The OUTPUT PROCEDURE follows the same rules as the INPUT PROCEDURE does. That is, if you are using an OUTPUT PROCEDURE, you must open, write to, and close the output file. The program will not automatically do any of the processing.

Once again the sort file, being a special type of file, requires special handling, this time not to get the records into the sort file, but rather to get them out of the sort file into the output file. We don't read the records of the sort file; we RETURN the records from the sort file. The form of the RETURN statement is simple:

RETURN file-name [AT END imperative statement]

Notice that we RETURN the file-name rather than the record-name. Since the RETURN statement is basically a READ statement (bringing data into the program), we must process the file, not the record. Also, when we RETURN the file, we can check for the end of the file—again, just like the READ statement. With the same file layouts we used in the last example, a sample SORT statement might look like the following:

```
SORT SORT-FILE
     ON ASCENDING KEY SORT-ZIP-CODE
     USING CUSTOMER-IN
     OUTPUT PROCEDURE IS 0900-ELIMINATE-ZIP-CODES.
```

If we were trying to eliminate zip codes in this OUTPUT PROCEDURE as we did in the INPUT PROCEDURE, the processing would vary only slightly:

```
0900-ELIMINATE-ZIP-CODES SECTION.

0910-ZIP-CODE-PARAGRAPH.

    OPEN OUTPUT CUSTOMER-OUT.

    RETURN SORT-FILE
         AT END MOVE 'YES' TO EOF.
    PERFORM 0920-ZIP-CODE-ROUTINE
         UNTIL EOF = 'YES'.

    CLOSE CUSTOMER-OUT.
    GO TO 0930-EXIT-ELIMINATE-ZIP-CODES.

0920-ZIP-CODE-ROUTINE.

    IF ZIP-CODE-IN = '79922' OR '79968'
        WRITE CUSTOMER-RECORD-OUT FROM SORT-RECORD.

    RETURN SORT-FILE
         AT END MOVE 'YES' TO EOF.

0930-EXIT-ELIMINATE-ZIP-CODES.
    EXIT
```

6-5-3 INPUT or OUTPUT PROCEDURE?

Even though we used the same zip code elimination routine for both procedure examples, it would make a lot more sense, for the reasons we discussed earlier, to eliminate the unneeded zip codes before they were sorted. But do we always want to do our processing before the records are sorted? And if we do, why is there an OUTPUT PROCEDURE in the first place?

To begin with, if the number of records is small, it really makes very little difference which procedure we use. But if there are a lot of records, it can prove important which method we choose. And no, we don't always want to process before the sort. Generally we do, but there are cases when it is more prudent to process the records after they have been sorted. A simple example would be records in which the sort key is blank in some of the records. Let's suppose that this is the case and that we want to eliminate those records rather than print them. We could set up an INPUT PROCEDURE to eliminate the records:

```
      SORT SORT-FILE
          ON ASCENDING KEY SORT-NAME
          INPUT PROCEDURE 0300-ERASE-BLANKS
          GIVING OUTPUT-FILE.
   : : :
   : : :

0300-ERASE-BLANKS SECTION.

0310-ERASE PARAGRAPH.

   OPEN INPUT INPUT-FILE.

   READ INPUT-FILE
        AT END MOVE 'YES' TO EOF.
   PERFORM 0320-ERASE-LOOP
        UNTIL EOF = 'YES'.

   CLOSE INPUT-FILE.
   GO TO 0330-ERASE-EXIT.

0320-ERASE-LOOP.

   IF NAME-IN NOT = SPACES
      RELEASE SORT-RECORD FROM INPUT-RECORD.

   READ INPUT-FILE
        AT END MOVE 'YES' TO EOF.

0330-ERASE-EXIT.
   EXIT.
```

In this routine, each record will be read and then the IF test will process them all before releasing only some of them to the sort routine. That means that all the records in the file will be processed through the IF test.

The OUTPUT PROCEDURE gives us a more efficient way of handling this situation. Since the records we are trying to eliminate have blanks in the sort key field, if we wait until after we sort the file, all the records with blank keys will end up at the front of the file. Then we can read through the blank ones, and all the records after the last blank one will be valid records that we will want to keep. We won't need to look at any more of the records because we will know that all the rest are valid.

This routine is only slightly more complicated to construct:

```
        SORT SORT-FILE
            ON ASCENDING KEY SORT-NAME
            USING INPUT-FILE
            OUTPUT PROCEDURE 0300-ERASE-BLANKS.
        : : :
        : : :

    0300-ERASE-BLANKS SECTION.

    0310-ERASE-PARAGRAPH.

        OPEN OUTPUT OUTPUT-FILE.

        RETURN SORT-FILE
            AT END MOVE 'YES' TO EOF.
        PERFORM 0320-ERASE-LOOP
            UNTIL SORT-NAME NOT = SPACES OR
                            EOF = 'YES'.
        PERFORM 0330-WRITE-THE-REST
            UNTIL EOF = 'YES'.

        CLOSE OUTPUT-FILE.
        GO TO 0340-ERASE-EXIT.

    0320-ERASE-LOOP.

        RETURN SORT-FILE INPUT-FILE
            AT END MOVE 'YES' TO EOF.

    0330-WRITE-THE-REST.

        WRITE OUTPUT-RECORD FROM SORT-RECORD.
        RETURN SORT-FILE INPUT-FILE
            AT END MOVE 'YES' TO EOF.

    0340-ERASE-EXIT.
        EXIT.
```

Now there are two loops instead of one. The first loop is executed until all the records with a blank key are returned. Then the second loop not only returns the records, but also writes them on the output file. Since the first loop doesn't write the records, the ones with the blank keys don't end up in the output file. Again, the important point is that only a part of the records are processed through a conditional. If there are a lot of records in the file, the OUTPUT PROCEDURE turns out to be much more efficient than the INPUT PROCEDURE we showed earlier.

6-6
The MERGE Statement

We mentioned earlier that the SORT statement can generally be used to sort one or more files. That is, we can merge the data of two files while we sort them. If that's true, one may wonder why COBOL has a separate **MERGE statement**. Well, the MERGE statement is constructed about the same way the SORT statement is, except that when you use the MERGE statement, the files are not sorted; they are simply merged. If you need to combine two large files, you can use the SORT statement, but if the files are already sorted and simply need to be put together, it would be faster and more efficient to simply merge them.

Earlier we looked at how a sort arranges a file, but how does a merge work? Suppose we have two files that are in sequence by their customer number:

```
FILE-1    FILE-2
1212      1251
2144      1416
2346      2112
3422      4355
5255      5126
5335
```

Now, if we merge the two files, they are simply joined in the same sequence that they are sorted in. The program will compare each element from each list and move them all to the sort file in the proper order. In our lists, the computer will look at the first two keys and move the record from FILE-1 into the sort file first:

```
FILE-1    FILE-2    SORT-FILE
1212      1251      1212

2144      1416
2346      2112
3422      4355
5255      5126
5335
```

Then the second key in FILE-1 will be compared against the first key in FILE-2 (since it wasn't moved). This time 1251 is less than 2144 so it is moved:

```
FILE-1         FILE-2    SORT-FILE
1212 (used)    1251      1212
                         1251
2144           1416
2346           2112
3422           4355
5255           5126
5335
```

Next come 1421 and 1416; since 1416 is the smallest, it is moved:

```
FILE-1        FILE-2        SORT-FILE
1212 (used)   1251 (used)   1212
2144          1416          1251
                          → 1416

2346          2112
3422          4355
5255          5126
5335
```

The comparison then moves on to 2144 and 2112. Again, the record in FILE-2 is smaller:

```
FILE-1        FILE-2         SORT-FILE
1212 (used)   1251 (used)    1212
2144          1416 (used)    1251
2346          2112           1416
                           → 2112

3422          4355
5255          5126
5335
```

The routine continues in this fashion until all the records from both files have been merged into the sort file, which then looks like this:

```
SORT-FILE
1212
1251
1416
2112
2346
3422
4355
5126
5255
5335
```

The MERGE statement itself is very much like the SORT statement, with three exceptions. We still use a sort file defined in an SD, we still use an ASCENDING KEY or a DESCENDING KEY with the field defined in the sort record, and we can still use the USING and GIVING clauses. The three exceptions are these:

- Obviously, we use the MERGE command instead of the SORT command.
- We must use at least two input files.
- The MERGE statement is not allowed to use an INPUT PROCEDURE. Since the computer has its own methods of joining the files (our example was merely an illustration), we are not allowed to use an INPUT PROCEDURE to tell the computer how to input the records (we might RELEASE the records in the wrong sequence). We can, however, use an OUTPUT PROCEDURE if we choose to.

A sample MERGE statement would look like

```
MERGE SORT-FILE
      ON ASCENDING KEY SORT-NAME
      USING CUSTOMER-FILE-1 CUSTOMER-FILE-2
      OUTPUT PROCEDURE IS 0900-ELIMINATE-BLANK-RECORDS.
```

The OUTPUT PROCEDURE above is constructed precisely the same way it was previously. The fact that we use two input files will have no bearing on an OUTPUT PROCEDURE because there will still be only one sort file.

6-7
The Record Rack Sort Program

The Record Rack has a record club in which albums and tapes are sold through the mail. Each month the company sends out a small magazine listing the albums currently available and any albums the store is selling at discount prices. Cindy has been assigned the job of writing a report program to list the current subscribers. Once a customer is a member of the club, that customer's name stays on the list but that person may no longer be sent copies of the magazine. Who receives a magazine is determined by how many months of subscription the record for a given name contains; if the number of months of subscription on that name is zero, that person is no longer sent the magazine.

The records are stored in the SUBSCRIB file (Figure 6-2) in customer number order, but Cindy's list needs to be printed in customer name order. It will have to be sorted. But since she doesn't want all the records (she needs to drop those with zero months of subscription), she will have to use an INPUT PROCEDURE on her sort.

SUBSCRIB File					
Field Description	*Position*	*Length*	:	*Dec*	*Type*
Customer number	1–4	4	:		Non-numeric
Customer name	5–24	20	:		Non-numeric
Address	25–39	15	:		Non-numeric
City	40–52	13	:		Non-numeric
State	53–54	2	:		Non-numeric
Zip code	55–59	5	:		Non-numeric
Months of subscription	60–61	2	:	0	Numeric
Filler	62–80	19	:		Non-numeric
Record Length = 80					

Figure 6-2 The record layout for the SUBSCRIB file.

The report she wants to print is shown in Figure 6-3. The systems chart for the program is in Figure 6-4. The flowchart design for her program is in Figure 6-5. The pseudocode follows:

```
Start
Sort the file by name
        Open input file
        Read a record at end mark end-of-file
        DO-WHILE not end-of-file
                IF months of subscription > 0 THEN
                        Release record to sort
                (ELSE)
                END-IF
                Read a record at end mark end-of-file
        END-DO
        Close input file
END-sort
Open print and sorted file
Print headings
Read record from sorted file at end mark end-of-file
DO-WHILE not end-of-file
        Print detail line
        Read record from sorted file at end mark end-of-file
END-DO
End
```

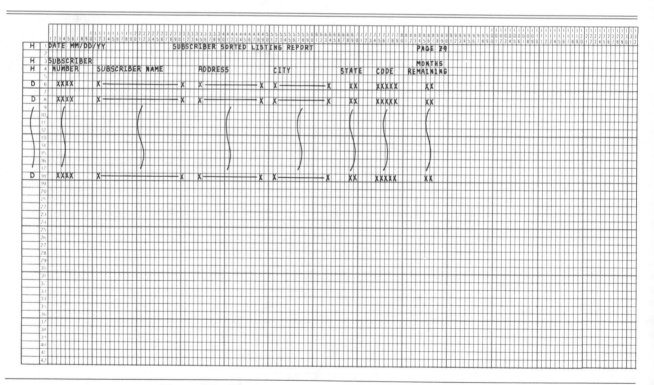

Figure 6-3   The report layout for *The Record Rack* magazine report.

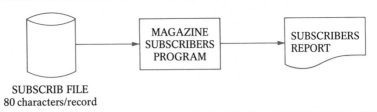

SUBSCRIB FILE
80 characters/record

Figure 6-4   The systems chart for *The Record Rack* magazine subscribers program.

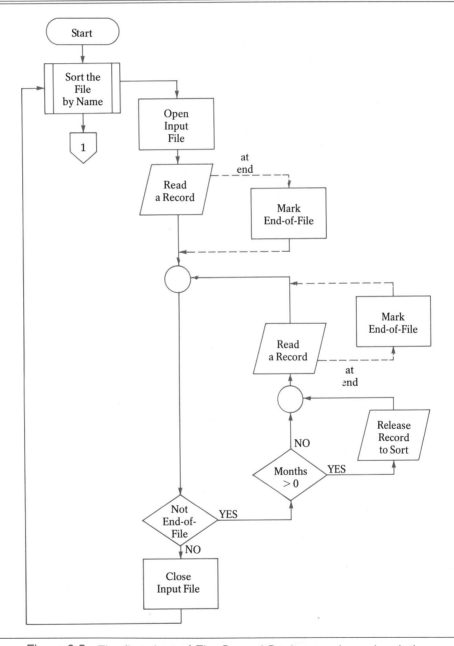

Figure 6-5   The flowchart of *The Record Rack* magazine subscription report.

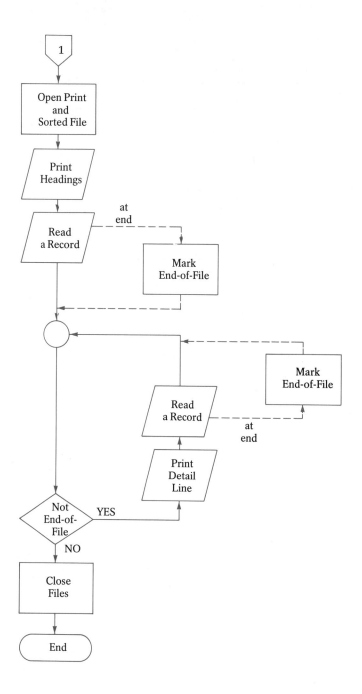

Figure 6-5 (continued)

Note that since she knew no standard way to design the sort, Cindy had to design a new one to convey what is happening.

Her program:

```
**************************************************************
**************************************************************
*
*
*
*   PROGRAM NAME: REC-SORT
*
*   PROGRAMMER NAME:  CINDY HARRISON
*
*   SOCIAL SECURITY NUMBER:  999-99-9999
*
*   DUE DATE: FEBRUARY 10, 1988
*
*   DESCRIPTION: THIS PROGRAM WILL SORT THE SUBSCRIB FILE AND
*                PRODUCE A LISTING OF CURRENT SUBSCRIBERS.
*
*
*
**************************************************************
**************************************************************

    IDENTIFICATION DIVISION.
    PROGRAM-ID.   REC-SORT.
    AUTHOR.       CINDY HARRISON.

    ENVIRONMENT DIVISION.

    CONFIGURATION SECTION.
    SOURCE-COMPUTER. IBM-4331.
    OBJECT-COMPUTER. IBM-4331.

    INPUT-OUTPUT SECTION.
    FILE-CONTROL.
        SELECT SORT-FILE       ASSIGN TO UT-S-SORTFILE.
        SELECT SUBSCRIBER-IN   ASSIGN TO UT-S-SUBSCRIB.
        SELECT SUBSCRIBER-OUT  ASSIGN TO UT-S-SORTSUB.
        SELECT LIST-OUT        ASSIGN TO UT-S-SYSPRINT.

    DATA DIVISION.
    FILE SECTION.

    SD  SORT-FILE
        RECORD CONTAINS 80 CHARACTERS.
    01  SORT-RECORD.
        05  FILLER                  PIC X(4).
        05  SORT-NAME               PIC X(20).
        05  FILLER                  PIC X(56).

    FD  SUBSCRIBER-IN
        LABEL RECORDS ARE OMITTED
        RECORD CONTAINS 80 CHARACTERS.
    01  SUBSCRIBER-RECORD.
        10  FILLER                  PIC X(59).
        10  SUBSCRIPTION-MONTHS     PIC 99.
        10  FILLER                  PIC X(19).
```

```
FD   SUBSCRIBER-OUT
     LABEL RECORDS ARE OMITTED
     RECORD CONTAINS 80 CHARACTERS.
01   SUBSCRIBER-OUT-RECORD.
     10   SUBSCRIBER-NUMBER         PIC X(4).
     10   SUBSCRIBER-NAME           PIC X(20).
     10   SUB-ADDRESS               PIC X(15).
     10   CITY                      PIC X(13).
     10   STATE                     PIC XX.
     10   ZIP-CODE                  PIC X(5).
     10   MONTHS-OF-SUBSCRIPTION    PIC 99.
     10   FILLER                    PIC X(19).

FD   LIST-OUT
     LABEL RECORDS ARE OMITTED
     RECORD CONTAINS 133 CHARACTERS.
01   LIST-OUT-RECORD               PIC X(133).


WORKING-STORAGE SECTION.

01   WORK-AREAS.
     05   EOF                      PIC XXX         VALUE 'NO '.
     05   LINE-CTR                 PIC 99          VALUE ZERO.
     05   PAGE-CTR                 PIC 99          VALUE 1.

     05   DATE-IN                  PIC X(6).
     05   DATE-WORK REDEFINES DATE-IN.
          10   DATE-YY             PIC XX.
          10   DATE-MM             PIC XX.
          10   DATE-DD             PIC XX.

01   PAGE-HEADING.
     05   FILLER                   PIC X(6)        VALUE ' DATE '.
     05   HEADING-MONTH            PIC XX.
     05   HEADING-DAY              PIC /XX/.
     05   HEADING-YEAR             PIC XX.
     05   FILLER                   PIC X(47)       VALUE
          '             SUBSCRIBER SORTED LISTING REPORT'.
     05   FILLER                   PIC X(23)       VALUE SPACES.
     05   FILLER                   PIC X(5)        VALUE 'PAGE '.
     05   PAGE-COUNTER-OUT         PIC Z9.

01   COLUMN-HEADING-1.
     05   FILLER                   PIC X(11)       VALUE
          ' SUBSCRIBER'.
     05   FILLER                   PIC X(67)       VALUE SPACES.
     05   FILLER                   PIC X(14)       VALUE
          'ZIP     MONTHS'.

01   COLUMN-HEADING-2.
     05   FILLER                   PIC X(42)       VALUE
          ' NUMBER     SUBSCRIBER NAME        ADDRESS'.
     05   FILLER                   PIC X(49)       VALUE
          '           CITY          STATE   CODE   REMAINING'.
```

```
01   DETAIL-LINE.
     05    FILLER                     PIC XXX          VALUE SPACES.
     05    NUMBER-OUT                 PIC XXXX.
     05    FILLER                     PIC X(5)         VALUE SPACES.
     05    NAME-OUT                   PIC X(20).
     05    FILLER                     PIC XXX          VALUE SPACES.
     05    ADDRESS-OUT                PIC X(15).
     05    FILLER                     PIC XX           VALUE SPACES.
     05    CITY-OUT                   PIC X(13).
     05    FILLER                     PIC XXXX         VALUE SPACES.
     05    STATE-OUT                  PIC XX.
     05    FILLER                     PIC XXXX         VALUE SPACES.
     05    ZIP-CODE-OUT               PIC XXXXX.
     05    FILLER                     PIC X(6)         VALUE SPACES.
     05    MONTHS-OUT                 PIC Z9.

PROCEDURE DIVISION.

0000-MAIN SECTION.

0100-MAIN-MODULE.

     SORT SORT-FILE
          ON ASCENDING KEY SORT-NAME
          INPUT PROCEDURE IS 0200-SORT-LOOP
          GIVING SUBSCRIBER-OUT.

     OPEN INPUT   SUBSCRIBER-OUT
          OUTPUT LIST-OUT.

     ACCEPT DATE-IN FROM DATE.
     MOVE DATE-YY TO HEADING-YEAR.
     MOVE DATE-MM TO HEADING-MONTH.
     MOVE DATE-DD TO HEADING-DAY.

     MOVE 'NO' TO EOF.

     PERFORM 0400-HEADINGS-ROUTINE.

     READ SUBSCRIBER-OUT
          AT END MOVE 'YES' TO EOF.
     PERFORM 0300-LIST-LOOP
             UNTIL EOF = 'YES'.

     CLOSE SUBSCRIBER-OUT
           LIST-OUT.
     STOP RUN.


0200-SORT-LOOP SECTION.

0210-SORT-PARAGRAPH.

     OPEN INPUT SUBSCRIBER-IN.
```

```
    READ SUBSCRIBER-IN
         AT END MOVE 'YES' TO EOF.
    PERFORM 0220-INPUT-LOOP
            UNTIL EOF = 'YES'.

    CLOSE SUBSCRIBER-IN.
    GO TO 0230-EXIT-LOOP.


0220-INPUT-LOOP.

    IF SUBSCRIPTION-MONTHS > 0
        RELEASE SORT-RECORD FROM SUBSCRIBER-RECORD.

    READ SUBSCRIBER-IN
         AT END MOVE 'YES' TO EOF.

0230-EXIT-LOOP.
    EXIT.


0300-LIST-LOOP SECTION.

0310-OUTPUT-LOOP.

    MOVE SUBSCRIBER-NUMBER       TO NUMBER-OUT.
    MOVE SUBSCRIBER-NAME         TO NAME-OUT.
    MOVE SUB-ADDRESS             TO ADDRESS-OUT.
    MOVE CITY                    TO CITY-OUT.
    MOVE STATE                   TO STATE-OUT.
    MOVE ZIP-CODE                TO ZIP-CODE-OUT.
    MOVE MONTHS-OF-SUBSCRIPTION TO MONTHS-OUT.

    WRITE LIST-OUT-RECORD FROM DETAIL-LINE
          AFTER ADVANCING 2 LINES.

    ADD 2 TO LINE-CTR.

    IF LINE-CTR IS GREATER THAN 59
        PERFORM 0400-HEADINGS-ROUTINE.

    READ SUBSCRIBER-OUT
         AT END MOVE 'YES' TO EOF.


0400-HEADINGS-ROUTINE SECTION.

0410-HEADINGS-PARAGRAPH.

    MOVE PAGE-CTR TO PAGE-COUNTER-OUT.
    WRITE LIST-OUT-RECORD FROM PAGE-HEADING
          AFTER ADVANCING PAGE.
    WRITE LIST-OUT-RECORD FROM COLUMN-HEADING-1
          AFTER ADVANCING 2 LINES.
    WRITE LIST-OUT-RECORD FROM COLUMN-HEADING-2
          AFTER ADVANCING 1 LINE.

    MOVE 6 TO LINE-CTR.
    ADD  1 TO PAGE-CTR.
```

Upon running the program using some sample data, Cindy got a report printed in last name sequence:

SUBSCRIBER NUMBER	SUBSCRIBER NAME	ADDRESS	CITY	STATE	ZIP CODE	MONTHS REMAINING
0040	BRENDA GIBBONS	5678 SOMEWHERE	EL PASO	TX	79956	10
0025	BURL ADDIS	4567 NOWHERE	EL PASO	TX	79945	7
0021	CHARLES HEADLEY	8798 AVE. A	DENVER	CO	23434	5
0015	DAVE ADDIS	425 CHISOM	ANTHONY	TX	88054	36
0008	FRANK CLAUSEN	234 WEST WAY	EL PASO	TX	79936	12
0016	JIM BREITBACH	1425 CHESTER	ANTHONY	TX	88076	24
0026	MERLE STIMONS	4677 MAIN	EL PASO	TX	79985	15
0038	RENE CARSNER	345 BUFFALO	CODY	WY	52546	15
0010	RICHARD COLLINS	9876 FINDUM	LAKERIDGE	NM	88569	5
0004	TONY PINON	2323 TRUTH	SARASOTA	FL	24234	4

DATE 01/08/87   SUBSCRIBER SORTED LISTING REPORT   PAGE 1

6-8
Summary

1. The sort, which is probably one of the most widely used techniques in data processing, is simply a process of arranging a list of data into sequential order. The list is ordered by the key field into ascending or descending sequence.
2. A computer puts lists in order using an internal collating sequence. The two collating sequences commonly used are ASCII and EBCDIC.
3. The COBOL SORT statement has four different parts: the SORT command; the KEY clause, which is used to designate what field is to be sorted on and whether the sort is to be ascending or descending; the USING clause, which designates the input file; and the GIVING clause, which names the output file.
4. The SORT statement will automatically open all the files, read the records from the input file, load them into the sort file, sort the records, read them from the sort file, write them to the output file, and close all files. Thus, the program doesn't do any of the file processing.
5. The sort file is defined using an SD statement, and the key field must be defined in the record definition of the SD.
6. In most COBOL versions, we can sort multiple files using the SORT statement, simply by listing more than one input file on the USING clause.
7. When we need to process the data *before* it is sorted, we can use the INPUT PROCEDURE, which takes the place of the USING clause in the SORT statement. In the INPUT PROCEDURE, the program does not automatically do the file processing, such as opening the file or reading the records. Your program must specify all the file manipulations.

8. Since the sort file is not an ordinary file, we don't write the data into the sort file. Instead, we RELEASE the records.

9. The INPUT PROCEDURE must call a section, rather than a paragraph, meaning that the routine called will have to either end the program or be followed immediately by another section. This action also causes us to program a GO TO and an EXIT paragraph at the end of out INPUT PROCEDURE section.

10. We use an OUTPUT PROCEDURE when we want to process the records *after* they have been sorted. The procedure generally follows the same rules as the INPUT PROCEDURE, except that it replaces the GIVING clause of the SORT statement instead of the USING. Also, instead of reading records from the sort file, you RETURN them to the output file.

11. The MERGE statement is similar to the SORT statement except that you must use at least two input files, they must already be sorted, and an INPUT PROCEDURE is not allowed—though an OUTPUT PROCEDURE can be used.

6-9
Glossary

Ascending sequence   The term for a list or file being in order from A to Z.

ASCII   The internal storage coding scheme used by all microcomputers and many mainframes. ASCII is an acronym for **A**merican **S**tandard **C**ode for **I**nformation **I**nterchange.

Collating   The process of putting things into sequence.

Collating sequences   The storage schemes used on all computers. Two different collating sequences are used: ASCII and EBCDIC.

Descending sequence   The term for a list or file being in order from Z to A.

EBCDIC   The internal storage coding scheme used by almost all IBM computers and a few others. EBCDIC is an acronym for Extended **B**inary **C**oded **D**ecimal **I**nterchange **C**ode.

EXIT paragraph   The paragraph that contains only the EXIT statement, which is used as a branch point to the end of the sort section.

GO TO statement   The statement that allows branching out of one paragraph to the beginning of the next paragraph or section.

INPUT PROCEDURE   In a SORT statement, a section of code that allows the input records to be processed before they are sorted.

Key field   The field that the file is to be sorted on.

MERGE statement   A modification of the SORT statement in which two or more files that are already in sequence can be joined together.

OUTPUT PROCEDURE   In a SORT statement, a section of code that allows the output records to be processed as they are returned from the sort and before they are written to the output file.

RELEASE statement   The statement used to write the records from the input file to the sort file.

RETURN statement   The statement used to read the records from the sort file after they have been sorted.

SD   The **S**ort **D**escription clause, used to define the sort file to the program.

Section A group of paragraphs that are executed in order until either the end of the program or another section is found.

Sort The arranging of a list or file into sequence.

SORT statement The COBOL statement that allows the sorting of a file of data into ascending or descending sequence by one or more designated keys.

6-10
Quick Quiz

Cover the answers with a blank sheet of paper and test yourself. Questions 1–15 are true or false questions, 16–20 are multiple choice, and 21–25 are fill-in-the-blank.

T F **1.** The field that is used to sort the file is called the key field.

T F **2.** If your computer system has a sort utility, it is always best to use it rather than waste your time writing a COBOL program to do the sorting.

T F **3.** *Ascending* means A-to-Z order.

T F **4.** The program will require more time to sort the file into descending order than into ascending sequence.

T F **5.** EBCDIC is most commonly used on IBM computers.

T F **6.** ASCII is known as a collating sequence.

T F **7.** In EBCDIC, the lowest character that can be keyed on the keyboard is the blank.

T F **8.** There is a limit to the number of KEY clauses we can use on the SORT statement.

T F **9.** The USING clause is used for the input file.

T F **10.** The sort can be used to sort the input file and then the same file can be used for the output file.

T F **11.** Most computers require special handling of the SELECT clause for the sort file.

T F **12.** Multiple sort output files are allowed on some computers.

T F **13.** We can have a USING and an INPUT PROCEDURE in the same SORT statement if we want to use multiple input files.

T F **14.** The last paragraph in an INPUT PROCEDURE must be some type of exit paragraph.

T F **15.** The RELEASE statement needs an AT END clause.

_____ **16.** Which of the following clauses is allowed on the SD statement?

(a) LABEL RECORDS   (c) RECORD CONTAINS
(b) BLOCK CONTAINS   (d) None of the them.

_____ **17.** In the INPUT PROCEDURE clause, which of the following do you not have to do?

(a) open the input file   (c) close the sort file
(b) read the input file   (d) release the input records

_____ **18.** Which of the following ends the execution of a section?

(a) another section   (c) another paragraph
(b) the end of the program   (d) either a or b

_____ 19. Which of the following situations would best be handled with an OUTPUT PROCEDURE?

    (a) the need to eliminate some records because they don't meet the criteria for the file

    (b) the need to eliminate some of the records because they contain a blank key

    (c) the need to calculate with the key field

    (d) None of them really makes any difference.

_____ 20. Which of the following is not true of the MERGE statement?

    (a) You must use more than one input file.

    (b) The input files must be sorted.

    (c) There must be more than one output file.

    (d) All are true.

21. The INPUT PROCEDURE must reference a _____ name rather than a paragraph-name.

22. When reading the records from the sort file, we use the _____ statement; when writing to the sort file we use the _____ statement.

23. We sort the file on a _____ .

24. The _____ sequence used on microcomputers is _____ .

25. We generally use the _____ statement at the end of an INPUT or OUTPUT PROCEDURE to indicate the end of the procedure.

≡≡≡ 6-11 ≡≡≡
Answers to Quick Quiz

1. T

2. F (Often, when you want to process the records before the sort, the COBOL sort utility is the only way to do it.)

3. T

4. F (There is no reason to believe that descending order would take longer. The sort process is the same either way. Which method you choose is simply a matter of need.)

5. T

6. T

7. T (The same is true in ASCII.)

8. T (However, for all practical purposes there is no limit, since more than two or three sort fields are really beyond the limit of usefulness in most sort situations.)

9. T

10. T (Though this is often not desirable.)

11. F (Only a few do.)

12. F (Multiple input files are allowed, but there is no need for multiple output files.)

13. F (The INPUT PROCEDURE must replace the USING statement. You can use multiple input files by reading and releasing them.)

14. T (It must be a branch point so the section can end.)

15. F (The RELEASE statement is basically a WRITE statement; the AT END is for a READ or READ-type statement.)
16. c (And, as always, it is a good idea to use it.)
17. c (You do not manipulate the sort file except to release the records.)
18. d (Either another section or the end of the program will end a section.)
19. b (This is the example we used in the chapter. Answer c probably would not matter.)
20. c
21. section
22. RETURN, RELEASE
23. key field
24. collating, ASCII
25. EXIT

6-12
Questions to Aid Understanding

1. Explain what a sort is and what it means for a sort to be ascending or descending.
2. Explain why it is cost effective to have a mailing list sorted by zip code when mailing a large amount of flyers.
*3. Explain what EBCDIC and ASCII are and what they have to do with a sort.
4. Describe the major parts of the SORT statement and how they are used by the program. Give an actual SORT statement as part of the explanation. Be sure to mention the key field.
5. Explain what an SD is and what significance it has to a sort. List and explain the differences between an SD and an FD.
*6. List the seven steps that are automatically handled by the computer for the USING and GIVING clauses.
7. Explain what INPUT and OUTPUT PROCEDUREs are and how they are used.
8. Explain the purpose of the RETURN and RELEASE statements, what other COBOL statements they are similar to, and where they are used in the sort procedure.
*9. Explain the purpose of the EXIT paragraph and why it is necessary. Explain what would probably happen in your program if you did not use an EXIT paragraph.
10. Give one example of when you would use an INPUT PROCEDURE and one example of when an OUTPUT PROCEDURE would be preferable.
11. Explain what the MERGE statement is and how it can prove useful. Explain why you would use the MERGE statement instead of the SORT since the sort will allow multiple input files.
12. Each of the following SORT statements has something wrong with it. Find the errors, explain what is wrong, and show how to fix it.

    (a) SORT SORT-FILE
    ```
            AT END PERFORM 0300-ERROR-ROUTINE
            USING INPUT-FILE
            GIVING OUTPUT-FILE.
    ```

```
(b) SORT SORT-FILE
        ON KEY SORT-FIELD
        USING INPUT-FILE
        GIVING OUTPUT-FILE.
(c) SORT SORT-FILE
        ON ASCENDING KEY SORT-FIELD
        GIVING OUTPUT-FILE
        USING INPUT-FILE.
(d) SORT SORT-FILE
        ON ASCENDING KEY SORT-FIELD
        INPUT PROCESSING 0300-EDIT-DATA
        GIVING OUTPUT-FILE.
(e) SORT SORT-FILE
        ON ASCENDING KEY SORT-FIELD
        INPUT PROCEDURE 0300-EDIT-DATA SECTION
        GIVING OUTPUT-FILE.
(f) SORT SORT-FILE
        ON ASCENDING KEY SORT-FIELD
        USING INPUT PROCEDURE 0300-EDIT-DATA
        GIVING OUTPUT-FILE.
(g) SORT SORT-FILE
        ON ASCENDING KEY SORT-FIELD
        INPUT PROCEDURE 0300-EDIT-DATA
        OUTPUT PROCEDURE 0300-EDIT-DATA.
```

13. Examine the following section of code carefully and then answer the questions below.

```
PROCEDURE DIVISION.

0000-MAIN SECTION.

0100-MAIN-MODULE.

    SORT SORT-FILE
        ON ASCENDING KEY SORT-LAST-NAME
        INPUT PROCEDURE IS 0200-SORT-LOOP
        GIVING SUBSCRIBER-OUT.

    OPEN INPUT SUBSCRIBER-OUT.

    READ SUBSCRIBER-OUT
        AT END MOVE 'YES' TO EOF.
    PERFORM 0300-PRINT-LOOP
            UNTIL EOF = 'YES'.

    CLOSE SUBSCRIBER-OUT
            LIST-OUT.
    STOP RUN.
```

```
0200-SORT-LOOP SECTION.

    OPEN INPUT SUBSCRIBER-IN.

    READ SUBSCRIBER-IN
        AT END MOVE 'YES' TO EOF.
    PERFORM 0220-INPUT-LOOP
            UNTIL EOF = 'YES'.

    CLOSE SUBSCRIBER-IN.
    GO TO 0230-EXIT-LOOP.

0220-INPUT-LOOP.

    IF MONTHS-OF-SUBSCRIPTION > 0
        RELEASE SORT-RECORD FROM SUBSCRIBER-RECORD.

    READ SUBSCRIBER-IN
        AT END MOVE 'YES' TO EOF.

0230-EXIT-LOOP.
    EXIT.

0300-PRINT-LOOP.

    MOVE   SUBSCRIBER-NUMBER TO NUMBER-OUT.
    MOVE   SUBSCRIBER-NAME   TO NAME-OUT.
    MOVE   ADDRESS           TO ADDRESS-OUT.
    MOVE   CITY              TO CITY-OUT.
    MOVE   STATE             TO STATE-OUT.
    MOVE   ZIP-CODE          TO ZIP-CODE-OUT.

    WRITE LIST-OUT-RECORD FROM DETAIL-LINE
            AFTER ADVANCING 2 LINES.

    READ SUBSCRIBER-OUT
        AT END MOVE 'YES' TO EOF.
```

(a) What is missing in the beginning of the 0200-SORT-LOOP SECTION? What would you use to correct the oversight?
(b) Explain the error in the 0200-INPUT-LOOP and show how to correct it.
(c) Immediately after the 0230-EXIT-LOOP is another paragraph. What is wrong with this setup and how can it be corrected? If the paragraph remained, what would happen upon execution of the program (if it worked to that point)?
(d) Could you move the statement CLOSE-SUBSCRIBER-IN to the 0230-EXIT-LOOP in place of the EXIT statement? If you could move it, explain why you would not want to.
(e) If you correct all the errors discussed above and execute the program, it will *not* output anything. Why not? How could you correct the problem?

6-13

Coding Exercises

1. Given a sort file of SORT-FILE, an input file of INPUT-FILE, and an output file of OUTPUT-FILE, write a SORT statement to sort the file into descending order by the address field.
2. Write the SD necessary to sort the PAYROLL file shown in Figure 6-6 into ascending order by the annual salary.
3. Write the SORT statement necessary to sort the PAYROLL file shown in Figure 6-6 down by hours worked and then by employee name. Include the SD for the sort file.
4. Write the SORT statement necessary to combine and sort the files CUST-IN and NEW-CUST-IN by the zip code.
5. Write the SORT statement and INPUT PROCEDURE necessary to sort the PAYROLL file shown in Figure 6-6 by employee number, eliminating those records with fewer than three deductions.
6. Combine the records from the SUBSCRIB (Figure 6-7) and MAGAZINE (Figure 6-8) files. As you can see, the layouts do not match. Write the SD and three FDs (two input, one output) necessary to set up the sort to combine the files. Then write the SORT statement to accomplish the task. In the INPUT PROCEDURE you will need to move the records from one of the files into the layout for the other file so that the two will have a common form.

PAYROLL **File**					
Field Description	*Position*	*Length*	:	*Dec*	*Type*
Employee number	1–4	4	:		Non-numeric
Employee name	5–24	20	:		Non-numeric
Hours worked	25–27	3	:	0	Numeric
Rate of pay	28–31	4	:	2	Numeric
Deductions	32–33	2	:	0	Numeric
Years of service	34–35	2	:	0	Numeric
Annual salary	36–41	6	:	0	Numeric
Union dues	42–47	6	:	2	Numeric
Hospital insurance	48–53	6	:	2	Numeric
Filler	54–80	27	:		Non-numeric
Record Length = 80					

Figure 6-6 The PAYROLL file for the coding exercises.

6-14

Maintenance Program

Roger Barnell, owner of *The Record Rack*, likes the sort program Cindy wrote (see section 6-7). He wants another program written that sorts the file the same way—except that instead of printing a report, he wants the program to be able to print four-across mailing labels.

SUBSCRIB File					
Field Description	*Position*	*Length*	:	*Dec*	*Type*
Customer number	1–4	4	:		Non-numeric
Customer name	5–24	20	:		Non-numeric
Address	25–39	15	:		Non-numeric
City	40–52	13	:		Non-numeric
State	53–54	2	:		Non-numeric
Zip code	55–59	5	:		Non-numeric
Months of subscription	60–61	2	:	0	Numeric
Filler	62–80	19	:		Non-numeric
Record Length = 80					

Figure 6-7   The SUBSCRIB file for the coding exercises.

MAGAZINE File					
Field Description	*Position*	*Length*	:	*Dec*	*Type*
Customer number	1–4	4	:		Non-numeric
Filler	5–8	4	:		Non-numeric
Name Last	9–18	10	:		Non-numeric
First & initail	19–28	1	:		Non-numeric
Filler	29–29	1	:		Non-numeric
Address	30–44	15	:		Non-numeric
City	45–57	13	:		Non-numeric
State	58–59	2	:		Non-numeric
Zip code	60–64	5	:		Non-numeric
Filler	65–80	16	:		Non-numeric
Record Length = 80					

Figure 6-8   The MAGAZINE file for the coding exercises.

It is your job to change the program so that it will print the mailing labels. The layout for the labels is shown in Figure 6-9. Pay particular attention to the first line of the labels, which will print the customer number and then the number of months left on the subscription. Naturally you will need to string the city, state, and zip code so that they will fit neatly on the bottom line of the label. Notice also that there are two blank lines between the labels.

You will need to redesign the program (flowchart and pseudocode) and redraw the systems chart for labels instead of a report. It is suggested that you use a table for storing the labels to be printed. See Chapter 5 for a review of how to do this.

6-15

Illustrative Program

The Hamster, a magazine dealing with the care and handling of hamsters, has been sending out samples of its publication to a large mailing list of hamster owners. Samples are sent only to those people on the list who have not received a sample for at least six months. After the labels are printed, another program is run to sequentially update the list with the current date in the date-of-sample field (see SUBSCRIB file layout in Figure 6-10). The labels have been prepared

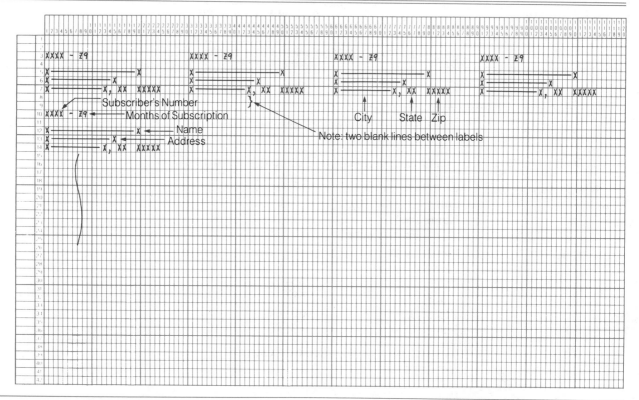

Figure 6-9 The report layout for the maintenance labels program.

by hand for the last few months, but the program to update the file has already been written.

It is your job, then, to write the program to print the labels for the samples. The program is to print two-across labels as shown in Figure 6-11.

SUBSCRIB File					
Field Description	*Position*	*Length*	:	*Dec*	*Type*
Customer number	1–4	4	:		Non-numeric
Customer name	5–24	20	:		Non-numeric
Address	25–39	15	:		Non-numeric
City	40–52	13	:		Non-numeric
State	53–54	2	:		Non-numeric
Zip code	55–59	5	:		Non-numeric
Filler	60–61	2	:		Non-numeric
Date of sample	62–67	6	:		Non-numeric
Filler	68–80	13	:		Non-numeric
Record Length = 80					

Figure 6-10   The record layout for the SUBSCRIB file.

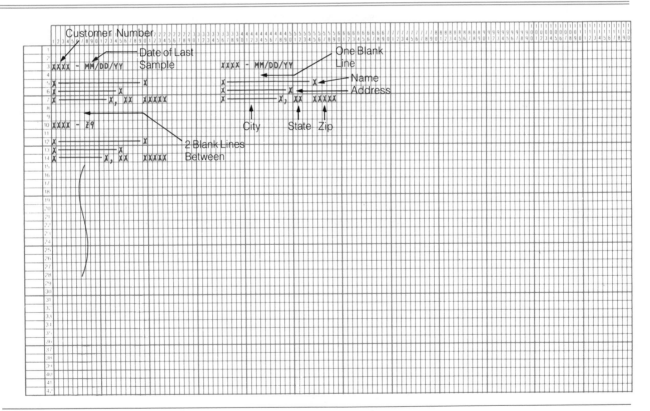

Figure 6-11   The labels layout for the illustrative program.

All records with a date earlier than six months prior to the current date (use "08/15/88" for the current date by using a literal) should be sent a sample. Be sure to turn the date around so it is YYMMDD and will be handled properly by the program. The file should be sorted into zip code sequence. The systems design of the program is shown in Figure 6-12. The flowchart design is in Figure 6-13. The pseudocode follows:

```
Start
Sort the file by zip code
       Open input file
       Initialize "current" date to "08/15/88" (or 880815)
       Read a record at end mark end-of-file
       DO-WHILE not end-of-file
              Turn date around
              IF record date < "current" date THEN
                   Release record to sort
              (ELSE)
              END-IF
              Read a record at end mark end-of-file
       END-DO
       Close input file
END-sort
Open print and sorted file
Read record from sorted file at end mark end-of-file
       DO-WHILE not end-of-file
              Store record in first label output area
              Read record from sorted file at end mark end-of-file
              IF not end-of-file THEN
                   Store record in second label output area
                   Read record from sorted file at end mark end-of-file
              (ELSE)
              END-IF
              Print labels (four lines printed)
              Blank out label areas
       END-DO
       End
```

Note that we used the new design for the structure of the sort. It is suggested that you use a table for storing the labels to be printed. See Chapter 5 for a review of how to do this.

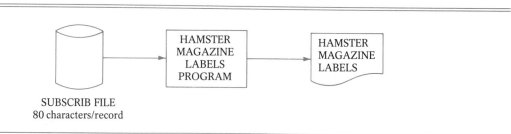

SUBSCRIB FILE
80 characters/record

Figure 6-12   The systems chart for the illustrative program.

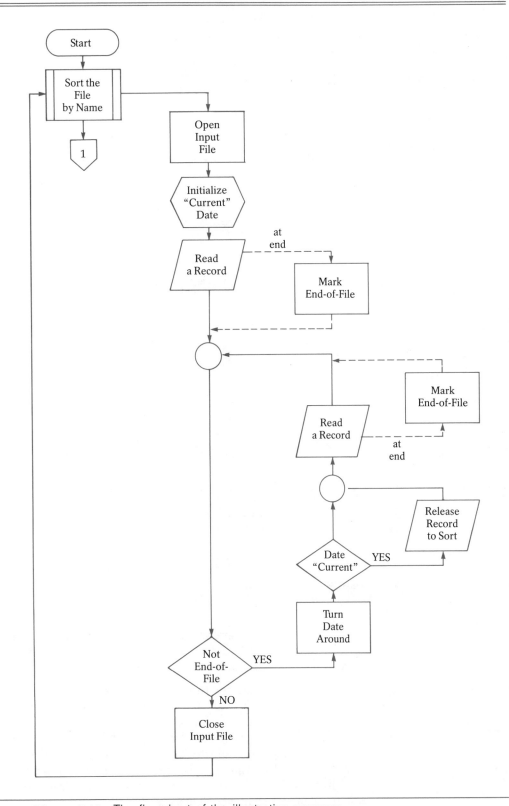

Figure 6-13   The flowchart of the illustrative program.

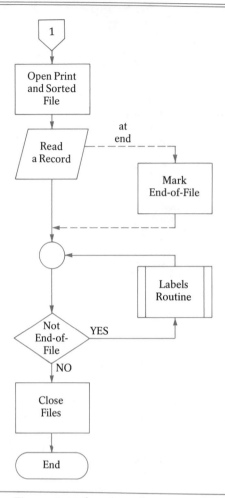

Figure 6-13 (continued)

6-16

System Designed Programs

For the following programs, all the design elements typically furnished to a programmer by the system analyst are furnished. It is up to you, as programmer, to design and code the program. The files to be used are found in Appendix A.

1. You are working for the *Rickety Rack Cabinet Company* and they need a special report prepared. Every month they reorder parts when the stock is below the reorder point. This month their cash flow is low, so they will not be able to order all the parts they otherwise might. Therefore, they need a report that will indicate which parts they need the most. You are assigned the task of writing a report program that will subtract the quantity-on-hand from the reorder point and then sort the file on the resulting number in descending sequence. This way the file will be sorted with those items that need ordering the most at the top (positive numbers; the ones with negative numbers, not needing reordering, will be at the bottom).

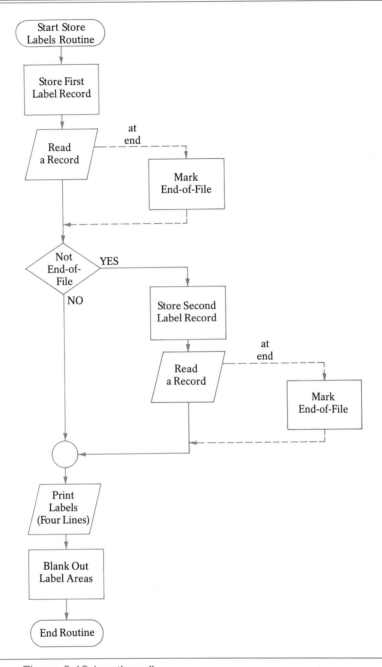

Figure 6-13 **(continued)**

Use the RRINVENT file (Figure 6-14) for the input file. You can use some of the filler area at the end of the record to store the amount that needs to be reordered (you will need to create a new field since the sort must have a field, not a calculation). The report you are to produce is shown in Figure 6-15. Notice that the difference field is indicated with a sign. Be sure you use the sign indicator in the record: if the inventory amount is larger than the reorder quantity, the difference will be negative, and the sort will work properly only if the sign is carried with the number. At the bottom of the report is the total of those differences that come out positive. Those that are zero or negative do not need reordering. The total is of the number of different products that need to be reordered, not of the quantity of each of those products. Thus, if product five needs to be reordered and the difference is 15, you would count 1 for product five, not 15. The systems chart for the program is shown in Figure 6-16.

RRINVENT **File**					
Field Description	*Position*	*Length*	:	*Dec*	*Type*
Product number	1–2	2	:		Non-numeric
Product type	3–5	3	:		Non-numeric
Product quantity	6–8	3	:	0	Numeric
Unit cost	9–12	4	:	2	Numeric
Reorder point	13–15	3	:	0	Numeric
Sales class	16–16	1	:		Non-numeric
Filler	17–80	64	:		Non-numeric
Record Length = 80					

Figure 6-14   The RRINVENT file layout for exercise 6-16-1.

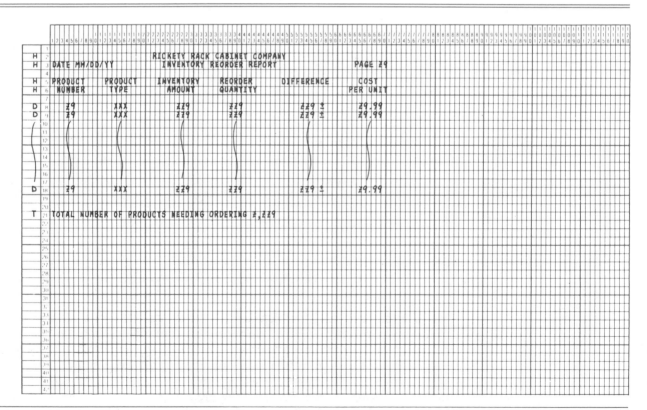

Figure 6-15   The report layout for the reorder report, exercise 6-16-1.

2. You are a programmer for a local construction company that is currently working on many different projects all over the country. The projects are classified according to type of project, for example, "PRIVATE HOME" or "GOLF COURSE." Company management would like a list of the current projects, printed in project type order, so that they can keep a close watch on how many of each type of project they are getting involved in. The list should show the budgeted amount for each project and the total budgeted amount for each type of project.

   You will need to sort the CNSTRUCT file (Figure 6-17) by the project type so that the control break report can be printed. You should print the file according to the report layout shown in Figure 6-18. The systems chart for the program is shown in Figure 6-19.

3. The company you work for employs many salesmen who sell to retail stores all over the country. You are assigned the task of printing a sales commission report organized according to sales territory order, so that the total amount of commission paid for sales in each territory can be discovered. You will need to sort the SALES file (Figure 6-20) by the sales territory and print the report shown in Figure 6-21. The report will have to perform a control break every time the sales territory changes and finally print a grand total. The total sales for the report is a total of the sales for the five products. The commission amount is the total sales multiplied by the percent of commission. The systems design for the program can be seen in Figure 6-22.

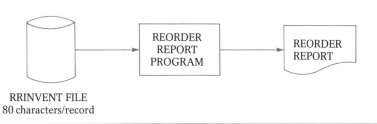

RRINVENT FILE
80 characters/record

Figure 6-16   The systems chart for the reorder report, exercise 6-16-1.

CNSTRUCT File					
Field Description	*Position*	*Length*	:	*Dec*	*Type*
Region	1–2	2	:	0	Numeric
Section	3–4	2	:	0	Numeric
Project number	5–9	5	:		Non-numeric
Type of project	10–24	15	:		Non-numeric
Budget amount	25–33	9	:	0	Numeric
Actual amount	34–42	9	:	0	Numeric
Filler	43–80	38	:		Non-numeric
Record Length = 80					

Figure 6-17   The record layout for the CONSTRUCT file, exercise 6-16-2.

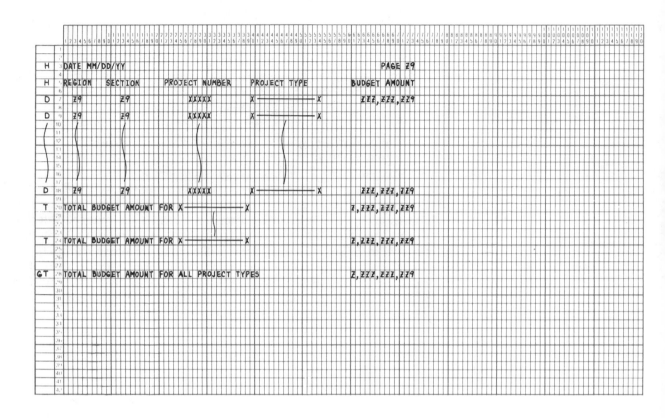

Figure 6-18 The report layout for the construction control break report, exercise 6-16-2.

CNSTRUCT FILE
80 characters/record

Figure 6-19 The systems chart for the construction control break report program, exercise 6-16-2.

SALES File					
Field Description	*Position*	*Length*	:	*Dec*	*Type*
Salesman number	1–4	4	:		Non-numeric
Salesman name	5–24	20	:		Non-numeric
Sales territory	25–26	2	:		Non-numeric
Percent of commission	27–28	2	:	0	Numeric
Sales of product 1	29–35	7	:	2	Numeric
Sales of product 2	36–42	7	:	2	Numeric
Sales of product 3	43–49	7	:	2	Numeric
Sales of product 4	50–56	7	:	2	Numeric
Sales of product 5	57–63	7	:	2	Numeric
Years of service	64–65	2	:	0	Numeric
Filler	66–80	15	:		Non-numeric
Record Length = 80					

Figure 6-20   The file layout for the SALES file for exercise 6-16-3.

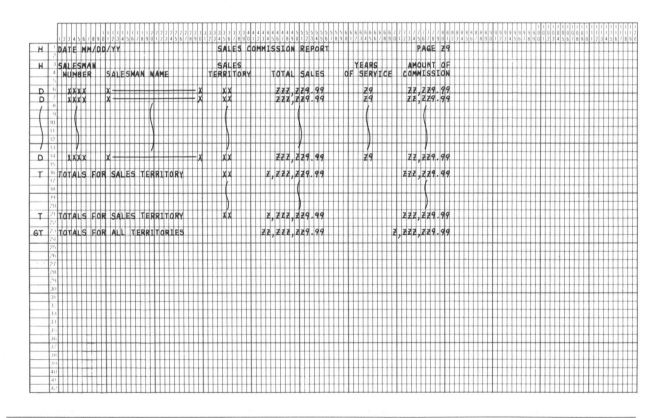

Figure 6-21   The report layout for the sales commissions report, exercise 6-16-3.

SALES FILE
80 characters/record

Figure 6-22   The systems chart for the sales commission report, exercise 6-16-3.

6-17

Interactive System Designed Programs

For the following programs, all the design elements typically furnished to a programmer by the systems analyst are furnished. It is up to you, as programmer, to design and code the program. The files to be used are found in Appendix A.

1. The local bank wants you to write an interactive program that will allow them to display various customer data on the screen. It will need to display all the records in a report format, sorted by the customer number, customer name, or charge card code. Use the BANK file as shown in Figure 6-23. You can design your own main menu, giving the user the choice among the options (list by number, name, or charge card code), but for the displayed report use the design shown in Figure 6-24. The charge card codes should be printed as 1 for MasterCard, 2 for Visa, and 3 for American Express. The systems chart for the program is shown in Figure 6-25.

BANK File					
Field Description	*Position*	*Length*	:	*Dec*	*Type*
Customer number	1–4	4	:		Non-numeric
Customer name	5–24	20	:		Non-numeric
Charge card code	25–25	1	:	0	Numeric
Balance	26–32	7	:	2	Numeric
Date of last payment	33–38	6	:		Non-numeric
Amount of last payment	39–39	7	:	2	Numeric
Credit limit	40–46	7	:	2	Numeric
Filler	47–80	34	:		Non-numeric
Record Length = 80					

Figure 6-23   The record layout for the BANK file, exercise 6-17-1.

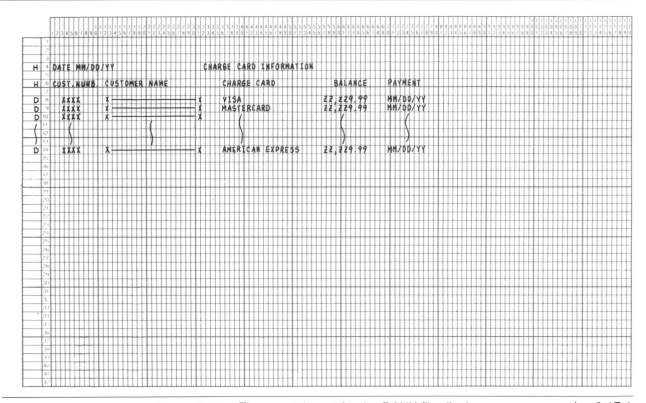

Figure 6-24   The report layout for the BANK file display program, exercise 6-17-1.

2. The company you work for needs a special type of interactive inventory program that will display a report of certain records of inventory on the screen. The INVENT file layout can be seen in Figure 6-26. You are to set up the program so that the user can print certain groups of records, based upon the unit price or unit cost. The program will need to input whether the displayed records are to be sorted on the unit cost or the unit price and then ask for a cost or price range (ask for the lowest and greatest acceptable amounts). It will then sort the file, eliminating all records except the ones that fit in the range.

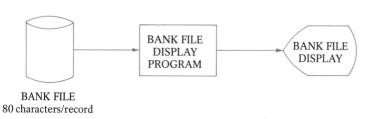

BANK FILE
80 characters/record

Figure 6-25 The systems chart for the BANK file display program, exercise 6-17-1.

INVENT **File**					
Field Description	*Position*	*Length*	:	*Dec*	*Type*
Item number	1–4	4	:		Non-numeric
Filler	5–10	6	:	0	Numeric
Current count	11–16	6	:	0	Numeric
Unit cost	17–24	8	:	2	Numeric
Unit price	25–32	8	:	2	Numeric
Amount received	33–38	6	:	0	Numeric
Amount sold	39–44	6	:	0	Numeric
Filler	33–80	48	:		Non-numeric
Record Length = 80					

Figure 6-26 The record layout for the INVENT file for exercise 6-17-2.

The display of the records you are to use is shown in Figure 6-27. The systems chart is shown in Figure 6-28.

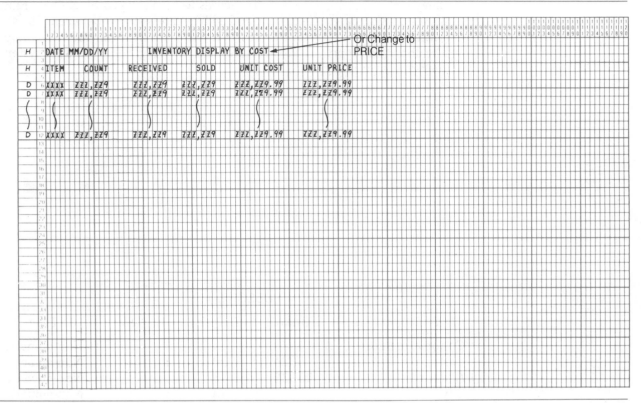

Figure 6-27   The report layout for the inventory display program, exercise 6-17-2.

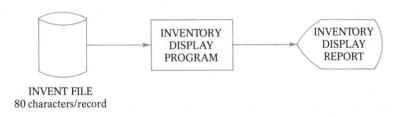

Figure 6-28   The systems chart for the inventory file display program, exercise 6-17-2.

3. The local newspaper you work for needs a program that will display subscriber information using the SUBSCRIB file (Figure 6-29). The users want the program to be able to display the data sorted by customer number or name, by customer's city of residence, or by date of subscription. On each of the listings, they want to be able to select the records to be displayed by giving a range of subscription dates--beginning and ending dates—to list between. The sort will need to eliminate the records that don't fall between the input dates. The displayed report you are to create is shown in Figure 6-30 and the systems chart is shown in Figure 6-31.

SUBSCRIB File					
Field Description	Position	Length	:	Dec	Type
Customer number	1–4	4	:		Non-numeric
Customer name	5–24	20	:		Non-numeric
Address	25–39	15	:		Non-numeric
City	40–52	13	:		Non-numeric
State	53–54	2	:		Non-numeric
Zip code	55–59	5	:		Non-numeric
Filler	60–61	2	:		Non-numeric
Date of subscription	62–67	6	:		Non-numeric
Filler	68–80	13	:		Non-numeric
Record Length = 80					

Figure 6-29   The record layout for the SUBSCRIB file for exercise 6-17-3.

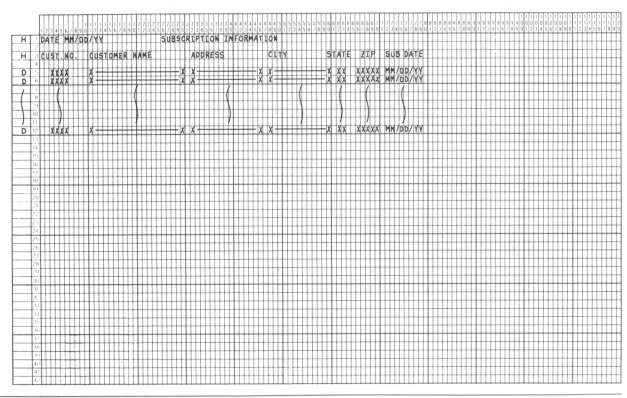

Figure 6-30   The report layout for the subscription display program, exericse 6-17-3.

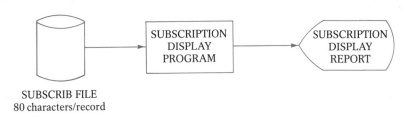

Figure 6-31   The systems chart for the subscription display program, exercise 6-17-3.

═══ 6-18 ═══
Non-designed Programs

In the following programs, you will need to design the systems chart, the input files (record layouts), the printer spacing chart, the program design, and the data with which to test the program.

1. You are to prepare a report of the products received by a particular warehouse. The report is to be sorted into sequence by the date on which the products were received. Be sure to turn the dates around (store them as MMDDYY) so they are YYMMDD when you sort them; otherwise, they may not come out in the proper order. Your report should detail such items as the company that the product was purchased from, the selling price, the price that was paid, and the cost of shipping the product.

2. Prepare a sales commission report. Your file should contain the salesman name and number, the years of service, and the sales amounts from several different products. Your report should detail only the total sales (add up the individual sales amounts). A sales commission is to be calculated on the total sales from the record and figured on the basis of years of service:

   ■ 1 year   = 3%
   ■ 2 years   = 5%
   ■ 3 years   = 6%
   ■ 4 to 6 years   = 8%
   ■ 7 to 9 years   = 9%
   ■ 10 years or more = 10%

   Sort the file down by the amount of commission. The commission rate is paid only if the total sales amount is at least $1,000. If it is less, no commission is paid. Eliminate any records in the sort that are paid no commission.

3. An employee file contains records that have, among other things, the fields of name, sex, date of birth, and date of hire. Write a program that will produce the following reports (depending upon a code input from the user):

   (a) a list of the entire file sorted into name sequence
   (b) a list of all employees who are over 50 years old
   (c) a list sorted by seniority

═══ 6-19 ═══
Interactive Non-designed Programs

In the following programs, you will need to design the systems chart, the input files (record layout), the printer spacing chart, the program design, and the data with which to test the program.

1. You work as a teacher's aide at the local high school. The teacher has assigned you the task of writing a program that will allow the students' grades to be displayed for easy reference. Each student has up to 15 grades and the teacher would like to be able to sort the display by any of the 15 different grades. The easiest way to do this type of program is to move the particular grade that the teacher wants the file sorted on to a spare field at the end of the record and then use one sort routine that will always sort on that field. Your display should allow all 15 grades, the student's name, and some message indicating which of the grades the file was sorted on.

2. Your company uses a fleet of vehicles and you need to write a program that will allow information about the vehicles to be shown on the display screen. Your file will need to include the vehicle ID, vehicle description (passenger car, pickup truck, 18-wheeler, and so on), miles traveled, and number of gallons of fuel used up to the current date. The program should be able to sort the records (upon user choice) by ID, vehicle description, and miles traveled (so the user can see which vehicles are getting the most use). When displayed, the records should show the miles per gallon for each vehicle and for the fleet as a whole, along with the average miles traveled and average gallons used for the whole fleet.

3. Prepare a program that will display general information about students. Your file should contain at least the student name, Social Security number, grade point average, classification (FR, SO, JR, SR, GR), credit hours taken, and residency classification (resident or non-resident). The program should be able to sort the records (by user choice) on any of the fields. It should also be able to display data on a certain student by either the name or the Social Security number. The display for the records as a whole should be in report format; the display for the individual records should be in display format.

OBJECTIVES After completing Chapter 7 you should be able to

1. explain why it is impractical to use sequential updating to process large files when other processing methods are available;

2. explain what files are used in sequential updating and how the files are processed;

3. explain how an ISAM file is structured, mentioning the main file, the index file, and the overflow areas;

4. explain why an indexed file cannot have duplicate keys in its main index;

5. explain how a record is accessed in an indexed file;

6. list the three ways the ACCESS IS statement is set up, explaining how each method is used in the program;

7. explain the purpose of the ALTERNATE RECORD KEY clause, mentioning the one possibility that is allowed with alternate keys but not with the main key;

8. explain the purpose of the FILE STATUS codes and show how the codes might be used;

9. explain the purpose of the INVALID KEY clause and show how the clause works on one of the statements it is used on;

10. explain the different method of using the OPEN statement necessitated by the indexed file;

11. explain the purpose of the REWRITE statement and illustrate the statement's use;

12. explain the purpose of the DELETE statement and illustrate the statement's use. Explain the different method used in the 1968 COBOL standards;

13. list the two files that are needed for an indexed update program and the third file that is normally used with them;

14. explain how ISAM differs from VSAM processing.

CHAPTER 7

INDEXED FILE PROCESSING

7-1
Introduction

We have discussed sequential file processing in the past. Although sequential file processing is acceptable for many applications, it is becoming more important to be able to access a particular record directly rather than having to look through an entire file to find the record of interest. A sequential file can be processed only sequentially, starting at the beginning of the file and examining each subsequent record until the desired one is found. But what if the file contains 10,000 records and we need to process only one that happens to lie somewhere in the middle of the file? We would have to process 5,000 or so records to get that one record we need. It would seem more practical to be able to look up that one record on the storage device, bring the record into the computer, process it, and then put the record back where it came from.

If we are processing a tape file or other medium that is only sequential, we have no choice but to process the file sequentially. But, if we store our files on disk, there are several ways we can process the records directly. In this book we will deal with two of the methods: **indexed file access** and **relative file access**. This chapter will deal with indexed files; in Chapter 9 we will discuss relative files.

7-2
Sequential File Updating

Before we begin our tour of indexed file processing, let's take a quick look at how a sequential file is constructed and updated. Doing so will give us a better perspective on the usefulness of indexed processing.

If we have a file stored on a strictly sequential device, such as a tape drive, the only way to update the file is sequentially. This requires the use of three files: the old master file, a new master file where the changed records can be stored, and a transaction file, which contains the records that cause the changes to the master file. Most of the time a print file is also used.

A record is read from the old master file and matched against a record from the transaction file. Based upon the results of this test, one of the three types of processing—add, delete, and change—is done. Since the master and transaction files are sequential, we have to read every record in both files to complete the processing. Every record from the old master file is written to the new master file (except those that are deleted, of course) and new records are added. This is a slow process, especially if the file is large and only a few of the records actually need processing.

7-3
ISAM File Processing

Sequential processing may be fine for small files and necessary for tape files, but when the files can be stored on a direct access device, such as a disk drive, indexed file processing is preferable. To update an indexed file, we need only two files (three if you count the print file) and we process only those records from the master file that the transaction file indicates.

The most commonly used file structure for indexed files is **ISAM**, or **Indexed Sequential Access Method**, which we will discuss next.

7-3-1   ISAM File Structure

A sequential file is simply a list of records stored one after the other, generally ordered by some key field. If the file is to be updated sequentially, it must be in key field order.

An ISAM file, on the other hand, is actually two files: the main file, containing all the data, and the index file, containing the highest value key in a **block** (one or more records) and a pointer to the corresponding block in the main file.

The main file of the ISAM set contains the data records themselves, which are stored in order by the keys. These records are normally blocked (arranged into groups), and the highest key value in each block is stored in the index file as the **record key**. An example of this structure follows:

Index File	Main File				Block #
Adams 001	Aaron	Abbot	Acorn	Adams	001
Beemer 002	Alcott	Baker	Barns	Beemer	002
Carson 003	Biaz	Blake	Brown	Carson	003
Drake 004	Coburn	Crest	Diaz	Drake	004
::::::	:::	:::	:::	:::	
Wright 255	Wirth	Wordworth	Worth	Wright	255
Zapada 256	Yanez	Yang	Yeates	Zapada	256

Notice that the main file is in alphabetic order by the key. This lets an ISAM file be accessed in sequential order in the same manner as a sequential file.

In the example, each line represents one block. Notice that the last key of each block is stored in the index along with the pointer to the particular block that the record is found in. Now, when a particular record is to be read, the key is looked up in the index. From it the computer determines which block the record should be in, and then it reads all the records in that block until the proper record is found.

The example above shows the main file with each block containing four records. Actually, blocks can contain virtually any number of records. They can contain as few as one or as many as the entire number of records in the file. Obviously, the best size of block would lie between these two extremes.

7-3-2 Overflow Area

The type of file layout just discussed has a problem. Since each block has a set number of records, there is no room to add a record to the block. Look again at the first line of the example:

Index File		Main File			Block #
Adams 001	Aaron	Abbot	Acorn	Adams	001

Suppose we need to add a record for Acosta to the file. The record will need to be inserted between the records for Acorn and Adams. But the block is already full (has four records); there is no room for the Acosta record. Adding records to an ISAM file requires that a special area called the **overflow area** be set up in the main file. This is simply the place where any records to be added are stored. Let's suppose that the overflow area for our file is in block 257 (right after the last block in the regular file). To add Acosta to the file, the computer would store it in the first record position in the overflow area block and write that information into the Acorn record. Then, when trying to locate the record, the computer would look through the block for the Acosta record, the Acorn record would point to the overflow area, and the computer would jump there to read that block and find the record.

After the addition of the Acosta record, the file (first block only) would look like

Index File		Main File			Block #
Adams 001	Aaron	Abbot	Acorn (257)	Adams	001
		Overflow Area			
		Acosta			257

If additional records are added to the file, they will be placed into the overflow area in block 257 until it is full. Then the next block will be utilized. As you can imagine, if there are a lot of additions to an ISAM file, the overflow area grows quickly, slowing down the processing of the file—which in turn requires us to reorganize the file so that all the records in the overflow area can be relocated into the proper sequential positions. The more additions there are to an ISAM file, the more often it has to be reorganized to avoid degrading the processing speed to an unmanageable level.

7-3-3 A Final Note

All of this processing is handled automatically by the computer. The COBOL programmer doesn't have to be concerned with how the files are maintained or accessed. In fact, the COBOL programmer doesn't even need to recognize the fact that there are two separate files involved. We have discussed all the various elements only to give you a better understanding of what is going on in the system.

Basically, all the COBOL programmer does is give the program the record to be stored, instruct the program where in the record the index key is, and then write the record to the file. The system takes care of extracting the key, writing the record into both files (overflow included), and setting up and sorting the indexes.

Now we need to look at just how the programming for an indexed file differs from that of a sequential file.

7-4
The SELECT Statement

One of the most significant differences between an indexed and a sequential file is in the SELECT statement. In the normal SELECT statement, you merely select an internal file-name to be used in the program and assign that to an external file-name that the computer uses as the name of the file that is stored. With indexed files, however, several additional clauses have to be added to the statement. The new form of the SELECT statement is

SELECT file-name ASSIGN TO external-file-name

ORGANIZATION IS INDEXED

$$ACCESS\ IS\ \begin{Bmatrix} SEQUENTIAL \\ RANDOM \\ DYNAMIC \end{Bmatrix}$$

RECORD KEY IS field-name-1

[ALTERNATE RECORD KEY IS field-name-2
              [WITH DUPLICATES]]

[FILE STATUS IS field-name-3]

We have already discussed the SELECT clause of the statement. We will now briefly discuss the external-file-name as it pertains to indexed files. There are basically three different ways the external-name is used:

■   First, it can simply be a file-name, such as

```
SELECT INPUT-FILE ASSIGN TO CUSTOMERS
```

■   Also, it can require some specification (of the type we have been using and will continue to use) that gives the type of device and type of access, such as

```
SELECT INPUT-FILE ASSIGN TO DA-I-CUSTOMERS
```

Here the DA tells the system that the file is stored on a direct access storage device. The I indicates that the program is going to process the file in indexed mode. The I can also be an R for random.

■   Finally, the form can include the SYS and device numbers, such as

```
SELECT INPUT-FILE ASSIGN TO SYS007-DA-3340-I-CUSTOMERS
```

where SYS007 is the SYS number and 3340 is the device number (3340 disk drive).

Now for a brief discussion of the other SELECT statement clauses:

■   ORGANIZATION IS INDEXED—This clause specifies the method that the computer uses to create the file. That is, it instructs the system to create or use an indexed file. As long as you are using an indexed file, this clause must be used exactly as is. There are no options on this clause. On some IBM systems, you don't need the ORGANIZATION clause at all when you use the DA-I-CUSTOMERS form of the external-name, because the I in the external-name indicates that the organization is indexed.

■   ACCESS IS SEQUENTIAL, RANDOM, or DYNAMIC—This clause is used to specify how the program is going to access the file. SEQUENTIAL is used to create the file or access it sequentially to print a report. RANDOM is used when you are going to access particular records directly (randomly) by key, without any sequential processing. DYNAMIC is used when your program is going to access the file both randomly and sequentially.

■   RECORD KEY IS field-name-1—This clause allows you to specify the field you are going to use as the record key. This field must be defined within the record layout of the file you are defining. When records are added to the indexed file, first the data, including the record key, is moved to the record layout; then the record is written to the file. Since the record key is a part of the record layout, the system can extract it to use for the index file.

■   ALTERNATE RECORD KEY IS field-name-2 [WITH DUPLICATES]

As we mentioned earlier, under ordinary circumstances, record keys must be unique. That is, when you want to update a record by using the key, you don't want five records in the file to have the same key because you won't know which of them should be updated. There are times, however, when it would be nice to be able to access records by some field other than the original key.

Suppose we create a file using the employee number as the key. Now we need to access one of the records, but we don't remember the employee number—though we do know the employee name. If we had the file set up with the employee name as an alternate key, we could search for the record by that key and would not have to remember the employee number. The problem with keys like this is that they are likely to have duplicates. If they do, we have to use the WITH DUPLICATES clause to warn the system. Otherwise, when your program tries to write the record and finds the duplicate key, you will have an error.

It is important to realize that an alternate key is just that—an alternate. You must specify an original key before you can specify an alternate, and the original key cannot have any duplicates.

The ALTERNATE KEY clause cannot be used on all versions of COBOL. It is actually an extension to the 1978 standards and not all systems have implemented it. You will have to check with your instructor or lab technician to determine if your computer will allow the use of alternate keys.

■ FILE STATUS IS field-name-3—As you are processing indexed files, there is always a possibility of an error. For example, you could try writing a record with a record key that already exists, or you could try to read a record with a key that does not exist on the file. With this clause, you can discover what type of error is occurring by capturing the file status code that the system returns to the program after every file access. In order for this to work, you must set up field-name-3 in WORKING-STORAGE as a numeric field with a length of 2. Then, after an error is captured, you can check that field for the particular type of error. The commonly discovered errors and their meanings are as follows.

Error Code	Meaning
00	No error—The I/O process was successfully completed.
02	Duplicate alternate record key—Not an error; simply a notification that a duplicate exists on either a read from the file or a write to the file.
10	The end of the file was found while reading sequentially.
21	Sequence error—Will occur on some systems when the file is opened for output and the record key of the record being written is not greater than the record key of the previously written record (most systems do not require that the records be added to the file in sequence).
22	Duplicate key—Occurs when you are trying to write a record that has the same record key as a record already stored in the file.
23	No record found—Occurs when you try to read the file or delete a record and the record key you used is not one that is in the file.
24	Boundary violation—This happens when the file limits set up in your JCL are exceeded.
30	Permanent error—This is a hardware error and should be reported to the operator or supervisory personnel. It is not indicative of a program problem.
9?	Compiler specific—Any error that is in the 90's is defined specifically by the developer of the compiler to cover any conditions that might not by covered by any of the other errors.

If we set up a field called ERROR-CODE, we can use a routine like the following to test the code. This routine comes after a READ statement, when the error will typically be for a record that is not found on the file:

```
IF ERROR-CODE = 23
    DISPLAY 'RECORD NOT FOUND. TRY AGAIN.'
ELSE
    DISPLAY 'AN UNKNOWN ERROR OCCURRED.'
    DISPLAY 'ERROR CODE IS ' ERROR-CODE.
    DISPLAY 'HALTING PROGRAM.'
    STOP RUN.
```

Notice that if the error code is 23, the routine displays a "Record not found" error. But if the code is not 23, which it should be, some unexpected type of error has occurred, whereupon the error code is printed so the programmer will be able to interpret the type of error and the program will stop. If unexpected errors are occurring, it is better to stop the program than risk damaging the file.

Putting together a SELECT statement like the ones normally used would yield

```
SELECT INDEXED-FILE ASSIGN TO DA-I-CUSTOMER
       ORGANIZATION IS INDEXED
       ACCESS IS DYNAMIC
       RECORD KEY IS CUSTOMER-NUMBER.
```

7-5

The PROCEDURE DIVISION Statements

The DATA DIVISION entries for setting up the file are exactly the same as those we have been using. There are some differences, however, in the statements used to read and write the records to the indexed file. We will discuss each of these statements briefly, but first we need to mention the INVALID KEY clause.

7-5-1 The INVALID KEY Clause

In the PROCEDURE DIVISION, the I/O statements used to process records in the indexed file are the same as the I/O statements used to process sequential files, except that when accessing the records directly by record key, we need to use the INVALID KEY clause to capture any errors. A sample use of the statement would be

```
READ INPUT-FILE
     INVALID KEY PERFORM 0900-ERROR-ROUTINE.
```

This statement would read the file and, if any problem occurred, would perform the error routine. In this error routine we could have error statements relating to the file status codes. Under ordinary circumstances, however, if the INVALID KEY clause gets executed we should know what type of error is occurring and set up the error routine to handle it.

For example, if the INVALID KEY clause is used on a READ statement, as our example shows, the error routine would need to produce some message stating that the record we tried to read was not found in the file. Since this is an indexed file, if we read the file and the record we are looking for is not there, the INVALID KEY clause would be executed.

A good technique for using the INVALID KEY clause is to use an error routine and in that routine check the error code as we did in our earlier example. If the code is what it is supposed to be, such as code 23 for a "Record not found " error when reading the file, you simply set up the program to print the appropriate error message. If the code is something different, however, you have the program print some other type of error message and stop the execution of the program. Stopping the execution of the program may seem a bit harsh, and in some cases it would be, but if the program is having unexpected problems accessing the file, it is generally a good idea to stop before serious file problems occur. It's simple to reexecute the program if it is stopped prematurely, but it's sometimes not so easy to fix errors that an errant program has caused.

7-5-2   The OPEN Statement

Naturally the first statement in the PROCEDURE DIVISION when processing data from a file is the OPEN statement. With an indexed file this statement can take three forms. If we are simply creating the file, we open the file for OUTPUT. If we are sequentially processing the file, we open it for INPUT. But, if we are accessing the records randomly, we want to read a record, change it as appropriate, and write the record back where it came from. This means we are doing both input and output, so we need to open the file for I-O. A sample statement would be

```
OPEN I-O    CUSTOMER-FILE
     OUTPUT PRINT-FILE.
```

If the file is opened for I-O, the ACCESS IS clause of the SELECT statement must be either RANDOM or DYNAMIC. ACCESS IS SEQUENTIAL will cause a compiler error.

7-5-3   The READ Statement

As we saw a few moments ago, the READ statement is basically the same as always except that there are now two auxiliary clauses available. If we are processing the indexed file sequentially, we use the AT END clause as we have in the past. If the access mode is dynamic, the READ statement must also include the **NEXT RECORD clause**.

If we are processing directly, however, we need to use the INVALID KEY clause. If we attempt to read a record that is not in the file and we do not have the INVALID KEY clause on the READ statement, a program ABEND will occur. A sample READ statement with the INVALID KEY clause and the NEXT RECORD clause is

```
READ INPUT-FILE NEXT RECORD
     INVALID KEY PERFORM 0900-READ-ERROR.
```

With this statement, if the record we are trying to access is not available, the 0900-READ-ERROR would be performed. In the error routine, we should print an error message stating that the record is not in the file.

The indexed file READ statement can also use the READ . . . INTO form, which allows us to read the data directly into an area in WORKING-STORAGE.

7-5-4   The START Statement

When you are reading an indexed file sequentially while in dynamic mode, most versions of COBOL allow you to begin reading at any record in the file rather than having to read all the records. This is accomplished by instructing the machine to search out the particular record you want to begin with by using the START **statement**. The form of the statement is

$$\underline{\text{START}}\text{ file-name }\left[\underline{\text{KEY}}\text{ IS }\begin{Bmatrix}\underline{\text{EQUAL}}\text{ TO}&(=)\\\underline{\text{GREATER}}\text{ THAN}&(>)\\\underline{\text{NOT}}\text{ }\underline{\text{LESS}}\text{ THAN}&(\underline{\text{NOT}}<)\end{Bmatrix}\text{ relative-key}\right]$$

[<u>INVALID</u> KEY imperative statement]

Notice that the START statement tells the program to search for a particular key that is equal to, greater than, or not less than a specified field (which is generally the record key of the file though it can be any field). The program will begin at the beginning of the file and look at all the records until it finds the one that meets the specified condition. Then, the subsequent READ statement will access the record where the computer stopped.

An example of the use of the START statement would be

```
MOVE 'SAM SMITH' TO NAME-IN.
START INPUT-FILE KEY IS EQUAL TO NAME-IN
      INVALID KEY PERFORM 300-ERROR-ROUTINE.
```

Here we move the name "SAM SMITH" to the record key (NAME-IN) and then tell the program to find the record using the equal condition on the START statement.

The INVALID KEY clause will be activated should no record in the file match the specified condition. If the KEY clause is omitted, the current contents of the field specified in the RECORD KEY clause of the SELECT statement is used and an equal condition is assumed.

7-5-5   The WRITE Statement

Again, the WRITE statement is virtually the same here as it has been all along. As with the READ statement, the difference is in the use of the INVALID KEY clause. A sample of the WRITE statement would be

```
WRITE CUSTOMER-RECORD
      INVALID KEY PERFORM 1000-WRITE-ERROR.
```

The WRITE statement is used to create the indexed file or to add records to it after it has been created. We do not use the WRITE statement to make changes to existing records in the file. There is another statement for that (discussed next—section 7-5-6).

The INVALID KEY clause on the WRITE statement is used to indicate whether we are trying to write a record to the file when the record already exists in the file. Our error routine, then, should print a message stating that the record is already on file. If you are using alternate keys and there is a duplicate on the alternate key, you will still get an invalid key, but the file status code will simply indicate that there is a duplicate on the alternate key, and the record will be written to the file anyway. If you look back at the file status codes, you'll see that 02 is used to indicate an alternate key duplication. So if you are using alternate keys, you definitely want to use the file status codes in your error routine. Otherwise, you might inadvertently indicate to the user that a record was not written into the file when, in fact, if was, and the invalid key was simply caused by the alternate key.

7-5-6   The REWRITE Statement

As we mentioned previously, the purpose of using an indexed file is to be able to make changes to a particular record without having to process any of the rest of the records in the file. In order to do this, we need to be able to read the record from the file, make our changes, and then put the record back in the file where it came from. That's the purpose of the **REWRITE statement.** It will write the record back at the disk location where it was originally stored. A sample statement would be

```
REWRITE CUSTOMER-RECORD
        INVALID KEY PERFORM 1100-REWRITE-ERROR.
```

Notice that we rewrite the record-name rather than the file-name, which we use in a READ statement. Since this is basically a WRITE statement, we must rewrite the *record*. Remember the saying READ A FILE, WRITE A RECORD.

This statement also uses the INVALID KEY clause, which is executed when we try to rewrite a record that is not there. The INVALID KEY clause on this statement should never be activated in a proper program. Records are processed by first being read from the file, updated and then rewritten back into the file. Since the record was simply read from the file, as long as your program doesn't modify the record key in any way, the program should be able to write it back into the file. This is a situation where you might want your INVALID KEY routine to stop the execution of the program so you can ferret out whatever is wrong.

7-5-7   The DELETE Statement

When we were doing a sequential update, we deleted records by simply not writing them to the new master file. Well, with indexed files, we need a special statement to delete the records, because updating is done to the same file, not to a new master file. Of course, deleting records simply means removing them from the file. A sample of the statement is

```
DELETE CUSTOMER-FILE
       INVALID KEY PERFORM 1200-DELETE-ERROR.
```

Notice that we use the file-name (CUSTOMER-FILE) rather than the record-name for this statement.

Once again we use the INVALID KEY clause, just in case there is some processing error. If we input the key we are to delete, move the key to the record layout, and then use the DELETE statement, there is a possibility that the record key we are trying to delete will not be in the file. The INVALID KEY clause is used to catch such situations.

The DELETE statement exists only in the 1974 and 1985 COBOL standards. In the 1968 version, a deletion flag is set instead. When you define the file, you must set up the first byte of the record as a special deletion flag, such as

```
01   CUSTOMER-RECORD.
     10   DELETION-FLAG          PIC X.
     10   RECORD-KEY             PIC X(5).
     : : :
     : : :
```

When the records are first written into the file, the DELETION-FLAG can be set to any value at all, though SPACES is typically used. Then, when the record is to be deleted, HIGH-VALUES is moved to the field and subsequent file access statements will ignore the record. The PROCEDURE DIVISION coding for doing this is simple:

```
MOVE HIGH-VALUES TO DELETION-FLAG.
REWRITE CUSTOMER-RECORD
        INVALID KEY
        DISPLAY 'UNKNOWN ERROR.  HALTING PROGRAM.'
        STOP RUN.
```

Notice we used an example that would stop the execution of the program if the INVALID KEY clause was activated. Since the record was just read from the file, there should be no problem rewriting the record. If the REWRITE statement encounters any problems, something is drastically wrong and the program should be stopped before any major damage is done to the file.

After records are deleted in this fashion, they are, of course, still in the file. We didn't actually delete them from the file; we merely marked them for deletion. Now we have to use a special program—a file update program—to remove the records from the file. We read the records from the first file and check the deletion code. Only if it is not HIGH-VALUES will the record be written to the new file. If the deletion code is HIGH-VALUES, the record will not be written, and in this way it will be deleted. This type of clean-up program needs to be run periodically to remove any deleted records.

7-6
Creating an Indexed File

Many computer systems have a utility program of some type to create your indexed files. You simply tell the program where the key is in the record and input all the records that are to be added to the file; the program will automatically create the file (actually two files) and put the records in it. Since not all systems have such utilities, however, it is necessary to look at how a program can be used to create an indexed file.

Creating an indexed file is identical to creating a sequential file except for the use of the INVALID KEY clause on the WRITE statement. Let's suppose we want to convert a sequential tape file to an indexed file so that we can access the records more easily. Our program would need two SELECT clauses, one for each file:

```
SELECT INPUT-FILE       ASSIGN TO UT-S-CUSTOMERS.
SELECT ISAM-OUTPUT-FILE ASSIGN TO DA-I-CUSOUT
        ORGANIZATION IS INDEXED
        ACCESS IS SEQUENTIAL
        RECORD KEY IS ISAM-CUSTOMER-NUMBER.
```

The organization of the indexed file is INDEXED, of course, but the access is SEQUENTIAL, which will allow us to add the records sequentially. The record key is the customer number and must be defined in the record layout for the ISAM-OUTPUT-FILE. The layout for the two files is

```
FD   INPUT-FILE
     LABEL RECORDS ARE OMITTED
     RECORD CONTAINS 80 CHARACTERS.
01   INPUT-RECORD                PIC X(80).

FD   ISAM-OUTPUT-FILE
     LABEL RECORDS ARE OMITTED
     RECORD CONTAINS 80 CHARACTERS.
01   ISAM-OUTPUT-RECORD.
     10   ISAM-CUSTOMER-NUMBER  PIC X(4).
     10   ISAM-DATA-RECORD      PIC X(75).
```

Since we are not going to be accessing any of the data, we don't need to define any of the fields in either file (with the exception of the record key, of course). We can simply move all the data from the INPUT-FILE to the ISAM-OUTPUT-FILE.

In the PROCEDURE DIVISION we will simply read the records from the INPUT-FILE, move them to the ISAM-OUTPUT-RECORD, and write the record. The coding will be

```
PROCEDURE DIVISION.

0100-MAIN-MODULE.

     OPEN INPUT   INPUT-FILE
          OUTPUT ISAM-OUTPUT-FILE.

     READ INPUT-FILE INTO ISAM-OUTPUT-RECORD
          AT END MOVE 'YES' TO EOF.
     PERFORM 0200-INPUT-LOOP
          UNTIL EOF = 'YES'.

     CLOSE INPUT-FILE
           ISAM-OUTPUT-FILE.
     STOP RUN.

0200-INPUT-LOOP.

     WRITE ISAM-OUTPUT-RECORD
           INVALID KEY
           DISPLAY 'RECORD KEY ' ISAM-CUSTOMER-NUMBER
                   'ALREADY ON FILE.'.
     READ INPUT-FILE INTO ISAM-OUTPUT-RECORD
          AT END MOVE 'YES' TO EOF.
```

Since the record layouts for both files match, we simply read the input file into the output file area. If the input file would have had extra fields or if we had wanted the output file to be organized differently, we would have had to move the fields individually from one record layout to the other.

As the records are written into the indexed file, the INVALID KEY clause simply displays a message on the screen each time the key is a duplicate. Then the user can check all the duplicates out. If there might be a lot of them, you might want to print the keys on the printer instead of the screen. That way there will be a more permanent record of the duplicates.

7-7
An Indexed Update Program

Now that we have created our indexed file, we can update it. We will use basically the same procedure we used when updating a sequential file, except that the program is simpler.

For the sequential update, we used four files: the old master file, the transaction file, the new master file, and the report file. To update an indexed file, we need only three—since we don't need the new master file. Also, since the indexed file is updated randomly, there is no matching of the keys from the transaction file with the keys from the master file. Thus, the transaction file does not have to be sorted. Even though it doesn't have to be, most users will still sort the transactions so that the update report will be in sequence. It's a lot easier to read through a report that is in some type of sequence.

7-7-1 The File Layouts

Just as with the sequential update procedure, there are three basic functions that we need to be concerned with when updating an indexed file:

- New records need to be added to the file.
- Unneeded records need to be deleted from the file.
- Current records need to be changed in some way, for example, replacing a name or increasing the value of one of the fields, such as the quantity-on-hand in an inventory file.

For our example program, assume that the file we are going to update has the following layout (shown in Figure 7-1):

```
FD  ISAM-FILE
    LABEL RECORDS ARE OMITTED
    RECORD CONTAINS 80 CHARACTERS.
01  ISAM-RECORD.
    10  CUSTOMER-NUMBER          PIC X(4).
    10  ISAM-DATA.
        20  CUSTOMER-NAME        PIC X(20).
        20  CUS-ADDRESS          PIC X(15).
        20  CITY                 PIC X(13).
        20  STATE                PIC XX.
        20  ZIP-CODE             PIC X(5).
        20  ACCOUNT-BALANCE      PIC 9(4)V99.
        20  FILLER               PIC X(15).
```

CUSTOMER File					
Field Description	*Position*	*Length*	:	*Dec*	*Type*
Customer number	1–4	4	:		Non-numeric
Name	5–24	20	:		Non-numeric
Address	25–39	15	:		Non-numeric
City	40–52	13	:		Non-numeric
State	53–54	2	:		Non-numeric
Zip code	55–59	5	:		Non-numeric
Account balance	60–65	6	:	2	Numeric
Filler	66–80	15	:		Non-numeric
Record Length = 80					

Figure 7-1   The record layout for the CUSTOMER file.

We set up the ISAM-DATA group item to make it easy to move the data from added records. You will see a similar layout for the add records in the transaction file.

The transaction records must first have the record key for the record that is to be added, deleted, or changed. Then, in order for the compiler to know which of these functions the program is to perform, the transaction record must have a transaction code. For our example program, we will assume that the transaction code is A for add, D for delete, and C for change. If our record key is five non-numeric characters long, our transaction record layout thus far is

```
FD   TRANSACTION-FILE
     LABEL RECORDS ARE OMITTED
     RECORD CONTAINS 80 CHARACTERS.
01   TRANSACTION-RECORD.
     10   TRANS-KEY              PIC X(4).
     10   TRANS-CODE             PIC X.
```

Now, depending upon what the transaction code is, the rest of the record can have one of three formats. If the record is an add, we need all of the fields for the rest of the record to be added (we already have the record key):

```
     10   TRANS-ADD-DATA         PIC X(75).
```

We could specify the individual fields, but there really is no need to since we will have to move all this data to the record layout for the indexed file (remember we set up the ISAM-DATA group item so this one could be moved there) and all the fields will be defined there. It will be easier to simply move all the data with a single MOVE statement rather than having to move all the fields individually.

If the transaction code is for a delete, nothing else is needed on the transaction record; all we need for a delete is the record key.

If the transaction is a change, we need a field code so we will know which field is to be changed. Look back at the record layout for the customer file we are updating and you will see that there are seven fields: CUSTOMER-NUMBER,

CUSTOMER-NAME, CUS-ADDRESS, CITY, STATE, ZIP-CODE, and ACCOUNT-BALANCE. Since this file is indexed, we cannot change the CUSTOMER-NUMBER because it is the key field, but we can change the other six fields. So, for the transaction change record, the next field needs to be a field-code.

Then we will need the new data that is to be loaded into the file. We can define the rest of the layout for the change record within the TRANS-ADD-DATA group item as

```
20   TRANS-FIELD-CODE            PIC X.
20   TRANS-DATA                  PIC X(74).
```

We could define each of the fields, but when they are all moved into the indexed record layout, the field TRANS-DATA with the length of 74 will be truncated to fit in the field lengths defined in the indexed record layout. Thus, when we move TRANS-DATA to CUSTOMER-NAME, only twenty characters of TRANS-DATA will be moved; the rest of the field, which would be blanks anyway, will be dropped. There is an exception to this, however. We have a numeric field that we need to be able to change. Since we cannot move a non-numeric field to a numeric one without running into problems, we will need to define the balance field by redefining the input record:

```
01   BALANCE-RECORD.
     10   FILLER                 PIC X(6).
     10   TRANS-BALANCE          PIC 9(4)V99.
     10   FILLER                 PIC X(68).
```

After this, the entire transaction layout would look like the following (layout in Figure 7-2):

TRANSIN **File**					
Field Description	*Position*	*Length*	:	*Dec*	*Type*
Customer number	1–4	4	:		Non-numeric
Transaction code	5–5	1	:		Non-numeric
Transaction data			:		
Field code	6–6	1	:		Non-numeric
Additional data	7–80	74	:		Non-numeric
Record Length = 80					

The additional data field is redefined to allow the use of the numeric balance field:

Transaction balance	7–12	6	:	2	Numeric
Filler	13–80	68	:		Non-numeric

Figure 7-2   The record layout for the transaction file.

```
FD  TRANSACTION-FILE
    LABEL RECORDS ARE OMITTED
    RECORD CONTAINS 80 CHARACTERS.
01  TRANSACTION-RECORD.
    10   TRANS-KEY                        PIC X(4).
    10   TRANS-CODE                       PIC X.
    10   TRANS-ADD-DATA.
         20   TRANS-FIELD-CODE            PIC X.
         20   TRANS-DATA                  PIC X(74).
01  BALANCE-RECORD.
    10   FILLER                           PIC X(6).
    10   TRANS-BALANCE                    PIC 9(4)V99.
         FILLER                           PIC X(68).
```

The final file we need to have defined is the report file. Its definition is simple:

```
FD  PRINT-OUT
    LABEL RECORDS ARE OMITTED
    RECORD CONTAINS 133 CHARACTERS.
01  PRINT-RECORD                          PIC X(133).
```

7-7-2 The Report Layout

Before we move on to the PROCEDURE DIVISION, let's take a brief look at the format we should use for the reports we are going to generate as the update procedure is executed. Recall from Chapter 3 that we usually print three reports: one before the update, one during the update, and one after the update. In an update to an indexed file, the first report is generally not printed because the update report will explain just what has happened and the number of records changed is generally only a small percentage of the records in the file. Because of the latter, the third report is often not printed either. In our example program, we will use both the update and the after update reports.

Generally the same report format is used for both reports, except that the update report prints additional information about the transaction. Figure 7-3 shows the report layout for both reports we would generate when updating the file we have been discussing.

Notice the area labeled "TRANSACTION INFORMATION," where we will print the information about what type of transaction we processed and how the data was affected. The information we will print for the transactions falls into four categories:

1. If the transaction is an add, we will print all the new fields being added to the file as if the transaction were already a record in the file. We will simply place a message in the "TRANSACTION INFORMATION" area that says "ADD."
2. If the transaction is a delete, all the fields from the record being deleted will be printed on the left side of the report and the "TRANSACTION INFORMATION" area will simply say "DELETE."
3. If the transaction is a change, we will print the record with the new data already in it on the left side of the report. Then, the "TRANSACTION INFORMATION" area will show the transaction type as "CHANGE," the name of the field being changed, and finally, the old data that was in the file before the change. For example, suppose the master record contains the name "SAM JONES" and we need to change it to "FRED SMITH." The transaction report detail line would look like the one shown in Figure 7-4.

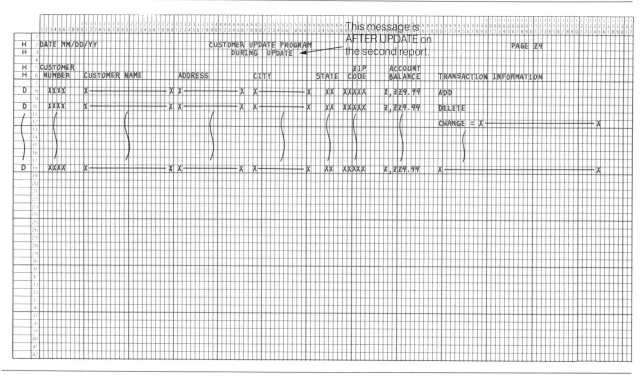

Figure 7-3 The report layout for the customer update report.

4. The fourth category of transaction detail is an error. Basically we can have three errors while processing these transactions:

∎ We can try to add a record that is already on file. The "TRANSACTION INFORMATION" for this error should look like

```
ADD = ERROR - RECORD ALREADY ON FILE
```

In the detail area (the left side of the report) you would print the data from the master record, not the data on the transaction record. Naturally, since the transaction code was for an add, the fields that were to be added will be on the transaction record. They will, unfortunately, just have to be ignored in favor of printing the current master record on the report.

∎ We can try to change a record that is not on file. Here the "TRANSACTION INFORMATION" should be

```
CHANGE = ERROR - RECORD NOT ON FILE = XXXXX (key)
```

Now we will print nothing on the left side of the report. The transaction record has only one field and that field is meaningless since the record we were supposed to change doesn't exist. The record key that we tried to match is printed on the end of the "TRANSACTION INFORMATION" so that we know which record we didn't find.

∎ We can try to delete a record that is not on file. We will print basically the same "TRANSACTION INFORMATION" and, again, no detail will be printed. The error message should be

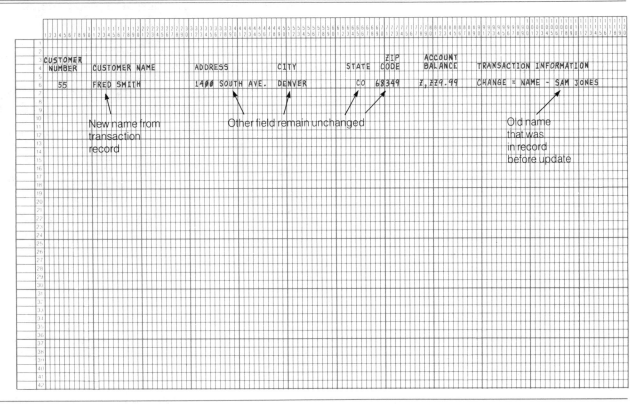

Figure 7-4   A sample of the transaction report detail.

```
DELETE = ERROR - RECORD NOT ON FILE = XXXXX (key)
```

Now that we have looked at the files and reports, let's look at how the PROCEDURE DIVISION coding is done.

7-7-3 The PROCEDURE DIVISION

First, of course, the files need to be opened and the report headings for the update report need to be printed:

```
PROCEDURE DIVISION.

0100-MAIN-MODULE.

    OPEN INPUT  TRANSACTION-FILE
         I-O    ISAM-FILE
         OUTPUT PRINT-OUT.

    ACCEPT DATE-IN FROM DATE.
    MOVE DATE-YY TO HEADING-YEAR.
    MOVE DATE-MM TO HEADING-MONTH.
    MOVE DATE-DD TO HEADING-DAY.

    PERFORM 0700-PRINT-HEADINGS.
```

Then we will read the first transaction record and perform the loop to do all the processing:

```
READ TRANSACTION-FILE
     AT END MOVE 'YES' TO EOF.
PERFORM 0200-TRANSACTION-LOOP
     UNITL EOF = 'YES'.
```

The 0200-TRANSACTION-LOOP will begin by moving the record key from the transaction record to the indexed file and attempting to read the indexed record. If the record is not found, the INVALID KEY clause will be executed and will move 'NO ' to the FOUND-KEY field. This will then be used to determine the type of transaction routine the program should perform. The loop will begin with

```
0200-TRANSACTION-LOOP.

     MOVE TRANS-KEY TO CUSTOMER-NUMBER.
     MOVE 'YES' TO FOUND-KEY.
     READ ISAM-FILE
          INVALID KEY MOVE 'NO ' TO FOUND-KEY.
```

Notice that we move 'YES' to the FOUND-KEY before we read the file. That way, if the record is found, the FOUND-KEY will still have 'YES' in it because the INVALID KEY clause will not be executed. If the record is not found (FOUND-KEY = 'NO '), adding the record would be the valid transaction, so the program will perform the add routine. If the record is found, however (FOUND-KEY remains 'YES'), the only valid transaction is change or delete. The test for the FOUND-KEY would be

```
IF FOUND-KEY = 'YES'
   PERFORM 0300-CHANGE-DELETE-ROUTINE
ELSE
   PERFORM 0400-ADD-ROUTINE.

READ TRANSACTION-FILE
     AT END MOVE 'YES' TO EOF.
```

Notice that the last action in this routine is to read the transaction file again. This keeps our loop going.

The 0300-CHANGE-DELETE-ROUTINE will test for the changing or deleting of the record based upon the transaction code in the transaction record. The test is actually the only element in this routine other than the error routine. You may notice that if the transaction code is not a 'C' for change or 'D' for delete, this routine does not assume that the code must be an 'A' for add (an error). Such an assumption would not be valid; someone could have keypunched the transaction code wrong and it would not necessarily be one of the three valid codes. Thus, this routine has two error messages: one for an add error and one for an invalid transaction code:

```
0300-CHANGE-DELETE-ROUTINE.

     IF TRANS-CODE = 'C'
        PERFORM 0310-CHANGE-ROUTINE
```

```
    ELSE
       IF TRANS-CODE = 'D'
          PERFORM 0320-DELETE-ROUTINE
    ELSE
       IF TRANS-CODE = 'A'
          MOVE ADD-ERROR-LINE TO TRANS-INFORMATION
          PERFORM 0600-WRITE-DETAIL
    ELSE
       MOVE TRANS-CODE      TO MISC-ERROR-CODE
       MOVE MISC-ERROR-LINE TO TRANS-INFORMATION
       PERFORM 0800-MOVE-FIELDS
       PERFORM 0600-WRITE-DETAIL.
```

Each of these error routines begins by performing the 0800-MOVE-FIELDS routine, which simply moves the data from the ISAM-FILE to the detail line. Then the add error routine moves the error message to the detail line (the TRANS-INFORMATION part of the detail line) and prints the detail line. The code error routine moves the transaction code to its error line and moves that error line to the detail line before printing it.

In the 0310-CHANGE-ROUTINE, we need to examine the transaction field code to determine which of the six fields we need to change. The codes relate to the fields as follows:

Field Code	Field to Change
2	CUSTOMER-NAME
3	CUS-ADDRESS
4	CITY
5	STATE
6	ZIP-CODE
7	ACCOUNT-BALANCE

There is no transaction code of 1 because the first field in the record is the key and we are not changing the key. Given these codes, our change routine will begin with

```
0310-CHANGE-ROUTINE.

    PERFORM 0800-MOVE-FIELDS.
    IF TRANS-FIELD-CODE = '2'
       MOVE CUSTOMER-NAME    TO NAME-CHANGE-TRANS
       MOVE NAME-CHANGE-LINE TO TRANS-INFORMATION
       MOVE TRANS-DATA       TO CUSTOMER-NAME
       MOVE TRANS-DATA       TO CUSTOMER-NAME-OUT
       PERFORM 0600-WRITE-DETAIL
       PERFORM 0330-REWRITE-ROUTINE
    ELSE

       IF TRANS-FIELD-CODE = '3'
```

The routine will continue through all six of the fields (2–7). Before we get into the IF test, we perform the routine to move all the fields to the detail line

(0800-MOVE-FIELDS). In each of the field routines, we set up the transaction information area of the report by moving the old data into the message area:

```
MOVE CUSTOMER-NAME     TO NAME-CHANGE-TRANS
```

Then we move that and the rest of the message to the transaction area of the report:

```
MOVE NAME-CHANGE-LINE TO TRANS-INFORMATION
```

Next we move the TRANS-DATA field to the indexed file

```
MOVE TRANS-DATA        TO CUSTOMER-NAME
```

and to the detail line

```
MOVE TRANS-DATA        TO CUSTOMER-NAME-OUT
```

Finally, we will print the detail line and rewrite the record (using a performed procedure):

```
PERFORM 0600-WRITE-DETAIL
PERFORM 0330-REWRITE-ROUTINE
```

The 0330-REWRITE-ROUTINE is simply a REWRITE statement:

```
0330-REWRITE-ROUTINE.

    REWRITE ISAM-FILE
            INVALID KEY
            DISPLAY 'UNKNOWN ERROR DURING REWRITE.'
            DISPLAY 'HALTING PROGRAM.'
            STOP RUN.
```

In the INVALID KEY clause for this REWRITE statement we print a message and stop the program. Since this record was just read, the INVALID KEY should not happen. If it does, something is drastically wrong and we want to stop the execution of the program.

   With some compilers, you cannot use an INVALID KEY clause on a statement that is within an IF test. This is why we put the one REWRITE statement in a procedure of its own. Normally, putting a single statement in a procedure is a waste of time, but since an INVALID KEY on an IF test sometimes causes problems, it is simply safer to put the REWRITE statement into a procedure. We will do the same with the WRITE statement we need for the add routine. To see the remainder of the IF test routines, check the completed program at the end of this section.

   The 0320-DELETE-ROUTINE is very basic. It will simply delete the record, move the fields, and print the detail line showing that the record was deleted:

```
0320-DELETE-ROUTINE.

    DELETE ISAM-FILE
           INVALID KEY
```

```
              DISPLAY 'UNKNOWN ERROR DURING DELETE.'
              DISPLAY 'HALTING PROGRAM.'
              STOP RUN.

          PERFORM 0800-MOVE-FIELDS.
          PERFORM 0600-WRITE-DETAIL.
```

Here too, if the INVALID KEY clause is executed, the program will display an error message and stop the run.

The last part of the program is the add routine. This, like the delete routine, is pretty simple. Since we have already read the file, we know the record is not in it. Therefore, we need to verify that the transaction is supposed to be an add by checking the transaction code and printing a change, delete, or transaction code error if the code is wrong. If the code is an A, for add, we simply move the data from the transaction record to the indexed record and the print area, print the detail line, and write the record in the file (again using a performed procedure for the WRITE statement):

```
  0400-ADD-ROUTINE.

      MOVE SPACES TO DETAIL-LINE.
      IF TRANS-CODE = 'C'
         MOVE TRANS-KEY          TO CHANGE-ERROR-KEY
         MOVE CHANGE-ERROR-LINE TO TRANS-INFORMATION
         PERFORM 0600-WRITE-DETAIL
      ELSE
         IF TRANS-CODE = 'D'
            MOVE TRANS-KEY          TO DELETE-ERROR-KEY
            MOVE DELETE-ERROR-LINE TO TRANS-INFORMATION
            PERFORM 0600-WRITE-DETAIL
      ELSE
         IF TRANS-CODE NOT = 'A'
            MOVE TRANS-CODE        TO MISC-ERROR-CODE
            MOVE MISC-ERROR-LINE TO TRANS-INFORMATION
            PERFORM 0800-MOVE-FIELDS
            PERFORM 0600-WRITE-DETAIL
      ELSE
         MOVE TRANS-ADD-DATA TO ISAM-DATA
         PERFORM 0800-MOVE FIELDS
         MOVE ADD-LINE TO TRANS-INFORMATION

         PERFORM 0600-WRITE-DETAIL
         PERFORM 0410-WRITE-ROUTINE.
```

The 0410-WRITE-ROUTINE is just the WRITE statement:

```
  0410-WRITE-ROUTINE.

      WRITE ISAM-RECORD
            INVALID KEY
            DISPLAY 'UNKNOWN ERROR DURING WRITE.'
            DISPLAY 'HALTING PROGRAM.'
            STOP RUN.
```

Again we use a routine to halt the program execution if the INVALID KEY clause is executed, since the record should not already be in the file.

This program is fairly complex already, but we're not finished yet. We still need to print the file sequentially after the update. Fortunately, printing an indexed file sequentially is no different than printing any other file. It does require several steps though. First the SELECT clause must be set up so the file can be accessed sequentially, which we do by using ACCESS IS DYNAMIC. Then, after we process the transaction records, we close the file (it was opened for I-O) and reopen it for INPUT. Last, we simply read the file and print the records, just as in any ordinary sequential file. The code we need will follow the transaction routine, which was called with

```
READ TRANSACTION-FILE
     AT END MOVE 'YES' TO EOF.
PERFORM 0200-TRANSACTION-LOOP
     UNTIL EOF = 'YES'.
```

We begin by closing and reopening the file:

```
CLOSE TRANSACTION-FILE
      ISAM-FILE.
OPEN  INPUT ISAM-FILE.
```

Then we read a record and perform the print routine (and end the program):

```
MOVE 'NO'           TO EOF.
MOVE SPACES         TO TRANS-INFORMATION, TRANS-HEAD.
MOVE 'AFTER UPDATE' TO HEAD-FILLER.
PERFORM 0700-PRINT-HEADINGS.
READ ISAM-FILE NEXT RECORD
     AT END MOVE 'YES' TO EOF.
PERFORM 0500-SEQUENTIAL-PRINT
     UNTIL EOF = 'YES'.

CLOSE ISAM-FILE
      PRINT-OUT.
STOP RUN.
```

Notice that in the above routine we move 'NO' to the EOF field. This is necessary since we used the same field when reading the sequential transaction file. Then we move SPACES to the two parts of the headings that deal with the transaction information since we don't need it anymore. Finally, we change the second page heading to reflect the new report before we print all the headings.

The print routine will look like most of the print routines we have written in the past with one minor difference:

```
0500-SEQUENTIAL-PRINT.

    PERFORM 0800-MOVE-FIELDS.
    PERORM 0600-WRITE-DETAIL.
    READ ISAM-FILE NEXT RECORD
         AT END MOVE 'YES' TO EOF.
```

Note the addition of the NEXT RECORD clause on the READ statement. Recall that when you use DYNAMIC access of an indexed file, the READ statement must use the NEXT RECORD clause.

Putting all these routines together, we get the entire program. Look through the program to examine the routines we have not yet discussed: the 0600-WRITE-DETAIL routine, the 0700-PRINT-HEADINGS routine, the 0800-MOVE-FIELDS routine, and the WORKING-STORAGE SECTION layouts for the error routines, the headings, and the detail line.

```
**************************************************************************
**************************************************************************
*
*
*
*   PROGRAM NAME: CUST-CHG
*
*   PROGRAMMER NAME:  ED COBURN
*
*   SOCIAL SECURITY NUMBER:  999-99-9999
*
*   DUE DATE: FEBRUARY 10, 1988
*
*   DESCRIPTION: THIS PROGRAM WILL PERFORMS AN ISAM FILE UPDATE
*               ALLOWING ADDITIONS, DELETIONS, AND CHANGES TO THE
*               ISAM MASTER FILE.
*
*
**************************************************************************
**************************************************************************

 IDENTIFICATION DIVISION.
 PROGRAM-ID.    CUST-CHG.
 AUTHOR.        ED COBURN.


 ENVIRONMENT DIVISION.

 CONFIGURATION SECTION.
 SOURCE-COMPUTER. IBM-4331.
 OBJECT-COMPUTER. IBM-4331.

 INPUT-OUTPUT SECTION.
 FILE-CONTROL.
     SELECT TRANSACTION-FILE ASSIGN TO UT-S-TRANSIN.
     SELECT PRINT-OUT         ASSIGN TO UT-S-SYSPRINT.
     SELECT ISAM-FILE ASSIGN TO DA-I-CUSTOMER
             ORGANIZATION IS INDEXED
             ACCESS IS DYNAMIC
             RECORD KEY IS CUSTOMER-NUMBER.


 DATA DIVISION.
 FILE SECTION.

 FD  ISAM-FILE
     LABEL RECORDS ARE OMITTED
     RECORD CONTAINS 80 CHARACTERS.
```

```
01   ISAM-RECORD.
     10   CUSTOMER-NUMBER              PIC X(4).
     10   ISAM-DATA.
          20   CUSTOMER-NAME           PIC X(20).
          20   CUS-ADDRESS             PIC X(15).
          20   CITY                    PIC X(13).
          20   STATE                   PIC XX.
          20   ZIP-CODE                PIC X(5).
          20   ACCOUNT-BALANCE         PIC 9(4)V99.
          20   FILLER                  PIC X(15).

FD   TRANSACTION-FILE
     LABEL RECORDS ARE OMITTED
     RECORD CONTAINS 80 CHARACTERS.
01   TRANSACTION-RECORD.
     10   TRANS-KEY                    PIC X(4).
     10   TRANS-CODE                   PIC X.
     10   TRANS-ADD-DATA.
          20   TRANS-FIELD-CODE        PIC X.
          20   TRANS-DATA              PIC X(74).
01   BALANCE-RECORD.
     10   FILLER                       PIC X(6).
     10   TRANS-BALANCE                PIC 9(4)V99.
     10   FILLER                       PIC X(68).

FD   PRINT-OUT
     LABEL RECORDS ARE OMITTED
     RECORD CONTAINS 133 CHARACTERS.
01   PRINT-RECORD                      PIC X(133).


WORKING-STORAGE SECTION.

01   WORK-AREAS.
     05   FOUND-KEY                    PIC XXX.
     05   EOF                          PIC XXX VALUE 'NO '.
     05   LINE-CTR                     PIC 99   VALUE ZERO.
     05   PAGE-CTR                     PIC 99   VALUE 1.

     05   DATE-IN                      PIC X(6).
     05   DATE-WORK REDEFINES DATE-IN.
          10   DATE-YY                 PIC XX.
          10   DATE-MM                 PIC XX.
          10   DATE-DD                 PIC XX.

01   NAME-CHANGE-LINE.
     05   FILLER                       PIC X(9)   VALUE
          'CHANGE = '.
     05   FILLER                       PIC X(7)   VALUE
          'NAME - '.
     05   NAME-CHANGE-TRANS            PIC X(20).

01   ADDR-CHANGE-LINE.
     05   FILLER                       PIC X(9)   VALUE
          'CHANGE = '.
     05   FILLER                       PIC X(10) VALUE
          'ADDRESS - '.
     05   ADDR-CHANGE-TRANS            PIC X(15).
```

```
01   CITY-CHANGE-LINE.
     05   FILLER                           PIC X(9)   VALUE
          'CHANGE = '.
     05   FILLER                           PIC X(7)   VALUE
          'CITY - '.
     05   CITY-CHANGE-TRANS                PIC X(13).

01   STATE-CHANGE-LINE.
     05   FILLER                           PIC X(9)   VALUE
          'CHANGE = '.
     05   FILLER                           PIC X(8)   VALUE
          'STATE - '.
     05   STATE-CHANGE-TRANS               PIC X(2).

01   ZIP-CHANGE-LINE.
     05   FILLER                           PIC X(9)   VALUE
          'CHANGE = '.
     05   FILLER                           PIC X(10)  VALUE
          'ZIP CODE - '.
     05   ZIP-CHANGE-TRANS                 PIC X(5).

01   BALANCE-CHANGE-LINE.
     05   FILLER                           PIC X(9)   VALUE
          'CHANGE = '.
     05   FILLER                           PIC X(10)  VALUE
          'BALANCE - '.
     05   BALANCE-CHANGE-TRANS             PIC Z,ZZ9.99.

01   ADD-ERROR-LINE.
     05   FILLER                           PIC X(36) VALUE
          'ADD = ERROR - RECORD ALREADY ON FILE'.

01   CODE-ERROR-LINE.
     05   FILLER                           PIC X(32) VALUE
          'TRANSACTION CODE ERROR - CODE = '.
     05   MISC-ERROR-CODE                  PIC X.

01   FIELD-ERROR-LINE.
     05   FILLER                           PIC X(26) VALUE
          'FIELD CODE ERROR - CODE = '.
     05   MISC-ERROR-FIELD                 PIC X.

01   CHANGE-ERROR-LINE.
     05   FILLER                           PIC X(38) VALUE
          'CHANGE = ERROR - RECORD NOT ON FILE = '.
     05   CHANGE-ERROR-KEY                 PIC X(4).

01   DELETE-ERROR-LINE.
     05   FILLER                           PIC X(38) VALUE
          'DELETE = ERROR - RECORD NOT ON FILE = '.
     05   DELETE-ERROR-KEY                 PIC X(4).

01   ADD-LINE                              PIC X(3)   VALUE
     'ADD'.

01   DELETE-LINE                           PIC X(6)   VALUE
     'DELETE'.
```

```
01   PAGE-HEADING-1.
     05   FILLER                              PIC X(6)   VALUE ' DATE '.
     05   HEADING-MONTH                       PIC XX.
     05   HEADING-DAY                         PIC /XX/.
     05   HEADING-YEAR                        PIC XX.
     05   FILLER                              PIC X(48) VALUE
     '                          CUSTOMER UPDATE PROGRAM'.
     05   FILLER                              PIC X(44) VALUE SPACES.
     05   FILLER                              PIC X(5)   VALUE 'PAGE '.
     05   PAGE-COUNTER-OUT                    PIC Z9.

01   PAGE-HEADING-2.
     05   FILLER                              PIC X(43) VALUE SPACES.
     05   HEAD-FILLER                         PIC X(14) VALUE
     'DURING UPDATE'.

01   COLUMN-HEADING-1.
     05   FILLER                              PIC X(9)   VALUE
     ' CUSTOMER'.
     05   FILLER                              PIC X(63) VALUE SPACES.
     05   FILLER                              PIC X(15)  VALUE
     'ZIP      ACCOUNT'.

01   COLUMN-HEADING-2.
     05   FILLER                              PIC X(40) VALUE
     '  NUMBER      CUSTOMER NAME         ADDRESS'.
     05   FILLER                              PIC X(47) VALUE
     '            CITY          STATE    CODE      BALANCE'.
     05   TRANS-HEAD                          PIC X(27) VALUE
     '     TRANSACTION INFORMATION'.

01   DETAIL-LINE.
     05   FILLER                              PIC X(2) VALUE SPACES.
     05   CUSTOMER-NUMBER-OUT                 PIC X(6).
     05   FILLER                              PIC X(4) VALUE SPACES.
     05   CUSTOMER-NAME-OUT                   PIC X(20).
     05   FILLER                              PIC X(1) VALUE SPACES.
     05   ADDRESS-OUT                         PIC X(15).
     05   FILLER                              PIC X(2) VALUE SPACES.
     05   CITY-OUT                            PIC X(13).
     05   FILLER                              PIC X(2) VALUE SPACES.
     05   STATE-OUT                           PIC XX.
     05   FILLER                              PIC X(4) VALUE SPACES.
     05   ZIP-OUT                             PIC X(5).
     05   FILLER                              PIC X(3) VALUE SPACES.
     05   BALANCE-OUT                         PIC Z,ZZ9.99.
     05   FILLER                              PIC X(4) VALUE SPACES.
     05   TRANS-INFORMATION                   PIC X(43).


PROCEDURE DIVISION.

0100-MAIN-MODULE.

     OPEN INPUT   TRANSACTION-FILE
          I-O     ISAM-FILE
          OUTPUT  PRINT-OUT.
```

```
ACCEPT DATE-IN FROM DATE.
MOVE DATE-YY TO HEADING-YEAR.
MOVE DATE-MM TO HEADING-MONTH.
MOVE DATE-DD TO HEADING-DAY.

PERFORM 0700-PRINT-HEADINGS.

READ TRANSACTION-FILE
     AT END MOVE 'YES' TO EOF.
PERFORM 0200-TRANSACTION-LOOP
        UNTIL EOF = 'YES'.

CLOSE TRANSACTION-FILE
      ISAM-FILE.
OPEN  INPUT ISAM-FILE.

MOVE 'NO'           TO EOF.
MOVE SPACES         TO TRANS-INFORMATION, TRANS-HEAD.
MOVE 'AFTER UPDATE' TO HEAD-FILLER.
PERFORM 0700-PRINT-HEADINGS.

READ ISAM-FILE NEXT RECORD
     AT END MOVE 'YES' TO EOF.
PERFORM 0500-SEQUENTIAL-PRINT
        UNTIL EOF = 'YES'.

CLOSE ISAM-FILE
      PRINT-OUT.
STOP RUN.


0200-TRANSACTION-LOOP.

    MOVE TRANS-KEY TO CUSTOMER-NUMBER.
    MOVE 'YES' TO FOUND-KEY.
    READ ISAM-FILE
         INVALID KEY MOVE 'NO ' TO FOUND-KEY.

    IF FOUND-KEY = 'YES'
       PERFORM 0300-CHANGE-DELETE-ROUTINE
    ELSE
       PERFORM 0400-ADD-ROUTINE.

    READ TRANSACTION-FILE
         AT END MOVE 'YES' TO EOF.


0300-CHANGE-DELETE-ROUTINE.

    IF TRANS-CODE = 'C'
       PERFORM 0310-CHANGE-ROUTINE
    ELSE
       IF TRANS-CODE = 'D'
          PERFORM 0320-DELETE-ROUTINE
    ELSE
       IF TRANS-CODE = 'A'
          PERFORM 0800-MOVE-FIELDS
          MOVE ADD-ERROR-LINE TO  TRANS-INFORMATION
          PERFORM 0600-WRITE-DETAIL
```

```
        ELSE
            MOVE TRANS-CODE        TO MISC-ERROR-CODE
            MOVE CODE-ERROR-LINE TO TRANS-INFORMATION
            PERFORM 0800-MOVE-FIELDS
            PERFORM 0600-WRITE-DETAIL.


    0310-CHANGE-ROUTINE.

        PERFORM 0800-MOVE-FIELDS.
        IF TRANS-FIELD-CODE = '2'
            MOVE CUSTOMER-NAME     TO NAME-CHANGE-TRANS
            MOVE NAME-CHANGE-LINE TO TRANS-INFORMATION
            MOVE TRANS-DATA        TO CUSTOMER-NAME
            MOVE TRANS-DATA        TO CUSTOMER-NAME-OUT
            PERFORM 0600-WRITE-DETAIL
            PERFORM 0330-REWRITE-ROUTINE
        ELSE
            IF TRANS-FIELD-CODE = '3'
                MOVE CUS-ADDRESS        TO ADDR-CHANGE-TRANS
                MOVE ADDR-CHANGE-LINE TO TRANS-INFORMATION
                MOVE TRANS-DATA        TO CUS-ADDRESS
                MOVE TRANS-DATA        TO ADDRESS-OUT
                PERFORM 0600-WRITE-DETAIL
                PERFORM 0330-REWRITE-ROUTINE
        ELSE
            IF TRANS-FIELD-CODE = '4'
                MOVE CITY              TO CITY-CHANGE-TRANS
                MOVE CITY-CHANGE-LINE TO TRANS-INFORMATION
                MOVE TRANS-DATA        TO CITY
                MOVE TRANS-DATA        TO CITY-OUT
                PERFORM 0600-WRITE-DETAIL
                PERFORM 0330-REWRITE-ROUTINE
        ELSE
            IF TRANS-FIELD-CODE = '5'
                MOVE STATE               TO STATE-CHANGE-TRANS
                MOVE STATE-CHANGE-LINE TO TRANS-INFORMATION
                MOVE TRANS-DATA          TO STATE
                MOVE TRANS-DATA          TO STATE-OUT
                PERFORM 0600-WRITE-DETAIL
                PERFORM 0330-REWRITE-ROUTINE
        ELSE
            IF TRANS-FIELD-CODE = '6'
                MOVE ZIP-CODE          TO ZIP-CHANGE-TRANS
                MOVE ZIP-CHANGE-LINE TO TRANS-INFORMATION
                MOVE TRANS-DATA        TO ZIP-CODE
                MOVE TRANS-DATA        TO ZIP-OUT
                PERFORM 0600-WRITE-DETAIL
                PERFORM 0330-REWRITE-ROUTINE
        ELSE
            IF TRANS-FIELD-CODE = '7'
                MOVE ACCOUNT-BALANCE      TO BALANCE-CHANGE-TRANS
                MOVE BALANCE-CHANGE-LINE TO TRANS-INFORMATION
                MOVE TRANS-BALANCE        TO ACCOUNT-BALANCE
                MOVE TRANS-BALANCE        TO BALANCE-OUT
                PERFORM 0600-WRITE-DETAIL
                PERFORM 0330-REWRITE-ROUTINE
        ELSE
            MOVE TRANS-FIELD-CODE TO MISC-ERROR-FIELD
            MOVE FIELD-ERROR-LINE TO TRANS-INFORMATION
```

```
        PERFORM 0800-MOVE-FIELDS
        PERFORM 0600-WRITE-DETAIL.


0320-DELETE-ROUTINE.

    DELETE ISAM-FILE
        INVALID KEY
        DISPLAY 'UNKNOWN ERROR DURING DELETE.'
        DISPLAY 'HALTING PROGRAM.'
        STOP RUN.

    PERFORM 0800-MOVE-FIELDS.
    MOVE DELETE-LINE TO TRANS-INFORMATION.
    PERFORM 0600-WRITE-DETAIL.


0330-REWRITE-ROUTINE.

    REWRITE ISAM-RECORD
        INVALID KEY
        DISPLAY 'UNKNOWN ERROR DURING REWRITE.'
        DISPLAY 'HALTING PROGRAM.'
        STOP RUN.


0400-ADD-ROUTINE.

    MOVE SPACES TO DETAIL-LINE.
    IF TRANS-CODE = 'C'
       MOVE TRANS-KEY          TO CHANGE-ERROR-KEY
       MOVE CHANGE-ERROR-LINE TO TRANS-INFORMATION
       PERFORM 0600-WRITE-DETAIL
    ELSE
       IF TRANS-CODE = 'D'
          MOVE TRANS-KEY          TO DELETE-ERROR-KEY
          MOVE DELETE-ERROR-LINE TO TRANS-INFORMATION
          PERFORM 0600-WRITE-DETAIL
    ELSE
       IF TRANS-CODE NOT = 'A'
          MOVE TRANS-FIELD-CODE TO MISC-ERROR-FIELD
          MOVE FIELD-ERROR-LINE TO TRANS-INFORMATION
          PERFORM 0800-MOVE-FIELDS
          PERFORM 0600-WRITE-DETAIL
    ELSE
       MOVE TRANS-ADD-DATA TO ISAM-DATA
       PERFORM 0800-MOVE-FIELDS
       MOVE ADD-LINE TO TRANS-INFORMATION

       PERFORM 0600-WRITE-DETAIL
       PERFORM 0410-WRITE-ROUTINE.


0410-WRITE-ROUTINE.

    WRITE ISAM-RECORD
        INVALID KEY
        DISPLAY 'UNKNOWN ERROR DURING WRITE.'
        DISPLAY 'HALTING PROGRAM.'
        STOP RUN.
```

```
0500-SEQUENTIAL-PRINT.

    PERFORM 0800-MOVE-FIELDS.
    PERFORM 0600-WRITE-DETAIL.
    READ ISAM-FILE NEXT RECORD
        AT END MOVE 'YES' TO EOF.


0600-WRITE-DETAIL.

    WRITE PRINT-RECORD FROM DETAIL-LINE
        AFTER ADVANCING 2 LINES.
    MOVE SPACES TO TRANS-INFORMATION.
    ADD 2 TO LINE-CTR.

    IF LINE-CTR > 55
       PERFORM 0700-PRINT-HEADINGS.


0700-PRINT-HEADINGS.

    MOVE PAGE-CTR TO PAGE-COUNTER-OUT.
    WRITE PRINT-RECORD FROM PAGE-HEADING-1
        AFTER ADVANCING PAGE.
    WRITE PRINT-RECORD FROM PAGE-HEADING-2
        AFTER ADVANCING 1 LINE.
    WRITE PRINT-RECORD FROM COLUMN-HEADING-1
        AFTER ADVANCING 2 LINES.
    WRITE PRINT-RECORD FROM COLUMN-HEADING-2
        AFTER ADVANCING 1 LINE.
    MOVE 6 TO LINE-CTR.
    ADD  1 TO PAGE-CTR.


0800-MOVE-FIELDS.

    MOVE CUSTOMER-NUMBER TO CUSTOMER-NUMBER-OUT.
    MOVE CUSTOMER-NAME   TO CUSTOMER-NAME-OUT.
    MOVE CUS-ADDRESS     TO ADDRESS-OUT.
    MOVE CITY            TO CITY-OUT.
    MOVE STATE           TO STATE-OUT.
    MOVE ZIP-CODE        TO ZIP-OUT.
    MOVE ACCOUNT-BALANCE TO BALANCE-OUT.
```

Based on this program and some of the data from Appendix A, the output from the program would be as shown on page 411. Notice that one record was deleted, one change was made to another record, several changes were made to still another record, and one record was added to the file.

DATE 06/29/87   CUSTOMER UPDATE PROGRAM   PAGE 1
                                      DURING UPDATE

CUSTOMER NUMBER	CUSTOMER NAME		ADDRESS	CITY	STATE	ZIP CODE	ACCOUNT BALANCE	TRANSACTION INFORMATION
1111	VIRAMONTE	ARNOLD	333 ROSEWOOD	SANTA TERESA	NM	88022	22.20	DELETE
2323	GRONDIN	SAM	1290 HAWKINS	EL PASO	TX	79936	9,999.90	CHANGE = NAME - GRONDIN GEO
2400	COBURN	EDWARD	1325 EAST	EMPORIA	KS	66801	11.22	ADD
2423	FIORETTI	GODDELL	1400 SOUTH ST.	EL PASO	TX	79936	4,242.24	CHANGE = ADDRESS - 234 WEST W
2423	FIORETTI	GODDELL	1400 SOUTH ST.	EL PASO	TX	79936	4,242.24	CHANGE = CITY - EL PASO
2423	FIORETTI	GODDELL	1400 SOUTH ST.	EL PASO	TX	79936	4,242.24	CHANGE = STATE - TX
2423	FIORETTI	GODDELL	1400 SOUTH ST.	EL PASO	TX	79922	4,242.24	CHANGE = ZIP CODE - 79936

- -

DATE 06/29/87   CUSTOMER UPDATE PROGRAM   PAGE 2
                                      AFTER UPDATE

CUSTOMER NUMBER	CUSTOMER NAME		ADDRESS	CITY	STATE	ZIP CODE	ACCOUNT BALANCE
0456	GEORGE	MONICA L	P. O. BOX 1610	ANTHONY	NM	88021	78.70
1234	PINON	TONY	234 TEXAS DR	EL PASO	TX	79935	50.00
2223	MCDOWELL	HARRY	2323 TRUTH	SARASOTA	FL	24234	2,412.42
2248	GESPIN	BRENDA	242 CHISHOLM	ANTHONY	TX	48234	2,432.44
2323	GRONDIN	SAM	1290 HAWKINS	EL PASO	TX	79936	9,999.90
2400	COBURN	EDWARD	1325 EAST	EMPORIA	KS	66801	11.22
2423	FIORETTI	GODDELL	1400 SOUTH ST.	EL PASO	TX	79922	4,242.24
3242	ADRIAN	DAVE	9887 JOSE WAY	MIDLAND	TX	23423	4,242.34
5677	AYALA	PAUL	4677 HERE	EL PASO	TX	79985	4,567.75
5687	ADDIS	ABABA	5677 MIDEAST	ARABIA	SO	56767	8,653.56
5688	BEELER	BOBBATT	6577 LOVE RD.	EL PASO	TX	79923	6,969.69
5753	DAVIS	JOHN	242 DAVIS ST.	DAVIS	CA	23423	4,234.23
6576	MORALES	LETICIA	3135 SOON TO BE	EL PASO	TX	97897	9,878.98

7-8
VSAM Files

If you are using an IBM OS/VS or IBM DOS/VS system, you are probably using **VSAM**, or Virtual Storage Access Method, instead of ISAM. VSAM is an IBM-only type of file structure that allows rapid record storage and retrieval. VSAM uses three different file organizations: **entry-sequenced organization**, which basically is sequential organization; **key-sequenced organization**, which is the counterpart of ISAM organization; and **relative organization**, which is used for direct access (as discussed in Chapter 9). Ordinary sequential files can be, and generally are, used on systems that use VSAM files; entry-sequenced files are not used too often. Also, relative files are not very popular. Thus, when we speak of VSAM files, we are generally referring to key-sequenced or indexed files.

VSAM provides some improvements over ISAM processing. First of all, VSAM processing is more efficient than regular ISAM processing. Also, some ISAM systems do not allow dynamic (sequential and random in the same program) processing, whereas VSAM does. The most important improvement, however, is that, unlike ISAM, VSAM doesn't use overflow areas for adding records to the file. The system automatically leaves empty spaces in the file and any records added later are put in these empty positions. This keeps the records in the file always in sequence and improves access time a great deal.

VSAM gives the programmer a few additional commands (which we won't discuss) but, basically, processing is the same with VSAM as it is with ISAM. The major difference between ISAM and VSAM as far as the programmer is concerned is the fact that the JCL necessary to operate in VSAM is much more complicated than the JCL used for ISAM. That's one of the reasons that regular OS sequential files are preferred over VSAM entry-sequenced files.

7-9
The Record Rack Customer Update Program

The Record Rack wants to maintain its customer records on an indexed file. Cindy has been assigned the job of creating an indexed update program that can be used to update the amount due every time a customer uses a charge account. The program will basically just make changes to the records, except that instead of simply substituting fields, the program will add the transaction amount to the record balance.

The layout for the file Cindy is to use is shown in Figure 7-5. As you can see from the record layout, not many of the fields in the file are needed for this program. The report to be printed is brief: it will print only the customer number and name, the original balance, the amount of the charge (from the transaction record Figure 7-6), and the new balance. There will also be totals on each of the three numeric fields. The report layout is shown in Figure 7-7. Notice that an error is printed if the record specified in the transaction record is not found on the indexed file. When that happens, the program will not print the old balance (BLANK WHEN ZERO is used) or the new balance but will still print the charge. Also, the charge will be totaled but the old and new balances will not since there was no record.

CUSTOMER File					
Field Description	*Position*	*Length*	:	*Dec*	*Type*
Customer number	1–4	4	:		Non-numeric
Name Last	5–14	10	:		Non-numeric
First & initial	15–24	10	:		Non-numeric
Filler	25–65	41	:		Non-numeric
Account balance	66–71	6	:	2	Numeric
Filler	72–80	9	:		Non-numeric
Record Length = 80					

Figure 7-5   The record layout for the CUSTOMER file.

BALTRANS File					
Field Description	*Position*	*Length*	:	*Dec*	*Type*
Customer number	1–4	4	:		Non-numeric
Charge amount	5–10	6	:	2	Numeric
Filler	11–80	70	:		Non-numeric
Record Length = 80					

Figure 7-6   The record layout for the BALTRANS file.

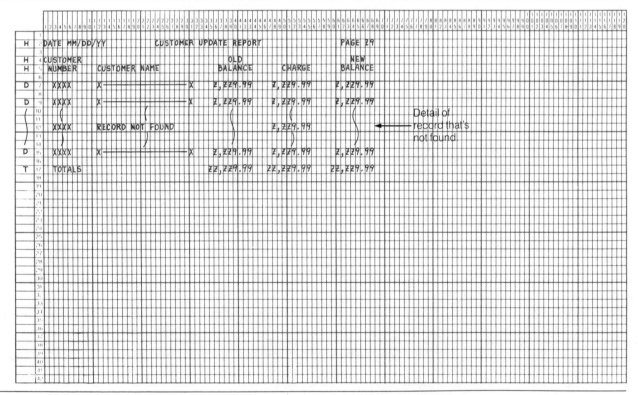

Figure 7-7   The report layout for *The Record Rack* customer update program.

The systems chart Cindy designed is shown in Figure 7-8. Since this program is not very difficult, Cindy had no trouble with the design, which is shown next (flowchart in Figure 7-9):

```
Start
Open files
Print headings
Initialize totals
Input transaction record at end mark end-of-file
DO-WHILE not end-of-file
        Input indexed record using transaction key
        IF record not found THEN
            Print error message
        ELSE
            Add transaction amount to balance
            Accumulate totals
            Write record back into file
            Print detail line
        END-IF
        Input transaction record at end mark end-of-file
END-SO
Print totals
Close files
End
```

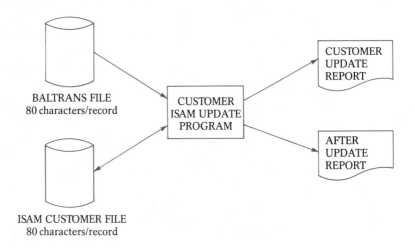

Figure 7-8 The systems chart for *The Record Rack* customer update report program.

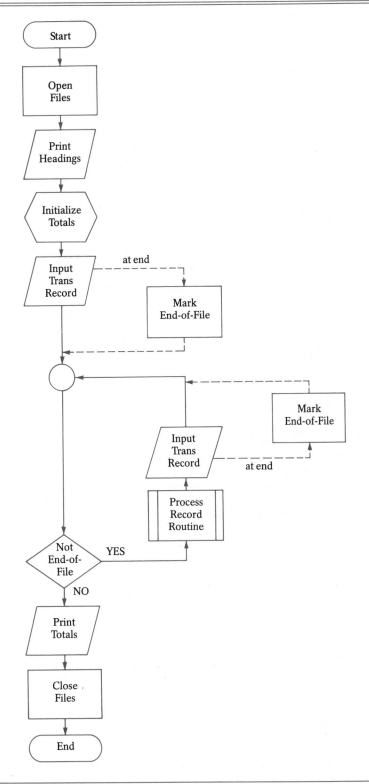

Figure 7-9   Flowchart of *The Record Rack* ISAM customer update (Main routine).

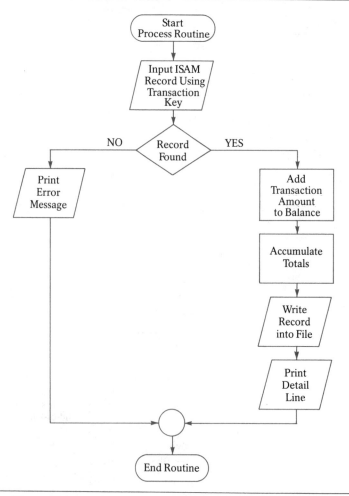

Figure 7-9 (continued)   Process routine.

Cindy's program:

```
****************************************************************
****************************************************************
*
*
*
*   PROGRAM NAME: CUST-UPD
*
*   PROGRAMMER NAME:   CINDY HARRISON
*
*   SOCIAL SECURITY NUMBER:   999-99-9999
*
*   DUE DATE: FEBRUARY 10, 1988
*
*   DESCRIPTION: THIS PROGRAM WILL PERFORM AN ISAM FILE UPDATE
*                ADDING THE TRANSACTION AMOUNT TO THE ACCOUNT
*                BALANCE.
*
*
****************************************************************
****************************************************************
```

```
IDENTIFICATION DIVISION.
PROGRAM-ID.    CUST-UPD.
AUTHOR.        CINDY HARRISON.

ENVIRONMENT DIVISION.

CONFIGURATION SECTION.
SOURCE-COMPUTER. IBM-4331.
OBJECT-COMPUTER. IBM-4331.

INPUT-OUTPUT SECTION.
FILE-CONTROL.
    SELECT TRANSACTION-FILE ASSIGN TO UT-S-TRANSIN.
    SELECT PRINT-OUT        ASSIGN TO UT-S-SYSPRINT.
    SELECT ISAM-FILE        ASSIGN TO DA-I-CUSTOMER
        ORGANIZATION IS INDEXED
        ACCESS IS DYNAMIC
        RECORD KEY IS CUSTOMER-NUMBER.

DATA DIVISION.
FILE SECTION.

FD  ISAM-FILE
    LABEL RECORDS ARE OMITTED
    RECORD CONTAINS 80 CHARACTERS.
01  ISAM-RECORD.
    10    CUSTOMER-NUMBER              PIC X(4).
    10    CUSTOMER-NAME                PIC X(20).
    10    FILLER                       PIC X(41).
    10    ACCOUNT-BALANCE              PIC 9(4)V99.
    10    FILLER                       PIC X(9).

FD  TRANSACTION-FILE
    LABEL RECORDS ARE OMITTED
    RECORD CONTAINS 80 CHARACTERS.
01  TRANSACTION-RECORD.
    10    TRANS-KEY                    PIC X(4).
    10    TRANS-AMOUNT                 PIC 9(4)V99.
    10    FILLER                       PIC X(70).

FD  PRINT-OUT
    LABEL RECORDS ARE OMITTED
    RECORD CONTAINS 133 CHARACTERS.
01  PRINT-RECORD                       PIC X(133).


WORKING-STORAGE SECTION.

01  WORK-AREAS.

    05    FOUND-KEY                    PIC XXX.
    05    EOF                          PIC XXX VALUE 'NO '.
    05    LINE-CTR                     PIC 99   VALUE ZERO.
    05    PAGE-CTR                     PIC 99   VALUE 1.
    05    NEW-BALANCE                  PIC 9(4)V99.
    05    OLD-TOTAL                    PIC 9(5)V99 VALUE 0.
    05    NEW-TOTAL                    PIC 9(5)V99 VALUE 0.
    05    CHARGE-TOTAL                 PIC 9(5)V99 VALUE 0.
```

```
         05   DATE-IN                        PIC X(6).
         05   DATE-WORK REDEFINES DATE-IN.
              10   DATE-YY                   PIC XX.
              10   DATE-MM                   PIC XX.
              10   DATE-DD                   PIC XX.

    01   PAGE-HEADING.
         05   FILLER                         PIC X(6)  VALUE ' DATE '.
         05   HEADING-MONTH                  PIC XX.
         05   HEADING-DAY                    PIC /XX/.
         05   HEADING-YEAR                   PIC XX.
         05   FILLER                         PIC X(32) VALUE
              '          CUSTOMER UPDATE REPORT'.
         05   FILLER                         PIC X(16) VALUE SPACES.
         05   FILLER                         PIC X(5)  VALUE 'PAGE '.
         05   PAGE-COUNTER-OUT               PIC Z9.

    01   COLUMN-HEADING-1.
         05   FILLER                         PIC X(9)  VALUE
              ' CUSTOMER'.
         05   FILLER                         PIC X(30) VALUE SPACES.
         05   FILLER                         PIC X(28) VALUE
              'OLD                      NEW'.

    01   COLUMN-HEADING-2.
         05   FILLER                         PIC X(25) VALUE
              ' NUMBER     CUSTOMER NAME'.
         05   FILLER                         PIC X(12) VALUE SPACES.
         05   FILLER                         PIC X(32) VALUE
              'BALANCE        CHARGE        BALANCE'.

    01   DETAIL-LINE.
         05   FILLER                         PIC X(2) VALUE SPACES.
         05   CUSTOMER-NUMBER-OUT            PIC X(4).
         05   FILLER                         PIC X(5) VALUE SPACES.
         05   CUSTOMER-NAME-OUT              PIC X(20).
         05   FILLER                         PIC X(4) VALUE SPACES.
         05   OLD-BALANCE-OUT                PIC Z,ZZ9.99
              BLANK WHEN ZERO.
         05   FILLER                         PIC X(4) VALUE SPACES.
         05   CHARGE-OUT                     PIC Z,ZZ9.99.
         05   FILLER                         PIC X(5) VALUE SPACES.
         05   NEW-BALANCE-OUT                PIC Z,ZZ9.99
              BLANK WHEN ZERO.

    01   TOTAL-LINE.
         05   FILLER                         PIC X(8)  VALUE
              ' TOTALS'.
         05   FILLER                         PIC X(26) VALUE SPACES.
         05   OLD-TOTAL-OUT                  PIC ZZ,ZZ9.99.
         05   FILLER                         PIC X(3)  VALUE SPACES.
         05   CHARGE-TOTAL-OUT               PIC ZZ,ZZ9.99.
         05   FILLER                         PIC X(4)  VALUE SPACES.
         05   NEW-TOTAL-OUT                  PIC ZZ,ZZ9.99.


PROCEDURE DIVISION.

0100-MAIN-MODULE.
```

```
        OPEN INPUT  TRANSACTION-FILE
             I-O    ISAM-FILE
             OUTPUT PRINT-OUT.

        ACCEPT DATE-IN FROM DATE.
        MOVE DATE-YY TO HEADING-YEAR.
        MOVE DATE-MM TO HEADING-MONTH.
        MOVE DATE-DD TO HEADING-DAY.

        PERFORM 0300-PRINT-HEADINGS.

        READ TRANSACTION-FILE
             AT END MOVE 'YES' TO EOF.
        PERFORM 0200-TRANSACTION-LOOP
             UNTIL EOF = 'YES'.

        MOVE CHARGE-TOTAL TO CHARGE-TOTAL-OUT.
        MOVE NEW-TOTAL    TO NEW-TOTAL-OUT.
        MOVE OLD-TOTAL    TO OLD-TOTAL-OUT.
        WRITE PRINT-RECORD FROM TOTAL-LINE.

        CLOSE TRANSACTION-FILE
              ISAM-FILE
              PRINT-OUT.
        STOP RUN.


    0200-TRANSACTION-LOOP.

        MOVE TRANS-KEY    TO CUSTOMER-NUMBER CUSTOMER-NUMBER-OUT.
        MOVE TRANS-AMOUNT TO CHARGE-OUT.
        ADD  TRANS-AMOUNT TO CHARGE-TOTAL.

        MOVE 'YES' TO FOUND-KEY.
        READ ISAM-FILE
             INVALID KEY MOVE 'NO ' TO FOUND-KEY.

        IF FOUND-KEY = 'NO '
           MOVE 'RECORD NOT FOUND' TO CUSTOMER-NAME-OUT
           MOVE ZERO TO OLD-BALANCE-OUT NEW-BALANCE-OUT
        ELSE
           MOVE CUSTOMER-NAME    TO CUSTOMER-NAME-OUT
           MOVE ACCOUNT-BALANCE TO OLD-BALANCE-OUT
           ADD  ACCOUNT-BALANCE TRANS-AMOUNT GIVING NEW-BALANCE
           ADD  ACCOUNT-BALANCE TO OLD-TOTAL
           MOVE NEW-BALANCE      TO NEW-BALANCE-OUT
           ADD  NEW-BALANCE      TO NEW-TOTAL
           MOVE NEW-BALANCE      TO ACCOUNT-BALANCE
           PERFORM 0400-REWRITE-ROUTINE.

        WRITE PRINT-RECORD FROM DETAIL-LINE
              AFTER ADVANCING 2 LINES.
        ADD 2 TO LINE-CTR.

        IF LINE-CTR > 55
           PERFORM 0300-PRINT-HEADINGS.

        READ TRANSACTION-FILE
             AT END MOVE 'YES' TO EOF.
```

```
0300-PRINT-HEADINGS.

    MOVE PAGE-CTR TO PAGE-COUNTER-OUT.
    WRITE PRINT-RECORD FROM PAGE-HEADING
        AFTER ADVANCING PAGE.
    WRITE PRINT-RECORD FROM COLUMN-HEADING-1
        AFTER ADVANCING 2 LINES.
    WRITE PRINT-RECORD FROM COLUMN-HEADING-2
        AFTER ADVANCING 1 LINE.
    MOVE 6 TO LINE-CTR.
    ADD  1 TO PAGE-CTR.


0400-REWRITE-ROUTINE.

    REWRITE ISAM-RECORD
        INVALID KEY
        DISPLAY 'UNKNOWN ERROR DURING REWRITE.'
        DISPLAY 'HALTING PROGRAM.'
        STOP RUN.
```

Having input some of the data from the CUSTOMER file in Appendix A, Cindy gets the following output:

```
DATE 06/29/87              CUSTOMER UPDATE REPORT              PAGE   1

CUSTOMER                              OLD                        NEW
NUMBER      CUSTOMER NAME           BALANCE       CHARGE       BALANCE

 0456     GEORGE    MONICA L        144.14        12.75        156.89

 2223     MCDOWELL  HARRY           239.31        10.00        249.31

 3242     ADRIAN    DAVE            162.65        14.23        176.88

 3242     ADRIAN    DAVE            176.88       154.98        330.86

 4000     RECORD NOT FOUND                        13.45

 6576     MORALES   LETICIA       1,007.65         9.76      1,017.41

 TOTALS                           1,716.40       215.17      1,918.12
```

═══ 7-10 ═══

Summary

1. When a sequential file is updated, all the records in the file must be processed—not a very efficient method if the number of changes is only a small percentage of the number of records in the file. Indexed file processing works much better in such situations.
2. Sequential updating requires two master files: the original and the one the updated records are written to. In an indexed file update, we need only one file because the changed records are written back to the original file. Then, in both the indexed and sequential cases, we use the transaction file and finally, the print file for generating any reports that are needed.

3. An indexed file is actually two files: the main file, containing all the data, and an index file, which contains only the index and a pointer back to the record in the main file.

4. When records are accessed in an indexed file, the system will find the appropriate index in the index file and then use the record pointer to retrieve the record from the main file.

5. There are only a few differences between the COBOL statements used for indexed processing and those used for sequential processing. The major difference is in the SELECT statement, for which additional clauses are either required or optional. First there is the ORGANIZATION IS INDEXED clause, which is required in exactly that form. Next is the ACCESS IS clause, which is required and must be completed by SEQUENTIAL, RANDOM, or DYNAMIC. The third required clause is the RECORD KEY clause, which specifies the field to be used for the index field. Optionally, you can set up an ALTERNATE RECORD KEY and use FILE STATUS codes to check for errors.

6. In indexed processing, the I/O statement should use an INVALID KEY clause to capture any possible errors. The READ statement gives an invalid key if the record is not on the file. The WRITE statement gives an invalid key if the record being written is a duplicate (the record key) of one already in the file.

7. In an indexed file, the OPEN statement has three forms: INPUT, OUTPUT, and I–O for accessing randomly.

8. In order to replace the record in the file after it has been read and updated, we use the REWRITE statement. We also use the INVALID KEY clause on the REWRITE statement. We usually stop the program if an error occurs because we should be able to rewrite the record since it was just read from the file.

9. To delete a record from an indexed file, we use the DELETE statement. We get an invalid key when deleting a record if that record is not in the file.

10. Some systems have a special utility program to create an indexed file. Otherwise, a program must be written to create the file and store the records in it.

11. An indexed update program requires the use of three files: the indexed file, a transaction file, and a print file to generate the report.

12. Modern IBM systems use a slightly different type of file processing called VSAM. It has three different types of file organization, but the one most commonly used is key-sequence, which is the VSAM method of indexed processing.

7-11
Glossary

Block On the disk, a storage group where the indexed records are stored. The highest key in the block is stored in the index.

Entry-sequenced organization A type of VSAM file organization that is similar to regular sequential file organization.

I-O The specification used in the OPEN statement when accessing an indexed file directly.

INVALID KEY clause A clause used on file access statements in an indexed file to detect processing errors.

ISAM, or Indexed Sequential Access Method   A type of file structure that is actually two files—a main file and an index file. The index file contains the record key and a pointer to the main file that can be used to retrieve the record from the main file.

Key-sequenced organization   A type of VSAM file organization that is similar to ISAM file organization.

NEXT RECORD clause   The clause needed on a READ statement when doing sequential access in dynamic mode.

Overflow area   On the disk, the area where records are placed when there is no room in the block to store them.

Record key   The field in the indexed file that is used as the index.

Relative file access   A type of file access that allows the compiler to access records by knowing their relative file position (to be discussed in Chapter 9).

Relative organization   A type of VSAM file organization that is similar to relative file organization (to be discussed in Chapter 9).

REWRITE statement   The I/O statement that lets a record that was just read be written back into the file at the same location it was read from.

START statement   The statement that lets the program begin reading records from an indexed file at a specified key.

VSAM, or Virtual Storage Access Method   An IBM-only type of access method that uses three different types of file organizations: entry-sequenced organization, key-sequenced organization, and relative organization.

═══ 7-12 ═══
Quick Quiz

Cover the answers with a blank sheet of paper and test yourself. Questions 1–15 are true or false questions, 16–20 are multiple choice, and 21–25 are fill-in-the-blank.

T   F   **1.** An indexed file is actually two files.

T   F   **2.** A sequential update program requires a minimum of three files.

T   F   **3.** An indexed update program requires a minimum of three files.

T   F   **4.** In a sequential update, every record in the file must be processed.

T   F   **5.** Indexed file processing can be used with tape files.

T   F   **6.** Only one record key in a block is stored in the index.

T   F   **7.** When a record is added to an indexed file, the record is inserted into the proper place in the file and the end record in the block is pushed off to the overflow area.

T   F   **8.** A pointer in the block is used to point to any record placed in the overflow area.

T   F   **9.** The index file consists of three items: the key field, the index, and the main file pointer.

T   F   **10.** An indexed file cannot have duplicate keys.

T   F   **11.** The INVALID KEY clause will not execute when you have a duplicate on the alternate key.

T   F   **12.** The file status code will have a value even when there is no file access error.

T   F   **13.** The INVALID KEY clause should always be used with a performed procedure.

T　F　**14.** When records are being written to an indexed file, the file must be opened for output.

T　F　**15.** If you use a file access statement without an INVALID KEY clause and an error occurs, your program will ABEND.

_____　**16.** Which of the following SELECT statement clauses is optional?

　　(**a**) ORGANIZATION IS INDEXED　　(**c**) RECORD KEY IS
　　(**b**) ACCESS IS　　(**d**) FILE STATUS IS

_____　**17.** Which of the following ACCESS options do you use when accessing the file directly and sequentially in the same program?

　　(**a**) SEQUENTIAL　　(**c**) RANDOM
　　(**b**) DYNAMIC　　(**d**) either b or c

_____　**18.** Which of the following ACCESS options do you use when creating an indexed file?

　　(**a**) SEQUENTIAL
　　(**b**) DYNAMIC
　　(**c**) RANDOM
　　(**d**) You must use a utility program to create an indexed file.

_____　**19.** Which of the following statements could be used most safely without the INVALID KEY clause?

　　(**a**) READ　　(**c**) WRITE
　　(**b**) REWRITE　　(**d**) The clause is required.

_____　**20.** Which of the following statements is not used for sequential updates?

　　(**a**) READ　　(**c**) DELETE
　　(**b**) WRITE　　(**d**) All are used.

21. The two files that make up an indexed file are called the _____ and the _____ .

22. The three types of processing typically done in an update procedure are _____ , _____ , and _____ .

23. If you want to use a record key with duplicates, you need to use the _____ clause.

24. The _____ clause is used to trap any errors that might occur on an I/O statement while an indexed file is being accessed.

25. We must open the file for _____ when using direct access of an indexed file.

≡ 7-13 ≡
Answers to Quick Quiz

　　1. T
　　2. T (Though a fourth, a print file, is also generally used.)
　　3. F (Only two are required: the indexed and the transaction files. The third file is the print file, which is optional though generally used.)
　　4. T (That's the main reason why indexed processing is preferable.)
　　5. F (Only with a direct access device such as a disk drive. A tape is strictly sequential.)

6. T (The highest record key in the block.)
7. F (The newly added record is placed into the overflow area.)
8. T (The pointer is put on the record sequentially in front of the record in the overflow area.)
9. F (The record key and the index are the same thing. The index file contains only the index and the main file pointer.)
10. T (Except in the alternate keys.)
11. F (It will execute and will give you a warning about the duplicate key, though the record will be written into the file.)
12. T (It will have a value of 00.)
13. F (Any imperative statement may be used. Our sample program did not use a performed procedure on all of them.)
14. F (Most of the time it is opened for I-O.)
15. T (Not on all systems, but on most.)
16. d (Though with some IBM systems, the ORGANIZATION clause is also optional.)
17. b (DYNAMIC allows both types of access.)
18. a.
19. b (Though it's a good idea to use the clause, your program would be unlikely to have any problem without it. The INVALID KEY clause is always optional.)
20. c (Sequential records are deleted simply by not being written to the file.)
21. main, index
22. add, change, delete
23. ALTERNATE KEY
24. INVALID KEY
25. I-O

7-14
Questions to Aid Understanding

1. Explain why sequential updating is impractical with large files when other processing methods are available. Why is indexed processing better?
*2. Explain what files are used and how the processing is done when a file is sequentially updated.
3. How is an ISAM file structured? Be sure to discuss the main and index files. How is a record accessed?
4. Why can't an indexed file have duplicate keys in the main index? How does an alternate key help with this?
*5. List the three different ways the ACCESS IS statement is used. Explain how each method is used in the program.
6. List the three types of processing done in an update and explain the difference in the way a sequential update and a random update accomplish each.
*7. Explain the purpose of the FILE STATUS codes and how the codes might be used.
8. Explain why an indexed file cannot be created using a tape file.
9. Explain the purpose of the INVALID KEY clause and show how the clause is used on a READ statement.
10. Illustrate the use of the INVALID KEY clause imperative statement by designing a performed procedure for the READ statement. Use the file status code as part of the procedure.

11. Explain the new method of using the OPEN statement necessitated by the indexed file. When would you use the new method and when would you use the other two methods?
12. Explain the purpose of the REWRITE and DELETE statements and illustrate the use of each.
13. List the two files that are needed for an indexed update program and the third file that is normally used with them.
14. Explain why it is imperative that you check the status codes when adding records to an indexed file that is using alternate keys.
15. Why do we sometimes use a STOP RUN statement at the end of an INVALID KEY clause?

7-15
Coding Exercises

1. Write a SELECT statement that could be used for a program that was creating the indexed file. Write one for an update program.
2. Write the PROCEDURE DIVISION code for creating an indexed file.
3. Suppose we use an update procedure that will just be used to delete records from an indexed file. Write the necessary PROCEDURE DIVISION code.
4. Suppose we use an update procedure that will be used simply to add records to an indexed file. Write the necessary PROCEDURE DIVISION code.
5. Suppose we use an update procedure to add to an account balance in the records in an indexed file. Write the necessary PROCEDURE DIVISION code.
6. We need to add records to an indexed file from a file with a different record layout. Design two record layouts that have similar fields in different places and create the necessary PROCEDURE DIVISION code.
7. Write a routine to read records from an indexed file and print a sequential listing.
8. We mentioned in the chapter that you don't normally allow changes to the record key of an indexed record. Well, changes can be made by deleting the original record and then writing the new record. Create a routine that will do this.

7-16
Maintenance Program

The Record Rack program written for this chapter assumes that all the transactions are charges. But Roger (the owner) now needs the program set up so that it can also handle returns. You will need to redesign the report layout to include another column for credits. Also, the program design will have to be modified slightly to incorporate the reduction of the account balance rather than there always being additions only. The rest of the program should remain basically unchanged.

7-17

Illustrative Program

Write a program that can be used to update the number of months left on a given subscription for *The Hamster*, a magazine about the care and feeding of hamsters. The SUBSCRIB file you are to use is shown in Figure 7-10. Notice that the only fields we are concerned about are the customer number and name and the months of subscription. The transaction file to update the records is very simple, as shown in the layout in Figure 7-11. The report to be printed is also simple and is shown in Figure 7-12. The systems chart for the program is shown in Figure 7-13 and the design of the program follows (flowchart in Figure 7-14):

SUBSCRIB File					
Field Description	*Position*	*Length*	:	*Dec*	*Type*
Customer number	1–4	4	:		Non-numeric
Customer name	5–24	20	:		Non-numeric
Filler	25–59	35	:		Non-numeric
Months of subscription	60–61	2	:		Numeric
Filler	62–80	19	:		Non-numeric
Record Length = 80					

Figure 7-10   The record layout for the SUBSCRIB file.

SUBTRANS File					
Field Description	*Position*	*Length*	:	*Dec*	*Type*
Customer number	1–4	4	:		Non-numeric
Number of months	5–6	2	:	0	Numeric
Filler	7–80	74	:		Non-numeric
Record Length = 80					

Figure 7-11   The record layout for the SUBTRANS file.

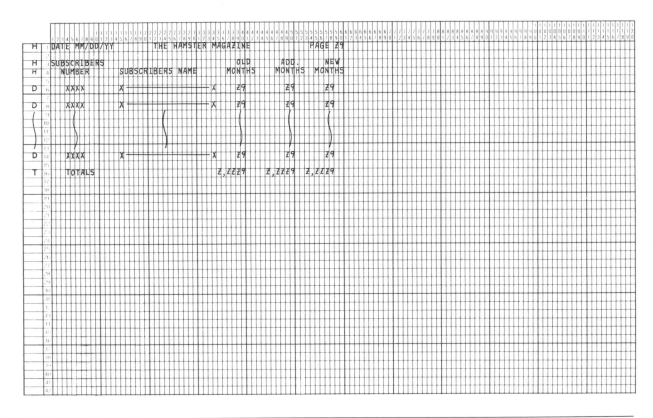

Figure 7-12 The report layout for the subscribers' update program.

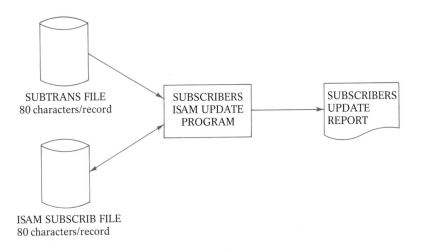

Figure 7-13 The systems chart for the subscriptions update program.

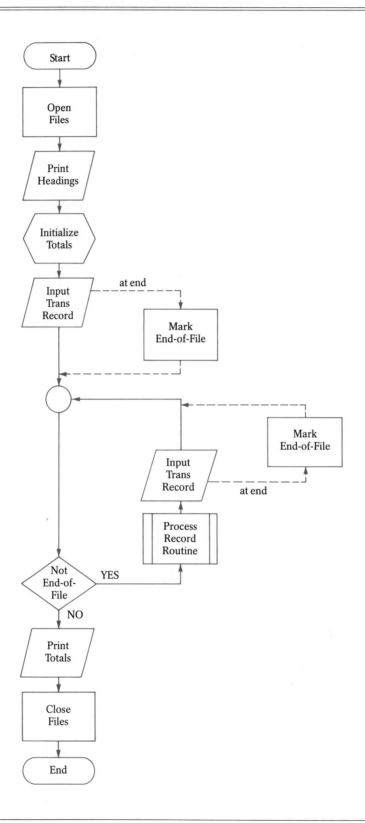

Figure 7-14   Flowchart of subscribers' ISAM update (Main routine.)

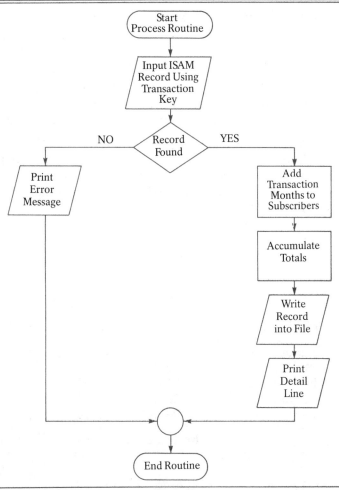

Figure 7-14 (continued)   Process routine.

Start
Open files
Print headings
Initialize totals
Input transaction record at end mark end-of-file
DO-WHILE not end-of-file
      Input indexed record using transaction key
      IF record not found THEN
        Print error message
      ELSE
        Add transaction months to subscribers months
        Accumulate totals
        Write record back into file
        Print detail line
      ELSE-IF
      Input transaction record at end mark end-of-file
END-DO
Print totals
Close files
End

7-18

System Designed Programs

For the following programs, all the design elements typically furnished to a programmer by the systems analyst are furnished. It is up to you, as programmer, to design and code the program. The files to be used are found in Appendix A.

1. Write a program to update an indexed PAYROLL file (layout in Figure 7-15). The program will need to input the record key and the hours worked (PAYTRANS, Figure 7-16) and then figure the gross pay to print on the report layout shown in Figure 7-17. The systems chart for the program is shown in Figure 7-18.

PAYROLL File					
Field Description	*Position*	*Length*	:	*Dec*	*Type*
Employee number	1–4	4	:		Non-numeric
Employee name	5–24	20	:		Non-numeric
Hours worked	25–27	3	:	0	Numeric
Rate of pay	28–31	4	:	2	Numeric
Filler	32–80	49	:		Non-numeric
Record Length = 80					

Figure 7-15　The payroll file for exercise 7-18-1.

PAYTRANS File					
Field Description	*Position*	*Length*	:	*Dec*	*Type*
Employee number	1–4	4	:		Non-numeric
Hours worked	5–7	3	:	0	Numeric
Filler	8–80	73	:		Non-numeric
Record Length = 80					

Figure 7-16　The PAYTRANS file for exercise 7-18-1.

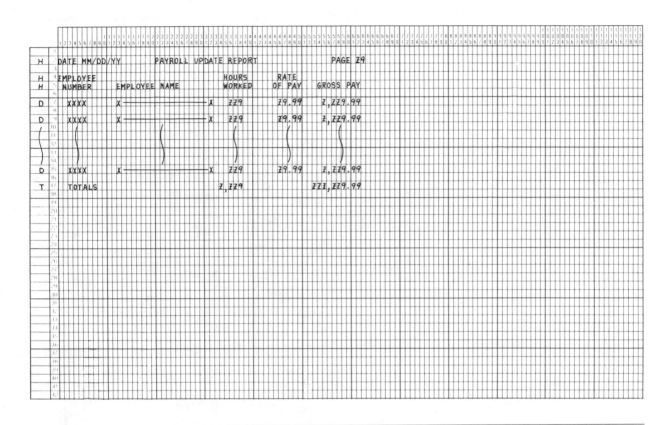

Figure 7-17   The report layout for the payroll update report, exercise 7-18-1.

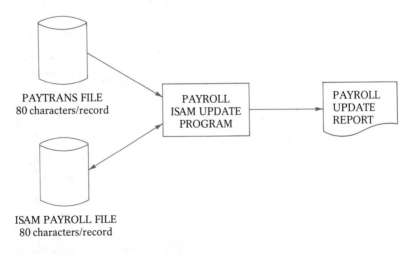

Figure 7-18   The systems chart for the payroll udpdate program, exercise 7-18-1.

2. The bank where you work needs you to change their sequential customer file to an indexed file. You will need to read the records from the sequential file and write them to the indexed file (create the file). As you do so, print the report shown in Figure 7-19. There will be one detail line printed for each record added to the file. The BANK file is shown in Figure 7-20. The systems chart for the program is shown in Figure 7-21.

H	DATE MM/DD/YY	BANK FILE CREATION PROGRAM						PAGE Z9

H	CUSTOMER		CARD		DATE OF	AMOUNT OF	CREDIT
H	NUMBER	CUSTOMER NAME	CODE	BALANCE	LAST PAY	LAST PAY	LIMIT
D	XXXX	X---------X	X	ZZ,ZZ9.99	MM/DD/YY	ZZ,ZZ9.99	ZZ,ZZ9.99
D	XXXX	X---------X	X	ZZ,ZZ9.99	MM/DD/YY	ZZ,ZZ9.99	ZZ,ZZ9.99
D	XXXX	X---------X	X	ZZ,ZZ9.99	MM/DD/YY	ZZ,ZZ9.99	ZZ,ZZ9.99
T	TOTALS			Z,ZZZ,ZZ9.99		Z,ZZZ,ZZ9.99	

Figure 7-19   The report layout for the creation of the BANK file, exercise 7-18-2.

BANK File				
Field Description	*Position*	*Length*	: *Dec*	*Type*
Customer number	1–4	4	:	Non-numeric
Customer name	5–24	20	:	Non-numeric
Charge card code	25–25	1	: 0	Numeric
Balance	26–32	7	: 2	Numeric
Date of last payment	33–38	6	:	Non-numeric
Amount of last payment	39–45	7	: 2	Numeric
Credit limit	46–52	7	: 2	Numeric
Filler	53–80	28	:	Non-numeric
Record Length = 80				

Figure 7-20   The record layout for the BANK file, exercise 7-18-2.

3. Write an indexed update program to update the INVENT file shown in Figure 7-22. The transaction file you need to use to update the file is shown in Figure 7-23. The layout for your report is shown in Figure 7-24. There will be two reports: one during the update and one after the update. Look back through the chapter for samples of the various messages that can be used for the "TRANSACTION INFORMATION." You will need to design your own messages. The systems chart for the program is shown in Figure 7-25.

7-19
Non-designed Programs

In the following programs, you will need to design the systems chart, the input files (record layout), the printer spacing chart, the program design, and the data with which to test the program.

1. Write a program to create an indexed file using at least six different fields. Have the program generate a report showing the records that are added to the file.
2. Write a program to print out the charges for tuition and fees at your school. The indexed file is to contain the student ID (Social Security number), student name, residency code (resident or non-resident), and credit hours. Since the indexed file will contain all the records for the entire school, and some of

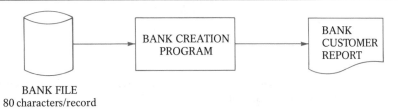

BANK FILE
80 characters/record

Figure 7-21   The systems chart for the BANK file creation program, exercise 7-18-2.

INVENT **File**					
Field Description	*Position*	*Length*	:	*Dec*	*Type*
Item number	1–4	4	:		Non-numeric
Last count	5–10	6	:	0	Numeric
Current count	11–16	6	:	0	Numeric
Unit cost	17–24	8	:	2	Numeric
Unit price	25–32	8	:	2	Numeric
Amount received	33–38	6	:	0	Numeric
Amount sold	39–44	6	:	0	Numeric
Filler	45–80	36	:		Non-numeric
Record Length = 80					

Figure 7-22   The record layout for the INVENT file, exercise 7-18-3.

INTRANS File					
Field Description	*Position*	*Length*	:	*Dec*	*Type*
Item number	1–4	4	:		Non-numeric
Transaction code	5–5	1	:		Non-numeric
Transaction data	6–80	75	:		Non-numeric
Record Length = 80					

The transaction code is A for add, C for change, and D for delete. When the transaction is an add, the transaction data will be

Last count	6–11	6	:	0	Numeric
Current count	12–17	6	:	0	Numeric
Unit cost	18–25	8	:	2	Numeric
Unit price	26–33	8	:	2	Numeric
Amount received	34–39	6	:	0	Numeric
Amount sold	40–45	6	:	0	Numeric
Filler	46–80	35	:		Non-numeric

When the transaction is a change, the transaction will be

Field code	6–6	1	:		Non-numeric
Numeric field	7–14	8	:	2	Numeric
Filler	15–80	65	:		Non-numeric

The numeric field will have a length of either 8 or 6 depending upon which field is being used. The field code will be 1–6: 1 for Last count, 6 for Amount sold.

Figure 7-23   The record layout for the INTRANS file, exercise 7-18-3.

those students may not currently be in school, you will need to use a transaction file to input the records for the current semester in order to print the report. The tuition is to be calculated as

    <   12 hours = $45 per credit for residents
    > = 12 hours = $540 total for residents
    <   12 hours = $118 per credit for non-residents
    > = 12 hours = $1416 total for non-residents

The fees are the same for residents or non-residents:

    <   12 hours = $3 per credit
    > = 12 hours = $36 per credit

Your report should list the student ID with dashes, the name, the hours, the tuition charge, the fees charge, and a total charge. There should be a report total of the hours and each of the charge columns. Also, you should have a count of the number of resident students and the average charge, the number of non-resident students and the average charge, and the total number of students and the average charge.

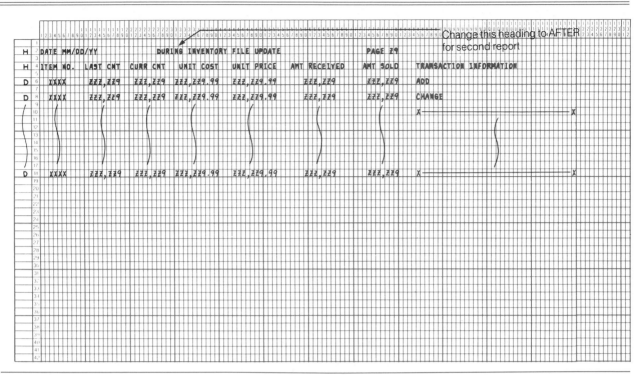

Figure 7-24   The report layout for the inventory file report, exercise 7-18-3.

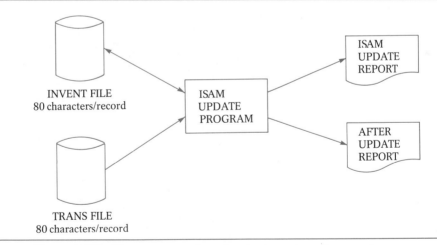

Figure 7-25   The systems chart for the inventory file report program, exercise 7-18-3.

3. Write a program that can be used to update a credit card file for the bank you work for. The transactions will need to be of four types: add new customers, cancel customers who no longer want their cards, change any data on the record, and transact charges or credits. You will need to generate a report showing the transactions as they are executed.

OBJECTIVES After completing Chapter 8 you should be able to
1. list and explain at least four of the screen handling techniques;
2. explain why, in an interactive indexed file, access is generally set up as DYNAMIC;
3. explain how to create an interactive indexed program, describing the various techniques necessary for each of the routines.

CHAPTER 8

INTERACTIVE PROGRAMMING USING INDEXED FILES

8-1
Introduction

A few chapters ago we introduced the idea of interactive programming, and we've been writing interactive programs ever since. Well, writing interactive programs for sequential files and writing interactive programs for indexed files require some different techniques. These differences are the subject of this chapter.

To be sure we are on a firm footing, we will have a quick review of interactive programming in general. Then we will move on to the special techniques necessary for indexed programs.

8-2
Interactive Techniques

When we were doing interactive processing of sequential files, most of the screen design techniques centered around making good use of menus and displayed data in report format. When using indexed files, however, we especially need to be concerned about displaying the data in a record format—that is, one record at a time. Most interactive programs that use indexed files will display one record on the screen so that the user can make modifications to the record and then store the record back into the file.

We originally discussed three different interactive program techniques: full screen I/O, cursor positioning I/O, and line-at-a-time processing. Since full-screen and cursor positioning are very machine specific, we will again stick with line-at-a-time processing. To begin, we will review some of the main points about how to set up screens so that they are easy to read and contain useful information.

1. When accepting data from the user, the program should display some type of marker so the user will know how long the entry should be. For example, when asking for a customer number, your program should prompt something like the following:

   ```
   ENTER THE CUSTOMER NUMBER
   ####
   ```

   Then the user would type the data right underneath the symbols and would know that the length of the field is four. Remember that, when inputting with the ACCEPT statement, most programs will allow the field entry to be only as long as the field itself. Thus, if the customer number field is four characters long, the entry accepted from the user can be only four characters long.

2. Using a menu system approach makes it very easy for the user to make choices from the available options. When you display the fields from the

record on the screen and want the user to indicate which field, if any, is to be changed, use letters or numbers:

```
    CUSTOMER NUMBER 1234
1.  CUSTOMER NAME . SAM SMITH
2.  ADDRESS ....... 1400 SOUTH STREET
3.  CITY .......... FORT DODGE
4.  STATE ......... IA
5.  ZIP CODE ...... 94857
```

Now, if the user wants to change the address, only the number 2 will have to be entered and the program will respond by prompting for the new address. Notice that the numbers begin with the CUSTOMER NAME, not the CUSTOMER NUMBER. It is important to remember that under normal circumstances a record key is not changed in an indexed file. Thus, for this example, we didn't put a number on the CUSTOMER NUMBER since we are not allowing changes to the field.

3. There should always be some type of heading on the screen so the user will not get confused as to what program is being executed and what function of the program is being used.
4. The screen display should not be cluttered. Use multiple screens if necessary. In Figure 8-1 the screen you see is very cluttered and difficult to interpret.

```
DATE 09/17/88           EMPLOYEE INFORMATION

    EMPLOYEE NUMBER... 12345            15.  M-T-D HEALTH INS.    $34.67
                                        16.  Q-T-D HEALTH INS.   $122.76
 1.  EMPLOYEE NAME..... SAM JONES       17.  Y-T-D HEALTH INS.   $254.76
 2.  ADDRESS.......... 1400 SOUTH STREET 18.  M-T-D LIFE INS...    $12.56
 3.  CITY............. NEW YORK          19.  Q-T-D LIFE INS...    $52.76
 4.  STATE............ NY               20.  Y-T-D LIFE INS...   $109.87
 5.  ZIP CODE......... 10016            21.  M-T-D UNION DUES.    $10.50
 6.  PHONE NUMBER..... 718-807-9876     22.  Q-T-D UNION DUES.    $42.50
 7.  BIRTH DATE....... 12/15/50         23.  Y-T-D UNION DUES.    $87.00
 8.  NUMBER OF DEP.... 3                24.  M-T-D FED. TAXES.   $464.88
 9.  HOURLY WAGE...... 12.45            25.  Q-T-D FED. TAXES.   $927.99
10.  INSURANCE CLASS... 2               26.  Y-T-D FED. TAXES  $1,987.98
11.  UNION CLASS...... 3                27.  M-T-D STATE TAXES    $34.76
                                        28.  Q-T-D STATE TAXES   $123.98
12.  M-T-D GROSS PAY...  $2,456.98      29.  Y-T-D STATE TAXES   $276.65
13.  Q-T-D GROSS PAY...  $7,328.98      30.  M-T-D CITY TAXES.    $11.54
14.  Y-T-D GROSS PAY... $16,387.87      31.  Q-T-D CITY TAXES.    $25.98
                                        32.  Y-T-D CITY TAXES.    $54.88
                                        33.  M-T-D FICA.......   $192.79
                                        34.  Q-T-D FICA.......   $348.76
                                        35.  Y-T-D FICA.......   $867.54

WHICH OPTION DO YOU WANT?
```

Figure 8-1   A congested screen display. Note how difficult it is to locate a particular field.

```
DATE 09/17/88              EMPLOYEE INFORMATION
                           INITIAL DISPLAY FOR

                           EMPLOYEE NUMBER 12345

 1. EMPLOYEE NAME..... SAM JONES          ******* GROSS PAY INFO *******
 2. ADDRESS........... 1400 SOUTH STREET  12. M-T-D GROSS PAY  $2,456.98
 3. CITY.............. NEW YORK            13. Q-T-D GROSS PAY  $7,328.98
 4. STATE............. NY                  14. Y-T-D GROSS PAY $16,387.87
 5. ZIP CODE......... 10016
 6. PHONE NUMBER...... 718-807-9876        ********** FICA INFO *********
 7. BIRTH DATE........ 12/15/50            15. M-T-D FICA.......  $192.79
 8. NUMBER OF DEP..... 3                   16. Q-T-D FICA.......  $348.76
 9. HOURLY WAGE....... 12.45               17. Y-T-D FICA.......  $867.54
10. INSURANCE CLASS... 2
11. UNION CLASS....... 3

18. SWITCH TO ADDITIONAL DATA

WHICH OPTION DO YOU WANT?
```

Figure 8-2   The first screen of the split display. Notice that option 18 will allow the user to switch to the second screen of information.

```
DATE 09/17/88              EMPLOYEE INFORMATION
                           ADDITIONAL DATA FOR

                           EMPLOYEE NUMBER 12345

    ********** INSURANCE **********     ********** TAXES *************
     1. M-T-D HEALTH INS.   $34.67      10. M-T-D FED. TAXES.   $464.88
     2. Q-T-D HEALTH INS.  $122.76      11. Q-T-D FED. TAXES.   $927.99
     3. Y-T-D HEALTH INS.  $254.76      12. Y-T-D FED. TAXES. $1,987.98

     4. M-T-D LIFE INS...   $12.56      13. M-T-D STATE TAXES    $34.76
     5. Q-T-D LIFE INS...   $52.76      14. Q-T-D STATE TAXES   $123.98
     6. Y-T-D LIFE INS...  $109.87      15. Y-T-D STATE TAXES   $276.65

                                        16. M-T-D CITY TAXES.    $11.54
    ********* UNION DUES **********      17. Q-T-D CITY TAXES.    $25.98
                                        18. Y-T-D CITY TAXES.    $54.88
     7. M-T-D UNION DUES.   $10.50
     8. Q-T-D UNION DUES.   $42.50      19. SWITCH TO INITIAL DISPLAY
     9. Y-T-D UNION DUES.   $87.00

    WHICH OPTION DO YOU WANT?
```

Figure 8-3   The second screen of the split display.

It is difficult to locate any one particular field because there are so many fields filling the screen. In Figures 8-2 and 8-3 we have split the screen displays so that the address and the gross pay information are on the first screen and the rest of the deduction information is on the second screen. Notice how much easier everything is to locate because of the group headings that were used.

If you look at the displayed data, you will see that there are groups of data for M-T-D, Q-T-D, and Y-T-D: month-to-date, quarter-to-date, and year-to-date. Since each of these three groupings shows up in each type of deduction, we could actually set up the second screen in a different fashion, as shown in Figure 8-4. Notice that the field numbers now run across the screen instead of down.

If you do split the data onto two or more screens, you need to make the transitions between the screen easy and quick. Perhaps a menu option on each screen that allows jumping back and forth would be appropriate. There is such an option in Figures 8-2, 8-3, and 8-4.

5. Be consistent in your use of screens. Always prompt in the same location on the screen (generally at the bottom) and always display error messages in the same location (again, generally at the bottom). If you display one message at the top and the next at the bottom, the user is likely to get confused and frustrated.

6. Use—but don't abuse—any available features of the terminal, such as highlighting, color, and field protection.

```
DATE 09/17/88                 EMPLOYEE INFORMATION
                  ADDITIONAL DATA FOR EMPLOYEE NUMBER 12345

* MONTH-TO-DATE *             QUARTER-TO-DATE       * YEAR-TO-DATE *

-------------------------------INSURANCE ----------------------------------

 1.  HEALTH   $34.67       2.  HEALTH $122.76    3.  HEALTH $254.76

 4.  LIFE     $12.56       5.  LIFE     $52.76    6.  LIFE    $109.87

------------------------------ TAXES ------------------------------------

 7.  FED.    $464.88       8.  FED.    $927.99    9.  FED. $1,987.98

10.  STATE    $34.76      11.  STATE  $123.98   12.  STATE   $276.65

13.  CITY     $11.54      14.  CITY    $25.98   15.  CITY     $54.88

16.  DUES     $10.50      17.  DUES    $42.50   18.  DUES     $87.00

19.  SWITCH TO INITIAL DISPLAY

WHICH OPTION DO YOU WANT?
```

Figure 8-4   The second screen of the split display redesigned to display the M-T-D, Q-T-D, and Y-T-D grouping together.

8-3

Creating a Program

Just as when we discussed interactive programs before, we will be concerned now with using the DISPLAY and ACCEPT statements. We will show the information on the screen with the DISPLAY statement and input the user's information with the ACCEPT statement. But we have more to be concerned about with an interactive indexed program. When creating an interactive program for use with a sequential file, we needed only a program that could add records and, possibly, list them. With an indexed file, we become concerned about the same techniques used in an update program: add, change, and delete. That is, we must have each of these routines in the program. In addition, we will generally use a sequential print routine.

To understand how to create such a program, we will build one, module by module. We will begin by looking at the file itself (we need only one file, the indexed file, because the transactions are entered interactively by the user.)

8-3-1 The Indexed File

For this example program, we will use the same file we used for the sample program in the previous chapter. We used the customer file with the layout shown in Figure 8-5. In the last chapter we didn't use all the fields from the file. This time we will use the entire file. The layout will look like the following:

```
FD   ISAM-FILE
     LABEL RECORDS ARE OMITTED
     RECORD CONTAINS 80 CHARACTERS.
01   ISAM-RECORD.
     10   CUSTOMER-NUMBER                PIC X(4).
     10   CUSTOMER-NAME.
          20   LAST-NAME                 PIC X(10).
          20   FIRST-NAME                PIC X(10).
     10   CUS-ADDRESS                    PIC X(15).
     10   CITY                           PIC X(13).
     10   STATE                          PIC XX.
     10   ZIP-CODE                       PIC X(5).
     10   SALE-AMOUNT                    PIC 9(4)V99.
     10   AMOUNT-DUE                     PIC 9(4)V99.
     10   CREDIT-LIMIT                   PIC X.
     10   SALESMAN-NUMBER                PIC X(4).
     10   FILLER                         PIC X(4).
01   RE-ISAM-RECORD.
     10   FILLER                         PIC X(59).
     10   NON-NUMERIC-SALE.
          20   SALE-DOLLARS              PIC X(4).
               JUSTIFIED RIGHT.
          20   SALE-CENTS                PIC XX.
     10   NON-NUMERIC-DUE.
          20   DUE-DOLLARS               PIC X(4)
               JUSTIFIED RIGHT.
          20   DUE-CENTS                 PIC XX.
     10   FILLER                         PIC X(9).
```

CUSTOMER File					
Field Description	*Position*	*Length*	:	*Dec*	*Type*
Customer number	1–4	4	:		Non-numeric
Name Last	5–14	10	:		Non-numeric
First & initial	15–24	1	:		Non-numeric
Address	25–39	15	:		Non-numeric
City	40–52	13	:		Non-numeric
State	53–54	2	:		Non-numeric
Zip code	55–59	5	:		Non-numeric
Amount of sale	60–65	6	:	2	Numeric
Amount due	66–71	6	:	2	Numeric
Credit limit	72–73	1	:		Non-numeric
Salesman number	74–77	4	:		Non-numeric
Filler	78–80	3	:		Non-numeric
Record Length = 80					

Figure 8-5   The record layout for the CUSTOMER file.

Notice that we redefined the two numeric fields in the second record layout so that they can be input and then edited around the decimal point, as we discussed in Chapter 3.

In order to use this file in our program, we will have to set up the SELECT statement:

```
SELECT ISAM-FILE ASSIGN TO DA-I-CUSTOMER
        ORGANIZATION IS INDEXED
        ACCESS IS DYNAMIC
        RECORD KEY IS CUSTOMER-NUMBER.
```

We set up the file as DYNAMIC rather than RANDOM because we intend to include a sequential print routine. Without the printing routine, we would have used RANDOM on the ACCESS clause.

8-3-2 The Initial Display

With most interactive programs, the first screen displayed is a menu from which the user chooses the program option needed. In our program, we are going to give the user five options:

1. add a new record
2. change an existing record
3. delete an existing record
4. print a list of the records
5. exit the program

The fifth option allows the user to exit the program. Interactive programs are not conventional programs that are finished when the end of the file is reached. They are finished only when the user indicates that no more entries are needed. In our program, that will be accomplished with a choice from the initial menu.

We will create the initial menu so that it looks like the following:

```
                      ***************************
DATE 09/17/88         * CUSTOMER UPDATE PROGRAM *    INITIAL MENU
                      ***************************

                      YOUR OPTIONS ON THIS MENU ARE:
                      1. ADD A NEW RECORD TO THE FILE
                      2. CHANGE AN EXISTING RECORD
                      3. DELETE AN EXISTING RECORD
                      4. DISPLAY A SEQUENTIAL LISTING OF THE FILE

                      9. EXIT THE PROGRAM

ENTER THE NUMBER FOR THE OPTION OF YOUR CHOICE:
```

We spaced out the exit option so it stands apart from the rest of the choices and is easier to see. We also numbered the option 9 so that it is not in the sequence of the other numbers. This lessens the likelihood that the user will press the exit key by accident.

The beginning of the PROCEDURE DIVISION would need to open the files and then display this initial menu:

```
PROCEDURE DIVISION.

0100-MAIN-MODULE.

    OPEN I-O ISAM-FILE.

    ACCEPT DATE-IN FROM DATE.
    MOVE DATE-YY TO DISPLAY-YY.
    MOVE DATE-MM TO DISPLAY-MM.
    MOVE DATE-DD TO DISPLAY-DD.

    MOVE SPACES TO OPTION.
    PERFORM 0200-INITIAL-DISPLAY
            UNTIL OPTION = '9'.

    CLOSE ISAM-FILE.
    STOP-RUN.
```

The display routine that we set up will be performed until the user enters '9', the exit option. Upon input of the '9', the program will end. The display routine will look like the following:

```
0200-INITIAL-DISPLAY.

    PERFORM 1400-DISPLAY-BLANK-LINE 12 TIMES.
    DISPLAY '                 ***************************'.
    DISPLAY 'DATE: ' DISPLAY-DATE
            '        * CUSTOMER UPDATE PROGRAM *    '
            'INITIAL MENU'.
```

```
DISPLAY '                              ***************************'.
DISPLAY ' '.
DISPLAY ' '.
DISPLAY '                    YOUR OPTIONS ON THIS MENU ARE:'.
DISPLAY ' '.
DISPLAY '                        1. ADD A NEW RECORD.'
DISPLAY ' '.
DISPLAY '                        2. CHANGE AN EXISTING RECORD.'
DISPLAY ' '.
DISPLAY '                        3. DELETE AN EXISTING RECORD.'
DISPLAY ' '.
DISPLAY '                        4. DISPLAY A SEQUENTIAL LISTING '
        'OF THE FILE.'.
DISPLAY ' '.
DISPLAY ' '.
DISPLAY ' '.
DISPLAY '                        9. EXIT THE PROGRAM'.
DISPLAY ' '.
DISPLAY ' '.
DISPLAY ' '.
DISPLAY 'ENTER THE NUMBER FOR THE OPTION OF YOUR CHOICE:'.
ACCEPT OPTION.

MOVE SPACES TO CUSTOMER-NUMBER.
IF OPTION = '1'
   PERFORM 0300-ADD-ROUTINE
          UNTIL CUSTOMER-NUMBER = '0000'
ELSE
   IF OPTION = '2'
      PERFORM 0700-CHANGE-ROUTINE
             UNTIL CUSTOMER-NUMBER = '0000'
ELSE
   IF OPTION = '3'
      PERFORM 0800-DELETE-ROUTINE
             UNTIL CUSTOMER-NUMBER = '0000'
ELSE
   IF OPTION = '4'
      MOVE 'NO' TO EOF
      CLOSE ISAM-FILE
      OPEN INPUT ISAM-FILE
      PERFORM 0900-DISPLAY-ROUTINE
             UNTIL EOF = 'YES'
ELSE
   IF OPTION NOT = '9'
      DISPLAY ' '
      DISPLAY 'ONLY 1, 2, 3, 4, OR 9 ARE VALID.  '
             'PLEASE TRY AGAIN ..'
      DISPLAY 'PRESS ANY KEY TO CONTINUE.'
      ACCEPT ANY-KEY.
```

The routine first displays the menu and then accepts the option entry. The IF test allows the performance of the appropriate routine; if the entry is wrong, an error message is printed. You will see shortly the purpose of the UNTIL clause on the three PERFORM statements. We will look at each of these routines separately, beginning with the add routine.

8-3-3   The Add Routine

In the add routine, we will input each of the fields necessary to make up the record. We begin by asking for the customer number, which is the record key:

```
0300-ADD-ROUTINE.

    PERFORM 1400-DISPLAY-BLANK-LINE 12 TIMES.
    DISPLAY '                        **************************'.
    DISPLAY 'DATE: ' DISPLAY-DATE
            '      * CUSTOMER UPDATE PROGRAM *    '
            'ADD ROUTINE'.
    DISPLAY '                        **************************'.
    DISPLAY ' '.
    DISPLAY ' '.
    DISPLAY 'ENTER THE CUSTOMER NUMBER FOR THE NEW RECORD:'.
    DISPLAY '####'.
    ACCEPT CUSTOMER-NUMBER.
```

Next the program will read the file to determine if the record is already in the file. We can wait until all the data for the record has been input and then try to write the record to the file, but if the record is already on file, we cannot write it (remember that this is an indexed file and as such does not allow duplicate keys). All the data will have been entered in vain. Thus, we check for the record at the beginning of the add routine:

```
    MOVE 'NO' TO FOUND-KEY.
    READ ISAM-FILE
        INVALID KEY MOVE 'YES' TO FOUND-KEY.
```

Now, let's assume that the record is found in the file. We cannot let the routine continue if the record is there, so the program needs to get another key from the user and try again. Unfortunately, the way we structured this routine, the program cannot do so. The routine will have to be restructured to loop until a valid record key is entered (one that is not already in the file).

But, if we set up the program to loop until a record key that is not on file is entered, we might cause another problem. Let's suppose the user enters a record key that is already on the file. We display an error message and then ask the user for another key. But the user was prepared to add the record for the key that was originally entered. Since the record key is in error, the user needs to determine what is wrong and so is not prepared to immediately add a different record. However, the program requires another key in order to continue. There is no way out of the situation.

The point is that we cannot set up the routine in a no-exit fashion. We must set up the entry of the record key so that the user can step out of the add routine should it become necessary.

The same problem will occur if the user gets into the add routine by mistake. The initial menu entry is supposed to be a 2 for a change, but what if a 1 is pressed? This would take the program into the add routine, but the user does not have a record to add. In each case there must be some way for the user to get out of the add routine.

We can set up the add routine so that it gets the record in a performed procedure. That's the easy part. More difficult is setting up the routine so that it will allow the user to get out without having to add a record. As it turns out, that's not too difficult either. We can redesign the add routine so that it begins with

```
0300-ADD-ROUTINE.

    PERFORM 0310-CHECK-ADD-RECORD
            UNTIL FOUND-KEY = 'NO ' OR
            CUSTOMER-NUMBER = '0000'.
```

Now it will continue to ask the user for a record key until the record is not found or the user enters the record key of all zeros. That means the 0310-CHECK-ADD-RECORD routine will need to read the record only if the CUSTOMER-NUMBER is not all zeros. The routine looks like this:

```
0310-CHECK-ADD-RECORD.

    PERFORM 1400-DISPLAY-BLANK-LINE 12 TIMES.
    DISPLAY '                       **************************'.
    DISPLAY 'DATE: ' DISPLAY-DATE
            '       * CUSTOMER UPDATE PROGRAM *   '
            'ADD ROUTINE'.
    DISPLAY '                       **************************'.
    MOVE SPACES TO CUSTOMER-NUMBER.
    PERFORM 0400-CUSTOMER-NUMBER-ROUTINE
            UNTIL CUSTOMER-NUMBER IS NUMERIC.

    IF CUSTOMER-NUMBER NOT = '0000'
       MOVE 'YES' TO FOUND-KEY
       PERFORM 0330-READ-ISAM-FILE
    ELSE
       MOVE 'NO ' TO FOUND-KEY.

    IF FOUND-KEY = 'YES'
       DISPLAY 'DUPLICATE RECORD KEY.  TRY AGAIN.'
       DISPLAY 'PRESS ANY KEY TO CONTINUE.'
       ACCEPT ANY-KEY.
```

Now, if the user enters a customer number of zeros, the program will not read the record. Rather, it will force FOUND-KEY to be 'NO ' so that the next IF test, in checking that FOUND-KEY won't print a duplicate record error message by mistake.

We use a performed procedure to input the customer number (0400-CUS-TOMER-NUMBER-ROUTINE) because we need to verify that it is all numeric. That input routine would look like the following:

```
0400-CUSTOMER-NUMBER-ROUTINE.

    PERFORM 1400-DISPLAY-BLANK-LINE 2 TIMES.
    MOVE SPACES TO CUSTOMER-IN.
    DISPLAY 'ENTER CUSTOMER NUMBER (PRESS JUST RETURN TO EXIT)...'.
    DISPLAY '####'.
    ACCEPT CUSTOMER-IN.

    STRING CUSTOMER-IN DELIMITED BY SIZE
           INTO CUSTOMER-NUMBER.

    INSPECT CUSTOMER-NUMBER REPLACING ALL SPACES BY ZEROS.

    IF CUSTOMER-NUMBER NOT NUMERIC
       DISPLAY ' '
       DISPLAY 'CUSTOMER NUMBER MUST BE ALL NUMERIC DIGITS.'
       DISPLAY ' '
       MOVE SPACES TO CUSTOMER-IN.
```

Remember that the add routine began as

```
0300-ADD-ROUTINE.

        MOVE 'YES' TO FOUND KEY.
        PERFORM 0310-CHECK-ADD-RECORD
                UNTIL FOUND-KEY = 'NO ' OR
                CUSTOMER-NUMBER = '0000'.
```

If the customer number is entered as zero (the user is getting out of the routine), the program should not continue on with the add routine (to input the data). Because of all the IF tests and ACCEPT statements, the easiest way to continue the add routine is with another performed procedure. Thus, the add routine continues with

```
    IF CUSTOMER-NUMBER NOT = '0000'
       PERFORM 0320-GET-DATA
       DISPLAY 'ADD ANOTHER RECORD (Y OR N)?'
       ACCEPT ANY-KEY
       IF ANY-KEY NOT = 'Y'
          MOVE '0000' TO CUSTOMER-NUMBER.
```

Remember that the IF test that originally performed the add routine looked like this:

```
    PERFORM 0300-ADD-ROUTINE
            UNTIL CUSTOMER-NUMBER = '0000'
```

We mentioned at that time that we would soon discover the reason for the UNTIL clause. If the user wants to get out of the add routine, a customer number of zeros is entered. Also, if the response is no ('N') when the program asks the user if an additional record is necessary, the program forces the customer number to zeros to allow for exiting from the routine. Otherwise, the PERFORM statement starts the procedure again.

The 0310-CHECK-ADD-RECORD contains another performed procedure, the one to get the data for the record (0320-GET-DATA). The routine is basically pretty simple. It inputs the fields from the user, verifies them for accuracy, and then writes the record into the file.

The routine begins by inputting the first name (the names are actually stored as last name, then first name, but it is generally more logical to ask the user for the first name first) and then all the rest of the fields. All of the fields are input using performed procedures, because all of these fields also need to be input during the change and editing routines at the end of this add routine (see the end of the routine). Using procedures saves a lot of keypunching. The routine will look like the following:

```
0320-GET-DATA.

        MOVE SPACES TO FIRST-NAME.
        PERFORM 0410-FIRST-NAME-ROUTINE.

        MOVE SPACES TO LAST-NAME.
        PERFORM 0420-LAST-NAME-ROUTINE.

        MOVE SPACES TO CUS-ADDRESS.
        PERFORM 0430-ADDRESS-ROUTINE.

        MOVE SPACES TO CITY.
        PERFORM 0440-CITY-ROUTINE.

        MOVE SPACES TO STATE.
        PERFORM 0450-STATE-ROUTINE.

        MOVE SPACES TO ZIP-CODE.
        PERFORM 0460-ZIP-CODE-ROUTINE
                UNTIL ZIP-CODE IS NUMERIC.

        MOVE SPACES TO NON-NUMERIC-SALE.
        PERFORM 0470-SALE-ROUTINE
                UNTIL NON-NUMERIC-SALE IS NUMERIC.

        MOVE SPACES TO NON-NUMERIC-DUE.
        PERFORM 0480-DUE-ROUTINE
                UNTIL NON-NUMERIC-DUE IS NUMERIC.

        MOVE SPACES TO CREDIT-LIMIT.
        PERFORM 0490-LIMIT-ROUTINE
                UNTIL CREDIT-LIMIT = '1'
                             OR = '2'
                             OR = '3'.

        MOVE SPACES TO SALESMAN-NUMBER.
        PERFORM 0495-SALESMAN-ROUTINE
                UNTIL SALESMAN-NUMBER IS NUMERIC.
```

These procedures are all basically the same, and we have looked at similar routines in the past. We will, however, examine one of the numeric procedures just to refresh your mind. The 0470-SALE-ROUTINE inputs the SALE-AMOUNT (using the dummy field SALE-IN) and then unstrings the field around the decimal point, editing each of the two fields that results. The routine would look like the following:

```
0470-SALE-ROUTINE.

    PERFORM 1400-DISPLAY-BLANK-LINE 5 TIMES.
    MOVE SPACES TO SALE-IN.
    DISPLAY 'ENTER AMOUNT OF SALE (INCLUDING DECIMAL POINT)...'.
    DISPLAY '#######'.
    ACCEPT SALE-IN.

    UNSTRING SALE-IN DELIMITED BY '.' OR SPACES
            INTO SALE-DOLLARS SALE-CENTS.

    INSPECT NON-NUMERIC-SALE REPLACING ALL SPACES BY ZEROS.

    IF NON-NUMERIC-SALE NOT NUMERIC
      DISPLAY ' '
      DISPLAY 'AMOUNT OF SALE INCORRECT.  TRY AGAIN.'
      DISPLAY ' '
      MOVE SPACES TO SALE-IN.
```

Now, after we have input all the fields, we need to display them so the user can look at them and decide if any are incorrect. Then we need to allow the user to change any of the fields if necessary. Thus, we need to perform another procedure, which begins by displaying the data:

```
    MOVE SPACES TO EDIT-OPTION.
    PERFORM 0500-EDIT-FIELDS
            UNTIL EDIT-OPTION = 'X'.
```

After the user is finished entering any necessary changes ('X' is the exit code), we write the record into the file:

```
    WRITE ISAM-RECORD
            INVALID KEY
            DISPLAY 'UNKNOWN ERROR DURING WRITE.'
            DISPLAY 'HALTING PROGRAM.'
            STOP RUN.
```

As always, we stop the execution of the program if an error occurs when we're writing the record into the file. We checked to be sure there were no such errors before we began inputting the data, so if this INVALID KEY clause is executed, we must have some drastic problem. We want to stop the program before we do some possibly irreparable harm to the file.

When we display all the data to the screen, using the 0500-DISPLAY-DATA routine, we will use a screen format like the following:

```
                    ***************************
DATE 09/17/88       * CUSTOMER UPDATE PROGRAM *   FIELD MAINTENANCE
                    ***************************


                    FOR CUSTOMER NUMBER 1234
A) FIRST NAME....... SAM
B) LAST NAME........ JONES
C) ADDRESS.......... 1400 SOUTH STREET
D) CITY............. NEW YORK
E) STATE............ NY
F) ZIP CODE......... 10016
G) AMOUNT OF SALE....   $12.34       H) AMOUNT DUE.......   $123.44
I) CREDIT LIMIT...... 1              J) SALESMAN NUMBER... 1123
ENTER LETTER OF FIELD TO CHANGE (OR X TO EXIT).
```

The routine to display this data is within the routine to allow the changes to the fields—the 0500-EDIT-FIELDS routine, which begins with

```
0500-EDIT-FIELDS.

    PERFORM 0600-DISPLAY-DATA.
```

The routine simply displays the data in the format we just examined, except for the prompt for the field change. We don't put that in the display routine because we are going to use the display routine later for the deletion routine and don't want it to automatically display the change prompt. Thus, the edit routine will have to prompt the user and then input the user's choice:

```
    DISPLAY ' '.
    DISPLAY 'ENTER LETTER OF FIELD TO CHANGE (OR X TO EXIT).'.

    ACCEPT EDIT-OPTION.
```

Next the routine will check EDIT-OPTION for the particular field to be edited. The nested IF test begins with

```
    IF EDIT-OPTION = 'A'
        MOVE SPACES TO FIRST-NAME
        PERFORM 0410-FIRST-NAME-ROUTINE

    ELSE
        IF EDIT-OPTION = 'B'
```

with the rest of the options following and performing the appropriate routines (as shown previously). At the end of the IF test is an error message that will display if the user has not entered a valid code.

This routine is constructed so that, after any field is changed, all the fields are redisplayed on the screen. This feature allows the user to re-examine all the data rather than trying to remember which of the fields was incorrect after viewing them only once.

8-3-4 The Change Routine

After covering all the elements in the add routine, we don't have much left that is new for the change routine because the two use many of the same routines. The change routine will, of course, start by performing a routine to ask the user for the customer number of the record that needs to be changed. The routine will allow the user to get out of the change routine by entering a customer number of all zeros, so the PERFORM statement will look like the one we used for the add routine:

```
0700-CHANGE-ROUTINE.

    MOVE 'NO ' TO FOUND-KEY.
    PERFORM 0710-CHECK-CHANGE-RECORD
           UNTIL FOUND-KEY = 'YES' OR
           CUSTOMER-NUMBER = '0000'.
```

The 0710-CHECK-CHANGE-RECORD routine will continue to work until either the record is found (FOUND-KEY = 'YES') or the customer number is zeros (to exit the routine). It will begin by getting the customer number:

```
0710-CHECK-CHANGE-RECORD.

    PERFORM 1400-DISPLAY-BLANK-LINE 12 TIMES.
    DISPLAY '                      **************************'.
    DISPLAY 'DATE: ' DISPLAY-DATE
           '      * CUSTOMER UPDATE PROGRAM *   '
           'CHANGE ROUTINE'.
    DISPLAY '                      **************************'.
    DISPLAY ' '.
    DISPLAY ' '.
    MOVE SPACES TO CUSTOMER-NUMBER.
    PERFORM 0400-CUSTOMER-NUMBER-ROUTINE
           UNTIL CUSTOMER-NUMBER IS NUMERIC.
```

Then it will read the record only if the customer number is not all zeros:

```
    MOVE 'YES' TO FOUND-KEY.
    IF CUSTOMER-NUMBER NOT = '0000'
       PERFORM 0330-READ-ISAM-FILE.

    IF FOUND-KEY = 'NO '
       DISPLAY 'RECORD NOT FOUND.  TRY AGAIN.'
       DISPLAY 'PRESS ANY KEY TO CONTINUE.'
       ACCEPT ANY-KEY.
```

Now, back to the change routine itself. It began by performing the check routine to get the customer number from the user and read the record. Next it needs to display all the data and allow it to be edited, if the user didn't enter all zeros:

```
    IF CUSTOMER-NUMBER NOT = '0000'
       MOVE SPACES TO EDIT-OPTION
       PERFORM 0500-EDIT-FIELDS
              UNTIL EDIT-OPTION = 'X'
```

Then it will rewrite the record (still within the IF test):

```
PERFORM 0720-REWRITE-ROUTINE.
```

Finally, we will need to have the routine prompt the user for another change:

```
IF CUSTOMER-NUMBER NOT = '0000'
   DISPLAY 'CHANGE ANOTHER RECORD (Y OR N)?'
   ACCEPT ANY-KEY
   IF ANY-KEY NOT = 'Y'
      MOVE '0000' TO CUSTOMER-NUMBER.
```

This routine first checks that the customer number is not already zeros. If it is, the program is already exiting the routine and doesn't need to ask the user any questions. Then it prompts the user and, if the user indicates that no other record is to be changed (a response of anything but 'Y'), the program moves zeros to the customer number so the program will exit from the PERFORM statement.

Again, this change routine is really pretty simple since all the routines it needs had already been created in the add routine. The delete routine is much the same.

8-3-5 The Delete Routine

When deleting records in interactive programs, we don't simply get the record key from the user and then delete the record. It's too easy for the user to enter the wrong record key. We must show the user the record and then verify (with a prompt) that the record is the correct one. If it is, we delete it; if it's not, we don't.

Since we are going to display the data for the user, we again use many of the routines we created for the add routine. We start by performing a routine to get the customer number

```
0800-DELETE-ROUTINE.

    MOVE 'NO ' TO FOUND-KEY.
    PERFORM 0810-CHECK-DELETE-RECORD
            UNTIL FOUND-KEY = 'YES' OR
            CUSTOMER-NUMBER = '0000'.
```

with the check routine virtually identical to the one we used in the change routine:

```
0810-CHECK-DELETE-RECORD.

    PERFORM 1400-DISPLAY-BLANK-LINE 12 TIMES.
    DISPLAY '               **************************'.
    DISPLAY 'DATE: ' DISPLAY-DATE
            '      * CUSTOMER UPDATE PROGRAM *   '
            'DELETE ROUTINE'.
    DISPLAY '               **************************'.
    DISPLAY ' '.
    DISPLAY ' '.
    MOVE SPACES TO CUSTOMER-NUMBER.
    PERFORM 0400-CUSTOMER-NUMBER-ROUTINE
            UNTIL CUSTOMER-NUMBER IS NUMERIC.
```

```
                 MOVE 'YES' TO FOUND-KEY.
                 IF CUSTOMER-NUMBER NOT = '0000'
                    PERFORM 0330-READ-ISAM-FILE.

                 IF FOUND-KEY = 'NO '
                    DISPLAY 'RECORD NOT FOUND.  TRY AGAIN.'
                    DISPLAY 'PRESS ANY KEY TO CONTINUE.'
                    ACCEPT ANY-KEY.
```

Next we verify from the user that this is the correct record to delete as long as the customer number is not zero:

```
IF CUSTOMER-NUMBER NOT = '0000'
   PERFORM 0600-DISPLAY-DATA
   DISPLAY ' '
   DISPLAY 'IS THIS THE RECORD YOU WANT TO DELETE (Y OR N)?'

   ACCEPT ANY-KEY

   IF ANY-KEY = 'Y'
      PERFORM 0820-DELETE-ROUTINE.

IF CUSTOMER-NUMBER NOT = '0000'
   DISPLAY 'DELETE ANOTHER RECORD (Y OR N)?'
   ACCEPT ANY-KEY
   IF ANY-KEY NOT = 'Y'
      MOVE '0000' TO CUSTOMER-NUMBER.
```

This routine first shows the record to the user (0600-DISPLAY-DATA) and then prompts the user about whether the record is the proper one; if it is, it is deleted (0820-DELETE-ROUTINE). Then the routine prompts the user again and, if the user indicates that another record is not to be changed (a response of anything but 'Y'), the program moves '0000' to the customer number as it did in the change routine.

8-3-6   The Display Routine

The last option we need to explore in this program is the one to display the file sequentially on the screen. About the only concern with this routine is that unless the file is extremely small, all the records cannot display on one screen. Thus, we need to set up the program so it will display 15 records and pause while the user examines them. Then, at an entry by the user, it will display 15 more records at a time until the end of the file is reached. We will also set the program up so that the user can exit the display routine before the end of the file if necessary.

We want to display on the screen as much data as possible. Unfortunately, there is no way all the fields will fit. Therefore we have to decide which fields are necessary and which can be left out. We decide upon the following format:

```
                    ***************************
DATE 09/17/88       * CUSTOMER UPDATE PROGRAM *   RECORDS DISPLAY
                    ***************************
```

NUMB	FIRST NAME	LAST NAME	ADDRESS	ZIP	SALE AMOUNT	AMOUNT DUE
1234	SAM	JONES	1400 SOUTH ST.	10016	$12.34	$123.44
2223	HARRY	MCDOWELL	2323 TRUTH	24234	$241.42	$2,393.12
2248	BRENDA	GESPIN	242 CHISHOLM	48234	$24.24	$4,077.78
2323	GEORGE	GRONDIN	1290 HAWKINS	79936	$9.90	$1,056.57
2345	FRANK	MUNIZ	24 OHARA RD	88021	$2.30	$3,800.00
2423	GODDELL	FIORETTI	234 WEST WAY	79936	$424.22	$4,022.56
2767	REBECCA	LYTER	4244 HOLLISTER	78966	$42.42	$440.00
2963	GOTCHA	FISHFINDER	9876 FINDUM	88569	$457.76	$6,111.66
3242	DAVE	ADRIAN	9887 JOSE WAY	23423	$424.23	$401.62
3345	JIM	BREITBACH	1507 CHARLES	79912	$813.42	$1,162.43
3455	STEPHEN	AYER	4566 FAROUT	56886	$746.75	$612.05
4234	JERRY	DUFOUR	303 N OREGON	86786	$1,668.68	$7,217.40
4466	MONICA L	FREDERICKS	425 CHISOM	88054	$566.88	$7,120.89
4565	CHRIS	GEORGE	1425 WEST AVE.	880J6	$54.66	$1,000.77
4566	JOHN	COOK	4566 NOEAST	79975	$457.88	$8,000.87
4578	EDITH ANN	RIGARILLO	3546 SOMEWHERE	88069	$56.75	$670.14

The display routine will have to begin by closing the file (since it had been opened for I-O) and reopening it for input. This is done when the routine is called during the menu selection:

```
IF OPTION = '4'
    MOVE 'NO' TO EOF
    CLOSE ISAM-FILE
    OPEN  INPUT ISAM-FILE
    PERFORM 0900-DISPLAY-ROUTINE
            UNTIL EOF = 'YES'
```

Then, within the routine itself, the heading will have to be displayed and a routine performed to read and display the records:

```
0900-DISPLAY-ROUTINE.

    PERFORM 1400-DISPLAY-BLANK-LINE 20 TIMES.
    DISPLAY '                    ***************************'.
    DISPLAY 'DATE: ' DISPLAY-DATE
            '      * CUSTOMER UPDATE PROGRAM *   '
    'RECORDS DISPLAY'.
    DISPLAY '                    ***************************'.
    DISPLAY ' '.
    DISPLAY 'NUMB  FIRST NAME  LAST NAME  ADDRESS            '
            'ZIP   SALE AMOUNT  AMOUNT DUE'.
    DISPLAY ' '.

    PERFORM 0910-DISPLAY-LOOP
            VARYING LOOP-COUNTER FROM 1 BY 1
            UNTIL LOOP-COUNTER > 15 OR EOF = 'YES'.
```

This PERFORM statement will execute the routine that will read the file and display the data to the screen. Then we will prompt the user to continue or quit, as long as we haven't already reached the end of the file:

```
IF EOF NOT = 'YES'
    DISPLAY ' '
    DISPLAY 'PRESS X TO END THE DISPLAY ROUTINE'
    DISPLAY 'OR ANY OTHER KEY TO CONTINUE'
    ACCEPT ANY-KEY

    IF ANY-KEY = 'X'
        MOVE 'YES' TO EOF
    ELSE
        NEXT SENTENCE

    ELSE
        DISPLAY ' '
        DISPLAY 'THE END OF THE FILE WAS REACHED.'
        DISPLAY 'PRESS ANY KEY TO RETURN TO THE MENU.'
        ACCEPT ANY-KEY.
```

Notice that if the user presses 'X' (to eXit), we force 'YES' into the end-of-file marker. This allows the PERFORM statement to stop executing the display routine.

We have not yet examined the routine that does the actual display. It is simple:

```
0910-DISPLAY-LOOP.

    READ ISAM-FILE NEXT RECORD
        AT END MOVE 'YES' TO EOF.
    IF EOF NOT = 'YES'
        MOVE SALE-AMOUNT TO SALE-AMOUNT-EDITED.
        MOVE AMOUNT-DUE  TO AMOUNT-DUE-EDITED.
        DISPLAY CUSTOMER-NUMBER
                        ' '     FIRST-NAME
                        ' '     LAST-NAME
                        ' '     CUS-ADDRESS
                        ' '     ZIP-CODE
                        '     ' SALE-AMOUNT-EDITED
                        ' '     AMOUNT-DUE-EDITED.
```

Notice that we display the data only if we have not reached the end-of-file. Why don't we use a READ statement in front of the PERFORM statement and then another at the end of the read routine like we usually do? If we do that and then don't reach the end of the file, when the PERFORM statement stops the printing because of 15 records, we will have already read the next record. When we restart the whole routine, if there is a READ statement in front of the PERFORM statement, another record will be read and the record we read at the end of the first display will be lost. Thus, we must use only one READ statement and it must be at the beginning of the routine so that we have a record to display the first time in the routine.

Notice also that we move the two numeric fields to edited fields so they will display in edited format. This is not actually necessary, but remember that we are constructing this program to be as useful for the user as possible, and making the data more readable is a great help.

8-3-7 The Entire Program

Now that we have examined all the various routines, it is time to put the entire program together. As you study it, pay particular attention to some of the things we have not examined, such as the routine to display the data to be edited and all the miscellaneous field definitions.

```
*******************************************************************
*******************************************************************
*
*
*
*    PROGRAM NAME: CUST-UP
*
*    PROGRAMMER NAME:  ED COBURN
*
*    SOCIAL SECURITY NUMBER:  999-99-9999
*
*    DUE DATE: FEBRUARY 10, 1988
*
*    DESCRIPTION: THIS INTERACTIVE PROGRAM WILL ALLOW THE USER
*                 TO ADD, CHANGE, DELETE, OR DISPLAY ON THE SCREEN
*                 THE ISAM CUSTOMER FILE.
*
*
*******************************************************************
*******************************************************************

     IDENTIFICATION DIVISION.
     PROGRAM-ID.   CUST-UP.
     AUTHOR.       ED COBURN.

     ENVIRONMENT DIVISION.

     CONFIGURATION SECTION.
     SOURCE-COMPUTER. IBM-4331.
     OBJECT-COMPUTER. IBM-4331.

     INPUT-OUTPUT SECTION.
     FILE-CONTROL.
         SELECT ISAM-FILE ASSIGN TO DA-I-CUSTOMER
                ORGANIZATION IS INDEXED
                ACCESS IS DYNAMIC
                RECORD KEY IS CUSTOMER-NUMBER.

     DATA DIVISION.
     FILE SECTION.
```

```
FD  ISAM-FILE
    LABEL RECORDS ARE OMITTED
    RECORD CONTAINS 80 CHARACTERS.
01  ISAM-RECORD.
    10   CUSTOMER-NUMBER                    PIC X(4).
    10   CUSTOMER-NAME.
         20   LAST-NAME                      PIC X(10).
         20   FIRST-NAME                     PIC X(10).
    10   CUS-ADDRESS                        PIC X(15).
    10   CITY                               PIC X(13).
    10   STATE                              PIC XX.
    10   ZIP-CODE                           PIC X(5).
    10   SALE-AMOUNT                        PIC 9(4)V99.
    10   AMOUNT-DUE                         PIC 9(4)V99.
    10   CRELIT-LIMIT                       PIC X.
    10   SALESMAN-NUMBER                    PIC X(4).
    10   FILLER                             PIC X(4).

01  RE-ISAM-RECORD.
    10   FILLER                             PIC X(59).
    10   NON-NUMERIC-SALE.
         20   SALE-DOLLARS                   PIC X(4)
              JUSTIFIED RIGHT.
         20   SALE-CENTS                     PIC XX.
    10   NON-NUMERIC-DUE.
         20   DUE-DOLLARS                    PIC X(4)
              JUSTIFIED RIGHT.
         20   DUE-CENTS                      PIC XX.
    10   FILLER                             PIC X(9).

WORKING-STORAGE SECTION.

01  WORK-AREAS.

    05   EOF                                PIC XXX.
    05   FOUND-KEY                          PIC XXX.
    05   LOOP-COUNTER                       PIC 99.

    05   DATE-IN                            PIC X(6).
    05   DATE-WORK REDEFINES DATE-IN.
         10   DATE-YY                        PIC XX.
         10   DATE-MM                        PIC XX.
         10   DATE-DD                        PIC XX.

    05   CUSTOMER-IN                        PIC X(4).
    05   ZIP-IN                             PIC X(5).
    05   SALE-IN                            PIC X(7).
    05   DUE-IN                             PIC X(7).
    05   EDIT-OPTION                        PIC X.
    05   OPTION                             PIC X.
    05   ANY-KEY                            PIC X.
    05   SALE-AMOUNT-EDITED                 PIC $$,$$9.99.
    05   AMOUNT-DUE-EDITED                  PIC $$,$$9.99.
```

```
       05  DISPLAY-DATE.
           10   DISPLAY-MM                    PIC XX.
           10   DISPLAY-DD                    PIC /XX/.
           10   DISPLAY-YY                    PIC XX.


   PROCEDURE DIVISION.

   0100-MAIN-MODULE.

       OPEN I-O ISAM-FILE.

       ACCEPT DATE-IN FROM DATE.
       MOVE DATE-YY TO DISPLAY-YY.
       MOVE DATE-MM TO DISPLAY-MM.
       MOVE DATE-DD TO DISPLAY-DD.

       MOVE SPACES TO OPTION.
       PERFORM 0200-INITIAL-DISPLAY
               UNTIL OPTION = '9'.

       CLOSE ISAM-FILE.
       STOP RUN.


   0200-INITIAL-DISPLAY.

       PERFORM 1400-DISPLAY-BLANK-LINE 12 TIMES.
       DISPLAY '                    **************************'.
       DISPLAY 'DATE: ' DISPLAY-DATE
               '          * CUSTOMER UPDATE PROGRAM *    '
               'INITIAL MENU'.
       DISPLAY '                    **************************'.
       DISPLAY ' '.
       DISPLAY ' '.
       DISPLAY '                        YOUR OPTIONS ON THIS MENU ARE:'.
       DISPLAY ' '.
       DISPLAY '                        1. ADD A NEW RECORD.'
       DISPLAY ' '.
       DISPLAY '                        2. CHANGE AN EXISTING RECORD.'
       DISPLAY ' '.
       DISPLAY '                        3. DELETE AN EXISTING RECORD.'
       DISPLAY '                        4. DISPLAY A SEQUENTIAL LISTING '
               'OF THE FILE.'.
       DISPLAY ' '.
       DISPLAY ' '.
       DISPLAY ' '.
       DISPLAY '                        9. EXIT THE PROGRAM'.
       DISPLAY ' '.
       DISPLAY ' '.
       DISPLAY ' '.
       DISPLAY 'ENTER THE NUMBER FOR THE OPTION OF YOUR CHOICE:'.
       ACCEPT OPTION.
```

```
      MOVE SPACES TO CUSTOMER-NUMBER.
      IF OPTION = '1'
         PERFORM 0300-ADD-ROUTINE
               UNTIL CUSTOMER-NUMBER = '0000'
      ELSE
         IF OPTION = '2'
            PERFORM 0700-CHANGE-ROUTINE
                  UNTIL CUSTOMER-NUMBER = '0000'
      ELSE
         IF OPTION = '3'
            PERFORM 0800-DELETE-ROUTINE
                  UNTIL CUSTOMER-NUMBER = '0000'
      ELSE
         IF OPTION = '4'
            MOVE 'NO' TO EOF
            CLOSE ISAM-FILE
            OPEN  INPUT ISAM-FILE
            PERFORM 0900-DISPLAY-ROUTINE
                  UNTIL EOF = 'YES'
      ELSE
         IF OPTION NOT = '9'
            DISPLAY ' '
            DISPLAY 'ONLY 1, 2, 3, 4, OR 9 ARE VALID.  '
                  'PLEASE TRY AGAIN ..'
            DISPLAY 'PRESS ANY KEY TO CONTINUE.'
            ACCEPT ANY-KEY.


  0300-ADD-ROUTINE.

      MOVE 'YES' TO FOUND-KEY.
      PERFORM 0310-CHECK-ADD-RECORD
            UNTIL FOUND-KEY = 'NO ' OR
            CUSTOMER-NUMBER = '0000'.

      IF CUSTOMER-NUMBER NOT = '0000'
         PERFORM 0320-GET-DATA
         DISPLAY 'WOULD YOU LIKE TO ADD ANOTHER RECORD (Y OR N)?'
         ACCEPT  ANY-KEY
         IF ANY-KEY NOT = 'Y'
            MOVE '0000' TO CUSTOMER-NUMBER.


  0310-CHECK-ADD-RECORD.

      PERFORM 1400-DISPLAY-BLANK-LINE 12 TIMES.
      DISPLAY '               *************************'.
      DISPLAY 'DATE: ' DISPLAY-DATE
            '     * CUSTOMER UPDATE PROGRAM *   '
            'ADD ROUTINE'.
      DISPLAY '               *************************'.
    MOVE SPACES TO CUSTOMER-NUMBER.
      PERFORM 0400-CUSTOMER-NUMBER-ROUTINE
            UNTIL CUSTOMER-NUMBER IS NUMERIC.
```

```
        IF CUSTOMER-NUMBER NOT = '0000'
            MOVE 'YES ' TO FOUND-KEY
            PERFORM 0330-READ-ISAM-FILE

        ELSE
            MOVE 'NO ' TO FOUND-KEY.

        IF FOUND-KEY = 'YES'
            DISPLAY 'DUPLICATE RECORD KEY.  TRY AGAIN.'
            DISPLAY 'PRESS ANY KEY TO CONTINUE.'
            ACCEPT ANY-KEY.


    0320-GET-DATA.

        MOVE SPACES TO FIRST-NAME.
        PERFORM 0410-FIRST-NAME-ROUTINE.

        MOVE SPACES TO LAST-NAME.
        PERFORM 0420-LAST-NAME-ROUTINE.

        MOVE SPACES TO CUS-ADDRESS.
        PERFORM 0430-ADDRESS-ROUTINE.

        MOVE SPACES TO CITY.
        PERFORM 0440-CITY-ROUTINE.

        MOVE SPACES TO STATE.
        PERFORM 0450-STATE-ROUTINE.

        MOVE SPACES TO ZIP-CODE.
        PERFORM 0460-ZIP-CODE-ROUTINE
                UNTIL ZIP-CODE IS NUMERIC.

        MOVE SPACES TO NON-NUMERIC-SALE.
        PERFORM 0470-SALE-ROUTINE
                UNTIL NON-NUMERIC-SALE IS NUMERIC.

        MOVE SPACES TO NON-NUMERIC-DUE.
        PERFORM 0480-DUE-ROUTINE
                UNTIL NON-NUMERIC-DUE IS NUMERIC.

        MOVE SPACES TO CREDIT-LIMIT.
        PERFORM 0490-LIMIT-ROUTINE
                UNTIL CREDIT-LIMIT = '1'
                             OR = '2'
                             OR = '3'.

        MOVE SPACES TO SALESMAN-NUMBER.
        PERFORM 0495-SALESMAN-ROUTINE
                UNTIL SALESMAN-NUMBER IS NUMERIC.

        MOVE SPACES TO EDIT-OPTION.
        PERFORM 0500-EDIT-FIELDS
                UNTIL EDIT-OPTION = 'X'.
```

```
WRITE ISAM-RECORD
        INVALID KEY
        DISPLAY 'UNKNOWN ERROR DURING WRITE.'
        DISPLAY 'HALTING PROGRAM.'
        STOP RUN.


0330-READ-ISAM-FILE.

   READ ISAM-FILE
        INVALID KEY MOVE 'NO ' TO FOUND-KEY.


0400-CUSTOMER-NUMBER-ROUTINE.

    PERFORM 1400-DISPLAY-BLANK-LINE 2 TIMES.
    MOVE SPACES TO CUSTOMER-IN.
    DISPLAY 'ENTER CUSTOMER NUMBER...'.
    DISPLAY '####'.
    ACCEPT CUSTOMER-IN.

    STRING CUSTOMER-IN DELIMITED BY SIZE
        INTO CUSTOMER-NUMBER.

    INSPECT CUSTOMER-NUMBER REPLACING ALL SPACES BY ZEROS.

    IF CUSTOMER-NUMBER NOT NUMERIC
        DISPLAY ' '
        DISPLAY 'CUSTOMER NUMBER MUST BE ALL NUMERIC DIGITS.'
        DISPLAY ' '
        MOVE SPACES TO CUSTOMER-IN.


0410-FIRST-NAME-ROUTINE.

    PERFORM 1400-DISPLAY-BLANK-LINE 5 TIMES.
    DISPLAY 'ENTER FIRST NAME...'.
    DISPLAY '**********'.
    ACCEPT FIRST-NAME.


0420-LAST-NAME-ROUTINE.

    PERFORM 1400-DISPLAY-BLANK-LINE 5 TIMES.
    DISPLAY 'ENTER LAST NAME...'.
    DISPLAY '**********'.
    ACCEPT LAST-NAME.


0430-ADDRESS-ROUTINE.

    PERFORM 1400-DISPLAY-BLANK-LINE 5 TIMES.
    DISPLAY 'ENTER ADDRESS...'.
    DISPLAY '***************'.
    ACCEPT CUS-ADDRESS.
```

```
0440-CITY-ROUTINE.

    PERFORM 1400-DISPLAY-BLANK-LINE 5 TIMES.
    DISPLAY 'ENTER CITY...'.
    DISPLAY '*************'.
    ACCEPT CITY.


0450-STATE-ROUTINE.

    PERFORM 1400-DISPLAY-BLANK-LINE 5 TIMES.
    DISPLAY 'ENTER STATE...'.
    DISPLAY '**'.
    ACCEPT STATE.


0460-ZIP-CODE-ROUTINE.

    PERFORM 1400-DISPLAY-BLANK-LINE 5 TIMES.
    DISPLAY 'ENTER ZIP CODE...'.
    DISPLAY '#####'.
    ACCEPT ZIP-CODE.

    IF ZIP-CODE NOT NUMERIC
        DISPLAY ' '
        DISPLAY 'ZIP CODE MUST BE ALL NUMERIC DIGITS.'
        DISPLAY ' '
        MOVE SPACES TO ZIP-CODE.


0470-SALE-ROUTINE.

    PERFORM 1400-DISPLAY-BLANK-LINE 5 TIMES.
    MOVE SPACES TO SALE-IN.
    DISPLAY 'ENTER AMOUNT OF SALE (INCLUDING DECIMAL POINT)...'.
    DISPLAY '#######'.
    ACCEPT SALE-IN.

    UNSTRING SALE-IN DELIMITED BY '.' OR SPACES
            INTO SALE-DOLLARS SALE-CENTS.

    INSPECT NON-NUMERIC-SALE REPLACING ALL SPACES BY ZEROS.

    IF NON-NUMERIC-SALE NOT NUMERIC
        DISPLAY ' '
        DISPLAY 'AMOUNT OF SALE INCORRECT.  TRY AGAIN.'
        DISPLAY ' '
        MOVE SPACES TO SALE-IN.
```

```
0480-DUE-ROUTINE.

    PERFORM 1400-DISPLAY-BLANK-LINE 5 TIMES.
    MOVE SPACES TO DUE-IN.
    DISPLAY 'ENTER AMOUNT DUE (INCLUDING DECIMAL POINT)...'.
    DISPLAY '#######'.
    ACCEPT DUE-IN.

    UNSTRING DUE-IN DELIMITED BY '.' OR SPACES
            INTO DUE-DOLLARS DUE-CENTS.

    INSPECT NON-NUMERIC-DUE REPLACING ALL SPACES BY ZEROS.

    IF NON-NUMERIC-DUE NOT NUMERIC
        DISPLAY ' '
        DISPLAY 'AMOUNT DUE INCORRECT.  TRY AGAIN.'
        DISPLAY ' '
        MOVE SPACES TO DUE-IN.


0490-LIMIT-ROUTINE.

    PERFORM 1400-DISPLAY-BLANK-LINE 5 TIMES.
    DISPLAY 'ENTER CREDIT LIMIT CODE (1, 2, OR 3)...'.
    DISPLAY '#'.
    ACCEPT CREDIT-LIMIT.

    IF CREDIT-LIMIT NOT = '1' AND
                    NOT = '2' AND
                    NOT = '3'
        DISPLAY ' '
        DISPLAY 'CREDIT LIMIT CODE MUST BE 1, 2, OR 3.'
        DISPLAY ' '.


0495-SALESMAN-ROUTINE.

    PERFORM 1400-DISPLAY-BLANK-LINE 5 TIMES.
    DISPLAY 'ENTER SALESMAN NUMBER...'.
    DISPLAY '####'.
    ACCEPT SALESMAN-NUMBER.

    IF SALESMAN-NUMBER NOT NUMERIC
        DISPLAY ' '
        DISPLAY 'SALESMAN NUMBER MUST BE ALL NUMERIC DIGITS.'
        DISPLAY ' '
        MOVE SPACES TO SALESMAN-NUMBER.


0500-EDIT-FIELDS.

    PERFORM 0600-DISPLAY-DATA.

    DISPLAY ' '.
    DISPLAY 'ENTER LETTER OF FIELD TO CHANGE (OR X TO EXIT).'.
```

```
ACCEPT EDIT-OPTION.

IF EDIT-OPTION = 'A'
    MOVE SPACES TO FIRST-NAME
    PERFORM 0410-FIRST-NAME-ROUTINE

ELSE
    IF EDIT-OPTION = 'B'
        MOVE SPACES TO LAST-NAME
        PERFORM 0420-LAST-NAME-ROUTINE

ELSE
    IF EDIT-OPTION = 'C'
        MOVE SPACES TO CUS-ADDRESS
        PERFORM 0430-ADDRESS-ROUTINE

ELSE
    IF EDIT-OPTION = 'D'
        MOVE SPACES TO CITY
        PERFORM 0440-CITY-ROUTINE

ELSE
    IF EDIT-OPTION = 'E'
        MOVE SPACES TO STATE
        PERFORM 0450-STATE-ROUTINE

ELSE
    IF EDIT-OPTION = 'F'
        MOVE SPACES TO ZIP-CODE
        PERFORM 0460-ZIP-CODE-ROUTINE
                UNTIL ZIP-CODE IS NUMERIC

ELSE
    IF EDIT-OPTION = 'G'
        MOVE SPACES TO NON-NUMERIC-SALE
        PERFORM 0470-SALE-ROUTINE
                UNTIL NON-NUMERIC-SALE IS NUMERIC

ELSE
    IF EDIT-OPTION = 'H'
        MOVE SPACES TO NON-NUMERIC-DUE
        PERFORM 0480-DUE-ROUTINE
                UNTIL NON-NUMERIC-DUE IS NUMERIC

ELSE
    IF EDIT-OPTION = 'I'
        MOVE SPACES TO CREDIT-LIMIT
        PERFORM 0490-LIMIT-ROUTINE
                UNTIL CREDIT-LIMIT = '1' OR '2' OR '3'

ELSE
    IF EDIT-OPTION = 'J'
        MOVE SPACES TO SALESMAN-NUMBER
        PERFORM 0495-SALESMAN-ROUTINE
                UNTIL SALESMAN-NUMBER IS NUMERIC
```

```
         ELSE
            IF EDIT-OPTION NOT = 'X'
               DISPLAY ' '
               DISPLAY 'ENTRY IS NOT CORRECT.   ENTER ONLY A - J OR X.'
               DISPLAY 'PLEASE TRY AGAIN.'
               DISPLAY ' '.


    0600-DISPLAY-DATA.

        MOVE SALE-AMOUNT TO SALE-AMOUNT-EDITED.
        MOVE AMOUNT-DUE  TO AMOUNT-DUE-EDITED.
        PERFORM 1400-DISPLAY-BLANK-LINE 12 TIMES.
        DISPLAY '                      **************************'.
        DISPLAY 'DATE: ' DISPLAY-DATE
                '      * CUSTOMER UPDATE PROGRAM *   '
                'FIELD MAINTENANCE'.
        DISPLAY '                      **************************'.
        DISPLAY ' '.
        DISPLAY '                       FOR CUSTOMER NUMBER '
                CUSTOMER-NUMBER.
        DISPLAY ' '.
        DISPLAY 'A) FIRST NAME........ ' FIRST-NAME.
        DISPLAY ' '.
        DISPLAY 'B) LAST NAME........ ' LAST-NAME.
        DISPLAY ' '.
        DISPLAY 'C) ADDRESS.......... ' CUS-ADDRESS.
        DISPLAY ' '.
        DISPLAY 'D) CITY............. ' CITY.
        DISPLAY ' '.
        DISPLAY 'E) STATE............ ' STATE.
        DISPLAY ' '.
        DISPLAY 'F) ZIP CODE......... ' ZIP-CODE.
        DISPLAY ' '.
        DISPLAY 'G) AMOUNT OF SALE.... ' SALE-AMOUNT-EDITED
                '       H) AMOUNT DUE........ ' AMOUNT-DUE-EDITED.
        DISPLAY ' '.
        DISPLAY 'I) CREDIT LIMIT...... ' CREDIT-LIMIT
        '           J) SALESMAN NUMBER... ' SALESMAN-NUMBER.


    0700-CHANGE-ROUTINE.

        MOVE 'NO ' TO FOUND-KEY.
        PERFORM 0710-CHECK-CHANGE-RECORD
                UNTIL FOUND-KEY = 'YES' OR
                CUSTOMER-NUMBER = '0000'.

        IF CUSTOMER-NUMBER NOT = '0000'
           MOVE SPACES TO EDIT-OPTION
           PERFORM 0500-EDIT-FIELDS UNTIL EDIT-OPTION = 'X'
           PERFORM 0720-REWRITE-ROUTINE.
```

```
    IF CUSTOMER-NUMBER NOT = '0000'
        DISPLAY 'CHANGE ANOTHER RECORD (Y OR N)?'.
        ACCEPT ANY-KEY.
        IF ANY-KEY NOT = 'Y'
            MOVE '0000' TO CUSTOMER-NUMBER.


0710-CHECK-CHANGE-RECORD.

    PERFORM 1400-DISPLAY-BLANK-LINE 12 TIMES.
    DISPLAY '                        **************************'.
    DISPLAY 'DATE: ' DISPLAY-DATE
            '        * CUSTOMER UPDATE PROGRAM *   '
            'CHANGE ROUTINE'.
    DISPLAY '                        **************************'.
    DISPLAY ' '.
    DISPLAY ' '.
    MOVE SPACES TO CUSTOMER-NUMBER.
  PERFORM 0400-CUSTOMER-NUMBER-ROUTINE
            UNTIL CUSTOMER-NUMBER IS NUMERIC.

    MOVE 'YES' TO FOUND-KEY.
    IF CUSTOMER-NUMBER NOT = '0000'
        PERFORM 0330-READ-ISAM-FILE.

    IF FOUND-KEY = 'NO '
        DISPLAY 'RECORD NOT FOUND.  TRY AGAIN.'
        DISPLAY 'PRESS ANY KEY TO CONTINUE.'
        ACCEPT ANY-KEY.


0720-REWRITE-ROUTINE.

        REWRITE ISAM-RECORD
            INVALID KEY
            DISPLAY 'UNKNOWN ERROR DURING REWRITE.'
            DISPLAY 'HALTING PROGRAM.'
            STOP RUN.


0800-DELETE-ROUTINE.

    MOVE 'NO ' TO FOUND-KEY.
    PERFORM 0810-CHECK-DELETE-RECORD
            UNTIL FOUND-KEY = 'YES' OR
            CUSTOMER-NUMBER = '0000'.

    IF CUSTOMER-NUMBER NOT = '0000'
        PERFORM 0600-DISPLAY-DATA
        DISPLAY ' '
        DISPLAY 'IS THIS THE RECORD YOU WANT TO DELETE (Y OR N)?'

        ACCEPT ANY-KEY
```

```
            IF ANY-KEY = 'Y'
                PERFORM 0820-DELETE-ROUTINE.

        IF CUSTOMER-NUMBER NOT = '0000'
            DISPLAY 'DELETE ANOTHER RECORD (Y OR N)?'
            ACCEPT ANY-KEY
            IF ANY-KEY NOT = 'Y'
                MOVE '0000' TO CUSTOMER-NUMBER.


    0810-CHECK-DELETE-RECORD.

        PERFORM 1400-DISPLAY-BLANK-LINE 12 TIMES.
        DISPLAY '                        *************************'.
        DISPLAY 'DATE: ' DISPLAY-DATE
                '     * CUSTOMER UPDATE PROGRAM *   '
                'DELETE ROUTINE'.
        DISPLAY '                        *************************'.
        DISPLAY ' '.
        DISPLAY ' '.
            MOVE SPACES TO CUSTOMER-NUMBER.
        PERFORM 0400-CUSTOMER-NUMBER-ROUTINE
                UNTIL CUSTOMER-NUMBER IS NUMERIC.

        MOVE 'YES' TO FOUND-KEY.
        IF CUSTOMER-NUMBER NOT = '0000'
            PERFORM 0330-READ-ISAM-FILE.

        IF FOUND-KEY = 'NO '
            DISPLAY 'RECORD NOT FOUND.  TRY AGAIN.'
            DISPLAY 'PRESS ANY KEY TO CONTINUE.'
            ACCEPT ANY-KEY.


    0820-DELETE-ROUTINE.

        DELETE ISAM-FILE
                INVALID KEY
                DISPLAY 'UNKNOWN ERROR DURING DELETE.'
                DISPLAY 'HALTING PROGRAM.'
                STOP RUN.


    0900-DISPLAY-ROUTINE.

        PERFORM 1400-DISPLAY-BLANK-LINE 20 TIMES.
        DISPLAY '                        *************************'.
        DISPLAY 'DATE: ' DISPLAY-DATE
                '     * CUSTOMER UPDATE PROGRAM *   '
                'RECORDS DISPLAY'.
        DISPLAY '                        *************************'.
        DISPLAY ' '.
        DISPLAY 'NUMB  FIRST NAME  LAST NAME  ADDRESS         '
                'ZIP    SALE AMOUNT  AMOUNT DUE'.
        DISPLAY ' '.
```

```
        PERFORM 0910-DISPLAY-LOOP
              VARYING LOOP-COUNTER FROM 1 BY 1
              UNTIL LOOP-COUNTER > 15 OR EOF = 'YES'.

    IF EOF NOT = 'YES'
       DISPLAY ' '
       DISPLAY 'PRESS X TO END THE DISPLAY ROUTINE'
       DISPLAY 'OR ANY OTHER KEY TO CONTINUE'
       ACCEPT ANY-KEY

       IF ANY-KEY = 'X'
          MOVE 'YES' TO EOF
       ELSE
          NEXT SENTENCE

    ELSE
       DISPLAY ' '
       DISPLAY 'THE END OF THE FILE WAS REACHED.'
       DISPLAY 'PRESS ANY KEY TO RETURN TO THE MENU.'
       ACCEPT ANY-KEY.


0910-DISPLAY-LOOP.

    READ ISAM-FILE NEXT RECORD
        AT END MOVE 'YES' TO EOF.
    IF EOF NOT = 'YES'
       MOVE SALE-AMOUNT TO SALE-AMOUNT-EDITED
       MOVE AMOUNT-DUE  TO AMOUNT-DUE-EDITED
       DISPLAY CUSTOMER-NUMBER
                    ' '     FIRST-NAME
                    ' '     LAST-NAME
                    ' '     CUS-ADDRESS
                    ' '     ZIP-CODE
                    '     ' SALE-AMOUNT-EDITED
                    '     ' AMOUNT-DUE-EDITED.


1400-DISPLAY-BLANK-LINE.

    DISPLAY ' '.
```

8-4

The Record Rack Interactive Indexed Program

Since *The Record Rack* recently installed interactive terminals, Roger Barnell wants Cindy to write an interactive program that can be used to update the indexed file that stores the subscriber information for the magazine the store publishes. The program should allow records to be added to the file, changed, and deleted when the subscription is canceled (no sequential display). Records are kept on the file even after subscriptions run out so that samples of the magazine can be sent to former subscribers in the hope that they will subscribe again.

The SUBSCRIB file to be used is shown in Figure 8-6. Cindy designed the main menu to look like the following:

```
                    SUBSCRIBERS UPDATE PROGRAM
                         DATE 09/17/88
                           MAIN MENU

              YOUR OPTIONS ON THIS MENU ARE:

              1. ADD A NEW RECORD TO THE FILE

              2. CHANGE AN EXISTING RECORD

              3. DELETE AN EXISTING RECORD

              9. EXIT THE PROGRAM

      ENTER THE NUMBER FOR THE OPTION OF YOUR CHOICE:
```

The field maintenance screen looks like this:

```
                    SUBSCRIBERS UPDATE PROGRAM
                         DATE 09/17/88
                        FIELD MAINTENANCE

                  FOR SUBSCRIBER NUMBER 1234

      A) NAME..................... SAM JONES

      B) ADDRESS................. 1400 SOUTH STREET

      C) CITY.................... NEW YORK

      D) STATE.................. NY

      E) ZIP CODE............... 10016

      F) MONTHS OF SUBSCRIPTION... 10

      ENTER LETTER OF FIELD TO CHANGE (OR X TO EXIT).
```

SUBSCRIB File					
Field Description	*Position*	*Length*	:	*Dec*	*Type*
Customer number	1–4	4	:		Non-numeric
Customer name	5–24	20	:		Non-numeric
Address	25–39	15	:		Non-numeric
City	40–52	13	:		Non-numeric
State	53–54	2	:		Non-numeric
Zip code	55–59	5	:		Non-numeric
Months of subscription	60–61	2	:		Non-numeric
Date of sample	62–67	6	:		Non-numeric
Filler	68–80	13	:		Non-numeric
Record Length = 80					

Figure 8-6   The record layout for the SUBSCRIB file for *The Record Rack* interactive indexed program.

Cindy's systems design for the program is shown in Figure 8-7. The program pseudocode design follows and the flowchart is in Figure 8-8.

```
Start
Open the file
Initialize choice
DO-WHILE choice < > exit
        Display menu of choices (add, change, delete, or exit)
        Input function from the user
        IF choice = add THEN
            Do add routine
        ELSE IF choice = change THEN
            Do change routine
        ELSE IF choice = delete THEN
            Do delete routine
        ELSE IF choice < > exit THEN
            Print error message
        END-IF
END-DO
```

Start add routine
DO-WHILE customer number not zeros or record found
     Input customer number
     IF customer number not zeros THEN
        Set record found code to yes
        Read indexed file invalid key set code to no
     ELSE
        Set record found code to no
     END-IF
END-DO
IF customer number not zeros THEN
     Input all fields
     Display all fields and allow editing
     Write the record to the file
     Prompt user for another add and input response
     IF response is no THEN
        Set customer number to zeros
     (ELSE)
     END-IF
(ELSE)
END-IF
End add routine

Start change routine
DO-WHILE customer number not zeros or record not found
     Input customer number
     Set record found code to yes
     IF customer number not zeros THEN
        Read indexed file invalid key set code to no
     (ELSE)
     END-IF
     IF record not found THEN
        Print error message
     (ELSE)
     END-IF
END-DO
IF customer number not zeros THEN
     Display all fields and allow editing
     Rewrite the record
     Prompt user for another add and input response
     IF response is yes THEN
        Set customer number to spaces
     (ELSE)
     END-IF
(ELSE)
END-IF
End change routine

Start delete routine
DO-WHILE customer number not zeros or record not found
      Input customer number
      Set record found code to yes
      IF customer number not zeros THEN
            Read indexed file invalid key set code to no
      (ELSE)
      END-IF
      IF record not found THEN
            Print error message
      (ELSE)
      END-IF
END-DO
IF customer number not zeros THEN
      Display all fields
      Ask user if record is correct and input response
      IF response is yes
            Delete the record
      (ELSE)
      END-IF
ELSE
      Set customer number to zeros
END-IF
Prompt user for another add and input response
IF response is yes THEN
      Set customer number to spaces
(ELSE)
END-IF
End delete routine

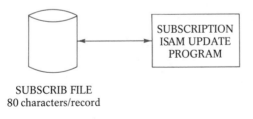

SUBSCRIB FILE
80 characters/record

Figure 8-7   The systems chart for *The Record Rack* program.

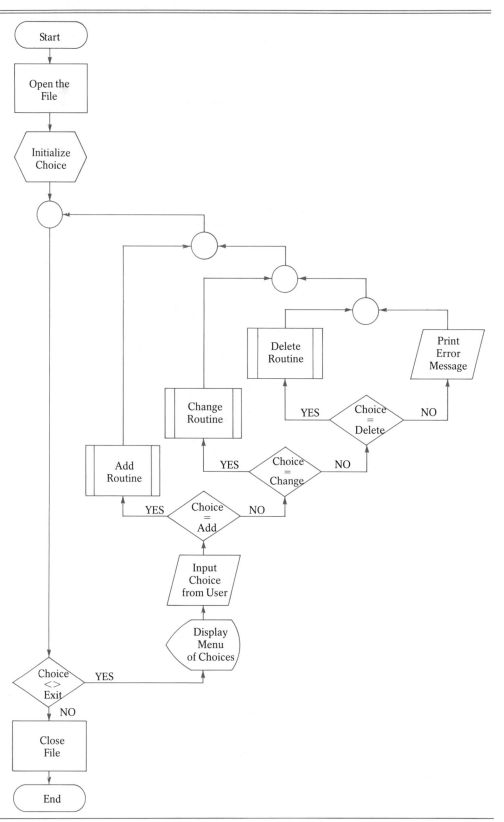

Figure 8-8 Flowchart of *The Record Rack* interactive indexed update program (Main module).

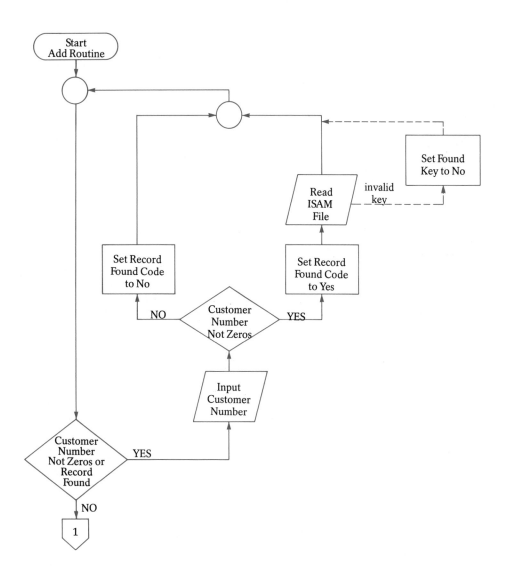

Figure 8-8 **(continued)**   Part 1 of add module.

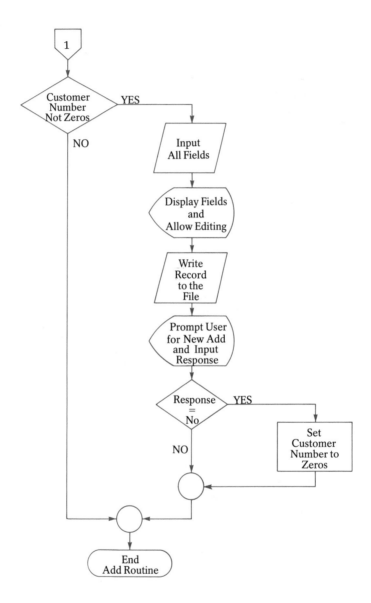

Figure 8-8 **(continued)**   Part 2 of add module.

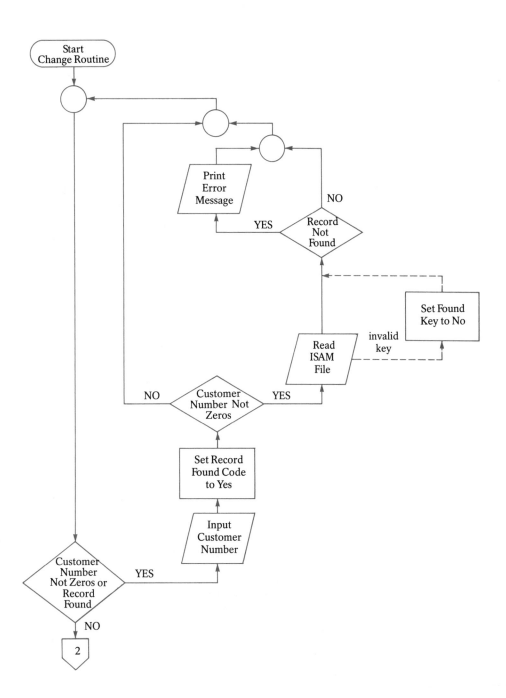

Figure 8-8 **(continued)**   Part 1 of change module.

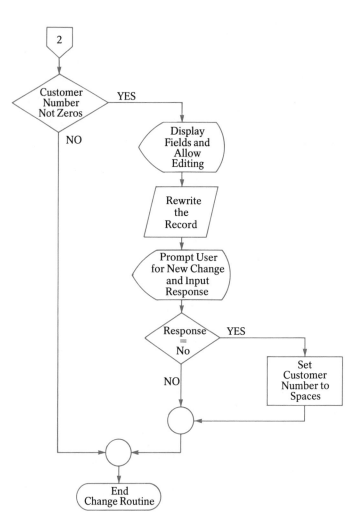

Figure 8-8 **(continued)** Part 2 of change module.

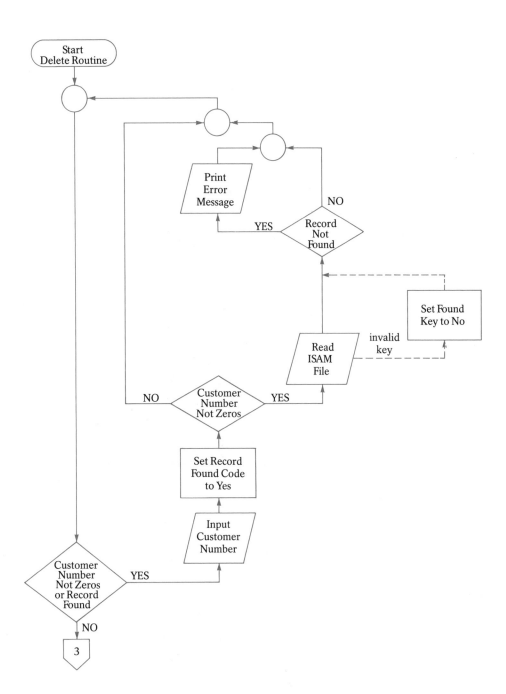

Figure 8-8 **(continued)**   Part 1 of delete module.

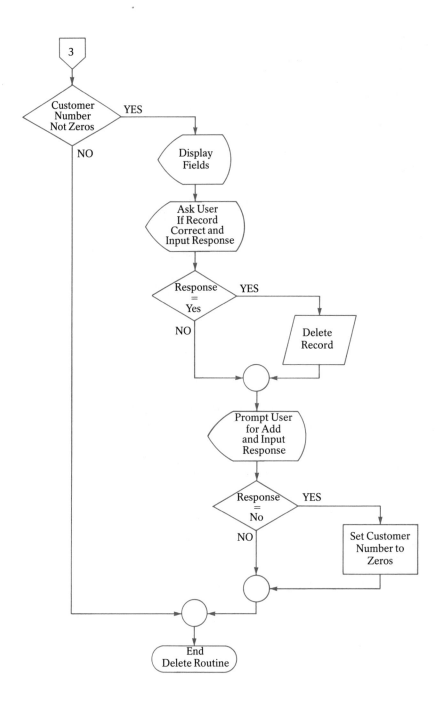

Figure 8-8 **(continued)** Part 2 of delete module.

Cindy's program looks like the following:

```
****************************************************************
****************************************************************
*
*
*
*   PROGRAM NAME: SUB-UP
*
*   PROGRAMMER NAME:  CINDY HARRISON
*
*   SOCIAL SECURITY NUMBER:  999-99-9999
*
*   DUE DATE: FEBRUARY 10, 1988
*
*   DESCRIPTION: THIS INTERACTIVE PROGRAM WILL ALLOW THE USER
*               TO ADD, CHANGE, OR DELETE ON THE SCREEN
*               THE ISAM SUBSCRIBERS FILE.
*
*
****************************************************************
****************************************************************
    IDENTIFICATION DIVISION.
    PROGRAM-ID.   SUB-UP.
    AUTHOR.       CINDY HARRISON.

    ENVIRONMENT DIVISION.

    CONFIGURATION SECTION.
    SOURCE-COMPUTER. IBM-4331.
    OBJECT-COMPUTER. IBM-4331.

    INPUT-OUTPUT SECTION.
    FILE-CONTROL.
        SELECT ISAM-FILE ASSIGN TO DA-I-SUBSCRIB
               ORGANIZATION IS INDEXED
               ACCESS IS DYNAMIC
               RECORD KEY IS CUSTOMER-NUMBER.

    DATA DIVISION.
    FILE SECTION.

    FD  ISAM-FILE
        LABEL RECORDS ARE OMITTED
        RECORD CONTAINS 80 CHARACTERS.
    01  ISAM-RECORD.
        10   CUSTOMER-NUMBER                PIC X(4).
        10   CUSTOMER-NAME                  PIC X(20).
        10   CUS-ADDRESS                    PIC X(15).
        10   CITY                           PIC X(13).
        10   STATE                          PIC XX.
        10   ZIP-CODE                       PIC X(5).
        10   SUB-MONTHS                     PIC 99.
        10   FILLER                         PIC X(19).
```

```
01   RE-ISAM-RECORD.
     10   FILLER                              PIC X(59).
     10   NON-MONTHS                          PIC XX.
     10   FILLER                              PIC X(19).


WORKING-STORAGE SECTION.

01   WORK-AREAS.

     05   EOF                                 PIC XXX.
     05   FOUND-KEY                           PIC XXX.
     05   LOOP-COUNTER                        PIC 99.

     05   DATE-IN                             PIC X(6).
     05   DATE-WORK REDEFINES DATE-IN.
          10   DATE-YY                        PIC XX.
          10   DATE-MM                        PIC XX.
          10   DATE-DD                        PIC XX.

     05   CUSTOMER-IN                         PIC X(4).
     05   ZIP-IN                              PIC X(5).
     05   MONTHS-IN                           PIC XX.
     05   EDIT-OPTION                         PIC X.
     05   OPTION                              PIC X.
     05   ANY-KEY                             PIC X.
     05   MONTHS-EDITED                       PIC Z9.

     05   DISPLAY-DATE.
          10   DISPLAY-MM                     PIC XX.
          10   DISPLAY-DD                     PIC /XX/.
          10   DISPLAY-YY                     PIC XX.


PROCEDURE DIVISION.

0100-MAIN-MODULE.

     OPEN I-O ISAM-FILE.

     ACCEPT DATE-IN FROM DATE.
     MOVE DATE-YY TO DISPLAY-YY.
     MOVE DATE-MM TO DISPLAY-MM.
     MOVE DATE-DD TO DISPLAY-DD.

     PERFORM 0200-INITIAL-DISPLAY
          UNTIL OPTION = '9'.

     CLOSE ISAM-FILE.
     STOP RUN.
```

```
0200-INITIAL-DISPLAY.

    PERFORM 1400-DISPLAY-BLANK-LINE 12 TIMES.
      DISPLAY '                    SUBSCRIBER UPDATE PROGRAM '.
      DISPLAY '                        DATE: ' DISPLAY-DATE.
      DISPLAY '                      MAIN MENU'.
      DISPLAY ' '.
      DISPLAY ' '.
      DISPLAY '                    YOUR OPTIONS ON THIS MENU ARE:'.
      DISPLAY ' '.
      DISPLAY '              1. ADD A NEW RECORD.'
      DISPLAY ' '.
      DISPLAY '              2. CHANGE AN EXISTING RECORD.'
      DISPLAY ' '.
      DISPLAY '              3. DELETE AN EXISTING RECORD.'
      DISPLAY ' '.
      DISPLAY ' '.
      DISPLAY '              9. EXIT THE PROGRAM'.
      DISPLAY ' '.
      DISPLAY ' '.
      DISPLAY ' '.
      DISPLAY 'ENTER THE NUMBER FOR THE OPTION OF YOUR CHOICE:'.

    ACCEPT OPTION.

    MOVE SPACES TO CUSTOMER-NUMBER.
    IF OPTION = '1'
        PERFORM 0300-ADD-ROUTINE
            UNTIL CUSTOMER-NUMBER = '0000'
    ELSE
     IF OPTION = '2'
         PERFORM 0700-CHANGE-ROUTINE
             UNTIL CUSTOMER-NUMBER = '0000'
    ELSE
     IF OPTION = '3'
         PERFORM 0800-DELETE-ROUTINE
             UNTIL CUSTOMER-NUMBER = '0000'
    ELSE
     IF OPTION NOT = '9'
         DISPLAY ' '
         DISPLAY 'ONLY 1, 2, 3, OR 9 ARE VALID.  '
             'PLEASE TRY AGAIN ..'
         DISPLAY 'PRESS ANY KEY TO CONTINUE.'
         ACCEPT ANY-KEY.


0300-ADD-ROUTINE.

    MOVE 'YES' TO FOUND-KEY.
    PERFORM 0310-CHECK-ADD-RECORD
            UNTIL FOUND-KEY = 'NO ' OR
            CUSTOMER-NUMBER = '0000'.
```

```
    IF CUSTOMER-NUMBER NOT = '0000'
        PERFORM 0320-GET-DATA
        DISPLAY 'ADD ANOTHER RECORD (Y OR N)?'
        ACCEPT  ANY-KEY
        IF ANY-KEY NOT = 'Y'
            MOVE '0000' TO CUSTOMER-NUMBER.


0310-CHECK-ADD-RECORD.

    PERFORM 1400-DISPLAY-BLANK-LINE 12 TIMES.
    DISPLAY '                    SUBSCRIBER UPDATE PROGRAM '.
    DISPLAY '                         DATE: ' DISPLAY-DATE.
    DISPLAY '                     ADD ROUTINE'.
    MOVE SPACES TO CUSTOMER-NUMBER.
    PERFORM 0400-CUSTOMER-NUMBER-ROUTINE
            UNTIL CUSTOMER-NUMBER IS NUMERIC.

    IF CUSTOMER-NUMBER NOT = '0000'
        MOVE 'YES ' TO FOUND-KEY
            PERFORM 0330-READ-ISAM-FILE
    ELSE
        MOVE 'NO ' TO FOUND-KEY.

    IF FOUND-KEY = 'YES'
        DISPLAY 'DUPLICATE RECORD KEY.  TRY AGAIN.'
        DISPLAY 'PRESS ANY KEY TO CONTINUE.'
        ACCEPT ANY-KEY.


0320-GET-DATA.

    MOVE SPACES TO CUSTOMER-NAME.
    PERFORM 0410-NAME-ROUTINE.

    MOVE SPACES TO CUS-ADDRESS.
    PERFORM 0430-ADDRESS-ROUTINE.

    MOVE SPACES TO CITY.
    PERFORM 0440-CITY-ROUTINE.

    MOVE SPACES TO STATE.
    PERFORM 0450-STATE-ROUTINE.

    MOVE SPACES TO ZIP-CODE.
    PERFORM 0460-ZIP-CODE-ROUTINE
            UNTIL ZIP-CODE IS NUMERIC.

    MOVE SPACES TO NON-MONTHS.
    PERFORM 0470-MONTHS-ROUTINE
            UNTIL NON-MONTHS IS NUMERIC.

    MOVE SPACES TO EDIT-OPTION.
    PERFORM 0500-EDIT-FIELDS
            UNTIL EDIT-OPTION = 'X'.
```

```
        WRITE ISAM-RECORD
             INVALID KEY
             DISPLAY 'UNKNOWN ERROR DURING WRITE.'
             DISPLAY 'HALTING PROGRAM.'
             STOP RUN.


    0330-READ-ISAM-FILE.

        READ ISAM-FILE
             INVALID KEY MOVE 'NO ' TO FOUND-KEY.


    0400-CUSTOMER-NUMBER-ROUTINE.

        PERFORM 1400-DISPLAY-BLANK-LINE 2 TIMES.
        MOVE SPACES TO CUSTOMER-IN.
        DISPLAY 'ENTER CUSTOMER NUMBER...'.
        DISPLAY '####'.
        ACCEPT CUSTOMER-IN.

        STRING CUSTOMER-IN DELIMITED BY SIZE
             INTO CUSTOMER-NUMBER.

        INSPECT CUSTOMER-NUMBER REPLACING ALL SPACES BY ZEROS.

        IF CUSTOMER-NUMBER NOT NUMERIC
             DISPLAY ' '
             DISPLAY 'CUSTOMER NUMBER MUST BE ALL NUMERIC DIGITS.'
             DISPLAY ' '
             MOVE SPACES TO CUSTOMER-IN.



    0410-NAME-ROUTINE.

        PERFORM 1400-DISPLAY-BLANK-LINE 5 TIMES.
        DISPLAY 'ENTER NAME...'.
        DISPLAY '********************'.
        ACCEPT CUSTOMER-NAME.


    0430-ADDRESS-ROUTINE.

        PERFORM 1400-DISPLAY-BLANK-LINE 5 TIMES.
        DISPLAY 'ENTER ADDRESS...'.
        DISPLAY '***************'.
        ACCEPT CUS-ADDRESS.


    0440-CITY-ROUTINE.

        PERFORM 1400-DISPLAY-BLANK-LINE 5 TIMES.
        DISPLAY 'ENTER CITY...'.
        DISPLAY '*************'.
        ACCEPT CITY.
```

```
0450-STATE-ROUTINE.

    PERFORM 1400-DISPLAY-BLANK-LINE 5 TIMES.
    DISPLAY 'ENTER STATE...'.
    DISPLAY '**'.
    ACCEPT STATE.


0460-ZIP-CODE-ROUTINE.

    PERFORM 1400-DISPLAY-BLANK-LINE 5 TIMES.
    DISPLAY 'ENTER ZIP CODE...'.
    DISPLAY '#####'.
    ACCEPT ZIP-CODE.

    IF ZIP-CODE NOT NUMERIC
        DISPLAY ' '
        DISPLAY 'ZIP CODE MUST BE ALL NUMERIC DIGITS.'
        DISPLAY ' '
        MOVE SPACES TO ZIP-CODE.


0470-MONTHS-ROUTINE.

    PERFORM 1400-DISPLAY-BLANK-LINE 5 TIMES.
    MOVE SPACES TO MONTHS-IN.
    DISPLAY 'ENTER MONTHS OF SUBSCRIPTION...'.
    DISPLAY '##'.
    ACCEPT MONTHS-IN.

    STRING MONTHS-IN DELIMITED BY SIZE
            INTO NON-MONTHS.

    INSPECT NON-MONTHS REPLACING ALL SPACES BY ZEROS.

    IF NON-MONTHS NOT NUMERIC
        DISPLAY ' '
        DISPLAY 'NUMBER OF MONTHS INCORRECT.  TRY AGAIN.'
        DISPLAY ' '
        MOVE SPACES TO MONTHS-IN.


0500-EDIT-FIELDS.

    PERFORM 0600-DISPLAY-DATA.
    DISPLAY ' '.
    DISPLAY 'ENTER LETTER OF FIELD TO CHANGE (OR X TO EXIT).'.

    ACCEPT EDIT-OPTION.

    IF EDIT-OPTION = 'A'
        MOVE SPACES TO CUSTOMER-NAME
        PERFORM 0410-NAME-ROUTINE

    ELSE
        IF EDIT-OPTION = 'B'
            MOVE SPACES TO CUS-ADDRESS
            PERFORM 0430-ADDRESS-ROUTINE
```

```
        ELSE
           IF EDIT-OPTION = 'C'
              MOVE SPACES TO CITY
              PERFORM 0440-CITY-ROUTINE

        ELSE
          IF EDIT-OPTION = 'D'
              MOVE SPACES TO STATE
              PERFORM 0450-STATE-ROUTINE

        ELSE
           IF EDIT-OPTION = 'E'
              MOVE SPACES TO ZIP-CODE
              PERFORM 0460-ZIP-CODE-ROUTINE
                   UNTIL ZIP-CODE IS NUMERIC

        ELSE
           IF EDIT-OPTION = 'F'
              MOVE SPACES TO NON-MONTHS
              PERFORM 0470-MONTHS-ROUTINE
                   UNTIL NON-MONTHS IS NUMERIC

        ELSE
           IF EDIT-OPTION NOT = 'X'
              DISPLAY ' '
              DISPLAY 'ENTRY IS NOT CORRECT.   ENTER ONLY A - F OR X.'
              DISPLAY 'PLEASE TRY AGAIN.'
              DISPLAY ' '.


    0600-DISPLAY-DATA.

        MOVE SUB-MONTHS TO MONTHS-EDITED.
        PERFORM 1400-DISPLAY-BLANK-LINE 12 TIMES.
        DISPLAY '                   SUBSCRIBER UPDATE PROGRAM '.
        DISPLAY '                        DATE: ' DISPLAY-DATE.
        DISPLAY '                   FIELD MAINTENANCE'.
        DISPLAY ' '.
        DISPLAY '                     FOR CUSTOMER NUMBER '
             CUSTOMER-NUMBER.
        DISPLAY ' '.
        DISPLAY 'A) NAME..................... ' CUSTOMER-NAME.
        DISPLAY ' '.
        DISPLAY 'B) ADDRESS.................. ' CUS-ADDRESS.
        DISPLAY ' '.
        DISPLAY 'C) CITY..................... ' CITY.
        DISPLAY ' '.
        DISPLAY 'D) STATE.................... ' STATE.
        DISPLAY ' '.
        DISPLAY 'E) ZIP CODE................. ' ZIP-CODE.
        DISPLAY ' '.
        DISPLAY 'F) MONTHS OF SUBSCRIPTION... ' MONTHS-EDITED.


    0700-CHANGE-ROUTINE.

        MOVE 'NO ' TO FOUND-KEY.
        PERFORM 0710-CHECK-CHANGE-RECORD
                UNTIL FOUND-KEY = 'YES' OR
                CUSTOMER-NUMBER = '0000'.
```

```
        IF CUSTOMER-NUMBER NOT = '0000'
            MOVE SPACES TO EDIT-OPTION
            PERFORM 0500-EDIT-FIELDS
                    UNTIL EDIT-OPTION = 'X'
          PERFORM 0720-REWRITE-ROUTINE.

        IF CUSTOMER-NUMBER NOT = '0000'
            DISPLAY 'CHANGE ANOTHER RECORD (Y OR N)?'
            ACCEPT ANY-KEY
            IF ANY-KEY NOT = 'Y'
                MOVE '0000' TO CUSTOMER-NUMBER.


    0710-CHECK-CHANGE-RECORD.

        PERFORM 1400-DISPLAY-BLANK-LINE 12 TIMES.
        DISPLAY '                    SUBSCRIBER UPDATE PROGRAM '.
        DISPLAY '                        DATE: ' DISPLAY-DATE.
        DISPLAY '                    CHANGE ROUTINE'.
        DISPLAY ' '.
        DISPLAY ' '.
        MOVE SPACES TO CUSTOMER-NUMBER.
        PERFORM 0400-CUSTOMER-NUMBER-ROUTINE
                UNTIL CUSTOMER-NUMBER IS NUMERIC.


        MOVE 'YES' TO FOUND-KEY.
        IF CUSTOMER-NUMBER NOT = '0000'
            PERFORM 0330-READ-ISAM-FILE.

        IF FOUND-KEY = 'NO '
            DISPLAY 'RECORD NOT FOUND.  TRY AGAIN.'
            DISPLAY 'PRESS ANY KEY TO CONTINUE.'
            ACCEPT ANY-KEY.


    0720-REWRITE-ROUTINE.

        REWRITE ISAM-RECORD
                INVALID KEY
                DISPLAY 'UNKNOWN ERROR DURING REWRITE.'
                DISPLAY 'HALTING PROGRAM.'
                STOP RUN.


    0800-DELETE-ROUTINE.

        MOVE 'NO ' TO FOUND-KEY.
        PERFORM 0810-CHECK-DELETE-RECORD
                UNTIL FOUND-KEY = 'YES' OR
                CUSTOMER-NUMBER = '0000'.
```

```
    IF CUSTOMER-NUMBER NOT = '0000'
        PERFORM 0600-DISPLAY-DATA
        DISPLAY ' '
        DISPLAY 'IS THIS THE RECORD YOU WANT TO DELETE (Y OR N)?'

        ACCEPT ANY-KEY

        IF ANY-KEY = 'Y'
            PERFORM 0820-DELETE-ROUTINE.

            IF CUSTOMER-NUMBER NOT = '0000'
                DISPLAY 'DELETE ANOTHER RECORD (Y OR N)?'
                ACCEPT ANY-KEY
                IF ANY-KEY NOT = 'Y'
                    MOVE '0000' TO CUSTOMER-NUMBER.


0810-CHECK-DELETE-RECORD.

    PERFORM 1400-DISPLAY-BLANK-LINE 12 TIMES.
    DISPLAY '                        SUBSCRIBER UPDATE PROGRAM '.
    DISPLAY '                            DATE: ' DISPLAY-DATE.
    DISPLAY '                        DELETE ROUTINE'.
    DISPLAY ' '.
    DISPLAY ' '.
    MOVE SPACES TO CUSTOMER-NUMBER.
    PERFORM 0400-CUSTOMER-NUMBER-ROUTINE
            UNTIL CUSTOMER-NUMBER IS NUMERIC.

    MOVE 'YES' TO FOUND-KEY.
    IF CUSTOMER-NUMBER NOT = '0000'
        PERFORM 0330-READ-ISAM-FILE.

    IF FOUND-KEY = 'NO '
        DISPLAY 'RECORD NOT FOUND.  TRY AGAIN.'
        DISPLAY 'PRESS ANY KEY TO CONTINUE.'
        ACCEPT ANY-KEY.


0820-DELETE-ROUTINE.

    DELETE ISAM-FILE
            INVALID KEY
            DISPLAY 'UNKNOWN ERROR DURING DELETE.'
            DISPLAY 'HALTING PROGRAM.'
            STOP RUN.


1400-DISPLAY-BLANK-LINE.

    DISPLAY ' '.
```

8-5
Summary

1. Updating an indexed file interactively is more difficult than updating a sequential file interactively, but only because there are a few more techniques to be concerned about. We not only add records, but also change and delete them.
2. Our major concern is displaying records one at a time in a display format so that the user can see the entire record at once. Full-screen processing is most commonly used, but because it is machine specific, we used line-at-a-time techniques in this chapter.
3. A review of screen design techniques shows the following:

   ■ The program should use markers to show how long the user's entry can be.
   ■ The program should use the menu approach when possible.
   ■ There should be some type of heading on the screen display.
   ■ The screen should not be cluttered.
   ■ The programmer should be consistent in the use of screens.
   ■ The programmer should use, but not abuse, any special features of the terminal.

4. An interactive program must use an exit routine that accepts its exit clue from the user. Since an indexed file is not read until the end of the file, the exit is the only clue to when the program is finished.
5. All the routines in an interactive program should provide some way for the user to get out of the routine without having to do any processing, just in case the user gets into the routine by mistake or decides that the record being accessed is not correct.
6. In an interactive program add, after all the data has been entered, the program should display the fields on the screen and let the user modify them as necessary. The user should not have to add the record and then change it later to fix any errors that were entered during the add routine.
7. When a record is being deleted, the program should display the record on the screen so the user can see it and verify that it is the one intended for deletion. This saves the user from making costly mistakes by deleting the wrong records.

8-6
Glossary

There are no new terms in this chapter.

══ 8-7 ══
Quick Quiz

Cover the answers with a blank sheet of paper and test yourself. Questions 1–10 are true or false questions.

T   F   **1.** We generally use more routines when creating an indexed interactive program than we do when creating a sequential interactive program.

T   F   **2.** We can always create an interactive indexed program that will print sequentially.

T   F   **3.** We should always display some type of prompt showing the user how long the entry can be.

T   F   **4.** When you use a menu system, it is a good idea to separate the exit item from the other items on the screen to make it stand out.

T   F   **5.** When you use multiple screens in a program, it is a good idea to use some type of message indicating how the user can move from the first screen to the second.

T   F   **6.** If you have a color terminal display, it is a good idea to display error messages in green so they stand out from the rest of the display.

T   F   **7.** The typical interactive indexed program not only adds records but also changes and deletes them.

T   F   **8.** When we have numeric fields with decimal points, we need to redefine them as non-numeric so we can edit the fields around the decimal points.

T   F   **9.** If we use a sequential print routine in an interactive indexed program, we must use DYNAMIC on the ACCESS IS clause.

T   F   **10.** When deleting records in an interactive indexed program, we always display the record to be deleted so the user doesn't inadvertently delete the wrong record.

══ 8-8 ══
Answers to Quick Quiz

1. T.

2. F (Some COBOL versions do not allow direct and sequential processing of an ISAM file in the same program.)

3. T (However, when the entry is only one character long or is a dummy entry, such as PRESS ANY KEY TO CONTINUE, the prompt really is not needed and sometimes is not used.)

4. T (Though this is not always possible. Sometimes the exit item is listed not on the screen but in the prompt.)

5. T

6. F (It is true that you should use color, but you should utilize normal color meanings. Normally, red, not green, means warning, so you should print error messages in red, not green.)

7. T

8. T

9. T (In any indexed program, whether interactive or not. We can, of course, just use SEQUENTIAL if we do not want to access the file randomly.)

10. T

8-9

Questions to Aid Understanding

*1. List the three commonly used methods of interactive programming and explain why we use the one we do.

2. List and explain at least four of the screen handling techniques.

3. Explain why an interactive indexed program file is generally set up with access as DYNAMIC.

4. When we set up the initial menu in the sample program on pages 459–471, we listed the options as 1 through 4 and the exit command as option 9. Explain the logic behind this.

*5. When we redesigned the second screen in the discussion of multiple screens, the layout of the screen was changed so that the numbers of the options no longer progressed down the screen but rather went across the screen. Explain why this might not be a good idea.

6. Explain why, in the sample program, we set up the amount fields so that they were redefined and split into dollars and cents.

7. Explain why it is important to have an exit out of a program function in an interactive program (such as a method of getting out of the add routine after it had been selected from the menu.)

8-10

Coding Exercises

1. In the sample program in the chapter, we set up a customer number of zeros for users to indicate that they had gotten into the routine by accident and wanted to exit. Devise some other method of getting out of the routine and code all the appropriate statements as they were used in the chapter.

2. Many times the user will want to list a user file in some order other than by index. Write a routine to sort the file we used in the chapter by customer name and list it on the screen (16 lines per screen as in the chapter).

3. The key of an indexed record cannot be changed, because changing the record would not change the index. We can, however, change the key if we first delete the record that has the old record key and then add the record that has the new record key. Write an interactive routine to do this. You can use the same record key we used for the sample program in the chapter.

8-11
Maintenance Program

Roger Barnell likes the indexed program Cindy wrote for the SUBSCRIB file. But he would like it to be able to list the file on the screen in customer number order. He also wants to be able to choose which record the display will begin with, such as key '1111.'

It is your job to change the program to meet these new requirements. You will need to change the initial menu to reflect the new options and change the design and the program so they will now produce the new listings.

8-12
Illustrative Program

The bank where you work keeps track of customer charge card accounts on an indexed file. You are assigned the task of writing a program that can be used to update the balance by inputting new charges and payments. Your program will need to prompt for the customer number and then for whether the transaction is a charge or a payment. If it is a payment, the program will need to input the payment amount and store it in the record along with the current date (date of payment) while updating the balance. If it is a charge, the program will need to simply update the balance. After the balance is updated, all the data in the file should be displayed in the following format:

```
                    THE FRIENDLY BANK
                    DATE: 10/15/88

          CUSTOMER NUMBER..... 1234

          CUSTOMER NAME....... JOHN SMITH

          CHARGE CARD......... MASTERCARD

          BALANCE.............     $34.65

          DATE OF LAST PAYMENT   09/15/88

          LAST PAYMENT........     $12.55

          CREDIT LIMIT........  $5,000.00

     PRESS ANY KEY FOR NEXT TRANSACTION............
```

On this display, the charge codes translate as 1 for Mastercard, 2 for Visa, and 3 for American Express. The file to be used in the program is the BANK file as shown in Figure 8-9. The systems design for the program is shown in Figure 8-10, the flowchart design in Figure 8-11, and the pseudocode here:

```
Start
Open the file
Initialize customer number to all 9's
DO-WHILE customer number not zeros
        DO-WHILE customer number not zeros or record not found
                Input customer number
                Set record found code to yes
                IF customer number not zeros THEN
                        Read indexed file invalid key set code to no and
                                                print error message
                (ELSE)
                END-IF
        END-DO
        IF customer number not zeros THEN
                Input transaction choice from user
                IF transaction is charge THEN
                        Input charge amount
                        Increase balance
                ELSE
                        Input payment amount
                        Reduce balance
                        Move current date into record
                END-IF
                Display data
                Write record to the file
        (ELSE)
        END-IF
END-DO
Close the file
End
```

BANK File					
Field Description	*Position*	*Length*	:	*Dec*	*Type*
Customer number	1–4	4	:		Non-numeric
Customer name	5–24	20	:		Non-numeric
Charge card code	25–25	1	:	0	Numeric
Balance	26–32	7	:	2	Numeric
Date of last payment	33–38	6	:		Non-numeric
Amount of last payment	39–39	7	:	2	Numeric
Credit limit	40–46	7	:	2	Numeric
Filler	47–80	34	:		Non-numeric
Record Length = 80					

Figure 8-9   The record layout for the BANK file.

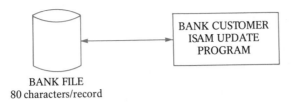

BANK FILE
80 characters/record

Figure 8-10   The systems chart for the indexed BANK update program.

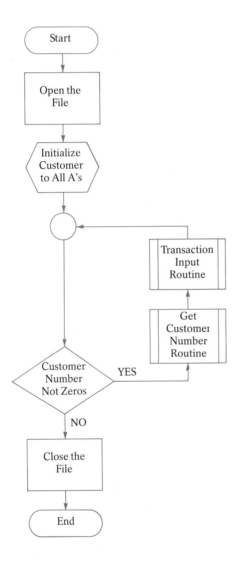

Figure 8-11   Flowchart of BANK interactive indexed update program (Main module).

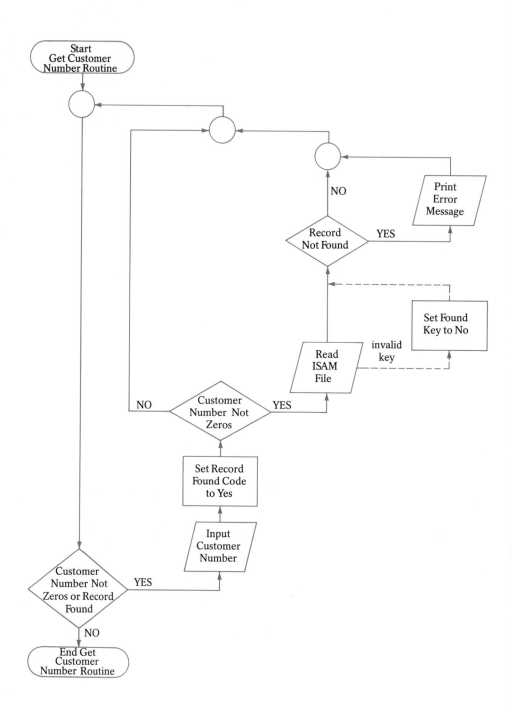

Figure 8-11 **(continued)**   Get customer number module.

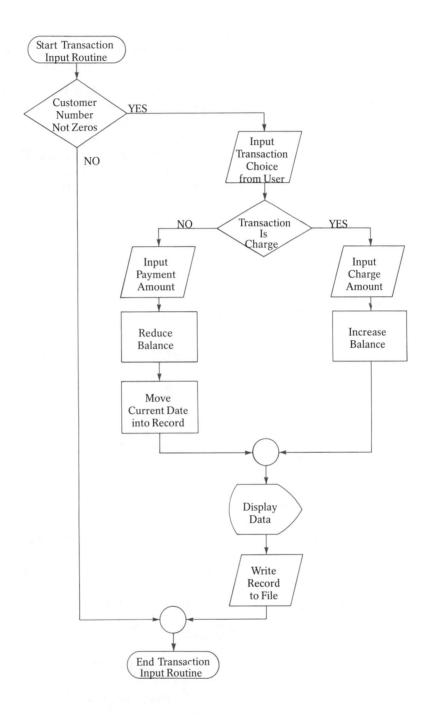

Figure 8-11 **(continued)** Change module.

8-13

Interactive System Designed Programs

For the following programs, all the design elements typically furnished to a programmer by the systems analyst are furnished. It is up to you, as programmer, to design and code the program. The files to be used are found in Appendix A.

1. The company you work for uses an indexed inventory file (INVENT) with the layout shown in Figure 8-12 (the item number is the record key). Your program should allow users to add new records, change existing ones, and delete ones no longer needed (no sequential printing). To get to the particular function, you should use the initial menu as shown in Figure 8-13. After the data for the record to be added is input, and when a record is accessed for changing or deleting, all the fields should be shown on the maintenance display, as in Figure 8-14. The systems chart for the program is shown in Figure 8-15.

INVENT **File**					
Field Description	*Position*	*Length*	:	*Dec*	*Type*
Item number	1–4	4	:		Non-numeric
Last count	5–10	6	:	0	Numeric
Current count	11–16	6	:	0	Numeric
Unit cost	17–24	8	:	2	Numeric
Unit price	25–32	8	:	2	Numeric
Amount received	33–38	6	:	0	Numeric
Amount sold	39–44	6	:	0	Numeric
Filler	45–80	36	:		Non-numeric
Record Length = 80					

Figure 8-12   The record layout for the INVENT file for exercise 8-13-1.

```
DATE MM/DD/YY          INVENTORY FILE UPDATE PROGRAM    INITIAL MENU

                    YOUR OPTIONS ON THIS MENU ARE:

                    1. ADD A NEW RECORD TO THE FILE

                    2. CHANGE AN EXISTING RECORD

                    3. DELETE AN EXISTING RECORD

                    9. EXIT THE PROGRAM

ENTER THE NUMBER FOR THE OPTION OF YOUR CHOICE:
```

Figure 8-13   The initial menu display for the indexed inventory program, exercise 8-13-1.

2. The company you work for has a large force of salesmen who travel all over the country. You have been assigned the task of writing an indexed program to keep the SALES file (Figure 8-16) up to date. Your program will need to allow records to be added, deleted, changed, and sequentially listed on the screen in salesmen number order (the record key). Figure 8-17 shows how the initial menu should look. Figure 8-18 illustrates the field maintenance display necessary after all the data has been input for the add and necessary to display the records for the change and delete functions. Figure 8-19 shows the layout for the sequential list. Note that there is only one product sales column, while the record contains five sales figures. The product column displays the total of the five sales figures. Figure 8-20 shows the systems chart for the program.

```
DATE MM/DD/YY          INVENTORY FILE UPDATE PROGRAM          FIELD MAINTENANCE

                       FOR ITEM NUMBER 1234
                  A)  LAST COUNT....... ZZZ,ZZ9

                  B)  CURRENT COUNT.... ZZZ,ZZ9

                  C)  UNIT COST........ ZZZ,ZZ9.99

                  D)  UNIT PRICE....... ZZZ,ZZ9.99

                  E)  AMOUNT RECEIVED.. ZZZ,ZZ9

                  F)  AMOUNT SOLD...... ZZZ,ZZ9

ENTER LETTER OF FIELD TO CHANGE (OR X TO EXIT).
```

Figure 8-14   The field maintenance display for the indexed inventory update program, exercise 8-13-1.

Figure 8-15   The systems chart for the inventory indexed update program, exercise 8-13-1.

SALES File					
Field Description	Position	Length	:	Dec	Type
Salesman number	1–4	4	:		Non-numeric
Sales name	5–24	20	:		Non-numeric
Sales territory	25–26	2	:		Non-numeric
Percent of commission	27–28	2	:	0	Numeric
Sales of product 1	29–35	7	:	2	Numeric
Sales of product 2	36–42	7	:	2	Numeric
Sales of product 3	43–49	7	:	2	Numeric
Sales of product 4	50–56	7	:	2	Numeric
Sales of product 5	57–63	7	:	2	Numeric
Years of service	64–65	2	:	0	Numeric
Filler	66–80	15	:		Non-numeric
Record Length = 80					

Figure 8-16   The record layout for the SALES file for exercise 8-13-2.

```
DATE MM/DD/YY          SALESMAN FILE UPDATE PROGRAM      INITIAL MENU

                    THE OPTIONS IN THIS PROGRAM ARE:

                    1. ADD A NEW RECORD TO THE FILE

                    2. CHANGE AN EXISTING RECORD

                    3. DELETE AN EXISTING RECORD

                    4. DISPLAY A SEQUENTIAL LIST

                    9. EXIT THE PROGRAM

          ENTER THE NUMBER FOR THE OPTION OF YOUR CHOICE:
```

Figure 8-17   The initial menu display for the indexed sales file update program, exercise 8-13-2.

```
DATE MM/DD/YY        SALESMAN FILE UPDATE PROGRAM     FIELD MAINTENANCE

                        SALESMAN NUMBER 1234

A) SALESMAN NAME.... X--------------------X

B) SALES TERRITORY.. XX

C) PERCENT OF COMM.. Z9 %

D) YEARS OF SERVICE. Z9

E) PRODUCT 1 SALES.. ZZ,ZZ9.99      F) PRODUCT 2 SALES.. ZZ,ZZ9.99

G) PRODUCT 3 SALES.. ZZ,ZZ9.99      H) PRODUCT 4 SALES.. ZZ,ZZ9.99

I) PRODUCT 5 SALES.. ZZ,ZZ9.99

ENTER THE LETTER OF FIELD TO CHANGE (OR X TO EXIT).
```

Figure 8-18   The field maintenance display for the indexed sales file update program, exercise 8-13-2.

```
DATE MM/DD/YY        SALESMAN FILE UPDATE PROGRAM      SEQUENTIAL LISTING

SALESMAN                          SALES  SALES      PRODUCT       YEARS
 NUMBER    SALESMAN NAME          TERR.  COMM.        SALES     OF SERVICE

  XXXX     X--------------------X  XX    Z9 %     ZZZ,ZZ9.99       Z9
  XXXX     X--------------------X  XX    Z9 %     ZZZ,ZZ9.99       Z9
  : ;          :     :     :       : :    : :       : : :          : :
  : ;          :     :     :       : :    : :       : : :          : :
  : ;          :     :     :       : :    : :       : : :          : :
  : ;          :     :     :       : :    : :       : : :          : :
  : ;          :     :     :       : :    : :       : : :          : :
  : ;          :     :     :       : :    : :       : : :          : :
  : ;          :     :     :       : :    : :       : : :          : :
  : ;          :     :     :       : :    : :       : : :          : :
  : ;          :     :     :       : :    : :       : : :          : :
  : ;          :     :     :       : :    : :       : : :          : :
  : ;          :     :     :       : :    : :       : : :          : :
  : ;          :     :     :       : :    : :       : : :          : :
  : ;          :     :     :       : :    : :       : : :          : :
  XXXX     X--------------------X  XX    Z9 %     ZZZ,ZZ9.99       Z9

PRESS ANY KEY TO SEE MORE RECORDS OR X TO QUIT.
```

Figure 8-19   The sequential listing display for the indexed sales file update program, exercise 8-13-2. Note that, at the end of the file, the message should read "END OF THE FILE . . . PRESS ANY KEY TO RETURN TO INITIAL MENU."

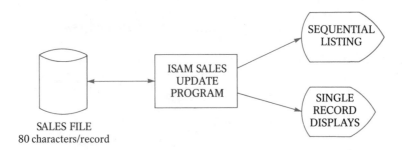

Figure 8-20   The systems chart for the indexed sales file update program, exercise 8-13-2.

3. The company you work for has its payroll data stored in an indexed file (Figure 8-21). You are assigned the task of writing an interactive program that can be used to update the file. The program needs to be able to allow new records to be added, old records to be deleted, and current records to be changed. The change routine must allow the employee number (the record key) to be changed. This is done by first deleting the current record and then adding a new one with the new record key. Your program should also allow the data to be displayed in several sequences: employee number order, employee name order, and years of service in descending sequence.

Payroll File					
Field Description	*Position*	*Length*	:	*Dec*	*Type*
Employee number	1–4	4	:		Non-numeric
Employee name	5–24	20	:		Non-numeric
Hours worked	25–27	3	:	0	Numeric
Rate of pay	28–31	4	:	2	Numeric
Deductions	32–33	2	:	0	Numeric
Years of service	34–35	2	:	0	Numeric
Annual salary	36–41	6	:	0	Numeric
Union dues	42–47	6	:	2	Numeric
Hospital insurance	48–53	6	:	2	Numeric
Filler	54–80	27	:		Non-numeric
Record Length = 80					

Figure 8-21   The payroll file for exercise 8-13-3.

The initial menu for the program should look like the one shown in Figure 8-22. The field maintenance display shown in Figure 8-23 is used to display the data after it has been input for an add or after the record has been read in for a change or delete. The sequential listings are to be shown

---

```
DATE MM/DD/YY        PAYROLL UPDATE PROGRAM      INITIAL MENU

THE OPTIONS IN THIS PROGRAM ARE:
                                   -- SEQUENTIAL LISTINGS --

1. ADD A NEW RECORD TO THE FILE    4. EMPLOYEE NUMBER ORDER

2. CHANGE AN EXISTING RECORD       5. EMPLOYEE NAME ORDER

3. DELETE AN EXISTING RECORD       6. YEARS OF SERVICE ORDER

               9. EXIT THE PROGRAM

ENTER THE NUMBER FOR THE OPTION OF YOUR CHOICE:
```

Figure 8-22 The initial menu display for the indexed payroll file update program, exercise 8-13-3.

```
DATE MM/DD/YY          PAYROLL FILE UPDATE PROGRAM      FIELD MAINTENANCE
                         EMPLOYEE NUMBER 1234

A) EMPLOYEE NAME.... X--------------------X

B) HOURS WORKED..... Z99

C) RATE OF PAY...... Z9.99

D) DEDUCTIONS....... Z9

E) YEARS OF SERVICE. Z9

F) ANNUAL SALARY.... ZZZ,ZZ9

G) UNION DUES....... Z,ZZ9.99    H) HOSPITAL INS... Z,ZZ9.99

ENTER THE LETTER OF FIELD TO CHANGE (OR X TO EXIT).
```

Figure 8-23 The field maintenance display for the indexed payroll file update program, exercise 8-13-3.

in the format given in Figure 8-24. Notice that the second page heading will have to change for each different listing. The headings should be

- EMPLOYEE NUMBER ORDER
- EMPLOYEE NAME ORDER
- YEARS OF SERVICE ORDER

The systems chart for the program is shown in Figure 8-25.

```
DATE MM/DD/YY          PAYROLL FILE UPDATE PROGRAM    SEQUENTIAL LISTING
                         EMPLOYEE NUMBER ORDER

EMPLOYEE                            HOURS   PAY          SERV.    ANNUAL
 NUMBER    EMPLOYEE NAME            WORKED  RATE  DED.    YEARS    SALARY

  XXXX     X--------------------X    ZZ9   Z9.99   Z9      Z9    ZZZ,ZZ9
  XXXX     X--------------------X    ZZ9   Z9.99   Z9      Z9    ZZZ,ZZ9
   ::          :      :      :        ::     ::    ::      ::      :::
   ::          :      :      :        ::     ::    ::      ::      :::
   ::          :      :      :        ::     ::    ::      ::      :::
   ::          :      :      :        ::     ::    ::      ::      :::
   ::          :      :      :        ::     ::    ::      ::      :::
   ::          :      :      :        ::     ::    ::      ::      :::
   ::          :      :      :        ::     ::    ::      ::      :::
   ::          :      :      :        ::     ::    ::      ::      :::
   ::          :      :      :        ::     ::    ::      ::      :::
   ::          :      :      :        ::     ::    ::      ::      :::
   ::          :      :      :        ::     ::    ::      ::      :::
  XXXX     X--------------------X    ZZ9   Z9.99   Z9      Z9    ZZZ,ZZ9

    PRESS ANY KEY TO SEE MORE RECORDS OR X TO QUIT.
```

Figure 8-24   The sequential listing display for the indexed payroll file update program, exercise 8-13-3. Note that, at the end of the file, the message should read "END OF THE FILE . . . PRESS ANY KEY TO RETURN TO INITIAL MENU."

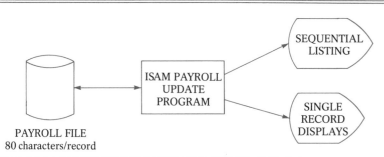

Figure 8-25   The systems chart for the indexed payroll file update program, exercise 8-13-3.

8-14
Non-designed Programs

In the following programs, you will need to design the systems chart, the input files (record layout), the printer spacing chart, the program design, and the data with which to test the program.

1. Write an interactive program that can be used to update a credit card file for the bank you work for. The program will need to allow addition of new customers, cancellation of customers who no longer want their cards, and changes to any data on the record. It will also need to allow charges or credits to the balance on the credit card.

2. Write a program to print out the charges for tuition and fees at your school. The indexed file is to contain the student ID (Social Security number), student name, residency code (resident or non-resident), and credit hours for each student. The program should allow a record to be called to the screen for verification and then, upon indication from the user, it should print the charges for that particular student on a form that can be mailed to the student. The tuition is to be calculated as follows:

$<$	12 hours	$=$	\$45 per credit for residents
$>=$	12 hours	$=$	\$540 total for residents
$<$	12 hours	$=$	\$118 per credit for non-residents
$>=$	12 hours	$=$	\$1416 total for non-residents

The fees are the same for residents and non-residents:

$<$	12 hours	$=$	\$3 per credit
$>=$	12 hours	$=$	\$36 total

The form should list, for each student, the student ID with dashes, the name, the hours, the tuition charges, the fees charge, and a total charge. Keep track of the total hours and all of the charges so that when the user exits the program, a list of all the totals can be printed (or displayed). In addition, keep track of the number of resident students and the average charge, the number of non-resident students and the average charge, and the total number of students and the average charge. This will also be printed (or displayed) at the end of the program.

3. Write a program that will allow the addition, deletion, and modification of records in a file containing records of books stored in a library. The records are stored in the indexed file by their book number (Library of Congress number). The file contains information on the name of the book, name of the author, subject of the book, date of publication, cost of the book, name of the publisher, date of purchase, and additional copies available, if any. The program will need to allow the changing of the record key. To do this, the original record must be deleted and a new record (with the new record key) added.

OBJECTIVES   After completing Chapter 9 you should be able to
1. explain what a relative file is and what advantages it has over an indexed file;
2. list and explain at least two problems associated with relative files;
3. explain the idea of hashing and show an example;
4. explain why a relative file that is to be used with a hashing technique is created with empty records;
5. explain how a record is added into a relative file when a hashing technique is used;
6. explain how a record is deleted in a relative file that is processed with a hashing technique;
7. explain what the START statement is and how it can be useful.

CHAPTER 9

RELATIVE FILES

Introduction

Thus far we have discussed two different types of file storage methods—sequential and indexed. Sequential files are useful if we are processing tape files and a few other specialized files that do not need to be accessed directly. With most files, however, having to access the records sequentially presents the user with severe handicaps. Indexed files overcome many of the disadvantages of sequential files, but indexed files have a couple of problems as well. First, they require storage space for the index file; second, because access is not directly to the records in the file but rather through the index, it is slowed down slightly.

There is a third type of storage that eliminates the two problems associated with indexed files. **Relative files** allow accessing of the records by specifying the location of the record in the file, similar to the way a table entry is accessed. In that respect, a relative file is similar to a table. But, unlike a table that is stored in memory, a relative file is stored on disk, making access to the information in the file much slower than access to the elements in a table. Relative files can be useful, however, because unlike tables they are not limited by the relatively small amount of memory available to a program.

Relative files can have problems also. If we have data to store as a relative file and the record key is a sequential number, such as an employee number, we simply write the records into the file using the employee number as the key and everything is fine. The records start with a key of 1 and continue until we reach the end of the employee numbers—200 or 500 or whatever the upper limit is. We have one record for every possible key.

The problem is that the actual number of files that can be created with a strictly sequential key is small. Most of the time, files are created with a key that is much more difficult to manipulate than a simple sequential key. Many employee files, for example, are created with the Social Security number as the record key. This means that the total number of records the file must be set up for is one shy of one billion (999,999,999) since the range of Social Security numbers is 000-00-0001 to 999-99-9999. We have to reserve a record for every possible Social Security number.

Obviously, this is not a workable solution. With such files, we need some method of reducing the number of possible keys. There are a number of different ways to do so, but one of the easiest is the **hash routine**. Hashing is simply a technique whereby the actual key is divided by the number of records in the file, and the remainder is used as the pointer into the file.

For example, let's suppose the key is a Social Security number of 123-45-6789 and we want the file to have enough room for 250 records. We divide the number 123,456,789 by 250 and get 493,827 with a remainder of 39. Now, since division will always yield a remainder that is, at the most, one less than the number we divide by (250 in this case), we need to add one to the remainder to be sure we use all the possible numbers for the file. This gives us a record pointer of 40, which is what we will use for the record key when we write the record into the file.

When we are trying to access a record, we simply reverse the process. We divide the Social Security number by 250, add 1 to the remainder, and use the result to read the record from the file.

This all seems pretty simple. But this technique causes another problem. Chances are quite good that this type of division will occasionally produce the same remainder for two different Social Security numbers. A simple way to prove this is to add 250 to the number we used, giving the following calculations:

$$123,456,789 + 250 = 123,457,039$$
$$123,457,039/250 \quad = 493,828 \text{ with a remainder of } 39$$

Of course, the odds of having two Social Security numbers that are exactly 250 apart is small. But we will come up with a duplicate remainder any time there are two Social Security numbers that are any multiple of 250 apart. The odds of that happening are quite high. When it happens, we have two record pointers that are the same. Of course, the first record will have already been put in the file, and when we try to put the second record in the file we will get an error. This is called a **collision**.

There are various ways of handling collisions, but one of the easiest and most often used is to begin examining records at the record where the collision occurred and continue until an empty record is found. The new record is then stored in this empty record.

As you might well expect, the more records there are in the file, the higher the odds are of collisions. Actually, when the file reaches about two-thirds full, the number of collisions increases dramatically. This results in a tremendous slow-down of the program as more and more accesses are necessary to locate the appropriate record.

There is one final problem with relative files. When we create the file, the records are in the file whether there is any data in them or not. Thus, we generally have a lot of wasted space in a relative file.

Given all the problems and necessary conditions, relative files are not used as often as other file types. There are certain applications, however, for which relative files can prove useful. For this reason we will examine how relative files are created and maintained.

9-2
Creating the Relative File

Creating a relative file is different than creating any other type of file. When a sequential file or indexed file is created, the records are written directly into the file when necessary. The file is only as large as the number of active records. A relative file, on the other hand, must be created with the appropriate number of records (we must know how many in order to use the hashing technique), and those records must be blanked out. The only way we know if a particular record has been used is to check to see if it is empty.

9-2-1 The SELECT Statement

Most of the statements used with relative files are the same as when they are used with indexed files, but there are a few subtle differences. We will begin by discussing the **SELECT statement**, the general form of which is

SELECT file-name ASSIGN TO external-file-name

ORGANIZATION IS RELATIVE

$$\left[\text{ACCESS IS} \left\{ \begin{array}{l} \text{SEQUENTIAL} \ \ [\text{RELATIVE KEY IS field-name-1}] \\ \text{RANDOM} \\ \text{DYNAMIC} \ \ \ \ \ \ \ \text{RELATIVE KEY IS field-name-1} \end{array} \right\} \right]$$

[FILE STATUS IS field-name-2]

If the file access is SEQUENTIAL, we can use the RELATIVE KEY clause if we need to, but it is optional. Remember that creating records in a relative file is different than writing records into an indexed file. For an indexed record, we needed the key because it was used to create the keys in the index file. With relative files, however, there is no index file and no real need to use the relative key when writing the records if all we want to do is write them sequentially. If we are accessing the file as either RANDOM or DYNAMIC, however, we must use the RELATIVE KEY clause.

When using a relative file, we don't usually write the records in the file by key. Since the file will be created with the maximum number of records already in the file and filled with blanks, writing an additional record into the file will cause a problem: there will now be additional records in the file and our hashing technique will no longer be valid. Thus, we generally don't use the RELATIVE KEY when writing the records in the file because they will merely be written in the file sequentially and blank. Then, when the actual records are put in the empty spots, they will be rewritten because they will already be in the file. We will simply be putting the actual data into the records.

In our sample file creation program, the SELECT statement we will use will look like the following:

```
SELECT RELATIVE-FILE ASSIGN TO DA-S-PATIENTS
       ORGANIZATION IS RELATIVE
       ACCESS IS SEQUENTIAL.
```

Again, since we are simply writing the records into the file sequentially, we will not need the RELATIVE KEY clause.

9-2-2 The Relative File Creation Program

The program to write the blank records into the file is extremely simple. We define the record layout with a single group item:

```
FD  RELATIVE-FILE
    LABEL RECORDS ARE OMITTED
    RECORD CONTAINS 80 CHARACTERS.
01  RELATIVE-RECORD                          PIC X(80).
```

Then the main routine in the PROCEDURE DIVISION contains

```
0100-MAIN-MODULE.

    OPEN OUTPUT RELATIVE-FILE.

    MOVE SPACES TO RELATIVE-RECORD.
    PERFORM 0200-WRITE-RECORDS 250 TIMES.

    CLOSE RELATIVE-FILE.
    STOP RUN.
```

The write routine is also simple:

```
0200-WRITE-RECORDS.

    WRITE RELATIVE-RECORD INVALID KEY
        DISPLAY 'UNKNOWN ERROR WRITING RECORDS.'
        DISPLAY 'HALTING PROGRAM.'
        STOP RUN.
```

Since we are merely writing blank records into the file, there should be no INVALID keys. We still choose to use the clause as a safeguard, however. If it is ever activated, the program will display a message and then stop.

The entire program:

```
****************************************************************
****************************************************************
*
*
*
*   PROGRAM NAME: REL-CRT
*
*   PROGRAMMER NAME:  ED COBURN
*
*   SOCIAL SECURITY NUMBER:  999-99-9999
*
*   DUE DATE: FEBRUARY 10, 1988
*
*   DESCRIPTION: THIS PROGRAM WILL CREATE A RELATIVE FILE
*                WITH 250 RECORDS.  ALL OF THE RECORDS WILL
*                BE EMPTY OF ANY DATA.
*
*
****************************************************************
****************************************************************

IDENTIFICATION DIVISION.
PROGRAM-ID.   REL-CRT.
AUTHOR.       ED COBURN.

ENVIRONMENT DIVISION.

CONFIGURATION SECTION.
SOURCE-COMPUTER. IBM-4331.
OBJECT-COMPUTER. IBM-4331.
```

```
            INPUT-OUTPUT SECTION.
            FILE-CONTROL.
            SELECT RELATIVE-FILE ASSIGN TO DA-S-PATIENTS
                    ORGANIZATION IS RELATIVE
                    ACCESS IS SEQUENTIAL.

            DATA DIVISION.
            FILE SECTION.

            FD  RELATIVE-FILE
                LABEL RECORDS ARE OMITTED
                RECORD CONTAINS 80 CHARACTERS.
            01  RELATIVE-RECORD                      PIC X(80).

        PROCEDURE DIVISION.

        0100-MAIN-MODULE.

            OPEN OUTPUT RELATIVE-FILE.

            MOVE SPACES TO RELATIVE-RECORD.
            PERFORM 0200-WRITE-RECORDS 250 TIMES.

            CLOSE RELATIVE-FILE.
            STOP RUN.


        0200-WRITE-RECORDS.

            WRITE RELATIVE-RECORD INVALID KEY
                    DISPLAY 'UNKNOWN ERROR WRITING RECORDS.'
                    DISPLAY 'HALTING PROGRAM.'
                    STOP RUN.
```

=== 9-3 ===
Updating a Relative File

To demonstrate how to use a relative file, we will write an interactive update program for the file we have just created. The processes used for updating a relative file are a bit different from those for an indexed file. We still need the capability of adding new records, but when adding them, we are actually rewriting the blank records that we have already created.

Changing records is still a matter of reading the record, changing it, and rewriting it back into the file. Now, however, when we read the record, not only do we use an INVALID KEY clause to determine if there is any problem, but we also check the record that we bring in to be sure that it actually has data in it and that it is, in fact, the record we are looking for. Remember that when we use a hashing technique, there can be collisions that might require us to look for the needed record further out in the file.

Deleting records is also different. We can't physically remove the record from the file because we have to retain a precise number of records in the file. Therefore, we need to blank out the record and rewrite it back into the file. This will effectively delete the record since it will now become just another of the blank records that have never been put into the file.

The final technique we might be interested in is a sequential list of the records. Since the records are stored in the file using a hashing technique, they are not in any type of sequence. To list them in some type of order, we will have to sort them first. Later in this chapter we will discuss how to sequentially print the records.

9-3-1 The File

We will set up our relative file to use a file of patients at a hospital. Our record key is the patient's Social Security number, and we have already created the file with 250 records in it. The record layout for the PATIENTS file is shown in Figure 9-1.

The SELECT clause we need for using this relative file will look like the following:

```
SELECT RELATIVE-FILE ASSIGN TO DA-R-PATIENTS
       ORGANIZATION IS RELATIVE
       ACCESS IS RANDOM
       RELATIVE KEY IS RELATIVE-KEY.
```

The RELATIVE-KEY field is not a field in the patient record layout. We do have the record key (the Social Security number) in the record, but remember that we are going to use a hashing technique to determine the relative position in the file so we need a temporary hash field in WORKING-STORAGE. That is what the RELATIVE-KEY field will be. Notice that this time we have assigned the access as RANDOM. If we had intended to do sequential access also, we would have used DYNAMIC.

PATIENTS **File**					
Field Description	*Position*	*Length*	:	*Dec*	*Type*
Patients number	1–9	9	:		Non-numeric
Name	10–29	20	:		Non-numeric
Address	30–44	15	:		Non-numeric
City	45–57	13	:		Non-numeric
State	58–59	2	:		Non-numeric
Zip code	50–64	5	:		Non-numeric
Amount due	65–70	6	:	2	Numeric
Last visit date	71–76	6	:		Non-numeric
Filler	77–80	4	:		Non-numeric
Record Length = 80					

Figure 9-1   The record layout for the PATIENTS file.

The file layout for the PATIENTS file is

```
FD  RELATIVE-FILE
    LABEL RECORDS ARE OMITTED
    RECORD CONTAINS 80 CHARACTERS.
01  RELATIVE-RECORD.
    10   SOCIAL-SEC-NUMBER            PIC X(9).
    10   PATIENT-NAME                 PIC X(20).
    10   PAT-ADDRESS                  PIC X(15).
    10   CITY                         PIC X(13).
    10   STATE                        PIC XX.
    10   ZIP-CODE                     PIC X(5).
    10   AMOUNT-DUE                   PIC 9(4)V99.
    10   LAST-DATE.
        20   LAST-MM                  PIC XX.
        20   LAST-DD                  PIC XX.
        20   LAST-YY                  PIC XX.
    10   FILLER                       PIC X(4).

01  RE-RELATIVE-RECORD.
    10   FILLER                       PIC X(64).
    10   NON-NUMERIC-AMOUNT.
        20   AMOUNT-DOLLARS           PIC X(4)
             JUSTIFIED RIGHT.
        20   AMOUNT-CENTS             PIC XX.
    10   FILLER                       PIC XX.
    10   NUMERIC-MM                   PIC 99.
    10   FILLER                       PIC X(8).
```

Notice that we subdefined the date so it can be input with slashes that can then be removed. We also used a second record layout to give us a second definition for the amount field so it can be input and edited around the decimal point as usual. At the same time we set up a second month field. We will reveal the use for this later.

9-3-2   The Relative Key Calculation Routine

Whether they are reading or rewriting (for all functions) the records, all the access routines will have to access the records in basically the same way. Thus it makes sense to use a performed procedure to calculate the relative key. We will also use one to input the Social Security number (using a second procedure).

We will begin by defining the RELATIVE-KEY field and the related fields in the WORKING-STORAGE SECTION. Since there are only 250 records in the file, the RELATIVE-KEY field needs to be defined for a length of only three:

```
WORKING-STORAGE SECTION.

01  WORK-AREAS.

    10   RELATIVE-KEY                 PIC 999.
    10   DIVISION-RESULT              PIC 9(7).
```

```
10   SOCIAL-IN.
     20   SOCIAL-IN-THREE              PIC XXX.
     20   FILLER                       PIC X.
     20   SOCIAL-IN-TWO                PIC XX.
     20   FILLER                       PIC X.
     20   SOCIAL-IN-FOUR               PIC XXXX.


10   CALCULATION-KEY.
     20   CALC-THREE                   PIC XXX.
     20   CALC-TWO                     PIC XX.
     20   CALC-FOUR                    PIC XXXX.
10   NUMERIC-KEY REDEFINES CALCULATION-KEY PIC 9(9).
```

Along with the relative key field, we set up the field to input the Social Security number so that the dashes may be removed (SOCIAL-IN). Then we set up the field into which we will move the pieces without the dashes (CALCULATION-KEY). The NUMERIC-KEY is the field we will use to calculate the RELATIVE-KEY. Naturally we need a numeric field, since it will be used in calculations. With the subdivisions and redefinition, we can remove the dashes and make one whole number. We also defined a field where we can store the results of the calculation to determine the relative key (DIVISION-RESULT).

Now the calculations to determine the RELATIVE-KEY will be fairly simple:

```
0300-CALCULATE-KEY.

     MOVE ALL 'A' TO CALCULATION-KEY.
     PERFORM 0310-GET-KEY UNTIL CALCULATION-KEY IS NUMERIC
                       OR   CALCULATION-KEY =  SPACES.

     IF CALCULATION-KEY NOT = SPACES
        DIVIDE NUMERIC-KEY BY 250 GIVING
              DIVISION-RESULT REMAINDER RELATIVE-KEY
        ADD 1 TO RELATIVE-KEY.
```

Just as we have done in the past, we will input the record key using a procedure that will let us make sure the key is all numbers. We will, however, allow the key to be input as all blanks as an exit message to the program. Thus, we check for the spaces before doing the calculations to determine the relative key. Also note that we force the CALCULATION-KEY to be all 'A' before we try to get the key. In the past we have blanked out the key we were looking up. Now, however, we allow the user to enter the key as blanks for an exit message; thus we have to force the key to be something other than numeric (including zeros) or blanks. We will make it A's, though any non-numeric character could be used.

The 0310-GET-KEY routine will look like the following:

```
0310-GET-KEY.

     DISPLAY ' '.
     DISPLAY ' '.
     DISPLAY 'ENTER THE PATIENTS SOCIAL SECURITY NUMBER.'
```

```
DISPLAY 'USE ALL 11 CHARACTERS INCLUDING THE DASHES.'
DISPLAY '(JUST PRESS RETURN TO EXIT.)'.
DISPLAY '###-##-####'.
MOVE SPACES TO SOCIAL-IN.
ACCEPT SOCIAL-IN.

MOVE SOCIAL-IN-THREE TO CALC-THREE.
MOVE SOCIAL-IN-TWO   TO CALC-TWO.
MOVE SOCIAL-IN-FOUR  TO CALC-FOUR.

IF CALCULATION-KEY NOT   NUMERIC AND
   CALCULATION-KEY NOT = SPACES
   DISPLAY 'INVALID SOCIAL SECURITY NUMBER.'
   DISPLAY 'PLEASE RE-ENTER.'.
```

After we input the Social Security number using the WORKING-STORAGE field, we move the pieces around the dashes to their appropriate places in the calculation key. This gives us the whole field, which we can then use for our calculations.

9-3-3 The Main Routine

Our initial menu will look like any number of other menus we have created in the past. We will need the usual three entries for adding, changing, and deleting, along with the exit entry. The menu will look like the following:

```
              PATIENTS UPDATE PROGRAM
                  DATE 09/17/88
                    MAIN MENU


         YOUR OPTIONS ON THIS MENU ARE:

         1. ADD A NEW RECORD TO THE FILE
         2. CHANGE AN EXISTING RECORD
         3. DELETE AN EXISTING RECORD

         9. EXIT THE PROGRAM

ENTER THE NUMBER FOR THE OPTION OF YOUR CHOICE:
```

The main module of the program will perform a procedure to display this screen and input the user's choice. This main module will look like

```
0100-MAIN-MODULE.

    OPEN I-O RELATIVE-FILE.

    ACCEPT DATE-IN FROM DATE.
    MOVE DATE-YY TO DISPLAY-YY.
    MOVE DATE-MM TO DISPLAY-MM.
    MOVE DATE-DD TO DISPLAY-DD.
```

```
PERFORM 0200-INITIAL-DISPLAY UNTIL OPTION = '9'.

PERFORM 1000-FINAL-DISPLAY.

CLOSE RELATIVE-FILE.
STOP-RUN.
```

The 0200-INITIAL-DISPLAY routine will display the initial menu, input the user's choice, and then use that choice to perform the appropriate routine. We will look at the routine in a few moments. Right now, however, we need to determine what the 1000-FINAL-DISPLAY procedure is for.

When an interactive program is used, it is difficult to determine what file modifications have been made; no report is printed as it was with a transaction file update program. (We could, of course, print a report with a detail line for every transaction done in the interactive program just as we do with the other program. This is virtually never done, however.) Thus, often we will want to keep a running count of how many additions, changes, and deletions have been made. If we do, we will need to print them out at some point. The end of the program seems the most appropriate place for this.

In order to keep track of the manipulations carried out in the program, we will need to have a field to store the counts of the number of additions, changes, and deletions. We will need to add those fields to the WORKING-STORAGE SECTION fields we have already used:

```
10   ADD-COUNT                   PIC 999 VALUE 0.
10   CHANGE-COUNT                PIC 999 VALUE 0.
10   DELETE-COUNT                PIC 999 VALUE 0.

10   ADD-COUNT-EDITED            PIC ZZ9.
10   CHANGE-COUNT-EDITED         PIC ZZ9.
10   DELETE-COUNT-EDITED         PIC ZZ9.
```

In each of the routines, when a record is rewritten into the file, we will simply add 1 to the appropriate counter. Then, when the user signals the end of the program, we will simply display the results on the screen:

```
1000-FINAL-DISPLAY.

    MOVE ADD-COUNT    TO ADD-COUNT-EDITED.
    MOVE CHANGE-COUNT TO CHANGE-COUNT-EDITED.
    MOVE DELETE-COUNT TO DELETE-COUNT-EDITED.
    PERFORM 1400-DISPLAY-BLANK-LINE 5 TIMES.
    DISPLAY 'THERE WERE ' ADD-COUNT-EDITED
            ' RECORDS ADDED.'.
    DISPLAY 'THERE WERE ' CHANGE-COUNT-EDITED
            ' RECORDS CHANGED.'.
    DISPLAY 'THERE WERE ' DELETE-COUNT-EDITED
            ' RECORDS DELETED.'.
```

As we mentioned, the 0200-INITIAL-DISPLAY routine will display the initial menu and then input the user's choice. This routine is virtually identical to ones we have used in the past:

```
0200-INITIAL-DISPLAY.

    DISPLAY '                    PATIENTS UPDATE PROGRAM'.
    DISPLAY '                      DATE ' DISPLAY-DATE.
    DISPLAY '                        MAIN MENU'.
    DISPLAY ' '.
    DISPLAY ' '.
    DISPLAY '                   YOUR OPTIONS ON THIS MENU ARE:'.
    DISPLAY ' '.
    DISPLAY '                      1. ADD A NEW RECORD'.
    DISPLAY ' '.
    DISPLAY '                      2. CHANGE AN EXISTING RECORD'.
    DISPLAY ' '.
    DISPLAY '                      3. DELETE AN EXISTING RECORD'.
    DISPLAY ' '.
    DISPLAY ' '.
    DISPLAY '                      9. EXIT THE PROGRAM'.
    DISPLAY ' '.
    DISPLAY ' '.
    DISPLAY ' '.
    DISPLAY 'ENTER THE NUMBER FOR THE OPTION OF YOUR CHOICE:'.

    ACCEPT OPTION.

    MOVE ALL 'A' TO CALCULATION-KEY.
    IF OPTION = '1'
       PERFORM 0400-ADD-ROUTINE
             UNTIL CALCULATION-KEY = SPACES
    ELSE
       IF OPTION = '2'
          PERFORM 0800-CHANGE-ROUTINE
                UNTIL CALCULATION-KEY = SPACES
    ELSE
       IF OPTION = '3'
          PERFORM 0900-DELETE-ROUTINE
                UNTIL CALCULATION-KEY = SPACES
    ELSE
       IF OPTION NOT = '9'
          DISPLAY ' '
          DISPLAY 'ONLY 1, 2, 3, OR 9 ARE VALID.  '
                  'PLEASE TRY AGAIN ..'
          DISPLAY 'PRESS ANY KEY TO CONTINUE.'
          ACCEPT ANY-KEY.
```

In this routine, we perform each of the other routines until the number entered is all blanks. Remember, this is the way the user will indicate a wish to exit the routine. We also begin by forcing the key to be all A's.

9-3-4   The Add Routine

The first of the routines we will discuss is the add routine. You need to learn a few things about this routine, as it is used for relative file processing, that are different from the routines we learned how to use in the previous chapter.

First, when we get the relative key, we need to read the record; if the record is there, we check the Social Security number to make sure it is not the same as the one we are trying to add. If it is the same, we have a duplicate key and an error. If it isn't, we need to read the records sequentially (using the relative record number plus 1 each time) from that point until we find an empty one. Each time we find a record with data in it, we must verify that the Social Security number is not the one we are trying to add. If it matches, again we have a duplicate.

If we do find a blank record that we can use, we input the data from the user and then *rewrite* the record instead of writing it. Remember that we have already written blank records into the file and are now simply putting the data into them.

The add routine begins by getting the relative record key:

```
0400-ADD-ROUTINE.

    PERFORM 0300-CALCULATE-KEY.
```

Then we read the file and determine if this is an empty record, which we can rewrite; a duplicate key; or a record with data already in it. We will put this procedure in a routine since all the add routine has to be in is an IF test so that we can skip it if the user has entered a blank Social Security number:

```
IF CALCULATION-KEY NOT = SPACES
    MOVE 'NO ' TO FOUND-RECORD
    PERFORM 0410-READ-THE-RECORD
        UNTIL FOUND-RECORD = 'YES'.
```

There is, of course, additional code in the add routine. But, since we are discussing record access, we will pause and examine the 0410-READ-THE-RECORD routine. Then we will look at the rest of the add routine. The 0410-READ-THE-RECORD routine begins with the READ statement:

```
0410-READ-THE-RECORD.

    READ RELATIVE-FILE
        INVALID KEY
        DISPLAY 'UNKNOWN ERROR DURING READ.'
        DISPLAY 'HALTING PROGRAM.'
        STOP RUN.
```

Notice that an INVALID KEY will print an error message and then stop the program. Since we are accessing records only within the established bounds of our file, we should not encounter any problems when reading the records. Thus, we will stop the program if there is an INVALID KEY.

The routine then continues by checking the Social Security number of the new record against the Social Security number that was entered by the user

(CALCULATION-KEY). If they match, we have a duplicate, and we will move spaces to the CALCULATION-KEY so the rest of the add routine can be skipped. We will also move 'YES' to FOUND-RECORD so the program can exit from the PERFORM statement that is executing this procedure. The beginning of the IF test is

```
IF SOCIAL-SEC-NUMBER = CALCULATION-KEY
   DISPLAY 'DUPLICATE KEY.  RECORD CANNOT BE ADDED.'
   DISPLAY 'TRY A DIFFERENT RECORD.'
   MOVE 'YES'  TO FOUND-RECORD
   MOVE SPACES TO CALCULATION-KEY
ELSE
```

If the Social Security numbers don't match, we need to be sure the record is blank. If it is, we are finished searching. If it isn't, we add 1 to the RELATIVE-KEY to move the file pointer to the next record (remember we have to look at each subsequent record until we find one that is empty). Since the number of records is finite (only 250 in our example), we also need to be sure the new RELATIVE-KEY does not extend beyond the end of the file. If it does, we will move the pointer back to the beginning of the file. The routine continues with

```
IF SOCIAL-SEC-NUMBER = SPACES
   MOVE 'YES' TO FOUND-RECORD
ELSE
   ADD 1 TO RELATIVE-KEY
   IF RELATIVE-KEY > 250
      MOVE 1 TO RELATIVE-KEY.
```

If we do increase the RELATIVE-KEY, this IF test will end, but since we don't change the FOUND-RECORD to 'YES', the PERFORM statement will simply send the program right back into this routine and the next record will be read. This loop continues until either a duplicate or a blank record is found.

Now that we have examined this routine, we need to finish explaining the add routine. If you recall, we had the following PERFORM for the routine:

```
IF CALCULATION-KEY NOT = SPACES
   MOVE 'NO ' TO FOUND-RECORD
   PERFORM 0410-READ-THE-RECORD
        UNTIL FOUND-RECORD = 'YES'.
```

After we come back from the 0410-READ-THE-RECORD routine, we have two possibilities: either there is a duplicate or we have found a record to use. Remember that the routine will move spaces to the CALCULATION-KEY upon a duplicate. Thus we need the next part to contain

```
IF CALCULATION-KEY NOT = SPACES
   PERFORM 0420-GET-DATA
   DISPLAY 'WANT TO ADD ANOTHER RECORD (Y OR N)?'
   ACCEPT ANY-KEY
   IF ANY-KEY NOT = 'Y'
      MOVE SPACES TO CALCULATION-KEY.
```

Now the 0420-GET-DATA routine is simply the input routine for the data. Of course, after the data is input it is displayed on the screen and verified. Finally, after the user is finished with the data, it is rewritten into the file and 1 is added to the counter that is keeping track of the number of records added. The routine will look like the following:

```
0420-GET-DATA.

    MOVE CALCULATION-KEY TO SOCIAL-SEC-NUMBER.

    MOVE SPACES TO PATIENT-NAME.
    PERFORM 0500-NAME-ROUTINE.

    MOVE SPACES TO PAT-ADDRESS.
    PERFORM 0510-ADDRESS-ROUTINE.

    MOVE SPACES TO CITY.
    PERFORM 0520-CITY-ROUTINE.

    MOVE SPACES TO STATE.
    PERFORM 0530-STATE-ROUTINE.

    MOVE SPACES TO ZIP-CODE.
    PERFORM 0540-ZIP-CODE-ROUTINE
            UNTIL ZIP-CODE IS NUMERIC.

    MOVE SPACES TO NON-NUMERIC-AMOUNT.
    PERFORM 0550-AMOUNT-ROUTINE
            UNTIL NON-NUMERIC-AMOUNT IS NUMERIC.

    MOVE SPACES TO LAST-DATE.
    PERFORM 0560-DATE-ROUTINE
            UNTIL LAST-DATE IS NUMERIC.

    MOVE SPACES TO EDIT-OPTION.
    PERFORM 0600-EDIT-FIELDS
            UNTIL EDIT-OPTION = 'X'.

    ADD 1 TO ADD-COUNT.

    PERFORM 0820-REWRITE-ROUTINE.
```

At one time or another, we have examined the samples of the various routines required to input a field. We will, however, examine the 0560-DATE-ROUTINE in detail because it is extensive. We will not only verify the entry to be sure it is numeric, but we will also make sure that the month is correct (not greater than 12) and the number of days are appropriate for the month (no more than 28 in February, etc.). For the date routine, we will need to begin with another group field, defined in WORKING-STORAGE, for inputting:

```
10  WORK-DATE.
    20   WORK-MM          PIC XX.
    20   FILLER           PIC X.
    20   WORK-DD          PIC XX.
    20   FILLER           PIC X.
    20   WORK-YY          PIC XX.
```

Then the date routine will begin with

```
0560-DATE-ROUTINE.

    DISPLAY ' '.
    DISPLAY ' '.
    DISPLAY 'ENTER THE DATE OF LAST VISIT (MM/DD/YY).'.
    DISPLAY '##/##/##'.

    ACCEPT WORK-DATE.

    MOVE WORK-MM TO LAST-MM.
    MOVE WORK-DD TO LAST-DD.
    MOVE WORK-YY TO LAST-YY.

    IF LAST-DATE NOT NUMERIC
        DISPLAY 'ALL CHARACTERS OF DATE NOT NUMERIC.'
        DISPLAY 'PLEASE RE-ENTER.'
```

After this we need to verify the month and days. We won't check the year, though generally you would check it for some range, such as not being less than the current year. Verifying the month is easy: we simply check to be sure it is greater than 00 and not greater than 12:

```
ELSE IF LAST-MM > '12' OR < '01'
        DISPLAY 'MONTH INCORRECT.  PLEASE RE-ENTER.'
        MOVE SPACES TO LAST-DATE
```

To check the days is a bit more tricky. We need to know the maximum number of days in each month. The easiest way to do this is to use a table (defined in WORKING-STORAGE again):

```
10  NUMERIC-TABLE                        PIC X(24) VALUE
    '312831303130313130313031'.
10  MONTH-TABLE REDEFINES NUMERIC-TABLE
            OCCURS 12 TIMES PIC XX.
```

Now you can see why earlier we used a second definition for the month field. Since we defined it as PIC 99, we can use it to point to the number of days in the month. Remember we defined it as

```
10  NUMERIC-MM        PIC 99.
```

Now we can use it to point to the months and test them:

```
ELSE IF LAST-DD < '01' OR > MONTH-TABLE (NUMERIC-MM)
        DISPLAY 'NUMBER OF DAYS INCORRECT FOR MONTH.'
        DISPLAY 'PLEASE RE-ENTER.'
        MOVE SPACES TO LAST-DATE.
```

The only things this routine does not test for are leap year and the number of days in February. Those are a little more complicated, and we will leave them for an exercise at the end of the chapter.

Incidentally, we move spaces to the LAST-DATE field when the date is wrong, so that the routine will be performed again. Remember that we accessed the routine with a PERFORM statement that ends when the date is numeric. If the user enters an incorrect date that is numeric, we print an error, but then the routine will end because the date could still be numeric even if it is incorrect. By forcing the date to be spaces, it will not be numeric and the routine will function again, forcing the user to enter a proper date.

With the date routine completed, all we have left to look at is the field edit routine. It too is similar to the ones we have used in the past. It uses the following display:

```
              PATIENTS UPDATE PROGRAM
                 DATE 09/17/88
                 FIELD MAINTENANCE

          FOR PATIENT NUMBER 123-45-6789
       A) NAME.................... SAM JONES
       B) ADDRESS................. 1400 SOUTH STREET
       C) CITY.................... NEW YORK
       D) STATE................... NY
       E) ZIP CODE............... 10016
       F) AMOUNT DUE.............     $11.22
       G) DATE OF LAST VISIT...... 10/15/87

       ENTER LETTER OF FIELD TO CHANGE (OR X TO EXIT).
```

The routine looks like the following:

```
0600-EDIT-FIELDS.

    PERFORM 0700-DISPLAY-DATA.

    DISPLAY ' '.
    DISPLAY 'ENTER LETTER OF FIELD TO CHANGE (OR X TO EXIT).

    ACCEPT EDIT-OPTION.

    IF EDIT-OPTION = 'A'
       MOVE SPACES TO PATIENT-NAME
       PERFORM 0500-NAME-ROUTINE

    ELSE
       IF EDIT-OPTION = 'B'
          MOVE SPACES TO PAT-ADDRESS
          PERFORM 0510-ADDRESS-ROUTINE

    ELSE
       IF EDIT-OPTION = 'C'
          MOVE SPACES TO CITY
          PERFORM 0520-CITY-ROUTINE
```

```
            ELSE
                IF EDIT-OPTION = 'D'
                    MOVE SPACES TO STATE
                    PERFORM 0530-STATE-ROUTINE

            ELSE
                IF EDIT-OPTION = 'E'
                    MOVE SPACES TO ZIP-CODE
                    PERFORM 0540-ZIP-CODE-ROUTINE
                            UNTIL ZIP-CODE IS NUMERIC

            ELSE
                IF EDIT-OPTION = 'F'
                    MOVE SPACES TO NON-NUMERIC-AMOUNT
                    PERFORM 0550-AMOUNT-ROUTINE
                            UNTIL NON-NUMERIC-AMOUNT IS NUMERIC

            ELSE
                IF EDIT-OPTION = 'G'
                    MOVE SPACES TO LAST-DATE
                    PERFORM 0560-DATE-ROUTINE
                            UNTIL LAST-DATE IS NUMERIC

            ELSE IF EDIT-OPTION NOT = 'X'
                DISPLAY ' '
                DISPLAY 'ENTRY IS NOT CORRECT.  ENTER ONLY A - G OR X.'
                DISPLAY 'PLEASE TRY AGAIN.'
                DISPLAY ' '.
```

The 0700-DISPLAY-DATA routine simply displays the data:

```
0700-DISPLAY-DATA.

        MOVE AMOUNT-DUE TO AMOUNT-EDITED.
        MOVE LAST-MM    TO PRINT-MM.
        MOVE LAST-DD    TO PRINT-DD.
        MOVE LAST-YY    TO PRINT-YY.
        PERFORM 1400-DISPLAY-BLANK-LINE 12 TIMES.
        DISPLAY '                   PATIENT UPDATE PROGRAM '.
        DISPLAY '                           DATE: ' DISPLAY-DATE.
        DISPLAY '                     FIELD MAINTENANCE'.
        DISPLAY ' '.
        DISPLAY '            FOR PATIENT NUMBER '
                SOCIAL-SEC-NUMBER.
        DISPLAY ' '.
        DISPLAY '            A) NAME.................... '
                PATIENT-NAME.
        DISPLAY ' '.
        DISPLAY '            B) ADDRESS................. '
                PAT-ADDRESS.
        DISPLAY ' '.
```

```
DISPLAY '              C) CITY.................... ' CITY.
DISPLAY ' '.
DISPLAY '              D) STATE................... ' STATE.
DISPLAY ' '.
DISPLAY '              E) ZIP CODE................ ' ZIP-CODE.
DISPLAY ' '.
DISPLAY '              F) AMOUNT DUE.............. '
        AMOUNT-EDITED.
DISPLAY ' '.
DISPLAY '              G) DATE OF LAST VISIT...... PRINT-DATE.
```

9-3-5 The Change Routine

When it comes to displaying the data and allowing the inputting of changes, this routine uses essentially the same elements as the add routine. The record accessing is virtually the same as we used for the add routine except that now we are not looking for a blank record. We are looking only for a match on the Social Security number. If we find a blank record before we find a match, we know the record doesn't exist in the file.

The change routine begins with the routine to get the RELATIVE-KEY:

```
0800-CHANGE-ROUTINE.

    PERFORM 0300-CALCULATE-KEY.
```

Then we need to read the file to determine if the record is the one we are looking for. There are two other possibilities: it could be an empty record, in which case our record doesn't exist, or it could be a different Social Security number. If it is different, we begin examining subsequent records until we either find a blank one—which means, again, that our record doesn't exist—or find the record we are looking for. As with the add routine, we will put this search procedure in a routine since we need to continue to process records until we find what we need:

```
IF CALCULATION-KEY NOT = SPACES
   MOVE 'NO ' TO FOUND-RECORD
   PERFORM 0810-READ-THE-RECORD
        UNTIL FOUND-RECORD = 'YES'.
```

This access routine begins with the READ statement:

```
0810-READ-THE-RECORD.

    READ RELATIVE-FILE
        INVALID KEY
        DISPLAY 'UNKNOWN ERROR DURING READ.'
        DISPLAY 'HALTING PROGRAM.'
        STOP RUN.
```

The routine then continues by checking the Social Security number of the new record against the Social Security number that was entered by the user

(CALCULATION-KEY). If they match, we have found the record we were looking
for and we have finished:

```
IF SOCIAL-SEC-NUMBER = CALCULATION-KEY
    MOVE 'YES' TO FOUND-RECORD
ELSE
```

If the Social Security numbers don't match, we need to see if the record is
blank. If it is, we have finished searching because we know our record doesn't
exist. Otherwise, we add 1 to the RELATIVE-KEY to move the file pointer to the
next record and check for the end of the file as before:

```
IF SOCIAL-SEC-NUMBER = SPACES
    MOVE 'YES' TO FOUND-RECORD
    MOVE SPACES TO CALCULATION-KEY
    DISPLAY 'RECORD DOES NOT EXIST ON FILE.'
    DISPLAY 'PLEASE TRY AGAIN.'
ELSE
    ADD 1 TO RELATIVE-KEY
    IF RELATIVE-KEY > 250
       MOVE 1 TO RELATIVE-KEY.
```

Remember that the change routine began simply enough:

```
0800-CHANGE-ROUTINE.

    PERFORM 0300-CALCULATE-KEY.

    IF CALCULATION-KEY NOT = SPACES
       MOVE 'NO ' TO FOUND-RECORD
       PERFORM 0810-READ-THE-RECORD
             UNTIL FOUND-RECORD = 'YES'
```

Now we need to finish it off by displaying the data (as long as the record was
found), letting the user make whatever changes are needed, and then finding out
if another change is wanted:

```
MOVE SPACES TO EDIT-OPTION
PERFORM 0600-EDIT-FIELDS
        UNTIL EDIT-OPTION = 'X'
ADD 1 TO CHANGE-COUNT
PERFORM 0820-REWRITE-ROUTINE

DISPLAY 'WANT TO CHANGE ANOTHER RECORD (Y OR N)?'
ACCEPT ANY-KEY
IF ANY-KEY NOT = 'Y'
    MOVE SPACES TO CALCULATION-KEY.
```

9-3-6 The Delete Routine

The delete routine uses the same display routine as the other two routines and uses the same method of finding the records as the change routine did. The essential difference is that the records aren't changed; we simply verify that the record is the proper one and then delete it. As discussed previously, we delete a record by putting blanks in the entire record in place of the previous data. Filled with blanks, the record is considered to be empty.

We begin the deletion routine by getting the relative key:

```
0900-DELETE-ROUTINE.

    PERFORM 0300-CALCULATE-KEY.
```

Then we read the file and determine if this is the record we are looking for, just as in the change routine. The routine continues with

```
IF CALCULATION-KEY NOT = SPACES
    MOVE 'NO ' TO FOUND-RECORD
    PERFORM 0810-READ-THE-RECORD
            UNTIL FOUND-RECORD = 'YES'
```

We already discussed the 0810-READ-THE-RECORD routine. It simply reads records until either the proper one or a blank one is found. If the record is not found, the CALCULATION-KEY is set to blanks and we need to exit the routine. Otherwise, we display the data and verify that the record is correct and the user wants it deleted:

```
PERFORM 0700-DISPLAY-DATA
DISPLAY ' '
DISPLAY 'IS THIS THE RECORD YOU WANT TO DELETE (Y OR N)?'
ACCEPT ANY-KEY
IF ANY-KEY = 'Y'
    MOVE SPACES TO RELATIVE-RECORD
    ADD 1 TO DELETE-COUNT
    PERFORM 0820-REWRITE-ROUTINE
```

Finally, we ask whether the user wants to continue with another delete:

```
DISPLAY 'WANT TO CHANGE ANOTHER RECORD (Y OR N)?'
ACCEPT ANY-KEY
IF ANY-KEY NOT = 'Y'
    MOVE SPACES TO CALCULATION-KEY.
```

9-3-7 The Whole Program

Now that we have seen the various routines, it is time to put the entire program together. It's always a good idea to examine the entire program because seeing how the routines fit together is just as important as learning how to write them individually. The program:

```
****************************************************************
****************************************************************
*
*
*
*  PROGRAM NAME: REL-UP
*
*  PROGRAMMER NAME:  ED COBURN
*
*  SOCIAL SECURITY NUMBER:  999-99-9999
*
*  DUE DATE: FEBRUARY 10, 1988
*
*  DESCRIPTION: THIS INTERACTIVE PROGRAM WILL ALLOW THE USER
*               TO ADD, CHANGE, OR DELETE RECORDS FROM THE
*               RELATIVE PATIENTS FILE.
*
*
****************************************************************
****************************************************************


    IDENTIFICATION DIVISION.
    PROGRAM-ID.   REL-UP.
    AUTHOR.       ED COBURN.

    ENVIRONMENT DIVISION.


    CONFIGURATION SECTION.
    SOURCE-COMPUTER. IBM-4331.
    OBJECT-COMPUTER. IBM-4331.

    INPUT-OUTPUT SECTION.
    FILE-CONTROL.

        SELECT RELATIVE-FILE ASSIGN TO DA-R-PATIENTS
               ORGANIZATION IS RELATIVE
               ACCESS IS RANDOM
               RELATIVE KEY IS RELATIVE-KEY.

    DATA DIVISION.
    FILE SECTION.

    FD  RELATIVE-FILE
        LABEL RECORDS ARE OMITTED
        RECORD CONTAINS 80 CHARACTERS.
    01  RELATIVE-RECORD.
        10   SOCIAL-SEC-NUMBER                    PIC X(9).
        10   PATIENT-NAME                         PIC X(20).
        10   PAT-ADDRESS                          PIC X(15).
        10   CITY                                 PIC X(13).
        10   STATE                                PIC XX.
        10   ZIP-CODE                             PIC X(5).
        10   AMOUNT-DUE                           PIC 9(4)V99.
```

```
    10   LAST-DATE.
         20   LAST-MM                         PIC XX.
         20   LAST-DD                         PIC XX.
         20   LAST-YY                         PIC XX.
    10   FILLER                               PIC X(4).

01  RE-RELATIVE-RECORD.
    10   FILLER                               PIC X(64).
    10   NON-NUMERIC-AMOUNT.
         20   AMOUNT-DOLLARS                  PIC X(4)
              JUSTIFIED RIGHT.
         20   AMOUNT-CENTS                    PIC XX.
    10   FILLER                               PIC XX.
    10   NUMERIC-MM                           PIC 99.
    10   FILLER                               PIC X(8).

WORKING-STORAGE SECTION.

01  WORK-AREAS.

    10   RELATIVE-KEY                         PIC 999.
    10   DIVISION-RESULT                      PIC 9(7).

    10   SOCIAL-IN.
         20   SOCIAL-IN-THREE                 PIC XXX.
         20   FILLER                          PIC X.
         20   SOCIAL-IN-TWO                   PIC XX.
         20   FILLER                          PIC X.
         20   SOCIAL-IN-FOUR                  PIC XXXX.

    10   CALCULATION-KEY.
         20   CALC-THREE                      PIC XXX.
         20   CALC-TWO                        PIC XX.
         20   CALC-FOUR                       PIC XXXX.
    10   NUMERIC-KEY REDEFINES CALCULATION-KEY PIC 9(9).

    10   FOUND-RECORD                         PIC XXX.
    10   ANY-KEY                              PIC X.
    10   OPTION                               PIC X.
    10   EDIT-OPTION                          PIC X.

    10   AMOUNT-IN                            PIC X(7).

    10   DATE-IN.
         20   DATE-YY                         PIC XX.
         20   DATE-MM                         PIC XX.
         20   DATE-DD                         PIC XX.

    10   DISPLAY-DATE.
         20   DISPLAY-MM                      PIC XX.
         20   DISPLAY-DD                      PIC /XX/.
         20   DISPLAY-YY                      PIC XX.

    10   PRINT-DATE.
         20   PRINT-MM                        PIC XX.
         20   PRINT-DD                        PIC /XX/.
         20   PRINT-YY                        PIC XX.
```

```
    10  ADD-COUNT                              PIC 999 VALUE 0.
    10  CHANGE-COUNT                           PIC 999 VALUE 0.
    10  DELETE-COUNT                           PIC 999 VALUE 0.

    10  ADD-COUNT-EDITED                       PIC ZZ9.
    10  CHANGE-COUNT-EDITED                    PIC ZZ9.
    10  DELETE-COUNT-EDITED                    PIC ZZ9.

    10  AMOUNT-EDITED                          PIC Z,ZZ9.99.

    10  WORK-DATE.
        20  WORK-MM                            PIC XX.
        20  FILLER                             PIC X.
        20  WORK-DD                            PIC XX.
        20  FILLER                             PIC X.
        20  WORK-YY                            PIC XX.

    10  NUMERIC-TABLE                          PIC X(24) VALUE
        '312831303130313130313031'.
    10  MONTH-TABLE REDEFINES NUMERIC-TABLE OCCURS 12 TIMES
                                               PIC XX.


PROCEDURE DIVISION.

0100-MAIN-MODULE.

    OPEN I-O RELATIVE-FILE.

    ACCEPT DATE-IN FROM DATE.
    MOVE DATE-YY TO DISPLAY-YY.
    MOVE DATE-MM TO DISPLAY-MM.
    MOVE DATE-DD TO DISPLAY-DD.

    PERFORM 0200-INITIAL-DISPLAY
          UNTIL OPTION = '9'.

    PERFORM 1000-FINAL-DISPLAY.

    CLOSE RELATIVE-FILE.
    STOP RUN.

0200-INITIAL-DISPLAY.

    DISPLAY '                     PATIENTS UPDATE PROGRAM'.
    DISPLAY '                         DATE ' DISPLAY-DATE.
    DISPLAY '                         MAIN MENU'.
    DISPLAY ' '.
    DISPLAY ' '.
    DISPLAY '                     YOUR OPTIONS ON THIS MENU ARE:'.
    DISPLAY ' '.
    DISPLAY '                     1. ADD A NEW RECORD.'
    DISPLAY ' '.
    DISPLAY '                     2. CHANGE AN EXISTING RECORD.'
    DISPLAY ' '.
    DISPLAY '                     3. DELETE AN EXISTING RECORD.'
    DISPLAY ' '.
    DISPLAY ' '.
    DISPLAY '                     9. EXIT THE PROGRAM'.
    DISPLAY ' '.
```

```
    DISPLAY ' '.
    DISPLAY ' '.
    DISPLAY 'ENTER THE NUMBER FOR THE OPTION OF YOUR CHOICE:'.

    ACCEPT OPTION.

    MOVE ALL 'A' TO CALCULATION-KEY.
    IF OPTION = '1'
       PERFORM 0400-ADD-ROUTINE
            UNTIL CALCULATION-KEY = SPACES
    ELSE
       IF OPTION = '2'
          PERFORM 0800-CHANGE-ROUTINE
               UNTIL CALCULATION-KEY = SPACES
    ELSE
       IF OPTION = '3'
          PERFORM 0900-DELETE-ROUTINE
               UNTIL CALCULATION-KEY = SPACES

    ELSE
       IF OPTION NOT = '9'
          DISPLAY ' '
          DISPLAY 'ONLY 1, 2, 3, OR 9 ARE VALID.  '
                  'PLEASE TRY AGAIN ..'
          DISPLAY 'PRESS ANY KEY TO CONTINUE.'
          ACCEPT ANY-KEY.


0300-CALCULATE-KEY.

    MOVE ALL 'A' TO CALCULATION-KEY.
    PERFORM 0310-GET-KEY
            UNTIL CALCULATION-KEY IS NUMERIC
            OR     CALCULATION-KEY =  SPACES.

    IF CALCULATION-KEY NOT = SPACES
       DIVIDE NUMERIC-KEY BY 250 GIVING
            DIVISION-RESULT REMAINDER RELATIVE-KEY
       ADD 1 TO RELATIVE-KEY.


0310-GET-KEY.

    DISPLAY ' '.
    DISPLAY ' '.
    DISPLAY 'ENTER THE PATIENTS SOCIAL SECURITY NUMBER.'
    DISPLAY 'USE ALL 11 CHARACTERS INCLUDING THE DASHES.'
    DISPLAY '(JUST PRESS RETURN TO EXIT.)'.
    DISPLAY '###-##-####'.
    MOVE SPACES TO SOCIAL-IN.
    ACCEPT SOCIAL-IN.

    MOVE SOCIAL-IN-THREE TO CALC-THREE.
    MOVE SOCIAL-IN-TWO   TO CALC-TWO.
    MOVE SOCIAL-IN-FOUR  TO CALC-FOUR.

    IF CALCULATION-KEY NOT   NUMERIC AND
       CALCULATION-KEY NOT = SPACES
       DISPLAY 'INVALID SOCIAL SECURITY NUMBER.'
       DISPLAY 'PLEASE RE-ENTER.'.
```

```
0400-ADD-ROUTINE.

    PERFORM 0300-CALCULATE-KEY.

    IF CALCULATION-KEY NOT = SPACES
        MOVE 'NO ' TO FOUND-RECORD
        PERFORM 0410-READ-THE-RECORD
                UNTIL FOUND-RECORD = 'YES'.

    IF CALCULATION-KEY NOT = SPACES
        PERFORM 0420-GET-DATA
        DISPLAY 'WANT TO ADD ANOTHER RECORD (Y OR N)?'
        ACCEPT ANY-KEY
        IF ANY-KEY NOT = 'Y'
            MOVE SPACES TO CALCULATION-KEY.


0410-READ-THE-RECORD.

    READ RELATIVE-FILE
            INVALID KEY
            DISPLAY 'UNKNOWN ERROR DURING READ.'
            DISPLAY 'HALTING PROGRAM.'
            STOP RUN.

    IF SOCIAL-SEC-NUMBER = CALCULATION-KEY
        DISPLAY 'DUPLICATE KEY.  RECORD CANNOT BE ADDED.'
        DISPLAY 'TRY A DIFFERENT RECORD.'
        MOVE 'YES'  TO FOUND-RECORD
        MOVE SPACES TO CALCULATION-KEY
    ELSE

        IF SOCIAL-SEC-NUMBER = SPACES
            MOVE 'YES' TO FOUND-RECORD
        ELSE
            ADD 1 TO RELATIVE-KEY
            IF RELATIVE-KEY > 250
                MOVE 1 TO RELATIVE-KEY.


0420-GET-DATA.

    MOVE CALCULATION-KEY TO SOCIAL-SEC-NUMBER.

    MOVE SPACES TO PATIENT-NAME.
    PERFORM 0500-NAME-ROUTINE.

    MOVE SPACES TO PAT-ADDRESS.
    PERFORM 0510-ADDRESS-ROUTINE.

    MOVE SPACES TO CITY.
    PERFORM 0520-CITY-ROUTINE.

    MOVE SPACES TO STATE.
    PERFORM 0530-STATE-ROUTINE.

    MOVE SPACES TO ZIP-CODE.
    PERFORM 0540-ZIP-CODE-ROUTINE
            UNTIL ZIP-CODE IS NUMERIC.
```

```
    MOVE SPACES TO NON-NUMERIC-AMOUNT.
    PERFORM 0550-AMOUNT-ROUTINE
          UNTIL NON-NUMERIC-AMOUNT IS NUMERIC.

    MOVE SPACES TO LAST-DATE.
    PERFORM 0560-DATE-ROUTINE
          UNTIL LAST-DATE IS NUMERIC.

    MOVE SPACES TO EDIT-OPTION.
    PERFORM 0600-EDIT-FIELDS
          UNTIL EDIT-OPTION = 'X'.

    ADD 1 TO ADD-COUNT.

    PERFORM 0820-REWRITE-ROUTINE.


0500-NAME-ROUTINE.

    PERFORM 1400-DISPLAY-BLANK-LINE 5 TIMES.
    DISPLAY 'ENTER NAME...'.
    DISPLAY '*******************'.
    ACCEPT PATIENT-NAME.


0510-ADDRESS-ROUTINE.

    PERFORM 1400-DISPLAY-BLANK-LINE 5 TIMES.
    DISPLAY 'ENTER ADDRESS...'.
    DISPLAY '***************'.
    ACCEPT PAT-ADDRESS.


0520-CITY-ROUTINE.

    PERFORM 1400-DISPLAY-BLANK-LINE 5 TIMES.
    DISPLAY 'ENTER CITY...'.
    DISPLAY '*************'.
    ACCEPT CITY.


0530-STATE-ROUTINE.

    PERFORM 1400-DISPLAY-BLANK-LINE 5 TIMES.
    DISPLAY 'ENTER STATE...'.
    DISPLAY '**'.
    ACCEPT STATE.


0540-ZIP-CODE-ROUTINE.

    PERFORM 1400-DISPLAY-BLANK-LINE 5 TIMES.
    DISPLAY 'ENTER ZIP CODE...'.
    DISPLAY '#####'.
    ACCEPT ZIP-CODE.

    IF ZIP-CODE NOT NUMERIC
       DISPLAY ' '
       DISPLAY 'ZIP CODE MUST BE ALL NUMERIC DIGITS.'
       DISPLAY ' '
       MOVE SPACES TO ZIP-CODE.
```

```
0550-AMOUNT-ROUTINE.

    PERFORM 1400-DISPLAY-BLANK-LINE 5 TIMES.
    DISPLAY 'ENTER AMOUNT DUE (INCLUDING DECIMAL POINT)...'.
    DISPLAY '######'.
    ACCEPT AMOUNT-IN.

    UNSTRING AMOUNT-IN DELIMITED BY '.' OR SPACES
            INTO AMOUNT-DOLLARS AMOUNT-CENTS.

    INSPECT NON-NUMERIC-AMOUNT REPLACING ALL SPACES BY ZEROS.

    IF NON-NUMERIC-AMOUNT NOT NUMERIC
        DISPLAY ' '
        DISPLAY 'AMOUNT DUE INCORRECT.  TRY AGAIN.'
        DISPLAY ' '
        MOVE SPACES TO AMOUNT-IN.


0560-DATE-ROUTINE.

    DISPLAY ' '.
    DISPLAY ' '.
    DISPLAY 'ENTER THE DATE OF LAST VISIT (MM/DD/YY).'.
    DISPLAY '##/##/##'.

    ACCEPT WORK-DATE.

    MOVE WORK-MM TO LAST-MM.
    MOVE WORK-DD TO LAST-DD.
    MOVE WORK-YY TO LAST-YY.

    IF LAST-DATE NOT NUMERIC
        DISPLAY 'ALL CHARACTERS OF DATE NOT NUMERIC.'
        DISPLAY 'PLEASE RE-ENTER.'

    ELSE
      IF LAST-MM > '12' OR < '01'
          DISPLAY 'MONTH INCORRECT.  PLEASE RE-ENTER.'
          MOVE SPACES TO LAST-DATE

    ELSE
      IF LAST-DD < '01' OR > MONTH-TABLE (NUMERIC-MM)
          DISPLAY 'NUMBER OF DAYS INCORRECT FOR MONTH.'
          DISPLAY 'PLEASE RE-ENTER.'
          MOVE SPACES TO LAST-DATE.


0600-EDIT-FIELDS.

    PERFORM 0700-DISPLAY-DATA.

    DISPLAY ' '.
    DISPLAY 'ENTER LETTER OF FIELD TO CHANGE (OR X TO EXIT).'.

    ACCEPT EDIT-OPTION.

    IF EDIT-OPTION = 'A'
        MOVE SPACES TO PATIENT-NAME
        PERFORM 0500-NAME-ROUTINE
```

```
        ELSE
            IF EDIT-OPTION = 'B'
                MOVE SPACES TO PAT-ADDRESS
                PERFORM 0510-ADDRESS-ROUTINE

        ELSE
            IF EDIT-OPTION = 'C'
                MOVE SPACES TO CITY
                PERFORM 0520-CITY-ROUTINE

        ELSE
            IF EDIT-OPTION = 'D'
                MOVE SPACES TO STATE
                PERFORM 0530-STATE-ROUTINE

        ELSE
            IF EDIT-OPTION = 'E'
                MOVE SPACES TO ZIP-CODE
                PERFORM 0540-ZIP-CODE-ROUTINE
                        UNTIL ZIP-CODE IS NUMERIC

        ELSE
            IF EDIT-OPTION = 'F'
                MOVE SPACES TO NON-NUMERIC-AMOUNT
                PERFORM 0550-AMOUNT-ROUTINE
                        UNTIL NON-NUMERIC-AMOUNT IS NUMERIC

        ELSE
            IF EDIT-OPTION = 'G'
                MOVE SPACES TO LAST-DATE
                PERFORM 0560-DATE-ROUTINE
                        UNTIL LAST-DATE IS NUMERIC

        ELSE
            IF EDIT-OPTION NOT = 'X'
                DISPLAY ' '
                DISPLAY 'ENTRY IS NOT CORRECT.  ENTER ONLY A - G OR X.'
                DISPLAY 'PLEASE TRY AGAIN.'
                DISPLAY ' '.


0700-DISPLAY-DATA.

        MOVE AMOUNT-DUE TO AMOUNT-EDITED.
        MOVE LAST-MM    TO PRINT-MM.
        MOVE LAST-DD    TO PRINT-DD.
        MOVE LAST-YY    TO PRINT-YY.
        PERFORM 1400-DISPLAY-BLANK-LINE 12 TIMES.
        DISPLAY '                    PATIENT UPDATE PROGRAM '.
        DISPLAY '                           DATE: ' DISPLAY-DATE.
        DISPLAY '                      FIELD MAINTENANCE'.
        DISPLAY ' '.
        DISPLAY '                 FOR PATIENT NUMBER '
                SOCIAL-SEC-NUMBER.
        DISPLAY ' '.
        DISPLAY '           A) NAME.................... '
                PATIENT-NAME.
        DISPLAY ' '.
        DISPLAY '           B) ADDRESS................. '
                PAT-ADDRESS.
```

```
        DISPLAY ' '.
        DISPLAY '             C) CITY.................... ' CITY.
        DISPLAY ' '.
        DISPLAY '             D) STATE................... ' STATE.
        DISPLAY ' '.
        DISPLAY '             E) ZIP CODE................ ' ZIP-CODE.
        DISPLAY ' '.

        DISPLAY '             F) AMOUNT DUE.............. '
             AMOUNT-EDITED.
        DISPLAY ' '.
        DISPLAY '             G) DATE OF LAST VISIT....... ' PRINT-DATE.


    0800-CHANGE-ROUTINE.

        PERFORM 0300-CALCULATE-KEY.

        IF CALCULATION-KEY NOT = SPACES
            MOVE 'NO ' TO FOUND-RECORD
            PERFORM 0810-READ-THE-RECORD
                    UNTIL FOUND-RECORD = 'YES'

            MOVE SPACES TO EDIT-OPTION
            PERFORM 0600-EDIT-FIELDS
                    UNTIL EDIT-OPTION = 'X'
            ADD 1 TO CHANGE-COUNT
            PERFORM 0820-REWRITE-ROUTINE

            DISPLAY 'WANT TO CHANGE ANOTHER RECORD (Y OR N)?'
            ACCEPT ANY-KEY
            IF ANY-KEY NOT = 'Y'
                MOVE SPACES TO CALCULATION-KEY.


    0810-READ-THE-RECORD.

        READ RELATIVE-FILE
            INVALID KEY
            DISPLAY 'UNKNOWN ERROR DURING READ.'
            DISPLAY 'HALTING PROGRAM.'
            STOP RUN.

        IF SOCIAL-SEC-NUMBER = CALCULATION-KEY
            MOVE 'YES'  TO FOUND-RECORD
        ELSE
            IF SOCIAL-SEC-NUMBER = SPACES
                MOVE 'YES' TO FOUND-RECORD
                MOVE SPACES TO CALCULATION-KEY
                DISPLAY 'RECORD DOES NOT EXIST ON FILE.'
                DISPLAY 'PLEASE TRY AGAIN.'
            ELSE
                ADD 1 TO RELATIVE-KEY
                IF RELATIVE-KEY > 250
                    MOVE 1 TO RELATIVE-KEY.
```

```
0820-REWRITE-ROUTINE.

    REWRITE RELATIVE-RECORD
            INVALID KEY
            DISPLAY 'UNKNOWN ERROR DURING REWRITE.'
            DISPLAY 'HALTING PROGRAM.'
            STOP RUN.


0900-DELETE-ROUTINE.

    PERFORM 0300-CALCULATE-KEY.

    IF CALCULATION-KEY NOT = SPACES
        MOVE 'NO ' TO FOUND-RECORD
        PERFORM 0810-READ-THE-RECORD
                UNTIL FOUND-RECORD = 'YES'

        PERFORM 0700-DISPLAY-DATA
        DISPLAY ' '
        DISPLAY 'IS THIS THE RECORD YOU WANT TO DELETE (Y OR N)?'
        ACCEPT ANY-KEY
        IF ANY-KEY = 'Y'
            MOVE SPACES TO RELATIVE-RECORD
            ADD 1 TO DELETE-COUNT
            PERFORM 0820-REWRITE-ROUTINE

        DISPLAY 'WANT TO CHANGE ANOTHER RECORD (Y OR N)?'
        ACCEPT ANY-KEY
        IF ANY-KEY NOT = 'Y'
            MOVE SPACES TO CALCULATION-KEY.


1000-FINAL-DISPLAY.

    MOVE ADD-COUNT    TO ADD-COUNT-EDITED.
    MOVE CHANGE-COUNT TO CHANGE-COUNT-EDITED.
    MOVE DELETE-COUNT TO DELETE-COUNT-EDITED.

    PERFORM 1400-DISPLAY-BLANK-LINE 5 TIMES.
    DISPLAY 'THERE WERE ' ADD-COUNT-EDITED
            ' RECORDS ADDED.'.
    DISPLAY 'THERE WERE ' CHANGE-COUNT-EDITED
            ' RECORDS CHANGED.'.
    DISPLAY 'THERE WERE ' DELETE-COUNT-EDITED
            ' RECORDS DELETED.'.


1400-DISPLAY-BLANK-LINE.

    DISPLAY ' '.
```

9-4

The DELETE Statement

When we set up the deletion routine in our program, we deleted the records by filling them with spaces. This way the data in the record was removed though the record was physically left on the file. There is, however, a regular **DELETE statement** for relative files. The form is the same as that for indexed files:

<u>DELETE</u> file-name [<u>INVALID</u> KEY imperative statement]

Though the statement is available, it is rarely used: relative files are typically built with a specified number of records, and it's preferable to blank out the record so it is still there to be used. If the record is physically deleted, instead of being replaced with blanks, the sequential numbers of the records are still intact. That is, if we delete record number 4, record number 5 is still record number 5, but record number 4 simply no longer exists on the file. This leaves us with one fewer record for storage of our data. If the file began with 250 records and we delete one, there will be only 249 records left for storage. Also, if we try to access record 4, we get an invalid key since the record no longer exists.

9-5

Printing a Relative File

Printing a relative file is basically the same as printing any other file. There are a few differences, however. We have already discussed the fact that relative files that are stored with a hashing technique are not going to be in any sorted order. Thus, if we want to list them in some sequence, we will have to sort them into the proper sequence. If, on the other hand, we want to list the file in its unordered sequence, we just open the file for sequential processing and read and print the records, skipping over the blank ones.

When records are to be read sequentially, most versions of COBOL allow the use of the START statement discussed in Chapter 7.

The statement can cause access to begin at a particular record by having the value of the relative key set to the appropriate number. An example of how the statement could be used is

```
MOVE 5 TO RELATIVE-KEY
START RELATIVE-FILE KEY IS = RELATIVE-KEY
      INVALID KEY PERFORM 0900-ERROR-ROUTINE.
```

To use the statement, we must always use the relative key that is defined in the SELECT statement. After the file sets the file pointer to the record specified in the START statement, the first READ statement automatically reads that record. With the START statement, the file must be opened for INPUT or I-O and the access must be SEQUENTIAL or DYNAMIC to allow for sequential access. If DYNAMIC access is used, the NEXT RECORD clause must be used on the READ statement.

9-6

The Record Rack Relative File Processing Program

Because *The Record Rack's* customers are filed by sequential customer number, Roger Barnell feels that processing will be improved if the file is made into a relative file rather than an indexed file. To test his theory, Roger assigns Cindy to write two programs, one to store the records in the file and the other to update the file from a transaction file that contains charges and payments for updating the customer balance.

The file containing the customer balances is called the BANK file (layout in Figure 9-2) since the bank is where the money will end up. Cindy's program to create the file is pretty simple. It reads the sequential file that has already been created with the data in it and stores the records into the relative file. The systems chart for the program is shown in Figure 9-3, the flowchart is in Figure 9-4, and the pseudocode design for the program follows:

```
Start
Open files
Read sequential file at end set end-of-file marker
DO-WHILE not end-of-file
        Write record in relative file by customer number
        Read sequential file at end set end-of-file marker
END-DO
Close files
End
```

BANK File					
Field Description	*Position*	*Length*	:	*Dec*	*Type*
Customer number	1–4	4	:		Non-numeric
Customer name	5–24	20	:		Non-numeric
Filler	25–25	1	:		Non-numeric
Balance	26–32	7	:	2	Numeric
Filler	33–80	48	:		Non-numeric
Record Length = 80					

Figure 9-2   The record layout for the BANK file.

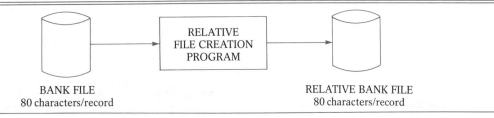

BANK FILE
80 characters/record

RELATIVE BANK FILE
80 characters/record

Figure 9-3   The systems chart for *The Record Rack* relative file processing program.

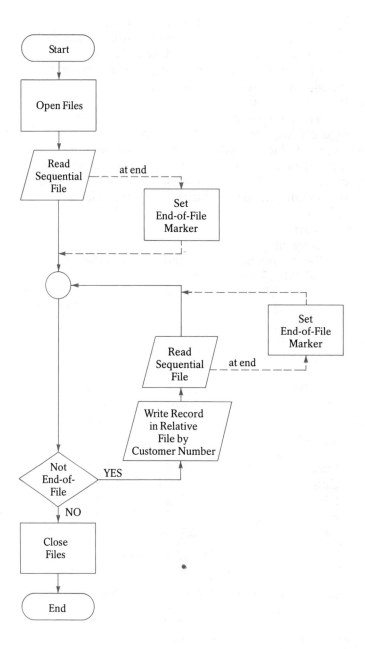

Figure 9-4   The flowchart for *The Record Rack* relative file processing program.

The program:

```
****************************************************************
****************************************************************
*
*
*
*   PROGRAM NAME: REL-CRT
*
*   PROGRAMMER NAME:  CINDY HARRISON
*
*   SOCIAL SECURITY NUMBER:  999-99-9999
*
*   DUE DATE: FEBRUARY 10, 1988
*
*   DESCRIPTION: THIS PROGRAM WILL READ THE SEQUENTIAL BANK
*                FILE AND WRITE IT BACK OUT AS A RELATIVE FILE.
*
*
*
****************************************************************
****************************************************************

    IDENTIFICATION DIVISION.
    PROGRAM-ID.    REL-CRT.
    AUTHOR.        CINDY HARRISON.

    ENVIRONMENT DIVISION.

    CONFIGURATION SECTION.
    SOURCE-COMPUTER. IBM-4331.
    OBJECT-COMPUTER. IBM-4331.

    INPUT-OUTPUT SECTION.
    FILE-CONTROL.

        SELECT BANK-IN        ASSIGN TO UT-S-BANK.
        SELECT RELATIVE-FILE ASSIGN TO DA-R-RELBANK.
            ORGANIZATION IS RELATIVE
            ACCESS IS SEQUENTIAL
            RELATIVE KEY IS RELATIVE-KEY.

    DATA DIVISION.
    FILE SECTION.

    FD  BANK-IN
        LABEL RECORDS ARE OMITTED
        RECORD CONTAINS 80 CHARACTERS.
    01  BANK-RECORD.
        10  KEY-IN                          PIC 9(4).
        10  FILLER                          PIC X(76).

    FD  RELATIVE-FILE
        LABEL RECORDS ARE OMITTED
        RECORD CONTAINS 80 CHARACTERS.
    01  RELATIVE-RECORD                      PIC X(80).
```

```
WORKING-STORAGE SECTION.

01   WORK-AREAS.

     10   EOF                                       PIC XXX.
     10   RELATIVE-KEY                              PIC 9(4).


PROCEDURE DIVISION.

0100-MAIN-MODULE.

     OPEN OUTPUT RELATIVE-FILE
          INPUT  BANK-IN.

     READ BANK-IN
          AT END MOVE 'YES' TO EOF.
     PERFORM 0200-WRITE-FILE
          UNTIL EOF = 'YES'.

     CLOSE RELATIVE-FILE
          BANK-IN.
     STOP  RUN.


0200-WRITE-FILE.

     MOVE BANK-RECORD TO RELATIVE-RECORD.
     MOVE KEY-IN       TO RELATIVE-KEY.
     WRITE RELATIVE-RECORD FROM BANK-RECORD
          INVALID KEY
          DISPLAY 'UNKNOWN ERROR DURING WRITE.'
          DISPLAY 'HALTING PROGRAM.'
          STOP RUN.

     READ BANK-IN
          AT END MOVE 'YES' TO EOF.
```

After using this program to create the relative file, Cindy began working on the second program. The file used to input the purchases and charges is the UPDATE file shown in Figure 9-5. The transaction type is either a P for payment or a C for charge. If the transaction is a payment, the amount is deducted from the balance. If the transaction is a charge, the amount is added to the balance. A brief report is to be written during the update program, as shown in Figure 9-6. The systems chart for this program is shown in Figure 9-7, the flowchart design is in Figure 9-8, and the the pseudocode follows here:

```
Start
Open files
Read a transaction record at end set end-of-file marker
DO-WHILE not end-of-file
        Use relative key to read relative file
        IF transaction is charge THEN
             Increment balance by charge amount
             Accumulate total charges
        ELSE
             Decrease balance by payment amount
             Accumulate total payments
```

```
                    END-IF
                    Rewrite record
                    Print detail line
                    Read a transaction record at end set end-of-file marker
              END-DO
              Print totals
              Close files
              End
```

UPDATE File					
Field Description	Position	Length	:	Dec	Type
Customer number	1–4	4	:		Non-numeric
Transaction type	5–5	1	:		Non-numeric
Amount	6–12	7	:	2	Numeric
Filler	13–80	68	:		Non-numeric
Record Length = 80					

Figure 9-5   The record layout for the UPDATE file.

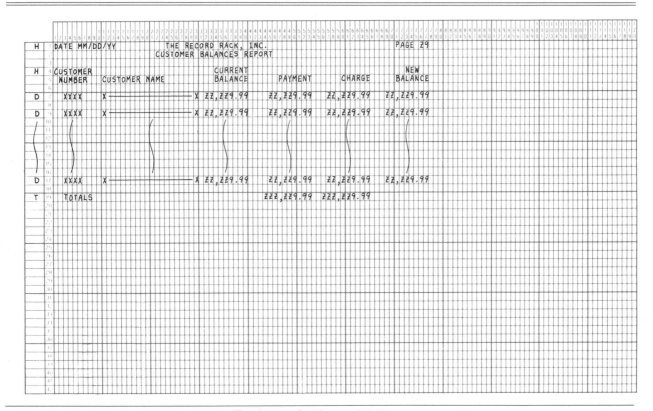

Figure 9-6   The layout for the update program report.

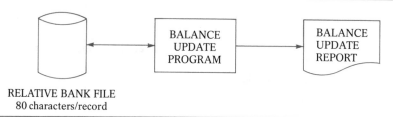

RELATIVE BANK FILE
80 characters/record

Figure 9-7   The systems chart for the update program.

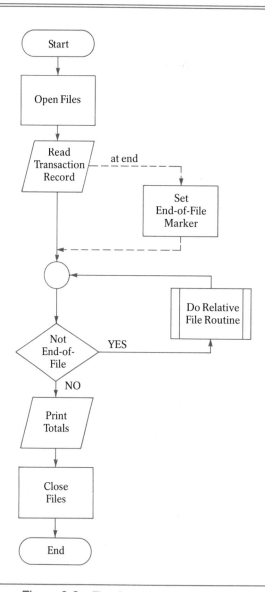

Figure 9-8   The flowchart for the update program.

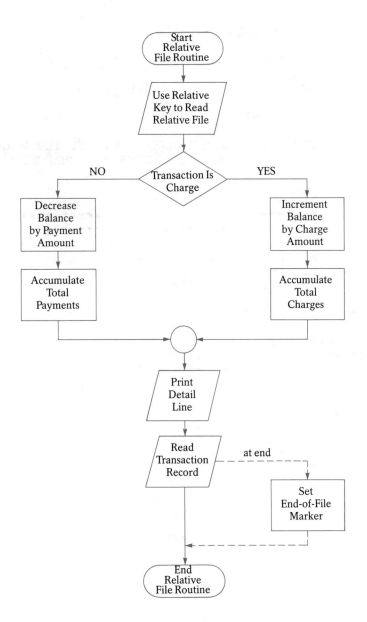

Figure 9-8 **(continued)**

The transaction update program will look like the following:

```
****************************************************************
****************************************************************
*
*
*
*   PROGRAM NAME: REL-UP
*
*   PROGRAMMER NAME:  CINDY HARRISON
*
*   SOCIAL SECURITY NUMBER:  999-99-9999
*
*   DUE DATE: FEBRUARY 10, 1988
*
*   DESCRIPTION: THIS PROGRAM WILL UPDATE THE RELATIVE CUSTOMER
*                FILE WITH PAYMENTS AND CHARGES.
*
*
*
****************************************************************
****************************************************************
    IDENTIFICATION DIVISION.
    PROGRAM-ID.   REL-UP.
    AUTHOR.       CINDY HARRISON.

    ENVIRONMENT DIVISION.

    CONFIGURATION SECTION.
    SOURCE-COMPUTER. IBM-4331.
    OBJECT-COMPUTER. IBM-4331.

    INPUT-OUTPUT SECTION.
    FILE-CONTROL.

        SELECT RELATIVE-FILE ASSIGN TO DA-R-RELBANK
               ORGANIZATION IS RELATIVE
               ACCESS IS RANDOM
               RELATIVE KEY IS RELATIVE-KEY.

        SELECT PRINT-FILE     ASSIGN TO UT-S-SYSPRINT.

        SELECT TRANS-FILE     ASSIGN TO UT-S-UPDATE.

    DATA DIVISION.
    FILE SECTION.

    FD  RELATIVE-FILE
        LABEL RECORDS ARE OMITTED
        RECORD CONTAINS 80 CHARACTERS.
    01  RELATIVE-RECORD.
        10  CUSTOMER-NUMBER         PIC 9(4).
        10  CUSTOMER-NAME           PIC X(20).
        10  FILLER                  PIC X.
        10  AMOUNT-DUE              PIC 9(5)V99.
        10  FILLER                  PIC X(48).
```

```
FD   PRINT-FILE
     LABEL RECORDS ARE OMITTED
     RECORD CONTAINS 133 CHARACTERS.
01   LIST-OUT-RECORD              PIC X(133).

FD   TRANS-FILE
     LABEL RECORDS ARE OMITTED
     RECORD CONTAINS 80 CHARACTERS.
01   TRANS-RECORD.
     10   TRANS-NUMBER            PIC 9(4).
     10   TRANS-CODE              PIC X.
     10   TRANS-AMOUNT            PIC 9(5)V99.
     10   FILLER                  PIC X(68).


WORKING-STORAGE SECTION.

01   WORK-AREAS.

     05   RELATIVE-KEY            PIC 9(4).
     05   EOF                     PIC XXX.
     05   FOUND-KEY               PIC XXX.

     05   LINE-CTR                PIC 999         VALUE ZERO.
     05   PAGE-CTR                PIC 999         VALUE 1.

     05   DATE-IN.
          10   DATE-YY            PIC XX.
          10   DATE-MM            PIC XX.
          10   DATE-DD            PIC XX.

     05   PAYMENT-TOTAL           PIC 9(6)V99     VALUE ZERO.
     05   CHARGE-TOTAL            PIC 9(6)V99     VALUE ZERO.

01   PAGE-HEADING-1.
     05   FILLER                  PIC X(6)        VALUE ' DATE '.
     05   HEADING-MONTH           PIC XX.
     05   HEADING-DAY             PIC /XX/.
     05   HEADING-YEAR            PIC XX.
     05   FILLER                  PIC X(33)       VALUE
     '              THE RECORD RACK, INC.'.
     05   FILLER                  PIC X(26)       VALUE SPACES.
     05   FILLER                  PIC X(5)        VALUE 'PAGE '.
     05   PAGE-COUNTER-OUT        PIC Z9.

01   PAGE-HEADING-2.
     05   FILLER                  PIC X(24)       VALUE SPACES.
     05   FILLER                  PIC X(24)       VALUE
     'CUSTOMER BALANCES REPORT'.

01   COLUMN-HEADING-1.
     05   FILLER                  PIC X(9)        VALUE
     ' CUSTOMER'.
     05   FILLER                  PIC X(26)       VALUE SPACES.
     05   FILLER                  PIC X(7)        VALUE
     'CURRENT'.
     05   FILLER                  PIC X(33)       VALUE SPACES.
     05   FILLER                  PIC X(3)        VALUE 'NEW'.
```

```
01   COLUMN-HEADING-2.
     05   FILLER                     PIC X(42)      VALUE
     '  NUMBER    CUSTOMER NAME           BALANCE'.
     05   FILLER                     PIC X(38)      VALUE
     '      PAYMENT      CHARGE      BALANCE'.

01   DETAIL-LINE.
     05   FILLER                     PIC XXX        VALUE SPACES.
     05   NUMBER-OUT                 PIC 9(4).
     05   FILLER                     PIC X(5)       VALUE SPACES.
     05   NAME-OUT                   PIC X(20).
     05   FILLER                     PIC X          VALUE SPACES.
     05   DUE-OUT                    PIC ZZ,ZZ9.99.
     05   FILLER                     PIC X(4)       VALUE SPACES.
     05   PAYMENT-OUT                PIC ZZ,ZZ9.99  BLANK WHEN ZERO.
     05   FILLER                     PIC X(4)       VALUE SPACES.
     05   CHARGE-OUT                 PIC ZZ,ZZ9.99  BLANK WHEN ZERO.
     05   FILLER                     PIC X(3)       VALUE SPACES.
     05   NEW-OUT                    PIC ZZ,ZZ9.99.

01   TOTAL-LINE.
     05   FILLER                     PIC X(9)       VALUE
     '   TOTALS'.
     05   FILLER                     PIC X(36)      VALUE SPACES.
     05   PAYMENT-TOTAL-OUT          PIC ZZZ,ZZ9.99.
     05   FILLER                     PIC XXX        VALUE SPACES.
     05   CHARGE-TOTAL-OUT           PIC ZZZ,ZZ9.99.


PROCEDURE DIVISION.

0100-MAIN-MODULE.

    OPEN I-O     RELATIVE-FILE
         INPUT   TRANS-FILE
         OUTPUT  PRINT-FILE.

    ACCEPT DATE-IN FROM DATE.
    MOVE DATE-YY TO HEADING-YEAR.
    MOVE DATE-MM TO HEADING-MONTH.
    MOVE DATE-DD TO HEADING-DAY.

    READ TRANS-FILE
         AT END MOVE 'YES' TO EOF.

    PERFORM 0200-PROCESS-TRANSACTIONS
         UNTIL EOF = 'YES'.

    PERFORM 0400-HEADINGS-ROUTINE.

    MOVE CHARGE-TOTAL  TO CHARGE-TOTAL-OUT.
    MOVE PAYMENT-TOTAL TO PAYMENT-TOTAL-OUT.

    WRITE LIST-OUT-RECORD FROM TOTAL-LINE
         AFTER ADVANCING 2 LINES.

    CLOSE RELATIVE-FILE
          TRANS-FILE
          PRINT-FILE.
    STOP  RUN.
```

```
0200-PROCESS-TRANSACTIONS.

    MOVE TRANS-NUMBER TO CUSTOMER-NUMBER RELATIVE-KEY.
    MOVE 'YES'       TO FOUND-KEY.
    READ RELATIVE-FILE
        INVALID KEY MOVE 'NO ' TO FOUND-KEY.

    IF FOUND-KEY = 'NO '
        MOVE ZEROS TO AMOUNT-DUE PAYMENT-OUT CHARGE-OUT NEW-OUT
        MOVE 'RECORD NOT FOUND' TO NAME-OUT
    ELSE

        MOVE AMOUNT-DUE TO DUE-OUT
        MOVE CUSTOMER-NUMBER TO NUMBER-OUT
        MOVE CUSTOMER-NAME   TO NAME-OUT
        IF TRANS-CODE = 'P'
            SUBTRACT TRANS-AMOUNT FROM AMOUNT-DUE
            MOVE ZERO         TO CHARGE-OUT
            MOVE TRANS-AMOUNT TO PAYMENT-OUT
            MOVE AMOUNT-DUE   TO NEW-OUT
            ADD TRANS-AMOUNT  TO PAYMENT-TOTAL
            PERFORM 0410-REWRITE-RECORD
        ELSE
            ADD TRANS-AMOUNT  TO AMOUNT-DUE
            MOVE ZERO         TO PAYMENT-OUT
            MOVE TRANS-AMOUNT TO CHARGE-OUT
            MOVE AMOUNT-DUE   TO NEW-OUT
            ADD TRANS-AMOUNT  TO CHARGE-TOTAL
            PERFORM 0410-REWRITE-RECORD.

    WRITE LIST-OUT-RECORD FROM DETAIL-LINE
        AFTER ADVANCING 2 LINES.

    ADD 2 TO LINE-CTR.
    IF LINE-CTR > 60
        PERFORM 0400-HEADINGS-ROUTINE.

    READ TRANS-FILE
        AT END MOVE 'YES' TO EOF.


0400-HEADINGS-ROUTINE.

    MOVE PAGE-CTR TO PAGE-COUNTER-OUT.
    WRITE LIST-OUT-RECORD FROM PAGE-HEADING-1
        AFTER ADVANCING PAGE.
    WRITE LIST-OUT-RECORD FROM PAGE-HEADING-2
        AFTER ADVANCING 1 LINE.
    WRITE LIST-OUT-RECORD FROM COLUMN-HEADING-1
        AFTER ADVANCING 2 LINES.
    WRITE LIST-OUT-RECORD FROM COLUMN-HEADING-2
        AFTER ADVANCING 1 LINE.

    MOVE 6 TO LINE-CTR.
    ADD  1 TO PAGE-CTR.
```

```
      0410-REWRITE-RECORD.

          REWRITE RELATIVE-RECORD
              INVALID KEY
              DISPLAY 'UNKNOWN ERROR DURING WRITE.'
              DISPLAY 'HALTING PROGRAM.'
              STOP RUN.
```

Upon running the program, Cindy got the following output:

| DATE 07/03/88 | THE RECORD RACK, INC. CUSTOMER BALANCES REPORT | | | | PAGE   1 |

CUSTOMER NUMBER	CUSTOMER NAME	CURRENT BALANCE	PAYMENT	CHARGE	NEW BALANCE
0001	JIM CLARK	44.67	14.07		30.60
0003	TOM ADDIS	38.74	27.86		10.88
0004	ABABA ADDIS	2.76		27.60	30.36
0007	JOHN DAVIS	14.76	7.61		7.15
0009	TOMMY MCNUTT	2.41		14.00	16.41
0011	SHARON RUSSEL	148.78		2,387.80	2,536.58
0011	SHARON RUSSEL	2,536.58		50.40	2,586.98
0013	PAT ANDERSON	34.82	18.20		16.62
0016	ISMAEL DE LEON	1,330.08		250.76	1,580.84
0016	ISMAEL DE LEON	1,580.84		42.80	1,623.64
0016	ISMAEL DE LEON	1,623.64	1,518.30		105.34
TOTALS			1,586.04	2,773.36	

9-7
Summary

1. In previous chapters we have dealt with sequential and indexed file processing. In this chapter we introduced a third type: relative file processing. In a relative file, the records are processed in the file by record pointer, much like a table pointer is used to access a table item.
2. If we have a file in which the record keys are simply sequentially numbered, we can use the keys as the file pointers for accessing the records. More often, though, the file keys are not so well behaved. When the number of possible keys exceeds the number of records needed for storage, we do a calculation on the key to produce the file pointer. The calculation technique is called hashing.

3. In one of the most commonly used hashing techniques the record key is divided by the number of records to be stored in the file, using the remainder of the division plus 1 as the file pointer.

4. This type of calculation occasionally will produce the same file pointer twice. Such duplication of pointers is known as a collision. When collisions occur, the computer stores the second record in the file by reading the record and then examining the subsequent records until it finds an empty record. The new record then replaces the empty one.

5. Relative files are created with the appropriate number of records, all filled with blanks. Then records are added to the file by simply putting the actual data into the file in place of the blanks.

6. When the SELECT statement is used to create a relative file, the ORGANIZATION clause is RELATIVE while the ACCESS IS clause can be SEQUENTIAL, RANDOM, or DYNAMIC. If SEQUENTIAL is used, the RELATIVE KEY clause can be used but is optional. If the other access methods are used, the RELATIVE KEY clause must be used.

7. In a relative file update procedure, the basic procedures of add, change, and delete are still used. The processing is slightly different, however.

8. When records are being added, if the key in the record is the same as the one used to read the record, the former is a duplicate. If there is different data in the file, the program must read subsequent records in the file until either a duplicate record or an empty one is found. If an empty one is found, the new record is rewritten there.

9. Changing records is done basically the same way it has been, except for the process of accessing the record. The record is first read by using the file pointer; if it is the correct record, the changes are made and the record is rewritten. Otherwise, subsequent records are read until either the proper record or a blank record is found. A blank one indicates that the record being searched for doesn't exist.

10. Records to be deleted are searched for in the same way as records to be changed. When they are deleted, however, they are merely rewritten into the file as blank records. Generally, they are not physically deleted because doing so will change the number of records in the file and mess up the hashing routine.

11. When accessing a relative file sequentially, we can use the START statement to begin processing the records at a point other than the first record in the file. We simply use the relative key to direct the computer to a particular record.

9-8
Glossary

Collision What happens when two relative keys produce duplicate record pointers.

DELETE statement The statement, rarely used, to delete a record in a relative file.

Hash routine A calculation routine used to produce the record pointer for a relative file.

Relative file   A file in which the records are accessed by a pointer indicating the relative position of the record in the file.

START statement   The statement that allows sequential access of a relative file to begin at a particular record rather than at the beginning of the file.

9-9
Quick Quiz

Cover the answers with a blank sheet of paper and test yourself. Questions 1–15 are true or false questions, 16–20 are multiple choice, and 21–25 are fill-in-the-blank.

T F   **1.** Indexed files require more storage than sequential files.

T F   **2.** Relative files require more storage than indexed files.

T F   **3.** A relative file is similar to a table.

T F   **4.** Access to the records in a relative file is faster than to those in an indexed file.

T F   **5.** We always use a hashing technique when creating relative files.

T F   **6.** Using the hashing technique discussed in the chapter, calculation of the record pointer is a simple process of division.

T F   **7.** Collisions are always a possibility when you are using relative files.

T F   **8.** Relative files are always created with blank records.

T F   **9.** The SELECT clause for relative files uses an error status code.

T F   **10.** If we are going to access the relative file both randomly and sequentially, we need to use ACCESS IS DYNAMIC on the SELECT statement.

T F   **11.** When we create a relative file filled with blank records, we use the ORGANIZATION IS SEQUENTIAL clause.

T F   **12.** We use INVALID KEY clauses on the I/O statements when using relative files, even though an invalid key should never happen.

T F   **13.** We cannot use a DELETE statement when using relative files.

T F   **14.** When calculating the file pointer with the hashing routine discussed in the chapter, we always add 1 to the remainder of the division.

T F   **15.** When using a hashing technique to add a record to a relative file, we first must locate a blank record to store the data into.

_____   **16.** Which of the following does not require the RELATIVE KEY clause on the SELECT statement?

     (a) ACCESS IS SEQUENTIAL   **(c)** ACCESS IS RANDOM
     (b) ACCESS IS DYNAMIC   **(d)** All require the clause.

_____   **17.** For which of the following transaction types do we rewrite the records into the relative file when using a hashing technique?

     (a) adding   **(c)** changing
     (b) deleting   **(d)** all of them

_____   **18.** If we are looking specifically for a blank record for our processing when using a hashing technique, we are doing what type of processing?

     (a) adding   **(c)** changing
     (b) deleting   **(d)** all of them

_____ **19.** When a date routine is used to edit an input date, which of the following is the least likely to be edited?

    (a) month   **(c)** day

    (b) year   **(d)** All of them require editing.

_____ **20.** Which of the following file types is most commonly used in modern COBOL installations?

    (a) sequential   **(c)** relative

    (b) indexed   **(d)** no way to know

21. When using a hashing technique for a relative file, we sometimes try to add a record where there already is one. This is called a _____ .

22. When creating a relative file to be accessed with a hashing technique, we create all the records filled with _____ .

23. If we want to begin sequentially accessing a relative file at a particular point, we can use the _____ statement.

24. There are three ways to access a relative file: _____ , _____ , and _____ .

25. If we rewrite a record into a relative files as blanks, we are _____ the record.

9-10
Answers to Quick Quiz

1. T (They require both the main file and the index file.)
2. F (But they generally have some empty records that are wasted space.)
3. T (It is similar in that the data is accessed by a pointer.)
4. T (At least for straight access, since the relative file does not have an index file. In reality, however, indexed access is often faster for certain records because in a relative file where the records were stored by hashing, several records may need to be read until the proper one is found.)
5. F (Hashing is only necessary when the record key cannot be used as the file pointer.)
6. T
7. F (Only when using a hashing technique. If we use the record key directly, there will be no duplicates.)
8. F (Again this is done only for files to be accessed by hashing. If we use the record key directly, we will write the records directly into the file.)
9. T (The codes generated relate to the same basic messages discussed in the ISAM chapter.)
10. T
11. F (The ORGANIZATION clause is always RELATIVE when we are using relative files.)
12. T (It is useful for capturing machine problems and it will give us an error under a few file conditions, for example, if we have physically deleted a record.)
13. F (Though it is not used often, there is a DELETE statement for relative files.)
14. T (Because the division will result in a maximum number that is one less than the total number records in the file.)

15. T (If we don't run into a duplicate record key first.)
16. a (It is optional because we sometimes write records into the file without using the key.)
17. d (All of them are rewritten when a hashing technique is used, because all the records are always there.)
18. a (We are looking for a blank record into which we can put the data of the record that is to be added.)
19. b (Though we will generally edit the year also, the month and day are obviously in need of checking. The year is not so necessary.)
20. b (By far, there are more indexed files used—at least files in constant use. If you count tape storage files, sequential might win out instead.)
21. collision
22. blanks
23. START
24. sequential, random, dynamic
25. deleting

9-11
Questions to Aid Understanding

*1. Explain what a relative file is and what advantages it has over indexed files.
2. List and explain at least two problems associated with relative files.
*3. Why is hashing necessary? Illustrate how it works by showing an example.
4. Why is a relative file created with empty records when it is to be used with a hashing technique?
5. Explain how a record to be changed is found when a hashing technique is used.
6. Explain how a record is added into a relative file when a hashing technique is used.
*7. Why is the WRITE statement not used with a relative file that is processed with a hashing technique?
8. Explain how a record is deleted from a relative file that is processed with a hashing technique.
9. Explain why the DELETE command is not used to remove records from a relative file that is processed with a hashing technique.
10. Explain what the START statement is and how it can be useful.
11. What was the purpose of printing the totals in the routine that we placed at the end of the sample program on pages 530–539?

9-12
Coding Exercises

1. In the sample program in the chapter, revise the routine used to input the amount due so that it will also check for a maximum amount of $3,000.00. That is, if the user tries to enter more than $3,000, the program should print an error.
2. In the sample program in the chapter, we wrote a date routine to verify the date entry. Revise the routine so it will verify the number of days in February during a leap year. (A year is a leap year when it is evenly divisible by four.)
3. Write the code necessary to read a record from a transaction file, get the record key (Social Security number) from the transaction record, calculate the relative key by using a hashing routine for 500 records in the file, and read the record from the relative file.

9-13
Maintenance Program

The Record Rack program works fine, but Roger has decided that he wants the program modified slightly so that it will also relate any credits to the customers' accounts. There will now be a third transaction code of D for credits (C cannot be used for credits since it is already being used for charges).

It is your job to redesign the program so that it will also have a column for credits. Credits are deducted from the balance just like payments are. The report generated should include a total of credits.

You will need to

- redesign the printer spacing chart to include the new column and total;
- redesign the program to match the new needs;
- modify the program to meet the new specifications.

9-14
Illustrative Program

You work for a lumber yard and your boss wants you to write a relative file update program to update the inventory of the lumber stock. The WOOD inventory file (layout in Figure 9-9) contains the last physical count of the inventory and the current count based upon sales and receipts. The received and sold figures are year-to-date figures. The relative key (item number) is made up of two separate numbers:

- The first two digits are the type of wood. Some types are not carried by the store but can be special-ordered. The types and codes are

  01—White pine   05—Birch
  02—Redwood   06—Walnut
  03—Beech   07—Cedar
  04—Oak   08—Fir

- The other two digits of the item number are for the sizes of the wood:

  01—1 × 2   06—2 × 4
  02—1 × 4   07—2 × 6
  03—1 × 6   08—2 × 8
  04—1 × 10   09—2 × 10
  05—2 × 2   10—3 × 4

There is to be a record in the file for every possible item number (80 records). You will need to write a file creation program to create the file with all the records (from Appendix A—your file needs 810 records).

Your update program is to use a transaction file (TRANWOOD) in Figure 9-10) to update the file according to board feet received or sold. The item number on the transaction record should be verified for accuracy before a record is read from the file. If the record is in error, an error message is to be printed.

The program should produce a report with the layout shown in Figure 9-11. The received and sold columns should show the transaction data, though the file data will need to be updated. Notice the totals on board feet received and sold.

WOOD File					
Field Description	*Position*	*Length*	:	*Dec*	*Type*
Item number	1–4	4	:		Non-numeric
Last count	5–10	6	:	0	Numeric
Current count	11–16	6	:	0	Numeric
Board feet received	17–22	6	:	0	Numeric
Board feet sold	23–28	6	:	0	Numeric
Filler	29–80	52	:		Non-numeric
Record Length = 80					

Figure 9-9 The record layout for the WOOD inventory file.

TRANWOOD File					
Field Description	*Position*	*Length*	:	*Dec*	*Type*
Item number	1–4	4	:		Non-numeric
Transaction type	5–5	1	:		Non-numeric
Board feet	6–11	6	:	0	Numeric
Filler	13–80	68	:		Non-numeric
Record Length = 80					

Figure 9-10 The record layout for the TRANWOOD file.

The systems chart for the program is shown in Figure 9-12, the program flowchart design is in Figure 9-13, and the pseudocode design follows:

```
Start
Open files
Read a transaction record at end set end-of-file marker
DO-WHILE not end-of-file
        IF relative key not correct THEN
            Print error message
        ELSE
            Use relative key to read relative file
            IF transaction is received THEN
                Increment current count by transaction amount
                Accumulate total received
            ELSE
                Decrease balance by transaction amount
                Accumulate total sold
            END-IF
            Print detail line
            Rewrite relative record
        END-IF
        Read a transaction record at end set end-of-file marker
END-DO
Print totals
Close files
End
```

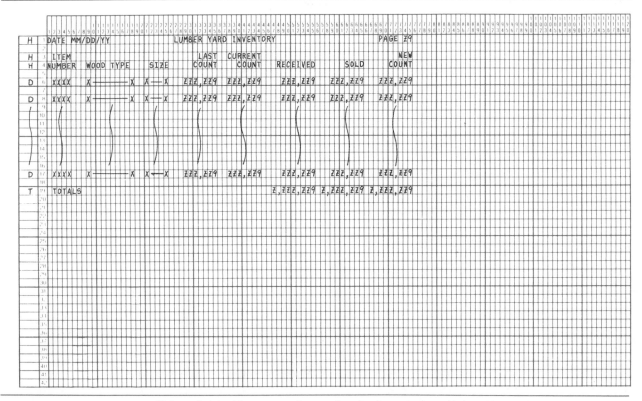

Figure 9-11   The report layout for the inventory update program.

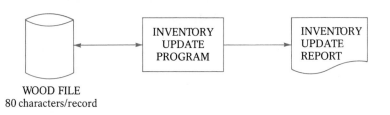

WOOD FILE
80 characters/record

Figure 9-12 The systems chart for the inventory update program.

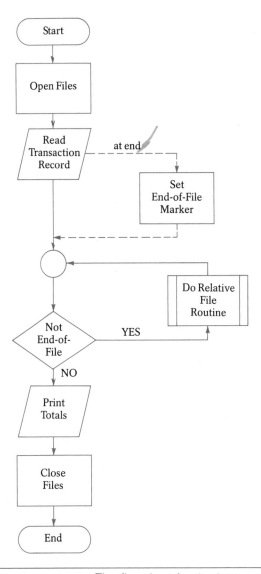

Figure 9-13 The flowchart for the inventory update program.

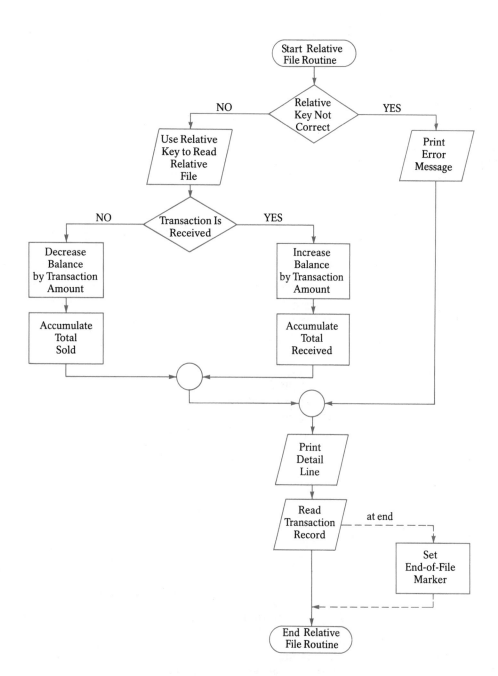

Figure 9-13 **(continued)**

9-15

System Designed Programs

For the following programs, all the design elements typically furnished to a programmer by the systems analyst are furnished. It is up to you, as programmer, to design and code the program. The files to be used are found in Appendix A.

1. Redo problem 1 of the System Designed Programs in Chapter 6 to use a relative file instead of an indexed file.
2. Write a relative file update program that will read a transaction file and update the SALES file shown in Figure 9-14 with the sales for one of the products. The transaction file layout (TRANSALE) is shown in Figure 9-15. All the transactions are additions to the sales; the transaction code determines which

SALES File					
Field Description	*Position*	*Length*	:	*Dec*	*Type*
Salesman number	1–4	4	:		Numeric
Salesman name	5–24	20	:		Non-numeric
Sales territory	25–26	2	:		Non-numeric
Percent of commission	27–28	2	:	0	Numeric
Sales of product 1	29–35	7	:	2	Numeric
Sales of product 2	36–42	7	:	2	Numeric
Sales of product 3	43–49	7	:	2	Numeric
Sales of product 4	50–56	7	:	2	Numeric
Sales of product 5	57–63	7	:	2	Numeric
Years of service	64–65	2	:	0	Numeric
Filler	66–80	15	:		Non-numeric
Record Length = 80					

Figure 9-14   The record layout for the SALES file, exercise 9-15-2.

TRANSALE File					
Field Description	*Position*	*Length*	:	*Dec*	*Type*
Salesman number	1–4	4	:	0	Numeric
Product number	5–5	1	:	0	Numeric
Amount of sales	6–12	7	:	2	Numeric
Filler	13–80	68	:		Non-numeric
Record Length = 80					

Figure 9-15   The record layout for the TRANSALE file, exercise 9-15-2.

product the transaction is to update. Your programs need to produce an update report like the one shown in Figure 9-16. The systems chart for the program is shown in Figure 9-17.

3. Redo problem 3 of System Designed Programs in Chapter 6 to use a relative file instead of an indexed file.

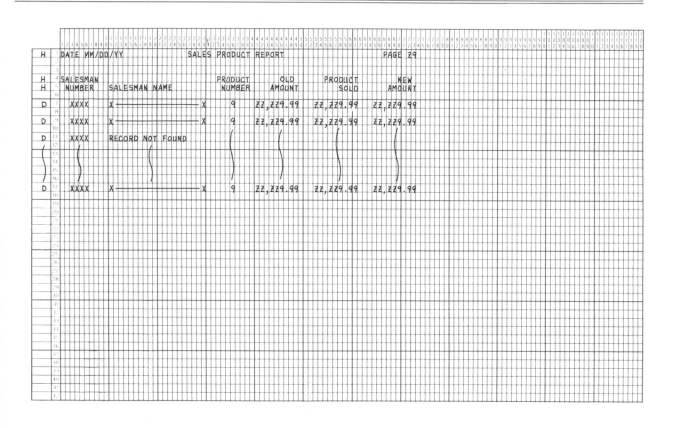

Figure 9-16   The report layout for the relative file update program, exercise 9-15-2.

Figure 9-17   The systems chart for the relative file update program, exercise 9-15-2.

3. You work for a sporting goods company that has its inventory file in the INVENT indexed file (layout in Figure 9-18). The company doesn't keep all the information in the one indexed file, however. There is also a relative SPORTTBL file that is used to store the name of the item and the current price (layout in Figure 9-19). Write a program that can input the inventory item number from the user and then read the indexed record and the relative record and display the data as shown here:

```
MM/DD/YY                  INVENTORY INFORMATION

                     ITEM NUMBER..... XXXX

                     DESCRIPTION..... X------------------X

                     PURCHASE PRICE.. Z,ZZ9.99

LAST COUNT...... ZZZ,ZZ9              COST OF INVENTORY.. ZZ,ZZZ,ZZ9.99

CURRENT COUNT... ZZZ,ZZ9              COST OF INVENTORY.. ZZ,ZZZ,ZZ9.99
```

INVENT File					
Field Description	*Position*	*Length*	:	*Dec*	*Type*
Item number	1–4	4	:		Non-numeric
Last count	5–10	6	:	0	Numeric
Current count	11–16	6	:	0	Numeric
Unit cost	17–24	8	:	2	Numeric
Filler	25–80	56	:		Non-numeric
Record Length = 80					

Figure 9-18   The record layout for the INVENT ISAM file, exercise 9-16-3.

SPORTTBL File					
Field Description	*Position*	*Length*	:	*Dec*	*Type*
Item number	1–4	4	:		Non-numeric
Item description	5–24	20	:		Non-numeric
Price	25–30	6	:	2	Numeric
Filler	31–80	50	:		Non-numeric
Record Length = 80					

Figure 9-19   The record layout for the SPORTTBL ISAM file, exercise 9-16-3.

The counts are from the indexed file, and the cost of inventory in each case is the purchase price times the inventory count. This program will do no maintenance of the records; it will simply display them. The systems chart is shown in Figure 9-20.

9-16
Interactive System Designed Programs

For the following programs, all the design elements typically furnished to a programmer by the systems analyst are furnished. It is up to you, as programmer, to design and code the program. The files to be used are found in Appendix A.

1. Redo problem 1 of the Interactive System Designed Programs in Chapter 8 to use a relative file instead of an indexed file.
2. Redo problem 3 of the Interactive System Designed Programs in Chapter 8 to use a relative file instead of an indexed file.

9-17
Non-designed Programs

In the following programs, you will need to design the systems chart, the input files (record layout), the printer spacing chart, the program design, and the data with which to test the program.

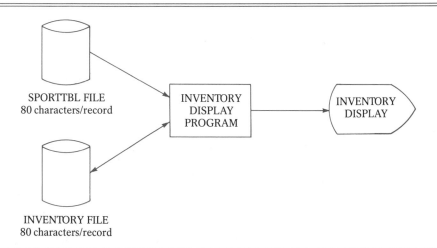

Figure 9-20   The systems chart for the inventory display program, exercise 9-16-3.

1. Write a program that can be modified easily so that a relative file with any number of blank records of any length can be created for use with maintenance programs.

2. Write a program that can update a relative master file, using transaction records to determine the adds, changes, and deletions. The data is to be salesman ID, name, commission code, amount of base pay, and total sales. Your program should allow all fields to be changed except the salesman ID, which is to be used as the relative key (directly, not through a hashing routine).

3. Write a program that can update a relative master file, using transaction records to determine the adds, changes, and deletions. Use a product number of eight digits for the record key and a hashing routine to store the records. Your file should be able to hold 350 records. The program should allow changes to all the fields except the record key. Other fields should include product type, description, cost, selling price, quantity-on-hand, and reorder quantity. The program should have a total at the end of all the transactions accomplished and should give the total number of records each that were changed, added, and deleted. The totals should also include a count of how many adds, changes, and deletions were tried but failed for some reason.

9-18
Interactive Non-designed Programs

In the following programs, you will need to design the systems chart, the input files (record layout), the printer spacing chart, the program design, and the data with which to test the program.

1. You work at an independent major appliance repair shop. Write an interactive program that can be used to determine the charges to be made on appliance repairs. Your program should ask for the customer name and address (street, city, state, and zip code) and then the appliance code for the appliance being repaired. This code is used to look up the appliance record in a relative file (you will have to put the records in the relative file). The appliance record contains the name of the appliance being repaired (refrigerator, etc.), the minimum charge, and the hourly repair charge, along with the markup on parts for that particular appliance. The user should then be asked to input the number of hours the appliance was worked on. If the hourly calculation (hours times hourly rate) is less than the minimum charge, the minimum charge is to be used. Then the user should be asked for the cost of parts used and that amount multiplied by the markup to determine the charge for parts. All this information is then displayed on the screen for the user to verify. After verification, a bill is to be printed and the record should be stored in a file.

2. Prepare a program that will use a relative file to display passenger information for a small commuter airline. The file will need to contain the ticket number, date of flight, passenger name, and origin and destination. The relative record key is to be the ticket number (simply sequentially numbered). Your program

should allow new tickets to be made out and current tickets to be changed as needed. Codes should be used for the origin and destination for user entry, though the code should be translated to city name to be displayed on the screen. The origin and destination should be used to determine the cost of the ticket from a table. The program should also be able to produce a list of the tickets purchased for each date (sort into date order).

3. The stationery store you work for needs you to write an interactive program to print sales slips. Your program will need to be able to automatically generate the receipt number (keep a sequential file on disk to store the current receipt number) and then input the product codes for the products sold. These codes are to be looked up in a relative file that is stored by these product codes, which are simply sequential inventory numbers. The relative file has the product name (to be printed on the receipt along with the code), the cost to the store of the product, and the sales price. Next the program should input (from the user) the quantity of that product. The program should continue inputting products until the user types in a stop code. After all the products have been entered, the program should calculate the gross total of the receipt, the taxes (5.125%), and then the final total. Finally, the receipt should be printed, after the user has been allowed to verify the receipt and change anything on it that is incorrect. The data should be displayed on the screen in the same form used to print the receipt.

OBJECTIVES After completing Chapter 10 you should be able to

1. explain the purpose of the COBOL Report Writer;
2. explain what is different about the FD for the printer output file when you use Report Writer;
3. explain what the REPORT SECTION is for;
4. explain what causes the PAGE-COUNTER and LINE-COUNTER to be automatically set up by the computer;
5. explain what the TYPE command is for;
6. list at least three of the different TYPE report groups and explain what each is for;
7. explain why the DETAIL clause generally requires the use of a group-name whereas the other TYPE clauses do not;
8. define the
   (a) LINE clause
   (b) NEXT GROUP clause
   (c) COLUMN clause
   (d) GROUP INDICATE clause
   (e) SOURCE clause
   (f) SUM clause
   (g) INITIATE statement
   (h) GENERATE statement
   (i) TERMINATE statement
9. explain what rolling forward totals are;
10. explain what declaratives are and why they are sometimes necessary in a report program.

CHAPTER 10

REPORT WRITER

10-1

Introduction

Writing reports is one of the COBOL user's most frequent tasks. We have been writing report programs since our very first COBOL program. We began with simple reports that listed only the detail lines. Then we learned how to format reports so they had page and column headings and how to format data fields and totals.

Constructing most of these report programs has been relatively easy, being basically a matter of reading records from a file, moving the data from an input area to an output area, and then printing that output area. The reports became more difficult to construct when we moved on to control break reports, but the basic report concepts were still adhered to: reading, moving, and printing. Since there generally is a common approach to creating reports, COBOL has a facility to allow us to create reports in a much simpler fashion than we have been using. We will still need to define all our headings and detail lines, but the processing of the data itself—from simply moving the data from the input area to the output area, to the more complicated needs of line and page counting and control breaks—can be done virtually automatically by the COBOL **Report Writer**.

Paradoxically, the Report Writer feature is an extremely useful tool that is seldom used in most installations. The reasons behind this lack of use vary, but the main reason is that many programmers simply don't know how to use Report Writer.

As we discuss Report Writer, you will discover how easy it is to use and how powerful it can be. We will begin by looking at the major features of Report Writer and then move on to some of its more complex uses.

10-2

The DATA DIVISION

There are a number of differences between a regular COBOL program and one that uses the Report Writer. We will begin by discussing the differences in the DATA DIVISION.

10-2-1   The FILE SECTION

We use the FILE SECTION to describe our files to the computer. If we expect the computer to do anything special with a particular file, we should describe it in the FILE SECTION. Use of the Report Writer is one of those special procedures.

On most machines, a normal FD has only one required clause, the LABEL RECORDS clause. For a file to be used with the Report Writer we need to add another clause, the **REPORT IS clause**. The format is

$$\left\{ \begin{array}{l} \text{REPORT} \quad \text{IS} \\ \text{REPORTS} \quad \text{ARE} \end{array} \right\} \text{report-name-1 [report-name-2]} \ldots$$

The "report-name-1" shown in the format is the name of the report, and we need to include it now so we can refer to it later in the program. Notice that the REPORT IS clause allows the specification of more than one report. When writing a program that creates more than one report, we use only one output file and simply move all data to that one print area, changing the headings and detail lines so they pertain to the report we are printing at the time. We will do the same thing when using the Report Writer: we will use one output file to print the Report Writer headings and detail lines through. When we finish with one report, we simply begin another, using different elements. We don't need multiple files.

An example of how the new clause would look in an FD is

```
FD   OUTPUT-FILE
     LABEL RECORDS ARE OMITTED
     RECORD CONTAINS 133 CHARACTERS
     REPORT IS DETAIL-REPORT.
```

A normal FD is followed by the record specification on an 01 level. The record specification is used to dictate the length of the record to be used, either as a single elementary item with a PIC clause or as a group with the length being the total of the elementary items contained within. A report FD does not use a record specification. Since the program is going to automatically handle the record processing for us, we don't need to specify the record itself. Instead we use the RECORD CONTAINS clause to specify the length of the record.

10-2-2 The WORKING-STORAGE SECTION

When we print our own reports, the WORKING-STORAGE SECTION is one of the largest areas of our program. When we use the Report Writer, the WORKING-STORAGE SECTION is one of the smallest. Since the Report Writer handles most of the normal report processing functions, we don't need to put any temporary fields, such as total fields, into WORKING-STORAGE. Also, none of the print layouts, such as headings and detail lines, is stored in the WORKING-STORAGE SECTION. The Report Writer has a section of its own for this storage.

The WORKING-STORAGE SECTION is still needed to define a few fields that we will still be in control of. Since we are printing a report, we will be reading a file and will need an end-of-file marker. This must be defined in the WORKING-STORAGE SECTION. We will also need to define the date areas for printing the date on our report.

10-2-3 The REPORT SECTION

We just mentioned that most of the elements needed for a report are stored in a section of their own: the REPORT SECTION. Within that section, each report we have designated in an FD must be defined in an RD or **Report Description**. All the various elements of the report are defined within the RD.

An RD is similar to an FD in that it uses several clauses to define the report, just as an FD uses clauses to define the file. The format of an RD is

```
RD   report-name
      [ { CONTROL   IS  }  { identifier-1 [identifier-2] . . .         } ]
      [ { CONTROLS ARE }   { FINAL identifier-1 [identifier-2] . . .   } ]
      [PAGE [ LIMIT  IS  ] INTEGER-1 [ LINE  ] ]
      [     [ LIMITS ARE ]           [ LINES ] ]
      [HEADING        integer-2]
      [FIRST DETAIL   integer-3]
      [LAST DETAIL    integer-4]
      [FOOTING        integer-5]
```

The RD statement begins in area A and the report-name begins in area B. The report-name specified on the RD must match a report-name used on a REPORT clause on a previous FD. For every report specified on an FD, there must be a separate RD. The FD and RD correspondence is illustrated as follows:

```
FD   OUTPUT-FILE
     LABEL RECORDS ARE OMITTED
     RECORD CONTAINS 133 CHARACTERS
     REPORT IS DETAIL-REPORT. ─────────────────────────┐
     : : :                                             │
     : : :                                             │
     : : :                                             │
RD   DETAIL-REPORT ◄───────────────────────────────────┘
```

                          same report name as used in FD

If the FD contains more than one report-name, there must be a separate RD for each one:

```
FD   OUTPUT-FILE
     LABEL RECORDS ARE OMITTED
     RECORD CONTAINS 133 CHARACTERS
     REPORTS ARE DETAIL-REPORT SUMMARY-REPORT.═══════┐
     : : :                                           │
     : : :                                           │
     : : :                                           │        both
RD   DETAIL-REPORT ◄─────────────────────────────────┘        reports
     : : :                                                    must be
     : : :                                                    on an
     : : :                                                    RD
     : : :
RD   SUMMARY-REPORT ◄──────────────────────────────────────────┘
```

Within the RD, there are several clauses that may be used to define how the report is to be formatted. We will cover each of these separately.

CONTROL Clause

The **CONTROL clause** defines the order of control breaks within the report. If your report is doing any control breaks, the CONTROL clause is required. If you are printing only a final total at the end of the report, you do not need a CONTROL clause, though you can specify the CONTROL clause with just the FINAL option if you desire.

You can use the CONTROL clause to specify several (as many as necessary) different control breaks simply by listing the fields in the record that are controlling the breaks. For example, a typical CONTROL clause might look like

```
CONTROLS ARE FINAL CUSTOMER-CODE DATE-OF-LAST-PURCHASE
```

In this case, the report would print final totals with the major control break on the CUSTOMER-CODE and the minor break on the DATE-OF-LAST-PURCHASE. If there were more fields on the clause, the levels of the breaks would be successively less as the fields were read from left to right.

The program will handle the control breaks just as if we were creating the routines ourselves. It will print the control totals when the values in the indicated fields change.

PAGE Clause

The **PAGE clause** defines the size and format of the printed page. The integer on the clause defines the length of the page. The following clauses are related to the use of the PAGE clause.

The **HEADING clause** defines the line on which the page heading is to be printed. Subsequent headings, such as any additional lines of the page heading and any column headings, are defined in reference to this heading line.

The **FIRST DETAIL clause** defines the first line where a detail line may be printed. This line number needs to be defined far enough down the page to allow room for the program to print all the headings.

The **LAST DETAIL clause** defines the last line where a detail line may be printed. If your report is to have page totals, the LAST DETAIL line will need to leave sufficient room to print them.

The page totals just mentioned are controlled with the **FOOTING clause**, which dictates the report line on which the footing can be printed. If your footing consists of more than one line, the FOOTING clause must be far enough from the physical bottom of the page to leave room for all the footing lines.

A simple example of how the PAGE clause might be used is

```
PAGE LIMIT        60
HEADING            3
FIRST DETAIL       8
LAST DETAIL       50
FOOTING           54.
```

This indicates that a maximum of 60 lines will be printed before a page break is automatically taken. The first heading line is printed on line 3 and the first detail is printed on line 8. That means that there can be five lines of headings and blank lines (lines 3, 4, 5, 6, and 7). The last detail line is printed on line 50, which will cause three blank lines to be left between it and the footing (lines 51, 52, and 53). Since the footing is printed on line 54, there can be seven lines of footing before the page limit of 60 is reached.

When the PAGE clause is used, COBOL automatically sets up, with reserved words, the two counters normally used to control reports: LINE-COUNTER and PAGE-COUNTER. The PAGE-COUNTER begins with a value of 1 and is incremented by 1 every time a page break is taken. It is an unsigned integer and can have a value as large as 999,999. The size of the field is actually specified in the program when the counter is used in your heading (we will look at this a bit later). Although the value of the PAGE-COUNTER is normally controlled by the program, it can be changed by a PROCEDURE DIVISION statement if necessary.

The LINE-COUNTER is used to determine when page breaks are to be taken and when the lines for the various headings, detail lines, and footings are to be printed. Its initial value is zero and it is reinitialized upon each page break. The Report Writer increments the LINE-COUNTER as dictated by the program. The size of the field and the rules for its use are the same as those for the PAGE-COUNTER.

As we have mentioned, many different types of lines are used for the typical report. A **report group** is the definition of one of these lines. Within an RD there may be many report groups, though only one is required. These report groups are defined on 01 levels (beginning in Area A) but, unlike the 01 levels for an FD, the record-name is optional on a report group. Instead, you specify the TYPE of print group you are defining. The form of a TYPE clause is

```
01  [identifier] TYPE IS
        { REPORT HEADING }
        { RH             }
        { PAGE HEADING }
        { PH           }
        { CONTROL HEADING }  { field-name-1 ...           }
        { CH              }  { FINAL                      }
                             { FINAL field-name-1 ...     }
        { DETAIL }
        { DE     }
        { CONTROL FOOTING }  { field-name-2 ...           }
        { CE              }  { FINAL                      }
                             { FINAL field-name-2 ...     }
        { PAGE FOOTING }
        { PF           }
        { REPORT FOOTING }
        { RF             }
```

Each of these TYPE clauses has special meaning to the program:

■ The **REPORT HEADING clause** specifies a heading that will be printed only once at the top of the first page of the report. If desired, it can be the only thing printed on the first page (a page feed can occur after the report heading is printed). The page heading is printed after the report heading. The REPORT HEADING clause is optional. If it is used, the PAGE LIMIT and the FIRST DETAIL clauses (of the RD) are required.

■ The **PAGE HEADING clause** causes a page heading to be printed at the top of each page of the report. The heading will be printed on the first page of the report after the report heading, if one is used, unless the REPORT HEADING is printed alone. You can print the page number on the page heading by using the automatically defined PAGE-COUNTER. If the page heading is printed on the first page of the report, the page number will be 1; if the report heading is printed by itself on the first page, the page number will be 2 on the first page heading.

- If your report is a control break report, the **CONTROL HEADING clause** can be used to print a heading in front of each control group. The field being used to control the break must be specified on the clause. If the optional FINAL clause is added, this special CONTROL HEADING is printed only once, at the end of the report, and the PAGE LIMIT clause is required.

- The **PAGE FOOTING clause** is used to print a footing at the bottom of each page of the report (except those that have separate report headings or footings). The PAGE LIMIT, LAST DETAIL, and FOOTING clauses are required.

- The **CONTROL FOOTING clause** is used to specify the information to be printed when a control break occurs. The field for the control break must be specified as part of the clause. When more than one control footing is used, minor footings are automatically generated as major ones are printed. When FINAL is added, the footing is printed only once, after the last control break. The PAGE LIMIT clause is the only one required.

- The **REPORT FOOTING clause** will print the summary lines only once, at the end of the report. The report footing can be printed on a page by itself. If it is, only the PAGE LIMIT clause is required; otherwise the clauses PAGE LIMIT, LAST DETAIL, and FOOTING are all required.

- The **DETAIL clause** is the only one of the clauses that is always under direct programmer control. As such, it must be preceded by an identifier so it can be referenced in the PROCEDURE DIVISION. Generating of the detail line is left to the programmer because it is sometimes necessary to have several different types of detail lines in one report. If the program were to automatically generate them, they might not appear in the proper sequence. When you use a DETAIL clause, the PAGE LIMIT clause is required.

A few examples of how the TYPE clause is used:

```
RD  TYPE IS PAGE HEADING.
RD  TYPE IS CONTROL HEADING CUSTOMER-CODE.
RD  TYPE IS CONTROL FOOTING FINAL CUSTOMER-CODE.
```

In addition to the TYPE on the report group, we can also designate the line that the particular group is to be printed on and, if it is a control group, the spacing to be done before the next group. The **LINE NUMBER clause**, which looks like

$$\left[\underline{\text{LINE}} \text{ NUMBER IS} \begin{Bmatrix} \text{integer-1 [ON } \underline{\text{NEXT}} \text{ PAGE]} \\ \underline{\text{PLUS}} \text{ integer-2} \end{Bmatrix} \right]$$

can be used to designate the specific line to be printed on by using integer-1, as in

```
LINE NUMBER IS 5.
```

It can also be used to skip to the top of the next page before printing with

```
LINE NUMBER IS 4 ON NEXT PAGE.
```

This is how a report footing is printed on a page by itself. The LINE clause can also skip lines by using the PLUS option:

```
LINE NUMBER PLUS 2.
```

The other clause is the NEXT GROUP

$$
\left[\ \underline{\text{NEXT}}\ \underline{\text{GROUP}}\ \text{IS} \left\{ \begin{array}{l} \text{integer-3} \\ \underline{\text{PLUS}}\ \text{integer-4} \\ \underline{\text{NEXT}}\ \underline{\text{PAGE}} \end{array} \right\} \right]
$$

which allows you to designate the spacing between one group and the next. You can arrange for the next group to be printed on the next page with the statement

```
NEXT GROUP IS NEXT PAGE.
```

which is the way to get a report heading to be printed alone on a page. The statement causes the next group, the page heading, to be printed on the next (second) page.

You can designate a specific line with

```
NEXT GROUP IS 5.
```

Finally, you can skip lines by using the PLUS option:

```
NEXT GROUP IS PLUS 6.
```

Report Description Entries

After we designate the report type, we still have to specify the actual report entries and the columns that everything is to appear in. The report description is listed on a lesser level number of 02 to 49 and can also show the line number if it wasn't given with the TYPE clause.

First, we need to discuss the COLUMN **clause** which designates the horizontal printing position of the left-most character of the field. Since we are describing the actual positioning of an item, the COLUMN clause is only valid on an elementary item. The form of the clause is

```
[COLUMN NUMBER IS integer]
```

This clause is used in conjunction with the PIC and VALUE (if there is one) clauses. For example,

```
COLUMN NUMBER IS 36      PIC X(16)
VALUE IS 'INVENTORY REPORT'.
```

would make INVENTORY REPORT begin printing in column 36.

When part of the detail line being printed needs to be printed only upon its first use within a group, the GROUP INDICATE **clause** can be used. For example, suppose we are printing a control report and want the control field to print only on the first line of the group:

```
CUST.           PAYMENT          PAYMENT
CODE            AMOUNT           DATE

01              156.75           12/15/88
                235.66           01/18/88
                122.93           03/17/88

02              156.76           11/15/88
                344.00           10/01/88
```

The GROUP INDICATE clause is simply added to the detail item description as such:

```
10   COLUMN NUMBER IS 6          PIC XX GROUP INDICATE
```

It's important to remember that the GROUP INDICATE clause is used only on detail line items.

Another clause used on detail line items, the SOURCE **clause**, indicates the field that the data being printed is coming from. Basically, it moves the data from a field outside the report description to the field being printed. We can finish the previous example by tacking on the SOURCE clause:

```
10   COLUMN NUMBER IS 6          PIC XX GROUP INDICATE
     SOURCE IS CUSTOMER-CODE.
```

The same clause (SOURCE IS) is needed when we print the PAGE-COUNTER in the page heading. The entire record description for the page heading might be

```
01   TYPE IS PAGE HEADING
     LINE NUMBER IS 1.
     10   COLUMN NUMBER IS 10        PIC X(5)  VALUE
          'PAGE '.
     10   COLUMN NUMBER IS 15        PIC Z9
          SOURCE IS PAGE-COUNTER.
     10   COLUMN NUMBER IS 60        PIC X(20) VALUE
          'CONTROL BREAK REPORT'.
```

We used the PAGE-COUNTER as the source for the second item printed. Notice that each successive field is simply listed with another similar level number. This is true anytime there is more than one field, just like with elementary items within a group item.

In order to print control totals, the program must know which fields we want totaled. We can indicate them with the SUM **clause**, a clause that is slightly more complicated than the last few we have looked at. Its form contains several pieces:

$$\left\{ \underline{\text{SUM}} \text{ IS field-name-1 [field-name-2]} \ldots \text{[}\underline{\text{UPON}}\text{ field-name-3]} \atop \left[\underline{\text{RESET}}\text{ ON } \left\{ \underline{\text{FINAL}} \atop \text{field-name-4} \right\} \right] \right\}$$

This clause is also attached to the end of the field description and is used only on control groups because they print the totals. Since it can be used in a variety of ways, we will examine each way separately.

■ It can be used as a straight sum, as in

```
01   TYPE IS CONTROL FOOTING
     LINE NUMBER PLUS 2.
     10   COLUMN NUMBER IS 50          PIC ZZ,ZZ9.99
          SUM PAY-AMOUNT.
```

In this example, the report group is a control footing and the field being summed is the PAY-AMOUNT. The PAY-AMOUNT field must, of course, have been defined previously, in either the detail line or a more minor control footing.

■ The SUM clause can be used to create a **crossfoot**, which is a horizontal total of several column totals. For example, suppose our report has several columns of numbers:

CUST. CODE	MAY CHARGES	JUNE CHARGES	JULY CHARGES	TOTAL CHARGES
01	155.65	122.60	134.56	412.81
02	1,234.87	34.50	12.54	1,281.91
TOTALS	1,390.52	157.10	147.10	1,694.72

The SUM clause can by used only on control groups, so the total charges on the detail lines will have to be calculated by the program in the PROCEDURE DIVISION. The total charges on the totals line, however, can be crossfooted with the SUM clause, as in

```
01   TYPE IS CONTROL FOOTING
     LINE NUMBER PLUS 2.
     10   COLUMN NUMBER IS 6            PIC X(6) VALUE
          'TOTALS'.
     10   MAY-SUM COLUMN NUMBER IS 18   PIC ZZ,ZZ9.99
          SUM MAY-AMOUNT.
     10   JUNE-SUM COLUMN NUMBER IS 28  PIC ZZ,ZZ9.99
          SUM JUNE-AMOUNT.
     10   JULY-SUM COLUMN NUMBER IS 38  PIC ZZ,ZZ9.99
          SUM JULY-AMOUNT.
     10   COLUMN NUMBER IS 49           PIC ZZZ,ZZ9.99
          SUM MAY-SUM JUNE-SUM JULY-SUM.
```

The column totals work the same as before, by totaling on one field. The crossfoot, on the other hand, totals all three of the column totals.

■ The UPON **clause** can cause the SUM to be accumulated when a certain detail group is printed, whether the group is related to the field being summed or not.

■ The summed field will automatically be reset to zero whenever the group total is printed. If, however, the field needs to be reset at a different time, the RESET **clause** can be used. The field can then be reset upon FINAL or upon the change of a different control field.

■ When we are creating a multi-level control break report, we need to have the minor subtotals totaled into intermediate ones and those into the major one. This is called **rolling forward totals**, and it can be handled easily with the SUM clause. Suppose our report is going to be printed so that there are daily, weekly, monthly, and quarterly totals. We would create the control footings like the following:

```
01   TYPE IS DETAIL LINE
     LINE NUMBER PLUS 1.
     10   COLUMN NUMBER IS 40                    PIC Z,ZZ9.99
          SOURCE IS DAILY-AMOUNT.

01   TYPE IS CONTROL FOOTING
     LINE NUMBER PLUS 2.
     10   DAILY-TOTAL COLUMN NUMBER IS 40        PIC ZZ,ZZ9.99
          SUM DAILY-AMOUNT.

01   TYPE IS CONTROL FOOTING
     LINE NUMBER PLUS 2.
     10   WEEKLY-TOTAL COLUMN NUMBER IS 40       PIC ZZZ,ZZ9.99
          SUM DAILY-TOTAL.

01   TYPE IS CONTROL FOOTING
     LINE NUMBER PLUS 2.
     10   MONTHLY-TOTAL COLUMN NUMBER IS 40      PIC ZZZ,ZZ9.99
          SUM WEEKLY-TOTAL.

01   TYPE IS CONTROL FOOTING
     LINE NUMBER PLUS 2.
     10   QUARTERLY-TOTAL COLUMN NUMBER IS 40    PIC ZZZ,ZZ9.99
          SUM MONTHLY-TOTAL.
```

Notice how the fields are used in subsequent totals: The daily total is used to calculate the weekly total and the weekly total is used to calculate the monthly total. Remember that all the calculations are going to be handled by the program without any commands in the PROCEDURE DIVISION. It is all set up with the SUM clauses.

10-3

The PROCEDURE DIVISION

Report processing in the PROCEDURE DIVISION is greatly simplified. We still open, read, and close the files, but most of the rest of the processing is handled automatically by the Report Writer. We do, however, need three new statements.

10-3-1   INITIATE Statement

The first special statement for the Report Writer is the INITIATE **statement**, which signals the beginning of the report processing. The form of the statement is simple:

<u>INITIATE</u> report-name [report-name] . . .

To use the statement, you use the name of the report that was defined on the RD and listed in the FD REPORT IS clause. When the statement is executed, all the SUM entries, the LINE-COUNTER, and the PAGE-COUNTER are initialized. The statement does not, however, open the files being used in the program. The program still must have an OPEN statement. You cannot use a second INITIATE statement until the first one has been terminated (see TERMINATE statement), but you can initiate multiple reports with one INITIATE statement.

10-3-2   GENERATE Statement

The GENERATE **statement**, which controls the printing of the report, has the form

$$\underline{\text{GENERATE}} \; \begin{Bmatrix} \text{detail-report-group-name} \\ \text{report-name} \end{Bmatrix}$$

Notice that there are two different ways the statement can be used. If the detail-report-group-name is used, a detail report is printed. If the report-name is used, the detail lines are not printed and a summary report is generated instead.

As the program executes, the first time the GENERATE statement is executed, all the headings—report, page, column, and control (or whichever ones are specified for the report)—are generated (along with the detail line if it is a detail report). Subsequent executions of the GENERATE statement will produce appropriate detail lines, control totals, and page breaks, increment the LINE-COUNTER and SUM operands, and reset SUM operands as specified.

10-3-3   TERMINATE Statement

When the program has read all the records in the file, the report must be finished with a TERMINATE **statement**, which will cause all the SUM operands to be totaled and all the control, FINAL, page, and report footings to be printed. Once a report has been terminated, another TERMINATE statement for the same report may not be used unless a second INITIATE statement, for that same report, has been used since the previous TERMINATE statement. Just as the INITIATE statement does not open any files, the TERMINATE statement does not close any files. You still must close your files with the CLOSE statement.

══════ 10-4 ══════════════════
A Sample Program

In order to demonstrate the use of the Report Writer features we have been discussing, we will create a sample program. We will begin with just a straight report that has no subtotals and will then make the report more complex (with control breaks) without overly complicating the program.

We need a file with which to generate control breaks. We will use a file of construction company information with the layout shown in Figure 10-1. The data for the file follows:

Reg.	Sect.	Proj. Number	Projerct Type	Budget Amount	Actual Amount
01	01	08187	BUILDING	010106812	002021884
01	01	07476	SHOPPING CENTER	021102719	001042552
01	03	25209	RR TERMINAL	002009638	030007425
01	03	11404	WAREHOUSE	020048446	020100164
03	01	06829	PRIVATE HOME	003008055	020040316
03	01	18107	PRIVATE HOME	021001949	002048776
03	01	17079	OFFICE BUILDING	020146212	011033892
03	04	31107	BUILDING DEMOL.	032000955	002144485
03	04	28193	HEATING PLANT	042108805	021144132
03	06	00048	TENNIS COURT	010036096	040010918
07	01	00359	PRIVATE HOME	030046438	000010074
07	01	03039	SHOPPING CENTER	001020570	001107836
07	04	13156	OFFICE BUILDING	000230931	000215395
10	03	00400	PRIVATE HOME	000210302	000046242
10	03	11774	STORE RENOV.	020047788	000115553
10	07	37331	SHOPPING CENTER	040143578	032007416
10	07	01269	PRIVATE HOME	040002583	002033024

The file is sorted into order by section within region. Using this file, we want to produce the report shown in Figure 10-2. As we mentioned earlier, this is going to be only a straight report. For the moment, we will ignore the control break lines shown in the report layout.

Since the SELECT clauses are the same for a Report Writer program as they are for a normal report program, we will begin with the DATA DIVISION. In the

CONSTCO File					
Field Description	*Position*	*Length*	:	*Dec*	*Type*
Region	1–2	2	:	0	Numeric
Section	3–4	2	:	0	Numeric
Project number	5–9	5	:		Non-numeric
Type of project	10–24	15	:		Non-numeric
Budget amount	25–33	9	:	0	Numeric
Actual amount	34–42	9	:	0	Numeric
Filler	43–80	38	:		Non-numeric
Record Length = 80					

Figure 10-1   The file layout for the CONSTCO file.

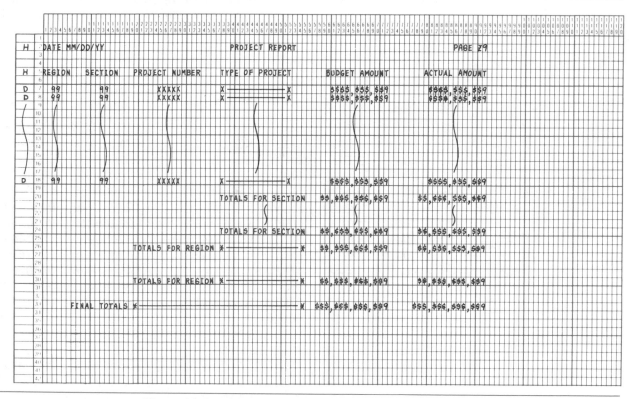

Figure 10-2   The report layout for the sample program.

FILE SECTION we will define the two files we need—the input file and the print file—beginning as follows:

```
DATA DIVISION.
FILE SECTION.

FD   CONSTRUCTION-FILE
     LABEL RECORDS ARE OMITTED
     RECORD CONTAINS 80 CHARACTERS.
01   CONST-RECORD.
     10   REGION-IN               PIC 99.
     10   SECTION-IN              PIC 99.
     10   PROJECT-IN              PIC X(5).
     10   TYPE-IN                 PIC X(15).
     10   BUDGET-IN               PIC 9(9).
     10   ACTUAL-IN               PIC 9(9).
     10   FILLER                  PIC X(38).

FD   PRINT-FILE
     LABEL RECORDS ARE OMITTED
     RECORD CONTAINS 133 CHARACTERS
     REPORT IS CONTROL-BREAK.
```

The CONSTRUCTION-FILE is defined in the usual fashion. The PRINT-FILE is defined for the Report Writer since it uses the REPORT IS clause and no record definition. These two entries are all that are necessary in the FILE SECTION.

The WORKING-STORAGE SECTION is very simple:

```
WORKING-STORAGE SECTION.

01   WORK-AREAS.
     05   EOF                          PIC XXX VALUE 'NO '.

     05   DATE-IN                 PIC X(6).
     05   DATE-WORK REDEFINES DATE-IN.
          10   DATE-YY            PIC XX.
          10   DATE-MM            PIC XX.
          10   DATE-DD            PIC XX.

     05   HEADING-DATE.
          10   HEADING-MONTH      PIC XX.
          10   HEADING-DAY        PIC /XX/.
          10   HEADING-YEAR       PIX XX.
```

As we discussed previously, all we need in this section is the end-of-file marker and the date areas.

The REPORT SECTION is where most of the program is to be found. It begins with the report definition:

```
REPORT SECTION.

RD   CONTROL-BREAK
     CONTROL IS FINAL
     PAGE LIMIT IS 55 LINES
     HEADING         1
     FIRST DETAIL    4
     LAST DETAIL     50
     FOOTING         53.
```

The name of the report is CONTROL-BREAK, which was first used on the FD. The first report group will be the page heading:

```
01   TYPE IS PAGE HEADING.
     05   LINE NUMBER IS 1.
          10   COLUMN NUMBER 1              PIC X(4)  VALUE
               'DATE'.
          10   COLUMN NUMBER 6              PIC X(8)
               SOURCE HEADING-DATE.
          10   COLUMN NUMBER 40             PIC X(14) VALUE
               'PROJECT REPORT'.
          10   COLUMN NUMBER 86             PIC X(4)  VALUE
               'PAGE'.
          10   COLUMN NUMBER 91             PIC Z9
               SOURCE PAGE-COUNTER.
     05   LINE NUMBER PLUS 3.
          10   COLUMN NUMBER 1              PIC X(33) VALUE
               'REGION    SECTION    PROJECT NUMBER'.
          10   COLUMN NUMBER 38             PIC X(35) VALUE
               'TYPE OF PROJECT      BUDGET AMOUNT'.
          10   COLUMN NUMBER 80             PIC X(13) VALUE
               'ACTUAL AMOUNT'.
```

Notice that we want the first heading to print on line 1 and that we used the PAGE-COUNTER. The next heading within the same group is defined by using another group with the same level number. This group is, of course, the column headings.

Next we need the detail line:

```
01  DETAIL-LINE TYPE IS DETAIL.
    05  LINE NUMBER PLUS 1.
        10  COLUMN NUMBER 3            PIC 99
            SOURCE REGION-IN.
        10  COLUMN NUMBER 13           PIC 99
            SOURCE SECTION-IN.
        10  COLUMN NUMBER 25           PIC X(5)
            SOURCE PROJECT-IN.
        10  COLUMN NUMBER 38           PIC X(15)
            SOURCE TYPE-IN.
        10  COLUMN NUMBER 61           PIC $$$$,$$$,$$9
            SOURCE BUDGET-IN.
        10  COLUMN NUMBER 80           PIC $$$$,$$$,$$9
            SOURCE ACTUAL-IN.
```

We give this group a group-name (DETAIL-LINE) so that it can be referenced in the GENERATE statement. All of the entries list the source field where the data is to be printed from.

Now all that we have left is the group for the final totals:

```
01  TYPE IS CONTROL FOOTING FINAL.
    05  LINE NUMBER PLUS 3.
        10  COLUMN NUMBER IS 7         PIC X(12) VALUE
            'FINAL TOTALS'.
        10  COLUMN NUMBER IS 20        PIC X(36) VALUE
            ALL '*'.
        10  COLUMN NUMBER IS 58        PIC $$$,$$$,$$$,$$9
            SUM BUDGET-IN.
        10  COLUMN NUMBER IS 78        PIC $$$,$$$,$$$,$$9
            SUM ACTUAL-IN.
```

Here we have spaced 3 lines down from the last detail line printed and have summed on the two amount fields.

Now we need to create the PROCEDURE DIVISION. Basically, we will have a standard processing loop, except that we don't have to worry about totaling the amount fields. The division begins as usual:

```
PROCEDURE DIVISION.

0100-MAIN-MODULE.

    OPEN INPUT  CONSTRUCTION-FILE
         OUTPUT PRINT-FILE.

        ACCEPT DATE-IN FROM DATE.
        MOVE DATE-YY TO HEADING-YEAR.
        MOVE DATE-MM TO HEADING-MONTH.
        MOVE DATE-DD TO HEADING-DAY.
```

Then we initiate the Report Writer:

```
INITIATE CONTROL-BREAK.
```

Now the normal file processing begins:

```
READ CONSTRUCTION-FILE AT END MOVE 'YES' TO EOF.
PERFORM 0200-PRINT-LOOP UNTIL EOF = 'YES'.
```

After the loop, we terminate the report and close the files:

```
TERMINATE CONTROL-BREAK.

CLOSE CONSTRUCTION-FILE
      PRINT-FILE.
STOP RUN.
```

In the 0200-PRINT-LOOP, we generate the report and then read another record as we would in a standard report loop:

```
0200-PRINT-LOOP.

    GENERATE DETAIL-LINE.
    READ CONSTRUCTION-FILE AT END MOVE 'YES' TO EOF.
```

Notice that we GENERATE the DETAIL-LINE, which will give us a detail report. The program, all put together, is as follows:

```
********************************************************************
********************************************************************
*
*
*
*   PROGRAM NAME: CONTBRK
*
*   PROGRAMMER NAME:  ED COBURN
*
*   SOCIAL SECURITY NUMBER:  999-99-9999
*
*   DUE DATE: FEBRUARY 10, 1988
*
*   DESCRIPTION: THIS PROGRAM WILL PRINT A CONTROL BREAK
*                REPORT USING THE REPORT WRITER FEATURE.
*
*
*
********************************************************************
********************************************************************

IDENTIFICATION DIVISION.
PROGRAM-ID.    CONTBRK.
AUTHOR.        ED COBURN.

ENVIRONMENT DIVISION.
```

```
      CONFIGURATION SECTION.
      SOURCE-COMPUTER. IBM-4331.
      OBJECT-COMPUTER. IBM-4331.

      INPUT-OUTPUT SECTION.
      FILE-CONTROL.
          SELECT CONSTRUCTION-FILE ASSIGN TO UT-S-CONSTCO.
          SELECT PRINT-FILE        ASSIGN TO UT-S-SYSPRINT.

      DATA DIVISION.
      FILE SECTION.

      FD  CONSTRUCTION-FILE
          LABEL RECORDS ARE OMITTED
          RECORD CONTAINS 80 CHARACTERS.
      01  CONST-RECORD.
          10  REGION-IN                   PIC 99.
          10  SECTION-IN                  PIC 99.
          10  PROJECT-IN                  PIC X(5).
          10  TYPE-IN                     PIC X(15).
          10  BUDGET-IN                   PIC 9(9).
          10  ACTUAL-IN                   PIC 9(9).
          10  FILLER                      PIC X(38).

      FD  PRINT-FILE
          LABEL RECORDS ARE OMITTED
          RECORD CONTAINS 133 CHARACTERS
          REPORT IS CONTROL-BREAK.


      WORKING-STORAGE SECTION.

      01  WORK-AREAS.
          05  EOF                         PIC XXX VALUE 'NO '.

          05  DATE-IN                     PIC X(6).
          05  DATE-WORK REDEFINES DATE-IN.
              10  DATE-YY                 PIC XX.
              10  DATE-MM                 PIC XX.
              10  DATE-DD                 PIC XX.

          05  HEADING-DATE.
              10  HEADING-MONTH           PIC XX.
              10  HEADING-DAY             PIC /XX/.
              10  HEADING-YEAR            PIC XX.

      REPORT SECTION.

      RD  CONTROL-BREAK
          CONTROL IS FINAL
          PAGE LIMIT IS 55 LINES
          HEADING        1
          FIRST DETAIL   4
          LAST DETAIL    50
          FOOTING        53.

      01  TYPE IS PAGE HEADING.
          05  LINE NUMBER IS 1.
              10  COLUMN NUMBER 1         PIC X(4)   VALUE
                  'DATE'.
```

```
        10      COLUMN NUMBER 6              PIC X(8)
                SOURCE HEADING-DATE.
        10      COLUMN NUMBER 40             PIC X(14) VALUE
                'PROJECT REPORT'.
        10      COLUMN NUMBER 86             PIC X(4)   VALUE
                'PAGE'.
        10      COLUMN NUMBER 91             PIC Z9
                SOURCE PAGE-COUNTER.
    05  LINE NUMBER PLUS 3.
        10      COLUMN NUMBER 1              PIC X(33) VALUE
                'REGION    SECTION    PROJECT NUMBER'.
        10      COLUMN NUMBER 38             PIC X(35) VALUE
                'TYPE OF PROJECT        BUDGET AMOUNT'.
        10      COLUMN NUMBER 80             PIC X(13) VALUE
                'ACTUAL AMOUNT'.

01  DETAIL-LINE TYPE IS DETAIL.
    05  LINE NUMBER PLUS 1.
        10      COLUMN NUMBER 3              PIC 99
                SOURCE REGION-IN.
        10      COLUMN NUMBER 13             PIC 99
                SOURCE SECTION-IN.
        10      COLUMN NUMBER 25             PIC X(5)
                SOURCE PROJECT-IN.
        10   COLUMN NUMBER 38                PIC X(15)
                SOURCE TYPE-IN.
        10      COLUMN NUMBER 61             PIC $$$$,$$$,$$9
                SOURCE BUDGET-IN.
        10      COLUMN NUMBER 80             PIC $$$$,$$$,$$9
                SOURCE ACTUAL-IN.

01  TYPE IS CONTROL FOOTING FINAL.
    05  LINE NUMBER PLUS 3.
        10      COLUMN NUMBER IS 7           PIC X(12) VALUE
                'FINAL TOTALS'.
        10      COLUMN NUMBER IS 20          PIC X(36) VALUE
                ALL '*'.
        10      COLUMN NUMBER IS 58          PIC $$$,$$$,$$$,$$9
                SUM BUDGET-IN.
        10      COLUMN NUMBER IS 78          PIC $$$,$$$,$$$,$$9
                SUM ACTUAL-IN.


PROCEDURE DIVISION.

0100-MAIN-MODULE.

    OPEN INPUT  CONSTRUCTION-FILE
         OUTPUT PRINT-FILE.

    ACCEPT DATE-IN FROM DATE.
    MOVE DATE-YY TO HEADING-YEAR.
    MOVE DATE-MM TO HEADING-MONTH.
    MOVE DATE-DD TO HEADING-DAY.

    INITIATE CONTROL-BREAK.

    READ CONSTRUCTION-FILE AT END MOVE 'YES' TO EOF.
    PERFORM 0200-PRINT-LOOP UNTIL EOF = 'YES'.
```

```
            TERMINATE CONTROL-BREAK.

            CLOSE CONSTRUCTION-FILE
                  PRINT-FILE.
            STOP RUN.


         0200-PRINT-LOOP.

            GENERATE DETAIL-LINE.
            READ CONSTRUCTION-FILE AT END MOVE 'YES' TO EOF.
```

The true test of any program is, of course, seeing if it works. When we execute this program, we get the following report:

```
DATE 04/15/87                          PROJECT REPORT


REGION     SECTION    PROJECT NUMBER    TYPE OF PROJECT       BUDGET AMOUNT

  01         01          08187         BUILDING              $10,106,812
  01         01          07476         SHOPPING CENTER       $21,102,719
  01         02          07251         OFFICE BUILDING       $22,025,699
  01         03          25209         RR TERMINAL            $2,009,638
  01         03          11404         WAREHOUSE             $20,048,446
  01         03          06875         PRIVATE HOME          $20,024,679
  03         01          06829         PRIVATE HOME           $3,008,055
  03         01          18107         PRIVATE HOME          $21,001,949
  03         01          17079         OFFICE BUILDING       $20,146,212
  03         02          25056         STORE RENOV.           $1,137,046
  03         04          31107         BUILDING DEMOL.       $32,000,955
  03         04          32992         SHOPPING CENTER       $40,200,981
  03         04          28193         HEATING PLANT         $42,108,805
  03         06          22544         GOLF COURSE               $39,631
  03         06          00048         TENNIS COURT          $10,036,096
  07         01          00359         PRIVATE HOME          $30,046,438
  07         01          08652         PRIVATE HOME          $20,030,881
  07         01          03039         SHOPPING CENTER        $1,020,570
  07         01          36130         OFFICE BUILDING        $2,121,281
  07         04          13156         OFFICE BUILDING          $230,931
  09         02          10864         PRIVATE HOME             $344,355
  09         02          07237         SHOPPING CENTER           $10,065
  09         03          00612         OFFICE BUILDING           $44,469
  09         03          15765         PRIVATE HOME          $21,325,449
  10         03          00400         PRIVATE HOME             $210,302
  10         03          11774         STORE RENOV.          $20,047,788
  10         05          00865         OFFICE BUILDING       $20,004,148
  10         05          00532         PRIVATE HOME          $32,108,904
  10         07          37331         SHOPPING CENTER       $40,143,578
  10         08          01269         PRIVATE HOME          $40,002,583


FINAL TOTALS  *************************************    $492,689,465
```

10-4-1 Using a Control Break in the Program

Now we want to change the report so it does a control break on the region field. To do so, we add a control footing on the region:

```
01   TYPE IS CONTROL FOOTING REGION-IN.
     05  LINE NUMBER PLUS 2.
         10  COLUMN NUMBER 20                   PIC X(36) VALUE
             'TOTALS FOR REGION ******************'.
         10  REGION-BUDGET COLUMN NUMBER 59   PIC $$,$$$,$$$,$$9
             SUM BUDGET-IN.
         10  REGION-ACTUAL COLUMN NUMBER 79   PIC $$,$$$,$$$,$$9
             SUM ACTUAL-IN.
```

Notice that we sum the budget and actual amounts to get the totals on the control footing.

Next we change the SUM clauses for the final total fields. The group is currently specified as

```
01   TYPE IS CONTROL FOOTING FINAL.
     05  LINE NUMBER PLUS 2.
         10  COLUMN NUMBER IS 7           PIC X(12) VALUE
             'FINAL TOTALS'.
         10  COLUMN NUMBER IS 20          PIC X(36) VALUE
             ALL '*'.
         10  COLUMN NUMBER IS 58          PIC $$$,$$$,$$$,$$9
             SUM BUDGET-IN.
         10  COLUMN NUMBER IS 78          PIC $$$,$$$,$$$,$$9
             SUM ACTUAL-IN.
```

Now, however, the SUM clauses should be summing on the region totals of REGION-BUDGET and REGION-ACTUAL. Thus, we change the group to

```
01   TYPE IS CONTROL FOOTING FINAL.
     05  LINE NUMBER PLUS 2.
         10  COLUMN NUMBER IS 7           PIC X(12) VALUE
             'FINAL TOTALS'.
         10  COLUMN NUMBER IS 20          PIC X(36) VALUE
             ALL '*'.
         10  COLUMN NUMBER IS 58          PIC $$$,$$$,$$$,$$9
             SUM REGION-BUDGET.
         10  COLUMN NUMBER IS 78          PIC $$$,$$$,$$$,$$9
             SUM REGION-ACTUAL.
```

Finally we change the RD CONTROL specifications. The RD is currently

```
RD   CONTROL-BREAK
     CONTROL IS FINAL
     PAGE LIMIT IS 55 LINES
     HEADING        1
     FIRST DETAIL   4
     LAST DETAIL    50
     FOOTING        53.
```

What we need to do is change the CONTROL IS statement so it reads

```
CONTROLS ARE FINAL REGION-IN
```

This informs the program that there are two controls, one for the final totals and one for the control break on the region.

The rest of the program would be unchanged. We will not relist the program, but we will examine the output. After we execute the new program, the output will look like the following:

DATE 04/15/87   PROJECT REPORT

REGION	SECTION	PROJECT NUMBER	TYPE OF PROJECT	BUDGET AMOUNT
01	01	08187	BUILDING	$10,106,812
01	01	07476	SHOPPING CENTER	$21,102,719
01	02	07251	OFFICE BUILDING	$22,025,699
01	03	25209	RR TERMINAL	$2,009,638
01	03	11404	WAREHOUSE	$20,048,446
01	03	06875	PRIVATE HOME	$20,024,679
		TOTALS FOR REGION	*****************	$95,317,993
03	01	06829	PRIVATE HOME	$3,008,055
03	01	18107	PRIVATE HOME	$21,001,949
03	01	17079	OFFICE BUILDING	$20,146,212
03	02	25056	STORE RENOV.	$1,137,046
03	04	31107	BUILDING DEMOL.	$32,000,955
03	04	32992	SHOPPING CENTER	$40,200,981
03	04	28193	HEATING PLANT	$42,108,805
03	06	22544	GOLF COURSE	$39,631
03	06	00048	TENNIS COURT	$10,036,096
		TOTALS FOR REGION	*****************	$169,679,730
07	01	00359	PRIVATE HOME	$30,046,438
07	01	08652	PRIVATE HOME	$20,030,881
07	01	03039	SHOPPING CENTER	$1,020,570
07	01	36130	OFFICE BUILDING	$2,121,281
07	04	13156	OFFICE BUILDING	$230,931
		TOTALS FOR REGION	*****************	$53,450,101
09	02	10864	PRIVATE HOME	$344,355
09	02	07237	SHOPPING CENTER	$10,065
09	03	00612	OFFICE BUILDING	$44,469
09	03	15765	PRIVATE HOME	$21,325,449
		TOTALS FOR REGION	*****************	$21,724,338
10	03	00400	PRIVATE HOME	$210,302
10	03	11774	STORE RENOV.	$20,047,788
10	05	00865	OFFICE BUILDING	$20,004,148
10	05	00532	PRIVATE HOME	$32,108,904
10	07	37331	SHOPPING CENTER	$40,143,578
10	08	01269	PRIVATE HOME	$40,002,583
		TOTALS FOR REGION	*****************	$152,517,303

FINAL TOTALS *********************************** $492,689,465

10-4-2   Doing a Second Control Break

We mentioned that we would ultimately end up with a program that would break on two fields, the region and the section. This second break is no more difficult to insert than the changes we just made. Once again, we begin with a new control break footing:

```
01   TYPE IS CONTROL FOOTING SECTION-IN.
     05   LINE NUMBER PLUS 2.
          10   COLUMN NUMBER 38              PIC X(18) VALUE
               'TOTALS FOR SECTION'.
          10   SECTION-BUDGET COLUMN NUMBER 59   PIC $$,$$$,$$$,$$9
               SUM BUDGET-IN.
          10   SECTION-ACTUAL COLUMN NUMBER 79   PIC $$,$$$,$$$,$$9
               SUM ACTUAL-IN.
```

Since we now sum the budget and actual amounts here, we need to change the region control footing to use the totals generated in this section footing. The footing was

```
01   TYPE IS CONTROL FOOTING REGION-IN.
     05   LINE NUMBER PLUS 2.
          10   COLUMN NUMBER 20              PIC X(36) VALUE
               'TOTALS FOR REGION *****************'.
          10   REGION-BUDGET COLUMN NUMBER 59   PIC $$,$$$,$$$,$$9
               SUM BUDGET-IN.
          10   REGION-ACTUAL COLUMN NUMBER 79   PIC $$,$$$,$$$,$$9
               SUM ACTUAL-IN.
```

We need to change the two sums so that the footing is

```
01   TYPE IS CONTROL FOOTING REGION-IN.
     05   LINE NUMBER PLUS 2.
          10   COLUMN NUMBER 20              PIC X(36) VALUE
               'TOTALS FOR REGION *****************'.
          10   REGION-BUDGET COLUMN NUMBER 59   PIC $$,$$$,$$$,$$9
               SUM SECTION-BUDGET.
          10   REGION-ACTUAL COLUMN NUMBER 79   PIC $$,$$$,$$$,$$9
               SUM SECTION-ACTUAL.
```

The final total fields don't need to be changed this time since they were already changed for the region totals. We do, however, need to change the RD CONTROL specification again. Remember that we changed the CONTROLS ARE clause to be

```
CONTROLS ARE FINAL REGION-IN
```

We need to add the minor control break on the end:

```
CONTROLS ARE FINAL REGION-IN SECTION-IN
```

This informs the program that there are now three controls.

We have one final change to make. We would like the region and section number to print in the detail line only upon the first occurrence. Remember, we can cause this by using the GROUP INDICATE clause on the detail line. The form of the detail group was

```
01   DETAIL-LINE TYPE IS DETAIL.
     05  LINE NUMBER PLUS 1.
          10  COLUMN NUMBER 3              PIC 99
              SOURCE REGION-IN.
          10  COLUMN NUMBER 13             PIC 99
              SOURCE SECTION-IN.
          10  COLUMN NUMBER 25             PIC X(5)
              SOURCE PROJECT-IN.
          10  COLUMN NUMBER 38             PIC X(15)
              SOURCE TYPE-IN.
          10  COLUMN NUMBER 61             PIC $$$$,$$$,$$9
              SOURCE BUDGET-IN.
          10  COLUMN NUMBER 80             PIC $$$$,$$$,$$9
              SOURCE ACTUAL-IN.
```

Now we add the GROUP INDICATE clause to the first two fields:

```
01  DETAIL-LINE TYPE IS DETAIL.

     05  LINE NUMBER PLUS 1.
          10  COLUMN NUMBER 3              PIC 99
              GROUP INDICATE SOURCE REGION-IN.
          10  COLUMN NUMBER 13             PIC 99
              GROUP INDICATE SOURCE SECTION-IN.
          10  COLUMN NUMBER 25             PIC X(5)
              SOURCE PROJECT-IN.
          10  COLUMN NUMBER 38             PIC X(15)
              SOURCE TYPE-IN.
          10  COLUMN NUMBER 61             PIC $$$$,$$$,$$9
              SOURCE BUDGET-IN.
          10  COLUMN NUMBER 80             PIC $$$$,$$$,$$9
              SOURCE ACTUAL-IN.
```

This final change will result in the following report:

```
DATE 04/15/87                          PROJECT REPORT


REGION     SECTION     PROJECT NUMBER     TYPE OF PROJECT         BUDGET AMOUNT

  01         01           08187           BUILDING                  $10,106,812
                          07476           SHOPPING CENTER           $21,102,719

                                          TOTALS FOR SECTION        $31,209,531

  01         02           07251           OFFICE BUILDING           $22,025,699

                                          TOTALS FOR SECTION        $22,025,699
```

01	03	25209	RR TERMINAL	$2,009,638
		11404	WAREHOUSE	$20,048,446
		06875	PRIVATE HOME	$20,024,679
			TOTALS FOR SECTION	$42,082,763
		TOTALS FOR REGION	******************	$95,317,993
03	01	06829	PRIVATE HOME	$3,008,055
		18107	PRIVATE HOME	$21,001,949
		17079	OFFICE BUILDING	$20,146,212
			TOTALS FOR SECTION	$44,156,216
03	02	25056	STORE RENOV.	$1,137,046
			TOTALS FOR SECTION	$1,137,046
03	04	31107	BUILDING DEMOL.	$32,000,955
		32992	SHOPPING CENTER	$40,200,981
		28193	HEATING PLANT	$42,108,805
			TOTALS FOR SECTION	$114,310,741
03	06	22544	GOLF COURSE	$39,631
		00048	TENNIS COURT	$10,036,096
			TOTALS FOR SECTION	$10,075,727
		TOTALS FOR REGION	******************	$169,679,730
07	01	00359	PRIVATE HOME	$30,046,438
		08652	PRIVATE HOME	$20,030,881
		03039	SHOPPING CENTER	$1,020,570
		36130	OFFICE BUILDING	$2,121,281
			TOTALS FOR SECTION	$53,219,170
07	04	13156	OFFICE BUILDING	$230,931
			TOTALS FOR SECTION	$230,931
		TOTALS FOR REGION	******************	$53,450,101
09	02	10864	PRIVATE HOME	$344,355
		07237	SHOPPING CENTER	$10,065
			TOTALS FOR SECTION	$354,420

DATE 04/15/87   PROJECT REPORT

REGION	SECTION	PROJECT NUMBER	TYPE OF PROJECT	BUDGET AMOUNT
09	03	00612	OFFICE BUILDING	$44,469
		15765	PRIVATE HOME	$21,325,449
			TOTALS FOR SECTION	$21,369,918
		TOTALS FOR REGION	******************	$21,724,338

```
10          03          00400       PRIVATE HOME               $210,302
                        11774       STORE RENOV.            $20,047,788

                                    TOTALS FOR SECTION      $20,258,090

10          05          00865       OFFICE BUILDING         $20,004,148
                        00532       PRIVATE HOME            $32,108,904

                                    TOTALS FOR SECTION      $52,113,052

10          07          37331       SHOPPING CENTER         $40,143,578

                                    TOTALS FOR SECTION      $40,143,578

10          08          01269       PRIVATE HOME            $40,002,583

                                    TOTALS FOR SECTION      $40,002,583

            TOTALS FOR REGION  *****************       $152,517,303


FINAL TOTALS  *********************************        $492,689,465
```

10-4-3   Changing to a Summary Report

We discussed earlier that we can change a detail report into a summary report by causing the GENERATE statement to use the report-name instead of the detail-report-group-name. Our GENERATE statement was

```
GENERATE DETAIL-LINE.
```

To make our detail report a summary report, all we have to do is change the statement to

```
GENERATE CONTROL-BREAK.
```

Or better yet, let's use DISPLAY and ACCEPT statements and let the user pick which type of report is needed. Right after the OPEN statement we will put the two statements

```
DISPLAY 'SUMMARY OR DETAIL REPORT (ENTER S OR D)?'.
ACCEPT REPORT-ANSWER.
```

Naturally, the REPORT-ANSWER field will need to be defined in the WORKING-STORAGE SECTION. With this response we can make an IF test for the GENERATE statement, giving the program two options:

```
IF REPORT-ANSWER = 'D'
    GENERATE DETAIL-LINE
ELSE
    GENERATE CONTROL-BREAK.
```

To be on the safe side, you would probably want to put your DISPLAY and ACCEPT statements into a loop to ensure that you got only a D or an S. Users wouldn't be happy if they pressed 'F' by accident and the program generated a summary report. Also, you might want to use different keys for the prompt since the 'S' and the 'D' are together on the keyboard. It would be very easy for the user to press the wrong key by accident.

10-5
Additional Report Writer Considerations

Now that we understand the basics of Report Writer, we need to look at a few more minor points. We will consider each of them separately.

10-5-1 Processing Conditionally

If we want to print only some of the records in the file, we can simply use an IF test on the GENERATE statement. Suppose, for example, we want our report to show only regions 8, 15, and 18. We simply create the conditional

```
IF REGION-IN = 8 OR 15 OR 18
    GENERATE DETAIL-LINE.
```

The conditional can be as simple or as complicated as any other conditional we might use.

10-5-2 DECLARATIVES

If we need to perform certain procedures based upon conditions happening automatically in the report program, we must specify these procedures as DE-CLARATIVES. Declarative procedures are coded together at the beginning of the PROCEDURE DIVISION. They must begin with the DECLARATIVES header and end with the END DECLARATIVES header. The declaratives themselves must be used within a section.

The particular type of process must be specified by a USE BEFORE REPORT-ING statement. The form of the statement is

USE BEFORE REPORTING group-name

The group-name dictates the group that the procedure is to effect, and it must be a control heading or footing.

After the USE BEFORE REPORTING sentence, there must be a paragraph to process the procedure. Within this paragraph we can use any valid COBOL statement except INITIATE, GENERATE, or TERMINATE. If we perform another section or paragraph, it must also be a declarative procedure. No nondeclarative procedure may be referenced by any declarative procedure. Nor can any declarative procedure be referenced in the nondeclarative portions of the PROCEDURE DIVISION.

A sample of the use of a declarative will help illustrate the procedures. Assume we have set up a control footing called REGIONAL-CONTROL-FOOTING and need to do some calculations on fields being printed in the footing. We would set up the declaratives as

```
PROCEDURE DIVISION.

DECLARATIVES.

0100-CONTROL-FOOTING SECTION.
    USE BEFORE REPORTING REGIONAL-CONTROL-FOOTING.

0200-CONTROL-FOOTING-PARAGRAPH.
    DIVIDE REGION-BUDGET BY REGION-ACTUAL GIVING REGION-VARIANCE.

END DECLARATIVES.
```

Now the division will be performed before the control footing is printed. Whenever the Report Writer is used, such calculations must be done as declaratives, not in the PROCEDURE DIVISION.

We discussed how to use an IF test to turn off the printing of a detail line. If for some reason we need to turn off the printing of a control heading or footing, however, we cannot do so with an IF test in the PROCEDURE DIVISION. We must do it as a declarative with the **SUPPRESS PRINTING statement**. Using the previous example to demonstrate the use of the SUPPRESS PRINTING statement, let's assume that we do not want the control footing to be printed if the variance is 1. That happens when the budgeted amounts and the actual amounts are the same. We would simply add another statement to the routine:

```
PROCEDURE DIVISION.

DECLARATIVES.

0100-CONTROL-FOOTING-SECTION.
    USE BEFORE REPORTING REGIONAL-CONTROL-FOOTING.

0200-CONTROL-FOOTING-PARAGRAPH.
    DIVIDE REGION-BUDGET BY REGION-ACTUAL GIVING REGION-VARIANCE.

    IF REGION-BUDGET = REGION-ACTUAL
        SUPPRESS PRINTING.

END DECLARATIVES.
```

Now, if the amounts match we will suppress the printing of the footing. We could have done the same thing with the IF test of

```
    IF REGION-VARIANCE = 1
        SUPPRESS PRINTING.
```

10-5-3 Combining Functions

We can do any other necessary procedures before we initiate the Report Writer. Suppose, for example, that we need to sort our file before we print the control break report. We can use a SORT statement before we INITIATE the Report Writer. The PROCEDURE DIVISION would look like the following:

```
PROCEDURE DIVISION.

    SORT SORT-FILE
        ON ASCENDING KEY SORT-REGION SORT-SECTION
        USING CONSTRUCTION-FILE
        GIVING OUTPUT-FILE.

    OPEN INPUT  OUTPUT-FILE
        OUTPUT PRINT-FILE.

    ACCEPT DATE-IN FROM DATE.
    MOVE DATE-YY TO HEADING-YEAR.
    MOVE DATE-MM TO HEADING-MONTH.
    MOVE DATE-DD TO HEADING-DAY.

    INITIATE CONTROL-BREAK.

    READ OUTPUT-FILE AT END MOVE 'YES' TO EOF.
    PERFORM 0200-PRINT-LOOP UNTIL EOF = 'YES'.

    TERMINATE CONTROL-BREAK.

    CLOSE OUTPUT-FILE
          PRINT-FILE.
    STOP RUN.

0200-PRINT-LOOP.

    GENERATE DETAIL-LINE.
    READ OUTPUT-FILE AT END MOVE 'YES' TO EOF.
```

Basically, all we did was use the sort routine at the beginning and then change the file-names in the rest of the division to fit the name OUTPUT-FILE, since we were no longer using CONSTRUCTION-FILE.

10-6
The Record Rack Report Writer Program

Roger Barnell is in the process of calculating the value of his inventory for the end-of-month balance sheet report. His inventory contains several products, and each product contains a different number of product types. He has instructed Cindy to prepare a control break report with the following details:

1. product number
2. product type

3. inventory amount of each product type
4. cost per unit of each product type
5. total cost of each product type
6. total cost for each product number (control total)
7. total cost of the inventory

She designed the program to print the report as shown in the printer spacing chart in Figure 10-3. Her systems design is shown in Figure 10-4. Since she has

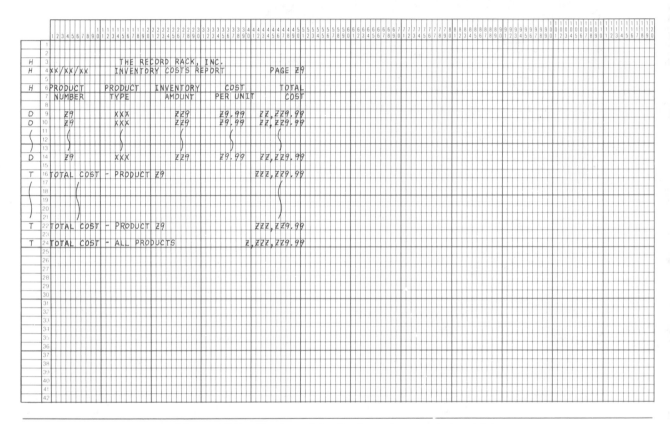

Figure 10-3   The layout for the inventory costs report.

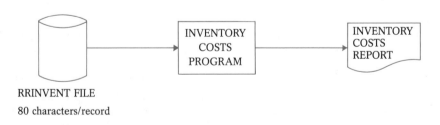

RRINVENT FILE

80 characters/record

Figure 10-4   The systems chart for *The Record Rack* costs report.

decided to use Report Writer, the computer will be doing all the work and there really isn't a program to design. Instead, she decides to simply list the pieces needed to write the Report Writer program:

1. RRINVENT input file
2. print file
3. end-of-file marker
4. page heading
5. detail line
6. control footing
7. final footing

The record layout for the RRINVENT file is shown in Figure 10-5. Cindy's sample data is

Product	Product Type	Inventory Amount	Cost per Unit
01	12C	453	2.00
01	14D	301	4.50
01	76F	90	11.99
01	81R	33	6.22
02	J09	700	10.00
02	KL1	43	34.67
02	MN5	27	15.48
02	PO8	51	17.99
02	TZ3	89	14.90
03	RT6	76	12.00
03	S6L	56	9.87
03	ZEF	84	4.09

RRINVENT **File**					
Field Description	*Position*	*Length*	:	*Dec*	*Type*
Product number	1–2	2	:	0	Numeric
Product type	3–5	3	:		Non-numeric
Product quantity	6–8	3	:	0	Numeric
Unit cost	9–12	4	:	2	Numeric
Filler	13–80	68	:		Non-numeric
Record Length = 80					

Figure 10-5   The RRINVENT file for the inventory costs report program.

Her program:

```
************************************************************
************************************************************
*
*
*  PROGRAM NAME: INV-BRK
*
*  PROGRAMMER NAME:  CINDY HARRISON
*
*  SOCIAL SECURITY NUMBER:  999-99-9999
*
*  DUE DATE: FEBRUARY 10, 1988
*
*  DESCRIPTION: THIS PROGRAM WILL PRODUCE A CONTROL BREAK INVENTORY
*               COST REPORT DETAILING THE QUANTITY, COST, AND TOTAL
*               COST OF THE INVENTORY.  THE REPORT WILL SHOW THE
*               CONTROL TOTAL ON THE PRODUCT NUMBERS.  THE PROGRAM
*               IS WRITTEN USING THE REPORT WRITER.
*
************************************************************
************************************************************
```

```
        IDENTIFICATION DIVISION.
        PROGRAM-ID.   INV-BRK.
        AUTHOR.       CINDY HARRISON.

        ENVIRONMENT DIVISION.

        CONFIGURATION SECTION.
        SOURCE-COMPUTER. IBM-4331.
        OBJECT-COMPUTER. IBM-4331.


        FILE-CONTROL.
            SELECT INVENTORY-IN ASSIGN TO UT-S-RRINVENT.
            SELECT LIST-OUT     ASSIGN TO UT-S-SYSPRINT.

        DATA DIVISION.
        FILE SECTION.

        FD  INVENTORY-IN
            LABEL RECORDS ARE OMITTED
            RECORD CONTAINS 80 CHARACTERS.
        01  INVENTORY-RECORD.
            05  PRODUCT-NUMBER                      PIC 99.
            05  PRODUCT-TYPE                        PIC XXX.
            05  PRODUCT-QUANTITY                    PIC 999.
            05  UNIT-COST                           PIC 99V99.
            05  FILLER                              PIC X(68).

        FD  LIST-OUT
            LABEL RECORDS ARE OMITTED
            REPORT IS INVENTORY-BREAK-REPORT
            RECORD CONTAINS 133 CHARACTERS.
```

```
WORKING-STORAGE SECTION.

01  WORK-AREAS.
    05  EOF                          PIC XXX VALUE 'NO '.
        88  WE-ARE-OUT-OF-DATA               VALUE 'YES'.
    05  TOTAL-COST                   PIC 9(6)V99 VALUE
        ZERO.
    05  MACHINE-DATE                 PIC X(6).
    05  DATE-WORK REDEFINES MACHINE-DATE.
        10  DATE-YY                  PIC XX.
        10  DATE-MM                  PIC XX.
        10  DATE-DD                  PIC XX.

REPORT SECTION.

RD  INVENTORY-BREAK-REPORT
    CONTROL IS FINAL PRODUCT-NUMBER
    PAGE LIMIT IS 55 LINES
    HEADING        1
    FIRST DETAIL   4
    LAST DETAIL    50
    FOOTING        53.

01  TYPE IS PAGE HEADING.
    05  LINE NUMBER IS 1.
        10  COLUMN NUMBER IS 15      PIC X(21) VALUE
            'THE RECORD RACK, INC.'.
    05  LINE NUMBER PLUS 1.
        10  COLUMN NUMBER IS 1       PIC XX
            SOURCE DATE-MM.
        10  COLUMN NUMBER 3          PIC /XX/
            SOURCE DATE-DD.
        10  COLUMN NUMBER 7          PIC XX
            SOURCE DATE-YY.
        10  COLUMN NUMBER 14         PIC X(22) VALUE
            'INVENTORY COSTS REPORT'.
        10  COLUMN NUMBER 45         PIC X(4)  VALUE
            'PAGE'.
        10  COLUMN NUMBER 50         PIC Z9
            SOURCE PAGE-COUNTER.
    05  LINE NUMBER PLUS 2.
        10  COLUMN NUMBER 1                   PIC X(51) VALUE
        'PRODUCT     PRODUCT    INVENTORY     COST         TOTAL'.
    05  LINE NUMBER PLUS 1.
        10  COLUMN NUMBER 2                   PIC X(50) VALUE
        'NUMBER      TYPE        AMOUNT    PER UNIT       COST'.
    05  LINE NUMBER PLUS 1.

01  DETAIL-LINE TYPE IS DETAIL.
    05  LINE NUMBER PLUS 1.
        10  COLUMN NUMBER 4          PIC Z9
            SOURCE PRODUCT-NUMBER.
        10  COLUMN NUMBER 14         PIC XXX
            SOURCE PRODUCT-TYPE.
        10  COLUMN NUMBER 26         PIC ZZ9
            SOURCE PRODUCT-QUANTITY.
        10  COLUMN NUMBER 35         PIC Z9.99
            SOURCE UNIT-COST.
        10  COLUMN NUMBER 43         PIC ZZ,ZZZ.99
            SOURCE TOTAL-COST.
```

```
01    TYPE IS CONTROL FOOTING PRODUCT-NUMBER.
      05   LINE NUMBER PLUS 2.
           10   COLUMN NUMBER 1                  PIC X(20) VALUE
                'TOTAL COST - PRODUCT'.
           10   COLUMN NUMBER 22                 PIC Z9
                SOURCE PRODUCT-NUMBER.
           10   SUB-TOTAL COLUMN NUMBER 42       PIC ZZZ,ZZ9.99
                SUM TOTAL-COST.

01    TYPE IS CONTROL FOOTING FINAL.
      05   LINE NUMBER PLUS 2.
           10   COLUMN NUMBER 1                  PIC X(25) VALUE
                'TOTAL COST - ALL PRODUCTS'.
           10   COLUMN NUMBER 40                 PIC Z,ZZZ,ZZ9.99
                SUM SUB-TOTAL.


PROCEDURE DIVISION.

0100-MAIN-MODULE.

    OPEN INPUT  INVENTORY-IN
         OUTPUT LIST-OUT.

    ACCEPT MACHINE-DATE FROM DATE.

    INITIATE INVENTORY-BREAK-REPORT.

    READ INVENTORY-IN AT END MOVE 'YES' TO EOF.
    PERFORM 0200-LIST-LOOP UNTIL WE-ARE-OUT-OF-DATA.

    TERMINATE INVENTORY-BREAK-REPORT.

    CLOSE INVENTORY-IN
          LIST-OUT.
    STOP RUN.


0200-LIST-LOOP.

    MULTIPLY UNIT-COST BY PRODUCT-QUANTITY GIVING TOTAL-COST.
    GENERATE DETAIL-LINE.
    READ INVENTORY-IN AT END MOVE 'YES' TO EOF.
```

The output generated by Cindy's program:

```
                         THE RECORD RACK, INC.
           05/23/88      INVENTORY COSTS REPORT          PAGE  1

           PRODUCT    PRODUCT    INVENTORY      COST        TOTAL
           NUMBER     TYPE        AMOUNT     PER UNIT        COST

                 1      12C          453         2.00      906.00
                 1      14D          301         4.50    1,354.50
                 1      76F           90        11.99    1,079.10
                 1      81R           33         6.22      205.26
```

```
TOTAL  COST  -  PRODUCT  1                               3,544.86

              2          J09          700      10.00      7,000.00
              2          KL1           43      34.67      1,490.81
              2          MN5           27      15.48        417.96
              2          P08           51      17.99        917.49
              2          TZ3           89      14.90      1,326.10

TOTAL  COST  -  PRODUCT  2                              11,152.36

              3          RT6           76      12.00        912.00
              3          S6L           56       9.87        552.72
              3          ZEF           84       4.09        343.56

TOTAL  COST  -  PRODUCT  3                               1,808.28

TOTAL  COST  -  ALL  PRODUCTS                           16,505.50
```

10-7
Summary

1. The COBOL Report Writer is one of the most powerful yet least used features of COBOL, simply because most programmers do not how to use it. In this chapter we learned just how easy it is to create and modify programs using Report Writer.
2. The SELECT clauses for Report Writer program files are the same as for normal reports. The differences in programming begin in the DATA DIVISION. In the FD for the print file, we use not a record description (the 01-level definition) but rather the RECORD CONTAINS clause to define the length of the record. We do, however, have to add the REPORT IS clause to give our report a name.
3. The WORKING-STORAGE SECTION of a Report Writer program is basically empty. About all we ever need to put in WORKING-STORAGE is an end-of-file marker and date fields for printing the date on the report. All the other total and miscellaneous fields, along with the print record layouts, are defined in the REPORT SECTION.
4. The REPORT SECTION begins with an RD, or Report Description, for each report being defined in the program. This RD is used to begin defining the report. It describes the types of control breaks in the report, if any, and the size and format of the printed page. The page description causes COBOL to automatically set up page- and line-counters.
5. Within the RD, the various lines to be printed are defined as report groups. They are specified as to the type of report feature they are, such as PAGE HEADING or CONTROL FOOTING.

6. In the definition of these groups, the line spacing is given and then each item to be printed is specified as to the column it starts in. The rest of the definition of each item includes the normal PIC clause; then it can have a VALUE clause for literals or a SOURCE clause if the data is to be printed from another field. Control fields are totaled with the SUM clause.

7. Fields totaled from one control field into another are known as rolling forward totals. These are handled easily by the Report Writer.

8. In the PROCEDURE DIVISION, we open, read, and close the files in the usual fashion. But all the rest of the processing, such as handling control breaks and printing headings, is handled automatically. Three new statements are required, however. The INITIATE statement marks the beginning of the processing of the report. The GENERATE statement causes the printing of the report itself and can be used to indicate to the program whether a detail report or a summary report is desired. Finally, the TERMINATE statement ends the printing of the report and causes the printing of all the footings.

9. If we need to modify the way control breaks are being automatically done in the program or if we need to do some extra calculations on the control totals, we can use DECLARATIVES.

10-8
Glossary

COLUMN clause   In the report description, the clause that indicates the column where an elementary item is to be printed.

CONTROL clause   The RD clause that specifies the order of the control breaks to be taken in the program.

CONTROL FOOTING clause   A footing line that will be generated upon the changing of the specified control field.

CONTROL HEADING clause   A heading that will be printed in front of a control group when the control field changes.

Crossfoot   A horizontal total of fields printed on a report.

DECLARATIVES   Procedures that are to be done based upon certain program conditions. All DECLARATIVES in a Report Writer program must be coded at the beginning of the PROCEDURE DIVISION.

DETAIL clause   The report group clause that specifies that the report group is a detail line.

END DECLARATIVES   The statement that marks the end of the declaratives used in a Report Writer program.

FIRST DETAIL clause   The RD clause that specifies the line where the first detail line is to be printed.

FOOTING clause   The RD clause that specifies the line where the page footing is to appear.

GENERATE statement   The PROCEDURE DIVISION statement that causes the printing (or simply the processing) of the record that is being read in.

GROUP INDICATE clause The elementary item clause that will cause the field to be printed only on the first detail line within a control group.

HEADING clause The RD clause that specifies the line on which the heading is to be printed.

INITIATE statement The PROCEDURE DIVISION statement that begins the printing of the named report.

LAST DETAIL clause The RD clause that specifies the report line on which the last detail line on the page is to be printed.

LINE-COUNTER The counter automatically set up by the Report Writer program to keep track of the number of lines printed.

LINE NUMBER clause The clause on the report group that tells how the line spacing is to be done.

NEXT GROUP The clause on the report group that indicates the type of spacing to be used before the next group is printed.

PAGE clause The RD clause that specifies the number of lines that are to be printed on the page.

PAGE-COUNTER The counter automatically set up by the Report Writer program to keep track of the number of the page being printed.

PAGE FOOTING clause The clause that indicates the report group to be a page footing. The page footing will print at the bottom of each page.

PAGE HEADING clause The clause that indicates the report group to be a page heading. The page heading will print at the beginning of each page.

RD, or Report Description The area of the REPORT SECTION that is used to describe the form and the layout of the report.

REPORT FOOTING clause The clause that indicates that the report group is to be a report footing that will print only one time, at the end of the report.

Report group The specification of how a printed line is to look on the report. The line spacing and positioning of all the elementary items are specified.

REPORT HEADING clause The clause that indicates that the report group is to be a report heading that will print only one time, at the beginning of the report.

REPORT IS clause The FD clause used to assign a name to the report to be printed.

REPORT SECTION The DATA DIVISION section in which the report is described.

Report Writer The COBOL feature that allows complex reports to be designed simply, with the Report Writer processing most of the data automatically.

RESET clause The control field clause that allows the control total to be reset at a time other than when there is a control break.

Rolling forward totals Subtotals that are accumulated from one control total to the next.

SOURCE clause The clause that specifies which field is to be used when an elementary item is being printed.

SUM clause The clause that specifies a total to be maintained on the named field.

SUPPRESS PRINTING statement The declarative statement that allows a control total to be suppressed upon a tested condition.

TERMINATE statement The PROCEDURE DIVISION statement that causes the report to be finished and all the control footings to be printed.

TYPE The report description clause that allows a report group to be designated as to the program purpose.

UPON clause The clause that can cause the accumulation of a control field under conditions other than the control breaking of the specified field.

USE BEFORE REPORTING statement The declarative statement used to initiate a declarative procedure.

10-9
Quick Quiz

Cover the answers with a blank sheet of paper and test yourself. Questions 1–15 are true or false questions, 16–20 are multiple choice, and 21–25 are fill-in-the-blank.

T   F   **1.** Most programmers know and use Report Writer.

T   F   **2.** Most of the coding of COBOL Report Writer programs is done in the DATA DIVISION.

T   F   **3.** For a print file to be used as a report file, nothing special is needed in the FD except a REPORT IS clause.

T   F   **4.** For the normal Report Writer program, we can eliminate the WORKING-STORAGE SECTION altogether.

T   F   **5.** The first thing used in the REPORT SECTION is the RD.

T   F   **6.** The report-name listed on the RD must match a report listed in the FD of the report file.

T   F   **7.** A page heading is automatically printed at the top of the first page and is printed at the top of all subsequent pages when specified.

T   F   **8.** The LINE NUMBER clause can be a part of the TYPE sentence or can be a level (sentence) of its own.

T   F   **9.** The LINE NUMBER clause can be used to send the next group to the next page.

T   F   **10.** The SOURCE clause specifies the field that the data is to be printed from.

T   F   **11.** Using multi-level control break totals is known as crossfooting.

T   F   **12.** The TERMINATE clause will close an open report file.

T   F   **13.** Printing only some of the detail lines of a report requires the use of declaratives.

T   F   **14.** The USE BEFORE REPORTING is part of the DECLARATIVES.

T   F   **15.** The SUPPRESS PRINTING command must be used in an IF test.

_____   **16.** Which of the following clauses is not related to the PAGE clause of the RD?

    (a) HEADING   **(c)** FIRST DETAIL

    (b) LINE-COUNTER   **(d)** FOOTING

_____   **17.** The term *crossfoot* is related to which clause?

    (a) GROUP INDICATE   **(c)** RESET

    (b) SUM   **(d)** SOURCE

_____   **18.** Which of the following commands is used to indicate whether the report is to be a detail report or a summary report?

    (a) GENERATE   **(c)** INITIATE

    (b) REPORT IS   **(d)** CONTROL IS

_____   **19.** Which of the following is not a report group TYPE?

    (a) HEADING   **(c)** PAGE FOOTING

    (b) CH   **(d)** DETAIL

_____   **20.** Which of the following is not related to the other three?

    (a) COLUMN clause   **(c)** LINE clause

    (b) NEXT GROUP clause   **(d)** HEADING clause

21. The _____ of the RD defines the order of the control breaks within the program.
22. The _____ and _____ are the counters automatically set up by the Report Writer.
23. The last footing that can appear on a report is the _____ .
24. To get a control break field to print only upon the first detail line after the control break, you use the _____ clause.
25. The statement used to begin the printing of a Report Writer report is the _____ .

10-10
Answers to Quick Quiz

1. F (Most programmers do not know how to use the Report Writer.)
2. T (More specifically, in the REPORT SECTION.)
3. T (A REPORT IS clause and the exclusion of the record description, the 01 level.)
4. F (We still need a few things in WORKING-STORAGE, such as the end-of-file marker and date storage.)
5. T
6. T
7. F (Not if there is also a report heading specified.)
8. T (You use it the way it seems the most appropriate.)
9. F (The NEXT GROUP clause is for that. The LINE NUMBER clause, however, can be used to print the current group on a new page.)
10. T (The clause is a sort of MOVE statement.)
11. F (It is called rolling forward totals.)
12. F (The TERMINATE statement denotes the end of the report, nothing else.)
13. F (Declaratives are used to control the control break report lines, not the detail lines.)
14. T
15. F (There is nothing that makes the command mandatory, but without an IF test, all the control breaks being controlled would be suppressed, not just the few you are trying to turn off.)
16. b (There is no LINE-COUNTER clause. LINE-COUNTER is merely the field that the computer automatically sets up to count the number of lines printed on the page.)
17. b (The SUM clause is used to create a crossfoot total.)
18. a (It is done by specifying the detail-report-group-name for a detail report or the report-name for a summary report.)
19. a (You must specify the type of heading as REPORT, PAGE, or CONTROL.)
20. d (The HEADING clause is part of the PAGE clause specifications. The other choices are part of the report record description entry.)
21. CONTROL clause
22. LINE-COUNTER, PAGE-COUNTER
23. REPORT FOOTING
24. GROUP INDICATE
25. INITIATE

════ 10-11 ════
Questions to Aid Understanding

1. Explain the purpose of the COBOL Report Writer.
*2. What is different about the FD for the printer output file when you use Report Writer rather than generating a report as we have in the past?
3. Explain what the REPORT SECTION is for.
*4. Explain what causes the PAGE-COUNTER and LINE-COUNTER to be automatically set up by the computer. What command would you use in the record description to print the PAGE-COUNTER?
5. What is the TYPE command used for?
6. List at least three of the different TYPE report groups and explain what each is for.
*7. Explain why the DETAIL clause generally requires the use of a group-name whereas the other TYPE clauses do not.
8. Define each of the following:

   (a) LINE clause
   (b) NEXT GROUP clause
   (c) COLUMN clause
   (d) GROUP INDICATE clause
   (e) SOURCE clause
   (f) SUM clause
   (g) INITIATE statement
   (h) GENERATE statement
   (i) TERMINATE statement

*9. What are rolling forward totals? What record description entry is needed to create rolling forward totals?
10. What is a crossfoot? Show how one could be set up.
11. What are declaratives and what are they used for?
12. Explain why virtually no coding is necessary in the WORKING-STORAGE SECTION when Report Writer is being used.

════ 10-12 ════
Coding Exercises

1. Write the RD specifications for a report with three control fields named MAJOR-FIELD, INTER-FIELD, and MINOR-FIELD. There should be no more than 40 lines per report page and the page heading must appear on line 10. There will be 5 lines of headings and the detail lines will be double-spaced. The control footings have two lines each.
2. Write an FD for a report file called PRINT-FILE with the report called REPORT-FILE.

3. Write the record description entries necessary to define the following headings (approximate the columns):

```
DATE MM/DD/YY              THE SAMPLE REPORT              PAGE Z9
                           THOMPSON AND SON


WORKER        HOURLY      HOURS         REGULAR     OVERTIME      GROSS
               WAGE       WORKED          PAY         PAY          PAY
```

4. Set up a report group record description for a detail line in which you print four fields with the sources CUST-CODE, CUST-NAME, AMOUNT-IN, and DATE-IN. Use whatever columns seem appropriate.
5. Set up two control footings with the names CUST-CODE for the major control field and CUST-ID for the minor control field. Use the amount field of CHARGES-IN for the control total. Use a final footing also.
6. Write the PROCEDURE DIVISION necessary to read records from the INPUT-FILE and write a detail report (DETAIL-LINE and DETAIL-REPORT) in which the detail lines are printed only when the AMOUNT-IN is greater than 20,000.

10-13
Maintenance Program

The Widget Works has several manufacturing facilities around the country that receive raw materials from several different warehouses. The company has a report that details these shipments as to what products are received and when they are received. You are assigned the task of modifying the Report Writer detail report into a control break program so that it breaks on the warehouse that the products are shipped from. The original systems chart is shown in Figure 10-6. The file layout that was used for the SHIPPING file is shown in Figure 10-7. The printer spacing chart in Figure 10-8 shows the way the report looks now, and Figure 10-9 shows the way it should look. Virtually the only difference is the use of the control totals. Since this is a Report Writer program and COBOL handles all the program details internally, there is no program design to examine.

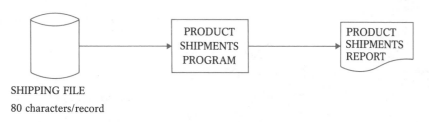

Figure 10-6   The systems chart for the maintenance program.

SHIPPING **File**					
Field Description	*Position*	*Length*	:	*Dec*	*Type*
Warehouse	1–2	2	:		Non-numeric
Product number	3–7	5	:		Non-numeric
Filler	8–33	26	:		Non-numeric
Product value	34–40	7	:	2	Numeric
Filler	41–45	5	:		Non-numeric
Date received	46–51	6	:		Non-numeric
Quantity received	52–56	5	:	0	Numeric
Filler	57–80	24	:		Non-numeric
Record Length = 80					

Figure 10-7   The file layout for the SHIPPING file.

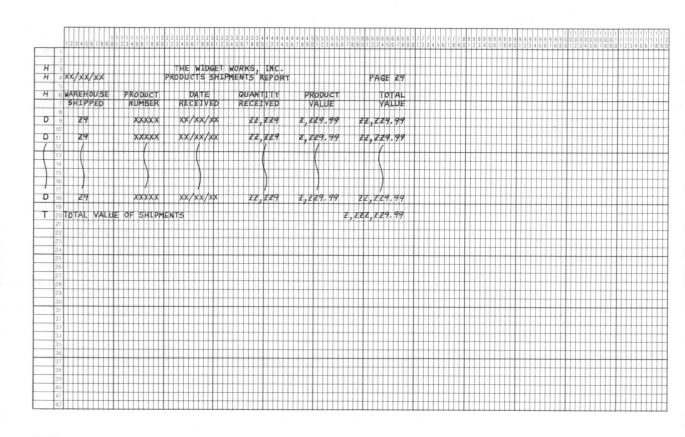

Figure 10-8   The original look of the products shipments report.

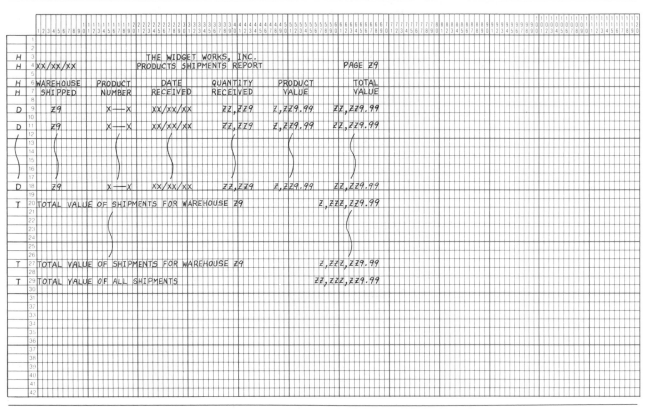

Figure 10-9 The layout of the products shipments report after it has been changed to a control break program.

The original program:

```
****************************************************************
****************************************************************
*
*
*
*    PROGRAM NAME: PROD-RPT
*
*    PROGRAMMER NAME:  EDWARD J. COBURN
*
*    SOCIAL SECURITY NUMBER:  999-99-9999
*
*    DUE DATE: FEBRUARY 10, 1988
*
*    DESCRIPTION: THIS PROGRAM WILL PRODUCE A REPORT SHOWING
*                 THE SHIPMENTS TO THE WAREHOUSE INCLUDING THE
*                 QUANTITY AND PRODUCT VALUES.  THE REPORT IS
*                 PRINTED WITH THE REPORT WRITER FEATURE.
*
****************************************************************
****************************************************************
```

```
        IDENTIFICATION DIVISION.
        PROGRAM-ID.    PROD-RPT.
        AUTHOR.        EDWARD J. COBURN.

        ENVIRONMENT DIVISION.

        CONFIGURATION SECTION.
        SOURCE-COMPUTER. IBM-4331.
        OBJECT-COMPUTER. IBM-4331.

        INPUT-OUTPUT SECTION.
        FILE-CONTROL.
            SELECT SHIPPING-IN ASSIGN TO UT-S-SHIPPING.
            SELECT LIST-OUT    ASSIGN TO UT-S-SYSPRINT.

        DATA DIVISION.
        FILE SECTION.

    FD  SHIPPING-IN
        LABEL RECORDS ARE OMITTED
        RECORD CONTAINS 80 CHARACTERS.
    01  SHIPPING-RECORD.
        05  WAREHOUSE              PIC 99.
        05  PRODUCT-NUMBER         PIC XXXXX.
        05  FILLER                 PIC X(26).
        05  PRODUCT-VALUE          PIC 9(5)V99.
        05  FILLER                 PIC X(5).
        05  DATE-RECEIVED          PIC X(6).
        05  QUANTITY-RECEIVED      PIC 9(5).
        05  FILLER                 PIC X(56).

    FD  LIST-OUT
        LABEL RECORDS ARE OMITTED
        REPORT IS DETAIL-REPORT
        RECORD CONTAINS 133 CHARACTERS.


    WORKING-STORAGE SECTION.

    01  WORK-AREAS.
        05  EOF                    PIC XXX        VALUE 'NO '.
            88  WE-ARE-OUT-OF-DATA                VALUE 'YES'.

        05  MACHINE-DATE           PIC X(6).
        05  DATE-WORK REDEFINES MACHINE-DATE.
            10  DATE-YY            PIC XX.
            10  DATE-MM            PIC XX.
            10  DATE-DD            PIC XX.


    REPORT SECTION.

    RD  DETAIL-REPORT
        CONTROL IS FINAL
        PAGE LIMIT IS 55 LINES
        HEADING        1
        FIRST DETAIL   4
        LAST DETAIL    50
        FOOTING        53.
```

```
01   TYPE IS PAGE HEADING.
     05   LINE NUMBER IS 1.
          10   COLUMN NUMBER 23    PIC X(22) VALUE
               'THE WIDGET WORKS, INC.'.
     05   LINE NUMBER PLUS 1.
          10   COLUMN NUMBER IS 1                PIC XX
               SOURCE DATE-MM.
          10   COLUMN NUMBER 3                   PIC /XX/
               SOURCE DATE-DD.
          10   COLUMN NUMBER 7                   PIC XX
               SOURCE DATE-YY.
          10   COLUMN NUMBER 21                  PIC X(25) VALUE
               'PRODUCTS SHIPMENTS REPORT'.
          10   COLUMN NUMBER 62                  PIC X(4)   VALUE
               'PAGE'.
          10   COLUMN NUMBER 67                  PIC Z9
               SOURCE PAGE-COUNTER.
     05   LINE NUMBER PLUS 2.
          10   COLUMN NUMBER 1                   PIC X(43) VALUE
               'WAREHOUSE    PRODUCT         DATE        QUANTITY'.
          10   COLUMN NUMBER 49                  PIC X(20) VALUE
               'PRODUCT          TOTAL'.
     05   LINE NUMBER PLUS 1.
          10   COLUMN NUMBER 2                   PIC X(43) VALUE
               'SHIPPED       NUMBER    RECEIVED    RECEIVED'.
          10   COLUMN NUMBER 50                  PIC X(19) VALUE
               'VALUE           VALUE'.

01   DETAIL-LINE TYPE IS DETAIL.
     05   LINE NUMBER PLUS 2.
          10   COLUMN NUMBER 4    PIC Z9
               SOURCE WAREHOUSE.
          10   COLUMN NUMBER 15   PIC X(5)
               SOURCE PRODUCT-NUMBER.
          10   COLUMN NUMBER 24   PIC XX/XX/XX
               SOURCE DATE-RECEIVED.
          10   COLUMN NUMBER 38   PIC ZZ,ZZ9
               SOURCE QUANTITY-RECEIVED.
          10   COLUMN NUMBER 47   PIC ZZ,ZZ9.99
               SOURCE PRODUCT-VALUE.
          10   COLUMN NUMBER 60   PIC ZZ,ZZ9.99
               SOURCE TOTAL-VALUE.

01   TYPE IS CONTROL FOOTING FINAL.
     05   LINE NUMBER PLUS 2.
          10   COLUMN NUMBER 1    PIC X(24) VALUE
               'TOTAL VALUE OF SHIPMENTS'.
          10   COLUMN NUMBER 55   PIC Z,ZZZ,ZZ9.99
               SUM TOTAL-VALUE.


PROCEDURE DIVISION.

0100-MAIN-MODULE.

     OPEN INPUT  SHIPPING-IN
          OUTPUT LIST-OUT.
```

```
          ACCEPT MACHINE-DATE FROM DATE.
          MOVE DATE-YY TO HEADING-YEAR.
          MOVE DATE-MM TO HEADING-MONTH.
          MOVE DATE-DD TO HEADING-DAY.

          INITIATE DETAIL-REPORT.

          READ SHIPPING-IN AT END MOVE 'YES' TO EOF.
          PERFORM 0200-LIST-LOOP UNTIL WE-ARE-OUT-OF-DATA.

          TERMINATE DETAIL-REPORT.

          CLOSE SHIPPING-IN
                LIST-OUT.
          STOP RUN.


      0200-LIST-LOOP.

          MULTIPLY QUANTITY-RECEIVED BY PRODUCT-VALUE
                  GIVING TOTAL-VALUE.

          GENERATE DETAIL-LINE.

          READ SHIPPING-IN AT END MOVE 'YES' TO EOF.
```

A sample of the output from the program:

```
                           THE WIDGET WORKS, INC.
05/23/88                 PRODUCTS SHIPMENTS REPORT                 PAGE  1

WAREHOUSE      PRODUCT       DATE      QUANTITY      PRODUCT         TOTAL
 SHIPPED       NUMBER      RECEIVED    RECEIVED       VALUE          VALUE

     1          A1345      01/25/88       1,225       426.18     22,070.50

     1          A3485      02/25/88       1,317        71.29     93,888.93

     1          BB908      02/12/88         176       418.59     73,671.84

     1          BR988      02/15/88         994       728.75     24,377.50

     7          A4569      02/18/88       1,377       931.78     83,061.06

     7          B8498      02/01/88         818     1,200.66     82,139.88

     7          DDD98      03/15/88          26       493.75     12,837.50

     8          B948R      04/12/88         216       364.84     78,805.44

     8          DD838      05/18/88         174        83.02     14,445.48

     8          R8477      01/18/88          20       473.27      9,465.40

     8          ZZ837      03/21/88         481       327.94     57,739.14

    12          AA948      04/25/88         742     1,190.42     83,291.64
```

12	AB948	05/16/88	268	1,007.04	69,886.72
12	ACC98	12/15/87	1,071	727.54	79,195.34
12	ACG99	01/14/88	551	785.14	32,612.14
12	BR88A	02/30/88	39	4.03	157.17
15	GHIH0	05/25/88	234	48.57	11,365.38

TOTAL VALUE OF SHIPMENTS   829,011.06

10-14
Illustrative Program

High-Tech College of Business needs a report to show the cash outlay necessary to purchase the required books for the next semester. Every department in the college offers several classes and each class requires a different book.

An inventory file (BOOKINV) has been prepared in sequence by department, with the record layout shown in Figure 10-10. Compare the existing inventory with the requested number of books needed to teach the classes. Compute the number of books that need to be purchased to meet the requirement. Then compute the necessary cash outlay to buy the books. Total the amount of cash outlay for each department (control break) and then total the overall cash outlay needed by *High-Tech College of Business* as shown in the printer spacing chart in Figure 10-11.

Note that the file contains a department code while the report shows the department name. The code given in the file is to be translated to a department name by the program. This is done with the following pairs (use a table for the translation process):

Department Code	Department Name
ACC	Accounting
BUS	Business
CHY	Chemistry
CIS	Computer Information Systems
ECN	Economics
EGN	Engineering
ENG	English
FRH	French
HIS	History
MTH	Mathematics
PE	Physical Education
PH	Physics

Figure 10-12 shows the systems design for the program. Since this is a Report Writer program, there is no design.

BOOKINV File					
Field Description	*Position*	*Length*	:	*Dec*	*Type*
Department code	1–3	3	:		Non-numeric
Class	4–18	15	:		Non-numeric
Book title	19–33	15	:		Non-numeric
Inventory amount	34–37	4	:	0	Numeric
Requested amount	38–41	4	:	0	Numeric
Cost of book	42–46	5	:	2	Numeric
Filler	47–80	34	:		Non-numeric
Record Length = 80					

Figure 10-10   The record layout for the BOOKINV file.

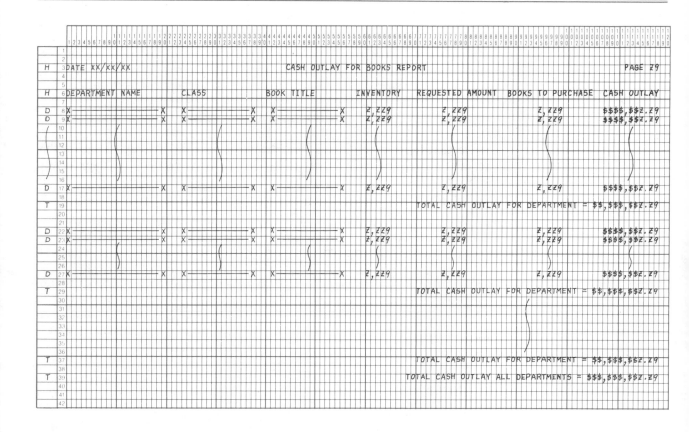

Figure 10-11   The layout for the cash outlay report.

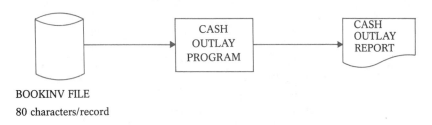

BOOKINV FILE

80 characters/record

Figure 10-12   The systems chart for the cash outlay program.

10-15

System Designed Programs

For the following programs, all the design elements typically furnished to a programmer by the systems analyst are furnished. It is up to you, as programmer, to design and code the program. The files to be used are found in Appendix A.

1. Write a program to determine the value of on-hand inventory. Using the file input layout shown in Figure 10-13 (file INVENT), you will add the beginning on-hand, to the amount received, deduct the amount sold, and thus come up with the current on-hand. Then multiply that amount by the unit price to arrive at the total value for that product. Of course, print the total value of the inventory at the end of the report. Do all this using Report Writer. The printer spacing chart is shown in Figure 10-14, and the system design for the program can be seen in Figure 10-15.

2. A credit card company is in the process of determining the total amount of debt charged by its card holders during a certain month. Write a program to show each card holder's charge account purchases during one month. Use the file input layout shown in Figure 10-16 for the CHARGE file. Print the date, place, type, and amount of purchase under the card holder's account number. At the end of each card holder's records, print the total amount for the purchases the card holder made. At the end of the report, print a grand total of all purchases made by all the card holders. The printer spacing chart is shown in Figure 10-17, and the system design is shown in Figure 10-18.

3. Because of advanced automation, a single factory can produce many varieties of products. A large factory in Kansas is divided into several manufacturing facilities, each containing a different number of machines. Each machine produces a different product. The factory wants a report showing the efficiency percent of each machine. This is computed by dividing the number of good products, which is the total products less those that are defective, by the total number of products produced by that machine. This number is then multiplied by 100 to give the efficiency percent. Also, the factory wants the efficiency percent for each manufacturing facility as well as the overall efficiency percent for the entire factory. The record layout for the MANUFACT file is shown in Figure 10-19, the printer spacing chart is shown in Figure 10-20, and the system design is shown in Figure 10-21. Arrange the program so that it can be used for printing either all the details or just a summary report.

INVENT File					
Field Description	*Position*	*Length*	:	*Dec*	*Type*
Item number	1–4	4	:		Non-numeric
Last count	5–10	6	:	0	Numeric
Filler	11–24	14	:		Non-numeric
Unit price	25–32	8	:	2	Numeric
Amount received	33–38	6	:	0	Numeric
Amount sold	39–44	6	:	0	Numeric
Filler	45–80	36	:		Non-numeric
Record Length = 80					

Figure 10-13   The record layout for the INVENT file, exercise 10-15-1.

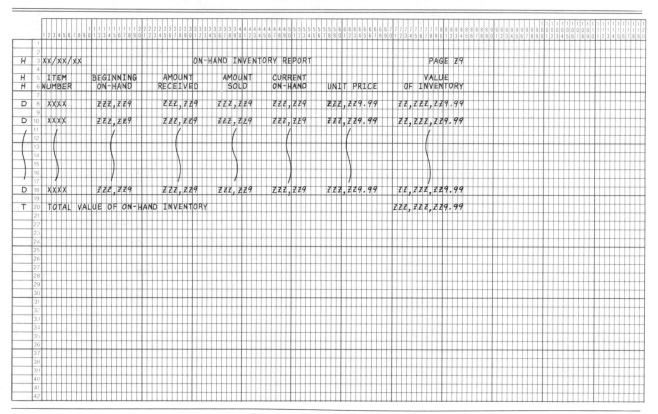

Figure 10-14   The layout for the on-hand inventory report, exercise 10-15-1.

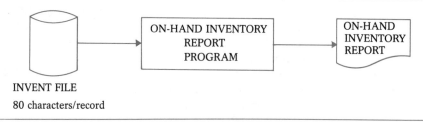

INVENT FILE

80 characters/record

Figure 10-15   The systems chart for the on-hand inventory report program, exercise 10-15-1.

CHARGE File					
Field Description	*Position*	*Length*	:	*Dec*	*Type*
Account number	1–5	5	:		Non-numeric
Date of purchase	6–11	6	:		Non-numeric
Place of purchase	12–31	20	:		Non-numeric
Description of purchase	32–46	15	:		Non-numeric
Amount of purchase	47–52	6	:	2	Numeric
Filler	53–80	28	:		Non-numeric
Record Length = 80					

Figure 10-16   The record layout for the CHARGE file, exercise 10-15-2.

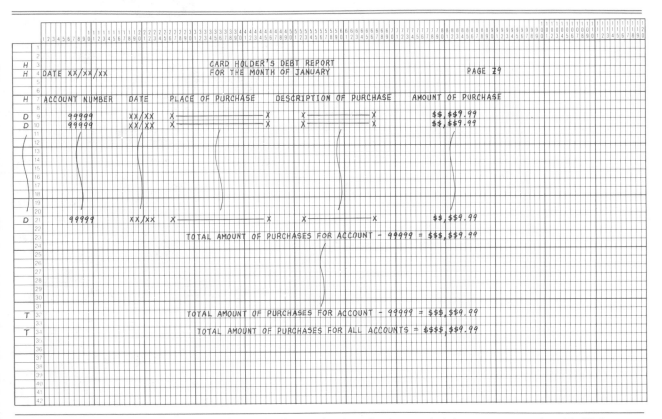

Figure 10-17   The layout for the charge card debt report, exercise 10-15-2.

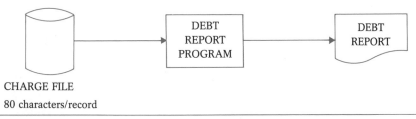

CHARGE FILE

80 characters/record

Figure 10-18   The systems chart for exercise 10-15-2.

MANUFACT File					
Field Description	*Position*	*Length*	:	*Dec*	*Type*
Facility	1–2	2	:	0	Numeric
Machine	3–4	2	:	0	Numeric
Total production	5–9	5	:	0	Numeric
Defective products	10–13	4	:	0	Numeric
Filler	14–80	67	:		Non-numeric
Record Length = 80					

Figure 10-19 The record layout for the MANUFACT file, exercise 10-15-3.

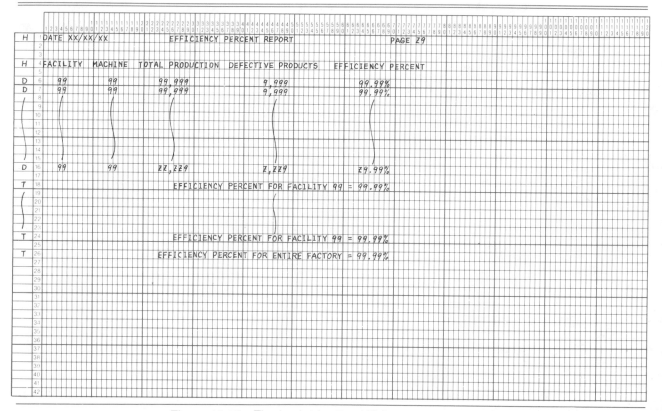

Figure 10-20 The layout for the efficiency report, exercise 10-15-3.

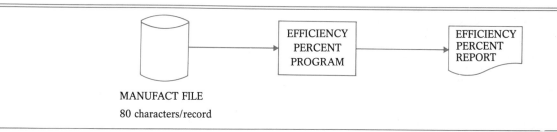

MANUFACT FILE

80 characters/record

Figure 10-21 The systems chart for exercise 10-15-3.

10-16
Non-designed Programs

In the following programs, you will need to design the systems chart, the input files (record layout), the printer spacing chart, the program design, and the data with which to test the program.

1. A large general merchandise store keeps track of the amount of sales each of its employees makes. Every time an employee makes a sale, a record is made showing the department number, employee number, and revenue from the sale. Each department has a different number of employees. Every employee is entitled to a 5% commission. Write a program that prints, by department, all the sales records, with a control total for each employee. Compute and print the commission during the printing of the control total. At the end of each department, print the total sales made and commissions earned. Also, print a grand total of both sales and commissions for the entire store.

2. A light bulb manufacturer has claimed that its light bulbs will burn not less than 95 percent of 1100 hours. A consumer activist TV show has decided to sample no more than ten but not fewer than five bulbs from every factory, in every region of the country the manufacturer operates in. A file containing the region number, the factory number, and the length of time each sample bulb burned has been prepared. The file is in sequence by region and factory number. Prepare a report showing the length of time each sample bulb burned, the percentage of time the bulb burned as compared to the manufacturer's claim, and whether or not the bulb passed the test. At the end of each factory, within each region, show the total number of bulbs that passed and the total number that failed. Do the same at the end of each region. Finally, at the end of the report, show the number of bulbs that passed and failed and the passing rate as a percentage of the total.

3. On the first day of every month, a newspaper company creates a file with all the home deliveries it expects to make in that month. Write a program that determines the amount of revenue the newspaper company expects to receive from its home deliveries in the month under study. The newspaper has divided its entire service area into zones. Each zone has a different number of areas, and each area is divided into a different number of routes. The file was created in sequence by zone, area, and route. The total number of houses in each route has already been totaled on the file. The newspaper charges a standard fee of $6.90 a month for Monday through Saturday deliveries. If a house receives a Sunday paper, an extra $1.50 per month is charged. The report should show the total number of houses in each route, the number of houses that receive the Sunday paper, and the total revenue expected from that route. Then, appropriate totals should show the expected revenue from each of the areas, within each zone. A total should also be generated for each zone and for the entire report.

OBJECTIVES   After completing Chapter 11 you should be able to
1. explain the purpose of the COPY statement;
2. explain the significance of a library;
3. explain why we might choose to use a subprogram rather than the COPY statement;
4. explain what a subprogram is;
5. list and explain at least three reasons for using subprograms;
6. explain how the CALL statement in the calling program and the PROCEDURE DIVISION statement in the subprogram are related;
7. explain the purpose of the LINKAGE SECTION;
8. list and explain at least two reasons why the traditional approach to creating files can cause problems and how a DBMS can overcome them;
9. list and explain the differences between the three types of DBMS;
10. explain what a schema and a subschema are.

CHAPTER 11

LIBRARIES, SUBPROGRAMS, AND DATA BASES

11-1
Introduction

In any COBOL installation, certain routines, such as date conversion, payroll tax calculations, and data editing functions, are used time after time. There are three general ways these common routines can be incorporated into the program where they are needed.

First of all, the routines can simply be coded into each program. This is what we have been doing throughout this text and your introductory one. Each time you needed a date routine to get the date from the computer and print it at the top of the report, you coded the needed routine. (Actually, you probably copied it from one program to the next the way most programmers do.) This is called "reinventing the wheel," and of course it's a waste of effort. Why should you spend valuable time writing routines or even simple file layouts that someone (yourself or someone else) has written before? Well, you don't have to.

The second method is to use a prewritten routine and have it *copied* into your program. This method is the subject of the next section.

The third method is to write a small (or sometimes large) program called a **subprogram** to accomplish the needed task and then tie that program into your new program where it is needed. We will deal with subprograms in the third section of this chapter.

One of the major problems for any computer installation is keeping track of all its data. We can help create uniform file layouts with copied routines or subprograms, but setting up the entire system using a **data base management system** can generally be of even greater benefit. We will examine data base management systems in the last section of the chapter.

11-2
The COPY Statement

Whenever you have multiple programs that are going to be accessing the same file, the file layout you use needs to be defined in precisely the same way in each program. COBOL allows the creation of libraries containing COBOL code. The library entries can be inserted directly into COBOL programs, and the result is the same as if the code had been written into the program to begin with. If file and record descriptions are placed in a library, then those definitions can simply be copied into any program that requires them. The files will automatically be defined with the established layouts.

The methods of placing the required definitions into the library differ, depending upon the computer and the specifics of the operating system. Some systems allow the creation of only one library, while others allow several libraries which can be given user-defined names.

Each entry in a library is identified by a **text name**, which the COBOL program uses in conjunction with the **COPY statement** to gain access to the library entry. The form of the COPY statement is

$$\underline{\text{COPY}} \text{ text-name} \left[\left\{ \begin{array}{l} \underline{\text{IN}} \text{ library-name} \\ \underline{\text{OF}} \end{array} \right\} \right]$$

The library-name shown on the COPY statement is used on only those systems that allow multiple libraries. Naturally, if there is more than one library, the specific library that the text-name is to be copied from will have to be shown.

When a COPY statement is used, the contents of the specified library entry replace the COPY statement in the program, though some compilers leave the COPY statement in the compiled source program for documentation purposes. This library replacement is done when the program is compiled. Once the program has been compiled, the copied code becomes a part of the object program.

Though a COPY statement may be used anywhere in a COBOL program, it is generally used in the DATA DIVISION and occasionally in the PROCEDURE DIVISION. About the only limitation to the COPY statement is that a library entry cannot contain a COPY statement.

To help get a feel for the use of a COPY statement, let's assume that we need to set up a layout for the file given in Figure 11-1 and that the layout is going to be needed for several programs. We will create a library entry like the following:

```
FD   ISAM-FILE
     LABEL RECORDS ARE OMITTED
     RECORD CONTAINS 80 CHARACTERS.
01   ISAM-RECORD.
     10   CUSTOMER-NUMBER          PIC X(4).
     10   CUSTOMER-NAME.
          20   LAST-NAME           PIC X(10).
          20   FIRST-NAME          PIC X(10).
     10   CUS-ADDRESS              PIC X(15).
     10   CITY                     PIC X(13).
     10   STATE                    PIC XX.
     10   ZIP-CODE                 PIC X(5).
     10   SALE-AMOUNT              PIC 9(4)V99.
     10   AMOUNT-DUE               PIC 9(4)V99.
     10   CREDIT-LIMIT             PIC X.
     10   SALESMAN-NUMBER          PIC X(4).
     10   FILLER                   PIC X(4).
```

CUSTOMER File					
Field Description	*Position*	*Length*	:	*Dec*	*Type*
Customer number	1–4	4	:		Non-numeric
Name Last	5–14	10	:		Non-numeric
First & initial	15–24	10	:		Non-numeric
Address	25–39	15	:		Non-numeric
City	40–52	13	:		Non-numeric
State	53–54	2	:		Non-numeric
Zip code	55–59	5	:		Non-numeric
Amount of sale	60–65	6	:	2	Numeric
Amount due	66–71	6	:	2	Numeric
Credit limit	72–72	1	:		Non-numeric
Salesman number	73–76	4	:		Non-numeric
Filler	77–80	4	:		Non-numeric
Record Length = 80					

Figure 11-1   The record layout for the CUSTOMER file.

The program segment into which we want to insert this file layout would normally be coded as follows:

```
ENVIRONMENT DIVISION.

CONFIGURATION SECTION.
SOURCE-COMPUTER. IBM-4331.
OBJECT-COMPUTER. IBM-4331.

INPUT-OUTPUT SECTION.
FILE-CONTROL.
    SELECT ISAM-FILE ASSIGN TO DISK.

DATA DIVISION.
FILE SECTION.

FD  ISAM-FILE
    LABEL RECORDS ARE OMITTED
    RECORD CONTAINS 80 CHARACTERS.
01  ISAM-RECORD.
    10  CUSTOMER-NUMBER              PIC X(4).
    10  CUSTOMER-NAME.
        20  LAST-NAME               PIC X(10).
        20  FIRST-NAME              PIC X(10).
    10  CUS-ADDRESS                 PIC X(15).
    10  CITY                        PIC X(13).
    10  STATE                       PIC XX.
    10  ZIP-CODE                    PIC X(5).
    10  SALE-AMOUNT                 PIC 9(4)V99.
    10  AMOUNT-DUE                  PIC 9(4)V99.
    10  CREDIT-LIMIT                PIC X.
    10  SALESMAN-NUMBER             PIC X(4).
    10  FILLER                      PIC X(4).

WORKING-STORAGE SECTION.

01  WORK-AREAS.
```

Notice that the library file entry is the only file defined in the program. In order to load the library entry, we would actually code the program (assuming a library-name of ISAM-LIBRARY and a text-name of CUSTOMER-ISAM) as follows:

```
ENVIRONMENT DIVISION.

CONFIGURATION SECTION.
SOURCE-COMPUTER. IBM-4331.
OBJECT-COMPUTER. IBM-4331.

INPUT-OUTPUT SECTION.
FILE-CONTROL.
    SELECT ISAM-FILE ASSIGN TO DISK.
```

```
DATA DIVISION.
FILE SECTION.

COPY CUSTOMER-ISAM OF ISAM-LIBRARY.

WORKING-STORAGE SECTION.

01 WORK-AREAS.
```

Then, after the program is compiled, our source listing will look like the program given previously (except that it might also still have the COPY statement in the code).

This library entry might also have been created using the SELECT statement and the DATA DIVISION and FILE SECTION headings. Thus, the library entry could have been

```
        SELECT ISAM-FILE ASSIGN TO DISK.

    DATA DIVISION.
    FILE SECTION.

    FD   ISAM-FILE
         LABEL RECORDS ARE OMITTED
         RECORD CONTAINS 80 CHARACTERS.
    01   ISAM-RECORD.
         10   CUSTOMER-NUMBER              PIC X(4).
         10   CUSTOMER-NAME.
              20   LAST-NAME               PIC X(10).
              20   FIRST-NAME              PIC X(10).
         10   CUS-ADDRESS                  PIC X(15).
         10   CITY                         PIC X(13).
         10   STATE                        PIC XX.
         10   ZIP-CODE                     PIC X(5).
         10   SALE-AMOUNT                  PIC 9(4)V99.
         10   AMOUNT-DUE                   PIC 9(4)V99.
         10   CREDIT-LIMIT                 PIC X.
         10   SALESMAN-NUMBER              PIC X(4).
         10   FILLER                       PIC X(4).
```

Then the entire code segment would have been loaded into the program upon the compile. The problem with doing this is that if the particular program using the library entry (remember that library entries are created to be used in multiple programs) had additional files, the SELECT clauses for these files would have to be in front of the SELECT clause for the ISAM-FILE and then the file definitions would have to follow the ISAM-FILE definition. This presents no real problem as long as the programmer is careful. But if more files are going to be combined with this one and we happen to define the DATA DIVISION with one of those files, then the two files would be copied into the same program and we would end up with the DATA DIVISION and FILE SECTION in the program twice. It is simply less confusing to always use in the library definitions only those pieces directly related to the file being defined.

As we mentioned, this type of library entry can also store PROCEDURE DIVISION routines that might need to be used in several programs. Such storage reduces the coding necessary since the routine would not need to be done several times. It also helps to maintain consistency in the coding used throughout the installation.

A definite advantage of using a library and copy system is that if any of the file layouts or PROCEDURE DIVISION coding needs to be changed, the changes need to be done only once and the programs simply recompiled to incorporate the new coding. This is certainly more efficient than recoding the changed procedure in all the affected programs. The problem with this is that all the affected programs must somehow be kept track of. That is, if your installation maintains 300 COBOL programs, only a few of them might be affected by the changes; you would want to recompile only the affected programs, not every one in your installation.

Because of the problem of having to recompile programs whenever the library entries change, **subprograms** are often used instead of the COPY statement.

11-3
Subprograms

A **subprogram** is simply a program that is executed by another program, called the **calling program**. In fact, a subprogram cannot be executed on its own; it must be combined with the calling program. A subprogram is generally compiled separately from the calling program and becomes a separate object module. Then, when a program requires the use of the subprogram, a **CALL statement** is coded in the program to load the subprogram.

Using subprograms in place of common routines eliminates needless recoding and testing of commonly used logic. It also (with most compilers) lessens the need to recompile the main program whenever the subroutine is modified. Use of subroutines also allows a large project to be broken into several separate units, so several different programmers may work on the project at the same time.

Some operating systems will allow subprograms to be coded in a language other than COBOL and then called into a COBOL program. For example, we may need to do some advanced calculations or complicated text manipulations that can be handled more easily in another language. We can code the needed routines in the other language, compile the routines to get the object code, and then call those routines into the COBOL program. However, the programmer involved must know how to write in both languages, and whoever maintains the program at a later date will also need to know how to program in both languages. For this reason, most coding, of both subprograms and main programs, is done in COBOL.

With many operating systems, more is involved than simply compiling the subprogram and then calling it in the main program. Some operating systems require that the calling program and any associated subprograms be **linked**. First, the calling program and the subprograms are compiled and the object programs are stored in a library. Then the operating system locates the calling program and any required subprograms and assigns memory locations to the programs that do not conflict with each other. Also, any references of one program to another are set up so that the memory addresses can be located. After the calling and sub-programs are linked, we have a whole unit called a **load module**. Whenever the program is executed, it is the load module that is executed, not any of the separate programs.

The problem with linking the programs is that anytime a subprogram is changed, any program that uses that module as part of its load module will have to be relinked. So we are back to the same problem we had with the COPY statement: we will have to keep track of all the affected programs so that they can all be relinked when a module is modified. Fortunately, most systems don't require linking. They allow all the programs that use a subprogram to be auto-matically changed when the subprogram is changed, since the subprogram is called into the calling program when the program is executed. Naturally, if a subprogram is modified it has to be recompiled, but if we don't have to recompile or relink all the affected programs, our work is much simpler.

11-3-1 The CALL Statement

The first statement we will look at for the use of subprograms is the **CALL state-ment**. Its form is

$$\text{CALL} \begin{Bmatrix} \text{field-name-1} \\ \text{literal} \end{Bmatrix} \text{[USING field-name-2 [field-name-3 . . .]]}$$
$$\text{[ON OVERFLOW imperative-statement]}$$

Remember we discussed that some compilers require the calling program and the subprograms to be linked together. The CALL statement for this type of system is called a **static CALL statement** because we must use a literal subprogram name in the CALL statement. For example, suppose we have a subprogram called DATERTN, which does some date calculations. We would need a CALL statement like the following:

```
CALL 'DATERTN'.
```

If we have a system that does not require subprograms to be linked, we can use a field-name for the name of the subprogram. This is called a **dynamic CALL statement**. Thus we might use two statements in the calling program:

```
MOVE 'DATERTN' TO SUBPROGRAM-NAME.
CALL SUBPROGRAM-NAME.
```

Here, the subprogram name DATERTN is moved to a field called SUBPROGRAM-NAME and then that field is used in the CALL statement. Since the calling program is being executed as the CALL is performed, SUBPROGRAM-NAME would have DATERTN in it and the proper subroutine could be located for execution. If the programs had to be linked, however, the requirements would be different. Since the linking is done before the programs are executed, a field-name on the CALL statement would not work: without the program execution, the field would not contain the name of the subprogram.

The ON OVERFLOW clause is only applicable when we are using a dynamic CALL statement. When the CALL statement is executed, if there is not enough memory to load the subprogram into, the ON OVERFLOW condition exists and the imperative-statement is executed. If your system uses static CALL statements, the ON OVERFLOW clause has no application.

The final part of the CALL statement is the USING clause, which specifies the fields needed to store any data that will be passed between programs. Subprograms are used when we need to do some common calculations or other routines that will cause some type of resultant field. This resultant field is what is passed between programs. Actually, the fields are not passed between the programs. The calling program sets up storage for the fields and then the subprogram simply uses these same storage locations for its data. Thus, the data is simply shared by both programs.

The entire CALL statement might look like

```
CALL DATERTN USING DATE-MM DATE-DD DATE-YY.
```

This statement would call in the subprogram DATERTN and use the DATE-MM, DATE-DD, and DATE-YY fields to pass any needed data.

The CALL statement is the only statement needed in the calling program to establish the link between the calling program and the subprogram. The subprogram, however, requires three modifications, as follows.

11-3-2 Writing the Subprogram

When writing a subprogram, you need to be concerned about three distinct features that are not used in other programs. Since we are linking the calling program to the subprogram, we use the **LINKAGE SECTION** to describe the fields that will be passed between the programs. Fields are defined in the LINKAGE SECTION the same way they are defined in the WORKING-STORAGE SECTION: either elementary items or group and elementary items. The difference is that the fields do not take any space in the subprogram. They are merely defined so that they can be referenced as if they were fields in the calling program. The defined lengths of the fields must be the same as the associated items in the calling program.

Just as we have a USING clause in the calling program, we have a **USING clause** in the subprogram. This time the USING clause is found on the PROCEDURE DIVISION statement; its form is

PROCEDURE DIVISION [USING field-name-1 [field-name-2] . . .]

Each of the fields named on the PROCEDURE DIVISION statement must be defined in the LINKAGE SECTION, though the reverse is not true. We can have fields defined in the LINKAGE SECTION without listing them on the PROCEDURE DIVISION statement. The order of the fields listed on this USING statement must be in precisely the same order as the fields listed on the CALL statement. The field-names don't have to be the same, so the only way the computer knows which fields are supposed to be the same is by their position on the USING clauses.

When a typical program is finished, we use a STOP RUN statement to tell the operating system that the processing of the program is over. With a subprogram, however, we don't want the processing to stop. We want the system to transfer back to the calling program and continue processing, so we use an **EXIT PROGRAM statement** instead. When the statement is encountered, control shifts from the subprogram back to the calling program. The EXIT PROGRAM statement is similar to the EXIT statement in that it must be in a paragraph and must be the only statement in that paragraph. A sample follows:

```
0300-EXIT-PARAGRAPH.
    EXIT PROGRAM.
```

11-3-3 A Sample Program Pair

In order to see how the various parts of the programs work together, we will write a subprogram and the needed parts of the calling program. Since subprograms generally are written to accomplish commonly needed routines, we will write ours to do a date translation. We want a program that will translate a date from the usual MM/DD/YY format into one that gives the months in words. For example, we want to translate 12/15/88 into December 15, 1988.

To accomplish this mission, we will write the subprogram first. The easiest way to get the month is to use a table. So, let's define a table of the months as

```
WORKING-STORAGE SECTION.

01   MONTH-NAMES.
     10   FILLER            PIC X(9) VALUE 'JANUARY'.
     10   FILLER            PIC X(9) VALUE 'FEBRUARY'.
     10   FILLER            PIC X(9) VALUE 'MARCH'.
     10   FILLER            PIC X(9) VALUE 'APRIL'.
     10   FILLER            PIC X(9) VALUE 'MAY'.
     10   FILLER            PIC X(9) VALUE 'JUNE'.
     10   FILLER            PIC X(9) VALUE 'JULY'.
     10   FILLER            PIC X(9) VALUE 'AUGUST'.
     10   FILLER            PIC X(9) VALUE 'SEPTEMBER'.
     10   FILLER            PIC X(9) VALUE 'OCTOBER'.
     10   FILLER            PIC X(9) VALUE 'NOVEMBER'.
     10   FILLER            PIC X(9) VALUE 'DECEMBER'.

01   MONTH-NAME-TABLE REDEFINES MONTH-NAMES
     10   MONTH-NAME-ENTRY OCCURS 12 TIMES          PIC X(9).
```

This table gives us easy access to the month names. You should recall that the subdefinition of the MONTH-NAME-TABLE is necessary because an OCCURS cannot be on an 01 level.

Now we need to define the date itself. This we will do in our normal fashion, with the exception that the DATE-MM field (the month) is numeric (so we can use it to point to the table element we need):

```
01   DATE-IN            PIC X(6).
01   DATE-WORK REDEFINES DATE-IN.
     10   DATE-YY        PIC XX.
     10   DATE-MM        PIC 99.
     10   DATE-DD        PIC XX.
```

Next we define our transfer field in the LINKAGE SECTION

```
LINKAGE SECTION.

01   DATE-TRANSFER      PIC X(18).
```

and specify the PROCEDURE DIVISION statement as

```
PROCEDURE DIVISION USING DATE-TRANSFER.
```

We put only one field on the USING clause since that one field is all we need to transfer from the subprogram to the calling program.

Now, in the PROCEDURE DIVISION itself we ACCEPT the date from the machine and set up the DATE-TRANSFER field:

```
PROCEDURE DIVISION USING DATE-TRANSFER.

0100-MAIN-MODULE.

    ACCEPT DATE-IN FROM DATE.
    MOVE SPACES TO DATE-TRANSFER.
    STRING MONTH-NAME-ENTRY (DATE-MM) DELIMITED BY SPACE
           " " DATE-DD ", 19" DATE-YY DELIMITED BY SIZE
           INTO DATE-TRANSFER.

0200-EXIT-MODULE.

    EXIT PROGRAM.
```

This program will blank the DATE-TRANSFER field and then string the month name (pointed to by the month number), a space, the day, a comma, a space, 19, and the year into that field.

When put together, the entire subprogram looks like the following:

```
******************************************************************
******************************************************************
*
*
*
*   PROGRAM NAME: DATERTN
*
*   PROGRAMMER NAME:  ED COBURN
*
*   SOCIAL SECURITY NUMBER:  999-99-9999
*
*   DUE DATE: FEBRUARY 10, 1988
*
*   DESCRIPTION: THIS SUBPROGRAM WILL TRANSLATE THE NORMAL DATE
*                TO ONE WITH THE MONTH IN WORDS.
*
*
*
******************************************************************
******************************************************************

IDENTIFICATION DIVISION.
PROGRAM-ID.    DATERTN.
AUTHOR.        ED COBURN.

ENVIRONMENT DIVISION.

CONFIGURATION SECTION.
SOURCE-COMPUTER. IBM-4331.
OBJECT-COMPUTER. IBM-4331.
```

```
DATA DIVISION.

WORKING-STORAGE SECTION.

01   MONTH-NAMES.
     10   FILLER            PIC X(9) VALUE 'JANUARY'.
     10   FILLER            PIC X(9) VALUE 'FEBRUARY'.
     10   FILLER            PIC X(9) VALUE 'MARCH'.
     10   FILLER            PIC X(9) VALUE 'APRIL'.
     10   FILLER            PIC X(9) VALUE 'MAY'.
     10   FILLER            PIC X(9) VALUE 'JUNE'.
     10   FILLER            PIC X(9) VALUE 'JULY'.
     10   FILLER            PIC X(9) VALUE 'AUGUST'.
     10   FILLER            PIC X(9) VALUE 'SEPTEMBER'.
     10   FILLER            PIC X(9) VALUE 'OCTOBER'.
     10   FILLER            PIC X(9) VALUE 'NOVEMBER'.
     10   FILLER            PIC X(9) VALUE 'DECEMBER'.

01   MONTH-NAME-TABLE REDEFINES MONTH-NAMES
     10   MONTH-NAME-ENTRY OCCURS 12 TIMES    PIC X(9).

01   DATE-IN               PIC X(6).
01   DATE-WORK REDEFINES DATE-IN.
     10   DATE-YY          PIC XX.
     10   DATE-MM          PIC 99.
     10   DATE-DD          PIC XX.


LINKAGE SECTION.

01   DATE-TRANSFER         PIC X(18).


PROCEDURE DIVISION USING DATE-TRANSFER.

0100-MAIN-MODULE.

     ACCEPT DATE-IN FROM DATE.
     MOVE SPACES TO DATE-TRANSFER.
     STRING MONTH-NAME-ENTRY (DATE-MM) DELIMITED BY SPACE
         " " DATE-DD ", 19" DATE-YY DELIMITED BY SIZE
         INTO DATE-TRANSFER.


0200-EXIT-MODULE.

     EXIT PROGRAM.
```

You will notice that this subprogram does not have any SELECT clauses or a FILE SECTION. Since it doesn't use any files, neither is necessary.

Now that we know what the subprogram looks like, we should examine the calling program. As it turns out, all we really need to look at is the CALL statement itself, since this statement is the only difference between an ordinary program and a calling program. We do need to define the DATE-TRANSFER field in the calling program (it is used on the CALL statement) but, other than that, the program is normal. The CALL statement would be

```
CALL DATERTN USING DATE-TRANSFER.
```

The subprogram name in the CALL statement is the same name that was used on the PROGRAM-ID statement in the subprogram. This is a requirement: the PROGRAM-ID is what gives the name of the program to the operating system, and if the system is to link the two programs, it needs to be able to associate the name in the CALL statement with some program in the subprogram library.

11-4
Data Base Management Systems

COPY statements and subprograms are tools that can help a computer department organize its programs into a more unified and useful system. Such systemization is not restricted to the programs, however. The data stored and used in the system also needs organization. All the data used in an installation has traditionally been known as the **data base**.

Since the first computer department came into existence, the normal practice for accomplishing any task has been to design a file and then write a program to process the data contained in it, which is what we have been doing throughout this book. This approach tends to organize the data base into a collection of distinct files, each designed around specified needs. Thus, the typical data base will have files relating to employees, inventory, accounting, payroll, and so on.

There are several problems with this traditional approach:

■ Such systems of files can become so large and complex that it becomes virtually impossible for any one person in the system to keep track of where all the data may be found. Maintaining accuracy and completeness of the data becomes a monstrous task.

■ There is usually a great deal of **redundancy** in the system. Take a typical sales business, for example. We may have a sales file that contains, along with other information, the names and addresses of all the sales staff. These same names will probably reappear in the accounts receivable system. Since the sales people will expect to be paid, their names will again show up in the payroll system. These are only three places. There are likely to be many more. The problem with data redundancy is that anytime a change is made to one of the fields that is reproduced in several locations, each of those field locations needs to receive the change. That is, if the name of one of the salespeople is changed, all the files that contain that name must be located and changed. This is difficult at best.

■ Each of the system files is typically accessed by many different programs. Anytime these files are changed, all the affected programs have to be located, modified, recompiled, possibly relinked (for subprograms), and retested (even if the file change is slight, changes should always be tested for accuracy).

■ A new request for information from the system may be difficult to respond to if the needed data is located in several different files. All of the data may not be recorded in compatible formats. Often the data will need to be organized or sorted, and when data comes from different files, such processing becomes a real challenge. Probably the worst problem is that the relationships among the data from the various files may not be clear, causing problems when users try to arrange the data in the needed format.

Because of these and other problems, the **Data Base Management System,** or **DBMS**, has emerged. A DBMS is a program system, designed to manage the data base by controlling the organization, access, security, and recovery of the data. The DBMS forces a single well-defined description of the data base in which all the logical relationships are precisely defined and the methods of access to the data are specified. The data base is no longer made up of a series of unrelated files. All the data is merged into one cohesive unit from which the data can be combined and accessed as needed.

This organization solves most of the aforementioned problems. Since there is only one definition of the data, data redundancy is eliminated. Any change to the data needs to be made only once. (Because of certain inherent limitations within the typical DBMS, a limited amount of redundancy is unavoidable.)

In a DBMS, definition of the data is not accomplished through the use of a program. All the data is defined independent of program logic. Therefore, little or no programming effort is required when there are changes to the data base (except when the lengths of the fields are changed).

Since all the applications in a system share a common view of the data, there are never any problems with inconsistent or incompatible data. In addition, the data can be combined in any way necessary because it is all one unit.

A DBMS is basically an interface between the data base and any application program that needs access to the data. It accepts requests for access to the data, handles the security controls (passwords and so forth), locates the data, and performs the I/O, including any error recovery. As a bonus, most DBMS have automatic statistic and audit trail facilities.

Also, most DBMS have generating facilities that, by eliminating the need to create a formal application program, can help reduce the time necessary to produce reports. Typically, the system will also provide some type of query system for nonprofessional users to gain access to the data. Such systems generally operate in an interactive environment, allowing the user to phrase access commands in an English-like language rather than in COBOL or some other computer language.

The DBMS has become an integral part of most data processing centers over the last decade. Understanding how it's organized has become a crucial part of programming knowledge.

11-4-1   DBMS Organization

There are three basic design philosophies for organizing data to reflect the logical relationships among the data items:

- hierarchical
- network
- relational

In a **hierarchical organization**, relationships are expressed in a top-down, one-to-one or one-to-many fashion. Each item at the top may have one or several subordinate items. For example, Figure 11-2 shows a one-to-many relationship in an invoicing system. Each customer will order many different times, and each time an order is placed an invoice will be generated with one or more items on it. As you can see from the illustration, customer A has placed three orders (three invoices) and has ordered different items each time. Notice, however, that there are no relationships among the items that are subordinate to customer A. That is, there is no direct connection from invoice #1 to invoice #2 or from item #1 to item #3.

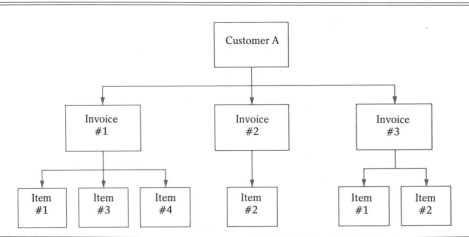

Figure 11-2 The hierarchical relationship among the customer, the invoices, and the items on the invoices. This diagram shows a one-to-many relationship.

Data is organized so that particular questions can be answered. The type of organization used in the data base dictates just what types of questions can be answered. A hierarchical organization would allow answers to the questions "How many invoices has customer A ordered?" and "How many of item #3 did customer A order on invoice #1?"

However, there are other questions that the hierarchical organization will not be able to answer directly (or sometimes not at all), such as "How many customers have ordered item #3?" or, even simpler, "How many times has customer A ordered item #3?"

This organization also cannot give us a true picture of the DBMS since, as you can see if you look back at Figure 11-2, there is redundancy in this picture (item #2 shows up twice).

For more inquiries to be handled, additional relationships need to be established. A system with these additional relationships uses a **network organization**. Figure 11-3 shows an example of a network system, which is organized a bit like a hierarchical system except that there are many additional relationships. Virtually every item is connected to every other item. Notice that item #2 is related to invoices #2 and #3.

This organization allows the more difficult questions to be answered since the relationships are more complex. The relationships between the various items are maintained by way of a series of pointers, pointing from one item to its related items. The problem with this organization is that these more complex relationships are difficult to implement and use. If a pointer would happen to be lost or forgotten, the entire system might be adversely affected.

The third commonly used DBMS organization is the **relational organization**, which arranges the data much as we visualize it. If we think of a file, we generally visualize it as a large table (square table, not COBOL table) made up of rows and columns with each record begin a row and each data item being at the intersection of a row and a column. The relational structure is this same table concept, each row being a relation. Figure 11-4 illustrates a relational organization.

It may seem that the relational organization is just like a series of records in a file. Well, that's true except that in an ordinary file there are no established relationships between the records and there may be a lot of redundancy (such as

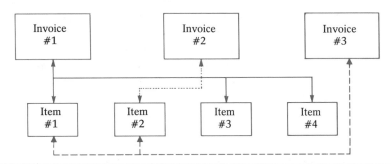

Figure 11-3 An illustration of a network organization. Notice that the relationship connections (the lines) indicate a dual relationship (by the use of the arrows).

Customer	Invoice #	Item #
A	1	1
A	1	3
A	1	4
A	2	2
A	3	1
A	3	2
B	4	1
B	4	4
B	5	3
B	5	2

Figure 11-4   Illustration of a relational organization.

the name of the customer on several invoice records). In the DBMS, however, relationships are established between the records by the use of key fields, so that redundancy is reduced or eliminated.

The primary advantage of the relational organization is its simplicity. It does have the disadvantage of requiring a lot of processing overhead to answer queries that are not implicit in the relations established. For example, it would be easy to answer the question "How many invoices did customer A order?" but much more difficult to answer "How many item #1's have been ordered?"

The current tendency in the use of the DBMS is towards the relational DBMS because of its simplicity. The processing overhead is becoming less of a problem because newer machines are gaining tremendously in processing power.

11-4-2   Components of a DBMS

A DBMS is made up of several distinct but related parts. The **Data Definition Facility** is used to define the data base to the system. For this definition, a **Data Definition Language** is used to describe the data in a language much like that used in the COBOL DATA DIVISION. After the data is defined, this definition is submitted to the **data definition processor**, which acts like a compiler to generate the internal data description, generally, called a **schema**.

The schema is the system definition of how the data is organized, what the validation procedures are, what operations are allowed, and how requests for information from the data base are to be handled. Using this schema, the Data Definition Language can also define **subschemas**, or the portions of the schema that are used in the applications programs. These subschemas are loaded into the applications programs using commands similar to the COPY statement we discussed earlier.

After the system is defined, we need to be able to access the data. This is where the **Data Manipulation Facility** comes in. It consists of a **Data Manipulation Language** and the **Data Base Manager**. The Data Base Manager is the program that actually controls access to the data base. The Data Manipulation Language, which is an interface to all the programming languages that might be used (COBOL or any other) to access the data base, provides special language commands for whatever language is being used. Special compilers are also provided, since an ordinary compiler would not recognize the special commands needed for the Data Manipulation Language.

Probably one of the most important components of the DBMS is the **Data Base Query Facility**. It has its own language, the **Data Base Query Language**, which is an interactive program interface, a query language that allows commands to be entered in an English-like language and responds by supplying either the requested data or an error message that will help guide the user to proper phrasing of the query. Such languages are designed to be as easy as possible to use, allowing virtually anyone access to the data base. This system is specifically designed for the casual user, who doesn't have the time to learn or use formal programming.

The **Report Generator Facility** consists (of course) of the **Report Generator Language** and a compiler that will translate the programs written in that language. This part of the system was designed to be used in a formal data processing environment to assist with the easy and orderly printing of routine reports from the data base.

Additional tools are typically available with the DBMS to aid in controlling the information. First, there is an initializer, which allocates the space, parameters, and tables for the data base when it is first created. Then there is the audit facility, to maintain a record of all the transactions processed by the system. Finally, so that management can monitor the DBMS usage and performance, there are statistical report generators.

11-5

The Record Rack Subprogram

Roger has decided that a lot of the programs used by *The Record Rack* should be converted to on-line programs. Since most of the programs will require entry of dates, Roger wants Cindy to write a subprogram that will verify the accuracy of the dates being entered without the routine having to be written each time it is needed. The program will need to verify that

- the date is numeric and none of the entries is zero;
- the month does not exceed 12;
- the number of days does not exceed the maximum in the month, such as 30 days for September. This part of the subprogram is to include a calculation for leap years (February has 29 days during leap years).

■ the year does not go below or above the minimum and maximum allowed. These minimums and maximums are to be passed to the subprogram from the main program.

If any part of the date entered is in error, the appropriate error message should be printed.

After she has written the subprogram, Roger wants Cindy to write a simple program to test the subprogram.

To get a firm handle on what she is to do, Cindy draws out the systems chart shown in Figure 11-5. Since this is a subroutine to do an edit only, there is no report to be printed and thus no printer spacing chart. The subprogram design (since the calling program will consist of a simple MOVE and CALL routine, Cindy didn't bother to design it) follows (see also Figure 11-6):

```
Start
Unstring around the slashes (dates will be entered with slashes)
IF month or day or year is less than or equal to zero THEN
      Print error message
ELSE IF year is less than minimum or greater than maximum THEN
      Print error message
ELSE IF month is greater than 12 THEN
      Print error message
ELSE IF month is 04 or 06, or 09, or 11
                  and day is greater than 30 THEN
      Print error message
ELSE IF month is not 02 or 04 or 06 or 09 or 11
                  and day is greater than 31 THEN
      Print error message
ELSE IF month is 02 THEN
      Divide month by 4 and get remainder
      IF remainder is not zero THEN
            IF day is greater than 28 THEN
                  Print error message
            (ELSE)
            END-IF
      ELSE IF day is greater than 29 THEN
            Print error message
            (ELSE)
            END-IF
      END-IF
END-IF
```

Cindy decides to make the subprogram as flexible as possible by using a table for the error messages and using precise error messages for every error possible.

Figure 11-5   The systems chart for *The Record Rack* subprogram.

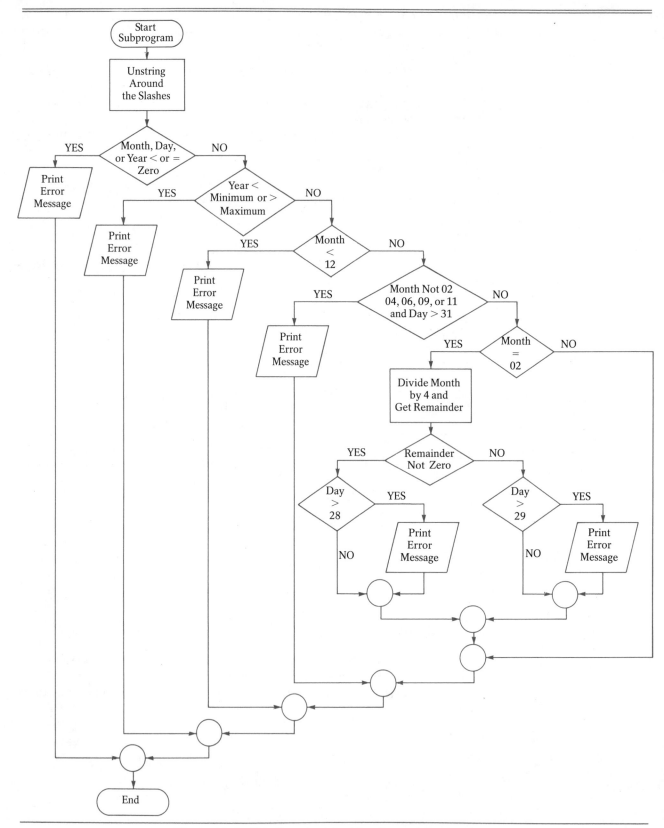

Figure 11-6 The flowchart for *The Record Rack* subprogram.

Her error messages are

- Month, day, or year less than one.
- Year exceeds maximum (and display maximum).
- Year is less than minimum (and display minimum).
- Month exceeds 12.
- Day exceeds maximum for month.
- Day exceeds maximum for February during non-leap year.

She also decides that the easiest way to figure the appropriate number of days in a month is to use a table, so she will simply use the month number to point to the table element. Her subprogram looks like the following:

```
****************************************************************
****************************************************************
*
*
*
*   PROGRAM NAME: DATEVER
*
*   PROGRAMMER NAME:  CINDY HARRISON
*
*   SOCIAL SECURITY NUMBER:  999-99-9999
*
*   DUE DATE: FEBRUARY 10, 1988
*
*   DESCRIPTION: THIS SUBPROGRAM WILL VERIFY A DATE ENTRY.
*
*
*
****************************************************************
****************************************************************
    IDENTIFICATION DIVISION.
    PROGRAM-ID.    DATEVER.
    AUTHOR.        CINDY HARRISON.

    ENVIRONMENT DIVISION.

    CONFIGURATION SECTION.
    SOURCE-COMPUTER. IBM-4331.
    OBJECT-COMPUTER. IBM-4331.

    DATA DIVISION.

    WORKING-STORAGE SECTION.

    01 DIV-RESULT          PIC 99.

    01 LEAP-YEAR           PIC 9.

    01  DAYS-TABLE.
        10   FILLER        PIC X(2) VALUE '31'.
        10   FILLER        PIC X(2) VALUE '29'.
        10   FILLER        PIC X(2) VALUE '31'.
        10   FILLER        PIC X(2) VALUE '30'.
        10   FILLER        PIC X(2) VALUE '31'.
        10   FILLER        PIC X(2) VALUE '30'.
        10   FILLER        PIC X(2) VALUE '31'.
```

```
         10   FILLER              PIC X(2) VALUE '31'.
         10   FILLER              PIC X(2) VALUE '30'.
         10   FILLER              PIC X(2) VALUE '31'.
         10   FILLER              PIC X(2) VALUE '30'.
         10   FILLER              PIC X(2) VALUE '31'.

      01  MONTH-DAYS-TABLE REDEFINES DAYS-TABLE.
         10   DAYS-OF-MONTH OCCURS 12 TIMES    PIC XX.

      01  ERROR-ENTRIES.
         10   FILLER            PIC X(30) VALUE
              'MONTH, DAY OR YEAR LESS THAN 1'.
         10   MAX-FIELD.
              20   FILLER       PIC X(24) VALUE
                   'YEAR EXCEEDS MAXIMUM OF '.
              20   MAX-YR-ERROR PIC XX.
              20   FILLER       PIC X(4)  VALUE SPACES.
         10   MIN-FIELD.
              20   FILLER       PIC X(26) VALUE
                   'YEAR LESS THAN MINIMUM OF '.
              20   MIN-YR-ERROR PIC XX.
              20   FILLER       PIC X(2)  VALUE SPACES.
         10   FILLER            PIC X(30) VALUE
              'MONTH EXCEEDS 12'.
         10   FILLER            PIC X(30) VALUE
              'DAY EXCEEDS MAXIMUM FOR MONTH'.
         10   FILLER            PIC X(30) VALUE
              '28 MAXIMUM IN NON-LEAP YEARS'.

      01  ERROR-TABLE REDEFINES ERROR-ENTRIES.
         10   ERROR-MESSAGES OCCURS 6 TIMES PIC X(30).

      01  WHOLE-DATE.
         10   MONTH-IN        PIC XX JUSTIFIED RIGHT.
         10   NUMERIC-MONTH REDEFINES MONTH-IN PIC 99.
         10   DAY-IN          PIC XX JUSTIFIED RIGHT.
         10   YEAR-IN         PIC XX JUSTIFIED RIGHT.
         10   NUMERIC-YEAR  REDEFINES YEAR-IN  PIC 99.

      LINKAGE SECTION.

      01  DATE-ERROR         PIC X(30).

      01  DATE-IN            PIC X(8).

      01  DATE-ERROR-FLAG    PIC X.

      01  YEAR-MAXIMUM       PIC XX.

      01  YEAR-MINIMUM       PIC XX.


      PROCEDURE DIVISION USING DATE-ERROR
                               DATE-IN
                               DATE-ERROR-FLAG
                               YEAR-MAXIMUM
                               YEAR-MINIMUM.
```

```
0100-MAIN-MODULE.

    MOVE '0' TO DATE-ERROR-FLAG.
    MOVE SPACES TO DATE-ERROR.
    UNSTRING DATE-IN DELIMITED BY '/'
         INTO MONTH-IN DAY-IN YEAR-IN.

    INSPECT WHOLE-DATE REPLACING ALL SPACES BY ZEROS.

    IF YEAR-IN  < '01' OR YEAR-IN  NOT NUMERIC OR
       MONTH-IN < '01' OR MONTH-IN NOT NUMERIC OR
       DAY-IN   < '01' OR DAY-IN   NOT NUMERIC
       MOVE '1' TO DATE-ERROR-FLAG
       MOVE ERROR-MESSAGES (1) TO DATE-ERROR
    ELSE IF YEAR-IN < YEAR-MINIMUM
         MOVE '1' TO DATE-ERROR-FLAG
         MOVE YEAR-MINIMUM TO MIN-YR-ERROR
         MOVE ERROR-MESSAGES (3) TO DATE-ERROR
    ELSE IF YEAR-IN > YEAR-MAXIMUM
         MOVE '1' TO DATE-ERROR-FLAG
         MOVE YEAR-MAXIMUM TO MAX-YR-ERROR
         MOVE ERROR-MESSAGES (2) TO DATE-ERROR
    ELSE IF MONTH-IN > '12'
         MOVE '1' TO DATE-ERROR-FLAG
         MOVE ERROR-MESSAGES (4) TO DATE-ERROR
    ELSE IF MONTH-IN NOT = '02' AND
         DAY-IN > DAYS-OF-MONTH (NUMERIC-MONTH)
         MOVE '1' TO DATE-ERROR-FLAG
         MOVE ERROR-MESSAGES (5) TO DATE-ERROR
    ELSE IF MONTH-IN = '02'
         DIVIDE NUMERIC-YEAR BY 4 GIVING DIV-RESULT
              REMAINDER LEAP-YEAR
         IF LEAP-YEAR = 0 AND DAY-IN > 29
            MOVE '1' TO DATE-ERROR-FLAG
            MOVE ERROR-MESSAGES (5) TO DATE-ERROR
         ELSE IF LEAP-YEAR > 0 AND DAY-IN > 28
                 MOVE '1' TO DATE-ERROR-FLAG
                 MOVE ERROR-MESSAGES (6) TO DATE-ERROR.

0200-EXIT-MODULE.

    EXIT PROGRAM.
```

You will notice that this subprogram links to the calling program with five different fields: DATE-ERROR, DATE-IN, DATE-ERROR-FLAG, YEAR-MAXIMUM, and YEAR-MINIMUM. The YEAR-MAXIMUM, YEAR-MINIMUM, and DATE-IN are transferred from the calling program to the subprogram. The other fields are transferred from the subprogram to the calling program. Of course, there is no true transferring since the fields actually exist in memory only once and are simply referenced in both programs.

Now, in order to test the subprogram, Cindy puts together a small program that will force the date to be many different values, each one designed to test one aspect of the edit subprogram. She will use a maximum year of 90 and a minimum year of 86. The dates used and the errors (or not) that should be produced are as follows:

Date	Error
12/15/87	No error—no error message
09/20/8A	MONTH, DAY, OR YEAR LESS THAN 1
0A/20/88	MONTH, DAY, OR YEAR LESS THAN 1
09/2A/88	MONTH, DAY, OR YEAR LESS THAN 1
09/20/98	YEAR EXCEEDS MAXIMUM OF 90
09/31/88	DAY EXCEEDS MAXIMUM FOR MONTH (31 in 09)
09/30/88	No error—checking for correct days (30)
02/29/88	No error—checking for 29 in leap year
02/29/87	28 MAXIMUM IN NON-LEAP YEARS
09/00/88	MONTH, DAY, OR YEAR LESS THAN 1
9/2/88	No error—checking for stringing

Cindy's program to call the subprogram will look like this:

```
****************************************************************
****************************************************************
*
*
*
*   PROGRAM NAME: PROG-CHK
*
*   PROGRAMMER NAME:  CINDY HARRISON
*
*   SOCIAL SECURITY NUMBER:  999-99-9999
*
*   DUE DATE: FEBRUARY 10, 1988
*
*   DESCRIPTION: THIS PROGRAM WILL CALL THE DATEVER SUBPROGRAM
*                AND TEST THE VERIFICATION ROUTINES.
*
*
****************************************************************
****************************************************************

    IDENTIFICATION DIVISION.
    PROGRAM-ID.   PROG-CHK.
    AUTHOR.       CINDY HARRISON.

    ENVIRONMENT DIVISION.

    CONFIGURATION SECTION.
    SOURCE-COMPUTER. IBM-4331.
    OBJECT-COMPUTER. IBM-4331.
```

```
DATA DIVISION.

WORKING-STORAGE SECTION.

01   DATE-ERROR              PIC X(30).

01   DATE-IN                PIC X(8).

01   DATE-ERROR-FLAG        PIC X.

01   YEAR-MAXIMUM           PIC XX VALUE '90'.

01   YEAR-MINIMUM           PIC XX VALUE '86'.


PROCEDURE DIVISION.

0100-MAIN-MODULE.

     MOVE '12/15/87' TO DATE-IN.
     PERFORM 0200-DATE-EDIT.
     MOVE '09/20/8A' TO DATE-IN.
     PERFORM 0200-DATE-EDIT.
     MOVE '0A/20/88' TO DATE-IN.
     PERFORM 0200-DATE-EDIT.
     MOVE '09/2A/88' TO DATE-IN.
     PERFORM 0200-DATE-EDIT.
     MOVE '09/20/98' TO DATE-IN.
     PERFORM 0200-DATE-EDIT.
     MOVE '09/31/88' TO DATE-IN.
     PERFORM 0200-DATE-EDIT.
     MOVE '09/30/88' TO DATE-IN.
     PERFORM 0200-DATE-EDIT.
     MOVE '02/29/88' TO DATE-IN.
     PERFORM 0200-DATE-EDIT.
     MOVE '02/29/87' TO DATE-IN.
     PERFORM 0200-DATE-EDIT.
     MOVE '09/00/88' TO DATE-IN.
     PERFORM 0200-DATE-EDIT.
     MOVE '9/02/88' TO DATE-IN.
     PERFORM 0200-DATE-EDIT.
     STOP RUN.

0200-DATE-EDIT.

     CALL 'DATEVER' USING DATE-ERROR
                          DATE-IN
                          DATE-ERROR-FLAG
                          YEAR-MAXIMUM
                          YEAR-MINIMUM.

     DISPLAY DATE-IN '   ' DATE-ERROR-FLAG '  ' DATE-ERROR.
```

After both programs are compiled, Cindy's program generates the following output on the screen:

```
12/15/87    0

09/20/8A    1   MONTH, DAY OR YEAR LESS THAN 1

0A/20/88    1   MONTH, DAY OR YEAR LESS THAN 1

09/2A/88    1   MONTH, DAY OR YEAR LESS THAN 1

09/20/98    1   YEAR EXCEEDS MAXIMUM OF 90

09/31/88    1   DAY EXCEEDS MAXIMUM FOR MONTH

09/30/88    0

02/29/88    1   28 MAXIMUM IN NON-LEAP YEARS

02/29/87    1   28 MAXIMUM IN NON-LEAP YEARS

09/00/88    1   MONTH, DAY OR YEAR LESS THAN 1

9/2/88      0
```

This list shows first the date, then the error code (a code 0 indicates no error), and then the message to be printed. If you look back at the error list we discussed before, you will discover that these errors mirror those listed.

11-6
Summary

1. All data processing installations have certain routines that are used over and over. There are three approaches to creating these routines. First, they can simply be written each time they are needed. Obviously, this is the most direct method, but also the most time-consuming one. It would probably be better to create the routine one time and then simply copy it into your program as needed, or possibly create a subprogram that can then be called into your program. Both of these approaches were discussed in this chapter.

2. You can create the needed file layout or PROCEDURE DIVISION routine and then store it in a library. Once it is stored there, you can use the COPY statement to load the code into your program. The command must include the text-name given to the code when it was stored in the library and, on some systems, the name of the library. The only limitation on the COPY statement is that the code being copied in cannot have a COPY statement. The problem with copying library entries is that if the entries ever change, every program they are in must be located and changed.

3. Such a problem doesn't (with most compilers) exist when subprograms are used. A subprogram is simply a program that is executed by another program. The execution is done with the CALL statement in the main (or calling) program. The subprogram is required to use a LINKAGE SECTION to set up

the fields that are going to contain data that needs to either come from or go to the calling program. Then the PROCEDURE DIVISION statement must specify which fields are to be used in the programs. Finally, the subprogram must have an EXIT PROGRAM statement to end the program.

4. The use of the COPY statement and subprograms fills the need for flexible programs. But we also have problems with our data files, ranging from simply finding the data we want to dealing with a lot of redundant data. A DBMS, or Data Base Management System, can help alleviate these problems by allowing the system to be in complete control of the entire data base.

5. There are basically three types of DBMS: hierarchical, network, and relational. Each has its strong points, but most people favor the use of a relational DBMS.

11-7
Glossary

CALL statement   In the main program, the statement that loads a subprogram into memory and executes it.

Calling program   The program that calls a subprogram.

COPY statement   The statement that copies code from a library into a program as the program is compiled.

Data base   The collection of all the data used in a computer system.

Data Base Management System, or DBMS   An interface program between the data base and any application programs that need access to the data.

Data Base Manager   The part of the DBMS that actually controls the access to the data.

Data Base Query Facility   The part of the DBMS that allows the user to gain interactive access to the data through use of an English-like language.

Data Base Query Language   The DBMS language that allows the user to get information from the data base by inquiring with English-language commands.

Data Definition Facility   The part of the DBMS that defines the data base to the system.

Data Definition Language   The DBMS language, similar to the COBOL DATA DIVISION language, that defines the data base.

Data Definition Processor   The DBMS compiler that translates the definition of the data base set up by the Data Definition Language.

Data Manipulation Facility   The part of the DBMS that allows the data to be manipulated for access.

Data Manipulation Language   The DBMS language that is an interface to all the programming languages that need access to the data base.

Dynamic CALL statement   A CALL statement that uses a variable subprogram name. Compilers that allow dynamic calling do not require the program to be linked.

EXIT PROGRAM statement   The program statement needed to end a subprogram.

Hierarchical organization   The type of DBMS organization that sets up the data items in a one-to-one or one-to-many hierarchy.

LINKAGE SECTION   The program section that defines the fields that are to be used to pass data from the subprogram to the calling program or vice versa.

Linking The process of combining a subprogram and a calling program after the two are compiled.

Load module The module created by linking a subprogram and the calling program.

Network organization The type of DBMS organization that sets up the data so that all the data items are linked.

Redundancy The process of having data items defined several times in the data base.

Relational organization The type of DBMS organization that sets up the data in relational form: each record is like a row of a table and the fields are the intersection of the rows and columns.

Report Generator Facility The part of the DBMS designed to allow easy and orderly printing of reports from the data base.

Report Generator Language The DBMS language that creates reports from the data base.

Schema The system definition of how the data is organized.

Static CALL statement A CALL statement in which the subprogram is listed by actual name. If a compiler requires the subprogram and the calling program to be linked, only static CALL statements are allowed.

Subprogram A program that can be executed by another program. The subprogram is called into the larger program for execution.

Subschema Portions of the schema that are loaded into the application programs.

USING clause The clause used on the PROCEDURE DIVISION statement in a subprogram and on the CALL statement in the calling program to pass fields between the programs. The fields listed on the USING clause must be in the same sequence in both programs.

11-8
Quick Quiz

Cover the answers with a blank sheet of paper and test yourself. Questions 1–15 are true or false questions, 16–18 are multiple choice, and 19–25 are fill-in-the-blank.

T F **1.** Using the COPY statement can be thought of as "reinventing the wheel."

T F **2.** When something is copied, it is copied from a library.

T F **3.** Some computer systems have a series of libraries and therefore require the use of the library-name on the COPY command.

T F **4.** Copy code stored in a library can copy other code.

T F **5.** A COPY statement can be used to copy any COBOL code desired.

T F **6.** The subprograms and calling program must be compiled before they can be linked.

T F **7.** If the compiler doesn't require linking, a subprogram that hasn't been compiled can be called in.

T F **8.** Subprograms must all be coded in the same programming language.

T F **9.** The ON OVERFLOW clause on the CALL statement is executed when the data for one of the fields on the USING clause does not fit in the field.

T F **10.** The LINKAGE SECTION is required in the subprogram.

T F **11.** It is imperative that the fields on the USING clauses in both the subprogram and the calling program be listed in the same order.

T F **12.** The COPY statement can reduce data redundancy.

T F **13.** Without a DBMS, if a file is changed, all the programs in which that file is used will have to be recompiled.

T F **14.** In a DBMS, data redundancy can be totally eliminated.

T F **15.** The schema is the system definition of the data base.

_____ **16.** Which of the following is the most commonly used type of DBMS?

  (a) hierarchical   **(c)** network
  (b) relational   **(d)** systematic

_____ **17.** Which of the following pieces is found only in the calling program?

  (a) CALL   **(c)** LINKAGE SECTION
  (b) EXIT PROGRAM   **(d)** PROCEDURE DIVISION USING

_____ **18.** Which of the following DBMS organizations contains the most relationship links?

  (a) hierarchical   **(c)** network
  (b) relational   **(d)** systematic

19. A _____ is executed by the calling program.

20. The COPY statement copies its code from a _____ .

21. When programs are linked, they form a unit called a _____ .

22. The USING clause is used on the _____ in the subprogram and on the _____ in the calling program.

23. The subprogram requires three parts not found in the typical program: _____ , _____ , and _____ .

24. Data redundancy can be overcome by the use of a _____ .

25. The part of the DBMS that actually defines the data base to the system is the _____ .

11-9
Answers to Quick Quiz

1. F (Rewriting the code each time is "reinventing the wheel.")

2. T (The library is where the code to be copied is stored.)

3. T

4. F (That's the one limitation of the COPY statement.)

5. T (Though it's usually used in the DATA and PROCEDURE DIVISIONs.)

6. T (Though only some compilers require linking.)

7. F (No, of course not. To be executed by another program, the subprogram must have been compiled so that the object code can be executed.)

8. F (Though this is most often true, most systems will let a calling program created in one language call subprograms created in a second language.)

9. F (The ON OVERFLOW takes effect on a dynamic CALL when there is not enough memory available to load the needed subprogram.)

10. T (It is required in all subprograms.)

11. T (That's the only way the system can determine which field is which.)

12. F (The COPY statement is used for reducing redundancy in coding, not in data.)
13. F (Not necessarily. It is possible that only one field is changed in the file and that that particular field is not used in some of the programs. Those programs would not need recompiling. But to keep track of which programs use which fields would be an even bigger nightmare than the lack of a DBMS already presents.)
14. F (A certain amount of redundancy is unavoidable.)
15. T
16. b (The relational organization is used the most often.)
17. a (Only the CALL statement is used in the calling program.)
18. c (The network has relational links between virtually every element.)
19. subprogram
20. library
21. load module
22. PROCEDURE DIVISION statement, CALL statement
23. LINKAGE SECTION, PROCEDURE DIVISION statement with USING clause, EXIT PROGRAM statement
24. DBMS
25. Data Definition Facility

11-10
Questions to Aid Understanding

*1. Explain the purpose of the COPY statement, mentioning the significance of the library.
2. When is the library-name needed on the COPY statement?
*3. Explain why we might choose to use a subprogram rather than the COPY statement.
4. Explain what a subprogram is.
5. List and explain at least three reasons for using subprograms.
*6. On some compilers, subprograms can be coded in languages other than COBOL and then called into a COBOL program. Explain why this is not necessarily a good idea.
7. Explain how the CALL statement in the calling program and the PROCEDURE DIVISION statement in the subprogram are related and why this relationship is necessary.
*8. Explain the purpose of the LINKAGE SECTION.
9. When does the ON OVERFLOW on the CALL statement get executed?
10. List and explain at least two reasons why the traditional approach to creating files can cause problems and how a DBMS can overcome them.
11. List the three types of DBMS and explain the differences among them.
12. Explain what a schema and a subschema are.

11-11

Coding Exercises

1. In your calling program, FIELD-1 has a PIC clause of 9(6)V99 that needs to be used in a subprogram. FIELD-2 and FIELD-3 are calculated in the subprogram with lengths of 9(5)V99 each and need to be used in the calling program. Write the statements needed to get FIELD-1 into the subprogram and FIELD-2 and FIELD-3 back into the main program. Don't concern yourself with what calculations are done in the subprogram or what FIELD-2 and FIELD-3 are going to be used for in the calling program. This is simply an exercise in setting up the transfer.

2. Set up a subprogram that calculates results using three fields from the calling program and then sends results back in the form of two additional fields. Design the various statements necessary to carry this out.

11-12

Maintenance Program

Roger likes the subprogram Cindy wrote in this chapter, but he decides he wants the subprogram to be able to translate the date into words if there are no errors. That is, if there is something wrong with the date, the program should return the error to the calling program. But if the date is valid, the program should return the date translated into words, as we showed in the sample program in the chapter. Your job is to combine both techniques into one program and then update Cindy's test program to verify the accuracy of the program's translations.

11-13

Illustrative Program

You should be familiar with the use of the ACCEPT statement to get the date from the computer. This statement can also be used to get the time from the computer using the keyword TIME. The form of the statement is

ACCEPT field-name FROM TIME.

The statement will place, in the field, the time as an eight-digit numeric value. This value can be expressed as HHMMSSHH, which is (all 2 digits each) hours, minutes, seconds, and hundredths of a second. The hours are expressed in military time format (we won't concern ourselves with seconds or hundredths):

Value of TIME	Normal Time
10150000	10:15 A.M.
13550000	1:55 P.M.
19220000	7:22 P.M.
23050000	11:05 P.M.

Write a subprogram to translate the time input from the computer to a string of characters like those shown in the lefthand column of the table just above. Then create a program to get the time string and display it on the screen.

Since there is no file the systems chart is not necessary; nor is the printer spacing chart since there is no report. The pseudocode for the subroutine is shown below (flowchart in Figure 11-7):

```
Start program
Accept the time from the computer into divided field
IF hours > 12 THEN
     Move P.M. to AM–PM field
     Subtract 12 from hours
     Move new hours to hours field in string
ELSE
     Move A.M. to AM–PM field
     Move hours to hours field in string
END-IF
End subprogram
```

11-14
System Designed Programs

For the following programs, all the design elements typically furnished to a programmer by the systems analyst are furnished. It is up to you, as programmer, to design and code the program. The files to be used are found in Appendix A.

1. Go back to exercise 1 in the System Designed Programs in Chapter 5 and use a library to store the two input file layouts needed for the program there. Then modify the program to use a COPY statement to load the file layouts into the program. Retest the program to be sure it works.
2. Go back to exercise 3 in the System Designed Programs in Chapter 7 and redo the program so that each of the functions (add, change, delete) is in a separate subroutine (as it would be if the program were assigned to three different programmers). The calling program should read the file and print the reports; only the needed calculations need to be in the subprogram. Compile and thoroughly test the program and subprograms.
3. Write a subroutine that will receive an 80-character record from the calling program and reverse the order of the characters in the field. Use only one field to pass the data—receiving the data in the subprogram, turning it around, and then passing it back to the calling program in the same field. The calling program should first display the original field and then display, right underneath, the reversed field.

11-15
Non-designed Programs

In the following programs, you will need to design the systems chart, the input files (record layout), the printer spacing chart, the program design, and the data with which to test the program.

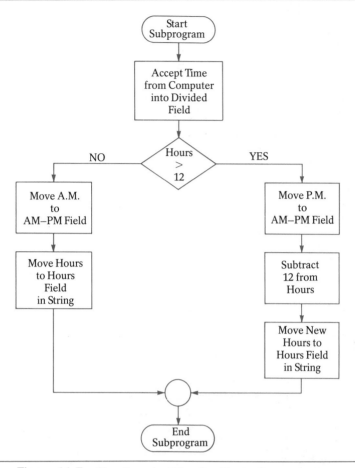

Figure 11-7   The flowchart for the illustrative program.

1. Go back to exercise 1 in the Non-designed Programs in Chapter 5 and use a library to store the input file layout needed for the program there. Then modify the program to use a COPY statement to load the file layouts into the program. Retest the program to be sure it works.
2. Go back to exercise 3 in the Non-designed Programs in Chapter 7 and redo the program so that each of the functions (four of them) is in a separate subroutine (as it would be if the program were assigned to three different programmers). The calling program should read the file and print the reports; only the needed calculations need to be in the subprogram. Compile and thoroughly test the program and subprograms.
3. Write a subprogram to calculate taxes and FICA deductions. Make up your own tax table figures (use a table, not a percentage calculation) and use a FICA deduction of 6.75%. In the calling program, input a data file with hours worked and rate of pay to calculate the gross pay. Then pass the gross pay to the subroutine. There the net pay and the two deductions should be calculated and passed back to the calling program, which then prints a report detailing name, hours worked, rate of pay, gross pay, taxes, FICA, and net pay. Use appropriate totals on the report.

A

Data Files Used

This Appendix contains the data for the files used in testing of programming assignments throughout the book. First is an alphabetical list of file names, and the exercises for which each is used. Then, for references purposes, follows a list of files for which the data is supplied within the chapter. The data for all other files follows.

File Name	Chapter and Figure	Exercise Number
BALLOT	5-9	Illustrative program
BALTRANS	7-6	*Record Rack* program
BANK	6-23	Interactive—1
	7-20	System designed—2
	3-26	System designed—2
	8-9	Illustrative program
	9-2	*Record Rack* program
BOOKINV	10-10	Illustrative program
CHARGE	2-18	System designed—2
	10-16	System designed—2
CNSTRUCT	5-17	System designed—2
	6-17	System designed—2
CONSTCO	10-1	Sample program
CUSTOMER	4-1	*Record Rack* program
	4-6	Maintenance program
	6-1	Sample program
	4-14	System designed—1
	7-1	Sample program
	7-5	*Record Rack* program

APPENDIXES

File Name	Chapter and Figure	Exercise Number
	8-5	Sample program
	11-1	Sample program
DONATE	2-11	Illustrative program
INVSALES	3-31	System designed—3
INTRANS	7-23	System designed—3
INVENT	6-26	Interactive—2
	4-21	System designed—3
	5-13	System designed—1
	7-22	System designed—3
	8-12	System designed—1
	3-30	System designed—3
	9-18	Interactive—3
	10-13	System designed—1
ITEMNO	5-14	System designed—1
MACHINE	5-20	System designed—3
MAGAZINE	6-8	Coding
MANUFACT	2-21	System designed—3
	10-19	System designed—3
PATIENTS	9-1	Sample program
PAYROLL	5-23	Interactive—1
	6-6	Coding
	7-15	System designed—1
	8-23	System designed—3
	3-12	*Record Rack* program
PAYTRANS	7-16	System designed—1
RRINVENT	2-5	*Record Rack* program
	6-14	System designed—1
	10-5	*Record Rack* program
SALES	2-15	System designed—1
	4-16	System designed—2

File Name	Chapter and Figure	Exercise Number
	5-1	*Record Rack* program
	8-16	System designed—2
	6-20	System designed—3
	3-22	System designed—1
	9-14	System designed—2
SALETRAN	3-23	System designed—1
SHIPPING	2-7	Maintenance program
	10-7	Maintenance program
SPORTTBL	9-19	System designed—3
SUBSCRIB	3-19	Illustrative program
	6-2	Maintenance program
	6-7	Coding
	6-10	Illustrative program
	6-29	Interactive—3
	7-10	Illustrative program
	8-6	*Record Rack* program
SUBTRANS	3-20	Illustrative program
	4-8	Illustrative program
	7-11	Illustrative program
TRANSALE	9-15	System designed—2
TRANSIN	7-2	Sample program
TRANWOOD	9-10	Illustrative program
UPDATE	3-27	System designed—2
	9-5	*Record Rack* program
WOOD	9-9	Illustrative program

Data for the following files is contained in the chapter. The files are listed here for reference only.

File Name	Chapter and Figure	Exercise Number
CONTRIB	3-8	Sample program
RRTRANS	3-13	*Record Rack* program
TRANS	3-9	Sample program

Here is the data necessary for completing all other programming assignments, as listed with each file.

The BALLOT **file** is used in Figure 5-9, Illustrative program. The data is

```
         1
1234567890
----------
11111
22333
35456
11234
15342
25455
32222
23333
34444
24455
35456
13333
13343
12232
22211
31111
31234
24321
22233
23322
14455
15456
24446
33326
22256
13356
22345
12456
32236
22221
```

The BALTRANS **file** is used in Figure 7-6, *Record Rack* program. The data is

```
         1
1234567890
----------
0456010422
1111002502
2248008875
2345017579
2423009000
3345005685
3455015402
4578010501
4597009127
4857006816
5465029710
5687005697
5753005519
6786010222
7655005815
7893017109
8678022500
```

The BANK **file** is used in Figure 3-26, System designed—2; Figure 6-23, Interactive—1; Figure 7-20, System designed—2; Figure 8-9, Illustrative program; and Figure 9-2, *Record Rack* program. The data is

```
          1         2         3         4         5
12345678901234567890123456789012345678901234567890 12
--------------------------------------------------
0001JIM CLARK           10004467011488001363400 10400
0002RONALD GEORGE       20030036020888002818100 02500
0003TOM ADDIS           30003874122088001080000 08800
0004ABABA ADDIS         10000276020288000142300 17500
0005BOBBETT BEELER      20006133022088001241200 09000
0006JIM COLLINS         30013713022788002522800 05600
0007JOHN DAVIS          10001476102688003675800 15400
0008MADGE HEADLEY       30028269031088003937400 10500
0009TOMMY MCNUTT        10000241020488001848900 09100
0010LETICIA MORALES     10012187101288000526400 06800
0011SHARON RUSSEL       10014878022588000769500 29700
0012ANGIE BEELER        20017554021588003590300 05600
0013PAT ANDERSON        10003482010288001929100 05500
0014LOU GONZALEZ        20000058111688000119400 10200
0015AGUSTIN DE LA CRUZ  30006762011288002682600 05800
0016ISMAEL DE LEON      20133008101688001160200 17100
0017WYNDETTA PEVEY      30010428011888000504300 22500
0018HELEN WEST          10025183010088001816700 05000
0019DAVID ADDIS         20019155120588001987001 0900
0020BOB ADDIS           20001259021488000282600 13300
```

The BOOKINV **file** is used in Figure 10-10, Illustrative program. The data is

```
          1         2         3         4
1234567890123456789012345678901234567890123456
----------------------------------------------
ACCBEG. ACCOUNTINGACCOUNTING I    0014006401812
ACCINT. ACCOUNTINGACCOUNTING II   0001005702719
BUSSMALL BUS. ADM.RUNNING SM. BUS0132001502699
BUSBUS. LAW       THE LAW BOOK    0020008510638
CHYORGANIC CHEM.  BEG. ORG. CHEM.0023004602446
CISINTRO. TO. COMPBUSINESS COMP.  0027014402679
CISADV. BUS. APP. INTRO. MICROS   0105001202055
CISCOBOL PROG.    BEG. COBOL       0037005202949
CISADV. COBOL PROGADV. COBOL       0000018002212
CISBEG. RPG II    PROG. IN RPG     0107009902046
CISDATA STRUCTURESFILES & DATA    0022004803955
CISDATA BASE THEO DB STRUCTURES   0005009002981
ECNECON. THEORY I THEORY OF ECON  0000040304805
ECNADV. ECON      FUTURE OF ECON  0111006501631
```

```
EGNCIRCUIT THEORY THE CIRCUIT    0016008801996
EGNASSEMB. LANG.  PROG IN ASSEMB 0101006002438
ENGBEG. ENGLISH   FIRST COURSE    0015023202881
ENGINT. ENGLISH   BETTER ENGLISH 0000012703570
ENGENGLISH ASL    SECOND LANG EN 0120005001281
FRHBEG. FRENCH    LEARN FRENCH    0021010202931
HISWORLD WAR I    1ST WORLD WAR  0007004004355
HISCIVIL WAR      BRO AGNST BRO  0018037204065
HISCURRENT HIST   WORLD TENSIONS 0130005202469
HISLIFE & TIMES   THE WORLD NOW  0011003702449
MTHBEG. ALGEBRA   ALGEBRA I       0120035502302
PE DANCE THEORY   MODERN DANCE   0000004802788
PE BEG. VOLLEYBALLUP IN ARMS     0007009802148
PE ELEM. PE       THE YOUNG STUD 0110001003904
PH PHYSICS I      INTRO TO PHYS. 0000012504578
PH INT. PHYSICS   MORE PHYSICS   0125003804583
```

The CHARGE **file** is used in Figure 2-18, System designed—2, and Figure 10-16, System designed—2. The data is

```
          1         2         3         4         5
1234567890123456789012345678901234567890123456789012
----------------------------------------------------
00001011488SWANSONS HARDWARE    MICROWAVE OVEN 014414
00001020888A-1 APPLIANCES       ROLL OF TAPE   000899
00001122088SEARS                LAWN TRACTOR   132037
00001020288JC PENNEY            VIDEO GAME     020210
00002022088SAM'S CAMERA         CAMERA         023931
00002022788KMART                TOASTER        007778
00002102688SEARS                LAMP           005657
00003031088BILL'S OFFICE SUPPLYDESK AND CHAIR  037011
00003020488STEREO CITY          TAPE DECK      010471
00003101288APPLE CITY           APPLE COMPUTER 107272
00010022588APPLE CITY           PRINTER        022560
00010021588SAM'S CAMERA         CAMERA CASE    005579
00010010288KMART                CAN OPENER     002204
00010111688SEARS                BLENDER        001664
00013011288KMART                DISH SET       016265
00013101688SOUTH SIDE APPLIANCEVACUUM          031624
00014011888FURNITURE WEST       RECLINER       035873
00015010088PETE'S HARDWARE      PLIERS         000380
00015120588JC PENNEY            AUTO REPAIRS   120524
00015021488SAM'S CAMERA         THREE-WAY LENS 021454
00015022288KMART                B&W TV         007217
00016010588SEARS                EXERCISE BIKE  018510
00016110888BILL'S OFFICE SUPPLYFILING CABINET  030841
00016011088STEREO CITY          CD PLAYER      011080
00017120888APPLE CITY           BOX OF PAPER   000894
00017010788APPLE CITY           PRINTER RIBBON 000777
00017011988SAM'S CAMERA         CLEANING KIT   000917
00017110888KMART                SET OF TIRES   010880
00018010888SEARS                SET OF TOOLS   000877
00020121288KMART                PROJECTION TV  125288
```

The CNSTRUCT **file** is used in Figure 5-17, System designed—2, and Figure 6-17, System designed—2. The data is

```
          1         2         3         4
1234567890123456789012345678901234567890 12
----------------------------------------------
070100359PRIVATE HOME    030046438000010074
010325209RR TERMINAL     002009638030007425
030118107PRIVATE HOME    021001949002048776
0102072510FFICE BUILDING022025699020010640
090315765PRIVATE HOME    021325449000040022
070103039SHOPPING CENTER001020570001107836
010306875PRIVATE HOME    020024679000018332
100737331SHOPPING CENTER040143578032007416
030225056STORE RENOV.    001137046001114418
100311774STORE RENOV.    020047788000115553
030432992SHOPPING CENTER040200981000017781
010108187BUILDING        010106812002021884
030428193HEATING PLANT   042108805021144132
090207237SHOPPING CENTER000010065000010388
030622544GOLF COURSE     000039631000112534
010107476SHOPPING CENTER021102719001042552
030600048TENNIS COURT    010036096040010918
070108652PRIVATE HOME    020030881020017984
030431107BUILDING DEMOL.032000955002144485
0701361300FFICE BUILDING002121281000213770
090210864PRIVATE HOME    000344355000111674
010311404WAREHOUSE       020048446020100164
100300400PRIVATE HOME    000210302000046242
030106829PRIVATE HOME    003008055020040316
1005008650FFICE BUILDING020004148030231757
0301170790FFICE BUILDING020146212011033892
100500532PRIVATE HOME    032108904030047014
0903006120FFICE BUILDING000044469010020432
100801269PRIVATE HOME    040002583002033024
0704131560FFICE BUILDING000230931000215395
```

The CONSTCO **file** is used in Figure 10-1, Sample program. The data is

```
          1         2         3         4
1234567890123456789012345678901234567890 12
----------------------------------------------
010108187BUILDING        010106812002021884
010107476SHOPPING CENTER021102719001042552
0102072510FFICE BUILDING022025699020010640
010325209RR TERMINAL     002009638030007425
010311404WAREHOUSE       020048446020100164
010306875PRIVATE HOME    020024679000018332
030106829PRIVATE HOME    003008055020040316
030118107PRIVATE HOME    021001949002048776
0301170790FFICE BUILDING020146212011033892
030225056STORE RENOV.    001137046001114418
030431107BUILDING DEMOL.032000955002144485
030432992SHOPPING CENTER040200981000017781
030428193HEATING PLANT   042108805021144132
030622544GOLF COURSE     000039631000112534
```

```
030600048TENNIS COURT   010036096040010918
070100359PRIVATE HOME   030046438000010074
070108652PRIVATE HOME   020030881020017984
070103039SHOPPING CENTER001020570001107836
070136130OFFICE BUILDING002121281000213770
070413156OFFICE BUILDING000230931000215395
090210864PRIVATE HOME   000344355000111674
090207237SHOPPING CENTER000010065000010388
090300612OFFICE BUILDING000044469010020432
090315765PRIVATE HOME   021325449000040022
100300400PRIVATE HOME   000210302000046242
100311774STORE RENOV.   020047788000115553
100500865OFFICE BUILDING020004148030231757
100500532PRIVATE HOME   032108904030047014
100737331SHOPPING CENTER040143578032007416
100801269PRIVATE HOME   040002583002033024
```

The CUSTOMER **file** is used in Figure 4-1, *Record Rack* program; Figure 4-6, Maintenance program; Figure 4-14, System designed—1; Figure 6-1, Sample program; Figure 7-1, Sample program; Figure 7-5, *Record Rack* program; Figure 8-5, Sample program; and Figure 11-1, Sample program. The data is

```
         1         2         3         4         5         6         7
1234567890123456789012345678901234567890123456789012345678901234567890123456
--------------------------------------------------------------------------
0456GEORGE    MONICA L  P. O. BOX 1610 ANTHONY     NM88021007870014414100001
1111VIRAMONTE ARNOLD    333 ROSEWOOD   SANTA TERESA NM88022002220132037200003
1234PINON     TONY      234 TEXAS DR   EL PASO     TX79935005000020210000004
2223MCDOWELL  HARRY     2323 TRUTH     SARASOTA    FL24234241242023931200005
2248GEORGE    BRENDA    242 CHISOM     ANTHONY     TX48234243244027778200012
2323GRONDIN   GEORGE    1290 HAWKINS   EL PASO     TX79936999990105657400014
2345MUNIZ     FRANK     24 OHARA RD    ANTHONY     NM88021023038000471200026
2423FIORETTI  GODDELL   234 WEST WAY   EL PASO     TX79936424224022560300016
2767LYTER     REBECCA   4244 HOLLISTER HOLLISTER   CA78966424244000204400025
2963FISHFINDERGOTCHA    9876 FINDUM    LAKERIDGE   NM88569457766111166400015
3242ADDIS     DAVE      9887 JOSE WAY  MIDLAND     TX23423424234016265100027
3345BREITBACH JIM       1507 CHARLES   EL PASO     TX79912981342101624300022
3455AYER      STEPHEN   4566 FAROUT    LONG BEACH  CA56886746756120524000001
4234DUFOUR    JERRY     303 N OREGON   SAN JOSE    CA86786766868007217400015
4466GEORGE    MONICA L  425  CHISOM    ANTHONY     TX88054566887120894400031
4565GEORGE    CHRIS     425  CHISOM    ANTHONY     TX880J654667700077720025
4566COOK      JOHN      4566 NOEAST    EL PASO     TX79975457888000877400075
4578RIGARILLO EDITH ANN 3546 SOMEWHERE LAS CRUCES  NM88069567567014935300030
4597FIORETTI  JAMES E   3939 EMORY     EL PASO     TX79901999999001518200020
4657ADDIS     DWAIN     5678 ADOBE     EL PASO     TX79985466777022466100010
4674BALSIGER  CHRIS     8798 CRI       JUAREZ      MX23434253235005955400001
4857SHAGNASTY OLIVER S  5867 IVEHADIT  RIVER-CITY  ND68457128554000034100005
5345CARSNER   RENE      4564 TOBIN PARKCHAPPARAL   NM88233234232025969300008
5465GEORGE    BRENDA    425  CHISOM    ANTHONY     TX88045768676026131000001
5467SANTOS    FRANK     4567 NOWHERE   EL PASO     TX79945876876014695400018
5677AYALA     PAUL      4677 HERE      EL PASO     TX79985456777502314800004
5687ADDIS     ABABA     5677 MIDEAST   ARABIA      SO56767865356200459000058
5688BEELER    BOBBETT   6577 LOVE RD.  EL PASO     TX79923696969011869000002
5709COLLINS   JIM       5709 CHEROKEE  EL PASO     TX79924200000100495300022
5753DAVIS     JOHN      242  DAVIS ST. DAVIS       CA23423423423000861100002
```

```
6576MORALES     LETICIA     3535 SOON TO BEEL PASO      TX9789798789810076500009
6756RUSSEL      SHARON      2435 GATEWAY     HOUSTON     TX2423563343401802430001
6786BEELER      ANGIE       7656 COLLEGE     COLLEGE ST  CO7665766568800066330002
7567DE LA CRUZAGUSTIN       1604 DARIN       EL PASO     TX7822243433403049300005
7655DE LEON     ISMAEL      243 NORTH WIND FT WORTH      TX8768686876700564610012
7859ADDIS       BOB         4566 EMORY       EL PASO     TX7990245787500090500035
7893PRATT       ADRIAN      5677 RICH        EL PASO     TX7998545677512191600016
8456WEST        BILL        345 BUFFALO      CODY        WY5254645535400615700017
8678SHEETS      GARY        234 HORIZON      HORIZON CITY TX4242342423300810510025
8906SMITH       BOBBY       5678 SOMEWHERE EL PASO       TX7995670564511368100015
```

The **DONATE file** is used in Figure 2-11, Illustrative program. The data is

```
                    1         2         3
          12345678901234567890123456789 0
          ------------------------------
          00010114880014414032288010916 4
          00020208880000899041988010735 7
          0S0313208801320371217880022815
          00040202880020210013988000798 5
          00050220880023931041588004244 6
          00060227880027778022488002204 4
          00071026880105657100188000311 2
          00080310880037011022888000785 2
          0009023488000A4710110880143180
          00101012880107272021988013619 9
          00110225880022560021988000304 8
          00120215880005579021188020609 0
          00330102880000204011988010200 3
          00141116880111664011888003486 5
          0A150112880016265011688003418 8
          00161016880101624141188004956 0
          00170118880015873011688003213 2
          00180100880000080100188002 1A27
          00191205880120524021 1.80125950
          00200214880021454100488023090 2
          00210222880007217011888034364 0
          00220105880018510100488001767 2
          00231108880130841010888004365 2
          0024011088001108001058803 2.937
          00251208880120894112688021055 5
          01260107880 0A0777100A880049648
          00270119880007917011088000899 8
          00281108880110880020688010891 0
          00290108880000877020288014562 5
          00301212880125288020888000803 8
```

The INVSALES **file** is used in Figure 3-31, System designed—3. The data is

```
                 1
        1234567890
        ----------
        0001008187
        0003007251
        0005011404
        0006006875
        0007006829
        0009017079
        0010025056
        0011031107
        0016000359
        0017008652
        0019036130
        0023000612
        0024015765
        0025000400
        0027000865
        0029037331
        0030001269
```

The INTRANS **file** is used in Figure 7-23, System designed—3. The data is

```
                 1         2         3         4         5
        12345678901234567890123456789012345678901234567890123456789012
        --------------------------------------------------------------
        0003C1001567
        0004C2002245
        0004C300007795
        0004C400010345
        0005C6002257
        0008A0370111001520000785200106916018107014162
        0012A00557910049500206090002161180329920213 60
        0013C1000356
        0014A1016241007650004956000113689000359005008
        0015D
        0018A120524000269011259500120491603613003949 1
        0021C1008345
        0021C2030453
        0021C401047201
        0021C5002345
        0022D
        0023D
```

The INVENT **file** is used in Figure 3-30, System designed—3; Figure 4-21, System designed—3; Figure 5-13, System designed—1; Figure 6-26, Interactive—2; Figure 7-22, System designed—3; Figure 8-12, System designed—1; Figure 9-18, Interactive—3; and Figure 10-13, System designed—1. The data is

```
          1         2         3         4
1234567890123456789012345678901234567890123 4
-------------------------------------------------
00010144140269400010916400149640008187013924
00020008990261310110735701018812007476014443
00031320370129500202281501149439007251029421
00040202100138010000798500113501025209000431
00050239310146950104244601052162011404004257
00060277780231480002204400010912006875023908
00071056570056600100311201011924006829024651
00080370111001520000785200106916018107014162
00090004710241480014318000216092017079000404
00101072722004590113619901212825025056008465
00110225600118690200304802110416031107029634
00120055791004950020609000216118032992021360
00130002040008610310200303126173028193018627
00150162652126350003418800048780000048004121
00161016241007650004956000113689000359005008
00170158730180240003213200235747008652000050
00191205240002690112595001204916036130039491
00200214540008520023090200336301013156033305
00210072170304930034364001037223010864015825
00220185100056460001767200037865007237011564
00231308410139470004365200122349000612000709
00240110800234930132693702002663015765003973
00251208940005150021055501016305000400010828
00260007770009050004964800129679011774024108
00270079171219160200899802117680000865028284
00281108800061570010891000230509000532010817
00290008770081050014562500219823037331035479
00301252881136810100803801139896001269005758
```

The ITEMNO **file** is used in Figure 5-14, System designed—1. The data is

```
          1
123456789012
------------
000101441402
000200089902
000502393101
000602777802
000900047102
001010727220
001610162410
001701587301
001800008000
002201851000
002512089400
002700791712
002900087700
003012528811
```

The MACHINE **file** is used in Figure 5-20, System designed—3. The data is

```
          1         2         3         4         5
123456789012345678901234567890123456789012345678901 2
-------------------------------------------------------
0101081870001
0304074760200
0702072510020
0901252090021
1004114040001
0905068750201
1006068290039
0705181070011
0305170790021
0706250563011
0102311070120
1002329920402
1001281930421
1003225440000
0302000480100
0303003590300
0103086520200
0104030390022
0701361300021
0904131560002
0708108640003
0306072370002
0105006120000
0107157650213
0108004000002
1007117740200
1003008650132
0307005320321
0704373310401
0902012690122
```

The MANUFACT **file** is used in Figure 2-21, System designed—3, and 10-19, System designed—3. The data is

```
          1
1234567890123
-------------
0101081870101
0101074760211
0102072510220
0103252090020
0103114040200
0103068750200
0301068290030
0301181070210
0301170790201
0302250560011
0304311070320
0304329920402
0304281930421
0306225440000
0306000480100
0701003590300
```

```
0701086520200
0701030390010
0701361300021
0704131560002
0902108640003
0902072370000
0903006120000
0903157650213
1003004000002
1003117740200
1005008650200
1005005320321
1007373310401
1008012690400
```

The PATIENTS **file** is used in Figure 9-1, Sample program. The data is created in an interactive fashion. Therefore, there are no records here.

The PAYROLL **file** is used in Figure 3-12, *Record Rack* program; Figure 5-23, Interactive—1; Figure 7-15, System designed—1; and Figure 8-23, System designed—3. The data is

```
            1         2         3         4         5
1234567890123456789012345678901234567890123456789 0123
-------------------------------------------------------
0001JOHN SMITH          4000512011001441400055 5000852
0002SAMANTHA JOHNSON    3550365041013203700964 8000493
0003CHRIS BALSIGER      2500874010202021000899 8005646
0004OLIVER SHAGNASTY    2900276010002393100891 0003947
0006RENE CARSNER        2800133020402777800562 5003493
0007JANE GREEN          2410713050210565700803 8000515
0008BRENDA GEORGE       3801476060003701100408 6000905
0009JOSEPH BORNMAN      4101269030010727200505 0001916
0010FRED HARRIS         4001085031402256000009 4006157
0011BOB FASHING         3711187021300557900527 2008105
0012FRANK SANTOS        3011878040011166400253 5003681
0013PAUL AYALA          4001554052001626500841 6004544
0014JIM CLARK           4801482081010162400832 7004016
0015ED COBURN           3651585070301587300729 5000563
0016RONALD GEORGE       3601762060312052400382 4000147
0017TOM ADDIS           3631008010402145400549 1000908
0018ABABA ADDIS         3010428050300721700964 0000601
0019BOBBETT BEELER      4001183020201851000881 2006075
0021JOHN DAVIS          4111155031213084100943 9000477
0025CINDY HARRISON      4001225032301108000350 1008157
```

The PAYTRANS **file** is used in Figure 7-16, System designed—1. The data is

```
         1
1234567890
----------
0001040
0002045
0003020
0004041
```

```
0006039
0007038
0008045
0009040
0010040
0011042
0012040
0013041
0014040
0015040
0016040
0017051
0018040
0019040
0021038
0025039
```

The RRINVENT **file** is used in Figure 2-5, *Record Rack* program; Figure 6-14, System designed—1; and Figure 10-5, *Record Rack* program. The data is

```
         1
1234567890123456
----------------
0112C45302003294
0114D30104502815
0176F09011992255
0181R03306220003
02J0970010000033
02KL104334670865
02MN502715480306
02P0805117993613
02TZ308914901311
03RT607612001086
03S6L05609870720
03ZEF08404090067
04KDJ08110101576
04LDO07421100043
040LO07222021173
0449K25202000086
04KJ411420040052
05LRK06820023736
05LF906803000125
05KL418121000663
05KFL17020140008
05JF825001133232
05KF031132000096
06HE732940200942
06AK928142103600
06KD822500030021
07KLD00010030371
07KD600330040051
08KM808620030232
09CJC03001020580
```

The **SALES file** is used in Figure 2-15, System designed—1; Figure 3-22, System designed—1; Figure 4-16, System designed—2; Figure 5-1, *Record Rack* program; Figure 6-20, System designed—3; Figure 8-16, System designed—2; and Figure 9-14, System designed—2. The data is

```
         1         2         3         4         5         6
123456789012345678901234567890123456789012345678901234567890123456789012345
-----------------------------------------------------------------------------
0001ROGER BARNELL        1801012445500544550035625240042914002620206
0002JOHN SMITH           2703008975501105120015466070254717004891302
0003SAMANTHA JOHNSON     2602015662500254660035500140880316193161103
0004FRED HARRIS          0603003552300155660000000021756326291840115
0005ED COBURN            2405003453302567990123433000901320071590206
0006TAWNY JACOBS         2604013456601233190245591000565607044620516
0007MONICA GEORGE        4005060446706067620318489071542014309273728
0008LLANI MRAZ           2908123003606330080205264170057107032671005
0009ARNOLD VIRAMONTE     2206250387400104282107695030914500009433420
0010TONY PINON           4007290027610251831235903050688309062780220
0011HARRY MCDOWELL       3907080613321191550019291012977208130710806
0012BRENDA GEORGE        4910041371300012590701194000561616016401110
0013GEORGE GRONDIN       4801380147614136340026826000558109287690514
0014FRANK CLAUSEN        0603112826900281810811602000026100008470918
0015FRANK MUNIZ          1005060024104108000005043060584816128640916
0016RICHARD COLLINS      3406171218715014232818167051715400149940706
0017GODDELL FIORETTI     2803201487800124121301987012251711177380710
0018REBECCA LYTER        4502001755407252281402826070509800035190111
0019DAVE ADDIS           0202280348204367582324268270092709002421502
0020JIM BREITBACH        4905090005828393740219757231331101025240610
```

The **SALETRAN file** is used in Figure 3-23, System designed—1. The data is

```
          1
12345678901
-----------
00010101244
00020300897
00030201566
00040300355
00050500345
00060401345
00070506044
00080812300
00090625038
00100729002
00110708061
00121004137
00130138014
00140311282
00150506002
00160617121
00170320148
00180200175
00190228034
00200509000
```

The SHIPPING **file** is used in Figure 2-7, Maintenance program, and Figure 10-7, Maintenance program. The data is

```
          1         2         3         4         5
123456789012345678901234567890123456789012345678901234 56
------------------------------------------------------------
01BJ817181BLUE WIDGET        012060446700818011488000 14
01G83K7001GREEN WIDGET       019123003600747020888000 25
01RJH12271RED WIDGET         099250387400725122088001 32
01RA12K269WIDGET RATCHET     038290027602520020288000 20
02GR23K063GREEN AND RED HOLDER046080613301140022088000 23
02BLS23244BLUE HOLDER        079041371300687022788000 27
02WTJ34267WIDGET TUB         055380147600682102688001 05
04PIEU6405PURPLE WIDGET      049112826901810031088000 37
04RJH12294RED WIDGET         212060024101707020488000 87
04WTJ34221WIDGET TUB         046171218702505101288001 07
08RA12K404WIDGET RATCHET     055201487803110022588000 22
15WW82K395WIDGET WRENCH      081001755403299021588000 05
15WCK23498WIDGET CLEANING KIT005280348202819010288000 33
15RJH12480RED WIDGET         031090005802254111688001 11
15NOJ89063NO-SLIP WIDGET TUB 096060676200004011288000 16
27WCK23109WIDGET CLEANING KIT038063300800035101688001 01
27WRJ8H343WIDGET ROD         081001042800865011888000 15
27WRTJ4288WIDGET REEL        070102518300303010288000 23
27WLJ87457WIDGET LIGHT       081211915503613120588001 20
27WP8H9028WIDGET PAINT       031000125901315021488000 21
27WC8IJ493WIDGET CHAIN       055141363401086022288000 07
35NOJ89435NO-SLIP WIDGET TUB 065002818100723010588000 18
35WRJ8H406WIDGET ROD         069041080000061110888001 30
35WLJ87046WIDGET LIGHT       049150142301576011088000 11
35WRK98244WIDGET REPAIR KIT  020012412000401208880012 0
35WDSJ9430WIDGET DESIGN SPECS.088072522801177010788000 15
35RJH12278RED WIDGET         148043675800086011988000 07
35BJ817214BLUE WIDGET        004283937400053110888001 10
35WP8H9390WIDGET PAINT       078031848903733010888000 22
35WCCJ9457WIDGET CARRYING CASE083020526400126121288001 25
35WCCJ9458WIDGET CARRYING CASE084210769500662032288000 32
35WC8IJ488WIDGET CHAIN       052123590300006041988000 46
45WDSJ9455WIDGET DESIGN SPECS.040001929103235121788001 24
55WRTJ4264WIDGET REEL        025070119400093011988000 14
55WRTJ4342WIDGET REEL        064002682600948041588000 21
55WCK23216WIDGET CLEANING KIT032081160203602022488000 22
67RJH12133RED WIDGET         016000504300026100188001 00
67BJ817231BLUE WIDGET        076281816700372022888000 05
67G83K7477GREEN WIDGET       092130198700654011088000 22
67WTJ34189WIDGET TUB         018140282601360021988000 25
```

The SPORTTBL **file** is used in Figure 9-19, System designed—3. The data is

```
          1         2         3
12345678901234567890123456789 0
------------------------------
0001BASEBALL           000700
0002BASEBALL GLOVE     001500
0003BASEBALL CAP       000650
0004BASEBALL BAT       003100
0005BASKETBALL         002000
0006SOCCER BALL        002600
0007FOOTBALL           002400
0008FOOTBALL HELMET    003275
```

```
0009KNEE PADS              000450
0010ELBOW PADS             000450
0011CHIN PADS              000500
0012BASEBALL GLOVE         001800
0013SWEAT BAND             000195
0014WRIST BANDS            000235
0015HOCKEY STICK           002295
0016ICE SKATES             006576
0017ICE SKATES             007592
0018ICE SKATES             009565
0019HOCKEY MASK            003585
0020SHOULDER PADS          009899
0021DART BOARD             000998
0022DART SET               000398
0023FISH KNIFE             000897
0024SUNNY BUNNY LURE       000297
0025BLUE MAGOO LURE        000485
0026SILLY SIDE LURE        000345
0027EAGLE HOOKS 1"         000200
0028EAGLE HOOKS 2"         000300
0029EAGLE HOOKS 1.5"       000250
0030FISHING LINE           000255
```

The SUBSCRIB **file** is used in Figure 3-19, Illustrative program; Figure 6-2, Maintenance program; Figure 6-10, Illustrative program; Figure 6-29, Interactive—3; Figure 7-10, Illustrative program; and Figure 8-6, *Record Rack* program. The data is

```
         1         2         3         4         5         6
1234567890123456789012345678901234567890123456789012345678901
---------------------------------------------------------------
0002LLANI MRAZ          333 ROSEWOOD   SANTA TERESA NM8802200011488
0003ARNOLD VIRAMONTE    234 TEXAS DR   EL PASO      TX7993500020888
0004TONY PINON          2323 TRUTH     SARASOTA     FL2423404122088
0006BRENDA GOLF         1290 HAWKINS   EL PASO      TX7993609020288
0008FRANK CLAUSEN       234 WEST WAY   EL PASO      TX7993612022088
0010RICHARD COLLINS     9876 FINDUM    LAKERIDGE    NM8856905022788
0011GODDELL FIORETTI    9887 JOSE WAY  MIDLAND      TX2342302102688
0012WALLY STOELZOL      1507 CHARLES   EL PASO      TX7991208031088
0013REBECCA LYTER       4566 FAROUT    LONG BEACH   CA5688614020488
0014GOTCHA FISHFINDER   303 N OREGON   SAN JOSE     CA8678626101288
0015DAVE ADDIS          425  CHISOM    ANTHONY      TX8805436022588
0016JIM BREITBACH       1425 CHESTER   ANTHONY      TX8807624021588
0018STEPHEN AYER        3546 SOMEWHERE LAS CRUCES   NM8806916010288
0021CHARLES HEADLEY     8798 AVE. A    DENVER       CO2343405111688
0022DOG FREEBE          5867 IVEHADIT  RIVER-CITY   ND6845700011288
0025BURL ADDIS          4567 NOWHERE   EL PASO      TX7994507101688
0026MERLE STIMONS       4677 MAIN      EL PASO      TX7998515011888
0027JOHN COOK           5677 MIDEAST   ARABIA       SO5676726010288
0028RIKKI GEORGE        6577 LOVE RD.  EL PASO      TX7992300120588
0029SHARON MC-CORMAK    5709 CHEROKEE  EL PASO      TX7992410021488
0030GEE RAMIREZ         242  DAVIS ST. DAVIS        CA2342322022288
0032EDITH ANNRIGARILLO  2435 GATEWAY   HOUSTON      TX2423523010588
0033JAMES FITZHUGH      7656 COLLEGE   COLLEGE ST   CO7665700110888
0034DWAIN HARLEN        1604 DARIN     EL PASO      TX7822203011088
0035SAUL PEDRIGON       243 NORTH WIND FT WORTH     TX8768626120888
0037OLIVER SHAGNASTY    5677 RICH      EL PASO      TX7998525010788
0038RENE CARSNER        345 BUFFALO    CODY         WY5254615011988
0039JANE GREEN          234 HORIZON    HORIZON CITY TX4242300110888
0040BRENDA GIBBONS      5678 SOMEWHERE EL PASO      TX7995610010888
```

The SUBTRANS **file** is used in Figure 3-20, Illustrative program; Figure 4-8, Illustrative program; and Figure 7-11, Illustrative program. The data is

```
         1         2         3         4         5         6
1234567890123456789012345678901234567890123456789012345678901 2
-------------------------------------------------------------
0001NMONICA GEORGE      P. O. BOX 1610 ANTHONY       NM8802112
0002R12
0004R12
0005R24
0007NGEORGE GRONDIN     24 OHARA RD     ANTHONY      NM8802102
0010C
0013R12
0015R24
0017C
0018R18
0019NJERRY DUFOUR       3939 EMORY      EL PASO       TX7990199
0021R12
0023NMONICA GEORGE      4564 TOBIN PARKCHAPPARAL      NM8823323
0024C
0028R12
0031R36
0035NED COBURN          1400 SOUTH ST. EL PASO        TX7992215
0036NCHRIS BALSIGER     4566 EMORY      EL PASO       TX7990245
```

The TRANSALE **file** is used in Figure 9-15, System designed—2. The data is

```
       1
123456789012
------------
000120070300
000130060201
000410040500
000630060401
000640098712
000650029287
000740050604
001040072900
001020082766
001130090708
001240091004
001250000919
001340101380
001510050600
001630106171
001840302001
002040805090
```

The TRANSIN **file** is used in Figure 7-2, Sample program. The data is

```
        1
1234567890
----------
0456001275
2223001000
3242001423
3242015498
4000001345
6576000976
```

The TRANWOOD **file** is used in Figure 9-10, Illustrative program. The data is

```
          1         2         3         4         5
1234567890123456789012345678901234567890123456789012
----------------------------------------------------
0101R001275
0103S001000
0107S001423
0110S015498
0110R001345
0110S000976
0208R001707
0209S002505
0210R003110
0305S003299
0305S002819
0402S002254
0402R000004
0410S000035
0503R000865
0505S000303
0601R003613
0601S001315
0601R008955
0601R036059
0610R046895
0705S007283
0706R037196
0706R005827
0802S031778
0804S038287
0807S047552
0809R017759
```

The UPDATE **file** is used in Figure 3-27, System designed—2, and Figure 9-5, *Record Rack* program. The data is

```
          1
123456789012
------------
0001C0008187
0001C0007476
0003P0007251
0003P0025209
0004C0011404
0005C0006875
0006P0006829
0006P0018107
0006C0017079
0009P0025056
0010P0031107
0010P0032992
0010C0028193
0014C0022544
0016C0000048
0016P0000359
0018P0008652
0018C0003039
0019P0036130
0020C0013156
```

The WOOD **file** is used in Figure 9-9, Illustrative program. The data is

```
          1         2         3         4         5
1234567890123456789012345678901234567890123456789012
----------------------------------------------------
01010345280485740376036027849
01020447560066940088730320577
01030003220231920340790416710
01040227230308940131210452750
01050374170399690193080474810
01060327730354450360290355950
01070434880058650376850102420
01080065070278210220450089550
01090187620372810235850360590
01100344090205720149820468950
02010031330229390052740072830
02020089280397450204520371960
02030352210234960009380058270
02040468670256470267950317780
02050348740051040247860382870
02060331760340680336580475520
02070362600016370405180177590
02080236380008360014660488520
02090114440099220059480106000
02100373020103360471900466340
03010397940096700118170374700
03020391440375900001580473040
03030374340055080203890174840
03040122700167680492820360860
03050287780282260210230277110
03060253110046230380910142010
03070095710466350310750083670
03080174760086250496080291610
03090335940459950469190422720
03100292740144130473340210770
04010436600143680321320163660
04020042040288960046850083560
04030275630101200336650486470
04040039590319430412070314910
04050017660028160326730266820
04060199970042640429450170860
04070254420014550303090193050
04080057290498900045110438060
04090157330490980307060319510
04100493980118310449380408600
05010372430370110293720439040
05020358370169920463080058760
05030156370151120357270331610
05040090430345570466160459190
05050422150144530193450272990
05060249010188060144720008840
05070342610422140110860072150
05080275620358890461970058290
05090103370259740284490006860
05100221030225790337160160460
06010211910123740197260247340
06020032650465520075530089620
06030111690313960495000357180
06040133550104480413400183800
06050126280119410193830142060
```

```
0606045088018968015602002376
0607012391042854048213013953
0608005130037690007388024291
0609015499006572015838031059
0610014746017259001672040022
0701032894035885019811016458
0702023193015234038453012161
0703026979048445045329002767
0704000587023332019304015775
0705027743014281021255010931
0706037938028168026850039680
0707022994049341019697033568
0708016097001983013461024251
0709044882018546018958026171
0710040556014448019355040136
0801011824015684030379014898
0802028537030510038618004863
0803005903030299004325016249
0804006754040526042258034371
0805011382004146019825000133
0806035670010796043694037114
0807025732037473041955029216
0808047240023124031920007633
0809021267018893041444014731
0810021059044325004301017566
```

The following files include their own data in the chapter. They are listed here for reference only.

The CONTRIB **file** is used in Figure 3-8, Sample program. The data is

```
          1         2         3
12345678901234567890123456789012345
-----------------------------------
002ABLE  BAKER         010188007000
003JOHN  CARTWELL      010188007712
004SAMUAL  DORSEY      010188033011
006JERMIA  NOLTE       010288012012
007LISA  REDFORD       010288083312
008FRED  JOHNKE        020188005512
010HARRISON  MARSHALL  020188004012
011TOM  EISEN          020188004013
013HARROLD  STERN      020288001008
014FREDERICK  SUMMERS  020288001003
016SALLY  JOHNSON      030188001014
017BARBARA  NOLAN      030188005005
018FRANCIS  CANTWELL   030288005600
019GEORGE  SMITH       030288005768
020MARK  HAMMEL        030288009012
```

The RRTRANS **file** is used in Figure 3-13, *Record Rack* program. The data is

```
          1         2         3
12345678901234567890123456789012
--------------------------------
0001A TONY  SMITH         013010
0002D
0004A JEFF  HAMMEL        084001
0010C 1260
0012A KAREN WHITE         075002
0030D
0035C 1075
0045D
```

The TRANS **file** is used in Figure 3-9, Sample program. The data is

```
          1         2         3
123456789012345678901234567890123456
------------------------------------
001A RICHARD ADAMSON    010188000200
002A ED COBURN           010188003500
002C2JAMIE STEVENS
002C4002222
004D
005A NICK HAMMOND        010288001500
006C2TOMMY TOMPSON
006C3061587
006C4006666
008D
009C2ED COBURN
011C4001234
012D
015A TOM JONES           030188000450
022C2ED COBURN
```

B

Major 1985 Changes

Throughout the book we have mentioned some significant changes that have been made in the 1985 version of the COBOL standards. In this Appendix we will summarize these revisions and introduce some other important changes that pertain to topics covered in the text. This list is by no means exhaustive.

ACCEPT Statement

The DAY-OF-WEEK phrase has been added to the ACCEPT statement so that the program can print out the day of the week without a lot of calculations. The statement will return a single-digit number representing the day of the week, as

1 for Monday
2 for Tuesday
3 for Wednesday
4 for Thursday
5 for Friday
6 for Saturday
7 for Sunday

ADD Statement

One problem many programmers have with the ADD statement is the use of the TO and GIVING clauses on the same statement. Using both is now allowed in the new standards. The form of the ADD statement has been expanded to

$$\underline{ADD} \left\{ \begin{array}{l} \text{field-name-1} \\ \text{literal-1} \end{array} \right\} \underline{TO} \left\{ \begin{array}{l} \text{field-name-2} \\ \text{literal-2} \end{array} \right\} \underline{GIVING} \text{ field-name-3}$$

An example of the statement now allowed would be

```
ADD FIELD-A TO FIELD-B GIVING RESULT-FIELD.
```

ALPHABETIC Class Test

When COBOL was first developed, lowercase letters were used rarely, if ever. Now, with more and more systems being used in an on-line capacity (the user communicating by typing data directly into the program from a terminal), the need to interpret lowercase letters has greatly increased. To help with this, the new standard has expanded the ALPHABETIC class test so that it is true not only for uppercase letters and blanks but also for lowercase letters. There are also two additional forms of the ALPHABETIC test: ALPHABETIC-LOWER to test lowercase letters and blanks and ALPHABETIC-UPPER to test uppercase letters and blanks.

ENVIRONMENT DIVISION Clauses

The CONFIGURATION SECTION and the SOURCE-COMPUTER and OBJECT COMPUTER paragraphs in the ENVIRONMENT DIVISION are optional and, what's more, are now considered obsolete. As such, on the next update of the standards they will be dropped. Thus, it is recommended that programmers stop using them so that future programs will be compatible with the next set of standards.

EVALUATE Statement

A new statement has been added to allow performance of a series of procedures based upon conditional tests. An example of the statement:

```
EVALUATE FIELD-A
        WHEN  0            PERFORM ERROR-ROUTINE
        WHEN  1 THRU 10 PERFORM ROUTINE-1
        WHEN 11 THRU 20 PERFORM ROUTINE-2
        WHEN 21 THRU 30 PERFORM ROUTINE-3
        WHEN 31 THRU 40 PERFORM ROUTINE-4
        WHEN OTHER         PERFORM DEFAULT-ROUTINE.
```

Field Reference

Field reference allows the referencing of a part of a field by specifying the location within the field and the length of the reference. For example, the reference (5:2) would begin at the fifth character and would be two characters in length. For example, given:

```
10  FIELD-A             PIC X(10)  VALUE  'ABCDEFGHIJ'.


    MOVE FIELD-A (4:3) TO FIELD-B.
```

FIELD-B would receive the characters DEF since D is the fourth character and the reference is for three characters.

FILLER

The word FILLER is now optional and may be left out when you are coding a record layout with unneeded fields. Normally we would code a record layout as

```
01  INPUT-RECORD.
    10  RECORD-KEY          PIC XXXX.
    10  FILLER             PIC XXXX.
    10  AMOUNT             PIC 9999V99.
```

With this revision, such code could be changed to

```
01  INPUT-RECORD.
    10  RECORD-KEY          PIC XXXX.
    10                     PIC XXXX.
    10  AMOUNT             PIC 9999V99.
```

IF Statement

We can now use the THEN clause as an optional indicator. Also, the END-IF scope terminator can be used (see SCOPE TERMINATORS).

INITIALIZE Statement

The INITIALIZE statement is a method for easily giving an initial value to numeric and non-numeric fields. It will automatically initialize numeric fields to zero and fill non-numeric fields with spaces.

LABEL RECORDS Clause

The LABEL RECORDS clause is now optional and is considered obsolete. It will be removed from the next COBOL revision.

Literals

The maximum size of non-numeric literals has been increased from 120 to 160 characters.

MOVE Statement

We can now move an edited numeric field to a unedited field. This move will remove the editing to result with an unedited number. This is called *de-editing*.

NOT Operator

The option to use the NOT operator has been added to all conditional statements including

- NOT ON-SIZE ERROR, for use with ADD, SUBTRACT, MULTIPLY, DIVIDE, and COMPUTE;
- NOT AT END, for use with the READ statement.

PERFORM Statement

The PERFORM statement has been upgraded to allow the use of the DO-UNTIL structure as well as the DO-WHILE. In the DO-WHILE, the test is the first procedure in the loop. In the DO-UNTIL, the test is the last procedure in the loop. The PERFORM statement now has a TEST AFTER clause that allows the processing to occur before the test is performed.

Another addition to the PERFORM statement allows the use of what are called *in-line* PERFORM statements: statements that are to be performed *with* the PERFORM statement instead of the programmer having to use a paragraph purely for syntax reasons. Here we can now use END-PERFORM to mark the end of the PERFORM statement. Using this form of the statement, we can write a statement like

```
PERFORM
     MOVE FIELD-A-IN TO FIELD-A-OUT
     MOVE FIELD-B-IN TO FIELD-B-OUT
     MOVE FIELD-C-IN TO FIELD-C-OUT
     WRITE OUTPUT-LINE AFTER ADVANCING 2 LINES
END-PERFORM.
```

Relational Operators

Two additional relation operators are now available:

GREATER THAN OR EQUAL TO

which can also be denoted as >=, and

LESS THAN OR EQUAL TO

which can also be expressed with the symbols <=.

Scope Terminators

In pseudocode we used the END-IF statement, even though COBOL has no such statement, because it helped to indicate visually the end of the IF structure. Now COBOL has an END-IF statement, along with many other END statements:

END-COMPUTE	END-MULTIPLY	END-WRITE
END-ADD	END-DIVIDE	END-READ
END-SUBTRACT	END-IF	END-PERFORM

STOP Statement

The STOP RUN statement will now automatically close any files that the programmer may have left open in the program. It is still much better specifically to close all open files, but this feature may save some files from being damaged because of programmer omission.

VALUE Clause

Tables can now be defined with the VALUE clause, so we don't have to REDEFINE a table to give it an initial value.

C

COBOL Language Formats

This Appendix contains complete 1974 ANS standard formats of all elements of the COBOL language. We have included all statements, whether they have been discussed previously in the text or not. We have also listed the statements as they are presented in the standard format, including semicolons and commas. Remember, however, that because of the chances of misinterpreting a comma as a period we recommend not using commas.

General Format for the IDENTIFICATION DIVISION

IDENTIFICATION DIVISION.

PROGRAM-ID.   program-name.

[AUTHOR.   [comment-entry] . . .]

[INSTALLATION.   [comment-entry] . . .]

[DATE-WRITTEN.   [comment-entry] . . .]

[DATE-COMPILED.   [comment-entry] . . .]

[SECURITY.   [comment-entry] . . .]

General Format for the ENVIRONMENT DIVISION

ENVIRONMENT DIVISION.

CONFIGURATION SECTION.

SOURCE-COMPUTER. computer-name [WITH DEBUGGING MODE].

OBJECT-COMPUTER. computer-name

$$
\left[\ ,\ \text{MEMORY SIZE integer}\ \left\{\begin{array}{l}\text{WORDS}\\\text{CHARACTERS}\\\text{MODULES}\end{array}\right\}\right]
$$

[, PROGRAM COLLATING SEQUENCE IS alphabet-name]

[, SEGMENT-LIMIT IS segment-number].

[SPECIAL-NAMES. [, implementor-name

$$
\left\{\begin{array}{l}\text{IS mnemonic-name [, ON STATUS IS condition-name-1}\\\qquad\qquad\qquad\text{[, OFF STATUS IS condition-name-2]]}\\\text{IS mnemonic-name [, OFF STATUS IS condition-name-2}\\\qquad\qquad\qquad\text{[, ON STATUS IS condition-name-1]]}\\\text{ON STATUS IS condition-name-1 [, OFF STATUS IS condition-name-2]}\\\text{OFF STATUS IS condition-name-2 [, ON STATUS IS condition-name-1]}\end{array}\right\}
$$

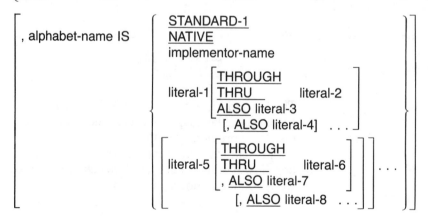

. . .

[, <u>CURRENCY</u> SIGN <u>IS</u> literal-9]

[, <u>DECIMAL-POINT</u> <u>IS</u> <u>COMMA</u>].

[<u>INPUT-OUTPUT</u> <u>SECTION</u>.

  <u>FILE-CONTROL</u>.

  {file-control-entry} . . .

  [<u>I-O-CONTROL</u>.

$$\left[\text{; }\underline{\text{RERUN}}\ \left[\underline{\text{ON}}\ \begin{Bmatrix} \text{file-name-1} \\ \text{implementor-name} \end{Bmatrix}\right]\right.$$

$$\text{EVERY}\ \left\{\begin{Bmatrix} \begin{Bmatrix} [\underline{\text{END}}\ \text{OF}] & \begin{Bmatrix} \underline{\text{REEL}} \\ \underline{\text{UNIT}} \end{Bmatrix} \end{Bmatrix}\ \text{OF file-name-2} \\ \text{integer-1 }\underline{\text{RECORDS}} \\ \text{integer-2 }\underline{\text{CLOCK-UNITS}} \\ \text{condition-name} \end{Bmatrix}\right\}\ \ldots$$

$$\left[\text{; }\underline{\text{SAME}}\ \begin{bmatrix} \underline{\text{RECORD}} \\ \underline{\text{SORT}} \\ \underline{\text{SORT-MERGE}} \end{bmatrix}\ \text{AREA FOR file-name-3 \{, file-name-4\}}\ \ldots\right]\ \ldots$$

    [; <u>MULTIPLE</u> <u>FILE</u> TAPE CONTAINS file-name-5 [<u>POSITION</u> integer-3]

    [, file-name-6 [POSITION integer-4]] . . .] . . .]]

General Format for the FILE CONTROL ENTRY

Format 1   <u>SELECT</u> [<u>OPTIONAL</u>] file-name

           <u>ASSIGN</u> TO implementor-name-1 [, implementor-name-2] . . .

$$\left[\text{; }\underline{\text{RESERVE}}\ \text{integer-1}\ \begin{bmatrix} \text{AREA} \\ \text{AREAS} \end{bmatrix}\right]$$

           [; <u>ORGANIZATION</u> IS <u>SEQUENTIAL</u>]

           [; <u>ACCESS</u> MODE IS <u>SEQUENTIAL</u>]

           [; FILE <u>STATUS</u> IS field-name-1].

Format 2   <u>SELECT</u> file-name

           <u>ASSIGN</u> TO implementor-name-1 [, implementor-name-2] . . .

$$\left[\text{; }\underline{\text{RESERVE}}\ \text{integer-1}\ \begin{bmatrix} \text{AREA} \\ \text{AREAS} \end{bmatrix}\right]$$

           [; <u>ORGANIZATION</u> IS <u>RELATIVE</u>]

$$\left[\text{; }\underline{\text{ACCESS}}\ \text{MODE IS}\ \begin{Bmatrix} \underline{\text{SEQUENTIAL}}\ \text{[, }\underline{\text{RELATIVE}}\ \text{KEY IS field-name-1]} \\ \begin{Bmatrix} \underline{\text{RANDOM}} \\ \underline{\text{DYNAMIC}} \end{Bmatrix}\ \ ,\ \underline{\text{RELATIVE}}\ \text{KEY IS field-name-1} \end{Bmatrix}\right]$$

           [; FILE <u>STATUS</u> IS field-name-2].

Format 3   SELECT file-name

ASSIGN TO implementor-name-1 [, implementor-name-2] . . .

$\left[\text{; } \underline{\text{RESERVE}} \text{ integer-1} \begin{bmatrix} \text{AREA} \\ \text{AREAS} \end{bmatrix} \right]$

; ORGANIZATION IS INDEXED

$\left[\text{; } \underline{\text{ACCESS}} \text{ MODE IS} \begin{Bmatrix} \underline{\text{SEQUENTIAL}} \\ \underline{\text{RANDOM}} \\ \underline{\text{DYNAMIC}} \end{Bmatrix} \right]$

; RECORD KEY IS field-name-1

[; ALTERNATE RECORD KEY IS field-name-2 [WITH DUPLICATES]]

[; FILE STATUS IS field-name-3].

Format 4   SELECT file-name ASSIGN TO implementor-name-1 [, implementor-name-2] . .

General Format for the DATA DIVISION

DATA DIVISION.

FILE SECTION.

FD file-name

$\left[\text{; } \underline{\text{BLOCK}} \text{ CONTAINS [integer-1 } \underline{\text{TO}} \text{] integer-2} \begin{Bmatrix} \underline{\text{RECORDS}} \\ \underline{\text{CHARACTERS}} \end{Bmatrix} \right]$

[; RECORD CONTAINS [integer-3 TO] integer-4 CHARACTERS]

$\text{; } \underline{\text{LABEL}} \begin{Bmatrix} \underline{\text{RECORD}} \text{ IS} \\ \underline{\text{RECORDS}} \text{ ARE} \end{Bmatrix} \begin{Bmatrix} \underline{\text{STANDARD}} \\ \underline{\text{OMITTED}} \end{Bmatrix}$

$\left[\text{; } \underline{\text{VALUE}} \underline{\text{ OF}} \text{ implementor-name-1 IS} \begin{Bmatrix} \text{field-name-1} \\ \text{literal-1} \end{Bmatrix} \right.$

$\left[\text{, implementor-name-2 IS} \begin{Bmatrix} \text{field-name-2} \\ \text{literal-2} \end{Bmatrix} \right] \left. \text{ . . .} \right]$

$\left[\text{; } \underline{\text{DATA}} \begin{Bmatrix} \underline{\text{RECORD}} \text{ IS} \\ \underline{\text{RECORDS}} \text{ ARE} \end{Bmatrix} \text{ field-name-3 [, field-name-4] . . .} \right]$

$\left[\text{; } \underline{\text{LINAGE}} \text{ IS} \begin{Bmatrix} \text{field-name-5} \\ \text{integer-5} \end{Bmatrix} \text{ LINES} \left[\text{, WITH } \underline{\text{FOOTING}} \text{ AT} \begin{Bmatrix} \text{field-integer-6} \\ \text{integer-6} \end{Bmatrix} \right] \right.$

$\left[\text{, LINES AT } \underline{\text{TOP}} \begin{Bmatrix} \text{field-name-7} \\ \text{integer-7} \end{Bmatrix} \right] \left[\text{, LINES AT } \underline{\text{BOTTOM}} \begin{Bmatrix} \text{field-name-8} \\ \text{integer-8} \end{Bmatrix} \right] \left. \right]$

[; CODE-SET IS alphabet-name]

$\left[\text{; } \begin{Bmatrix} \underline{\text{REPORT}} \text{ IS} \\ \underline{\text{REPORTS}} \text{ ARE} \end{Bmatrix} \text{ report-name-1 [, report-name-2] . . .} \right].$

[record-description-entry] . . .] . . .

[SD file-name

    [; RECORD CONTAINS [integer-1 TO] integer-2 CHARACTERS]

$$\left[; \text{DATA} \begin{Bmatrix} \text{RECORD} & \text{IS} \\ \text{RECORDS} & \text{ARE} \end{Bmatrix} \text{field-name-1 [, field-name-2]} \ldots \right].$$

{record-description-entry} ...] ...]

[WORKING-STORAGE SECTION.

$$\begin{bmatrix} \text{77-level-description-entry} \\ \text{record-description-entry} \end{bmatrix} \ldots$$

[LINKAGE SECTION.

$$\begin{bmatrix} \text{77-level-description-entry} \\ \text{record-description-entry} \end{bmatrix} \ldots$$

[COMMUNICATION SECTION.

[communication-description-entry

[record-description-entry] ...] ...]

[REPORT SECTION.

[RD report-name

    [; CODE literal-1]

$$\left[; \begin{Bmatrix} \text{CONTROL} & \text{IS} \\ \text{CONTROLS} & \text{ARE} \end{Bmatrix} \begin{Bmatrix} \text{FINAL} & \text{field-name-1 [, field-name-2]} \ldots \\ & \text{[, field-name-1 [, field-name-2]} \ldots] \end{Bmatrix} \right]$$

$$\left[; \text{PAGE} \begin{bmatrix} \text{LIMIT} & \text{IS} \\ \text{LIMITS} & \text{ARE} \end{bmatrix} \text{integer-1} \begin{bmatrix} \text{LINE} \\ \text{LINES} \end{bmatrix} \text{[, HEADING integer-2]} \right]$$

    [, FIRST DETAIL integer-3] [, LAST DETAIL integer-4]

    [, FOOTING integer-5].

{report-group-description-entry} ...] ...]

General Format for Data Description Entry

Format 1   level-number $\begin{Bmatrix} \text{field-name-1} \\ \text{FILLER} \end{Bmatrix}$

    [; REDEFINES field-name-2]

$$\left[; \begin{Bmatrix} \text{PICTURE} \\ \text{PIC} \end{Bmatrix} \text{IS character-string} \right]$$

$$\left[; \text{[USAGE IS]} \begin{Bmatrix} \text{COMPUTATIONAL} \\ \text{COMP} \\ \text{DISPLAY} \\ \text{INDEX} \end{Bmatrix} \right]$$

$$\left[\ ; [\underline{SIGN}\ IS]\ \left\{\begin{array}{l}\underline{LEADING}\\\underline{TRAILING}\end{array}\right\}\ [\underline{SEPARATE}\ CHARACTER]\ \right]$$

$$\left[\ ; \underline{OCCURS}\ \left\{\begin{array}{l}integer\text{-}1\ \underline{TO}\ integer\text{-}2\ TIMES\ \underline{DEPENDING}\ ON\ field\text{-}name\text{-}3\\integer\text{-}2\ TIMES\end{array}\right\}\right.$$

$$\left[\left\{\begin{array}{l}\underline{ASCENDING}\\\underline{DESCENDING}\end{array}\right\}\ KEY\ IS\ field\text{-}name\text{-}4\ [,\ field\text{-}name\text{-}5]\ \ \ldots\ \right]\quad.$$

$$\left[\underline{INDEXED}\ BY\ index\text{-}name\text{-}1\ [,\ index\text{-}name\text{-}2]\ \ \ldots\ ]\right]$$

$$\left[\ ;\left\{\begin{array}{l}\underline{SYNCHRONIZED}\\\underline{SYNC}\end{array}\right\}\left[\begin{array}{l}\underline{LEFT}\\\underline{RIGHT}\end{array}\right]\ \right]$$

$$\left[\ ;\left\{\begin{array}{l}\underline{JUSTIFIED}\\\underline{JUST}\end{array}\right\}\ RIGHT\ \right]$$

$$[\ ;\ \underline{BLANK}\ WHEN\ \underline{ZERO}]$$

$$[\ ;\ \underline{VALUE}\ IS\ literal].$$

Format 2 66 field-name-1; $\underline{RENAMES}$ field-name-2 $\left[\left\{\begin{array}{l}\underline{THROUGH}\\\underline{THRU}\end{array}\right\}\ field\text{-}name\text{-}3\ \right].$

Format 3 88 condition-name; $\left\{\begin{array}{ll}\underline{VALUE}&IS\\\underline{VALUES}&ARE\end{array}\right\}$ literal-1 $\left[\left\{\begin{array}{l}\underline{THROUGH}\\\underline{THRU}\end{array}\right\}\ literal\text{-}2\ \right]$

$$\left[\ ,\ literal\text{-}3\ \left[\left\{\begin{array}{l}\underline{THROUGH}\\\underline{THRU}\end{array}\right\}\ LITERAL\text{-}4\ \right]\ \right]\ \ \ldots\ .$$

General Format for Communication Description Entry

Format 1 $\underline{CD}$ cd-name;

$$FOR\ [\underline{INITIAL}]\ \underline{INPUT}\quad\left[\begin{array}{l}[[\ ;\ SYMBOLIC\ \underline{QUEUE}\ IS\ field\text{-}name\text{-}1]\\ \quad[\ ;\ SYMBOLIC\ \underline{SUB\text{-}QUEUE\text{-}1}\ IS\ field\text{-}name\text{-}2]\\ \quad[\ ;\ SYMBOLIC\ \underline{SUB\text{-}QUEUE\text{-}2}\ IS\ field\text{-}name\text{-}3]\\ \quad[\ ;\ SYMBOLIC\ \underline{SUB\text{-}QUEUE\text{-}3}\ IS\ field\text{-}name\text{-}4]\\ \quad[\ ;\ \underline{MESSAGE}\ \underline{DATE}\ IS\ field\text{-}name\text{-}5]\\ \quad[\ ;\ \underline{MESSAGE}\ \underline{TIME}\ IS\ field\text{-}name\text{-}6]\\ \quad[\ ;\ SYMBOLIC\ \underline{SOURCE}\ IS\ field\text{-}name\text{-}7]\\ \quad[\ ;\ \underline{TEXT}\ \underline{LENGTH}\ IS\ field\text{-}name\text{-}8]\\ \quad[\ ;\ \underline{END}\ \underline{KEY}\ IS\ field\text{-}name\text{-}9]\\ \quad[\ ;\ \underline{STATUS}\ \underline{KEY}\ IS\ field\text{-}name\text{-}10]\\ \quad[\ ;\ MESSAGE\ \underline{COUNT}\ IS\ field\text{-}name\text{-}11]]\\ [field\text{-}name\text{-}1,\ field\text{-}name\text{-}2,\ \ \ldots\ ,\ field\text{-}name\text{-}11]\end{array}\right]$$

Format 2   <u>CD</u> cd-name; FOR <u>OUTPUT</u>

[; <u>DESTINATION</u> <u>COUNT</u> IS field-name-1]

[; <u>TEXT</u> <u>LENGTH</u> IS field-name-2]

[; <u>STATUS</u> <u>KEY</u> IS field-name-3]

[; <u>DESTINATION</u> <u>TABLE</u> <u>OCCURS</u> integer-2 TIMES

[; <u>INDEXED</u> BY index-name-1 [, index-name-2] . . .]

[; <u>ERROR</u> <u>KEY</u> IS field-name-4]

[; SYMBOLIC <u>DESTINATION</u> IS field-name-5].

General Format for Report Group Description Entry

Format 1   01   [field-name-1]

$$\left[\; ; \underline{LINE} \text{ NUMBER IS } \begin{Bmatrix} \text{integer-1} & [\text{ON } \underline{NEXT} \underline{PAGE} \\ \underline{PLUS} \text{ integer-2} \end{Bmatrix} \right]$$

$$; \; \underline{NEXT} \text{ } \underline{GROUP} \text{ IS } \begin{Bmatrix} \text{integer-3} \\ \underline{PLUS} \text{ integer-4} \\ \underline{NEXT} \text{ } \underline{PAGE} \end{Bmatrix}$$

$$; \underline{TYPE} \text{ IS } \begin{Bmatrix} \begin{Bmatrix} \underline{REPORT} \text{ } \underline{HEADING} \\ \underline{RH} \end{Bmatrix} \\ \begin{Bmatrix} \underline{PAGE} \text{ } \underline{HEADING} \\ \underline{PH} \end{Bmatrix} \\ \begin{Bmatrix} \underline{CONTROL} \text{ } \underline{HEADING} \\ \underline{CH} \end{Bmatrix} \begin{Bmatrix} \text{field-name-2} \\ \underline{FINAL} \end{Bmatrix} \\ \begin{Bmatrix} \underline{DETAIL} \\ \underline{DE} \end{Bmatrix} \\ \begin{Bmatrix} \underline{CONTROL} \text{ } \underline{FOOTING} \\ \underline{CF} \end{Bmatrix} \begin{Bmatrix} \text{field-name-3} \\ \underline{FINAL} \end{Bmatrix} \\ \begin{Bmatrix} \underline{PAGE} \text{ } \underline{FOOTING} \\ \underline{PF} \end{Bmatrix} \\ \begin{Bmatrix} \underline{REPORT} \text{ } \underline{FOOTING} \\ \underline{RF} \end{Bmatrix} \end{Bmatrix}$$

[; [<u>USAGE</u> IS] <u>DISPLAY</u>].

Format 2   level-number [field-name-1]

$$\left[\; ; \underline{LINE} \text{ NUMBER IS } \begin{Bmatrix} \text{integer-1} & [\text{ON } \underline{NEXT} \underline{PAGE}] \\ \underline{PLUS} \text{ integer-2} \end{Bmatrix} \right]$$

[; [<u>USAGE</u> IS] <u>DISPLAY</u>].

Format 3   level-number [field-name-1]

[; <u>BLANK</u> WHEN <u>ZERO</u>]

[; <u>GROUP</u> INDICATE]

$$\left[; \left\{ \begin{array}{l} \underline{\text{JUSTIFIED}} \\ \underline{\text{JUST}} \end{array} \right\} \text{RIGHT} \right]$$

$$\left[; \underline{\text{LINE}} \text{ NUMBER IS} \left\{ \begin{array}{l} \text{integer-1} \quad [\text{ON } \underline{\text{NEXT}} \ \underline{\text{PAGE}}] \\ \underline{\text{PLUS}} \text{ integer-2} \end{array} \right\} \right]$$

[; <u>COLUMN</u> NUMBER IS integer-3]

$$; \left\{ \begin{array}{l} \underline{\text{PICTURE}} \\ \underline{\text{PIC}} \end{array} \right\} \text{IS character-string}$$

$$\left\{ \begin{array}{l} ; \underline{\text{SOURCE}} \text{ IS field-name-1} \\ ; \underline{\text{VALUE}} \text{ IS literal} \\ \{; \underline{\text{SUM}} \text{ field-name-2 [, field-name-3] } \ldots \\ \quad \underline{\text{UPON}} \text{ field-name-2 [, field-name-3] } \ldots]\} \ldots \\ \quad \left[\underline{\text{RESET}} \text{ ON} \left\{ \begin{array}{l} \text{field-name-4} \\ \underline{\text{FINAL}} \end{array} \right\} \right] \end{array} \right\}$$

[; [<u>USAGE</u> IS] <u>DISPLAY</u>].

General Format for PROCEDURE DIVISION

Format 1   <u>PROCEDURE</u> <u>DIVISION</u> [<u>USING</u> field-name-1 [, field-name-2] . . .].

[<u>DECLARATIVES</u>.

{section-name <u>SECTION</u> [segment-number]. declarative-sentence

[paragraph-name. [sentence] . . .] . . . } . . .

<u>END</u> <u>DECLARATIVES</u>.]

{section-name <u>SECTION</u> [segment-number].

[paragraph-name. [sentence] . . .] . . . } . . .

Format 2   <u>PROCEDURE</u> <u>DIVISION</u> [<u>USING</u> field-name-1 [, field-name-2] . . .].

{paragraph-name. [sentence] . . . } . . .

General Format for Verbs

<u>ACCEPT</u> field-name [<u>FROM</u> mnemonic-name]

$$\underline{\text{ACCEPT}} \text{ field-name } \underline{\text{FROM}} \left\{ \begin{array}{l} \underline{\text{DATE}} \\ \underline{\text{DAY}} \\ \underline{\text{TIME}} \end{array} \right\}$$

<u>ACCEPT</u> cd-name MESSAGE <u>COUNT</u>

$$\underline{\text{ADD}} \left\{ \begin{array}{l} \text{field-name-1} \\ \text{literal-1} \end{array} \right\} \left\{ \begin{array}{l} \text{, field-name-2} \\ \text{, literal-2} \end{array} \right\} \ldots \text{TO field-name-m [\underline{ROUNDED}]}$$

[, field-name-n [<u>ROUNDED</u>]] . . . [; ON <u>SIZE</u> <u>ERROR</u> imperative-statement]

$$\underline{\text{ADD}} \left\{ \begin{array}{l} \text{field-name-1} \\ \text{literal-1} \end{array} \right\}, \left\{ \begin{array}{l} \text{field-name-2} \\ \text{literal-2} \end{array} \right\} \left[\begin{array}{l} \text{, field-name-3} \\ \text{, literal-3} \end{array} \right] \ldots$$

GIVING field-name-m [ROUNDED] $\left[$, field-name-n [ROUNDED] $\right]$ . . .

[; ON SIZE ERROR imperative-statement]

ADD $\left\{\begin{array}{l}\text{CORRESPONDING}\\\text{CORR}\end{array}\right\}$ field-name-1 TO field-name-2 [ROUNDED]

[; ON SIZE ERROR imperative-statement]

ALTER procedure-name-1 TO [PROCEED TO] procedure-name-2

[, procedure-name-3 TO [PROCEED TO] procedure-name-4] . . .

CALL $\left\{\begin{array}{l}\text{field-name-1}\\\text{literal-1}\end{array}\right\}$ [USING field-name-1 [, field-name-2] . . .]

[; ON OVERFLOW imperative-statement]

CANCEL $\left\{\begin{array}{l}\text{field-name-1}\\\text{literal-1}\end{array}\right\}$ $\left[\begin{array}{l}\text{field-name-2}\\\text{, literal-2}\end{array}\right]$ . . .

CLOSE file-name-1 $\left[\begin{array}{l}\left[\left\{\begin{array}{l}\text{REEL}\\\text{UNIT}\end{array}\right\}\right]\left[\begin{array}{l}\text{WITH NO REWIND}\\\text{FOR REMOVAL}\end{array}\right]\\\text{WITH}\ \left\{\begin{array}{l}\text{NO REWIND}\\\text{LOCK}\end{array}\right\}\end{array}\right]$

$\left[\begin{array}{l}\text{, file-name-2}\ \left[\begin{array}{l}\left\{\begin{array}{l}\text{REEL}\\\text{UNIT}\end{array}\right\}\left[\begin{array}{l}\text{WITH NO REWIND}\\\text{FOR REMOVAL}\end{array}\right]\\\text{WITH}\ \left\{\begin{array}{l}\text{NO REWIND}\\\text{LOCK}\end{array}\right\}\end{array}\right]\end{array}\right]$

CLOSE file-name-1 [WITH LOCK] [, file-name-2 [WITH LOCK]] . . .

COMPUTE field-name-1 [ROUNDED] , field-name-2 [ROUNDED] . . .

= arithmetic-expression [; ON SIZE ERROR imperative-statement]

DELETE file name RECORD [; INVALID KEY imperative-statement]

DISABLE $\left\{\begin{array}{l}\text{INPUT}\ \ [\text{TERMINAL}]\\\text{OUTPUT}\end{array}\right\}$ cd-name WITH KEY $\left\{\begin{array}{l}\text{field-name-1}\\\text{literal-1}\end{array}\right\}$

DISPLAY $\left\{\begin{array}{l}\text{field-name-1}\\\text{literal-1}\end{array}\right\}$ $\left[\begin{array}{l}\text{, field-name-2}\\\text{, literal-2}\end{array}\right]$ . . . [UPON mnemonic-name]

DIVIDE $\left\{\begin{array}{l}\text{field-name-1}\\\text{literal-1}\end{array}\right\}$ INTO field-name-2 [ROUNDED]

[, field-name-3 [ROUNDED]] . . . [; ON SIZE ERROR imperative-statement]

DIVIDE $\left\{\begin{array}{l}\text{field-name-1}\\\text{literal-1}\end{array}\right\}$ INTO $\left\{\begin{array}{l}\text{field-name-2}\\\text{literal-2}\end{array}\right\}$ GIVING field-name-3 [ROUNDED]

[, field-name-4 [ROUNDED]] . . . [; ON SIZE ERROR imperative-statement]

DIVIDE $\left\{\begin{array}{l}\text{field-name-1}\\\text{literal-1}\end{array}\right\}$ BY $\left\{\begin{array}{l}\text{field-name-2}\\\text{literal-2}\end{array}\right\}$ GIVING field-name-3 [ROUNDED]

[, field-name-4 [ROUNDED]] . . . [; ON SIZE ERROR imperative-statement]

DIVIDE $\left\{\begin{array}{l}\text{field-name-1}\\\text{literal-1}\end{array}\right\}$ INTO $\left\{\begin{array}{l}\text{field-name-2}\\\text{literal-2}\end{array}\right\}$ GIVING field-name-3 [ROUNDED]

$$\underline{\text{REMAINDER}} \text{ field-name-4} \quad \ldots \quad [; \text{ON } \underline{\text{SIZE}} \ \underline{\text{ERROR}} \text{ imperative-statement}]$$

$$\underline{\text{DIVIDE}} \begin{Bmatrix} \text{field-name-1} \\ \text{literal-1} \end{Bmatrix} \underline{\text{BY}} \begin{Bmatrix} \text{field-name-2} \\ \text{literal-2} \end{Bmatrix} \underline{\text{GIVING}} \text{ field-name-3 } [\underline{\text{ROUNDED}}]$$

$$\underline{\text{REMAINDER}} \text{ field-name-4} \quad \ldots \quad [; \text{ON } \underline{\text{SIZE}} \ \underline{\text{ERROR}} \text{ imperative-statement}]$$

$$\underline{\text{ENABLE}} \begin{Bmatrix} \underline{\text{INPUT}} \\ \underline{\text{OUTPUT}} \end{Bmatrix} [\underline{\text{TERMINAL}}] \text{ cd-name WITH } \underline{\text{KEY}} \begin{Bmatrix} \text{field-name-1} \\ \text{literal-1} \end{Bmatrix}$$

$$\underline{\text{ENTER}} \text{ language-name [routine-name].}$$

$$\underline{\text{EXIT}} \ [\underline{\text{PROGRAM}}].$$

$$\underline{\text{GENERATE}} \begin{Bmatrix} \text{detail-name} \\ \text{report-name} \\ \text{group-name} \end{Bmatrix}$$

$$\underline{\text{GO}} \text{ TO [procedure-name-1]}$$

$$\underline{\text{GO}} \text{ TO procedure-name-1 [, procedure-name-2]} \quad \ldots,$$
$$\text{procedure-name-n } \underline{\text{DEPENDING}} \text{ ON field-name}$$

$$\underline{\text{IF}} \text{ condition;} \begin{Bmatrix} \text{statement-1} \\ \underline{\text{NEXT}} \ \underline{\text{SENTENCE}} \end{Bmatrix} \begin{Bmatrix} ; \underline{\text{ELSE}} \text{ statement-2} \\ ; \underline{\text{ELSE}} \ \underline{\text{NEXT}} \ \underline{\text{SENTENCE}} \end{Bmatrix}$$

$$\underline{\text{INITIATE}} \text{ report-name-1 [, report-name-2]} \quad \ldots$$

$$\underline{\text{INSPECT}} \text{ field-name-1 } \underline{\text{TALLYING}}$$

$$\begin{Bmatrix} \text{, field-name-2 } \underline{\text{FOR}} \begin{Bmatrix} , \begin{Bmatrix} \begin{Bmatrix} \underline{\text{ALL}} \\ \underline{\text{LEADING}} \end{Bmatrix} \begin{Bmatrix} \text{field-name-3} \\ \text{literal-1} \end{Bmatrix} \\ \underline{\text{CHARACTERS}} \end{Bmatrix} \\ \left[\begin{Bmatrix} \underline{\text{BEFORE}} \\ \underline{\text{AFTER}} \end{Bmatrix} \text{INITIAL} \begin{Bmatrix} \text{field-name-4} \\ \text{literal-1} \end{Bmatrix} \right] \end{Bmatrix} \ \ldots \end{Bmatrix} \ \ldots$$

$$\underline{\text{INSPECT}} \text{ field-name-1 } \underline{\text{REPLACING}}$$

$$\begin{Bmatrix} \underline{\text{CHARACTERS}} \ \underline{\text{BY}} \begin{Bmatrix} \text{field-name-6} \\ \text{literal-4} \end{Bmatrix} \left[\begin{Bmatrix} \underline{\text{BEFORE}} \\ \underline{\text{AFTER}} \end{Bmatrix} \text{INITIAL} \begin{Bmatrix} \text{field-name-7} \\ \text{literal-5} \end{Bmatrix} \right] \\ \begin{Bmatrix} , \begin{Bmatrix} \underline{\text{ALL}} \\ \underline{\text{LEADING}} \\ \underline{\text{FIRST}} \end{Bmatrix} \begin{Bmatrix} , \begin{Bmatrix} \text{field-name-5} \\ \text{literal-3} \end{Bmatrix} \underline{\text{BY}} \begin{Bmatrix} \text{field-name-6} \\ \text{literal-4} \end{Bmatrix} \\ \left[\begin{Bmatrix} \underline{\text{BEFORE}} \\ \underline{\text{AFTER}} \end{Bmatrix} \text{INITIAL} \begin{Bmatrix} \text{field-name-7} \\ \text{literal-5} \end{Bmatrix} \right] \end{Bmatrix} \ \ldots \end{Bmatrix} \end{Bmatrix} \ \ldots$$

$$\underline{\text{INSPECT}} \text{ field-name-1 } \underline{\text{TALLYING}}$$

$$\begin{Bmatrix} \text{, field-name-2 } \underline{\text{FOR}} \begin{Bmatrix} , \begin{Bmatrix} \begin{Bmatrix} \underline{\text{ALL}} \\ \underline{\text{LEADING}} \end{Bmatrix} \begin{Bmatrix} \text{field-name-3} \\ \text{literal-1} \end{Bmatrix} \\ \underline{\text{CHARACTERS}} \end{Bmatrix} \\ \left[\begin{Bmatrix} \underline{\text{BEFORE}} \\ \underline{\text{AFTER}} \end{Bmatrix} \text{INITIAL} \begin{Bmatrix} \text{field-name-4} \\ \text{literal-2} \end{Bmatrix} \right] \end{Bmatrix} \ \ldots \end{Bmatrix} \ \ldots$$

REPLACING

$$\left\{ \begin{array}{l} \underline{\text{CHARACTERS}} \ \underline{\text{BY}} \left\{ \begin{array}{l} \text{field-name-6} \\ \text{literal-4} \end{array} \right\} \left\{ \begin{array}{l} \underline{\text{BEFORE}} \\ \underline{\text{AFTER}} \end{array} \right\} \text{INITIAL} \left\{ \begin{array}{l} \text{field-name-7} \\ \text{literal-5} \end{array} \right\} \\[3em] \left\{ \left\{ \begin{array}{l} \underline{\text{ALL}} \\ \underline{\text{LEADING}} \\ \underline{\text{FIRST}} \end{array} \right\} \left\{ \begin{array}{l} \text{field-name-5} \\ \text{literal-3} \end{array} \right\} \underline{\text{BY}} \left\{ \begin{array}{l} \text{field-name-6} \\ \text{literal-4} \end{array} \right\} \right. \\[3em] \left. \left[\left\{ \begin{array}{l} \underline{\text{BEFORE}} \\ \underline{\text{AFTER}} \end{array} \right\} \text{INITIAL} \left\{ \begin{array}{l} \text{field-name-7} \\ \text{literal-5} \end{array} \right\} \right] \right\} \ \ldots \end{array} \right\} \ \ldots$$

$$\underline{\text{MERGE}} \ \text{file-name-1 ON} \left\{ \begin{array}{l} \underline{\text{ASCENDING}} \\ \underline{\text{DESCENDING}} \end{array} \right\} \text{KEY field-name-1} \ [\text{, field-name-2}] \ \ldots$$

$$\left[\text{ON} \left\{ \begin{array}{l} \underline{\text{ASCENDING}} \\ \underline{\text{DESCENDING}} \end{array} \right\} \text{KEY field-name-3} \ [\text{, field-name-4}] \ \ldots \right] \ \ldots$$

[COLLATING <u>SEQUENCE</u> IS alphabet-name]

<u>USING</u> file-name-2, file-name-3 [, file-name-4] ...

$$\left\{ \begin{array}{l} \underline{\text{OUTPUT}} \ \underline{\text{PROCEDURE}} \ \text{IS section-name-1} \left[\cdot \left\{ \begin{array}{l} \underline{\text{THROUGH}} \\ \underline{\text{THRU}} \end{array} \right\} \text{section-name-2} \right] \\[2em] \underline{\text{GIVING}} \ \text{file-name-5} \end{array} \right\}$$

$$\underline{\text{MOVE}} \left\{ \begin{array}{l} \text{field-name-1} \\ \text{literal} \end{array} \right\} \underline{\text{TO}} \ \text{field-name-2} \ [\text{, field-name-3}] \ \ldots$$

$$\underline{\text{MOVE}} \left\{ \begin{array}{l} \underline{\text{CORRESPONDING}} \\ \underline{\text{CORR}} \end{array} \right\} \text{field-name-1} \ \underline{\text{TO}} \ \text{field-name-2}$$

$$\underline{\text{MULTIPLY}} \left\{ \begin{array}{l} \text{field-name-1} \\ \text{literal-1} \end{array} \right\} \underline{\text{BY}} \ \text{field-name-2} \ [\underline{\text{ROUNDED}}]$$

$$\left[\text{, field-name-4} \ [\underline{\text{ROUNDED}}] \right] \ \ldots \ [\text{; ON } \underline{\text{SIZE}} \ \underline{\text{ERROR}} \ \text{imperative-statement}]$$

$$\underline{\text{MULTIPLY}} \left\{ \begin{array}{l} \text{field-name-1} \\ \text{literal-1} \end{array} \right\} \underline{\text{BY}} \left\{ \begin{array}{l} \text{field-name-2} \\ \text{literal-2} \end{array} \right\} \underline{\text{GIVING}} \ \text{identifier-3} \ [\underline{\text{ROUNDED}}]$$

, field-name-4 [<u>ROUNDED</u>] ... [; ON <u>SIZE</u> <u>ERROR</u> imperative-statement]

$$\underline{\text{OPEN}} \left\{ \begin{array}{l} \underline{\text{INPUT}} \qquad \text{file-name-1} \left[\begin{array}{l} \underline{\text{REVERSED}} \\ \text{WITH } \underline{\text{NO}} \ \text{REWIND} \end{array} \right] \\[1.5em] \qquad \left[\text{, file-name-2} \left[\begin{array}{l} \underline{\text{REVERSED}} \\ \text{WITH } \underline{\text{NO}} \ \text{REWIND} \end{array} \right] \right] \ \ldots \\[2em] \underline{\text{OUTPUT}} \quad \text{file-name-3 [WITH } \underline{\text{NO}} \ \text{REWIND} \\ \qquad \text{[, file-name-4 [WITH } \underline{\text{NO}} \ \text{REWIND]] } \ \ldots \\[1em] \underline{\text{I-O}} \ \text{file-name-5 [, file-name-6] } \ \ldots \\[1em] \underline{\text{EXTEND}} \ \text{file-name-7 [, file-name-8] } \ \ldots \end{array} \right\} \ \ldots$$

$$\underline{\text{OPEN}} \left\{ \begin{array}{l} \underline{\text{INPUT}} \quad \text{file-name-1 [, file-name-2] } \ \ldots \\ \underline{\text{OUTPUT}} \ \text{file-name-3 [, file-name-4] } \ \ldots \\ \underline{\text{I-O}} \qquad \text{file-name-5 [, file-name-6] } \ \ldots \end{array} \right\} \ \ldots$$

$$\underline{\text{PERFORM}} \text{ procedure-name-1} \left[\begin{Bmatrix} \underline{\text{THROUGH}} \\ \underline{\text{THRU}} \end{Bmatrix} \text{procedure-name-2} \right]$$

$$\underline{\text{PERFORM}} \text{ procedure-name-1} \left[\begin{Bmatrix} \underline{\text{THROUGH}} \\ \underline{\text{THRU}} \end{Bmatrix} \text{procedure-name-2} \right] \begin{Bmatrix} \text{field-name-1} \\ \text{integer-1} \end{Bmatrix}$$

$$\underline{\text{PERFORM}} \text{ procedure-name-1} \left[\begin{Bmatrix} \underline{\text{THROUGH}} \\ \underline{\text{THRU}} \end{Bmatrix} \text{procedure-name-2} \right] \underline{\text{UNTIL}} \text{ conditi}$$

$$\underline{\text{PERFORM}} \text{ procedure-name-1} \left[\begin{Bmatrix} \underline{\text{THROUGH}} \\ \underline{\text{THRU}} \end{Bmatrix} \text{procedure-name-2} \right]$$

$$\underline{\text{VARYING}} \begin{Bmatrix} \text{field-name-2} \\ \text{index-name-1} \end{Bmatrix} \underline{\text{FROM}} \begin{Bmatrix} \text{field-name-3} \\ \text{index-name-2} \\ \text{literal-1} \end{Bmatrix}$$

$$\underline{\text{BY}} \begin{Bmatrix} \text{field-name-4} \\ \text{literal-3} \end{Bmatrix} \underline{\text{UNTIL}} \text{ condition-1}$$

$$\left[\underline{\text{AFTER}} \begin{Bmatrix} \text{field-name-5} \\ \text{index-name-3} \end{Bmatrix} \underline{\text{FROM}} \begin{Bmatrix} \text{field-name-6} \\ \text{index-name-4} \\ \text{literal-3} \end{Bmatrix} \right.$$

$$\underline{\text{BY}} \begin{Bmatrix} \text{field-name-7} \\ \text{literal-4} \end{Bmatrix} \underline{\text{UNTIL}} \text{ condition-2}$$

$$\left[\underline{\text{AFTER}} \begin{Bmatrix} \text{field-name-8} \\ \text{index-name-5} \end{Bmatrix} \underline{\text{FROM}} \begin{Bmatrix} \text{field-name-9} \\ \text{index-name-6} \\ \text{literal-5} \end{Bmatrix} \right.$$

$$\left. \left. \underline{\text{BY}} \begin{Bmatrix} \text{field-name-10} \\ \text{literal-6} \end{Bmatrix} \underline{\text{UNTIL}} \text{ condition-3} \right] \right]$$

$\underline{\text{READ}}$ file-name RECORD [$\underline{\text{INTO}}$ field-name] [; AT $\underline{\text{END}}$ imperative-statement]

$\underline{\text{READ}}$ file-name [$\underline{\text{NEXT}}$] RECORD [$\underline{\text{INTO}}$ field-name]
[; AT $\underline{\text{END}}$ imperative-statement]

$\underline{\text{READ}}$ file-name RECORD [$\underline{\text{INTO}}$ field-name]
[; $\underline{\text{INVALID}}$ KEY imperative-statement]

$\underline{\text{READ}}$ file-name RECORD [$\underline{\text{INTO}}$ field-name]
[; $\underline{\text{KEY}}$ IS field-name]
[; $\underline{\text{INVALID}}$ KEY imperative-statement]

$$\underline{\text{RECEIVE}} \text{ cd-name} \begin{Bmatrix} \underline{\text{MESSAGE}} \\ \underline{\text{SEGMENT}} \end{Bmatrix} \underline{\text{INTO}} \text{ field-name-1}$$
[; $\underline{\text{NO}}$ $\underline{\text{DATA}}$ imperative-statement]

$\underline{\text{RELEASE}}$ record-name [$\underline{\text{FROM}}$ field-name]

$\underline{\text{RETURN}}$ file-name RECORD [$\underline{\text{INTO}}$ field-name]; AT $\underline{\text{END}}$ imperative-statement

$\underline{\text{REWRITE}}$ record-name [$\underline{\text{FROM}}$ field-name]

$\underline{\text{REWRITE}}$ record-name [$\underline{\text{FROM}}$ field-name] [; $\underline{\text{INVALID}}$ KEY imperative-statemen

SEARCH field-name-1 $\left[\text{VARYING} \begin{Bmatrix} \text{field-name-2} \\ \text{index-name-1} \end{Bmatrix}\right]$

[; AT END imperative-statement-1]

; WHEN condition-1 $\begin{Bmatrix} \text{imperative-statement-2} \\ \text{NEXT SENTENCE} \end{Bmatrix}$

$\left[\text{; WHEN condition-2} \begin{Bmatrix} \text{imperative-statement-3} \\ \text{NEXT SENTENCE} \end{Bmatrix}\right]$ ...

SEARCH ALL field-name-1 [; AT END imperative-statement-1]

; WHEN {field-name-1} $\begin{Bmatrix} \text{IS EQUAL TO} \\ \text{IS =} \end{Bmatrix}$ $\begin{bmatrix} \text{field-name-1} \\ \text{field-name-3} \\ \text{literal-1} \\ \text{arithmetic-expression-1} \\ \text{condition-name-1} \end{bmatrix}$

$\left[\text{AND {field-name-2}} \begin{Bmatrix} \text{IS EQUAL TO} \\ \text{IS =} \end{Bmatrix} \begin{bmatrix} \text{field-name-4} \\ \text{literal-2} \\ \text{arithmetic-expression-2} \\ \text{condition-name-2} \end{bmatrix} \cdots\right]$ ...

$\begin{Bmatrix} \text{imperative-statement-2} \\ \text{NEXT SENTENCE} \end{Bmatrix}$

SEND cd-name FROM field-name-1

SEND cd-name [FROM field-name-1] $\begin{matrix} \text{WITH field-name-2} \\ \text{WITH ESI} \\ \text{WITH EMI} \\ \text{WITH EGI} \end{matrix}$

$\left[\begin{Bmatrix} \text{BEFORE} \\ \text{AFTER} \end{Bmatrix} \text{ADVANCING} \begin{Bmatrix} \begin{Bmatrix} \text{field-name-3} \\ \text{integer} \end{Bmatrix} \begin{bmatrix} \text{LINE} \\ \text{LINES} \end{bmatrix} \\ \begin{Bmatrix} \text{mnemonic-name} \\ \text{PAGE} \end{Bmatrix} \end{Bmatrix}\right]$

SET $\begin{Bmatrix} \text{field-name-1 [, field-name-2]} \\ \text{index-name-1 [, index-name-2]} \end{Bmatrix} \cdots$ TO $\begin{Bmatrix} \text{field-name-3} \\ \text{index-name-3} \\ \text{integer-1} \end{Bmatrix}$

SET index-name-4 [, index-name-5] ... $\begin{Bmatrix} \text{UP BY} \\ \text{DOWN BY} \end{Bmatrix} \begin{Bmatrix} \text{field-name-4} \\ \text{integer-2} \end{Bmatrix}$

SORT file-name-1 ON $\begin{Bmatrix} \text{ASCENDING} \\ \text{DESCENDING} \end{Bmatrix}$ KEY field-name-1 [, field-name-2] ...

$\left[\text{ON} \begin{Bmatrix} \text{ASCENDING} \\ \text{DESCENDING} \end{Bmatrix} \text{KEY field-name-3 [, field-name-4]} \cdots\right]$ ...

[COLLATING SEQUENCE IS alphabet-name]

$\begin{Bmatrix} \text{INPUT PROCEDURE IS section-name-1} \left[\begin{Bmatrix} \text{THROUGH} \\ \text{THRU} \end{Bmatrix} \text{section-name-2}\right] \\ \text{USING file-name-2 [, file-name-3]} \cdots \end{Bmatrix}$

$$\left\{\begin{array}{l}\underline{\text{OUTPUT}}\ \underline{\text{PROCEDURE}}\ \text{IS section-name-3}\ \left[\left\{\begin{array}{l}\underline{\text{THROUGH}}\\\underline{\text{THRU}}\end{array}\right\}\ \text{section-name-4}\right]\\\underline{\text{GIVING}}\ \text{file-name-4}\end{array}\right.$$

$$\underline{\text{START}}\ \text{file-name}\ \left[\text{KEY}\ \left\{\begin{array}{l}\text{IS}\ \underline{\text{EQUAL}}\ \text{TO}\\\text{IS}\ =\\\text{IS}\ \underline{\text{GREATER}}\ \text{THAN}\\\text{IS}\ >\\\text{IS}\ \underline{\text{NOT}}\ \underline{\text{LESS}}\ \text{THAN}\\\text{IS}\ \underline{\text{NOT}}\ <\end{array}\right\}\ \text{field-name}\right]$$

[; INVALID KEY imperative-statement]

$$\underline{\text{STOP}}\ \left\{\begin{array}{l}\underline{\text{RUN}}\\\text{literal}\end{array}\right\}$$

$$\underline{\text{STRING}}\ \left\{\begin{array}{l}\text{field-name-1}\\\text{literal-1}\end{array}\right\}\ \left[\begin{array}{l}\text{, field-name-2}\\\text{, literal-2}\end{array}\right]\ \ldots\ \underline{\text{DELIMITED}}\ \text{BY}\ \left\{\begin{array}{l}\text{field-name}\\\text{literal-3}\\\underline{\text{SIZE}}\end{array}\right\}$$

$$\left[\left\{\begin{array}{l}\text{field-name-4}\\\text{literal-4}\end{array}\right\}\ \left[\begin{array}{l}\text{, field-name-5}\\\text{, literal-5}\end{array}\right]\ \ldots\ \underline{\text{DELIMITED}}\ \text{BY}\ \left\{\begin{array}{l}\text{field-name}\\\text{literal-6}\\\underline{\text{SIZE}}\end{array}\right\}\right]\ \ldots$$

$\underline{\text{INTO}}$ field-name-7 [WITH $\underline{\text{POINTER}}$ field-name-8]

[; ON $\underline{\text{OVERFLOW}}$ imperative-statement]

$$\underline{\text{SUBTRACT}}\ \left\{\begin{array}{l}\text{field-name-1}\\\text{literal-1}\end{array}\right\}\ \left[\begin{array}{l}\text{, field-name-2}\\\text{, literal-2}\end{array}\right]\ \ldots\ \underline{\text{FROM}}\ \text{field-name-m}\ [\underline{\text{ROUN}}$$

[, field-name-n [$\underline{\text{ROUNDED}}$]] ... [; ON $\underline{\text{SIZE}}$ $\underline{\text{ERROR}}$ imperative-statement]

$$\underline{\text{SUBTRACT}}\ \left\{\begin{array}{l}\text{field-name-1}\\\text{literal-1}\end{array}\right\}\ \left[\begin{array}{l}\text{, field-name-2}\\\text{, literal-2}\end{array}\right]\ \ldots\ \underline{\text{FROM}}\ \left\{\begin{array}{l}\text{field-name-m}\\\text{literal-m}\end{array}\right\}$$

$\underline{\text{GIVING}}$ field-name-n [$\underline{\text{ROUNDED}}$], field-name-o [$\underline{\text{ROUNDED}}$] ...

[; ON $\underline{\text{SIZE}}$ $\underline{\text{ERROR}}$ imperative-statement]

$$\underline{\text{SUBTRACT}}\ \left\{\begin{array}{l}\underline{\text{CORRESPONDING}}\\\underline{\text{CORR}}\end{array}\right\}\ \text{field-name-1}\ \underline{\text{FROM}}\ \text{field-name-2}\ [\underline{\text{ROUNDED}}$$

[; ON $\underline{\text{SIZE}}$ $\underline{\text{ERROR}}$ imperative-statement]

$\underline{\text{SUPPRESS}}$ PRINTING

$\underline{\text{TERMINATE}}$ report-name-1 [, report-name-2] ...

$\underline{\text{UNSTRING}}$ field-name-1

$$\left[\underline{\text{DELIMITED}}\ \text{BY}\ [\text{ALL}]\ \left\{\begin{array}{l}\text{field-name-2}\\\text{literal-1}\end{array}\right\}\ \left[,\ \underline{\text{OR}}\ [\underline{\text{ALL}}]\ \left\{\begin{array}{l}\text{field-name-3}\\\text{literal-2}\end{array}\right\}\right]\ \ldots\right]$$

$\underline{\text{INTO}}$ field-name-4 [, $\underline{\text{DELIMITER}}$ IN field-name-5]
[, $\underline{\text{COUNT}}$ IN field-name-6]

[, field-name-7 [, $\underline{\text{DELIMITER}}$ IN field-name-8]
[, $\underline{\text{COUNT}}$ IN field-name-9] ...

[WITH $\underline{\text{POINTER}}$ identification-10] [$\underline{\text{TALLYING}}$ IN field-name-11]

[; ON $\underline{\text{OVERFLOW}}$ imperative-statement]

USE AFTER STANDARD $\left\{\begin{array}{l}\underline{\text{EXCEPTION}}\\\underline{\text{ERROR}}\end{array}\right\}$

PROCEDURE ON $\left\{\begin{array}{l}\text{file-name-1 [file-name-2]} \ldots\\\underline{\text{INPUT}}\\\underline{\text{OUTPUT}}\\\underline{\text{I-O}}\\\underline{\text{EXTEND}}\end{array}\right\}$

USE AFTER STANDARD $\left\{\begin{array}{l}\underline{\text{EXCEPTION}}\\\underline{\text{ERROR}}\end{array}\right\}$

PROCEDURE ON $\left\{\begin{array}{l}\text{file-name-1 [file-name-2]} \ldots\\\underline{\text{INPUT}}\\\underline{\text{OUTPUT}}\\\underline{\text{I-O}}\end{array}\right\}$

USE BEFORE REPORTING field-name.

USE FOR DEBUGGING ON $\left\{\begin{array}{l}\text{cd-name-1}\\\text{[ALL REFERENCES OF] field-name-1}\\\text{file-name-1}\\\text{procedure-name-1}\\\underline{\text{ALL}}\ \underline{\text{PROCEDURES}}\end{array}\right\}$

$\left[\begin{array}{l}\text{cd-name-2}\\\text{[ALL REFERENCES OF] field-name-2}\\\text{, file-name-2}\\\text{procedure-name-2}\\\underline{\text{ALL}}\ \underline{\text{PROCEDURES}}\end{array}\right] \ldots$

WRITE record-name [FROM field-name-1]

$\left[\left\{\begin{array}{l}\underline{\text{BEFORE}}\\\underline{\text{AFTER}}\end{array}\right\} \text{ADVANCING} \left\{\begin{array}{l}\text{field-name-2}\\\text{integer}\\\text{mnemonic-name}\\\text{PAGE}\end{array}\right\} \left[\begin{array}{l}\text{LINE}\\\text{LINES}\end{array}\right]\right]$

$\left[; \text{AT} \left\{\begin{array}{l}\underline{\text{END-OF-PAGE}}\\\underline{\text{EOP}}\end{array}\right\} \text{imperative-statement}\right]$

WRITE record-name [FROM field-name] [INVALID KEY imperative-statement]

General Format for Conditionals

Relation Condition

$\left\{\begin{array}{l}\text{field-name-1}\\\text{literal-1}\\\text{arithmetic-expression-1}\\\text{index-name-1}\end{array}\right\} \left\{\begin{array}{l}\text{IS [NOT] } \underline{\text{GREATER THAN}}\\\text{IS [NOT] } \underline{\text{LESS}} \text{ THAN}\\\text{IS [NOT] } \underline{\text{EQUAL}} \text{ TO}\\\text{IS [NOT] } >\\\text{IS [NOT] } <\\\text{IS [NOT] } =\end{array}\right\} \left\{\begin{array}{l}\text{field-name-2}\\\text{literal-2}\\\text{arithmetic-expression-2}\\\text{index-name-2}\end{array}\right\}$

Class Condition

field-name IS [NOT] $\left\{\begin{array}{l}\underline{\text{NUMERIC}}\\\underline{\text{ALPHABETIC}}\end{array}\right\}$

Sign Condition

$$\text{arithmetic-expression IS [\underline{NOT}]} \begin{Bmatrix} \underline{\text{POSITIVE}} \\ \underline{\text{NEGATIVE}} \\ \underline{\text{ZERO}} \end{Bmatrix}$$

Condition-Name
Condition

condition-name

Switch-Status Condition

condition-name

Negated Simple
Condition

<u>NOT</u> simple-condition

Combined Condition

$$\text{condition} \left\{ \begin{Bmatrix} \underline{\text{AND}} \\ \underline{\text{OR}} \end{Bmatrix} \text{condition} \right\} \; \ldots$$

Abbreviated Combined
Relation Condition

$$\text{relation-condition} \left\{ \begin{Bmatrix} \underline{\text{AND}} \\ \underline{\text{OR}} \end{Bmatrix} \text{[\underline{NOT}] [relation-operator] object} \right\} \; \ldots$$

Miscellaneous Formats

Qualification

$$\begin{Bmatrix} \text{field-name-1} \\ \text{condition-name} \end{Bmatrix} \left[\begin{Bmatrix} \underline{\text{OF}} \\ \underline{\text{IN}} \end{Bmatrix} \text{field-name-2} \right] \; \ldots$$

Subscripting

$$\text{paragraph-name} \left[\begin{Bmatrix} \underline{\text{OF}} \\ \underline{\text{IN}} \end{Bmatrix} \text{section-name} \right]$$

Indexing

$$\text{text-name} \left[\begin{Bmatrix} \underline{\text{OF}} \\ \underline{\text{IN}} \end{Bmatrix} \text{library-name} \right]$$

Format 1

$$\begin{Bmatrix} \text{field-name} \\ \text{condition-name} \end{Bmatrix} \text{(subscript-1 [, subscript-2, [, subscript-3]])}$$

Format 2

$$\begin{Bmatrix} \text{field-name} \\ \text{condition-name} \end{Bmatrix} \left(\begin{Bmatrix} \text{index-name-1 [\{±\} literal-2]} \\ \text{literal-1} \end{Bmatrix} \right.$$

$$\left. \left[, \begin{Bmatrix} \text{index-name-2 [\{±\} literal-4]} \\ \text{literal-3} \end{Bmatrix} \left[, \begin{Bmatrix} \text{index-name-3 [\{±\} literal-6]} \\ \text{literal-5} \end{Bmatrix} \right] \right] \right)$$

Identifier

$$\text{field-name-1} \left[\begin{Bmatrix} \underline{\text{OF}} \\ \underline{\text{IN}} \end{Bmatrix} \text{field-name-2} \ldots \right] \text{[(subscript-1 [, subscript-2 [, subscript-3]])]}$$

$$\text{field-name-1} \left[\begin{Bmatrix} \underline{\text{OF}} \\ \underline{\text{IN}} \end{Bmatrix} \text{field-name-2} \right] \; \ldots \; \left[\left(\begin{Bmatrix} \text{index-name-1 [\{±\} literal-2]} \\ \text{literal-1} \end{Bmatrix} \right. \right.$$

$$\left. \left. \left[, \begin{Bmatrix} \text{index-name-2 [\{±\} literal-4]} \\ \text{literal-3} \end{Bmatrix} , \left[\begin{Bmatrix} \text{index-name-3 [\{±\} literal-6]} \\ \text{literal-5} \end{Bmatrix} \right] \right] \right) \right]$$

General Format for COPY Statement

COPY text-name $\left[\left\{ \begin{matrix} \underline{OF} \\ \underline{IN} \end{matrix} \right\} \text{library-name} \right\}$

$$\left[\underline{\text{REPLACING}} \left\{ , \left\{ \begin{matrix} ==\text{pseudo-text-1}== \\ \text{field-name-1} \\ \text{literal-1} \\ \text{word-1} \end{matrix} \right\} \underline{\text{BY}} \left\{ \begin{matrix} ==\text{pseudo-text-2}== \\ \text{field-name-2} \\ \text{literal-2} \\ \text{word-2} \end{matrix} \right\} \right\} \ldots \right]$$

D

ANS COBOL Reserved Words

This list of reserved words contains all those of the 1974 standard. Your particular COBOL compiler may have additional or fewer entries. If you inadvertently use a reserved word incorrectly in your program, your compiler will give you an error message. When in doubt, check your COBOL manual.

ACCEPT	CH	DAY
ACCESS	CHARACTER	DE
ADD	CHARACTERS	DEBUG-CONTENTS
ADVANCING	CLOCK-UNITS	DEBUG-ITEM
AFTER	CLOSE	DEBUG-LINE
ALL	COBOL	DEBUG-NAME
ALPHABETIC	CODE	DEBUG-SUB-1
ALSO	CODE-SET	DEBUG-SUB-2
ALTER	COLLATING	DEBUG-SUB-3
ALTERNATE	COLUMN	DEBUGGING
AND	COMMA	DECIMAL-POINT
ARE	COMMUNICATION	DECLARATIVES
AREA	COMP	DELETE
AREAS	COMPUTATIONAL	DELIMITED
ASCENDING	COMPUTE	DELIMITER
ASSIGN	CONFIGURATION	DEPENDING
AT	CONTAINS	DESCENDING
AUTHOR	CONTROL	DESTINATION
	CONTROLS	DETAIL
BEFORE	COPY	DISABLE
BLANK	CORR	DISPLAY
BLOCK	CORRESPONDING	DIVIDE
BOTTOM	COUNT	DIVISION
BY	CURRENCY	DOWN
		DUPLICATES
CALL	DATA	DYNAMIC
CANCEL	DATE	
CD	DATE-COMPILED	EGI
CF	DATE-WRITTEN	ELSE

EMI
ENABLE
END-OF-PAGE
ENTER
ENVIRONMENT
EOP
EQUAL
ERROR
ESI
EVERY
EXCEPTION
EXIT
EXTEND

FILE
FILE-CONTROL
FILLER
FIRST
FOOTING
FOR
FROM

GENERATE
GIVING
GREATER
GROUP

HEADING
HIGH-VALUE
HIGH-VALUES

I-O
I-O-CONTROL
IDENTIFICATION
INDEX
INDEXED
INDICATE
INITIAL
INITIATE
INPUT
INPUT-OUTPUT
INSPECT
INSTALLATION
INTO
INVALID

JUST
JUSTIFIED

KEY

LABEL
LAST
LEADING
LEFT
LENGTH
LESS
LIMIT
LIMITS
LINAGE
LINAGE-COUNTER
LINE
LINE-COUNTER
LINES
LINKAGE
LOCK
LOW-VALUE
LOW-VALUES

MEMORY
MERGE
MESSAGE
MODE
MODULES
MORE-LABELS
MOVE
MULTIPLE
MULTIPLY

NAMED
NEGATIVE
NEXT
NOT
NUMBER
NUMERIC

OBJECT-COMPUTER
OCCURS
OMITTED
OPEN
OPTIONAL
ORGANIZATION
OVERFLOW

PAGE
PAGE-COUNTER
PASSWORD
PERFORM

PF
PH
PIC
PICTURE
PLUS
POINTER
POSITION
POSITIVE
PRINTING
PROCEDURE
PROCEDURES
PROCEED
PROCESSING
PROGRAM
PROGRAM-ID

QUEUE
QUOTE
QUOTES

RANDOM
RD
READ
READY
RECEIVE
RECORD
RECORDING
RECORDS
REDEFINES
REEL
REFERENCES
RELATIVE
RELEASE
RELOAD
REMAINDER
REMOVAL
RENAMES
REPLACING
REPORT
REPORTING
REPORTS
RERUN
RESERVE
RESET
RETURN
RETURN-CODE
REVERSED
REWIND
REWRITE
RF
RH
RIGHT
ROUNDED
RUN

SAME	SUB-QUEUE-1	UNTIL
SD	SUB-QUEUE-2	UP
SEARCH	SUB-QUEUE-3	UPON
SECTION	SUBTRACT	USAGE
SECURITY	SUM	USE
SEGMENT	SUPPRESS	USING
SEGMENT-LIMIT	SYMBOLIC	
SELECT	SYNC	VALUE
SEND	SYNCHRONIZED	VALUES
SENTENCE		VARYING
SEPARATE	TABLE	
SEQUENCE	TALLYING	WHEN
SEQUENTIAL	TAPE	WITH
SET	TERMINAL	WORDS
SIGN	TERMINATE	WORKING-STORAGE
SIZE	TEXT	WRITE
SORT	THAN	
SORT-MERGE	THROUGH	ZERO
SOURCE	THRU	ZEROES
SOURCE-COMPUTER	TIME	ZEROS
SPACE	TIMES	
SPACES	TO	+
SPECIAL-NAMES	TOP	−
STANDARD	TRAINING	*
STANDARD-1	TYPE	/
START		**
STATUS		>
STOP	UNIT	<
STRING	UNSTRING	=

The following list represents the reserved words that have been added in the 1985 standard.

ALPHABET	END-DELETE	GLOBAL
ALPHABETIC-LOWER	END-DIVIDE	
ALPHABETIC-UPPER	END-EVALUATE	INITIALIZE
ALPHANUMERIC	END-IF	
ALPHANUMERIC-EDITED	END-MULTIPLY	NUMERIC-EDITED
ANY	END-PERFORM	
	END-READ	ORDER
CLASS	END-RECEIVE	OTHER
COMMON	END-RETURN	
CONTENT	END-REWRITE	PADDING
CONTINUE	END-SEARCH	PURGE
CONVERSION	END-START	
CONVERTING	END-STRING	REFERENCE
	END-SUBTRACT	REPLACE
DAY-OF-WEEK	END-UNSTRING	
DEBUG-SUB-NUM	END-WRITE	STANDARD-2
	EVALUATE	
END-ADD	EXTERNAL	TEST
END-CALL		THEN
END-COMPUTE	FALSE	TRUE

E

Answers to Selected Exercises

Several of the Questions to Aid Understanding in each chapter are marked with an asterisk. These questions are answered for you in this Appendix.

Chapter 1

3. To get the first record from the file, there must be an input before the loop. Then there must be another input at the end of the loop to keep the loop going.
5. Structured programming allows all programs to be written using standardized structures that all programmers can understand and follow. The structures allow the programs to be cleaner and more straightforward.
7. In structured programming it is important that the flow of the program continue directly from the beginning of the program to the end without any branching (SIMPLE SEQUENCE). If all structures (not just the IF) are considered as elements of the simple sequence, then the flow of the program is from top to bottom.
10. When desk checking your programs, you will find logic errors as well as syntax errors. You will also develop a better understanding of the program itself.

Chapter 2

4. (a) Correct.
   (c) Incorrect—There is no ZIP-CODE-OUT field.
   (e) Incorrect—You write a record.
   (g) Incorrect—(Probably) Since EOF is given an initial value of NO, you will probably need to PERFORM the routine until EOF is YES, not NO.
   (i) Incorrect—There is no UNTIL clause on the WRITE statement.
5. Data editing simply allows the programmmer to output the data in a more presentable fashion. Dollar signs on money, decimal positions lined up, and zeros suppressed are a few of the editing features.
6. (a) 12.44
   (b) ZZZZ9.9
   (c) $.06
   (d) $123.00
   (e) -
   (f) $123.45
   (g) Z9
   (h) Z9BDB
   (i) $.01
   (j) $$$9.90
   (k) --,--9.99
   (l) $1,234.00
   (m) 12/34
   (n) 12/34 5
   (o) $22.22-

(p) $1.00

(q) $ƀƀƀƀƀ.13CR

(r) $$.99 (since additional blanks are not shown in front)

(s) ++9.99

(t) ƀƀ

(u) ƀ-

8. When several calculations must be done to get the desired results, it is sometimes easier to code one statement using the COMPUTE statement rather than coding several statements using the keyword calculations.

10. **(a)** FIELD-C = 35

(c) FIELD-A = 005V00

(e) FIELD-D = 8

(g) FIELD-A = 000V08 (10 − 18 = −8 but FIELD-A has no sign designation and so will lose the fact that the 8 is negative)

11. **(a)** Correct.

(c) Incorrect—No result field given.

(e) Correct.

(g) Correct.

(i) Incorrect—INTO is incorrect usage.

(k) Correct.

(m) Incorrect—ROUNDED is in the wrong place.

(o) Correct.

(q) Incorrect—REMAINDER is used incorrectly.

(s) Incorrect—No result field is given.

(u) Incorrect—REMAINDER is in the wrong location.

13. Logic errors allow the program to continue to function but will cause it to produce the wrong output. They are difficult to find because the machine won't find them for you, often you don't even know they are there, and, most of the time, there is no indication of where in the program the error is occurring, so the program has to be searched in order for the error to be found.

18. The three logical operators are AND, OR, and NOT. The AND operator makes the entire conditional true only if both simple conditionals are true. The OR operator makes the entire conditional true if either or both of the single conditionals are true. The NOT operator simply negates a test. If an AND and an OR are used together in the same statement, the AND will be tested first unless the natural order is changed by the use of parentheses.

20. The NEXT SENTENCE clause allows an exit out of an IF test without the test being inadvertently tied to incorrect statements. It could be used in a nested IF test:

```
IF FIELD-A = FIELD-B
    IF FIELD-C = FIELD-D
        PERFORM CHECK-ROUTINE
    ELSE
        NEXT SENTENCE
ELSE
    PERFORM BUILD-ROUTINE.
```

21. The statement is correct.

23. Incorrect. One correct interpretation would be

```
IF FIELD-A NOT = FIELD-B AND
   FIELD-A = FIELD-C
   PERFORM ROUTINE-1.
```

25. Incorrect. One correct interpretation would be

```
IF FIELD-A = 5 OR
   FIELD-B = 5
   PERFORM ROUTINE-1.
```

28. After the first record is read, the control field is moved into the hold field; then, after each record is read, the two fields are compared to see if the control field has changed. If it has, the control break is generated.

Chapter 3

3. The file could be updated without anything being printed but, since errors are common in updating, a written record allows you to check your input so that errors can be found and corrected.

7. If the master key is less than the transaction key, we know we are finished with the master record because it can never match the transaction key. Therefore, the master record can be written to the new master file.

Chapter 4

2. The three methods are full-screen I/O, I/O done with cursor positioning commands, and I/O done with line-at-a-time processing. We used line-at-a-time processing only since the other two methods are specific to the type of computer being used. The information we used is general and the knowledge can be transferred to any other machine.

5. The DISPLAY statement is used to display information on the screen. We can set up the data to be displayed in the WORKING-STORAGE SECTION as a single field that could be displayed with one DISPLAY statement. We can also display each line on the screen with a separate DISPLAY statement, again from the WORKING-STORAGE SECTION. The third method is to DISPLAY all the data on the screen by using literals in the PROCEDURE DIVISION. This last method is the preferred one because of the way the computer memory is used when there is more than one user.

8. The STRING statement or UNSTRING statement can be used for verifying non-numeric data, but the UNSTRING statement is needed for verifying numeric data (especially if the data includes a decimal point). When a field has a decimal point, we UNSTRING the integer and the decimal portions around the decimal (using the decimal point as the delimiter); then each of these fields can be verified separately.

11. (a) FIELD-4 = AB-C12-3b4
   (c) FIELD-4 = AB-CXYbABb
   (e) FIELD-4 = AB12XYb-Z-

12. (b) FIELD-1 = ABC
      FIELD-2 = ƀƀƀƀ
      FIELD-3 =Dƀ1*
   (d) FIELD-1 =ABC
      FIELD-2 = -Dƀ1
      FIELD-3 = ƀƀƀƀ

Chapter 5

2. A single-level table is just a single column of entries. A two-level table is that same column of entries, except that the entries are not simply entries but are tables themselves. Thus we have a single-level table of single-level tables.

5. In order for information in one table to match information in another table, the two tables must be used concurrently.

8. A subscript can be used with any table, but a table that is to be searched with the SEARCH statement must be defined with an index. A subscript is programmer-defined, while an index is automatically defined by the computer as it is designated with the table.

Chapter 6

3. EBCDIC and ASCII are two coding methods used to store the data in computers (a computer uses only one method). To be able to arrange the data into the proper sequence, the computer must know how it is stored.

6. (a) Open the input and output files.
   (b) Read the records from the input file.
   (c) Write the input records into the sort file.
   (d) Sort the sort file according to the directions given in the KEY clause(s).
   (e) Read the sorted records back from the sort file.
   (f) Write the sorted records to the output file.
   (g) Close the input and output file and erase the sort file.

9. Since the INPUT PROCEDURE (or OUTPUT) must be a SECTION, and a SECTION continues until the computer finds another SECTION, we must have a way to branch around the read (or write) loop (which is a paragraph and would be performed in sequence) after we have read all the records. Without the EXIT paragraph (or one rigged with another method) the program will continue on into the read loop again and will ABEND when it tries to read another record from the closed file.

Chapter 7

2. The files are the old master file, the transaction file, the new master file, and the print file (although the print file is optional). The old master and the transaction file are matched on the key. Depending upon the result of that match, records are added, changed, or deleted from the old master as the records are transferred to the new master.

5. The three methods are SEQUENTIAL, RANDOM, and DYNAMIC. SEQUENTIAL is used for files being read sequentially or created for the first time. RANDOM is used to access the file randomly rather than sequentially. DYNAMIC is used when the file needs to be accessed both randomly and sequentially.

7. The FILE STATUS codes are returned by the computer each time a file is accessed. They are used to determine what type of error, if any, has occurred.

Chapter 8

1. The three methods are full-screen I/O, I/O done with cursor positioning commands, and I/O done with line-at-a-time processing. We used only line-at-a-time processing since the other two methods are specific to the type of computer being used. The information we used is general and the knowledge can be transferred to any other machine.
5. It might be confusing for the user to see two different screen layouts in the same program.

Chapter 9

1. Similar to tables, relative files allow accessing of the records by specifying the location of the record in the file. The advantages of relative files over indexed files are that they save storage space because they do not require an index file and they are faster because they do not have to access the index file to get the address of the record.
3. Hashing allows the user to arrive at the address of the records in the file without having to make the file large enough to accommodate every possible address. If we create a file with room for 250 records and use a Social Security number as the key, we divide the number by 250 and then use the remainder of the division as the pointer into the file.
7. A WRITE statement is not used because all the records are already written into the file as blanks. When we put the records into the file, all we actually do is rewrite the blank records that are already there.

Chapter 10

2. A normal FD contains only the LABEL RECORDS clause, but a Report Writer FD must also use the REPORT IS clause.
4. Use of the PAGE clause on the RD causes the computer to set up the counters. To print the PAGE-COUNTER, we must use the SOURCE IS clause.
7. To generate the detail line, we must use the GENERATE statement and call for the DETAIL line by name.
9. Rolling forward totals are simply subtotals. They are created by using the SUM clause.

Chapter 11

1. The COPY statement is used to load file layouts from a library into the program. These layouts are inserted into the program as regular code.
3. COPY statement code is loaded into the program when the program is compiled, so if the copied code ever needs changing, all the affected programs will have to be recompiled. But a subprogram is called into the calling program when the program is executed. Any changes made in a subprogram are automatically included every time the calling program is executed.
6. When the code is written, the programmer will have to understand both programs. Later, if changes are needed, the programmer making those changes will also have to know both languages.
8. The LINKAGE SECTION is used to describe any fields that are going to be passed between the calling program and the subprogram.

BIBLIOGRAPHY

A. Chai Winchung and Henry W. Chai. *Programming Standard* COBOL. New York: Academic Press, 1976.

Robert T. Grauer. *Structured COBOL Programming*. Englewood Cliffs: Prentice-Hall, 1985.

A. S. Philippakis and Leonard J. Kazmier. *The New COBOL: An Illustrated Guide*. New York: McGraw-Hill, 1986.

J. K. Pierson and Jeretta A. Horn. *Structured COBOL Programming*. Glenview: Scott, Foresman, 1986.

Gary S. Popkin. *Introductory Structured COBOL Programming*. Boston: Kent, 1985.

Gary B. Shelly, Thomas J. Cashman, and Steven G. Forsythe. *Structured COBOL*. Brea: Anaheim, 1985.

Nancy Stern and Robert A. Stern. *Structured COBOL Programming*, 4th ed. New York: John Wiley, 1985.

Steve Teglovic, Jr., and Kenneth D. Douglas. *ANSI Structured COBOL: An Introduction*. Homewood: Richard D. Irwin, 1986.

INDEX

This index has some special listings to help you find the precise type of text you are looking for. If the reference is simply a number, the entry can be found in the regular textual material. If the reference is marked with an S, it will be found in a Chapter Summary, and if it is marked with a G, it will be found in a Chapter Glossary.

A 8
B 9
C 0
D 1
E 2
F 3
G 4
H 5
I 6
J 7